HISTORY OF THE POPES
VOL. XIV

THE
HISTORY OF THE POPES,

FROM THE CLOSE OF THE MIDDLE AGES

DRAWN FROM THE SECRET ARCHIVES OF THE VATICAN AND OTHER
ORIGINAL SOURCES

FROM THE GERMAN OF

LUDWIG, FREIHERR VON PASTOR

EDITED BY

RALPH FRANCIS KERR

OF THE LONDON ORATORY

VOLUME XIV

MARCELLUS II. (1555)
PAUL IV. (1555-1559)

KRAUS REPRINT
Nendeln / Liechtenstein
1969

Reprinted by permission of the original publisher

KRAUS REPRINT
A Division of
KRAUS-THOMSON ORGANIZATION LIMITED
Nendeln/Liechtenstein
1969
Printed in Germany

CONTENTS OF VOLUME XIV.[1]

[1] For Bibliography see Volume XIII.

TABLE OF CONTENTS OF VOLUME XIV.[1]

CHAPTER I.

ELECTION OF MARCELLUS II.—HIS FAMILY AND PREVIOUS CAREER.

[1] Unpublished documents are marked by an asterisk (*) ; documents to be published in the " Acta Pontificum Romanorum " are designated by two asterisks (**).

CHAPTER II.

THE PONTIFICATE OF MARCELLUS II.

CHAPTER III.

ELECTION OF PAUL IV.—HIS CHARACTER AND PROJECTS. —THE CARAFA.

CHAPTER IV.

COMMENCEMENT OF THE STRUGGLE OF PAUL IV. AGAINST THE SUPREMACY OF SPAIN.

CHAPTER X.

PAUL IV. AND THE ROMAN INQUISITION.

CHAPTER XI.

THE TRIAL OF CARDINAL MORONE.

CHAPTER XII.

SPREAD OF PROTESTANTISM IN THE NETHERLANDS, FRANCE AND POLAND.

CHAPTER XIII.

THE CONSUMMATION OF THE SCHISM IN GERMANY.—DISPUTE OF PAUL IV. WITH FERDINAND I.

CHAPTER XIV.

MARY THE CATHOLIC AND THE LEGATION OF CARDINAL POLE.

CHAPTER XV.

ACCESSION OF ELIZABETH, AND THE ESTABLISHMENT OF THE
ENGLISH STATE CHURCH.—LAST DAYS OF PAUL IV.

LIST OF UNPUBLISHED DOCUMENTS IN APPENDIX.

CHAPTER I.

ELECTION OF MARCELLUS II.—HIS FAMILY AND PREVIOUS CAREER.

Discussions on the subject of the Papal election had already begun among the Cardinals even before a fatal termination of the illness of Julius III. was expected,[1] whereas the Imperial as well as the French diplomatists, who had been seriously occupied with the possibility of a conclave a year earlier,[2] were now caught unawares and could take no decisive steps.[3] On the morning after the death of the Pope the Sacred College assembled in the Vatican ; Ascanio della Corgna was entrusted with the protection of the city and the conclave, while Girolamo Federici, Bishop of Sagona, who had been appointed Governor of Rome by Julius III., was confirmed in his office.[4]

For the sake of safety, the College of Cardinals had 2000 additional men enrolled, besides the usual troops. The tumult which broke out on March 27th, 1555, proved that this precautionary measure was not unnecessary ; after

[1] *Questa infermità del Papa anchor che non si giudicasse mortale nondimeno ha mosso di molti humori intorno al papato . . . Bellai si lascia intendere che gli pare di poter pensar così bene al papato come fa Morone, Ferrara, Mignanelli et Farnese. . . . Ferrara non perde punto di tempo. . . . Carpi, S. Jacomo non dormono. *C. Capilupi to Cardinal Gonzaga, dat. Rome, March 19, 1555 (Gonzaga Archives, Mantua).

[2] Cf. the reports in DRUFFEL, IV., 380.

[3] Cf. the letter of Charles V. to Ferdinand I. on April 11, 1555, in DRUFFEL, IV., 651 ; see also RIESS, 4.

[4] Cf. MASSARELLI, 248.

this was settled, however, there was no further disturbance,[1] nor were there any risings of any importance in the provinces.[2]

It is characteristic of the worldly view of the Papacy which was still taken at that time in important circles in Rome, that the probable result of the conclave formed now, as on previous occasions, the subject of betting in the banks ; but even in these circles the distinguished Cardinal Cervini was considered to have the best prospects of success.   After him came the rich Ippolito d'Este of Ferrara.[3]   It is clear from the dispatches of the diplomatists how very excellent the prospects of Cervini were.   Camillo Capiluli summed up his views on March 30th, 1555, in the following terms : " Although it is difficult to predict anything, on account of the position, which changes almost every hour, still Cervini, Bertano and Puteo appear to have the best chances ; if Pole were here, he would stand by far in the first place, but his absence, and the fact that he must, just at this time, remain in England, have been disadvantageous to him ; should Morone arrive in time,he would stand a chance ; Este is doing everything in his power to secure his own election."[4]

Cervini, Este and Bertano also figure as the most likely candidates in the reports of the other Mantuan agents on April

[1] Cf. besides MASSARELLI, 248, and J. v. MEGGEN in the Archiv für schweiz. Ref.-Gesch., III., 515, the *letters of Bernardino Pia to Calandra, dated Rome, March 27, 1555, and of C. Capilupi, dated March 28 and 30 (Gonzaga Archives, Mantua), and of Ulisse Gozzadini of March 28 and 30, and April 3, 1555 (State Archives, Bologna).

[2] See the Portuguese report of April 6, 1555, in SANTAREM, XII., 424.

[3] See the statements of the *Avvisi (Vatican Library) in SEGMÜLLER in the Zeitschr. für schweiz. Kirchengesch., III., 1 ; cf. also the report of Cocciano in DRUFFEL, IV., 625, and the *report of C. Titio of April 4, 1555, in the State Archives, Florence.

[4] See the *letter of C. Capilupi to the Duke of Mantua dated Rome, March 30, 1555 (State Archives, Mantua).

4th and 5th, 1555.[1] Giovanni Francesco Arrivabene remarked on April 6th that the position was such that no one
party could forward their aims without the others, and that
the conclave would therefore either be very short or of very
long duration.[2] This opinion was so far justified in that the
sharply opposed Imperial and French parties were equally
strong ; the former worked for Bertano, the latter for Este.
The Cardinals of Julius III. had at first fixed their choice on
Puteo, but when his election appeared impossible, they were
willing to support Bertano. The decision lay with the neutrals, and to these belonged the older Cardinals, who, however,
had a candidate of their own.[3]

During the obsequies of Julius III., which were celebrated
in the simplest manner, owing to the want of money,[4] the
Cardinals assembled each day for consultation. Before the
beginning of the conclave the important question had to be
settled, whether the recent Bull of Julius III. had binding
force upon the Papal election. Opinions varied considerably
with regard to this. Those who held the affirmative view
justified themselves by the fact that the Bull of Julius III. had
been sanctioned and signed by all the Cardinals, and had
already been provided with the leaden seal. Those who
denied that it had the force of law laid stress on the fact that
the document had not, as was customary, been affixed in the
Campo di Fiore, and on the doors of the Roman basilicas. As
the Cardinals could come to no agreement, experienced canonists, at whose head was the Dean of the Rota, were called upon
for an opinion. Their view was that the Bull was not binding
on the Cardinals. The Dean of the Sacred College, Cardinal

---

[1] See the *reports of B. Pia to Calandra of April 4, and of
Ipp. Capilupi to the Duchess of Mantua of April 5, 1555 (Gonzaga
Archives, Mantua).

[2] **Original in the Gonzaga Archives, Mantua.

[3] *Cf.* the reports in PETRUCELLI, II., 67, and DRUFFEL, IV.,
625, as well as Ghisi's letter of April 8, 1555, in Appendix No. 3
(Gonzaga Archives, Mantua) ; see also MASIUS, Briefe, 199.

[4] *Report of U. Gozzadïni of March 27, 1555 (State Archives,
Bologna).

Carafa, announced this decision to his colleagues on April 3rd, the day on which the obsequies, which had begun on March 26th, came to an end.[1] The Mass of the Holy Ghost was celebrated two days later, after which the learned scholar and jurist, Uberto Foglietta, delivered the usual discourse. Then the Cardinals proceeded to the conclave, which had been prepared in the Vatican.[2]

At the death of Julius III. the Sacred College consisted of fifty-seven members, of whom thirty were resident in Rome. Only a few of the twenty-seven who were absent were able to reach Rome in time. On March 28th, Crispi and Savelli arrived, on April 1st, Cervini and Ranuccio Farnese, on April 3rd, Ercole Gonzaga, and on April 4th, Madruzzo and Pisani.[3] No less than twenty Cardinals, therefore, would be absent from the conclave. Of these, besides Alessandro Farnese, Bourbon, Tournon, Givry, Lenoncourt, Meudon, Annebaut, Charles and Louis of Lorraine, Vendôme and Châtillon, in all no less than ten Cardinals devoted to the interests of Henry II., were in France.[4] It was not to be wondered at, therefore, that the French party strove to defer the beginning of the conclave.[5]

As the thirty-seven Cardinals present in Rome had already entered the conclave on April 5th, the French members of the

---

[1] *Cf.* MASSARELLI, 249 *seq.* and Acta consist. in SÄGMÜLLER, Papstwahlbullen, 35, as well as SCHWEITZER, Reform unter Julius III., 63.

[2] Plan of the cells of the Cardinals in the *Conclave factum in Vaticano post mortem p. Julii III.* A publication of the same period in the Secret Archives of the Vatican ; there is a second publication (Romae apud Valerium et Aloisium Doricos fratres, Brixien. 1555), which gives more detailed particulars.

[3] These dates are given more exactly in the publications quoted in the previous note than in Panvinio (MERKLE, II., 249 n. 2). Cardinal Gonzaga came with a train of 300 horses ; see *Ghisi's report to the governor of the castle at Mantua, dated Rome, April 3, 1555 (Gonzaga Arch. Mantua).

[4] Morone and Truchsess were staying in Germany ; see MASSARELLI, 251 *seq.*

[5] Legaz. di Serristori, 347.

Sacred College, as well as the instructions of Henry II., came too late.[1] The ambassador of Charles V., Juan Manrique de Lara, was delayed in Siena, and chose to come by sea to avoid falling into the hands of the French, and on April 5th no one even knew wheré he was.[2] His absence was especially regretted by those Cardinals, such as Carpi, who were devoted to the Imperial interests, and by the Florentine ambassador, Averardo Serristori. Duke Cosimo I. was a strong opponent of the French candidate, Cardinal d'Este.[3] In this respect he allied himself with the reform party, whose strictly ecclesiastical principles had, on this occasion, for the first time obtained a decided influence on the Papal election.[4] The time had now come, in the opinion of these men—as Cardinal Cervini openly declared in Perugia, during his journey to the conclave—when, with the help of God, a Pope would be given to the afflicted Church, who would vie with the holy and learned Popes of former times, and be a true representative of Christ.[5]

The early opening of the conclave, in spite of the opposition of the French, was in itself a victory for the men who desired, in these days of grave danger, to give a new head to the Church as soon as possible, and in so doing, only to look to the qualities

[1] The instructions of Henry II. of April 4, 1555, to support Este in the first place, then Tournon, du Bellay, Armagnac and lastly Pole, in RIBIER, II., 604 seqq.

[2] See the *letter of lpp. Capilupi to the Duchess of Mantua, dated Rome, April 5, 1555 (Gonzaga Archives, Mantua).

[3] See PETRUCELLI, II., 70 seqq. Philip II., like the Emperor, desired the election of Pole in the first place ; after him Bertano or Morone would have been agreeable to them. On this occasion Cervini was not expressly excluded by the Emperor. But in any case all instructions from Brussels arrived too late (cf. SÄGMÜLLER, Papstwahlen, 202 seq.). Manrique did not reach Rome until April 8 ; see the *report of B. Pia to Calandra, dated Rome, April 8, 1555 (Gonzaga Archives, Mantua).

[4] See RANKE, I.[6], 182 ; SÄGMÜLLER, loc. cit. 204 ; HERRE, 15 ; WAHRMUND, Das Ausschliessungsrecht, Vienna, 1888, 73.

[5] PANVINIO, Vita Marcelli II. ; cf. also the expression in CIACONIUS, III., 801.

of the candidate, without considering whether his elevation would be agreeable either to the French king or to the Emperor. No one pursued this object with so much zeal as Cardinal Carafa, who, in this respect as in other things, maintained his place as the leader of the Catholic Reformation. As Carafa was not popular on account of his abrupt manner, Cervini, Pole and Morone had the best prospects of being elected, should a purely ecclesiastical point of view be taken into consideration. Carafa expressed himself in the strongest terms against the clandestine meetings and attempts at bribery by which Este endeavoured to secure his election.[1]

His remonstrances did not fail in having an effect. It is evident that a change had taken place since the last conclave, as well from the exclusion of all intruders from the enclosure,[2] as from Serristori's report of April 4th, 1555, in which he describes how earnestly the unseemly interference of the secular princes, in the election of Julius III., was now deprecated. This feeling was so pronounced that the shrewd Florentine thought it advisable to exercise the greatest caution on this occasion.[3] Very characteristic also of the reform movement was the election capitulation, which declared that the Pope would wage war with no Christian princes, nor enter into any alliance against them, but would rather prove himself a common father to all and preserve a strict neutrality.[4]

Quite unlike the ambitious Este, who promoted his own election by every means in his power,[5] Cervini, who, after him, was the most likely candidate for the tiara, maintained a modest reserve. He declared that his only wish was that a good Pope should be raised to the throne of St. Peter. This

[1] See the report of A. Cocciano to Seripando in DRUFFEL, IV., 624 *seq*.

[2] *Cf.* Lett. de' princ., III., 233.

[3] *Cf.* in Appendix No. 1 the *letter of April 4, 1555 (State Arch. Florence).

[4] See LULVES in the Quellen und Forschungen des Preuss. Histor. Inst., XII., 225.

[5] The Portuguese ambassador also says in his report of April 6, 1555, that money was not spared. Corpo dipl. Port., VII., 383.

dignified behaviour gained for the representative of the reform party the respect of all, and made it clearer than ever that he was the man chosen by God to be the ruler of the Church.[1] His elevation, however, was not effected without considerable difficulties. It was commonly known that he was favoured neither by the French King nor by the Emperor, though the Imperialists could not deny that Cervini possessed the most excellent qualities, and that, as he was poor, the Emperor had nothing to fear from him in Italy.[2] It is not, therefore, surprising that Serristori reports on April 6th that Cervini, on account of his blameless mode of life, was favoured by many of the Imperialist Cardinals, as well as by those of Julius III. Besides the Frenchmen, the Italian Cardinals Capodiferro, Sermoneta, Giulio della Rovere, del Monte, and the other younger Cardinals trembled before the severity of such a representative of ecclesiastical reform and were steadily opposed to Cervini.[3] These worldly Cardinals kept firmly to Este. Cardinal Ercole Gonzaga had also been won over to his side by the Duke of Ferrara, while Cardinal Madruzzo, who, on other grounds, was on bad terms with Cardinal Cervini, did not appear inimical to Este. The prospects of the latter were also improved because the Imperial Cardinals were at variance with one another, and had not been able to fix on a definite candidate. Este was therefore able to indulge in high hopes at the beginning of the conclave, as it was exceedingly probable that he would be able to attain to the necessary two-thirds majority if, after the first scrutiny, the accession should be allowed.[4]

[1] *Cf.* in Appendix No. 2 the *letter of Serristori of April 6, 1555 (State Archives, Florence).

[2] *Cf.* SÄGMÜLLER, Papstwahlen, 202, 205.

[3] See the *letter quoted *supra* n. 1

[4] The principal source for the conclave of Marcellus II. was hitherto the very detailed report of G. Fr. Lottini in the *Conclavi de' pontefici*, I., 135 *seqq.* (French edition, Cologne, 1703, I., 110 *seq.*), the details of which cannot be verified, but concerning which SÄGMÜLLER (Papstwahlen, 208) justly observes that he describes the political side of the conclave on the whole correctly.

Fully recognizing the danger which a victory of the French candidate would mean for the interests of Charles V. in Italy, the leader of the Imperialists, the Camerlengo, Guido Ascanio Sforza of Santa Fiora and Cardinal Ranuccio Farnese resolved to strain every nerve to prevent the election of a candidate with French sympathies. It was of great importance that the Dean of the Sacred College, Cardinal Carafa, was, on ecclesiastical grounds, a strong opponent of the worldly-minded Este, and at once set to work against him. The voting papers had hardly been read on the morning of April 9th when Carafa announced that in accordance with the ancient custom, no accession would take place after the first scrutiny. Nobody dared to gainsay him.

This first success against Este encouraged Cardinals Guido Ascanio Sforza and Ranuccio Farnese to further proceedings. In order to prevent Este from forcing his way to success, they proposed two candidates who, although always inclined to French interests, were at the same time known as excellent, thoroughly trustworthy and blameless men : Carafa and Cervini. It is not astonishing that Cervini should have met with more favour than the fiery Neapolitan. Savelli, Carpi, Juan Alvarez de Toledo, de Silva, Cueva, Medici, Crispi and

To this may be added, as a most valuable supplement, the description of Panvinio, which is founded on the testimony of eye-witnesses and must be regarded as of supreme importance. SÄGMÜLLER (Papstwahlbullen, 35) has since edited this description and it is now published in MERKLE, II., 253 seq. With regard to the initiative given to the election of Cervini, SÄGMÜLLER (loc. cit.) believes that Lottini has represented the matter wrongly, in favour of his master, Card. G. A. Sforza. It is, however, worthy of note, on the other hand, that Agostino Gonzaga, in a *letter sent on April 9, 1555 (see Appendix No. 5, Gonzaga Archives, Mantua) also names Sforza as having brought about the change in favour of Cervini. C. Capilupi also names Sforza in the first place in his *letter of April 10 (see Appendix No. 7, loc. cit. and also the report in the Lett. de' princ., III., 234, and Serristori in the *letter of April 10, 1555, given infra p. 9, n. 2. (State Arch. Florence).

Fulvio della Corgna at once declared themselves for him ; to these was also added, somewhat later, Carafa, who at first felt hurt by the universal preference shown for the younger man, but who afterwards accepted the situation and indeed warmly recommended his rival. It also weighed heavily in the scale that Cervini, as far as the purity of his faith was concerned, stood above suspicion, while Carafa was not free from it in the opinion of several of the Cardinals who were zealous for reform.[1] Soon afterwards, Cesi, Verallo, Saraceni, Crispi, Tagliavia, Puteo, Mignanelli, Poggio, Cicada, Dandino, Pisani, Cornaro and Nobili were also won over to Cervini. Finally Madruzzo also allowed himself to forget the unpleasantness which had made him a personal opponent of Cervini in Trent. In company with Carafa he betook himself on April 9th, at break of day, to Cervini's cell, to conduct him to his assembled supporters in the Pauline Chapel. A dramatic scene then followed : Este personally confronted Madruzzo and violently reproached him with breaking his word.[2]

[1] *Cf.* the *report of B. Pia of April 8, 1555, in Appendix No. 4 (Gonzaga Archives, Mantua).

[2] *Sendosi declarati publicamente Mantova, Urbino et Monte per Ferrara si messe inanzi gagliardo per tutti i versi che poteva, il che visto Carpi et il camarlingo ristrinsero la parte imperiale con le creature di papa Julio et si congregarono in capella avanti che Ferrara et la fattione Franzese ne intendesse cosa alcuna, quali con tutto che si aiutassero et facessero ogni forza per rompere la pratica fin col opporsi Ferrara in persona, mentre che il Teatino (Panvinio here means the Camerlengo) et il car[al] di Trento menavano S.St[à] in capella, dicendo : " che volete fare " et al car[al] di Trento intendo che disse : " a questo modo sig[re] ? questa è la fede che mi havete data ?" al qual dicono che S.S.R.[ma] rispose essere vero, che gl' haveva promesso di non lo fare Papa, ma che adesso non poteva fare altro, comandandognene lo Spirito S[to], in modo che visto che in capella erano già circa 30 voti, tutti si risolveron a andare adorarlo et in questo atto il car[al] camarlingo, Carpi, Perugia, San Vitale, San Clemente, Cornaro et Saraceno si sono portati valorosamente nell' opporsi a' Franzesi. Però l' E. V. non lasci di scrivere loro et alli altri amorevolmente, reconoscendo questa loro prontezza che hanno mostrata per il

The Cardinals assembled in the Pauline Chapel were determined to proclaim Cervini as Pope ; they were only waiting
for Ranuccio Farnese and della Corgna, who had gone to the
adherents of Este in order to obtain from among them some
additional votes.   As, after some time, they had not yet
returned, the cardinals assembled in the Pauline Chapel grew
weary of waiting and declared that they would immediately
proceed to the elevation of Cervini.   Thereupon Farnese and
della Corgna hurried on to the scene, while the adherents of
Este followed them.   These came just at the right time to
witness the election of Cervini.   In the general excitement
the conclavists had also rushed into the place of voting, where
the usual honours were paid to Cervini as Pope.   Cardinal
Medici, however, who had also come forward at the drawing
up of the election capitulation,[1] opposed such tumultuous proceedings in the most determined way.   Although an adherent
of Cervini, he declared that the election must be carried out
with due regard to legal procedure, and that the conclavists
must be removed.   When this had been done, the Dean,
Carafa, arose first and declared that he elected the Cardinal of
Santa Croce as Pope.   His vote and those of the others were
then recorded by a secretary.   At seven o'clock in the evening,
when the voting had come to an end, the bell for the Ave
Maria was rung, and all said the Angelus.   Thereupon Cervini,
in a fine Latin address, declared that he accepted the election,
although he felt that he was unworthy to wear the tiara, and
that his powers were hardly equal to bearing so great a burden.
He would, however, strive to do his duty, and would always
keep nothing but the general well-being of the Church before

servitio et honore di Dio, di S. M^{ta} et suo, perchè invero, per
quello che si intende, le cose di Ferrara erano tanto inanzi, che
se non pigliavano queste partito, portava pericolo di riuscire
Papa.   Dio sia rigratiato, etc.   *Letter of Serristori of April
10, 1555 (State Archives, Florence).   Cf. also the letter of
Madruzzo to Ferdinand I. in the Studien aus dem Bene-
diktinerorden, II., 3 (1884), 457.

[1] Cf. as to this Quellen und Forschungen des Preuss. Histor.
Inst., XII., 224 ; see also MÜLLER, Konklave Pius' IV., 234.

his eyes. Carafa then declared that, in order to comply with the old regulation, the written " Scrutinium " with open voting papers must be taken on the following morning, though without prejudice to the election already made. This accordingly took place early on April 10th.

With one exception all the papers bore the name of Cervini. He himself gave his vote for Carafa, thereby clearly proclaiming that he adhered to the strict ecclesiastical reform movement. Without changing his name, he announced that he would be known as Marcellus II.[1]

The reform party, which in the conclave of 1549-1550 had not been able to withstand the intrigues of Spain and France, had now won a decisive victory, for he who had now been chosen to succeed Julius III. was the most eminent man that the College of Cardinals contained.

The family of Cervini originally came from Montepulciano, in the territory of Siena, and was one of the noblest of that beautiful little town, which had produced so many very distinguished men.[2]

---

[1] PANVINIO *loc. cit.* 255. MASSARELLI, 253. FIRMANUS, 507 *seq.* POLANCO (*cf. infra* p. 37, n. 1), 153. Lett. de' princ., III., 234. Cardinal Nobili's account in CIACONIUS, III., 804 *seq.* U. Gozzadini gives the hour of the election in his *report of April 10, 1555, as : " fra le 23 hore et 24 fu fatto papa per adoratione " ; the confirmatory scrutiny took place on the morning of April 10, between 9 and 10 o'clock (State Archives, Bologna). Concerning his refusal to change his name, *cf.* PALLAVICINI, 13, 11, 2.

[2] *Cf.* BENCI, Storia di Montepulciano, Firenze, 1641, 101 *seq.* ; BUSCHBELL in the Histor. Jahrbuch, XXI., 423 *seqq.* ; see also the still useful monograph of P. POLLIDORUS, De Vita Marcelli II. (Romae 1744), written at the instigation of Benedict XIV., which is taken from all the published sources available at that time, as well as from several manuscript sources, among others the Life of Marcellus II. composed by his brother Alessandro. Pollidorus complains that of this valuable authority only the first part (up to 1538) remained, in consequence of a fire which broke out in the palace of the Cervini at Montepulciano in 1598. Pollidorus has rightly made frequent use of this *Vita*

The father of the Pope, Ricciardo Cervini, born in 1454, had received a most excellent education in Florence, of which city his mother, Elisabetta Machiavelli, was a native, and he had afterwards served Innocent VIII. as scriptor of the Apostolic Penitentiary.[1] His connection with the noble family of the Spannocchi in Siena was of far-reaching importance for his future career.

Ricciardo stayed so long and so frequently with Antonio and Giulio Spannocchi that Siena became a second home to him.[2] The influence of the Spannocchi with Alexander VI, procured for him the position of vice-treasurer of the March of Ancona. For nine years he managed this territory, which was administered by the Spannocchi, in the most admirable manner, and also took part, in other ways, in everything that concerned

di Marcello II. scritta di propria mano del sig. Alessandro Cervini, suo fratello. RANKE (Päpste, III., Appendix 28) cites a copy of the Vita in the Albani Library, Rome, but he only takes from it one passage relating to the improvement of the calendar under Leo X. The Albani library was lost in 1857 with the ship that was conveying it to Prussia (cf. PASTOR, Le Bibliotheche private di Roma, Roma, 1906, 5). We are therefore limited to the copy of the Vita in Ferrara, from which some information was given in 1849 in the Arch. stor. Ital., App. VII., 248 seqq., though without any details as to the manuscript. I was enabled, by the assistance of Prof. Agnelli to find it again in the Communal library in Ferrara in the Miscellanea Riminaldi, t. 1 (Ms. Cl.,. I., n. 264). Cf. besides PANVINIO, Vita Marcelli II. (as a supplement to the editions of Platina), which is valuable and reliable on account of the close connection between the author and hero. A short summary is in MERKLE, II., 255 seqq. The *Vita di Marcello II. by A. Cervini is also to be found in the Carte Cervini in the State Archives, Florence. Cf. BUSCHBELL in the Histor. Jahrb., XXI., 424.

[1] He appears as such in 1487 ; see DEL LUNGO, Florentia, Florence, 1897, 269 n. 2.

[2] He was received into the ranks of the Sienese nobility in 1493, through the Spannocchi. (See GIGLI, Diario Sanese, Lucca, 1723, 113, 141), hence the name Cardinal Spannocchi Cervini.

the well-being of the province. In Macerata and elsewhere one could long afterwards see the sign of his care in the arms of the Cervini affixed to public buildings and the city walls. Ricciardo Cervini took successful measures against internal disputes, and also against the disorders caused by the bandits, who were a real plague in that part of the country.[1] While he was at Montefano,[2] not far from Macerata, in the year 1501, his wife Cassandra, who belonged to the noble family of the

[1] *" Esercitò quell' offizio con honore e fama e benevolenza grandissima di que' popoli, di che si vede in Macerata, Montefano et altri luoghi di quella provincia ancora segno e l'arme d' Cervini ne torrioni delle muraglie et altri luoghi publici in pietre bianche elegantemente scolpite. Questo offizio esercitò m. Ricciardo nove anni continui per se et per la ragione delli Spannocchi . . . per mezzo de' quali m. Ricciardo hebbe principi a questra grandezza . . . " A. Cervini further on again returns to Ricciardo's activity in the March of Ancona, and states " oltre l'haver pacificato que' popoli che da gravi inimizizi e sanguinose erano vessati, frenato le incursioni de banditi haveva nel castigo de' rei et esaltazione de' buoni lassato di se memoria e benevolenza grande in quel paese " (Library in Ferrara).

[2] L. Cardauns has lately (Nuntiaberichte, V., xxii.) thrown doubts on the statement made by most of his biographers that Marcellus was born at Montefano, on grounds, however, which are not very trustworthy. The passage in the dispatch in GENTILE, Politica di Paolo III.: " il rev^mo Marcello da Montepulciano " as well as the word " Politianus " on the tomb, are explained by the fact that the family came from Montepulciano : the passage in Panvinio, in his Epitome Pontif. Rom. of 1557, is contradicted by the text of his Vita Marcelli II. (loc. cit.) where it is expressly stated : " in agro Piceno oppido Montis Fano natus." Two other contemporaries, who were on intimate terms with Marcellus II., Massarelli (MERKLE, II., 261) and A. Cervini (*Vita di Marcello II. loc. cit.) say the same. In the letter about the election of Marcellus in the Lett. de' princ., III., 234, it is said : " Il Papa, benche sia nato a Monte Fano . . . pure è da Montepulciano." In addition to all this, there is also the testimony of Marcellus II. himself in his letter to the inhabitants of Montefano, in POLLIDORUS, 130.

Benci in Montepulciano, bore him, on May 6th, a son who
received the name of Marcello. An astrologer predicted, at
the hour of his birth, that the child would one day be a great
light of the Church. The fulfilment of this prediction, in which
his father believed[1] (a thing not to be wondered at, considering
the views of those days), seemed at first very unlikely, as
Marcello's health as an infant was so delicate that his family
besieged heaven with masses, alms and fasting, to preserve the
life of the little one.[2] Their constant prayer was heard, and
Marcello in time developed exceedingly, not only in body, but
also in mind. He showed at a very early age that mixture of
seriousness and gaiety which won all hearts to him. Lively,
without being talkative, he was at once friendly and modest ;
the love of God and his neighbour, qualities which also distinguished his excellent parents, were his in an eminent degree.
After the early death of his mother, who was well known for
her great piety, he clung with rare affection to his father.
His biographer tells us that even when he was a man of thirty
years of age he never took a step outside the door without
asking his father's permission and receiving his blessing, and
presenting himself before him on his return. This intimate
relationship between them owed its origin to the fact that the
father himself had directed the first steps of his son's education.
In Castiglione d'Orcia, near Montepulciano, where the family
possessed an estate, he gave him his first lessons in grammar,
rhetoric, arithmetic, geometry and astronomy. The father
possessed so great a knowledge of astronomy that Leo X.

[1] " Ancorche poco attendesse alle cose pertinenti alla divin-
azione " (not devozione, as in the copy in the Arch. stor. Ital.,
App. VII., 250) is to be read in the *Vita di Marcello II.

[2] *Oltre a ogni costume ordinario de putti, relates A. Cervini
of his step-brother, non voleva in modo alcuno gustare latte,
pero la madre infinitamente dogliosa et il padre similmente non
si quietarono ne giorno ne notte sempre pensando e cercando,
come potessero aiutare il povero figliuolo che non mancasse
per diffeto di cibo, a fra gli altri rimedi si ricorse a Dio nostro
signore e con messe e sacrifizi e con elemosine et orazioni e digiuni
(Library in Ferrara).

sought his advice to improve the calendar.[1] Methodical instruction for practical work in the mechanical arts and agriculture was also imparted to him by his versatile father. Marcello proved himself the most diligent pupil imaginable. By a most careful arrangement of his day, and the cutting down of his intercourse with society, which he seldom cultivated, and then only in so far as his health required recreation, he succeeded in finding the time necessary for his studies, as well as for his religious duties. He began his day by prayer ; intercourse with the dead, he used to say, by which he meant their writings, was the most useful pursuit and the safest.[2] He used the greatest moderation in play, in drinking and in pleasure. One never saw him idle, and he knew how to fill in his leisure hours with useful occupation, such as drawing, carving, modelling, book-binding or forestry.[3]

Marcello was sent to Siena by his father for his further education, and there he studied Greek dialectics and mathematics with great success. During the Renaissance period this city was notorious for the licentious manner of life which was prevalent there. Marcello remained, however, quite untouched by this, for he only sought out good company. He was just as particular with regard to his studies ; in philosophy, as in astronomy, he carefully avoided all that was evil. This model student, staid beyond his years, gained universal love and respect in Siena ; if his friends and contemporaries sometimes indulged in frivolous or loose talk for amusement, they at once ceased when Marcello came into their presence.[4]

[1] *Cf.* Arch. stor. Ital., App. VII., 248 ; see also Vol. VIII. of this work, p. 398 *seq.*

[2] *Dicendo il ragionare con i morti era il più utile e più sicuro esercizio. *Vita, etc. (Library in Ferrara).

[3] The passage in the *Vita di Marcello II., in the Arch. stor, Ital., App. VII., 250, has escaped CARDAUNS (Nuntiaturberichte. V., xxiv., n. 6.

[4] In Siena, so says A. Cervini, *sotto la disciplina di m. Ugo imparò lettere greche e sotto m. Giov. Batt. Politi dialettica e mattematica. Quivi trovandosi il giovine libero et in città licenziosa mostrò grandissimo segno della sua natural prudenza.

Marcello's studies in Siena included astronomy, mathematics, architecture and archæology, but, above all, he devoted himself to the classics, so that he was soon able to express himself in prose and verse with equal ease and elegance.[1]

After the election of Clement VII., Marcello was sent to Rome for the completion of his studies, and there an opportunity for distinguishing himself soon presented itself. At that time the whole of Italy was greatly disturbed by the fear of an approaching flood. A long spell of rainy weather, no less than the predictions of celebrated astrologers, led even serious men to share this belief ; even Clement VII. himself was sufficiently impressed to be already thinking of taking flight to Tivoli. Marcello alone, whose father had always combated this bugbear, was able to make the Pope understand how groundless the general fear was. Clement VII. commanded him, in conjunction with his learned father, to complete the treatise concerning the reform of the calendar which had already been begun in the reign of Leo X. Marcello returned to Rome with the completed work at the beginning of 1525.[2] He was treated

Prima fu alli precettori carissimo, alli compagni carissimo. Avertito a fuggire la converzazione de tristi etiam di alcuni noti e dalla patria sua, che in quel tempo si trovarono a Siena sapendo che la prattica e la consuetudine suol dare occasione al vizio ed alla virtu, però sempre conversò con uomini ottimi e letterati . . . Dell' astrologia e filosofia lasciando quel che era particolarmente pericoloso quel solo che era utile elesse (Library in Ferrara). *Cf.* also Panvinio in MERKLE, II., 255. That Marcellus was not, however, free from the false astrological beliefs of the age is shown in the letter in CARDAUNS in the Nuntiaturberichte, V., xxiii., n. 1.

[1] *Negli studi di humanità fu veramente eccellente come ne fanno ampia fede quelli che vivono e le sue scritture in prosa et in versi con summa facilità et eleganza da lui formate. *Vita etc. (Library, Ferrara).

[2] *Cf.* Arch. stor. Ital., App. VII., 249, 254 *seq.*, and MARZI in the Atti del congresso stor. di Roma, III. (1906), 649. Concerning the predictions for 1524, see Vol. IX. of this work, p. 378, n. 4.

with distinction by the Pope, who took a lively interest in the reform of the calendar, and was repeatedly allowed to assist at the learned disputations which took place at the Pope's table.[1] Marcello also took advantage of this stay in the Eternal City to continue his scientific studies with eagerness. He visited the libraries, and was on terms of social intercourse with the numerous humanists and scholars who lived in the Curia. It was at this time that he formed an intimate friendship with Lampridio, Tebaldeo, Lascari, Bembo, Angelo Colocci and other humanists,[2] which he kept up with the fidelity which was part of his character. In view of these relationships, and the particular favour which the Pope always showed him, an honourable position in the Curia seemed to be assured to him, when the outbreak of the plague in Rome caused his anxious father to call him home in May, 1526.[3]

[1] Cf. the passages quoted by CARDAUNS in the Nutiaturberichte, V., xxiii., from the letters of Cervini (Carte Cerv. in the State Archives, Florence) which are here drawn upon for the first time to write his life. Buschbell's question (Histor. Jahrbuch, XXI., 423 n. 5), as to whether the whole of the family archives had been brought to Florence, must be answered in the negative, for there are several manuscripts in the Siena Library which certainly belong to these archives, especially, for example, Codex B.V. 18 and D.V. 13 (cf. ILARI, Bibl. di Siena, VI., 274, 491). They probably got there with the literary remains of Archbishop Aless, Cervini ; cf. DRUFFEL, Mon. Trid., I., 4. The hypothesis here advanced, that Cervini intentionally gave up his papers to his relative when he was elected Pope, is difficult to believe. Their coming into the hands of his family is explained in the most natural way, by the death of Marcellus II. before he could carry out his intended reform of the Papal Chancery (see LAEMMER, Mon. Vatic., 461), in connection with which a reform of the archives was also intended.

[2] Cf. A. CERVINI, *Vita di Marcello II. (Library in Ferrara).

[3] According to POLLIDORUS, 12, Marcellus had left the Eternal City after having gained the Jubilee Indulgence of 1525. This is certainly wrong, as a letter of his from Rome of May 5, 1526, is. in existence, concerning which all documentary evidence is wanting until 1528 (see CARDAUNS, loc. cit., xxiii.). The worst

This unwelcome period of leisure Marcello employed in literary work. He translated Cicero's De Amicitia into Italian, as he had already translated words of Euclid and other Greek authors into Latin, and he also composed a poem about baths and medicinal springs. He likewise assisted his now ageing father in the management of his estates, a work in which he proved himself to be an excellent farmer, as well as a careful protector of the poor labourers.[1]

During the time of war, which followed the sack of Rome, no return to the Eternal City was possible. The troubled times caused Cardinal Alessandro Farnese to make long stays in Castro. When he visited the Farnese family estates from there he met Ricciardo Cervini, who had once been his fellow student in Florence at the Academy of Lorenzo de' Medici, and whose distinguished work in the March of Ancona he still bore in remembrance. The old friendship between the two, which was now renewed, was to bear good fruit for the son of Riccardo. Marcello returned to Rome in 1531, with a new work by his father on the reform of the calendar, and was received in the most friendly manner by Cardinal Farnese, with whom he stayed for about a year. The following years, except for a short stay in Rome in 1533, Marcello again spent at home.[2] It is evident from one of his letters to his father, in February, 1534, that he had no intention of marrying ; he then proposed to his father to leave him in his will a capital sum of 1000 ducats, as well as to give him an annual income of 100 ducats, so that he could devote himself to science without pecuniary anxieties, and live in a place suitable for that purpose, such as Rome or Venice.[3] It is not known, however, whether his father made arrangements in accordance with this request,

---

time of the plague, which is expressly stated by A. Cervini to have been the reason of his recall, can be determined by SANUTO, Diarii XLI., 346, to have been after May 13, 1526.

[1] See A. CERVINI, *Vita di Marcello II. (Ferrara Library). Concerning the translation of Cicero cf. POLLIDORUS, 13.

[2] See CARDAUNS, loc. cit. xxiv.

[3] Ibid.

before his death, which took place on April 2nd, 1534.[1]

Soon after Ricciardo's death, his second wife, Leonora Egidi
Cacciaconti, who had borne him five daughters and two sons,
also died. The whole care of this large family now fell to
Marcello, as eldest son. He fulfilled this duty most con-
scientiously, but still held to his resolution of again betaking
himself to Rome, where his patron, Cardinal Farnese, had been
elected Pope in October, 1534. After the settlement of his
family affairs, Marcello entrusted his step-brothers, Alessandro
and Romolo, with the management of the estates, at the same
time arranging for the future of his sisters, one of whom
entered the Order of Poor Clares, while three married, one of
them, Cintia, becoming the mother of the celebrated Cardinal
Bellarmine. The most favourable prospects awaited Marcello
in the Eternal City ; Paul III. received the son of his old friend
all the more joyfully, as he was well aware of his admirable
qualities. Marcello was admitted into the intimate circle
surrounding His Holiness, who entrusted him with the training
and education of his nephew, the youthful Cardinal Farnese.[2]
In this position he gained in an increased degree the confidence
and affection both of his pupil and of Paul III. When the
latter, at the beginning of 1538, entrusted the Cardinal-nephew
with the management of the affairs of state, Cervini received,
as his principal secretary, one of the most influential posts in
the Curia, and was now appointed a Protonotary.[3] Although,
up to this time, Cervini had had absolutely nothing to do with
political affairs, he took a very short time in acquiring a practical knowledge of his new sphere of work, which was as exten-

[1] The statement of CARDAUNS (loc. cit.) that Ricciardo died at
the end of March is erroneous. Besides A. Cervini, *Vita di
Marcello II. (Ferrara Library), see also a *Biographia di Ricciardo
Cervini (Carte Cerv. [State Archives, Florence] ; cf. concerning
this work BUSCHBELL in the Histor. Jahrbuch, XXI., 424) who
give the date as in the text.

[2] Besides A. CERVINI, *Vita di Marcello II., cf. the extracts
from letters in CARDAUNS, loc. cit. xxvi., n. 1.

[3] See EHSES, Conc. Trid., IV., 145, n. 2 ; cf. Vol. XI. of this
work, p. 34.

sive as it was important.   As secretary of the Cardinal-nephew,
he soon became also the most intimate secretary of the Pope.
The diplomatic correspondence was, it is true, addressed to
the Cardinal, and signed by him, but the drafting of it was
entirely in the hands of Cervini.   How carefully he examined
the documents emanating from the Curia is proved by the
numerous corrections in his fine and characteristic hand-
writing.   As adviser of the young Cardinal he was, at the same
time, the right hand of the Pope, for the furtherance of his
plans.   In the Chancery his influence was unlimited ; in this
department he formed a school of able officials and diplomatists, upon whom a conscientious performance of their official
duties as well as the careful preservation of all documents was
impressed as the strictest of obligations.   The carelessness
with which the documents received had been treated in the
negligent days of the Renaissance now came to an end, a thing
which was of the greatest advantage from the point of view
of historical research.[1]

The direction of the affairs of state made constant intercourse
with the Pope imperative, and Cervini therefore took up his
residence in the immediate neighbourhood of the private
apartments of Paul III., with whom he discussed current
affairs every morning.[2]   When Cardinal Alessandro Farnese

---

[1] Cf. SICKEL, Römische Berichte, I., in the Sitzungsberichte
der Weiner Akademie, CXXXIII., 13 ; RICHARD in the Rev.
d'hist. eccl., XI., 518 ; cf. also FRIEDENSBURG, Das Preuss.
Histor. Institut : Abhandlungen der Berliner Akad., 1903,
74 seq.

[2] *Hora così vivendo era molto grato a S.S.^{tà} e già nell' opinione
universale stimato fra i favoriti di questa corte, dove dovendo
continuamente per l'officio, ch' egli esercitava e per la tenera
età del cardinale suo padrone trattare col papa negozi gravissimi
gli fù dato per camera proprio luogo da pochi scalini separato
da quello dove dormiva S.S.^{tà} d'ordine dello quale ogni mattina
andava mentre S.B. era in letto a trattenerla ragionando di
varie cose per certo spazio di tempo.   A. Cervini, *Vita di Marcello II. (Ferrara Library).   Cf. also I. Pogiani Oratio in funere
Marcelli II. ; Pogiani, Epist., I., 106.

undertook his first legation to Spain in May, 1539, on the occasion of the death of the Empress, he was accompanied by Cervini. From this time onwards he devoted himself to diplomacy instead of to the affairs of the Chancery, and in this capacity proved himself to be one of the most active, able and disinterested servants of the Holy See.[1]

How very much the Pope valued his services is shown by the fact that he bestowed on him the administration of the bishopric of Nicastro, in Calabria, at the end of August, 1539, which Cervini exchanged for that of Reggio in September, 1540.[2] He had already received the purple on December 10th, 1539.[3] Rapid as had been his advance in the course of a few years from a simple scholar to the supreme senate of the Church, there was, nevertheless, no jealousy displayed against him. Nobody grudged the Cardinal of Santa Croce, as he was now called, after his titular church, S. Croce in Gerusalemme, his good fortune. Contarini, Sadoleto, Pole, Aleander, and Bembo congratulated him in the warmest terms, in which is evident the universal conviction that Paul III., with his penetrating knowledge of character, had, in this appointment, raised merit and devotion to duty to the place to which they had a right.[4]

One reason for this appointment was that Cervini, as the companion of Cardinal Alessandro Farnese, when he was appointed legate to Francis I. and Charles V. in November, 1539, might have unrestricted personal intercourse with those monarchs. The youthful legate left the management of the actual negotiations to his former secretary. It is clear from the reports of Cervini how difficult he felt this task to be. His greatest talents did not lie in the sphere of politics, yet he endeavoured by his diligent devotion to duty and his con-

[1] The opinion of CARDAUNS (V., xxvii.).

[2] See Acta consist. in CARDAUNS, *loc. cit.* xxvii. *Cf.* TACCONE GALLUCCI, Regest. d. pontif. Rom. per le chiese della Calabria, Reggio, 1902, 272 *seq.*

[3] *Cf.* Vol. XI. of this work, pp. 191, 366.

[4] See CIACONIUS, III., 806 ; POLLIDORUS, 26 *seq.* ; CARDAUNS, *loc. cit.* ; HEFNER, App. 4.

scientiousness to make up for his lack of diplomatic finesse.[1]

Even before Paul III. granted to Cardinal Farnese his wished-for recall on April 24th, 1540, the report was current that Cervini was to remain at the Imperial court. The Cardinal sought by means of urgent representations to his friends, Bernardino Maffei and Dandino, to prevent this, but Paul III. would not change his mind, nor would he grant a further request for recall until the determination of the Emperor concerning the final decision at Hagenau was made known.

Cervini, therefore, could only leave Brussels, where the Emperor was then staying, on September 18th, 1540, and he did not reach Rome until the middle of October. In his final dispatch he gave a report of the negotiations with the Emperor concerning the religious question, and the position of the Church in Germany. With characteristic frankness he assigns the reason for the marked estrangement of the German nation from Rome to the neglect of the very things which once had won the Germans for the Church : the apostolic manner of life which the Holy See had formerly followed, fervent and reverent public worship in the churches, the performance of the duties of Christian charity and of zealous preaching. Finally he emphasizes the degeneracy of the German episcopate, men who, chosen merely on account of worldly considerations, left their flocks to look after themselves.[2]   While he had been away Cervini had done all that was in his power to bring about a change in the ecclesiastical manner of life. It was owing to him that Farnese took no money for the exercise of his very extensive faculties, and he also gave warning, in his reports to Rome, of the bad impression which the collection for the building of St. Peter's was making, while at the same time he urged the reform of the Curia.[3]

Cardinal Farnese had once jokingly remarked that Cervini

---

[1] Cf. CARDAUNS, loc. cit.

[2] See Nuntiaturberichte, pub. by CARDAUNS, V., xxx., 246 n. 1, 405 n. 1, 408 seq.

[3] See Nuntiaturberichte, V., xxix.; cf. concerning Cervini's legation, Vol. XI., of this work, pp. 366, 368 seq., 380, 385 seqq.

was even more of a Theatine than Carafa,[1] and this was an absolute fact. Since Cervini had received Holy Orders, he had been a model priest. He said mass with the most touching devotion, recited the divine office on his knees, and his morning and evening prayers with outstretched arms. Spiritual reading, daily examination of conscience, strict fasting, generous alms-giving, and above all, constant prayer, were his rule of life, which he did not allow to be interfered with by the most urgent business or the most inopportune occurrences.[2]

Although Cervini could not reside in his bishopric of Nicastro, he nevertheless administered it with zeal and vigilance. He appointed the best priest he could find to be his vicar-general, and, not content with this, he placed his diocese under the supervision of the neighbouring bishops and of other reliable men, and more especially of Galeazzo Florimonte, whom he particularly valued on account of his love of the truth, since for Cervini the truth came before everything else. His arch-priest had feared at first to tell him everything openly, but Cervini impressed upon him that much as wickedness might displease him, he was nevertheless grateful to whoever pointed it out to him.[3] As Bishop of Reggio, in the Emilia, Cervini at once summoned the Jesuit Lainez to undertake the reform of the clergy, as afterwards he sent Broet to Montepulciano[4]; in the year 1543 he also ordered a strict visitation of the diocese, as a result of which he afterwards issued statutes of reform which were approved by Paul III.[5]

In the spring of 1544 Cervini exchanged the bishopric of Reggio for that of Gubbio; here also he worked in the interests

[1] See Nuntiaturberichte, V., 269, n. 1.

[2] *Cf.* POLLIDORUS, 20 *seq.*

[3] See POLLIDORUS, 22-24, who made use of the episcopal archives at Nicastro. How Cervini regarded the office of bishop is reflected in a dedication to him by Gentianus Hervetus; see S. CHRYSOSTOMI, Opera I., Venetiis, 1583, 232.

[4] See TACCHI VENTURI, I., 578, and Vol. XII. of this work, p. 84.

[5] See Vol. XI. of this work, p. 587, from the episcopal archives, Reggio.

of reform.   The diocese owed to him the extirpation of heresy
and a new division of the parishes, as well as the restoration
and decoration of the cathedral.   He kept a book of his own
concerning everything that was done or that he intended to do,
and also, from time to time, obtained exact information with
regard to the carrying out of his orders.   His ceaseless activity
met with such recognition among the citizens of Gubbio that
they erected a marble statue of him as a token of their gratitude.[1]

An especially fine trait in the character of Cervini was that
he preserved the greatest humility in the midst of all the honours that were conferred on him.   He wrote to his brother that
he looked upon every good thing that happened to him as a
benefit for which he had to thank God, the Church and the
Pope, and as a call to fulfil his duties faithfully and conscien-
tiously.   " You, however," he continues, " if you love me
truly, must constantly pray to God that He may grant me
light and help where I need it most, so that I may not be found
guilty and unworthy of my hire, after I have received so much
for which I can never sufficiently thank the Giver of all good
things."[2]

It is no wonder that such a man enjoyed the favour of Paul
III.   In the autumn of 1541 the Pope took him with him to
Lucca to meet Charles V.   Before the conference at Busseto

[1] See POLLIDORUS, 49 seqq.; BUSCHBELL, 14, 207 seq.   In
the chapter-room of the cathedral at Gubbio the silk chasuble
is still preserved which Marcellus II. presented to the church ;
it is an artistic piece of work, executed in Flanders, having
the Passion of Christ embroidered on it in circles.   The division
of the parishes of January 1, 1545, is entered in the *Lib. delle
Riforme in the communal archives in Gubbio ; ibid. Miscell,
II., a *Bando del luogotenente del duca d'Urbino of 1549, issued
at the instigation of Cervini for enjoining rests on Sundays,
and against disrespectful behaviour in church.   The *Synodales
constitutiones Eugubinae per card. S. Crucis (Episcopal Archives
in Gubbio) which are of value for the history of the Catholic
reformation, I intend to publish in another place.

[2] POLLIDORUS, 42-43.

in June 1543 he sent him as legate to the Emperor, while two years later there followed his appointment as legate at the Council of Trent.[1] With this, a new period of ecclesiastical and diplomatic activity began for Cervini ; his task of representing the Head of the Church at the General Council, together with Cardinals Pole and del Monte, was the most difficult that can be imagined, but Cervini proved himself equal to it. His pre-eminently ecclesiastical views, his learning and his uprightness of character, soon caused him to take the first place. With a versatility that was characteristic of him, he gave thought to the most various questions, and worked upon each subject with as much zeal as though it were his only task. He attacked the uncatholic Constance-Basle theory of the superiority of the Council over the Pope with remarkable firmness,[2] while he knew how to settle the disputes which arose, and which aroused the anger of his colleague del Monte, with mildness and sagacity ; at the same time he devoted himself to the theological questions with the thoroughness, the conscientiousness and the knowledge of the expert. In all questions of dogma he stood out as the leading personality of the Council, while del Monte seemed rather to devote himself to the sphere of ecclesiastical law and the question of reform.[3] Authentic documents bear witness to Cervini's share in the drawing up of the decrees concerning the Canon of Scripture and Tradition, as well as to his very prominent share in that relating to Justification. His activity was very marked with regard to this most important question, which affected the very nerve centre of the religious division, especially after the draft of September 23rd, 1546, and he devoted all his powers to the framing of this decree.[4]

The delicate health of the Cardinal suffered from all these

[1] Cf. Vol. XII. of this work, pp. 162, 174, 209 seq.

[2] Cf. EHSES' interesting essay in the third issue of the association of the Görres-Gesellschaft for 1911, Cologne, 1911, 13 seq.

[3] See the testimony in EHSES, Conc. Trid., V., 780, 961.

[4] Cf. Ibid. 4, 8 seq., 11, 26 seq., 36, 420 seqq., 500 seqq. ; cf. also Vol. XII. of this work, p. 315 ; HEFNER, 33 ; LAUCHERT, 542 n.

exertions, particularly as he had a disease of the kidneys in
the summer of 1545, and he was again ill in May, 1546.[1] During the difficult state of affairs which resulted from the attitude
of the Imperialists in the summer of 1546 Cervini adhered to
the strictly ecclesiastical point of view ; he was determined
to remove the Council to another place where its safety would
not be threatened.[2]   Charles V. had formerly tried to win the
Cardinal over by the grant of a large pension, but had received
a decisive rebuff from the incorruptible Cardinal.[3] Now the
Emperor vainly endeavoured to intimidate Cervini by threats
of violence.   The Emperor might, the Cardinal declared, do
violence to his body, but he had no power over his soul, while
he calmly left the judgment upon his attitude to God alone.[4]
When, accordingly, the Council was removed to Bologna,[5]
Cervini was looked upon in many quarters as the future Pope,
but, in order to prevent his election, the Emperor declared him
to be excluded from the candidates after the death of Paul III.[6]
    Although Cervini impressed upon the new Pope, Julius III.,

[1] See Massarelli in MERKLE, I., 202 seq., 545, 548.   Concerning
his later illnesses cf. ibid. 743, 869.

[2] Cf. Vol. XII. of this work, p. 269 seq.

[3] A. Cervini says, in an *account of Marcello's legation to the
Emperor, 1538-1539 : " Contro quello leggesi nel Platina nuova-
mente stampato, dove pare si voglia dar a Marcello qualche
taccia d'interesse, stimo bene d'opporre oltre le qualita del suo
vivere sempre lontano di ogni sorte di studio d'accumular richezze
i refiuti di ricchi doni fatti da esso in piu occasioni sapendo per
cosa certa che nell' abboccamento che fece Carlo V. imperadore
col pontefice Paolo III. avendo il detto imperadore destinato a
Marcello allora cardinale una pensione di 10,000 scudi esso la
riscusò constantemente e solo ne accettò scudi 1000 sopra la
chiesa di Vagliadolid di commandemento espresso del pontefice."
In the Codex of the Ferrara library mentioned supra p. 11, n. 2.

[4] Cf. the list of authorities in MERKLE, I., 565 seq. ; see also
PANVINIO, Vita Marcelli, II.

[5] Cervini openly declares his reason for the removal of the
Council to Bologna on March 10, 1547 ; see EHSES, Conc. Trid.,
V., 1024.

[6] Cf. Vol. XIII. of this work, p. 10.

with the greatest freedom, a serious view of his duties, Julius nevertheless valued him highly and made an intimate friend of him ; he constantly accepted his advice and help, especially in questions of reform.[1] In 1552 he entrusted Cervini with the presidentship of the reform commission, in the work of which the Cardinal took an active part.[2] In other respects, however, he withdrew himself as much as possible, and did not attempt to conceal his disapproval of much that Julius III. did. His sorrow was very great when the Pope, by assigning Camerino to his brother, introduced an element of nepotism into his government ; Cervini had done everything in his power to prevent this, and in order openly to show his disapproval, he at once retired to his diocese of Gubbio.[3]

Cervini belonged to the Congregation of the Roman Inquisition under Julius III., as he had already done under Paul III. He devoted himself to this office with great zeal,[4] but, although he proved himself strict with those who spread the new doctrines, he nevertheless avoided all exaggeration. The burden of Cervini's duties was still further increased by his protectorate of the Servite Order, a thing which he did not look upon as merely a position of honour, any more than his protectorate of the Augustinian Hermits, but which he carried out with that careful attention which he bestowed on everything with which he was connected. His services to the Augustinians were recognized in the terms of the highest praise by no less a person than the General of the Order, Seripando.[5]

---

[1] See Vol. XIII., p. 159, and MASSARELLI, 171 seq., 174, 193, 197 seqq., 202 seq., 207, 209, 211, 215, 216. Concerning the part taken by the Cardinal in the reform of the regulars, see *Concilio, LXXVIII., 188 seq. (Secret Archives of the Vatican).

[2] Cf. Vol. XIII., p. 165.

[3] See PANVINIO, loc. cit. ; POLLIDORUS, 92 seq., 101.

[4] See, besides Vol. XII. of this work, p. 505 seq., Vol. XIII., p. 217 ; especially the fundamental work of BUSCHBELL : Ref. und Inquisition in Italien, 174 seq., 210 seq. ; cf. also TACCHI VENTURI, I., 523 seq.

[5] Cf. Massarelli in MERKLE. I., 845 ; POLLIDORUS, 93 seq., 103 seq.

A special feature in the portrayal of the character of Cervini would be wanting if no mention were made of his love of learning. It was above all things as a scholar that he had been attracted to Rome, and though he had been placed there in quite other circumstances, he had always returned again to his studies. Paul III., with the penetration that was characteristic of him, had seen this and entrusted the learned Cardinal with the care of the Vatican Library in 1548.[1] Even as a private scholar he had been a keen collector of manuscripts and books, and now as Cardinal he profited by every opportunity of adding to his library.[2] After the long years during which he had been obliged to devote himself to ecclesiastical and diplomatic affairs, it was like a renewal of his youth for him to find himself once more among the interests of former days, although these were now on a much more extensive scale than before. He now devoted himself to the great collection under his care with a truly burning zeal ; new catalogues of the Greek and Latin manuscripts were a result of his enterprise.[3] As custodian of the most extensive library of that time, he did not lose sight of his own idea of making the most important of the Greek manuscripts still unprinted available to scholars by means of publication.[4] The register of expenditure for the

[1] *Cf.* Vol. XII. of this work, p. 545 *seq.*, and the literature mentioned there.

[2] A. Cervini says concerning the time before 1534 (*loc. cit.* Ferrara Library) : *" E sebbene Marcello era allora in privata fortuna non mancava di ricercare libri rari e farne ricerca per ogni via possibile."* Concerning the purchase of books and manuscripts made by Cervini as Bishop of Gubbio, see POLLIDORUS, 51 *seq.* Cervini's manuscripts afterwards came to the Vatican Library ; see TIRABOSCHI, VII., I, 210.

[3] See Vol. XII. of this work, p. 546 *seq.*

[4] *Cf.* DOREZ, Le card. M. Cervini et l'imprimerie a Rome : Mél d'archéol. XII., 289 *seqq.* Dorez' monograph on Cervini, announced as long ago as 1895, which will deal with all the points mentioned with the author's characteristic thoroughness, has, unfortunately, not yet appeared. The essays in the Mél. d'archéol. (*supra*) and the Rev. d. Bibl., V., 14 *seq.* (L'exemplaire de Pline), 139 *seqq.*, 153 *seqq.* (Romolo Cervini), are precursors of this work.

Vatican Library shows with what zeal and understanding Cervini sought, not only to preserve and increase the treasures entrusted to him, but also to make them available for others.[1] Julius III., as an acknowledgment of his labours, confirmed him in his appointment, and further decided that it should be for life.[2] Cervini had rendered such important services in the Vatican Library, had shown such wide discrimination, and had displayed such great generosity, that he far surpassed all his predecessors. As he added to the collection of manuscripts in many different directions, including the acquisition of Oriental manuscripts, so did he increase the number of officials ; at the same time he looked after the preservation of damaged manuscripts. A decree of 1554 assured the opening of the library to scholars at fixed hours.[3] He repeatedly assisted the collection from his own means, and never content with all that he had done, unceasingly thought of ways of improving the " Vaticana," which he looked upon as the greatest treasure which the Apostolic See possessed.[4]

Cervini had as great a love for good books as he had a horror of those that were bad, and it is related that in the year 1541 the Cardinal bought up obscene books in order to have them burned.[5]

A man of such varied interests and wide erudition that even

---

[1] *Cf.* DOREZ in the Fasciculus Io. W. Clark dicatus, Cantabrigae, 1909, 142 *seqq.* The far-reaching wisdom of the Cardinal is shown by his plan of publishing the complete original documents of the Council of Trent, especially those of the Sessions ; see EHSES, Conc. Trid., V., xiii., xxvii.

[2] See Vol. XIII. of this work, p. 327 and Appendix No. 5 (Secret Archives of the Vatican).

[3] *Cf.* DOREZ in the Fasciculus, *loc. cit.*, 158 *seq.* ; MERCATI, Bibl. Apost., 38, 44, 57. According to TIRABOSCHI, VII., 1, 221 (Roman edition), Cervini also laid the foundations of the collection of antiquities connected with the Vatican Library ; *cf.* POLLIDORUS, 48.

[4] Letter to Card. Farnese of September 17, 1554, in the Mél. d'archéol., XII., 311.

[5] *Cf.* GORI, Arch. stor., III., 40.

such persons as Sangallo and Michael Angelo valued his attainments in the sphere of architecture and archæology,[1] Cervini by no means limited himself to the collection of books and manuscripts ; he had also gathered together an important collection of antiquities, ancient inscriptions and medals.[2] His house, which contained these treasures, was open to everyone who gave promise of accomplishing anything of note. The Cardinal especially loved to encourage youthful talent ; without any pretension or condescension, and without allowing the superiority of his own knowledge to appear, he would talk with young students about their work. He often looked through the work of young writers and found a publisher for them ; he was generous where he saw signs of earnest endeavour, not only by pointing out books and manuscripts, but also by giving valuable suggestions and advice. A whole number of scholars, with whom he was in communication, either personally or by letter, were indebted to the Cardinal for similar kindnesses. He took a special interest in the theological works of Sirleto and Seripando ; he encouraged Luigi Lippomano to publish the Lives of the Saints, and the learned Pier Vettori to prepare an improved edition of the works of Clement

[1] A. Cervini says : " Nell' architettura e cognizione delle cose antiche non fu a nessuno de' suoi tempi secondo e sanno ancora molti che oggi vivono che ne 'l San Gallo ne il Buonarrotti si sdegnava d'intendere il suo consiglio." Vita di Marcello II. (Ferrara Library) ; cf. also MERKLE, Il., xxv. Cervini was also a member of the Academy of Vitruvius, founded in 1542, and had entrusted Sangallo with the plans of his villa at Monte Amiata (see MÜNTZ, III., 109, 240). His knowledge of architecture tempted Cervini to mix himself up with the building of St. Peter's, an action which Michael Angelo resented in his abrupt way (see Vol. XIII. of this work, p. 334). In the time of Clement VII. Cervini was so devoted to the study of archaeology that he nearly lost his life in a visit to the subterranean ruins of the Thermae of Trajan ; see the notice in CONTELORIUS, Vita Marcelli II. (Secret Archives of the Vatican, XI., 48, p. 291).

[2] Cf. POLLIDORUS, 155 ; REUMONT, III., 2, 695 ; DOREZ, A. Eparque : Mél. d'archéol., XIII., 322.

of Alexandria, while he encouraged Niccolo Beni in an Italian translation of the celebrated Commonitorium of Vincent of Lerins. He also persuaded Annibale Caro and Pier Francesco Zeno to translate the Homilies of Gregory Nazianzen and John Damascene into Italian ; Genziano Erveto composed, at his instigation, a Latin translation of the Commentaries of Chrysostom on the Psalms. It was owing to Cervini that Onofrio Panvinio turned to the study of Christian antiquities and Church History. The indefatigable Cardinal must also be thanked for the translation of the four Gospels into Ethiopian, as well as for translations of Theodoret, Metaphrastes and others. Cervini shrank from no sacrifice to secure the publication of the Commentaries of Eustathius on Homer, while a proof of his versatility is to be found in the fact that he assisted Ippolito Salviani in the production of his work on fish.[1]

Among scholars Cervini loved most of all those of earnest character, who united true piety with sound knowledge. Very characteristic of him in this respect were his intimate relations with Guglielmo Sirleto. Cervini had always been most careful in choosing the members of his household ; he used to say that people should be just as particular about having good servants as they were about their own reputation and honour.[2] He showed in this respect that he not only preached reform but also practised it. He presented a strict manner of life in its most effective and attractive form ; to the purest morality, the truest piety, and the strictest orthodoxy, he united a large-hearted patronage of profane as well as of theological learning, and to a shrewd moderation he joined a burning zeal for reform. What hopes then, were not called forth by the elevation of such a man to the Chair of Peter ! The good and

---

[1] Cf. besides TIRABOSCHI, VII., 1, 30 seq. (Roman edition) and POLLIDORUS, 75 seqq., DOREZ in the Mél. d'archéol., XII., 291 seq. ; MERKLE, II., xxvii., seq., cxxiv. seq. ; MAI, Spiceleg., IX., xvi. ; Freiburger Kirchenlex. XI., 359 seq. ; MERCATI in the Theol. Revue, VIII. (1909), 61 seq. ; HEFNER, 32.

[2] See POLLIDORUS, 22.

pious members of the Curia were filled with joyful expectations, while the others trembled with fear.[1]

[1] As early as April 9, 1555, Ghisi writes : *Par che Roma poco si rallegri di questa elezione. Agost. Gonzaga, Bishop of Reggio, writes on April 12, 1555 : *It is hoped that Marcellus II. will be a good Pope for the Christian religion, but at the court they fear his strictness. (Gonzaga Archives, Mantua). See also Montesa in DRUFFEL, IV., 652 n. 3. The great joy of those who had the interests of the Church really at heart is made clear in numerous utterances ; cf. besides the extracts in POLLIDORUS, 112 seqq., the Corpo dipl. Port., VII., 385 ; letters in GATTICUS 332 n ; L. ALAMANNI, Canzone a Marcello II. in the collection of ATANAGI, II., Venezia, 1565, 172. Pollidorus mentions other poems (p. 113). Concerning the joy in Venice see Studi stor., XVII., 528. The nuncio at the imperial court, G. Muzzarelli, *wrote on April 22, 1555, to the Cardinals from Brussels : " Marcellus, velut alter Aaron," will look after the " afflicta et desolata ecclesia. Benedictus Deus, etc." (Lett. de' princ. XV., n. 71. Secret Archives of the Vatican).

CHAPTER II.

THE PONTIFICATE OF MARCELLUS II.

IT had seldom been the case that such unanimity of opinion had been shown concerning a new Pope as was the case with Marcellus II. The whole world was agreed that the most worthy and most suitable man had been chosen to steer the storm-tossed ship of the Church through the tempestuous waves of the times.[1] Even the French, to whom Cervini's election had not been agreeable, could not do enough to acknowledge his excellent qualities.[2] In consequence of this the result of the conclave was well received at the court of Henry II. The Emperor also forgot his former displeasure, and his representative in Rome expressed himself in terms of high praise of the new Pope.[3]

The loudest jubilation of all, however, came, as may easily be understood, from the representatives of Catholic reform, for they knew from the experience of many years, that Cervini was the right man, by his example as well as by his firmness, so tempered by mildness, to carry out the long desired reform of ecclesiastical conditions.[4] Never, wrote Seripando, had he thought that the choice would fall on a Cardinal whose principles were so inflexible, that they were far more likely to bar

---

[1] See, besides the testimony quoted *supra* p. 32, n. 1, MASIUS, Briefe, 200, the letter of congratulation of P. Manutius (Epist. I., 7). HOSII epist., II., 1025, and the letter of Seripando s.d. in the Miscell. Arm. 2, t. 60, p. 320 *seq.* (Secret Archives of the Vatican).

[2] *Cf.* RIBIER, II., 607; DRUFFEL, IV., 660 *seq.*

[3] *Cf.* BROWN, VI., 1, n. 62, 64; DRUFFEL, IV., 652 *seq.*

[4] *Cf.* the letter of Dionisio Atanagi in the Lett. de' princ., I., 185.

33

for him the way to the highest authority than to smooth it.
Seripando therefore saw in the elevation of Cervini a special
dispensation of divine grace, which had directed the votes to
the man who would " save Israel." He had prayed that a
Pope might arise who would remove from the ideas of Church,
Council, and Reform, the despicable interpretation which had
become attached to these otherwise beautiful words. His
hopes had now been realized and his desires fulfilled.[1]

The representatives of the Catholic reformation could now
look forward with confidence to the completion of the important and difficult task which Paul III. and Julius III. had
begun, but had left unfinished because, apart from other
considerations, so much of the worldly spirit of the Renaissance
had still lingered in their hearts. But now, the man whose
name had become proverbial for the work of ecclesiastical
renewal was absolutely free from any such thing.[2]

The members of the Sacred College were also unanimous in
declaring that if Cervini remained the man he had always been,
everything would turn out for the best.

A valuable and beautiful testimony to this effect is contained
in a letter from Cardinal Ercole Gonzaga which was addressed
to Ferrante Gonzaga immediately after the close of the conclave. The Cardinal had been an adherent of Este, and had
spent a sleepless night between the 9th and 10th of April, and
was dead tired when he wrote the letter. " If Cervini," he
said, "only remains as Pope what he has been as Cardinal, then
we may expect the greatest blessings for the Church ; on the
other hand, to those who wish to lead a dissolute life his election
must be most unwelcome. His pure manner of life is known
to everyone, as are his love of learning, his earnestness and his
dignity. It is but seldom that one has seen him merry ; as
soon as he sees or hears anything ridiculous he only smiles
faintly and passes it over in silence, with true Catonian gravity.

---

[1] Lett. de' princ., III., 187[b] seq.

[2] Cf. the *letter of G. Florimente to Marcellus II., dated Sessa,
April 15, 1555 (Castel S. Angelo, VIII., ii., p. 160. Secret
Arch. of the Vatican).

He never takes any pleasure in magnificent banquets, feasts or gay company ; he has always disapproved of the dissolute life of the clergy, hated the vagrant monks, punished all who were suspected of false doctrines, and always, under Paul III. as well as under Julius III., carried on the work of reform. He is the opposite of his predecessor, and God, in His mercy, has given him to the Church so that there may be a hope of abolishing countless abuses."[1] Everybody in Rome who knew the newly elected Pope at all intimately was of the same opinion.[2] The Florentine ambassador, Serristori, a dispassionate diplomatist, wrote as early as April 11th that although Marcellus II. would allow no interference on the part of secular persons in the affairs of the Church, and would be very slow in the bestowal of favours, he believed that in all other respects everyone would be contented, for his whole behaviour, to put it shortly, was that of a saint.[3]

Even on the first day of his pontificate Marcellus II. showed himself to be a true representative of the cause of Catholic Reform. As soon as the scrutiny was over, there followed his consecration as bishop, and then the coronation in St. Peter's, which ceremony he caused to be very much curtailed, in order that he might carry out the functions of Holy Week, which had already begun ; at the same time the unnecessary expenses of the coronation festivities were to be saved.

All the Renaissance Popes had allowed the celebrations which were customary at the coronation to develop into a carefully prepared feast which cost the large sum of from

----

[1] See the text (University Library, Bologna) in Appendix No. 6.

[2] See above all MASSARELLI (p. 255 *seq.*)

[3] *Credo bene che habbi a essere acerrimo defensore dell' autorità sua et cose ecclesiastiche et che chi vorrà stare bene seco, bisognerà che non metta mano nell' offitio suo, nè si impacci molto di benefitii et cose di chiesa, et in quanto alle gratie sia per andare assai più stretto che non hanno fatto molti dei suoi antecessori et nel resto credo che ogn' huomo da bene se n'harà da contentare. In sustantia il modo, l'apparentia et demostrationi sono come d'un santo (State Archives, Florence).

20,000 to 30,000 scudi. Marcellus rightly looked upon this as extravagance ; he wished to receive the tiara in apostolic simplicity, and without the usual ostentatious display. He even forbade the loud manifestations of joy, such as the thunder of the cannon from the Castle of St. Angelo, and the fire-works, so much loved by the Roman people, out of consideration for Holy Week. Half of the money that was saved he devoted to the needs of the Holy See, the other half to the relief of the poor, for whom the day of his elevation was to be a day of joy.[1]

The first actions of the Pope afforded further proof that he intended to avoid all outward pomp, and that he wished to do nothing which was not of benefit to the Church. He had already, as Cardinal, allowed no doubt to exist as to his zeal for reform ; he had always been convinced that this was a work which would allow of no delay, and now that he had been raised to the highest dignity, he wished to set to work at once. Deeds not words was to be the programme of his reign.[2]

Until now it had been the custom for the newly elected Pope, in the joy of his accession, to grant with lavish generosity all the requests of the members of the conclave for privileges and favours. When Marcellus II. was presented with these petitions for signature, he excused himself in his modest way, with the reply that he could in no way act contrary to the reform decrees, but that he had the intention, after careful considera-

---

[1] Besides MASSARELLI, 253, *cf.* Avanson's report in RIBIER, II., 606 ; L. LATINII Lucubrat., II., 29 ; the account in GORI, Arch., IV., 255 ; MASIUS, Briefe, 200 ; J. v. MEGGEN in the Archiv für schweiz. Ref. Gesch., III., 516 ; *Letter of Passini, dated Rome, April 10, 1555 (Gonzaga Archives, Mantua), and the detailed report of Polanco of April 16, 1555, to the Superior of the Society of Jesus, in the Cartas de S. Ignacio V., Madrid, 1889, 152 *seq.* This report, which SPONDANUS (ad. a. 1555, n. 5-7) seems to have had before him, appears in the following, simply quoted by Polanco. In POLANCO, Chron. V., 14 *seq.*, there are several additions.

[2] *Cf.* MASSARELLI, 254 *seq.*, 261 ; PANVINIO, Vita Marcelli II ; POLLIDORUS. 115.

tion, of showing himself benevolent in all that was right. The same answer was given to the Cardinals, the conclavists, and indeed to his most intimate friends. He would not sign a single petition, but promised to consider everything carefully. When a very prominent personage handed the Pope paper and pen and urged him vehemently to confirm by his signature several concessions, Marcellus replied : " If what you ask is just, you will receive it after I have thought it over, if, however, it is not, you will neither receive it now nor in the future."[1]

The Pope received the congratulations seriously and sedately. When someone wished him long life, he answered : "If my life should prove useful to the Church of God, may He preserve it, if not, then I wish for a short life, so as not to increase the number of my sins."[2] Marcellus made use of the congratulations of the Cardinals to work for reform. Worthy members of the Sacred College, if they were young, like Nobili, were, he said encouragingly, to continue in the good path they had already entered on, while he reminded the worldly Cardinals, with paternal earnestness, of their duties ; the unworthy Cardinal del Monte was sharply reproved for his previous conduct, and Marcellus warned him that he would do everything in his power to force him to reform his life.[3]

The Pope also admonished the members of his household to preserve a virtuous and modest demeanour ; they must not assume airs of superiority because they were now servants of the Pope, and at the least transgression he would dismiss them. There would, moreover, be no change in the arrangements of his household for the time being. Marcellus wished to examine the financial position of the Holy See before he embarked upon further expenditure. As this investigation proved most unsatisfactory, he resolved to organize his household in the

---

[1] See POLANCO, 155 *seq.* ; Avanson in RIBIER, II., 608 *seq.* and the letters of U. Gozzadini, dated Rome, April 10 and 24, 1555 (State Archives, Bologna).

[2] POLANCO, 156.

[3] See in Appendix No. 6 the *letter of Card. E. Gonzaga of April 10, 1555 (University Library, Bologna).

simplest manner ; very few new officials were appointed, and
those already in office were kept with such simplicity and
economy that many complained of hardships. According to
Massarelli, the following arrangements were decided upon for
the maintenance of the officials : everyone, without regard to
their position or rank, must have only one attendant (except a
few higher officials, who were allowed two), they received every
day a certain quantity of wine and bread. Besides this, the
officials of the first class were paid a seventh part, those of the
second class a sixteenth part, and those of the third class a
thirty-fifth part of a gold florin. Barley was to be given to no
one, and hay only to a very few, and at most for two horses.
The common kitchen was done away with, as was the supply
of salt, oil, vinegar, barley and wood, which had hitherto been
customary. The Pope's table also was to be in no way different from what it had been while he was a Cardinal, when he
had been distinguished for its simplicity. Luxury, Marcellus
was accustomed to say, was a source of great evils, and even
of the worst. Gold plate, which had hitherto been customary,
was no longer to appear at his table, while instead of the silver
kitchen utensils he ordered that copper ones should be procured. He was anxious to cut down expenses in every way,
in order to be able to pay the debts of the Holy See by his
economies. That he might be successful in doing so, he
declared that he would avoid war and all unnecessary building,
as well as the bestowal of princely revenues on his relatives.
In his humility he dreaded the temptations which had assailed
even the Saints when they had reached the height of power, and
had, in the case of many of his predecessors, rendered their
best intentions quite futile ; he well knew, as he told Cardinal
Gonzaga, that to be slow in speech and active in works was
the wisest course, although he, nevertheless, made many
promises,so that his word might from the beginning be associa-
ated with the right course and that the shame of breaking his
promises might save him from any vacillation.[1]

[1] Besides MASSARELLI, 261 *seq.*, see also POLANCO, 153 *seq.*, as
well as Chron., V., 14 *seq.*, and especially PANVINIO, Vita Marcelli

It was not in words alone, however, but in deeds also, that he sought to carry his resolutions into effect. Angelo Massarelli was summoned to the Pope's presence as early as April 11th and was commissioned to look out all the documents relating to reform which had been drawn up during the pontificate of Julius III, and especially the recent Bull concerning the conclave ; these were to be once more thoroughly examined, and to this end Massarelli was to put himself at once into communication with Cardinal Puteo. Two days later Massarelli again received orders to bring to the Pope Cardinal Puteo's opinion, as well as that of Cardinals Madruzzo and Gonzaga, who were just about to set out on a journey, for the Bull was to be published as soon as possible.[1] It was also made known during the first days of the pontificate that Marcellus II. intended to require all bishops to fulfil their duty of residence, and many of them were already preparing to return to their dioceses after Easter.[2] The Dataria was informed by the Pope that he would allow no further compositions except in the case of fines.[3] The Jews and prostitutes were to be ban-

II. Antonio Lorenzini, who was highly valued by the Pope (see Cocciano in DRUFFEL, IV., 662), became "Maestro di Camera." Ant. Helius (Elio) Bishop of Pola, became his first secretary, and under him, Aug. Masserelli ; Serristori announces these appointments in his *letter of April 13, 1555 (State Archives, Florence). P. P. Gualterius was confirmed as secretary of Latin letters (see MERKLE, II., xxxviii.). Sirleto became "referendario," Commendone was placed among the officers of the household, and P. Vettori was also summoned to Rome. POLLIDORUS, 120.

[1] MASSARELLI, 256 seq. ; cf. the *letter of A. Gonzaga to the governor of Mantua, dated Rome, April 12, 1555 (Gonzaga Archives, Mantua).

[2] *Cf. the *letter of Card. Gonzaga of April 10, 1555 (University Library, Bologna), and Lett. de' princ., III., 235.

[3] *Questa sera ho inteso che ha imposto al Datario che non vuole che pigli compositione alcuna salvo di quelle cose dove fussi colpa. Serristori's report of April 11, 1555 (State Archives Florence).

ished to a corner of the city on the other side of the Tiber, and
the Jews were also to wear a yellow hat ; those of the prostitutes who were married would have to return to their husbands
or be sent to a convent. Marcellus also spoke of placing the
crime of sodomy under the Inquisition.[1] That still further
reform regulations were to be expected could be drawn from
the fact that Cardinal Carafa had apartments assigned to him
in the Vatican.[2] The impression that was made by all this
was so deep that many at once changed their manner of life of
their own accord, without waiting for the appearance of any
regulations,[3] which was certainly the best and most enduring
kind of reform.

Marcellus took part in the ceremonies of Holy Week with
the greatest devotion ; people were astonished to see that he
always went on foot to St. Peter's and to the chapel in the
Vatican where he said mass with great fervour.[4] After the
function on Good Friday (April 12th) the Pope made it clear
that he also proposed a reform in church music ; he had the
singers of the choir summoned to his presence and ordered them
to be careful in future that the music was suitable to a day of
mourning and was not of a joyful, noisy character ; he also
required of them such a performance of the vocal music that
the words could be understood.[5]

On Easter Sunday the Pope celebrated High Mass in St.
Peter's, at which he distributed Holy Communion to the Cardinals and other prominent persons ; then followed the be-

---

[1] POLANCO, Chron., V., 14 seq.

[2] *Al card. S. Agnolo ha dato in palazzo le stantie di torre
Borgia, dove stava il s. Baldovino, et al Teatino quelle di guard-
arobba, dove stava il card. di Monte. Serristori on April 13, 1555
(State Archives, Florence).

[3] Cf. the letter of Raverta in the Archiv für schweiz. Ref.-
Gesch., III., 518.

[4] POLANCO, 154.

[5] MASSARELLI, 256 seq. This testimony proves that in the
view which the learned writer of the essay " Die Kirchenmusik
und das Tridentinische Konzil " (Histor. polit. Bl., XLII.,
895 seq.) combats, there is nevertheless a grain of truth.

stowal of the solemn blessing. It had hitherto been the custom on this occasion that coins should be thrown among the assembled crowds, but when one of the reform party happened to remark that it would be more pleasing to God if this money were to be used for charitable works or given to the poor, than that the people should scramble for it and many be disappointed, the Pope at once approved of the suggestion and acted upon it. On the same day he drew the attention of the bishops to the rule that they should have spiritual reading at their tables, a regulation that was hardly anywhere observed. He was himself the first to carry out this rule, and after the reading he introduced spiritual disputations.[1]

On the Monday and Tuesday of Easter week (April 15th and 16th) Massarelli received orders to obtain the opinions of Cardinals Carafa, Morone, Truchsess, Medici, Mignanelli, Saraceni, Cicada, and Bertano with regard to the new conclave Bull, for the Pope thought that the more this document was discussed the better it would prove.[2]

The ideal personality of the new Pope had made such an impression on the Romans that, as an ambassador reports, they laid down their arms at once after his election.[3] People were exceedingly anxious to see how Marcellus would behave towards his numerous relations. The recollection of the excesses of the Renaissance Popes was still so vivid that many feared lest the love of his own flesh and blood, as well as the great number of his relatives, should lead the Pope away from the true path.[4] These fears were increased when Marcellus, clearly for the sake of his personal safety, appointed two members of his family to important positions. Giovan Battista Cervini was made governor of the Castle of St. Angelo and Biagio Cervini captain of the Vatican guard.[5] The idea that

[1] See POLANCO, 154; MASSARELLI, 257.

[2] MASSARELLI, 257.

[3] Second *letter of U. Gozzadini, dated Rome, April 10, 1555 (State Archives, Bologna).

[4] POLANCO, 154.

[5] MASSARELLI, 258. PAGLIUCCHI, Castellani, 127. Concerning G. B. Cervini cf. BUSCHBELL in the Histor. Jahrb., XXI., 423 seq.

he was about to introduce a régime of nepotism was, however,
completely erroneous. Marcellus knew only too well the
disastrous effect of such weakness in the case of many of his
predecessors ; as Cardinal he had repeatedly admonished
Paul III. and Julius III. as to the evils of nepotism, and he
now wished all the more to apply in his own case the advice
he had given to others. He therefore declared`from the first
that he would not allow his brother Alessandro to come to
Rome ; it was his desire, he said, that he should remain at home
and live there, not as a great noble, but as a simple citizen, as
he had hitherto done.[1] He wrote to Montepulciano that
neither Alessandro nor any others of his relatives should come
to Rome under the pain of his severe displeasure.[2] When a son
of one of his sisters, then in Orvieto, in spite of this prohibition,
appeared in the Eternal City in order to congratulate the Pope,
he was informed that he might return home, as no audience
would be given him.[3] The two youthful nephews of the Pope,
Ricciardo and Erennio Cervini, the sons of Alessandro, who had
till this time been very strictly brought up in Rome by Sirleto,
and who gave promise of much talent, had no hopes of undue
preferment. In answer to the question whether they should
now take up their residence in the Vatican, the Pope answered :
" What have they to do with the Apostolic palace ? Have
they inherited it ? " Nor would he grant them the smallest
benefice until they had attained the age required by the
Church, and they were obliged to live in the same modest and
retired way as before, appointing no new servants and receiving
no visits. It troubled the Pope little that people reproached
him with being too strict, and even harsh with his family ;
when he learned that these two nephews had allowed themselves to be so far led astray as to put on purple hose and
silken mantles, he at once ordered these to be laid aside. In

[1] Legaz. di Serristori, 350.
[2] See Lett. de' princ., III., 235 ; POLANCO, 154 *seq.* ; MAS-
SARELLI, 261.
[3] *Letter of Serristori of April 13, 1555 (State Archives,
Florence).

order to render all nepotism impossible, both now and in the future, Marcellus resolved on drawing up a Bull which should make any bestowal of church property on relations liable to the severest penalties. Since Adrian VI. no Pope had shown such a contempt of the ties of blood, and it was only on the representation of the Cardinals that several of the Cervini family who were in really necessitous circumstances received a little help, and this only after their worthiness had been carefully looked into. Merit alone, and not the ties of blood, was to turn the scales in their favour.[1]

The Pope gave a proof of the manner in which he intended to administer justice in Rome on the very first day of his pontificate. The Spanish ambassador had begged mercy for a murderer of high rank, but Marcellus refused this with great decisiveness, remarking that he did not wish to inaugurate his reign with the pardon of a murderer. Strict orders were given to the Presidents of the civil and criminal courts that, in the administration of justice, they were to allow themselves to be influenced by no considerations whatever, even in the case of relatives of the Pope, and that a strict account of their proceedings would be required of them. To the Auditors who came to pay their respects, in accordance with the old custom, the Pope said that in future such forms of politeness were unnecessary, and that they would do much better to devote themselves to their business.[2]

This attitude had such an effect that one writer reports that the appearance of the city was quite changed, and that one might now hope that justice would be the rule instead of favour.[3] Marcellus II. at once turned his attention to the wishes and needs of the Roman people. In order that he might listen to all complaints, he granted audience to everyone, even the least important, although the pressure of business was

[1] *Cf.* POLANCO, 155; Lett. de' princ., III., 235; Legaz. di Serristori, 350; MASSARELLI, 261.

[2] *Cf.* POLANCO, 155; PANVINIO, Vita Marcelli, II.

[3] POLANCO, 155. *Cf.* also the *letter of Filippo Zoboli to A. Cervini, dated Rome, April 13, 1555, and that of Ottavio Graccho to A. Cervini, dated Rome, April 23, 1555 (Carte Cerv. 52, State Archives, Florence).

crushing in the first days of his reign. Five Cardinals, Carafa, Carpi, Morone, Cicada, and Sforza di Santa Fiora, the Camerlengo, were commissioned to see that Rome was supplied with grain and other provisions, and to deliberate about a mitigation of the taxes.[1] After such beginnings, it can easily be understood that the complete abolition of all the abuses which had crept into the government of the States of the Church was looked for from such a " saintly Pope."[2] As the money which he saved, however, was insufficient to cover the requirements of the Holy See and to pay off its heavy debts, Marcellus was unfortunately obliged to revive the so-called " Sussidio " which had been introduced by Paul III.   He ordered that the tax on the Jews, the so-called " twentieth " should be devoted to the support of the poorer Cardinals.[3]

[1] Cf. MASSARELLI, 258 ; Lett. de' princ., I., 185. Two *briefs to the Emperor and the nuncio Muzzarelli, dated Rome, April 26, 1555, are concerned with the alleviation of the scarcity of corn in Rome by procuring grain from Sicily (Arm. 44, t. 6, n. 94, 95. Secret Archives of the Vatican). Concerning the audiences, Serristori reports on April 11 : *Hieri stette tutto il giorno fra la sala di Constantino et la prima camera che gl' è canto a porte aperta, dove ciascuna persona di qualunque qualità ancorche minima gli possete parlare che furono infinite ; on April 13 he says : *Ha detto volere due volte la settimana dare audientia publica in modo che qual si vogli minima persona gli possa parlare (State Archives, Florence).

[2] *Poiche non ho che dire molto a V.V.S.S. con questo spazzo dirò solo della grande aspettatione nella quale si sta per il buon nome et l'ottima fama sparta ch'ogni giorno più augmenta con gli effetti della bontà, benignità, clementia, virtu, justitia, et santità di N.S.re, dalle quale cose tutte si puo sperare ch'ogni abuso, mala introduttione posta nelle città del stato ecclesiastico per qual si voglia causa et accidente sia per riformarsi et ridursi ad una meta et ordine ottimamente salutifero et satisfattorio a tutti li sudditi di S.B.ne. U. Gozzadini on April 20, 1555 (State Archives, Bologna).

[3] See PANVINIO, Vita Marcelli, II., who remarks : " Sedis enim Apostolicae stabiles redditus sunt CL millia aureorum, ex hoc subsidio reliqui et triginta millia qui ex censibus hauriuntur." Concerning the " Sussidio " of Paul III., cf. Vol. XI., of this work, p. 262.

As far as the attitude of Marcellus II. towards great political questions is concerned, the Imperial ambassador at once reported that the Pope would take no further part in them than to admonish the Christian princes to peace.[1] Marcellus himself spoke to the ambassadors in this sense,[2] and the briefs in which he announced his election to the Emperor, the King of France and the other Christian princes, were to the same effect.[3] He exhorted the nuncio in France, and Pole, the legate in England, to do everything in their power for the preservation of peace.[4] In the question of Siena, which was daily becoming more acute, he endeavoured to mediate between the two parties. He refused to grant the request of the besieged for help against the Duke of Florence and the Imperialists, and explained that as the common father of all Christian nations it was impossible for him to take any side, still less could he allow himself to be mixed up with any warlike plans. The Sienese should not refuse to accept easy terms of surrender, for necessity knows no law. The Pope then exhorted Duke Cosimo in several letters to show leniency. When Siena fell, without any rioting or plundering, the satisfaction of the Pope was very great.[5]

[1] See the letters of April 11 and 19, 1555, in DRUFFEL, IV., 652.

[2] *Cf.* RIBIER, II., 606.

[3] See the **Letters to Charles V., Henry II., Philip II., and Mary (Secret Archives of the Vatican).

[4] The *injunction to the French nuncio (in Italian), dated April 16, 1555, contains the admonition : " batter a la porta de la pace finche ci sia aperta," and always to harp upon this point and to pray and have prayers said for peace. (Arm 44, t. 6, p. 213. Secret Archives of the Vatican). Concerning Pole see PIEPER, 73, and *infra*, cap.

[5] Besides Serristori's letter of April 14 (Legaz. di Serristori 351), *cf.* his *Report of April 25, 1555 (State Archives, Florence) See also the brief to Cosimo I. of April 19, 1555, in RAYNALDUS 1555, n. 19. Marcellus II., by the *brief of April 16, 1555 (Arm 44, t. 4, n. 79) recommended his old friend Bart. Cavalcant to the Duke of Florence (concerning its success see the Att Mod., IV., 145) ; t. 4, n. 82, *brief for Manlio Marignani of Apri 19 ; warm commendation of Siena. See also ADRIANI, XII. POLLIDORUS, 118.

It is characteristic of the Pope's love of peace and his high ideals that the plan of entirely doing away with the Swiss Guard is attributed to him. He repeatedly said that many Christian princes are better protected against their enemies by the sign of the Cross than by arms, and that the Vicar of Christ requires no swords for his defence ; it would be better, he said, if such a misfortune were to occur, that he should be murdered by wicked men than that he should give an unseemly example to the Christian world. Panvinio, who records this remark, also reports an example of the strict neutrality of Marcellus II. Cardinal Madruzzo was very desirous of obtaining the legation of Bologna ; the Pope refused this, as the Cardinal was a devoted adherent of the Emperor, and an enemy of the French. Instead of granting him his request, he allowed him, on the advice of Cardinal Gonzaga, ten thousand ducats to indemnify him for his expenses during the Council ; the legation would not, in two years, have brought him a greater sum.[1]

It is worthy of note that Marcellus united to his efforts to observe neutrality, as being more advantageous to the cause of reform, the greatest exertions for the promotion of ecclesiastical interests. He begged and exhorted the Emperor as well as the King of France to assist his efforts for reform on their part, by proposing only worthy and suitable candidates for bishoprics, and by seeing that the duty of residence was duly observed.[2]

Marcellus II. showed great strictness with regard to all

[1] PANVINIO, Vita Marcelli, II. It seems doubtful whether Marcellus really entertained the plan about the Swiss, as the captain of the guard, J. v. Meggen, reports on April 20, 1555, that the Pope had said to him that they were to serve as before ; see Archiv für schweiz. Ref-Gesch., III., 517.

[2] The laconic observation of Serristori in his letter of April 14, 1555 (Legaz. di Serristori, 350 seq.) is supplemented by his *report of April 22, 1555, in which he says : " Intendo come il Papa ha mandato il Montemerlo (cf. CARO-FARNESE, Lettere, II., 161 seq.) in Francia con un breve al Rè per far complimenti et per pregarlo volere ordinare che i vescovi che sono in quel regno vadino a le loro chiese, et quanto ai car[ll] harà piacere che S.M.[tà] mandi a Roma, dove è la stantia loro, pur in questo non le la

appointments to spiritual offices, declaring from the very first, quite clearly and openly, that he would favour no one except on the sole ground of merit. A very characteristic example of this is quoted. When Giovan Battista Cervini asked the Pope for a parish which had become vacant in the Spanish diocese of Cuenca, he was refused with contumely, and the parish was conferred on a Spaniard who had been born there, and who had never attempted to obtain it, and indeed, had never even thought of it.[1] The members of the Curia, meanwhile, became very much depressed ; everything was sad, gloomy and disheartening, writes Massarelli in his diary, while a few lines later he says that all in Rome are in great sorrow, for the relations of the Pope, as well as his intimate friends, have recognised that they have little or nothing to hope for from him. Many members of the Curia, indeed, feared the Pope's reform measures so much that they sold the offices which they had bought at a high price for a mere trifle.[2]

The thoughts of the Pope were not only occupied with plans of reform of all kinds, but he also entertained the idea of again summoning the Council. He remarked that his predecessors had been wrongly informed that reform would lessen the esteem in which the Papacy was held, and that he was of opinion that it could only gain by it. The best way, moreover, of closing the mouths of the Lutherans was by reform ; he would, therefore, not allow himself to be turned aside by anything, and would, above all, require from those who had the care of souls, that they should fulfil their duty of residence and keep themselves free from the profane interests of the world.[3]

In the carrying out of his plans for reform, Marcellus thought

vuol gravare più che tanto, volendo che lei se ne sodisfaccia et che S.M.^{tà} non habbi riguardo all'aspettarsi a S.S.^{tà} la dispositione dei benefitii de' car^{li} che morissino in questa corte, perchè occorrendo il caso ne provederebbe secondo la volontà di S.M.^{tà} Christ^{ma}, pure che la proponessi persona idonea et conveniente " (State Archives, Florence).

[1] See MASSARELLI, 261 seq.

[2] Ibid. 262.

[3] Cf. POLLIDORUS, 122.

above all of making use of that new Order, which had already
spread so far, and which was so closely united with the Holy
See, the Jesuits. Cervini's connection with them was of long
standing. He loved the disciples of his friend, Ignatius of
Loyola, because he had known them in Rome in their early
days, because he had become convinced at Trent of their zeal
for reform, and because, as Polanco says, he knew what God
had effected by their means, even as far away as the Indies.
Jesuits had frequently been his confessors, and only a short
time before he arrived in Rome for the conclave he had been
to confession to the rector of the Jesuit college in Loreto, had
said mass there and had given communion with his own hands
to the fathers, and encouraged them to advance in virtue.
When Ignatius visited the new Pope with another father he
received a warm welcome ; Marcellus embraced them both
and gave them the kiss of peace. Then he discussed plans
of reform with Ignatius, expressing at the same time the wish
that two priests of the Society of Jesus should take up their
residence in the Vatican, so that he could always have the
benefit of their advice. In this audience the Pope expressly
bade the General of the Order always to tell him quite freely
anything he considered advantageous for the glory of God.[1]

While the reputation of Marcellus II.[2] for love of duty and
holiness was spreading all over Christendom,[3] and ever raising
greater hopes, the friends of reform in Rome were becoming
anxious about the life of the Pope.

[1] See POLANCO, 157. The following are the words, as reported
by later writers, which Marcellus is supposed to have addressed
to Ignatius : Tu milites collige et bello tuos instrue, nos utemur
(CIACONIUS, III., 804). which GOTHEIN (Ignatius, 473 seq.) has
not accepted. Gothein always puts Marcellus III.

[2] A. Gonzaga *writes from Rome to the governor of Mantua
on April 17, 1555 : " Dio laudato poiche noi havemo un bono
et santissimo pastore." (Gonzaga Archives, Mantua). U. Gozzadini also describes Marcellus II. as " pontefice santo " in a
letter of April 20, 1555 (State Archives, Bologna).

[3] Cf. besides the testimony in POLLIDORUS, 133, OLDECOP,
Chronik, 382 seq.

The health of Marcellus II. had been very delicate from his earliest years, and his weak body had repeatedly shown signs of not being able to endure the hardships which he demanded of it. It was easy to see in the slight and wasted figure with the pale and serious countenance, framed by a long black beard, how weak was the bodily frame in which this strong spirit had its dwelling.[1] The labours of his office and his frequent severe illnesses had brought Cardinal Cervini to the brink of the grave. During the conclave which resulted in the election of Julius III., he was already in a very suffering state, and in May, 1550, he became so seriously ill that his death was looked upon as certain. A long stay amid his native mountains restored him, but his strength was permanently impaired.[2] There was, therefore, grave danger lest the strong emotions and the great physical and mental exertions which his elevation to the Papacy made inevitable, should wear out his weak and delicate body. Marcellus was repeatedly urged to preserve his strength and to take care of his health. The Pope answered Cardinal

---

[1] *Cf.* the remarks in the *letter of E. Gonzaga of April 10, 1555 (University Library, Bologna; see Appendix No. 6), and in Lett. de' princ., III., 234[b]. A splendid portrait by Pontormo (Borghese Gallery, Rome, No. 408) shows Cardinal Cervini seated at a table with an open book before him, very serious, and with penetrating eyes (see BURCKHARDT, Beitrage, 332). A second portrait of him as a Cardinal is preserved in the Vatican Library. The face, which is full of expression, shows that the picture belongs to his earlier years. On his medal as Pope, Marcellus appears as bald (MÜNTZ, III., 240). The portrait of Marcellus by Vasari was in the cathedral at Naples (see CIACONIUS, III., 808; POLLIDORUS, 152). Another portrait was in the council chamber of the castle at Caprarola. A marble statue in the cathedral at Siena shows the Pope seated in the act of blessing. The beautiful seal of Cardinal Cervini is reproduced by PASINI FRASSONI, 37. Medals (see CIACONIUS, III., 808; VENUTI, 99 *seq.*) and coins of Marcellus II. (*cf.* SERAFINI, 263 *seq.*) are exceedingly rare.

[2] *Cf.* MASSARELLI, 10, 12, 44, 71 *seq.*, 172, 174; Lett. de' princ., I., 185.

Sforza, who had taken the liberty of making such representations to him, in the following terms : " From the day on
which I took upon myself the charge of the whole Christian
Church, I consecrated myself entirely to the flock of Christ.
The high priesthood involves the highest obligations ; it is no
dignity and sovereign authority, but a burden and a servi-
tude."[1]

Marcellus II. not only felt exceedingly the burden of affairs,
but also the responsibility which his high office brought with it.
Weighed down by such thoughts, the zealous and earnest Head
of the Church cried out that he did not understand how a man
who held this highest of offices could save his soul. He repeatedly quoted the words of Adrian IV. that no one was more
to be pitied than the Pope, no one more miserable ; the Papal
throne was filled with thorns and stings, the joy of a Pope's
life was bitterness, and the weight of the tiara so great that it
would crush the strongest shoulders.[2] It was especially his
efforts for the reform of the clergy, with which Marcellus was
occupied day and night, under which his frail body threatened
to succumb. He had to contend with obvious weakness even
in the first days of his reign, but he nevertheless took part in
the long ceremonies of Holy Week, observing with his usual
conscientiousness the strict fasts and unceasingly granting
audiences. Even as soon as Maundy Thursday, April 11th,
when he undertook the ceremony of the washing of the feet,
he was observed to be suddenly overcome with a feverish
trembling and to change colour.[3] In spite of this he in no
way spared himself on the following days, but took part in all
the services of the Church, and celebrated the High Mass on
Easter Sunday, while working all the time on questions of
reform. On April 18th he blessed the Agnus Dei in the Hall of

[1] POLLIDORUS, 131.

[2] See PANVINIO, Vita Marcelli II.

[3] Cf. the report of Jacobus Riballus to A. Cervini about the
mortal illness of Marcellus II. in POLLIDORUS, 134 seq. Ant.
Lorenzini *reported on April 13, 1555, to A. Cervini that the
Pope was so " affannato che è una compassione a vederlo. "(Carte
Cerv. 52, State Archives, Florence).

Constantine, but on the 19th he felt himself so exhausted and ill that on the 20th he could not undertake the ceremony of their distribution.[1] He was also obliged, on the advice of his doctors, to cease giving the audiences of which he had been so lavish. He was now suffering from a violent catarrh and cough, to which was soon added a fever. On April 21st blood-letting seemed to afford him some relief,[2] but as soon as he felt better he would take no rest, although the fever and catarrh had not left him, for the duties of his office, as Massarelli said, occupied him day and night. On April 25th he had Massarelli summoned and commissioned him to inform Cardinals Puteo and Cicada that it was the Pope's wish that they should, during his illness, make a further examination of all the reform work which had been prepared under Julius III., so that he might be able to conclude the matter with them on his recovery. In the matter of the Signatura, the Pope, on the following day, impressed on the officials that the reform regulations which he had given them were to be observed most exactly.[3]

The doctors had forbidden the granting of audiences, but Marcellus could not refrain from occupying himself with urgent matters. He hoped to move in a short time to the palace of S. Marco and to be completely cured by the change of air.[4] On the 27th his condition was again considerably worse, and the doctors forbade all serious work ;[5] they did not yet think of

[1] See MASSARELLI, 258.

[2] See the detailed *report of U. Gozzadini of April 22, 1555 (State Archives, Bologna) and *that of A. Lorenzini of April 20, 1555 (State Archives, Florence).

[3] See MASSARELLI, 259; cf. also the *report of Gozzadini of April 24, 1555 (State Archives, Bologna) ; the *letter of O. Gracchi of April 23, 1555 (see supra p. 43, n. 3) ; SCHWEITZER, Zur Gesch. der Reform, 65.

[4] Cf. the *letters of A. Lorenzini of April 22 and 24, 1555, loc. cit. the *report of Serristori of April 25, 1555 (State Archives, Florence) concerning the physicians of Marcellus II. see MARINI, I., 418 seq.

[5] *Letter of U. Gozzadini of April 27, 1555 (State Archives, Bologna).

danger, nor did the Pope himself, though he felt very unwell
and was much troubled by the catarrh,[1] but in consequence of
pressing business he soon again completely neglected his health.
On April 29th he not only received the Dukes of Urbino and
Ferrara, who had come to Rome to pay homage, but also
Cardinals Farnese, Guise, Este and Sforza, and other persons,
among them Massarelli, upon whom he enjoined the reform of
the Penitentiary.[2] The exertions of this day, during which
Marcellus had given audiences until evening,[3] were too great.
On April 30th an unusual feeling of weakness overcame him
while he was at work, so he took a restorative and lay down.
As he was sleeping peacefully the doctors thought that the
danger was over, but at last the long sleep made the Pope's
attendants anxious, and they sought to revive him, at first with
mild measures but afterwards by stronger ones, but in vain.
A stroke of apoplexy had deprived him of consciousness. In
the evening Marcellus came to himself, but his condition re-

[1] *Per ancora il Papa non si truova libero dal catarro, ma
l'hanno atteso a purgare in modo, che sperano fra quattro o
sei giorni si habbi esser fuori, e poter dare audientia. Dicono
bene che si sente debole et stracco et in tutto senza febre et si
è di poi inteso che il mal suo è stato molto maggiore di quel che
si è detto. Piaccia a N.S.re Dio renderli l'intera salute la quale
recuperata che harà intendo che vuol spedire all' Impre et al
Re d'Inghilterra il signor Hiermo da Coreggio per rallegrarsi con
quelle Mtà dell' assuntione sua et per fare altri complimenti . . .
Serristori on April 27, 1555 (State Archives, Florence).

[2] MASSARELLI, 260. Lett. de' princ., I., 187. CARO-FARNESE,
Lett., II., 180. Cardinal A. Farnese had arrived in Rome on
April 16, 1555, and it was expected that he would play an im-
portant part in affairs of state (cf. Lett. de' princ., I., 185, and the
*letter of Ipp. Capilupi of April 16, 1555, in Gonzaga Archives,
Mantua). According to Avanson, Marcellus offered him the post
of secretary of state, which, however, Farnese refused (see
RIBIER, II., 608). Several authorities, including J. v. Meggen
(Archiv für schweiz. Ref.-Gesch., III., 517), place the audience
of the Duke of Urbino on April 28, thus differing from Massarelli.

[3] See the *Memorie* of Jacobo delli Herculani in the Cod. Gesuit.
170, p. 796 of the Vittoria Emanuele Library, Rome.

mained hopeless, and in the early morning of May 1st, he gave up his noble soul to God.[1]

The paralysing effect which the sudden death of this admirable Pope had on his contemporaries is reflected in numerous characteristic utterances. People could not understand why such a man, from whom the much needed reformation was confidently to be expected, should only have had a reign of twenty-two days, during which he had not enjoyed good health for more than ten. Panvinio applied to him the words spoken by Virgil of another Marcellus " Fate wished only to show him."[2] Seripando saw in the sudden calling away of Marcellus an indication that God did not mean to bring about the reformation of His Church by means of human help, but by His own divine power, at a time and by means of which mortal men knew nothing.[3] Another contemporary saw in the death of the Pope a divine punishment for the wickedness of the age, which was so great that God would not allow the good to live long in it.[4] " Oh, unhappy Pope, who hast hardly touched the tiara," writes Massarelli in his diary, " unhappy we, his servants, who have been so soon robbed of so admirable a

---

[1] Besides MASSARELLI, 260, cf. J. Riballus loc. cit. ; Cocciano in DRUFFEL, IV. 668 seq. ; Lett. de' princ., I., 187 ; the two *letters of U. Gozzadini of April 30, 1555 (State Archives, Bologna); the *reports of Camillo Titio and Serristori of April 30, 1555 (State Archives, Florence ; ibid. *letter of A. Lorenzini of May 1, 1555) and Avanson's report in RIBIER, II., 609. The hour of the Pope's death, " hora 7½ noctis " (FIRMANUS, 508 and most of the reports of the ambassadors), is expressed by J. v. Meggen after the German fashion, " dritthald stunden vor tag " (Archiv für schweiz. Ref-Gesch., III., 517). The supposition that Marcellus II. was poisoned is groundless (DRUFFEL, IV., 679. OLDE-COP, 383) ; see POLLIDORUS, 137.

[2] In the *correspondence of Olaus Magnus with Cardinal Madruzzo there is an **account of the death of Marcellus II. with the remark : " qui poterit dicere : dum adhuc ordirer succidit me " (Vice-regal Archives, Innsbruck).

[3] Lett. de' princ., III., 189.

[4] Lat. Latinius in POLLIDORUS, 145.

master, unhappy all Christians, who justly expected from such
a holy Pope wonderful and great things for the honour of God ;
the restoration of the authority and majesty of the Apostolic
See, the reform, splendour and unity of the Catholic Church,
the spread of the faith, the furtherance of everything that is
good.   Unhappy century, that was not permitted to rejoice
over such a shepherd, nor, indeed, even to see him ! "[1]   The
nuncio at the court of the Emperor describes the deep sorrow
which Charles V. experienced at the news of the death of the
Pope.   The hopes which were buried with him in the grave
had been founded on his well-known holiness and his practical
talents, and had been strengthened at the beginning of his
pontificate by his zeal for the advancement of God's service
and the furtherance of morality.[2]

Marcellus II. had lived in apostolic simplicity, and so was he
buried.   The Canons of St. Peter's bore his body into the
basilica,[3] where a grave had been made ready for him, so modest
that the poet Faustus Sabaeus could write :

Non ut Pontificem Summum, Sanctumque decebat
MARCELLE ; indigno conderis hoc tumulo ;
Parce ; ubicumque iaces, semper celebrabere : honorat
Non tumulus cinerem, sed cinis ipse locum.[4]

---

[1] MASSARELLI, 260.   Greek distichs on the death of Marcellus
II. in the Cod. Ottob. gr., 228, p. 76-82.   Vatican Library.

[2] See the beautiful *letter in Appendix No. 8 (Secret Archives
of the, Vatican).   Cf. also the letter of the Swiss nuncio Raverta
in the Archiv für schweiz. Ref-Gesch., III., 518 ; REINHARDT,
VIII. ; CARO-FARNESE, Lett., II., 179, 180, 188 ; POLLIDORUS,
144 seq.

[3] Cf. MASSARELLI, 260 ; FIRMANUS, 508 ; PANVINIO, Vita
Marcelli II. ; POLLIDORUS, 160 seq.   The following inscription
was put up in the town hall of Montepulciano : Marcello II.
Cervino Politiano Pont. Max. Terris tantum ostenso, coelis
repente asserto urbe et orbe prae desiderio lugente.   *Miscell.
in the Ricci Archives, Rome.

[4] CIACONIUS, III., 805 ; see BRUNNER, Italien, II., 8.

In the autumn of 1606, at the re-opening of St. Peter's under Paul V., the remains of Marcellus II. were removed to the crypt, where they are buried in a simple early Christian sarcophagus of marble, and only the short inscription, " Marcellus II." indicates who lies there.[1] Nevertheless the memory of this admirable Pope still lives to the present day. He is assured of an honourable place in the history of the Catholic struggle for reform. He occupies a high place in the esteem of all scholars on account of the services he rendered to the Vatican Library, and to the devotees of music his name will always be familiar through the wonderful mass which Palestrina composed in honour of his memory.[2]

[1] Bellarmine's report on the finding of the body and its translation on September 15, 1606, in the Römischen Quartalschrift, XV., 192. Concerning the tomb see CIACONIUS *loc. cit.*; FORCELLA, VI., 71; Katholik, 1901, II., 543 *seq.*; DUFRESNE, 97 *seq.*, with illustration.

[2] Concerning the *Missa papae Marcelli* see AMBROS, IV.[2], 19 *seq.*; HABERL, Musikkatalog der päpstlichen Kapelle, Leipzig, 1888, 9, 58 *seq.*; Stimmen aus Maria-Laach, XLVII., 125.

CHAPTER III.

ELECTION OF PAUL IV.—HIS CHARACTER AND PROJECTS. —THE CARAFA.

AT the death of Marcellus II., the Sacred College consisted of fifty-six members, of whom thirty-nine were in Rome, while of the seventeen absent members, only four arrived in Rome in time for the beginning of the election proceedings ; Cardinal Mendoza on the 3rd, Doria on the 9th, Madruzzo on the 12th, and Tagliavia on the 13th of May.[1]

The obsequies for Marcellus II., which had been begun on May 6th, on a very simple scale, on account of the want of money,[2] were concluded on the 14th. On the following morning the Mass of the Holy Ghost was celebrated, after which Uberto Foglietta delivered the usual discourse, in which he exhorted the members of the Sacred College to make a wise choice. After this the forty-three Cardinals entered the conclave, for which the same apartments were used as at the previous election. The number of electors was increased to forty-five by the arrival of Cardinals Gonzaga and Pacheco on May 16th and 17th. The guarding of the conclave was entrusted to the Duke of Urbino,[3] and the greatest tranquillity prevailed in the city.[4]

[1] See besides Panvinio in MERKLE, II., 263, the contemporary : *Conclave factum in Vaticano post mortem papae Marcelli II.*, preserved in the Secret Archives of the Vatican.

[2] See the *report of U. Gozzadini, dated Rome, May 7, 1555 (State Archives, Bologna).

[3] *Cf.* MASSARELLI, 263 *seq.* According to the *letter of Camillo Capilupi of May 15 (Gonzaga Archives, Mantua) Cardinal E. Gonzaga reached Rome on that date. Concerning the discourse of Foglietta see I. POGIANI epist. I., 103 n. An exact plan of the conclave, in which the cells of the Cardinals present are shown, is in the publication cited *supra* n. 1.

[4] See the *reports of U. Gozzadini, dated Rome, May 4, 8, and 11, 1555 (State Archives, Bologna), and the *letter of C. Capilupi of May 8, 1555 (State Archives, Mantua).

56

In consequence of the many different parties in the Sacred College, the Romans were prepared for a long conclave, but the general opinion was that the representatives of the Catholic reform party, Carafa, Morone and Pole had once more the best prospects of success.[1]

The decision was again on this occasion in the hands of the neutrals, for the Imperial party, led by Santa Fiora and Madruzzo, was only twenty strong, while the French had at most only fifteen votes, and they were not even united, as their most distinguished members, Cardinals d'Este, du Bellay and Alessandro Farnese, all had quite different objects in view.[2]

Cardinal d'Este had already done everything in his power, even before the beginning of the conclave, to secure the tiara at last. He met with the greatest opposition, however, on the part of the Imperialists, for the Emperor objected to the elevation of Este to the Papal throne as heartily as Henry II. desired it. Duke Ercole II., in particular, worked on behalf of his brother, Cardinal d'Este ; he had come to Rome to pay homage to Marcellus II., and was still staying there. Both of the brothers sought, above all, to win the favour of Cardinal Alessandro Farnese, who stood so high in the estimation of all the members of the Sacred College that a great deal depended upon his influence.[3]

---

[1] See the *report of U. Gozzadini of May 7, 1555 (*loc. cit.*) and the *letter of Ippolito Capilupi of May 9, 1555 (Gonzaga Archives, Mantua). *Cf.* the reports in L. LATINIUS, Lucubr. II., 32 ; RIBIER, II., 609 ; Legaz. di Serristori, 354 ; COGGIOLA, Conclave, 68 *seq.*, 79 *seq.* ; SEGMÜLLER, Wahl Pauls IV., 3 ; MASIUS, Briefe, 201. The opinion of REUMONT (III., 2, 513) that no one had thought of Carafa being elected, is quite erroneous. Atanagi says expressly in his letter of May 1 : " Teatino è in maggior predicamento di tutti " (TARDUCCI, 73). Carafa is mentioned even in the " Pasquille " as the most likely candidate ; see PADIGLIONE, La Bibl. del Museo naz. di S. Martino, Naples, 1876, 308.

[2] *Cf.* the report of Avanson in Ribier, II., 612.

[3] *Cf.* the numerous contemporary reports in COGGIOLA, Conclave, 81 *seq.* Concerning the intrigues of Este see also the Portuguese report in SANTAREM, XII., 425.

Farnese's candidate was his friend Pole, from whom he
looked for the advancement of his family interests. When
Farnese had started from France for the conclave of Marcellus II. he had succeeded in winning over even Henry II.
for the English Cardinal, but he had arrived too late in Rome
on that occasion. All the more eagerly, then, did he now
wish to promote Pole's candidature, since he was also agreeable
to Philip II. and the Emperor.[1] He remained true to him
even though immediately before the beginning of the conclave
instructions arrived from the French king that he should
work in the first place for Este.[2] The intrigues of the two
Este brothers to win over Farnese by tempting promises and
an agreement about an alliance between the two families
were also unsuccessful. In the same way an attempt of the
Este to win over, through Cosimo I., the Cardinals of Julius
III., to their side proved vain.[3] The prospects of the Cardinal
of Ferrara were thus practically destroyed even before the
beginning of the conclave.

The candidature of Pole also soon proved to be impossible.
The fact that he was still in England, and that they did not
care to elect an absentee, stood in his way on this occasion as
it had done at the last election, and it soon became apparent
that some of the Imperialists, as well as the French, were
opposed to him. In this Cardinals Carpi, Alvarez de Toledo
and Carafa were especially prominent, as they doubted Pole's
orthodoxy, and accused him of erroneous opinions as to certain
controverted points of faith, such as the doctrine of justification. This, which had already destroyed Pole's chances in
the conclave of Julius III., was not without effect on this
occasion also, even though the accusation was by no means
proved.[4]

[1] See SÄGMÜLLER, Papstwahlen,211 ; COGGIOLA, Conclave,209 seq.

[2] Farnese had counter-representations made to Henry II.
through his agent in Paris ; see CARO-FARNESE, Lettere, II.,
188 seq. ; SÄGMÜLLER, loc. cit. 215.

[3] See the reports in COGGIOLA, Conclave, 83 seqq., 205 seqq.

[4] See the reports in COGGIOLA, Conclave, 212 seqq. ; cf. RIBIER,
II., 610 and the report of the Portuguese ambassador concerning

The candidate with the best prospects of success, therefore, was the Dean, Cardinal Carafa, whose orthodoxy could be as little called in question as his distinguished qualities and his blameless life, although he was generally feared, if not hated, by the worldly Cardinals, such as Este and Santa Fiora, on account of his great severity. Some of the stricter Cardinals also took offence at his peculiar character and abrupt manner.[1] The fact that the other candidates had no chance of success was in his favour, as was the goodwill of the reform party and of the French. Henry II. had placed Carafa second among his favoured candidates ;[2] the Emperor, on the other hand, had given instructions to the Spanish party to prevent the election of this man, whom he had never liked.[3] Juan de Mendoza, who was the ambassador-extraordinary for the " obedientia " of Charles V. to Marcellus II., is said to have gone so far as to tell Carafa to his face that he might as well give up all thoughts of the tiara, as the Emperor had excluded him. To this Carafa made the dignified answer that the

the conclave dated Rome, June 18, 1555, in the Corpo dipl. Port., VII., 414. Coggiola (*loc. cit.*) emphasizes the fact that Carafa *bona fide* doubted the orthodoxy of Pole, but that the other two Cardinals were only actuated by selfish motives.

[1] See L. *Firmani Diaria caerem.* in MERKLE, II., 509.

[2] See the report of Avanson in RIBIER, II., 612.

[3] The statement of PETRUCELLI (II., 94), that the Imperial ambassador, Juan Manrique, had instructions to exclude Carafa, but was not to make the fact public except in case of need and at the right moment, seems quite worthy of belief (see SÄGMÜLLER, Papastwahlen, 212 *seqq.*) Manrique informed the Imperialist Cardinals of the wishes of Charles V., and named the four candidates of Philip II. and the Emperor (see his letter of May 15 in DRUFFEL-BRANDI, IV., 674 *seqq.*) ; a number of the Imperialist Cardinals did not act in accordance with this communication, of which fact Manrique bitterly complained (see his letter of May 24 in DRUFFEL-BRANDI, IV., 674, n. 3, and a second letter from Manrique to Charles V., dated Rome, May 25, 1555, in which he says : *Hemos acordado el Camarlengo e yo de embiar una viva voz presente a todo lo que passo en conclavi. [The ambassador was Lottino ; see RIBIER, II., 612 ; BROWN, VI., 1,

Emperor could not prevent his election if God wished it, and that in such a case, he would have the advantage of having only God to thank for his elevation.[1]

It was of decisive importance that Cardinal Alessandro Farnese, in view of the difficulties which made the election of Pole impossible, showed himself more and more favourable to Carafa, and at last used all his influence and skill on his behalf.

Any united action on the part of the Imperialists was prevented by the fact that Cardinals Alvarez de Toledo and Carpi were working with the greatest energy for their own election. These ambitious men, however, were soon obliged to give up their hopes, as they did not possess the support of Farnese, and, in addition, had a dangerous rival in the person of Morone. Farnese absolutely refused to favour these candidates;[2] thereupon the Camerlengo, Guido Ascanio Sforza di Santa Fiora, the acknowledged leader of the Imperialist party, and Madruzzo, turned their attention to one of the Cardinals of Julius III., the very distinguished Puteo, who was eminent alike for his learning and his moral life, and who, although he was a Provençal by birth, was nevertheless

n. 130; COGGIOLA, Conclave, 472; Nonciat., II., 582 seqq.]) After a short account of the course of the election, Manrique especially accuses Alvarez de Toledo and Carpi (cf. infra n. 2) and praises Lottino, *el qual es persona que a estado en los dos conclaves y en dambos a servido quanto a podido de bien y solicitamente y ingeniosamente (Archives at Simancas, Leg. 882, n. 30).

[1] See CIACONIUS, III., 824; RIESS, 6, n. 14.

[2] Cf. the reports in COGGIOLA, Conclave, 460 seqq., and Corpo dipl. Port., VII., 414 seq. B. Pia reported on May 18, 1555: *La prattica di Morone va strettissima da questa sera in qua et in banche le sue polize sono andate a 40 (Gonzaga Archives, Mantua). The fault of Cardinal Alvarez de Toledo and Carpi is sharply commented on by Manrique in the *letter to Charles V. on May 25, 1555, mentioned above: *Estos dos fueron los que hizieron todo el danno y dieron el exemplo y comensaron a romper los nostros (Archives at Simancas, loc. cit.) Cf. also Pacheco's letter in DRUFFEL-BRANDI, IV., 674.

devoted to the Emperor, so that he appeared to be agreeable to all parties.[1] Not only all the Imperialists, but also the older neutral Cardinals declared themselves in favour of Puteo. Finally, Madruzzo informed Farnese of this plan, pointing out that Pole was made impossible by his absence while Morone and Carpi had been excluded by the French, and Carafa by the Spaniards. The shrewd Farnese would not, however, make any promise ; he declared that he must, at anyrate, await the arrival of Cardinal Bourbon ; otherwise he considered Puteo very worthy of the triple crown, though he would prefer Pole.

While the twenty-five Cardinals who had been won over to the cause of Puteo were making preparations for the elevation of their candidate to the throne of St. Peter, without the agreement of the French, great excitement prevailed among the rival party. This group, which had assembled in the Pauline Chapel, consisted, apart from the Frenchmen, du Bellay, Armagnac, Guise, and Lenoncourt,[2] of Cardinals d'Este, Giulio della Rovere, Capodiferro, Dandino, Sermoneta, Innocenzo del Monte, Nobili, Mignanelli, and Ranuccio Farnese. Their fears were further increased when it was rumoured that Alessandro Farnese had gone over to the side of Puteo. This, however, was not the case ; on the contrary,

---

[1] For the following *cf.* the description by Panvinio in MERKLE, II., 268 n. who received very accurate information from those who had taken part in the conclave ; his account was later confirmed by the letter of the Bishop of Pola to Duke O. Farnese on May 23, 1555, published by COGGIOLA (Conclave, 466 *seqq.*) The decisive part taken by Farnese in the election of Paul IV. had already been emphasized by SEGNI (Storie fiorent., IV., 898). The report of Lucretio Tassone to the Marchese Sigismondo d'Este, published by MOTTA in the Miscell. d. stor. Lomb., *Castello Sforzesco*, 1903, 112 *seq.*, maintain quite erroneously that Este had been the principal person in deciding the election in favour of Carafa ; there is not even mention of Farnese in this biassed account !

[2] Lenoncourt had arrived in the conclave on May 22 ; *cf.* MASSARELLI, 265 and COGGIOLA, Conclave, 467.

Farnese was deeply offended by the attempt of the Imperialists
to make Puteo Pope without his co-operation, and he declared
to the Cardinals assembled in the Pauline Chapel that there
could be no question of his agreement to his candidature.
He said, at the same time, that the only way of preventing
Puteo's election was for Este to give up his own candidature
and to set up a rival candidate; which Este himself eventually
admitted. Farnese then proposed his old friend, the worthy
Cardinal Pietro Bertano. Capodiferro, however, declared
that Bertano would not accept the election, to which Farnese
replied : " Then elect Carafa, the holy and venerable Dean of
the Sacred College, who is worthy of being Pope." Everyone present declared that they would agree to this. Although
the proposal seemed, in view of the great unpopularity of
Carafa, even among those of French sympathies, and of the
open enmity of the Spanish-Imperial party, added to his
exclusion by Charles V., to have hardly any prospect of
success, he nevertheless received the tiara. The author of
the history of the Papal elections[1] can only explain this by
declaring that we must see in it a striking example of " the
wonders of the conclaves, and how true it is that God makes
the Popes."

Saraceni was sent to Carafa to ask if he would accept the
election. He declared himself willing to do so, but only if
the proceedings were all in due order. He was then conducted to the Pauline Chapel, and during the next two hours
Farnese was feverishly employed in obtaining for him the
votes still required. He succeeded first in winning over
Truchsess and Morone, and then others, such as Doria, Cornaro, Carpi, Alvarez de Toledo, Savelli and Medici.[2] At last

---

[1] *Conclavi de' pontefici Rom.*, I., Colonia 1691, 264 *seq.*

[2] For these changes to the other side, *cf.* besides Panvinio *loc.
cit.* the letters of Truchsess in the Histor. Jahrbuch, VII., 195
seqq., and the letter of the Bishop of Pola quoted *supra* p. 61, n. 1,
in which likewise Truchsess is named in the first place. See also
L. FIRMANUS, *loc. cit.* GOTHEIN (Ignatius, 475) lays great stress
on the fact that the " Spaniards of the Congregation of the Inquisition " declared themselves for Carafa. This is, however,

Farnese had collected twenty-eight votes, so that only three more were wanting to make the required majority of two-thirds. The sixteen who remained true to Puteo (Madruzzo, Santa Fiora, Mendoza, Cueva, Pacheco, Cristoforo del Monte, Corgna, Ricci, Mercurio, Bertano, Poggio, Cicada, Tagliavia, Gonzaga, Cornaro and Simoncelli) had assembled in the Hall of Consistories and unanimously persisted in their opposition to Carafa. Pacheco would rather, he said, give his vote even to a Frenchman than to this enemy of the Emperor ![1] The two parties remained obstinately opposed to one another during the night between May 22nd and 23rd, and negotiations were carried on in all directions without any result. At this critical moment Carafa showed himself the strict churchman he had always been. Dignified and free from ambition, he exhorted his adherents to refrain from all disorderly proceedings ; he would rather, he said, relinquish his hopes of election than consent to anything that was not in accordance with the law.[2] In the meantime, Carafa's opponents, and especially Madruzzo, Santa Fiora and Pacheco, were again making a supreme effort against the hated candidate.[3] They endeavoured in every way to bring Farnese round to their way of thinking. The Imperialists even declared themselves ready to elect Farnese himself, or his friend Pole ; they pointed to the numerous relations of Carafa, and to his connection with the Neapolitan and Florentine exiles. It was all, however, in vain, for Farnese would not give way.

wrong, for only one Spaniard (Alvarez de Toledo) belonged to the Inquisition.

[1] See the report of Avanson of May 24, 1555, in FAVRE, Olivier de Magny, 436.

[2] See *L. Firmani Diaria caerem.* in SEGMÜLLER, 6, n. 1, and the Portuguese report in the Corpo dipl. Port., VII., 415.

[3] For this *cf.* besides PANVINIO *loc. cit.* the reports in COGGIOLA, Conclave, 465. Manrique, in his *report to Charles V. of May 25, 1555, gives the highest praise to Madruzzo : Noñ ay que hablar que jamas huvo hombre tan declarado, que tan travajasse y se afatigasse en que V.M.ᵈ fuesse servido (Archives at Simancas, *loc. cit.*)

On the morning of May 23rd, Farnese and Morone were
sent to the Imperialists, who consented, on the threatening
representations of the former, to open the door of the Hall of
Consistories.　Morone then entreated the minority, in order
to avoid a schism, to give their votes to the candidate for
whom the majority of the Sacred College had declared them-
selpes.　His entreaties were supported by Farnese, but
remained without success, while Corgna and Cicada in particular answered him in the most violent terms.　Farnese
and Morone thus had to return to their party without having
gained their object.　They now resolved to make an attempt
to gain the three votes still necessary by means of private
negotiations.　Este was to go to Bertano, Pisani to his relative, Cornaro, and Farnese to Poggio.　Bertano and Cornaro
were soon won over, but Farnese had greater difficulty with
Poggio, though he at last succeeded in getting him also to
agree.

The necessary majority of two-thirds was now reached,
but Farnese desired, if possible, a unanimous vote.　He
applied therefore to Ricci, and induced him to hold a consultation with Carafa.　Ricci then besought the Cardinal
Dean to pardon Santa Fiora and his other opponents, which
Carafa at once agreed to do.　Then Farnese once more begged
the remaining members of the Spanish-Imperial party to
concur with the choice of the other Cardinals, but refused the
hour for consideration asked for by Santa Fiora.　The Imperialists then at last agreed to withdraw their opposition.　At
noon on May 23rd, the Feast of the Ascension, the election of
Carafa was confirmed by a unanimous " adoration."[1]　Out
of gratitude to Paul III. and Cardinal Farnese he assumed
the name of Paul IV.　He announced that he wished to

---

[1] See PANVINIO loc. cit. 270.　The Cardinals had already deliberated before the conclave concerning the legality of an election
per adorationem (cf. as to this WURM, Papstwahl, Cologne, 1902,
113) without, however, coming to any decision (see MASSARELLI,
263 seq.)　On May 22, it was already current in the city that
Carafa had been elected ; see the *letter of U. Gozzadini of May
22, 1515 (State Archives, Bologna).

devote the first day of his reign entirely to prayer and spiritual exercises, and that then only should the festival of his coronation take place.[1]

The new Pope, whose election was contrary to the general expectation,[2] enjoyed great vigour, in spite of his seventy-nine years. Tall and spare, he was, as the Venetian ambassador, Bernardo Navagero, points out, full of activity, and still so strong and healthy that he seemed scarcely to touch the ground with his elastic step.[3] It was said that he had never taken any medicine in his life;[4] rheumatism and catarrh were the only troubles of which he had sometimes to complain. His massive head was sparsely covered with hair, and his face, framed in a heavy beard, although not beautiful, was of expressive gravity; lines indicative of an unbending will-power lay round about his mouth, while out of his deeply sunk dark eyes there shone the glow of the fires of southern Italy.[5]

[1] See the *letter of C. Olivo of May 23 (State Archives, Mantua) and that of U. Gozzadini, dated Rome, May 25, 1555 (*volendo S.S.ta celebrare et confessarsi questa mattina et stare tutto hoggi in spirito). State Archives, Bologna.

[2] " Contra la comune opinione," says the Bishop of Reggio in his *report of May 25, 1555, speaking of Este : " Il. buon Ferrara non è ne sarà papa mai, ma ne farà de questi et a questo modo." Gonzaga Arch. Mantua).

[3] See for the following Navagero's narrative of 1558, one of the principal sources for the character of Paul IV., in ALBÈRI, Ser 2, III., 379 seq. Cf. besides the *Apologia alla relatione del Navagero by Antonio Carafa, commented on in Appendix No. 61-62 (National Library, Naples), Panvinio in MERKLE, II., 333. ANDREAS (Die venezianischen Relationen, Leipsic, 1908, 114–115) shows that he greatly misunderstands Navagero when he says that Paul IV. said " Mass as far as Vespers " in the forenoon, and " the rest of the Mass, Vespers and Compline " after dinner.

[4] See in Appendix No. 9 the *letter of Camillo Olivo to Sabino Calandra, dated Rome, May 23, 1555 (Gonzaga Archives, Mantua).

[5] The best known portrait of Paul IV. is that of the third year of his reign. Through the engraving by Nicholas Beatrizet (Romae, 1558. Cf. concerning this artist HÜBNER, I., 35) it

The very arrangement of his day betrayed his hot-blooded temperament.   He did not like to be disturbed in the morning, as he wished to say mass and recite his office slowly and with great devotion.   He would not be tied down to any fixed hours for his meals,[1] though he wished his table to be served very generously, in accordance with his high position.   He himself ate very little, and in spite of his advanced age, kept the rules of fasting and abstinence in the strictest manner.   Of the different wines which were served he always took one glass only of the dark, thick Neapolitan wine, and at the end of the repast a little malvoisie to rinse his mouth.[2]   After dinner he liked to sit for a time in animated conversation with his guests ;   these were for the most part only the Cardinals, though, as an exception, the Venetian ambassador would sometimes be invited.   In such conversations after dinner, things sometimes escaped the lips of the youthfully lively old

passed into most of the works containing portraits, as, for example, the continuation of Platina and Ciaconius.   The portrait of Carafa at the time when he was raised to the cardinalate is admirably true to life ; it is in the council-chamber of the castle of Capra-rola.   The beautiful bronze bust of Paul IV. in the passage to the sacristy of St. Peter's, is a pious bequest of the Canons there, but is not yet reproduced (see FORCELLA, VI., 71).   The statue on his tomb in the church of the Minerva is somewhat idealized. A later bust of Paul IV. is in the cloisters of St. Paolo Maggiore at Naples.   Fine examples of the bronze medals of Paul IV. are in the Vatican collection of coins, and in the Kaiser Friedrich Museum Berlin (Hall, 16, Case 3).   The medal of the de Rossi collection of coins in the National Library, Paris in GOYAU-PERATÉ-FABRE, Der Vatikan, Einsiedeln, 1898, 141.

[1] Up to his last illness, says Navagero, loc. cit.   Cf. MASIUS, Briefe, 235.

[2] According to the remark of Navagero it might seem (see RANKE, I⁶., 186) that Paul IV. had been a great drinker.   This has been correctly contradicted in the *essay of Antonio Carafa, quoted supra p. 63, n. 3.   On the contrary, all contemporaries praise the great moderation of Paul IV. in eating and drinking. The Pope only gave banquets on account of his position, and did not himself even touch most of the dishes.   Cf. BROMATO, II., 219.

man which would have been better unsaid. At this hour also, audiences were granted, which were, however, of very limited duration, for Paul IV. was always fond of retirement, and did not like to see many people.[1] He received the Cardinals and ambassadors in the course of the afternoon ; they alone were permitted to enter the private apartments, but it sometimes happened that even such highly placed personages were not received, or only permitted to enter after midnight, when they had been waiting for four, five, six or seven hours.[2] This was the result of the irregularity in his division of the day, for the Pope allowed himself the necessary time for repose at quite different hours. Paul IV. frequently got up at night when he could not sleep, and set about reading or writing until fatigue forced him again to seek his bed. The coming of day did not disturb him in the least, for no one was allowed to enter his room until he gave the signal with a bell. It was considered a sign of his asceticism that he despised the help of a valet in dressing, a thing that seldom occurred in the case of one of the princes of the Church, and was quite unheard of in the case of a Pope.[3]

To those who dealt with him, Paul IV. proved very difficult to manage ; the more anyone begged him to do a thing, the less inclined he was to do it, but when he was not urged he would yield quickly and easily.[4] He could endure no contradiction and lost his temper very readily. It was in keeping with the majestic, stern and peremptory manner which was characteristic of him,[5] that he always took the leading part in a

[1] *Item qualiter d. Paulus de sua natura erat secretus et, ut vulgo dicitur, ritirato nec in eius cameram et cubiculum admittebat multos homines, says a defender of the Cardinal of Naples (Cod. Barb. lat., 2630, p. 3. Vatican Library). See also SEGMÜLLER, 26.

[2] See MOCENIGO-ALBÈRI 49 ; cf. MASIUS, Briefe, 235, 267, and the *report of Navagero of February 22, 1556 (Cod. Marc., 9445, f. 123b· Library of St. Mark's, Venice).

[3] See BROMATO, II., 221.

[4] Cf. the ambassadorial reports in RIBIER, II., 815.

[5] *Ha una mirabil gravità et grandezza. Questa grandezza et gravità l'ha mostrata in tutti gli stati. *Apologia cit. (National Library, Naples), where striking examples are given.

conversation, and whoever wished to get anything from him
had to be very careful not to interrupt him ; on the other hand,
he was very fond of interrupting others, and in so doing gave
free expression to his natural eloquence, which Hosius compared to that of Cicero.[1] Navagero says : " In dealing with
him, as much patience as adroitness is necessary ; if one is
successful in soothing him, he does not lightly refuse anything." Those attained most who could adapt themselves
to his ways, and the shrewd representative of Venice never
went to an audience with a definite object in view, but each
time adapted himself to the circumstances.

In the matter of his dress, Paul IV. laid great stress on
everything being in exact accordance with the ceremonial, as
he attached great importance to official display.[2] He had
always had a very high idea of the ecclesiastical office, and he
had a still higher one of the Papal dignity ; now that he sat
on the throne of St. Peter, the self-assurance which the remembrance of his always blameless priestly life, and his unswerving
severity and activity as a churchman, as well as the experience
of many years had given him, was visibly increased. He
repeatedly declared that he would rather be torn in pieces than
do anything unworthy of his exalted office,[3] and all who knew
him could testify that these were not mere words.

Cardinal Pacheco, at a critical moment, drew the attention
of the Duke of Alba to the fact that Paul IV. would never allow
himself to be influenced by fear, for he was a man who would
rather permit the destruction of the city of Rome and suffer
death himself than do anything unworthy of his high position.[4]

[1] See the report in RIBIER, II., 715 seq. ; cf. MASIUS, Briefe, 271.

[2] See Navagero in BROWN, VI., 2, n. 766, 768. The famiglia
of Paul IV. consisted, according to his " Ruolo " of 421 actual
famigliari, and 313 servi, in all 734 persons, besides 247 horses
(see MORONI, XXIII., 66–73). This was by no means excessive,
for every great house had, at that time, about 100 famigliari ; see
MÜNTZ, Art., III., 78.

[3] See the report of Navagero of June 4, 1557 in BROWN, VI., 2,
n. 919.

[4] Ibid., n. 1030.

Cardinal Morone expresses himself in similar terms in a letter to his friend Pole. In this he declares that the Pope would rather suffer martyrdom than allow the dignity and honour of the Holy See, for which he felt himself responsible before God and Christendom, to suffer in the slightest degree ; in the opinion of Morone, he was so penetrated with the idea of being the representative of Christ, that he considered an offence against his own dignity as an insult to God.[1]

The consciousness that, as the representative of Christ, he stood above everyone, made itself very noticeable in his attitude towards the princes. Fully conscious of his own dignity, he did not regard them as his sons, but as his subjects.[2] He was so far removed from the world in his ideas, that he was accustomed to look at political questions from a very one-sided point of view, and to judge of them very harshly. He told the ambassadors that the place of kings and emperors was at the feet of the pope, from whom they should receive their laws as if they were his pupils.[3] His rigid ecclesiastical principles rebelled against the tendency, at that time very prevalent even among Catholic sovereigns, to assume control even in the domestic concerns of the Church. He declared that he would put an end to the shameful subservience of his predecessors to the princes. He therefore considered it right to make no secret of his deep distrust of them, and to act towards them with increasing irritability, as well as with extreme severity and inflexibility. The conflicts into which such sentiments, joined to the vivacity and impetuosity of his nature, led this old man, who was still filled with youthful ardour, may easily be imagined.

As a true son of Naples, Paul IV. was very susceptible to

[1] See the original text of the *letters of November 28 and December 12, 1556, in Appendix Nos. 34 and 35 (Secret Archives of the Vatican).

[2] See the report of the French ambassador in RIBIER, II., 716 ; cf. in Appendix No. 18, the *letter of Navagero of January 18th, 1556 (Library of St. Mark's, Venice).

[3] See NAVAGERO-ALBÈRI, 380, 409, and MOCENIGO-ALBÈRI, 48 ; cf. RIBIER, II., 716 seq.

sudden impressions, hasty and changeable in his decisions, and not infrequently impolitic in his expressions, as well as unnecessarily sharp and abrupt. Just as he bound himself by no fixed rules in his daily life, so was he also fond of giving way to the impulses of the moment, and bestowed his confidence as easily as he withdrew it. The utterances of his volcanic nature were as sudden as the eruptions of Vesuvius ; like all his fellow-countrymen, he spoke eagerly and at great length, and the words flowed like a torrent from his lips. Whenever any event stirred his blood, he broke out, after the manner of southern Italians, into the most violent and rough language, which he accompanied with highly descriptive gestures ; sometimes he so far forgot his dignity as to permit himself to proceed to actual acts of violence.[1] All his asceticism had not been able to teach him moderation in the expression of his passionate feelings, or calmness and self-possession in his actions. Consequently, as Cardinal, he had had disputes with many people, and had also been at variance with men who, like Ignatius of Loyola, were struggling for the same object as himself, the regeneration of the Church. He grappled with each task with iron energy and passionate fire ; there was nothing underhand and no trace of hypocrisy in his character. His piety was genuine, as were his love for Church and country, his wide view of life and his idealism ; equally genuine were his stormy eloquence and his extensive knowledge. He was well versed in the most varied branches of learning, but above all in theology. He spoke Italian, Greek and Spanish fluently ; unusually well read, he remembered everything he had ever learned, and was intimately acquainted with the Latin and Greek classics, while the Scriptures he knew almost by heart. Among theologians his favourite author was St. Thomas Aquinas.[2]

[1] *Cf*. Serristori's report of July 6, 1555 in COGGIOLA, Capitolazione, 27 n.

[2] *Cf*. NAVAGERO *loc. cit.* Carafa's letters show his familiarity with the Holy Scriptures, as they consist almost entirely of passages from the Bible. Many of them are still unprinted ; see especially *Cod. Barb. lat. 5697. Vatican Library.

For sixty years Gian Pietro had devoted all the gifts of his intellect, the strength of his iron will, and the firmness of a character which brooked no opposition to one aim alone : to infuse new life into the authority, the power, the purity and the dignity of the Church, which was now so sorely beset by enemies, both from within and without. This aim had been steadily before his eyes as Bishop of Chieti, as nuncio in England and Spain, as a member of the Oratory of Divine Love, as head of the Theatine Order, which he had founded in conjunction with S. Gaetano di Tiene, as a member of the reform commission of Paul III., and as Cardinal.[1] In all these offices he had shown himself to be a man of strong and decided character, and an indefatigable fighter in the interests of the Church, as well as the strictest of the strict, especially in all that concerned the purity of morals and of the faith. No respect of persons could restrain his frankness ; he always declared his opinions openly and without reserve, before Cardinals and Pope alike. The history of Paul III. as well as that of Julius III. often tells of cases when measures had to be carried out, even by those in the highest positions, which were not in accordance with the interests and dignity of the Holy See. On such occasions Cardinal Carafa was to be found, either in direct opposition, or, if further resistance appeared to have no prospect of success, at any rate protesting by his absence from the consistory.[2] If, in such cases, Carafa drew down upon himself the displeasure of the Pope, he troubled as little about it as he did about the actual material disadvantages which he had to suffer.[3] He bore it all in silence and calmness of spirit, and kept unswervingly to his own strict principles.

[1] *Cf.* Vol. X. of this work pp. 401 *seqq.* and Vol. XI., pp. 147, 155, 157, 161, 169.

[2] *Cf.* Panvinio in MERKLE, II., 271 n. ; see also SILOS, I., 310 seq and Vol. XII. of this work, p. 232 *seqq.*, and Vol. XIII., p. 71.

[3] A. Carafa relates in the *Apologia* the opposition of Carafa to the bestowal of Parma and Piacenza on Pier Luigi Farnese (see Vol. XII. of this work, p. 233) : *Onde venne in disgratia del papa et gli tolse la provisione di cento scudi il mese, che se li

Whereas most people relax in old age and begin to feel
inclined to rest, Carafa's energy, fire, and strength of will
seemed to increase from year to year.[1] " The Pope," writes
the Florentine ambassador, " is a man of iron, and the very
stones over which he walks emit sparks which cause a con-
flagration should his wishes not be carried out."[2]

It is easy to understand that such a man had few friends
and adherents ; people recognized his pure life, his incorruptible honesty, and his learning, but all blamed and feared his
exaggerated severity, his abruptness and his obstinacy.   There
had been no lack of titles and honours in the life of this man,
who had risen to the dignity of Dean of the Sacred College, but
he had won the affection and love of very few.[3]

The new Pope was quite aware of this, and he felt the
necessity of making some little concession to public opinion,
if he was not to make himself hated from the outset, and thus
destroy all his influence.   The more the Romans had feared
the ascetic Theatine, the more agreeably astonished were they
when Paul IV. also brought into prominence the brilliant and
princely side of the Papacy.   They learned with satisfaction
how this man, who as Cardinal had led such a frugal and retired
life,[4] had ordered the officials of the palace, when they asked

dava come cardinale povero, restandogli da vivere mille soli scudi
d'entrata l'anno.   Nè perciò ne fece mai parola o alcuno risenti-
mento.   Anzi perchè quando usciva a palazzo negli atti publici
non era salutato, come si suole fare con cardinali, dalle musiche
di castello et trombe di palazzo, se ne rideva con ogni serenità
d'animo (Cod. X., F. 55, p. 6., National Library, Naples).

[1] *Cf.* Panvinio *loc. cit.*

[2] Legaz. di Serristori, 375.

[3] See MOCENIGO-ALBÈRI, 46.

[4] One of the Cardinal's defenders, Alfonso Carafa says : *Item
ponit et . . . probare intendit qualiter praedictus Paulus quartus fe. re. ante papatum fuerat per viginti annos in circa cardinalis,
habebat redditus competentes adeo quod tempore sue assumptionis ad pontificatum habebat in redditibus circa duodecim
milia scuta annua, et erat parcus in expedendo et non amplam
familiam retinebat, adeo quod verisimiliter et unus quisque recti

for instructions, to make arrangements " on as magnificent a scale as is fitting for a great prince."[1] No expense was spared for the feast of the coronation, which took place on May 26th. The banquet which was given on this occasion to the Cardinals and ambassadors was exceedingly brilliant. " Although only four days have elapsed since the election," writes Angelo Massarelli in his diary, " the new Pope has already given so many proofs of his generosity, benevolence, magnanimity and splendour, that one can easily form an opinion about the new reign."[2] The Bolognese ambassador expressed himself in a similar manner in a letter of May 29th, 1555 : " His Holiness will be an excellent Pope, full of goodness and magnanimity."[3] When Paul IV. left the Castle of St. Angelo on June 4th, for his summer residence at the palace of S. Marco, such magnificence was displayed that it might have been thought that the days of Leo X. had again returned.[4]

This beginning, which no one had expected from the stern, ascetic Pope, was undoubtedly intended to make an impression on the Romans, who were dazzled by the outward pomp and

iuditii ita diceret et iudicaret, quod deductis expensis quolibet anno potuerat conservare et congregare quatuor aut quinque milia scuta (Cod. Barb. lat., 2630, f. 3 b., Vatican Library).

[1] See H. Seripandus, ed. HÖFLER 53 ; cf. BROMATO, II., 218.

[2] See MERKLE, II., 270. Concerning the coronation, cf. the *report of Franchino to Ottavio Farnese, dated Rome, May 27, 1555 (State Archives, Parma).

[3] *Letter of U. Gozzadini (State Archives, Bologna). Cf. also the reports in L. LATINIUS, Lucubrat., II., 35, and SEGMÜLLER, Wahl Pauls IV., 9.

[4] Besides MASSARELLI, 272 seq. L. Firmanus, *Diaria XII., 29 (Secret Archives of the Vatican) and Corpo dipl. Port., VII., 423 seq., the *report of U. Gozzadini, dated Rome, June 5, 1555, who remarks in his description of the brilliant procession : *et da Leone in qua non si è fatto una tal cosa (State Archives, Bologna). Concerning the Possesso of Paul IV. see Cola Coleine in CANCELLIERI, 108 ; MASSARELLI, 284 ; MASIUS, Briefe, 232 ; L. Firmanus, *Diaria loc. cit.

lavishness ; besides this, the high conception of the Papal dignity which animated Paul IV. did not fail to have an effect. He had not sought for this, the highest position of which ambition could dream, and the astonishing fact that he, the hated and dreaded Cardinal, who had always displayed the greatest severity, and had never shown the least favour to anyone, should, in spite of his exclusion by the Emperor, have received the tiara, could, he felt, only be explained by seeing in it the intervention of a higher power. He was, and he remained, firmly convinced that, not the Cardinals, but God Himself had chosen him for the furtherance of His designs.[1] He was also as firmly persuaded that these designs could be none other than those upon which the whole of his previous aims and thoughts had ever been fixed : the defence and revivi- fying of the Church, her liberation from the domination of every secular power, and her victory over heresy. He was entirely permeated with these ideas, and now that he was raised to the supreme pontificate, he intended to carry them out with all the inconsidered idealism which had always been characteristic of him, and to employ all his powers in restoring to the Catholic religion its former splendour and might.[2]

The Church, and above all her centre, the Holy See, had for a whole generation suffered unheard-of attacks and great humiliations. Now that he was in possession of the supreme power, Paul IV. meant to reverse this state of affairs, and once more to restore to the Holy See its old position of domination. With his ideas rooted, as were all his views, in the Middle Ages, he saw the ecclesiastical ideal in the century of Innocent III., when the Papal power was at its zenith. Nothing, therefore, was so far opposed to his ideas as the great drifting apart of the spiritual and the temporal which had come to pass in later times ; to him, everything should be looked at from the point of view of the Church. He accordingly considered it to be his

[1] See MOCENIGO-ALBÈRI, 46-47.
[2] Cf. the coronation day *brief (May 26, 1555) to the Kings of Portugal and of the Romans (Arm. 44, t. 4, n. 104 and 106, Secret Archives of the Vatican).

duty to take up once more the attitude which the Holy See had adopted at that time towards princes and peoples, and again, with all the power of his will, and quite regardless of the consequences, to revive it, even in the domain of politics. In his fiery enthusiasm, it quite escaped[1] him that all the rights to which in the course of centuries the Popes had laid claim did not arise from the divine law or from the nature of the primacy, but that many of them, and especially the political ones, were the result of historical development and were human in their origin, and might therefore once more have to be relinquished. No less did it escape the notice of this idealist, who thought only of what ought to be, that the vast changes in the ecclesiastical and political condition of Europe rendered a vindication of such Papal authority over the Christian princes as had existed during the centuries of the Middle Ages an utter impossibility. Untroubled by the falling away of half the world, and regardless of the far-reaching changes which had taken place even in those states which had remained Catholic, Paul IV. lived and worked in those days when the Popes, as fathers and leaders of Christendom, had also exercised a widespread power, even in the sphere of politics. Although there existed no ecclesiastical definition with regard to the power of the Holy See in secular matters,[2] he clung rigidly to all the claims which his predecessors had made under quite different conditions and in quite other circumstances.

With such views, matters might very easily come to a hostile encounter with the great power of the House of Hapsburg, all the more as the Spanish-Hapsburg monarchy was as great a menace to the freedom of Italy as to that of the Papacy. Not only was the remembrance of the one-time independence and extensive power of the Holy See firmly rooted in Carafa's soul, but so also was the memory of the splendour of Italy, of which he had received the deepest impressions in his early youth. He compared this Italy of the past to a perfectly tuned instru-

---

[1] The statements made to the French ambassador are very characteristic of this in RIBIER, II., 716, *seq.*

[2] HERGENRÖTHER, Staat und Kirche, 749.

ment, of which the four strings were the States of the Church,
Naples, Milan and Venice. He detested the memory of
Alfonso of Aragon and Ludovico Moro, through whom this
harmony had been thrown into discord.[1] The domination of
the Spaniards in the Appenine peninsula, the yoke which they
had imposed on his beloved Naples, and the heavy pressure
which they had brought to bear on the Holy See, appeared
to him all the more intolerable, as he entertained the gravest
doubts as to the Catholic sentiments of Charles V.[2] Already
as a Cardinal he had watched with growing indignation the
numerous encroachments of this monarch in the domain of
domestic ecclesiastical affairs, and it had even then become
a fixed idea with him that the possessor of the Imperial
authority secretly favoured the German Protestants, in order
to destroy the temporal power of the Holy See, and thus rule
alone in Italy. To this policy he ascribed the sweeping progress which the enemies of the Church were now making.
Above all, the recollection of the horrible devastation which
Rome, the capital of Christendom, had had to suffer from
the troops of the Emperor, was indelibly fixed in his memory,
nor could he ever forget that attempt of this prince to set up,
by his own power, an " Interim " religion in Germany, without
the consent of the Holy See. He therefore detested and
opposed[3] this monarch as a Neapolitan, as an Italian, and above
all as a Catholic, and had regarded the complaisance of Julius
III. towards him with ever-increasing displeasure.

Now that he was in possession of the supreme power, Paul
IV. made no secret of his dislike for the Spaniards, and of his

[1] Navagero in ALBÈRI, Ser. 2, III., 389.

[2] Navagero repeatedly made reports concerning this ; see
especially BROWN, VI., 1, 392, 453, 622, 669, 674, 798 ; cf. also
infra, Cap. IV.

[3] The well-informed maintain that Cardinal Carafa advised
Paul III. in the year 1547 to an undertaking against the Spanish
domination in Naples (see GIANNONE, Storia di Napoli, 33, 1 ;
cf. the note to NORES, 304 and the remarks of several Cardinals,
which Bruzzone published in the Cultura N.S.1 [1891] 434 seq.)
Julius III. officially disavowed the matter ; see SILOS, I., 311 seq.

leaning towards France, whose king had promoted his election.[1] The thought of opposing the domination of the Spaniards in Italy urged him to take action all the more strongly as the political situation appeared to be very favourable to his purpose. The Emperor's star was no longer in the ascendant, but was irresistibly set on the downward path. The haughty monareh, on whose dominions the sun never set, felt, in view of the menace to his domination in Germany and the Netherlands, and his far from assured position in Italy, the failure of his far-reaching plans all the more deeply as his bodily infirmities weighed more and more upon him.

Under such circumstances it was very tempting to make use of this moment to free Italy and the Papacy from the pressure of the Spanish power. Men now saw the rare spectacle of a man who had hitherto been exclusively occupied with the reform of the clergy, the struggle against heresy, and with works of Christian charity, plunging with all the impetuosity of his fiery nature into international politics and embarking on a great war. Anyone else would have drawn back in fear before the rashness of an encounter with the Colossus of the Spanish power, but not so Paul IV. He, who had never known fear, was now filled with a double confidence, and was persuaded that God would assist him, an idea which he expressed in the words of his motto,[2] where it was written : " Thou shalt walk upon the asp and the basilisk, and thou shalt trample under foot the lion and the dragon."[3] The monarch who had allowed Rome to be devastated, and had attempted to introduce a mixed religion into Germany, he considered as abetting the worst enemies of the Church in an even greater degree than a schismatic and a heretic. It was unbearable to him that the Spaniards, whom he looked upon as a mixture of Jews and Marani, should rule the north and south of Italy and thereby threaten the freedom and the great position in the world of

---

[1] See the letter of Avanson of May 24, 1555, in FAVRE, Olivier de Magny, 436 ; cf. also the report in SEGMÜLLER, Wahl Pauls IV., 6.

[2] " Dominus mihi adjutor " ; see CIACONIUS, III., 813.

[3] Psàlm XC., 13. Cf. NAVAGERO-ALBÈRI, 390.

the Holy See.   He would no longer tolerate a state of affairs, to end which his great predecessor had undertaken a mortal combat with the Hohenstaufen.

Besides these ecclesiastical reasons, Paul IV. was no less animated by national motives when he resolved to enter upon a struggle with the tremendous power of Spain.   This poor Italy which, even though the golden age of the Renaissance was now over, still stood at the head of the European nations as supreme in literature and art, should no longer languish under the yoke of a foreign power, the ancient home of culture must be freed from the "barbarians."   Not as masters, thought the Pope, must these strangers be suffered in the Hesperides, but rather as stable-boys and cooks, or, at the most, as shop-keepers.[1]   The idea of freeing Italy from every foreign influence was so deeply engrained in Paul IV. that he regarded the help of the French in driving out the Spaniards as a merely temporary expedient.   He once said to the Venetian ambassador, Navagero, in whom he had special confidence: " They are all barbarians, and it would be a good thing if they remained at home, and nothing but Italian were spoken in our country."[2]   On another occasion he reminded the same ambassador of a Neapolitan proverb, to the effect that the Spaniards were good as a beginning, but the French for later on, as the Spaniard was very polite, and with hat in hand was lavish in compliments and flattery, but as soon as he had obtained a grip he would play the host ; the Frenchman, on the other hand, in accordance with his hot-headed nature, was impudent at first, but calmed down later on, so that one could at last get on with him very well.[3]

This idea of liberating the Holy See from foreign influences by bringing about the downfall of the Spanish domination in Naples and Milan reminds us of the plans of Julius II.   Indeed

---

[1] *Cf.* Navagero in BROWN, VI., 2, n. 813.

[2] See the letter of Navagero in the Appendix to NORES, 308 ; *cf.* NAVAGERO-ALBÈRI, 405 *seq.*

[3] See the report of Navagero in ANCEL, Sienne, 28, n. 4, and also BROWN, VI., 2, n. 813.

there was something of the spirit of the Rovere Pope in Paul IV., and a contemporary[1] described the entrance of the new Pope into diplomatic affairs by the same word " terrible "— powerful, grand, which the Venetian ambassador of the time had used in speaking of Julius II.[2] However, quite apart from the political and ecclesiastical differences between the two times, Paul IV. could not undertake such a bold enterprise as the expulsion of the Spaniards from Italy with any prospect of success, because he was entirely lacking in the political and military capacity which had been characteristic, in such a marked degree, of his great predecessor. In consequence of the direction which the development of his powers had always taken, Paul IV. had more and more lost touch with political matters, while of military affairs he had never had any experience. The difficulties, therefore, with which his colossal undertaking would confront him, the new condition of political affairs caused by the religious divisions, the insufficient number of the troops at the disposal of the States of the Church, and the unwarlike nature of the Italians, were as little realized by him as the unfavourable state of the Papal treasury.[3] To all this must be added his own temperament, which was as little suited to a diplomatist as to a commander of armies.

The nature of the Pope was also to a great extent responsible for the silence of those who would have warned him before beginning a conflict with Spain. It is especially the fate of princes that they seldom or never hear the truth, and much more is this the case with those of hasty disposition. Anyone who frankly explained the true state of affairs to Paul IV. fell

[1] It is thus expressed in a *letter of a Mantuan agent, dated Rome, September 1, 1555 (Gonzaga Archives, Mantua).

[2] Cf. Vol. VI. of this work, 274 seq.

[3] See, concerning the financial state of affairs, the complaints in the *brief to the vice-legate of the provinces of the States of the Church of June 4, 1555 (Arm. 44, t. 4, n. 116. Secret Archives of the Vatican). Cf. NAVAGERO-ALBÈRI, 375 ; BROSCH, I., 202 seq. Abundant details of the receipts and expenditure in the States of the Church under Paul IV. are collected in a volume in the Secret Archives of the Vatican, Miscell. Arm. II., t. 45.

into disfavour, while, on the other hand, he willingly lent his ear to those who agreed with his ideas, although they often withheld from him just what was most important.[1] Consequently the Pope lived, as far as political and military matters were concerned, in a world of phantasy, which was in glaring contrast to the actual state of affairs.

It was a great misfortune that such a man should have entered into the maze of politics, a misfortune alike for the Papal States and for the Church, which was in need of nothing so much as a thorough reformation. To neglect this for political activity was by no means the intention of Paul IV., all the more so as the liberation of the Holy See from the Spanish yoke was also part of his plan of reform. In accordance with this, in his first consistory, on May 29th, 1555, he laid stress on his fixed intention of maintaining his own dignity and the authority of the Holy See, as well as of reforming the bad moral state of the clergy, and he besought the Cardinals to assist him in this, and to give an example by their own good lives. The same members of the Sacred College were appointed to deliberate upon the necessary reforms as had been chosen for this task by Marcellus II.[2] The Pope expressed himself in such a manner on this occasion that it was generally recognized that he intended to devote his first care to this difficult task.[3] It was announced at the same time that the seventy-nine-year-old Pope would depute Cardinals for the government

---

[1] Cf. NAVAGERO-ALBÈRI, 405 seq. Even P. Strozzi, who was able to speak very openly to Paul IV. (see ibid. 407), often had to conceal the full truth from him ; an example of this in ANCEL, Disgrâce, 20, n. 5.

[2] Besides MASSARELLI, 272 see *Acta consist. (Consistorial Archives) and the report of U. Gozzadini, dated Rome, May 29, 1555 (State Archives, Bologna).

[3] U. Gozzadini reported in a *letter of May 29, 1555 : S.S.tà ha fatto una exortatione a tutti li cardinali a dovere vivere da cardinali et con molta efficacia con accennare che vuole che si attendi alla reformatione et che ha delle prime cose che si facciano al darle fine (State Archives, Bologna).

of the States of the Church and for the administration of political business.[1]

This last plan was soon after carried into effect in a manner that was as fateful for Paul IV. as it was for the Church. Filled with distrust of the Cardinals who had elected him almost against their wills, the Pope thought that he would find the necessary qualities for the direction of political affairs—the later secretaryship of state—more surely in a member of his own family. In a consistory on June 7th, 1555, Carlo Carafa, the youngest son of Giovan Alfonso, Count of Montorio, the deceased elder brother of the Pope, was appointed a Cardinal Deacon.[2] On July 15th Carlo Carafa received the position which Alessandro Farnese had filled under Paul III., and Innocenzo del Monte under Julius III. ; the nuncios were enjoined to have the same confidence in him as in the Pope himself.[3]

The Pope looked upon such an arrangement, which was similar to that of so many of his predecessors, as a matter of course, without having been led to this choice by any exaggerated love for his family, for his nepotism was not founded on personal or family affection, as had been the case with so many of the Renaissance Popes.[4]

It is, therefore, all the more tragic that his choice should have

[1] See the *letter of U. Gozzadini of May 29, 1555 (State Archives, Bologna).

[2] See *Acta consist.* in GULIK-EUBEL, III., 38 and MASSARELLI, 273. Carata did not receive ordination as a priest, and he knew nothing of Latin. See Nonciat., II., 362.

[3] See the **brief to Cardinal Carafa of July 15th, 1555, which has escaped the notice even of ANCEL (Secrét. pontif., 6). Secret Archives of the Vatican, Arm. 44, t. 4, n. 168.

[4] RANKE (Päpste, I.[6], 195) and SUSTA (Mitteil. des Osterr. Instituts, Erg.-Bd., VI., 551) are justified in emphasizing this. I cannot, however, estimate the consideration for the anti-Spanish policy as highly as they do. Šusta shows very clearly how the unfortunate system of nepotism was in a certain sense inevitable in the States of the Church. *Cf.* also FELTEN in the Freib Kirchenlex., IX., 104 *seq.*

fallen on one who could not have been more unsuited for the dignity. Carlo Carafa was the type of an Italian " condottiere " ; an able but unprincipled man, he had had a very stirring and adventurous career.

Born in the year 1517 or 1519, he had been, as a boy, page to Cardinal Pompeo Colonna, and had then entered the service of Pier Luigi Farnese, finally devoting himself entirely to the military profession, since, as the youngest son, and having no prospect of the family possessions, he had to carve out his own way with his sword. He fought for many years under the banner of the Emperor, in Piedmont under Vasto, and in the Schmalkaldic war under Ottavio Farnese. Disappointed in his hopes, and badly treated by the Spaniards, he at last abandoned the cause of the Emperor and fought for the French under Strozzi in the Sienese war. At the time of the conclave he was in Rome.[1]

At first sight it appears impossible to understand how the Pope, so austere with regard to morals, could suddenly summon this rough soldier, whose scandalous and licentious life was known to him,[2] into the supreme senate of the Church. It was therefore supposed that the cunning nephew had deceived the old Pope by a comedy of conversion.[3] The truth, however, was quite different. The bestowal of the purple on Carlo Carafa was the result of a cleverly devised intrigue of his elder brother Giovanni, Count of Montorio.[4] Concerned above everything else with the splendour and greatness of the

---

[1] NAVAGERO-ALBÈRI, 383. PETRAMELLARIUS, 91 seq. CIACONIUS, III., 842 seq. DURUY, 7 seq., 345 seq. RIESS, 19 seq. ANCEL, Disgrâce, 12 seq. Nonciat., II., 258.

[2] Cf. the Motu Proprio by which Carafa was absolved from his former crimes, in CHRISTOFORI, Paolo IV. (Miscell. stor. Romana, 1888, I., Ser. 2, p. 56), and ANCEL, Disgrâce, 15, n. 3.

[3] The story of Carafa's comedy of conversion, which has been widely circulated, chiefly through RANKE, (Päpste, I⁶., 188), is also repudiated by RIESS (p. 23 seq.)

[4] The source of proof for this has been furnished by ANCEL (Disgrâce, 14 seq.) Cf. also COGGIOLA, Farnesi, 74, 75, and Corpo dipl. Port., VII., 424.

family, Giovanni Carafa saw the means of promoting this by a close connection with Spain. It is characteristic of the man and his times that he could conceive the plan of detaching his brother Carlo from the French service, which might cause serious embarrassments, and withdrawing this experienced soldier from the calling of arms, by procuring for him the dignity of Cardinal. Carlo himself, though it may be doubted whether he was in earnest, showed but little inclination for the change. At first the Pope would not hear of such a promotion, but in spite of this Giovanni Carafa contrived to bring it about ; he was eagerly encouraged in his plan by the French Ambassador, Avanson, who, fearing the great influence of Cardinal Alessandro Farnese, favoured the cause of the nephew in every way.[1] At last Giovanni won over the representative of the Emperor to his plan, and the Pope, after some hesitation, finally gave way to the general pressure put upon him.[2] He was destined, however, to regret nothing more bitterly than this choice, which remains a great slur upon his reputation.

The first, however, to repent of the elevation of Carlo was his brother Giovanni.[3] In a very short time Carlo was able to ingratiate himself to such an extent with the Pope that the latter, after a few weeks, entrusted him with the entire direction of secular politics. Giovanni, who, since the beginning of

[1] *Cf.* COGGIOLA, Conclave, 474 *seqq.* Avanson also feared the influence of the Imperialist Cardinal Carpi, who was very intimate with Paul IV., see his letter of May 24, 1555, in FAVRE, 436.

[2] * It is quite in accordance with the truth when Paul IV., in a *brief to Pole of July 16, 1555, says that he has appointed C. Carafa as Cardinal : " non solum omnium consensu, sed hortatu." (Min. brev. Arm. 44, t. 4, n. 169. Secret Archives of the Vatican).

[3] The second brother, Antonio, Marchese di Montebello, was a passionate man and not of any great talent, but, in spite of this he was appointed to the command of the Papal troops (see the *brief to him of August 31, 1555 ; Brev. ad princ. Arm. 44, t. 4, n. 226. Secret Archives of the Vatican). Antonio played no part in the time that followed. On the other hand his son Alfonso became a favourite of the Pope (*cf. infra* p. 202).

June, had had a decisive influence[1] in this matter, found himself, to his great surprise, completely supplanted. The
change found outward expression in the fact that Carlo Carafa
now moved to the Borgia apartments, which had hitherto been
occupied by his brother.[2] The ambassadors and envoys of
the powers now crowded these rooms, especially as Paul IV.
granted audiences very unwillingly. The only person who saw
His Holiness every day was Carlo Carafa ; in his new position
as head of the actual secretaryship of state, he could confer
with the Pope as often and as long as he wished. The whole
of the political correspondence with the nuncios and other
representatives of the Holy See, as well as with the kings and
princes, was directed by him. He alone had the right to open
and answer all letters, even those addressed directly to the
Pope. In addition to this, all political business, as well as
everything that concerned finance, law, and the administration
of the city of Rome and the States of the Church, was placed
under the superintendence of the Cardinal-nephew.[3]

In order to carry on such an amount of work Carlo Carafa
surrounded himself with a numerous and well-trained staff of
officials, who were entirely devoted to him. Giovanni della
Casa, his principal secretary, worked under him as his confidential assistant and representative (segretario intimo or
maggiore). This Florentine humanist and open enemy of
the Medici was the most distinguished of the numerous Floren-
tines who had left their home and come to Rome. He alone
had cognizance of all the projects of the Cardinal-nephew, and
the whole of the diplomatic correspondence passed through his

[1] See in Appendix No. 10 the *brief of June 2, 1555 (Secret
Archives of the Vatican) and the Portuguese report in the Corpo
dipl. Port., VIII., 431. As early as June 20, 1555, an agent of
Cardinal Madruzzo *reported from Rome : the new Cardinal
Carafa was indeed, " privato del papa," but : " Chi adesso fa
tutte le cose è il conte di Montorio." Correspondence of Madruzzo in the Vice-Regal Archives, Innsbruck.

[2] See ANCEL, Disgrâce, 17 seq. and Secrétairie, 10 ; cf. COGGIOLA,
Farnesi, 77n.

[3] See ANCEL, Secrét., 7 seq.

hands ; indeed, he alone was aware of the existence of many of these documents.[1]

Positions similar to that held by Giovanni della Casa for political affairs, were held by Annibale Bozzuto for the affairs of the States of the Church, and by the celebrated jurist, Silvestro Aldobrandini, for fiscal and criminal causes. Every morning, with the exception of that given over to the reception of the ambassadors, Carlo Carafa received these men for the delivery of their reports, and important questions were dealt with by all four.[2] Aldobrandini, who belonged to a noble Florentine family, had been banished in 1531 as an opponent of the Medici. Bozzuto was a banished Neapolitan, and the appointment of these exiles who, full of spite and passion, were awaiting their return home by means of the fall of the Spanish power, counted for much in the warlike turn which affairs took in Rome.[3]

[1] See ANCEL, Secrét. 5 *seqq.* Della Casa (see concerning him Vol. XII. of this work, p. 525) had already known Paul IV., in Venice ; he owed his new position to Cardinal Farnese (CARO-FARNESE, Lettere, II., 221). He was summoned to Rome by a *brief of May 30, 1555 (Min. brev. Arm. 44, t. 4, n. 110. Secret Archives of the Vatican) and definitely appointed on July 13 (see Studi storici, XVII., 592). After his death (November 14, 1556) he was succeeded by S. Aldobrandini. After the fall of the latter in 1557 (see *infra* p. 154) A. Lippomano succeeded to his important post, which he united to that of a " secretarius domesticus " ; see ANCEL, Secrét., 15 *seq.*

[2] See the *Summario dell' attioni di Mons. Illmo in the minutes of the trial of Carafa (State Archives, Rome), of which Ancel justly remarks (*loc. cit.*) that it should not be attributed to Antonio Carafa, as Coggiola has it (Sull' anno della morte di m. della Casa, Pistoia, 1901, 8 *seqq.*) Passarini had already remarked (Aldobrandini, 118) this error of Nores (p. 272). Concerning the fall of Bozzuto F. Pasoto reports from Rome on September 1, 1557 *Domenica mattina si disse la notte inanci N.S. havea fatto levar di letto Monsig. Bozzuto cosi amalato com' era et fattolo mettere prigione in castello, dove è ancora. La causa non si dice. His successor was Annibale Bràncaccio (Gonzaga Archives, Mantua.)

[3] See NAVAGERO-ALBÈRI 391, 405. The apologetic counter-remarks of Passarini (Aldobrandini, 118) prove nothing.

Five secretaries were appointed in addition to della Casa
to carry on the Italian correspondence. Of these, Antonio
Elio, Bishop of Pola, and Giovanni Francesco Commendone,
Bishop of Zante, held the first place. There were also three
other secretaries, Girolamo Soverchio, Angelo Massarelli and
Trifone Bencio, the latter for the cypher letters. All of these
highly placed officials of the department of the secretary of
state had a corresponding number of lesser officials at their
disposal. Besides these, Cardinal Carafa employed various
private secretaries and agents, who were partly made use of
for purposes of his own. Among these a great part was played
by Annibale Rucellai, although he had no special title ; he
was a nephew of Giovanni della Casa, and was initiated into
many secrets of the policy of his master.[1]

The secretariate of briefs was strictly separated from the
secretariate of state, and had its own archives. This department, which was exclusively occupied with ecclesiastical affairs
and the administration of the States of the Church, was
directly under the Pope. Giovanni Barengo held, as first
" segretario domestico," a similar position in this department
to that of della Casa in that of the secretariate of state. Like
Barengo, who composed all the important briefs and bulls, a
second " segretario domestico," Giovanni Francesco Bini,
lived in the Vatican. The latter, a humanist of the school of
Sadoleto, had to draw up the briefs to the princes. Besides
those mentioned, there also appear, as highly placed officials
of the secretariate of briefs, Antonio Fiordibello, once secretary
to Sadoleto, and Cesare Grolierio. All of these, who in their
turn had many officials under them, are distinguished from
the great functionaries of the secretariate of state principally
by the fact that they did no independent work of their own,
but had only to carry out the orders they received, these being
given by the Pope himself, or by those to whom the head of
the Church had transferred some part of his authority.[2]

[1] See the thorough investigations of ANCEL, Secrét., 14 seqq.
25 seqq., 32 seqq. ; concerning Elio cf. MERKLE, I., 377.

[2] See ANCEL, Secrét., 47 seqq. Concerning Barengo cf. MASIUS,
Briefe, 244,251 for Bini (died September, 1556) see MERKLE, II.,

It is characteristic of Paul IV. that he placed a limit to the powers of Carlo Carafa, as far as the actual inner administration of the Church was concerned.[1] The nephew, however, ruled all the more freely in the matter of politics ; in this department he eventually got such a grip that he managed the Pope like a child.[2] Cardinal Alessandro Farnese, in whom the Pope, at the beginning of his reign, had shown, in the fullness of his gratitude, an almost unlimited confidence, was now put on one side, as had been the case with Giovanni Carafa.[3] The crafty and intriguing Carlo, who could adapt himself to every situation, understood perfectly how to lead the unwary old Pope.

The unusual capabilities of his nephew, and his hatred of the Spaniards, had made Paul IV. forget everything which he had formerly blamed in him. He bore all the more willingly with the warlike nature of Carlo, which was quite opposed to his principles as a strict churchman, because their characters were in reality much akin ; both were true Neapolitans, passionate, credulous and rash in their resolves.[4] Carlo possessed, moreover, a wonderful skill in managing his old uncle, and in accomodatiig himself to his weaknesses and favourite theories. Paul IV. became more and more persuaded that the Holy See possessed no more faithful, honest and capable servant than his nephew. So completely was he

xxii. Bini's successor was A. Lippomano ; when Barengo died in June, 1559, he was suceeded by Francesco Aragonia.

[1] See NAVAGERO-ALBÈRI, who twice emphasizes this limitation of authority (384 and 411). It cannot therefore be said with RANKE (I.[6], 188) that the Pope entrusted his nephew with " the whole, not only of secular, but also of ecclesiastical affairs." In the report of Salvago (Atti Lig., XIII., 755) he says distinctly that Cardinal Carafa had possessed the " suprema authorità et cura de' negotii appartenenti a stato et a giustitia."

[2] See MASIUS, Briefe, 222.

[3] Cf. COGGIOLA, Conclave, 476 seq., and FARNESI, 81 seq. ; ANCEL, Secrét, 14 seq. Concerning the great influence of Farnese at the beginning see also the report of the Portuguese ambassador of June 18, 1555, in the Corpo dipl. Port., VIII., 420.

[4] Cf. the opinion of Cardinal Farnese in RIESS, 53.

beguiled, that he did not hesitate repeatedly to assure the Venetian ambassador that Carlo excelled all his predecessors as a statesman. The nephew, who was soon overwhelmed with tokens of favour,[1] was able to make himself so indispensable that the Pope longed for him when he was absent, and put off all important business until his return. As Navagero points out, Carlo was able, with wonderful sagacity, to find out exactly what pleased the Pope, and to make use of every circumstance for the attainment of his own ends. He was exceedingly jealous of his own influence, and wanted to be recognized everywhere as the master, and to see others in a position of dependence ; he also treated the representatives of the powers with abrupt self-assurance. In the same way as he promoted his friends and adherents, he revenged himself on his rivals and opponents. He had reached an age when he had come to the full vigour of his powers, and he devoted himself with indefatigable energy to the affairs of state. Sagacious and skilled in all manner of plots and intrigues, a master of the art of always having irons in the fire, unprincipled, double-faced and calculating, like a true follower of Machiavelli, full of bold and far-reaching schemes, which he was exceedingly skilful in carrying into effect, and entirely possessed by an insatiable ambition, Carafa's fiery nature was more and more inflamed by his unexpected good fortune, of which he was determined to make full use as long as his aged uncle lived. It was only in appearance that he was working for the noble end of liberating the Holy See and Italy from the oppressive yoke of foreign rule, in reality his activities

---

[1] C. Carafa received the legation of Bologna, as well as all the offices connected with it on October 26, 1555 (see the *brief of that date in the Secret Archives of the Vátican, Arm. 44, t. 4, p. 143). This office brought in to the nephew 8000 ducats. Concerning this and other revenues see NAVAGERO-ALBÈRI, 384-385. In February, 1556 Cardinal Carafa also received the ' governo d'Ancona ' (see the *letter of Card. Medici to Card. Carafa of February 5, 1556. Cod. Barb. lat. 5698, p. 8. Vatican Library), in July, 1556 he received the bishopric of Comminges ; see Mél. d' archéol., XXII., 101 seq.

were wholly selfish and unscrupulous, and directed to his own advancement and that of his family.[1] Such was the man who, in these exceedingly dangerous times, was to direct the secular policy of the Holy See.

[1] For a character sketch of Cardinal Carafa, *cf.* of contemporaries, especially NAVAGERO-ALBÈRI, 384 *seq.*, and Charles Marillac in VAISSIÈRE, Charles de Marillac, Paris, 1896, 327 ; of later historians PALLAVICINI, 13, 12, 6 ; MARCKS, Coligny, 81, and especially ANCEL, Secrét, 11 *seqq.*, and Disgrâce, 13 *seq.* In his admirable work, La question de Sienne, ANCEL remarks : " Entre les bas calculs de Carlo Carafa et l'idéal du pape qui voudrait soustraire l'Église et l'Italie a la tutelle qui va désormais peser si lourdement sur elles, il y a un abîme." (p. 90).

CHAPTER IV.

COMMENCEMENT OF THE STRUGGLE OF PAUL IV.
AGAINST THE SUPREMACY OF SPAIN.

ON the same May 29th, 1555, on which Paul IV. had announced his intentions concerning reform in his first consistory, he signed a Bull in which he solemnly promised to devote the whole of his powers to the restoration of peace in Christendom and the renewal of the ancient discipline in the Church.[1]

The Pope had already taken steps towards securing peace,[2] and he now set about putting his plans for reform into immediate execution. A decree was therefore issued in a consistory on June 5th that in future, those who had the right of patronage should only present for bishoprics and abbeys those who were thoroughly fitted for such positions, and who were absolutely free from any suspicion of ambition or simony.[3]

A decree of July 17th forbade dispensations being granted for the occupation of bishoprics by those who had not reached the canonical age.[4] On the same day an important consistory was held, in which three bulls were published ; the first concerned the proclamation of a Jubilee Indulgence for all those who prayed for the peace of Christendom ; the second imposed the severest restrictions on the Jews in the

---

[1] See MASSARELLI, II., 272 ; BROMATO, II., 224.

[2] See the briefs to the Emperor and Ferdinand I. of May 24 and 26, 1555, in RAYNALDUS, 1555, n. 24 seq., the *letters to the nuncio G. Muzzarelli, to *Philip II. and Queen Mary, as well as to *Cardinal Pole, all of May 24, 1555. Brevia ad princ., Arm. 44, t. 4, n. 98, 99, 100 (Secret Archives of the Vatican).

[3] Cf. *Acta consist. (Consistorial Archives) ; see Appendix, No.11.

[4] Cf. *Acta consist. (Consistorial Archives) ; see Appendix No. 12 and Bull., VI., 496 seq. ; cf. *Report of Camillo Titio to C. Pagni, dated Rome, July 18, 1555 (State Archives, Florence).

90

States of the Church; the third was directed against all alienation of the property of the Roman Church. After these documents had been read, the Pope exhorted the Cardinals to reform, blamed such as had not lived up to their high dignity, and repeated his intention of employing all his powers for the improvement of the condition of the whole Church.

He accordingly appointed five Cardinals who were to superintend the work of reform in the different countries. These were : du Bellay for France, Pacheco for Spain, Truchsess for Germany, and Puteo and Cicada for Italy.[1] A constitution of August 7th provided for the strictest regulations against heresy.[2] A few days later a correspondent, who was inimical to Paul IV., reported that the Pope was thinking day and night of the amendment of morals of all classes, and that a great reform and a thorough purification were awaiting the clergy.[3] Ignatius of Loyola expressed a similar opinion when writing to the rectors of the Jesuit colleges.[4] With how little consideration Paul IV. proceeded is shown by the painful dismissal of Palestrina from the Papal choir, which took place on July 30th, 1555, on the ground that married members would, in future, no longer be allowed.[5] In a consistory of August 23rd, Paul IV. spoke about the appointment of a commission of Cardinals for the examination

---

[1] How incomplete the official *Acta consist. are is best shown by the fact that the important events which we learn from MASSARELLI (p. 276) are not even mentioned. *Cf.* also the report of G. Grandi of August 7, 1555 in ANCEL, Concile, 9.

[2] See RAYNALDUS, 1555, n. 54.

[3] Report from Rome on August 10 to Kurpfalz, in DRUFFEL-BRANDI, IV., 704 *seq. Cf.* also the letter of Cardinal du Bellay of July 26, 1555 in RIBIER, II., 613, that of Carafa of July 27 and of Serristori of August 27, 1555 (State Archives, Florence) ; Nonciat. I., lxi., n. 248 ; MASIUS, Briefe, 515. A brief of August 2, 1555 concerning the reform of monasteries in Ferrara in FONTANA, 433.

[4] Of August 13, 1555. Cartas, V., 288 *seq.* Mon. Ign. Ser. I., IX., 463 *seq.*

[5] *Cf.* AMBROS, IV., 9.

of those who were to receive bishoprics.[1] At the beginning
of September he expressed his displeasure in the sharpest
terms against those princes who delayed in making appointments to vacant bishoprics.[2]

It can therefore be seen that the beginning of the reign of
the new Pope was fully in accordance with the idea of the
strict zealot, from whom the whole world, good as well as bad,
had been led to expect an era of ecclesiastical reform. Unfortunately, a state of affairs was soon to supervene which
seriously endangered the work so auspiciously begun, entirely
turned the thoughts of the head of the Church away from the
attempts at securing peace, which had hardly been begun,
and entangled him in a disastrous war.[3]

It was a thing quite trifling in itself which first fanned the
ill-will which Paul IV. had for years entertained against the
Spaniards, to such an extent that at length a disastrous break
occurred.

The Count of Santa Fiora, the head of the Sforza family,
had, as well as his brother Alessandro and the Cardinal, Guido
Ascanio, always belonged to the Imperial party. After the
occupation of Siena by the Spaniards, the Count succeeded
in prevailing on his other two brothers, Carlo and Mario, to
give up their military service with the French and enter that
of Charles V. They both treacherously resolved to hand over
the two galleys which they commanded into the hands of the
Imperialists ; they succeeded in inducing the French captain
of the galleys to put into Civitavecchia in order to have some
repairs carried out, but hardly had they arrived there when
Alessandro Sforza took forcible possession of the vessels.
The Papal harbour-master opposed the departure of the ships,
as he would take no responsibility for this act of violence
committed before his very eyes. The Sforza, however, found

---

[1] *Acta consist. (Consistorial Archives).

[2] See the report in SANTAREM, XII., 431.

[3] The clear sighted C. Olivo expressed apprehension about the
future as early as May 23, 1555. See Appendix No. 9 (Gonzaga
Archives, Mantua).

a way out, for Alessandro at once informed his brother the
Cardinal, who procured, through his crafty secretary, Giovan
Francesco Lottini, a letter from the Count of Montorio to the
harbour-master, who then allowed the vessels to sail. Alessandro could now get his spoils in safety to Naples; to a
counter-command from the Pope (who had meantime learned
the true state of affairs), which reached him while he was on
the way, he paid no attention at all.[1]

While the Imperialists in Naples and Rome were rejoicing,
the French ambassador complained to the Pope of this breach
of neutrality, and represented to him the insult which his
authority had suffered at the hands of the Sforza. Such
representations were not required to put Paul IV. into the
greatest state of excitement. He had already, at the beginning of his reign, formed the plan of breaking down the arrogance of the powerful nobles, and especially of the Sforza.
This family had been accustomed, as being near relatives of
Paul III., and on account of their importance to Julius III.
in his struggle with France, to observe no other law than their
own will.[2]

---

[1] Cf. CASA, Opere, II., 17, 31 ; CARO-FARNESE, Lettere, III.,
19 seq. ; Legaz. di Serristori, 358 ; Pacheco's letter of August 17,
1555 in DÖLLINGER, Beiträge, I., 209 ; DRUFFEL-BRANDI, IV.,
308, n. 2 ; Doc. ined., II., 446 ; Arch. stor. Ital., XII., 372 seq. ;
Nonciat., II., 259 seq. ; see also the letter of the Count of Santa
Fiora of August 11, 1555 in the Bollet. Senese, X., 124 seq., and
that from Rome of August 17 in the *reports of Lasso to
Ferdinand I. (State Archives, Vienna). Concerning G. F. Lottini
cf. MAFFEI in the Rassegna mensile di storia per la città di Volterra, I. (1898), 10 seq., 41 seqq., 56 seq., 83 seq. This work, which
is unfortunately incomplete, is based principally on the documents preserved in the State Archives in Rome of the legal proceedings against Lottini, concerning which Bruzzone was the first
to make several extracts in the Fanfulla della Domenica, II.,
n. 28, and also on Acta in the rich Inghirami Archives at Volterra.

[2] A Sforza had murdered a financial official in the middle of
Rome ; see RIBIER, II., 617 ; cf. PALLAVICINI 13, 14.

Paul IV., who, just at that time, was taking proceedings[1] against some unworthy officials of Julius III., eagerly seized upon this opportunity of beginning to subdue the insubordinate nobles. Lottini, upon whom the Count of Montorio succeeded in fixing the guilt, was imprisoned in the Castle of St. Angelo on August 10th, while Carlo Carafa was ordered to inform the Cardinal of Santa Fiora that if the vessels were not brought back to Civitavecchia within three days, legal proceedings would be taken against him also. Santa Fiora sought advice from the Spanish Cardinals and from the representative of Charles V., Fernando Ruiz de Castro, Marquis de Sarria, who had arrived in Rome on July 6th.[2] The latter, an honest Basque, but quite without experience in politics,[3] had requested an immediate audience with the Pope, but had received the answer that he was to present himself on the following day. The Imperialists then resolved that Sarria should, at all costs, endeavour to secure an immediate audience and represent to the Pope that he had no reason to feel himself offended; he was also to complain of the imprisonment of Lottini and of the order given to Cardinal Santa Fiora, which the Emperor would not readily endure.[4]

[1] Besides MASSARELLI, 278 seq., cf. the *letter mentioned supra p. 93, n. 1, dated Rome, August 7, 1555 : " Francesco d'Aspra thesoriere sotto papa Giulio III. mercodi serà fu menato in torre di Nona dal bargello et hieri andò in castello, al qual sono imputate grandissime rubbarie fatte nella thesoreria " (State Arch., Vienna).

[2] See MASSARELLI, 276; cf. DRUFFEL-BRANDI, IV., 702. The *letter of credence of Charles V. for Sarria, dated Brussels, June 4, 1555, in the Arch. S. Angelo, VIII.-II., Vol. I., the letter to Paul IV., Secret Archives of the Vatican; ibid. also a *letter of Philip II.of June 7, in which he also accredited Sarria for his affairs.

[3] Cf. SOMMARIO, 350; DRUFFEL-BRANDI, IV., 707 n.; COGGIOLA, Farnesi. 149.

[4] See the report of Serristori of August 10, 1555 (Legaz. 358 seq.) Concerning the proceedings against Lottini see GORI, Archivio, I., 209 seq. ; cf. BRUZZONE in the Turin Stampa, 1900, n. 51.

Arrived at the Vatican, Sarria penetrated as far as the anti-camera, and renewed his request in an excited manner. The Pope, however, remained inflexible, and did not permit the entrance of the ambassador. The excitement among the Imperialists now knew no bounds; they deliberated as to whether, not Sarria only, but Santa Fiora as well, should leave Rome.[1] The character of Paul IV. was so little understood by them that they believed they could force him by threats to withdraw from his position.

That very night Cardinal Santa Fiora arranged a meeting of protest at his palace, of the adherents of the Imperialist party, at which, besides the Colonna, Cesarini and other barons, Sarria and the " obedientia " envoy of Philip II., Count Chinchon, were present.[2] They then proceeded to attack the dignity and honour of the Pope in the most violent and unworthy terms, Marcantonio Colonna declaring himself ready to stir up a revolt with his followers, for which purpose a collection was actually made.[3]

This meeting of protest was not concealed from the Pope, but, instead of frightening him, as the Imperialists had hoped, it enraged him more than ever. The documents found in the house of Lottini had also given him grounds for serious thought with regard to the intentions of Spain; in these he found mention of the calling together of a Council and other things which deeply offended the head of the Church,[4] who had

---

[1] See Legaz. di Serristori, 360.

[2] The autograph *letter of Philip II. of June 8, 1555, by which Chinchon was accredited, is in the above-mentioned (p. 94, n. 2) collection of letters in the Secret Archives of the Vatican.

[3] See the report of Farnese to Henry II. of August 14 (not 24, as PALLAVICINI, 13, 14 gives it) in CARO-FARNESE, Lettere, III., 20 seq.

[4] Cf. the *brief to Charles V. of July 15 and that to *Alba of July 20, 1555 (Brevia ad princ. Arm. 44, t. 4, n. 164 and 170. Secret Archives of the Vatican). See also Nonciat. de France, I., lxi. seq.

hitherto, officially at anyrate, been on friendly terms with Charles V. and Alba.[1]

It is no wonder that Cardinals Carpi and Mendoza, who repaired to the Pope on August 11th, could come to no arrangement with him, although they negotiated with him for four hours. Paul IV. was determined that the ships seized must be returned to Civitavecchia. In the event of this not having been done within three days, he threatened Alessandro Sforza in a monitorium with the loss of his position as a chamberlain and a fine of 20,000 scudi ; the Pope, however, declared that he would see that the ships did not get into the hands of the French.[2]

In face of this determined attitude, the representatives of the Emperor had misgivings about plunging their master into a conflict, the consequences of which could not be foreseen, about a comparative trifle, and they requested the Neapolitan authorities to return the ships. The Sforza, however, would only give up their booty on condition that Lottini should be set at liberty, and Alessandro Sforza escape all punishment. This demand only embittered the Pope still further ; he felt it intolerable that those whose duty it was to obey him as their lawful master should make such conditions. He understood, moreover, that the Sforza had secret designs of their own, from the fact that they were putting their fief in the States of the Church into a state of defence, while, at the same time, he heard of suspicious movements of the Imperial partisans on the southern boundaries of the Papal dominions.[3]

Paul IV. was, as Cardinal Farnese points out, exceedingly hot-tempered and extraordinarily strong-willed, especially when his honour and dignity were concerned, yet he realized his helplessness, in view of the exhaustion of his treasury, and the limited number of troops at his disposal in Rome. It is just such fiery natures as his which often break down after the first outburst. Cardinal Carafa and the French

---

[1] See " Extráctus processus card, Caraffae " in RIESS, 35.

[2] See Serristori's report of Aug. 12, 1555. Legaz. 364 seq.

[3] Cf. COGGIOLA, Farnesi, 113.

knew this very well, and they, therefore did all in their power to encourage him. The ambassador of Henry II. promised him assistance to the amount of 100,000 scudi ; the old friend of France, Cardinal Farnese, came to an understanding with Carlo Carafa ; he appeared before the Pope on August 12th, and assured him of the support of his whole house, at the same time specially pointing out that an alliance with France would offer perfect security to the Pope. Paul IV. received this significant encouragement with great pleasure. Farnese, who immediately reported matters to Henry II., declared that although he could not promise that the Pope would decide on such a course, the inclination to do so was present in his mind to such a degree, that he considered it advisable that his majesty should, in any case, send full authority to act in accordance with it. When the Imperial ambassador, who had an audience on the same day, presented the conditions demanded by the Sforza, he received a decided refusal to accept them.[1]

During the time that followed, the Imperialists took no serious steps to settle the affair ; accustomed to the weakness of Julius III., they were unable to realize the character of the new Pope, whom they thought to put off with empty promises.

Under these circumstances, it was not difficult for Carlo Carafa to obtain permission from his master to proceed with the preparation of an extensive armament. As early as August 15th Carafa was able to call upon the Duke of Urbino, as Captain-General of the Church, to hold himself in readiness to appear at once in Rome, when summoned, with from 5,000 to 6,000 infantry and a corresponding number of cavalry.[2]

The fact that Marcantonio Colonna was fortifying Paliano, not far from the Neapolitan frontier, and Paolo Giordano Orsini the fortress of Bracciano, seemed to point to a renewed

---

[1] See CARO-FARNESE, Lettere, III., 19 seqq. ; cf. RIESS, 36 seq. and COGGIOLA, Farnesi, 109 seq.

[2] CASA, II., 19. The appointment of the Duke as *Capitaneus generalis* of the Church was made in a *brief of June 20, 1555 (Brevia ad. princ. *loc. cit.*, 132. Secret Archives of the Vatican).

outbreak of the old party struggles in Rome and its neighbourhood.[1]

The Pope informed the Bolognese ambassador on August 28th that he was to raise troops, the number of which might amount to about 3,000 men. He had already surrounded himself with a special bodyguard for the defence of his own person ;[2] it was also said that Ottavio Farnese would provide an additional body of 3,000 men. The Imperial ambassador was so imprudent as then to say that if the Pope raised ten men he would raise twenty. The Florentine envoy declared that Paul IV. had said after dinner that he intended to administer justice in his States, and that in punishing the evildoers, he would take care that the big fish did not swallow the small ones ; should the Emperor dare to interfere with him in so doing, he would have cause to repent it.[3]

The news that the Sforza were continuing to make preparations for war, was bound to strengthen the Pope's resolve to protect himself. When Cardinal Mendoza took the liberty of remarking in an audience that armaments were unnecessary, as there was nothing to be feared from the Emperor, he received the angry answer that he, the Pope, intended to maintain his authority, and to punish those who were disobedient. "No one" writes the Florentine ambassador, "dares to contradict His Holiness, but everyone keeps silent."[4]

Cardinals Carafa and Farnese, who were so friendly to the French, had reason to be pleased. "The honour of His Holiness," wrote Farnese on August 28th to his trusted friend Tiburzio, who was then at the court of Henry II., "no longer allows him to turn back. As events are themselves driving us to war, we may calmly await further developments, while we are fanning the righteous anger of His Holiness." Farnese, confident of victory, then proceeds to

---

[1] See Legaz. di Serristori, 373.

[2] *Letter of U. Gozzadini, dated Rome, August 28, 1555 (State Archives, Bologna).

[3] Report of Serristori of August 31, 1555.　Legaz. 372 *seq.*

[4] *Ibid* 371.

discuss in detail the manner of such an alliance. He also further advises that a pension of from 3,000 to 4,000 scudi should be settled on Cardinal Carafa, who is as zealous in the cause of France as he is powerful with the Pope ; should the influential Datary be won over in the same manner, then they would have the advisers of the Pope at their disposal. The actual decision, indeed, was dependent on the Emperor, to whom the Pope had applied in the matter of the ships, but whatever his answer might be, friendly relations between the Pope and Charles V. were impossible, since their aims were so different, and if a breach did not take place now, it would not be long before it occurred.[1]

As appears from the report of the French ambassador, Lanssac, of August 28th, the latter promised the Pope, in the name of the king, energetic help against his rebellious subjects, and encouraged him in every way in making a determined stand against the Spaniards. The Franco-Papal alliance, and the inclusion of Venice in the league, were then discussed in great detail.[2]

Nothing was more opposed to the Pope's character than to yield to rebellious subjects. As soon as the time fixed for the return of the ships by Cardinal Santa Fiora had passed without result, he took a decisive step. On August 31st, the Cardinal was taken to the Castle of St. Angelo ; his fate was shared by Camillo Colonna, who had expressed himself in a very threatening manner against Paul IV. The Colonna and other suspected barons, such as Giuliano Cesarini, received orders not to leave the city.[3]

[1] CARO-FARNESE, Lettere, III., 51 seqq.
[2] See RIBIER, II., 615 seq. ; Corresp. de Lanssac 473 seqq.
[3] See MASSARELLI, 279-280 ; CARO-FARNESE, Lettere III., 57 seq., and RIESS, 38 seq., who rightly repudiates the statement that Santa Fiora was taken by surprise ; also Nonciat. II., 261 n. 1 (report of Serristori). Cf. also Docum. ined., II., 448 and the *Diario di Cola Coleine Romano, which is to be found in many copies, as in the Corsini Library, Cod. 128 (see LÄMMER, Zur Kirchengesch., 143), in the Archivio Capitolino, XIV., 7, and in the Chigi Library, N. II., 32. The copy in the Chigi Library was before me. C. Coleine is mentioned in FORCELLA, V., 253.

Paul IV. was quite aware of the difficulties which he had to
face, in consequence of his attack on the relatives and followers
of the masters of the Campagna, the Colonna and Orsini.   In
order to assure his own safety, he ordered that the castles
which these families possessed in the neighbourhood of the city
should be delivered up to him.   While the Orsini submitted,
and gave up Bracciano, the Colonna refused to admit the
Papal troops, trusting in the Emperor's protection ; this
powerful Ghibelline family was therefore now mixed up in
the dispute between the Pope and the Sforza.   Marcantonio
Colonna, who was also to have been arrested, intended to
fortify himself at Paliano, but eventually, not venturing to
make any resistance, he took to flight.   Monitoria were issued
against him and his father, Ascanio Colonna, on account of
various acts of violence of which they were accused, and when
they failed to appear, judgment was given against them by
default, according to which they forfeited their estate.   This
sentence was immediately put into execution by force of arms,
and Papal troops invested Paliano, Genazzano, and other
fortresses belonging to them.   All the adherents of the Imperial party, as well as those who were merely suspects, were
expelled from the Papal dominions ; this measure affected
even several relatives of the Pope.[1]

" As far as His Holiness is concerned," Cardinal Farnese
triumphantly announced on August 31st, " the die is cast.
We must now keep quiet, and await the next move of the
Imperialists."   A Mantuan correspondent in a letter of
September 1st thought that very little more would have led
to the arrest of even the ambassador of Charles V.[2]

Relations with the Imperial ambassador were still further
strained just at this moment, because the latter refused to

---

[1] See MASSARELLI, 280 *seq.* ; BROMATO, II., 300 n. ; COGGIOLA,
Farnesi, 118 ; *cf.* also the letters of Marcantonio Colonna in the
Delizie degli eruditi bibliof. ital., VII, Florence, 1865, and GORI,
Archivio, I., 221 *seq.* The *Acta of the process against M. Col-
onna are in the Colonna Archives, Rome.

[2] *Letter of Ippolito Capilupi in the Gonzaga Archives, Mantua.

deliver three fortresses of the Colonna, of which he was administrator, in consequence of a law-suit then pending between the Colonna and the Prince of Sulmona. Letters from Alba were also intercepted at this time, in which he advised the retention of the ships which had been seized, as energetic measures should be adopted in dealing with such a Pope.[1] This language was quite in keeping with the news of extensive preparations for war on the part of the Spaniards in the Neapolitan territory.[2] Rome seemed to be threatened from the South.[3]

In spite of all this, Paul IV., at that time, had by no means made up his mind to such a hazardous enterprise as a break with the great world power of Spain. The best proof of this is that Cardinal Carafa thought it advisable to conceal from his uncle a political move of the greatest importance which was made at that time. Quite on his own initiative, the nephew on September 14th and 15th, dispatched envoys, invested with full powers, to Ferrara and France, in order to win over those states to an anti-Imperial league. In order that the old Pope should hear nothing of this before the proper time, the crafty Carafa concealed the true object of this mission, and even kept the fact of his having sent it from the French nuncio and his friend Cardinal Farnese.[4]

How little the Pope was aware of what his nephew was doing behind his back, is best seen from the fact that he banished Cardinal d'Este from the Papal dominions on September 5th[5] for simoniacal intrigues concerning the Papal election, thereby

---

[1] CARO-FARNESE, Lettere, III., 70 seq.

[2] Cf. COGGIOLA, Farnesi, 120 seq.

[3] See CAVALCANTI, Lettre, 105.

[4] See RIESS, 54 seqq.; cf. COGGIOLA, Farnesi, 124 and Arch. stor. Ital., Ser. 3, XXV., 56 seq.

[5] * See, MASSARELLI 281; Masius, Briefe, 222; COGGIOLA, Asc. d. Cornia, 140 n. 1 and Farnesi, 123 seq. Duke Ercole of Ferrara sent a special envoy to intercede for his brother with the Pope; see the autograph *letter of Ercole, dated Ferrara, October 2, 1555, in the second volume of the collection of letters in the Secret Archives of the Vatican mentioned supra p. 94, n. 2.

doing, as far as he was concerned, everything in his power to make an alliance with Ferrara impossible.

Annibale Rucellai, the envoy sent on September 14th on a secret mission to the French court, was to decide Henry II. to undertake the protection of the Holy See against the Imperialists. The king was begged to confirm immediately the promises of his ambassador with regard to troops and money, and also to draw up instructions giving full authority for the conclusion of a defensive and offensive alliance. Besides this, Henry II. was begged to induce Ferrara and Venice to enter this anti-Imperialist league.[1] Carafa had expressly instructed his envoy to make the proposals quite independently of the settlement of the disputes then pending, as he could foresee that sooner or later a rupture would inevitably come.

The ships that had been seized were, as a matter of fact, at last brought back to Civitavecchia on September 15th, and the Pope then released Cardinal Santa Fiora from his imprisonment on September 19th, after he had given a security of 200,000 scudi, and promised not to leave Rome without permission. Three days later Camillo Colonna was also set at liberty.[2]

The restoration of the ships removed the actual cause of dispute ; this, however, had been so long delayed that a strong feeling of resentment remained in the mind of the Pope, and there was in addition to this, the great massing of the Spanish troops on the southern frontier of the States of the Church. As Duke Cosimo I. of Florence was a firm adherent of the

---

[1] The memorandum and instructions for Rucellai in the Nonciat, II., 255 seq., 267 seq. ; cf. CASA, II., 27 seqq. ; ibid. 21 seqq. the instructions for Andrea d'Agubbio, who was sent to Ferrara, which, in the Neapolitan edition V., 48 and in the *Inf. polit. XXIV., 269 (Royal Library, Berlin) as well as in the *Cod. 33—E. 18, p. 7-11 of the Corsini Library, bears the date of September 10. The brief to the Duke of Ferrara of September 15, 1555 in the Arch. stor. Ital., Ser. 3, XXV., 57 seq. Concerning Rucellai in France see Nonciat., I., xxxvii., lxix. ; II., 277 seqq., 286 seqq.

[2] MASSARELLI 281-282. COGGIOLA, Farnesi, 122, 262. Nonciat. II., 278 seq.

Emperor, Paul IV. feared, more than ever, to find himself between two fires.[1] Cardinal Carafa made use of this state of affairs to work upon the excitable Pope to come to an open break with Spain. "Matters," reports Cardinal Farnese on September 27th, " are advancing even more quickly than we could wish, as they are being hurried on by Carafa with a zeal which nothing can surpass."[2] On the same day Farnese represented to the Pope that neither Alba nor the other officials of Charles V. were the cause of the enmity between them, but no one else than the Emperor himself, who was intent on gradually destroying the power of the Holy See. The soil on which these remarks fell was all the more fruitful as Paul IV. had heard reports, just at this time, which filled the lively imagination of the old man with terrifying visions, giving him the impression that his life was threatened by the Imperialists, and leading him to form the desperate resolve to break with the all-powerful Spaniards. It was said that a plot of the Imperialists to poison the Pope and Cardinals Carafa and Farnese had been discovered. This affair, in spite of legal proceedings which were instituted later on, has never been satisfactorily cleared up. It is highly probable, however, that the whole story of the plot was only a cunning intrigue on the part of Carafa, in order to win over his uncle more easily to his disastrous plans.[3]

Old people are readily inclined to mistrust and suspicion, and so was it in the case of Paul IV. He had always had a prejudice against the Spaniards, and had been repeatedly and greatly irritated by them. He therefore believed all that he was told

[1] *Cf.* Serristori's report of September 17, 1555 in the Nonciat., I., lxix. *seq.*

[2] CARO-FARNESE, Lettere, III., 89.

[3] This view, already expressed by PALLAVICINI (13, 15), is confirmed by RIESS' investigations (p. 48 *seqq.*) LAMANSKI (Secrets d'état de Venise, St. Petersburg, 1884, 363) still believes in the truth of the poisoning story ; PLATZHOFF (Die Theorie von der Mordbefugniss, Berlin, 1906) thinks (p. 75-76) that the truth cannot be stated with certainty. Concerning the legal proceedings taken with regard to the matter, see GORI, Arch. I., 218 *seqq.*

about them, and that all the more readily as, just at that time,
letters from Brussels told of threatening remarks of the
Imperialists, which had been made with regard to the arrest
of Santa Fiora and Camillo Colonna.[1] On September 30th the
Pope summoned the French ambassador and Cardinals Farnese
and Carafa to his presence, and deliberated with them as to
how he could best defend himself against the plots of the
Imperialists.[2]

The Pope was so busy and so fatigued on this day that all
audiences were refused.[3] On October 20th he held a consistory, in which he informed the Cardinals that he had resolved
on war, so that he might not be taken by surprise. Cardinal
Medici thought it his duty to make counter-representations
and to urge him to preserve peace. Paul IV. answered :
" What business is it of the Emperor's, if I punish one of my
subjects ? " Medici answered that consideration must be
shown to princes, and advised him to appoint a commission
of Cardinals to consider the difficulties.[4] Realizing the weakness of his military position, the Pope agreed to this proposal,
and at once named a commission of seven members, who were
all adherents of the Emperor, with the exception of Carafa.
He himself assisted at the first meeting ; he defended his
position in a long speech, permitted the commission to deliberate with the Imperial ambassador, and declared that if the

[1] *Cf.* COGGIOLA, Farnese 127 ; Nonciat. I., lxx.

[2] *Cf.* CARO-FARNESE, Lettere, III., 93 ; CASA, II., 39 *seqq. ;*
RIBIER, II., 618 *seqq. ;* COGGIOLA, Farnesi, 127 *seqq.* DURUY
(p. 72 *seqq.*) has already compared the sonorous speech of the Pope,
given in NORES (63 *seqq.*) with the rhetorical essays in the style
of the ancient historians, which does not prevent BROSCH (Mitteil.
des Österr. Inst., XXV., 475) from considering the address as
authentic ! RIESS (p. 45, n. 11) points out, with perfect justice,
that one must not believe with Duruy, that there were ten hearers
(instead of three).

[3] *Letter of G. Aldrovandi, dated Rome, October 2, 1555
(State Archives, Bologna).

[4] See the report of Navagero in BROWN, VI., 1, n. 234 and the
report of Serristori in COGGIOLA, Farnesi, 144 *seqq.*

Imperialists showed themselves inclined to meet him half way, they would find him also ready to forgive, but that if they should take up a hostile attitude, he would fear no monarch, as God would be on his side.[1]

The Duke of Urbino also worked for the preservation of peace. In an audience on October 4th, he made earnest representations to the Pope. He soon saw, however, that it was impossible to prevail against the influence of Carafa and his clique, which was made up almost entirely of Neapolitan and Florentine exiles, such as Bozzuto, della Casa and Silvestro Aldobrandini, who were working with all the power and means at their disposal to bring about a rupture.[2] The alleged attempt at poisoning had given Carafa a better pretext for inducing the Pope to begin hostilities than any other that he could have devised. The demands of the Imperialists, as well as news of the continued preparations for war in Naples, where Marcantonio Colonna was zealously inciting the people against the Pope, finally overcame his reluctance, and he resolved on taking decisive steps.[3]

On October 8th the Pope summoned Cardinals Mendoza, Carpi, Mignanelli, Saraceni, Medici, Cueva, Truchsess, Puteo, Juan Alvarez de Toledo and Carafa, as well as the ambassadors of England, Portugal and Venice, to his private apartments, and made the following announcement to them in fluent Latin : it had always been his first thought, as it still was, to endeavour, with the help of the Cardinals, to find the means of carrying out the much needed reform of the Church, but that while he was devoting himself with his whole heart to this object, the devil had set all the powers of evil to work, and had

[1] Besides Navagero, *loc. cit.* see also MASSARELLI 283 ; *cf.* also COGGIOLA, Farnesi, 145 *seq.*

[2] See the report of Navagero in BROWN, VI., 1, n. 236. Concerning the instigation to war made by the exiles see NAVAGERO-ALBÈRI, 391, 405 *seq.*, 427 and SOMMARIO, 352 *seq.* ; *cf.* also BAGUENAULT DE PUCHESSE, J. de Morvillier (Orléans, 1870), 87.

[3] *Cf.* COGGIOLA, Farnesi, 151, and Nonciat. de France, 1., lxxi. Concerning the incitements of M. Colonna see his ** letters to Madruzzo of October 4, 1555 (Vice-Regal Archives, Innsbruck).

hatched plots, not only against the Holy See, but also against his own life and that of his relatives. " We cannot say this, my lords ambassadors," he continued, " without pain and grief, but it is the actual state of affairs, which admits of no doubt, and which will be revealed at the proper time. They have forced us to take up arms, and nothing will induce us to lay them down again, as we well remember what happened to Pope Clement, to whom the Emperor's ministers that day had made fine promises, but who had hardly disbanded his troops when the terrible capture of Rome, with all its terrible and frightful devastation took place, which, indeed, was the most awful and godless that ever occurred." The Pope then drew a vivid picture of the atrocities then committed in Rome. " This example," he cried, " moves us deeply, and is ever before our eyes, and we do not intend, like Pope Clement, to be taken unawares and deceived. We are well aware of the weakness of our army, but our cause is the cause of God, Who has founded this Holy See, and Who will defend it." He said he was firmly resolved to maintain the ecclesiastical supremacy of Rome, but that he would not begin a war unless challenged and forced by necessity to do so. He then requested the ambassadors to communicate all this to their masters. The reasons which the Portuguese ambassador then brought forward in defence of the Imperialists, he would not listen to.[1]

This sensational declaration proves how greatly Paul IV. feared an attempt on his life. Nevertheless, some days elapsed before Carafa and the ambassador of Henry II. succeeded in inducing the Pope, who was again wavering before taking the last decisive step, to sign the draft of an alliance with France. The imprudence of the Imperialists, however, rendered the attainment of the nephew's aim much easier. They demanded information from the Pope as to the number

---

[1] See the *report of Navagero of October 8, 1555 (State Archives, Venice, translated in BROWN, VI., I, n. 242, and used by SEGRE in the Mem. d. Accad. di Torino, Ser. 2, LV., 388) and the Portuguese report in SANTAREM, XII., 434 ; cf. CARO-FARNESE, Lettere, III., 105, and Serristori in COGGIOLA, Farnesi, 151.

of troops he intended to raise. " As many as I choose ; " answered the Pope angrily, " I shall not allow myself to be dictated to ; I am free, and acknowledge no master over me save God alone."[1] The Pope signed the draft of the alliance on October 14th, and on the same day it was also signed by the French ambassador, a period of forty days being allowed for its confirmation by Henry II.[2]

All this was done with the greatest secrecy, and even Cardinal Farnese learned nothing of it. The Pope did not seem to have fully realized the importance of this too hasty signing of the draft. When the situation temporarily improved on October 15th, owing to the agreement of the commission of Cardinals with the Imperialists,[3] it disturbed Carafa as greatly as the fact that Paul IV. got on very well with the unassuming ambassador-extraordinary of the Hapsburgs, Garcilasso de la Vega, and again seemed inclined to peace.[4] The final decision, however, did not lie in Rome, but in Paris and Ferrara. Should the alliance with Henry II. and Duke Ercole become an accomplished fact, then affairs would develop of themselves in the sense desired by Cardinal Carafa.

In this, however, the patience of the nephew was sorely tried, for it was not until November 20th that Cardinal Guise and two days later, Cardinal Tournon, arrived in Rome with full authority for the conclusion of the alliance. Both took up their residence in the Vatican.[5] They were able to announce

---

[1] See in Appendix No. 13 the *report of Navagero of October 12, 1555 (Library of St.Mark's, Venice). *Cf*.CAVALCANTI, Lettere, 126 *seq.*

[2] CASA, Opere, V., 77 (Neapolitan edition). NORES, 35. DURUY' 78 *seqq.* RIESS, 60 *seqq.* COGGIOLA, Farnesi, 158 *seqq.* Nonciat., II., 325 *seq.*

[3] See MASSARELLI, 284.

[4] See Legaz. di Serristori, 378 *seq.* The instructions for Garcilasso de la Vega, who was to announce the abdication of the Netherlands in favour of Philip II., in the Archives of Simanca, Leg. 882 *seq.*, 193 *seq.*, and an extract in RIESS, 69 *seq.*

[5] See CARO-FARNESE, Lettere, III., 115 ; Navagero in BROWN, VI., 3, App. n. 134 ; *Avviso di Roma de 23 Nov., 1555 (Cod. Vat. 8223, p. 23. Vatican Library) ; *cf.* RIESS, 72 *seq.* and Nonciat., I., lxxiv ; II., 278, 298.

that Duke Ercole II. also had been won over to a Franco-
Papal alliance against Spain.[1] During the course of the
negotiations, which were held in profound secrecy, they came
to an agreement as to an offensive and defensive alliance,
which was signed on December 15th by the Pope and both
the Cardinals.

By this treaty, which was signed by the Pope's own hand,[2]
and contained several changes from the text agreed upon in
October, the French king pledged himself to assist the Holy
See against everyone ; he should only have the right to withdraw from the league in the event of his own dominions being
attacked. Henry II. took Cardinal Carafa and his brothers
Giovanni and Antonio under his protection, and promised
that, for the property which they would lose in Naples, he
would grant them corresponding indemnification, either in
Italy or in France The defensive and offensive league
between the King and the Pope should only be entered upon
with regard to Italy, exclusive of Piedmont A sum of
500,000 gold scudi, of which the Pope was to pay 150,000, was
to be deposited in Venice or Rome within three months, to
defray the expenses of the war. The French auxiliary army
which was to be sent to Italy was fixed at 12,000 men, and, in
addition to this, the Pope was to provide 10,000 infantry and
1,000 cavalry. The war was to be directed, according to the
desire of the Pope, either against Naples or Tuscany, from
which the Medici were to be expelled. With regard to the
conquests that were to be made, it was decided that Siena and
its territory should fall to the Holy See, or, if the inhabitants
should be agreeable, to the Count of Montorio or another ruler

[1] See MURATORI, Antichità Estens., II., 381 ; Arch. stor. Ital.,
Ser. 3, XXV., 52 *seqq.* ; BAGUENAULT DE PUCHESSE in the Rev.
des quest. hist., V., 501 ; Nonciat. II., 313 n. ; *cf.* Ercole d'Este,
Due lettere al rè Enrico II. di Francia e al conestabile di Francia
del 22 Novembre, 1555, relative alla convenzione stipulata in
Ferrara il 16 (15) Novembre 1555 fra il duca di Ferrara e il rè di
Francia per unirsi insieme col papa ai danni della Spagna (*Per
nozze* Sarro Ferraguti con A. Menegatti, Agenta, 1896).

[2] See the report of G. Soranzo in BROWN, VI., 1, n. 343.

of the Pope's appointment ; Naples and Milan were to belong to the sons of Henry II., but not to the Dauphin. The French prince who received Naples was to hold it as a fief of the Church, was to pay an annual subsidy to the amount of 20,000 gold scudi, and was not to interfere in ecclesiastical matters ; all the territory to the west of the line which runs from S. Germano to the mouth of the Garigliano, the right bank of this river, the town of Gaeta, and that part of the Abruzzi which is north of the river Pescara, were to be incorporated into the States of the Church. The Count of Montorio and Antonio Carafa were to receive endowments in the Neapolitan territory which would yield them 25,000 and 15,000 gold scudi respectively. Entrance into the league was to be kept open for the Duke of Ferrara, the Venetians and the Swiss.[1]

This treaty was concluded with so much secrecy that Cardinal Farnese, with all his craft and skill, was not able to learn anything about it. The Imperialists were completely deceived and their suspicions were not even aroused.[2]

The good terms on which Paul IV. stood with the Romans, who were highly delighted at the reduction of the taxes, found expression at the beginning of December,· when they offered the Pope a body-guard[3] of 100 young men of good family, for the defence of his person. On November 3rd a review of the Roman troops, consisting of about 8000 men, had been held in St. Peter's Square, and an immense sensation was caused

[1] See SUMMONTE, Hist. di Napoli, IV., Naples, 1675, 278 seq. ; CASA, Opere, V., 73-83 (Neapolitan edition) ; NORES, 36 seq. 41 ; DURUY, 88 seq. ; GORI, Archivio, I., 26 seq., 193 seq. (with wrong date). The decision regarding Siena was made in a separate article, which could, according to circumstances, be kept secret ; see Nonciat. I., lxxvii seq., II., 368 seq.

[2] Cf. Nonciat., I., lxxiv. seqq., lxxviii. seq.

[3] See MASSARELLI, 289, 285. This guard was the origin of the so-called " Lanze spezzate " (see MORONI, XLV., 111 ; see also CROSTAROSA, Le milizie urbane di Roma, Roma, 1897, 31). Concerning the reduction of the taxes see Navagero's *letter of November 30, 1555 (Library of St. Mark's, Venice).

at the beginning of December by the arrest of the Datary, Giovan Battista Osio, who had hitherto been a man of very great influence ; it was said that he was accused of having an understanding with the Imperialists.[1]

The anti-Hapsburg feelings of Paul IV. were still further increased by the news of the far-reaching concessions granted by Ferdinand I. to the Protestants, in the religious peace at Augsburg, and of the intention of Charles V. to abdicate in favour of his brother, without having first obtained the consent of the Holy See.. The Pope, who adhered strictly to the mediæval idea of the Imperial dignity, saw in this intention of Charles V. a serious encroachment upon his rights.   Charles had, on October 22nd, 1555, surrendered the government of the Netherlands to his son, Philip II., and on January 16th, 1556, he prepared the documents by which he also resigned the kingdoms of Leon, Castile and Aragon in Philip's favour. Charles, who was still only fifty-five years of age, but was worn out by trouble and illness, was also firmly resolved to resign the title of Emperor.

A document, dated December 29th, 1555, conferred the office of Captain-General of the Church on the Pope's eldest nephew, Giovanni Carafa, Count of Montorio, which office the Duke of Urbino, who did not approve of the war, had just resigned.   The preamble of this document explained in detail the necessity for arming the Holy See, on the ground that many only obeyed from motives of fear.[2]   The Count of Montorio, as to whose military capacity grave doubts were entertained, received the bâton of commander-in-chief on January 1st,

---

[1] See the *report of Navagero of December 3, 1555, which emphasizes the " meraviglia d'ognuno sendo (il Datario) di quella autorità che era appresso di lui che potea quasi al pari et più del card. Carafa " (Library of St. Mark's, Venice).   RODOCANACHI (St. Ange, 159) gives a wrong date for the arrest.   The Dataria was now placed under Cardinals Scotti, Motula and Reumano ; see Navagero's *report of January 4, 1556, loc. cit.

[2] See *Brevia ad princ. Arm. 44, t. 4, n. 312 (Secret Archives of the Vatican).

1556, in the Sixtine Chapel, from the hands of the Pope, and then rode in solemn procession to the Capitol.[1]

In the midst of the great festivities which were then held in honour of the Pope's nephew,[2] the news arrived that the consort of Ascanio Colonna, the once famous beauty Giovanna d'Aragona, who had been forbidden to leave Rome on her own initiative, or to celebrate the betrothal of one of her daughters, had fled from the palace adjoining the Church of S.S. Apostoli. Giovanna escaped in disguise with her daughters by the Porta S. Lorenzo, through Tivoli into the Abruzzi.[3] As she was very much beloved by the people, who were adherents of the Colonna family, the Pope feared a rising and took military measures of precaution for the night. The captain of the gate paid for his carelessness or his corruptibility with his life, while the soldiers of the guard were sent to the galleys, and Giuliano Cesarini was imprisoned in the Castle of St. Angelo, on suspicion of complicity.[4] At the same time the most severe measures were adopted towards the insurgent nobles in the States of the Church, and Marcantonio Colonna was summoned to appear in Rome under pain of being declared a rebel.[5]

When Sarria and Garcilasso de la Vega once more spoke on behalf of Colonna in an audience on January 7th, 1556, a

---

[1] See MASSARELLI, 268 and the letter of G. Aldrovandi, dated Rome, January 1, 1556 (State Archives, Bologna). Card. Medici congratulated the Count of Montorio in an autograph* letter of January 7, 1556 (Cod. Barb. lat., 5698, p. 7). Concerning the difference with the Duke of Urbino see DURUY, 101, 406 seqq.

[2] Cf. the report of G. Aldrovandi, dated Rome, December 28, 1555 (State Archives, Bologna).

[3] See, besides Navagero in the Atti. Mod., Ser. 3, II., 158 seqq., and MASIUS, Briefe, 233, the detailed statements in the *Avviso di Roma 1556, Gennaio I. (Cod. Urb., 1038, p. 119, Vatican Library).

[4] See Navagero in BROWN, VI., I, n. 337, 347 and the *Avviso of January 11, 1556 loc. cit., 121 ; cf. also Arch. d. Soc. Rom., IV., 333 seqq.

[5] See Navagero in BROWN, VI., I, n. 347 and the *Avvisi of January 18 and 25, 1556 loc. cit., 124 b, 128.

violent scene took place. The Pope would brook no interference with his affairs, and declared that the Colonna had always
been the enemies of the Holy See. The Marquis de Sarria
then also adopted a haughty tone and requested a plain answer,
as he had so far only had fair words, with which the Pope's
actions did not agree. Thereupon Paul IV. next morning
instructed his nephew to send fourteen officers out to enlist
3000 men.[1]

It was every day becoming more evident that things were
drifting towards war. On February 7th, 1556, the Pope said
to the Venetian ambassador, Navagero, in whom he had full
confidence, that he would speak openly to him. " We are
obliged," he continued, " to put up with so many and such
great insults from these Imperialists, that we have surpassed
Job in patience. We possess so many proofs of their plots and
traitorous practices that we could astonish you with their
recital, if we had the time." He then again referred to the
poisoning story, in which he firmly believed. The Pope finished with the significant declaration " We greatly fear that
we must have recourse to that most dreadful measure (ad
ultimum terribilium)—war. We shall wage it against our
will, but it may, perhaps, be the best way of punishing our
enemies for their sins, and of freeing poor, unhappy Italy.[2]

On February 12th, 1556, followed the dispatch of Antonio
Carafa to the Duke of Ferrara, for whom was destined the
position of a general in the anti-Imperial league.[3] Before

[1] See the report of Navagero of January 11, 1556 in the Atti
Mod., Ser. 3, II , 160.

[2] See the letter of Navagero of February 8, 1556 in BROWN, VI.,
1, n. 381 ; cf. also Navagero's report of December 19th, 1555 in
ANCEL, Sienne, 27.

[3] The instructions for A. Carafa in CASA, II., 60 seq., the *letter
of credence for Carafa of February 7, 1556 in the State Archives,
Modena. The appointment of Ercole as dux et capitaneus generalis was made in a secret brief of February 26, 1556 (see PIEPER,
81, n. 4 ; cf. BROMATO, II., 293 ; DURUY, 106 seq. ; ANCEL,
Secrét., 18), which the Duke received on March 2 ; he immediately thanked the Pope (see FONTANA, II., 417 seq.) By the

this, on January 20th, the Duke of Somma, a relative of the Pope, had been sent to the French court, to beg Henry II. to lose no time in carrying out the terms of the treaty of alliance, which he had ratified on January 18th ; he was also commissioned to find out definitely what were the real intentions of the French sovereign, concerning which some anxiety was felt in Rome.[1]

*brief of March 14, 1556, Paul IV. ratified the directions of Henry II. for Ercole as a general of the league (State Archives, Modena). *Ibid* the *brief of September 15, 1556 by which the appointment was made public, and a *brief of December 30, 1556, which announces the dispatch of the consecrated *stocco et cappello*.

[1] * See the instructions in CASA, II., 48 *seq.* ; *cf.* PIEPER, *loc, cit.* and Nonciat., I., lxxx. ; II., 324 *seq.* The *brief, dated January 22, 1556, then addressed to Henry II. in the Brevia ad princ. *loc, cit.*, n. 317 (Secret Archives of the Vatican).

CHAPTER V.

EVENTS LEADING TO THE WAR WITH SPAIN.

WHILE everything in Rome was assuming a warlike appearance,[1] a dispatch sent by special courier from the nuncio in France, Sebastiano Gualterio, arrived during the night of February 14th, 1556, with the news that an armistice for five years had been concluded at Vaucelles between the French, the Emperor and Philip II.[2] The far-reaching plans of Carafa were thereby completely upset, and the States of the Church delivered over to the revenge of an irritated and powerful enemy. The dismay at the Vatican was all the greater as Henry II.'s ratification of the league had only arrived a few days before.[3]

The French ambassador only received news of the great change effected by the Constable de Montmorency on February 21st; on the same day a letter from Henry II. reached the Pope, who received the communication with very mixed

---

[1] Cf. MASIUS, Briefe, 233, 234 seq. An *Avviso of February 15, 1556, announces the strengthening of the Papal army; 12,000 infantry and 1,000 cavalry had been raised, all the gates were closed except four, and nobody was allowed to pass without strict inquiry. (Cod. Urb. 1038, p. 138. Vatican Library).

[2] See the *report of Bongianni Gianfigliazzi to Cosimo I., dated Rome, February 18, 1556 (State Archives, Florence); the despatch of Seb. Gualterio to Cardinal Carafa, dated Blois, February 6, 1556 (Nonciat., II., 337). The text of the armistice (in GORI, Arch., I., 193 seq.; cf. also DURUY, De pactis a. 1556 apud Volcellas indutis, Paris, 1883) was made known in Rome on March 4, 1556, in a pamphlet; see *Diario di Cola Coleine (Chigi Library, N. II., 32).

[3] On February 11, according to the instructions for A. Carafa of February 12, in CASA, Opere, V., 102 (Neapolitan edition).

feelings.[1] Cardinal Carafa felt the blow most keenly, for all
his plans and all his schemes had rested on the alliance with
France. The astute politician was, however, able to pull
himself together very quickly. He considered the changed
situation in detail with his trusted friend, Giovanni della
Casa, and a new plan was soon formed, which shows that the
freedom and independence of the Holy See was not the
lofty aim which the Cardinal had in view in his dangerous
policy, but only the aggrandisement of his own family. In
order to gain Siena for his house, no effort was to be spared
to induce Henry II. to repudiate what had been arranged at
Vaucelles ; if, however, he would not agree to this, the negotiations were to be continued all the same, and everything done
to form an anti-Imperial coalition. After the anxiety of
the Imperialists had been aroused by this scare, Carafa intended to whisper to them that the best way to put an end
to these dangerous proceedings would be to cede a state, for
example, Siena, to the family of the Pope's nephew.[2]

Such were the aims, and such was the course of the Machiavellian policy of the man to whom Paul IV., ignorant as he was
of the ways of the world, had imprudently entrusted the
secular affairs of the Holy See. While the Pope looked upon

[1] S.Sta ne haveva fatta allegrezza con le lagrime," we are
told in the *Avviso of February 22, 1556 (Cod. Urb. 1038, p.
131, Vatican Library). Cf. NAVAGERO-ALBÈRI, 392. We learn
from Navagero's reports of February 15 and 21, 1556, in BROWN,
VI., I., n. 392 and 405, that Paul IV. persuaded himself that
he had, by his unbending attitude, forced the arrangement
of an armistice which was unfavourable to the Imperialists.
G. Aldrovandi mentions the arrival of Henry II.'s letter in his
*report of February 22, 1556 (State Archives, Bologna).

[2] See the Discorso all' ill. et rev. Card. Caraffa per impetrare
dalla M^ta dell' Imp. Carlo V. lo stato et dominio di Siena, first
printed in CASA, Opere, IV., 35 seq. (Neapolitan edition). ANCEL
(Sienne, 3 seqq. and Nonciat., I., lxxxii. seq.) explained the
circumstances under which Casa drew up this record and published it in the Nonciat. II., 593 seq., after the original in the Secret
Archives of the Vatican.

the liberty of the Church and Italy as his highest aim, his nephew was only thinking of the advantage of the house of Carafa. What the Borgia, the Medici and the Farnese had attempted with more or less success, the acquisition of principalities for their families, Carafa also wished to accomplish, quite regardless of the dangers into which he would plunge the States of the Church and the Holy See. It is indeed a tragedy that he succeeded in leading his uncle, who, in virtue of his whole character and his former activities, belonged to the strictly ecclesiastical party, to enter upon such a tragic course.

Carafa felt himself, at that time, so completely master of the situation, that he had no doubt of being able to manage the Pope, in a political sense, in this new state of affairs. One thing is very significant in this connection. The document drawn up by della Casa, containing an outline of the above political programme of Carafa, shows that Paul IV. was not initiated into the secrets of his nephew. It is, on the contrary, clear from this document, to what an extent Carafa looked upon the head of the Church, in political matters, as a factor which he could pass over with impunity.[1] Indeed, Carafa knew so well how to take advantage of the weaknesses of his uncle that, thanks to his cunning and skill, his most daring enterprises succeeded only too well.

He also showed the greatest craftiness in his dealings with the French. As soon as he had recovered from his indescribable astonishment at the conclusion of the armistice of Vaucelles, he pretended to accept it as an accomplished fact, but all the time worked secretly and with all his power, to have it annulled, and also, in the event of his not being successful in this, to attain, all the same, his principal aim, the acquisition of Siena.[2]

Carafa was of opinion that such a difficult task could neither be accomplished by tedious negotiations in writing, nor by the

---

[1] See the excellent details in ANCEL, Sienne, 8.

[2] See the instructions for the Duke of Somma of March 5, 1556, in CASA, II., 67 seq. and also ANCEL, Sienne, 11 seq.

use of intermediaries. A successful issue seemed to him possible if he were to go himself as ambassador, and come into direct contact with Henry II. He therefore very soon decided upon a French legation, and it was only necessary to obtain the Pope's consent to such a plan ; this he easily succeeded in getting.

It had troubled Carafa very little when Paul IV., who was very susceptible to sudden impressions, had embraced the Imperial ambassador on February 17th, 1556, and had congratulated him on the armistice,[1] for he knew very well how easily his long and deeply rooted anti-Spanish sentiments would be again aroused at the slightest imprudence on the part of the Imperialists.[2] This feeling was so strong that Paul IV. took no offence at the secret negotiations which Carafa was carrying on with a confidant of the Protestant Albert Alcibiades of Brandenburg, who was known as the bitter enemy of the Emperor, and it was only when Cardinal Truchsess unmasked the agent as a Lutheran and an intriguer, that the Pope ordered him to leave.[3] The position is again reflected in a report of the Venetian ambassador on March 14th. " The Pope," explains Navagero, " wishes to remain armed, for he is convinced that this is the only way to keep the Imperialists in check. It is known in the Vatican that during a conference of the Imperial generals the cry was raised : ' To Rome ! ' to which the more thoughtful answered : ' To what purpose ? ' Do you not know that the Pope is armed, and that everyone in Rome would fight for

[1] See the report of Gianfigliazzi of February 18, 1556, in ANCEL, Sienne, 3.

[2] *Cf.* for this, Navagero's letters of February 15 and 28, 1556, in BROWN, VI., 1, n. 392, 415.

[3] *Cf.* RIESS, 87 *seqq.*, 425 *seqq.*, in which, however, the important statements which ANCEL (Disgrâce, 115 *seq.*) had already made with regard to this matter are overlooked. The disagreements in which Carafa entangled the Pope through his machinations can be seen from the **brief of September 5, 1555 (Secret Archives of the Vatican).

him ? "[1] The strictness with which the Pope maintained his authority in Rome had made the deepest impression ; no one dared to move, not even the Cardinals.[2]

Instead of taking into account the self-assurance of the Pope, the Imperialists, just at that moment, committed another of their imprudent actions. The Marquis de Sarria, who was an ardent sportsman, had obtained the privilege, through the Count of Montorio, of leaving the city during the time that the gates were closed. When he was about to make use of this permission, before daybreak on March 25th, he met with determined opposition. The officer who was in command of the Porta S. Agnese had not been informed, through carelessness, of the permission granted to the ambassador, and refused to open the gate. Thereupon the arrogant suite of Sarria used force, disarmed the guard and broke open the gate.[3] While the weak Count of Montorio

---

[1] BROWN, VI., 1, n. 425. Concerning the preparations for war by the Pope who feared a new Sack see HOSII epist. II., n. 1568, and PRAY, Epist. proc. regni Hung., III., Posen, 1806, 85. The strict control exercised at the gates is emphasized by Lasso in his *letter to Ferdinand I. on April 11, 1556 (State Archives, Vienna).

[2] See MASIUS, Briefe, 241, 243, 258.

[3] *Cf.* concerning this occurrence, the *report of Gianfigliazzi of March 30, 1556 (State Archives, Florence) ; also the letter of E. Carne (ed. TURNBULL, n. 494) and Navagero (BROWN, VI., 1, n. 447) and *Summarii* 350. Sarria protested (see Nonciat. I., lxxxv. n. 3) against Carafa's version of the event (in CASA, II., 75 *seq.*). According to Carne the circumstance took place on the " Wednesday before Palme Sunday," but RIESS (p. 96) gives it as March 18, in doing which he takes it for granted that the Easter of 1556 fell on March 29. This is, however, a mistake, for Easter in that year fell on April 5, Palm Sunday on March 29, and the occurrence, therefore, on March 25. Ipp. Capilupi reports in a *letter to Cardinal E. Gonzaga dated Rome, March 25, 1556, concerning the discovery of a plot to murder Cardinal Carafa, for which a German was executed (Gonzaga Archives, Mantua).

was endeavouring to arrange the affair amicably, Cardinal Carafa very skilfully made use of it to bring to the Pope's notice the arrogance and insolence of the Spaniards. Paul IV., who held jealously to the maintenance of his authority, took a serious view of the matter, and when Sarria came to the Papal chapel on Palm Sunday to take part in the function, he was ordered out of the palace. In order to make his peace with the Pope, he begged for an audience, which was granted to him for March 31st, but when some one (probably the Count of Montorio, who wished to avoid a scandal) told him that he would, this time, be taken to the Castle of St. Angelo, he failed to appear at the audience. In the meantime, legal proceedings were instituted against the guilty parties, and several members of the ambassador's suite were arrested.[1] All the attempts of Sarria to soothe the irritated pontiff proved vain, as we are informed by a correspondent on April 11th, 1556.[2] On the same day the suit against Cesarini was also brought to an end.[3]

On the previous day, April 10th, the Pope had astonished the Cardinals and the whole world by appointing two legates for the arrangement of peace.[4] Cardinal Carafa was destined for France, and Scipione Rebiba, who had recently been raised to the purple, for the Emperor and Philip II. It was rumoured that Cardinal Farnese would also go to France.[5]

---

[1] See Navagero's report in BROWN, VI., 1, n. 459; cf. RIESS, 97.

[2] *Avviso di Roma of April 11, 1556 (Cod. Urb. 1038, p. 133, Vatican Library).

[3] Ibid.

[4] See Acta consist. cancell. VII. (Consistorial Archives). Cf. reports from the Carteggio Farnesiano in the State Archives, Parma, in COGGIOLA, A. d. Cornia, 234, and the *letter of Lasso to Ferdinand I. of April 11, 1556 (State Archives, Vienna).

[5] See the *Avviso cited supra note 2. On May 30, 1556, Andrea Calegari wrote to Commendone, then staying in Venice . *Si dice chel card. Farnese non andrà più in Francia, che N.S. non gli ha voluto dar licentia con dirli che non vole che l'abbandoni (Lett. de' princ. XXIII., n. 1. Secret Archives of the Vatican).

The verbose instructions for the legates announced the intention of the Pope to summon a General Council to Rome, to deal with the question of reform, and contained orders to work for the bringing about of peace, as a necessary preliminary to such an assembly. The French king had made over to Paul IV. the right of arbitration in all matters, and he trusted that a corresponding readiness to meet his advances would be shown by the other side.[1] Should the Imperialists really refuse peace—and that was the Pope's firm conviction, in view of Charles V.'s pride and thirst for new territory— then there would be plain proof that it was they who had destroyed the tranquillity of Christendom.[2]

While preparations were being made for the mission of Carafa, who was to proclaim by his outward pomp the greatness of the sovereign whom he represented, on May 2nd

---

[1] See PIEPER, 194 seqq.; cf. ANCEL, Sienne, 15 seqq. and Nonciat. I., lxxxvii. seq. concerning the secret *Instruttione vulgare del card. Carafa* (published in Nonciat., II., 603 seq.), a memorandum drawn up by Casa in May, 1556, with regard to the legation of his master, which has already been printed, a fact which has escaped the notice of Ancel, by MARTINETTI in the Riv. Europ., 1877, IV., 228 seqq. There are also two instructions for Rebiba. The first, beginning: "Quamvis antequam pontificatum inivimus" (Secret Archives of the Vatican, Varia Polit,. LXXVIII., 145 seq., and Court Library, Vienna, 6621, p. 21 seq.), this is the one from which PALLAVICINI has made extracts (13, 17). The second, in which the Council is not mentioned, but which in many places exactly coincides verbally with the first, had been published by CAMPANA in the work A.V. Cian i suoi scolari, Pisa, 1909, 125 seq.; the first instruction, however, is not known to this investigator, although not only Pallavicini, but Pieper also (*loc. cit*) discuss it. In the *Brevia ad princ., Arm. 44, t. 4, n. 347 seqq.*, the briefs to the respective princes regarding the dispatch of the legates, all dated April 22, 1556 (Secret Archives of the Vatican). The Bull for Carafa of April 10, is now printed in the Nonciat., II., 599 seq.; this was only intended for the public; see *ibid*. I., lxxxvii.

[2] See Navagero's report of April 11, 1556, in BROWN, VI., 1, n. 453; cf. also Nonciat. I., lxxxvi.

further friction arose between the Papal officials and the
members of the Imperial embassy ; the anger of the Pope
against Sarria, which was already violent enough, was so
much increased by this that he even spoke of having him
executed.[1]

Two days after this occurrence, the Cardinals were informed
in a Bull that, as the final result of the long drawn out suit
against Ascanio and Marcantonio Colonna, these nobles were
declared to be excommunicated and their estates forfeited.
In the preamble to this document, mention was made of the
anti-Papal proceedings of the Colonna family since the time
of Boniface VIII., and the misdeeds of Pompeo and Ascanio
under Clement VII., Paul III. and Julius III.   Marcantonio,
it stated, had followed in their footsteps, opposing the orders
of the present Pope since the beginning of his reign, hindering
the importation of grain into Rome, and entering into a plot
with the enemies of the Holy See.[2]

On May 9th all the Cardinals were summoned in the Vatican
for the following day.   The Pope then informed them, in few
and terse words, that he had resolved to bestow Paliano, and
the remainder of the fiefs of the Colonna, together with the
title of Duke, on the Count of Montorio, who would certainly
prove himself a true and obedient vassal of the Holy See.
He had not summoned the Cardinals in order to ask their
consent and advice, for he was determined to drive the enemy
out of his house, so that, in future, no one would have any
cause for fear.   The members of the Sacred College received
in silence this declaration, so pregnant with direful consequences, of a Pope who, at one time, when he was a Cardinal,

[1] See Navagero's report of May 5, 1556, in BROWN, VI., 1,
n. 475 ; cf. RIESS, 103 seqq. ; MASIUS, Briefe, 279.

[2] See the text of the bull in PASSARINI, 189 seqq. and in DURUY,
359 seqq. ; cf. ibid., 130 seqq. and Navagero's report in the Atti
Mod. Ser. 3, II., 165 seq. In the *Acta consist. cancell. VII.
it says : " Romae die lunae 4 Maii, 1556, fuit consistorium, in
quo lecta fuit sententia privationis Paliani et aliarum terrarum
Ascanii et Marci Antonii de Colonna assistentibus ibidem rev[mi]."
(Consistorial Archives).

could not say enough in condemnation of the nepotism of the Popes, but who now had himself fallen into exactly the same fault. They then proceeded to Mass in the Sixtine Chapel, where Giovanni Carafa, already clothed in the gold embroidered mantle of a duke, had taken his place at the foot of the throne. The Pope blessed him, and handed him the sword and spurs, the red velvet cap, richly set with pearls and jewels, and the gilded sceptre. He touched the shoulder of his nephew three times with the sword and received from him the oath of fealty and the tribute for the fief. Those assembled gathered from the bull of investiture, which was very indistinctly read by the secretary, Barengo, that the Count of Montorio and his descendants were raised to the dignity of Dukes of Paliano, and that the eldest son, in this case Diomede, should bear the title of Marchese di Cave. The annual tribute to be paid on the feast of St. Peter and St. Paul, was fixed at 1,000 ducats.

After this ceremony, the new duke, accompanied by the notabilities of Rome, and part of the Papal troops, repaired to the Capitol, the thunder of the cannon welcoming him on his arrival at the Castle of St. Angelo. Rome was illuminated in the evening and a banquet was held at the Vatican, to which the Venetian and Polish ambassadors were invited, as well as the Cardinals. When the guests had risen from the table, the Pope declared, in a speech which he made to them, the very great pleasure which it afforded him that God should have inspired him to this act just in this month, and almost on the very day of the sack of Rome in 1527. " Your countrymen," he added, turning towards Cardinals Pacheco and Cueva, " were the scoundrels who committed that ruthless deed." He said that he would next day deliver the cross to the peace legates, and declared that, on the whole, he had confidence in the French king. " I do not know," he continued, again turning to the Spanish Cardinals, " what is to be expected from your nation ; I shall, however, clear up all doubt on this point, and I shall not fail to do my duty." Then the Pope proceeded to enlarge, in his rhetorical manner, on the unhappy times, in which heresy was always bringing

new kingdoms into danger.   The ambassador of the King of
Poland, who very well understood the reference to his sovereign, now became as embarrassed as the Spanish Cardinals,
who scarcely dared to raise their eyes.   We also learn from
the report of the Venetian ambassador, who describes this
painful scene, that when he was signing the bull of investiture,
Cardinal Tournon remarked that his signature would not be
considered valid in France, as he had not taken part in any
of the deliberations concerning the matter.   Cardinal Juan
Alvarez de Toledo refused to sign, as he had not been present
at the meeting of the Cardinals, and, moreover, did not think
the act was salutary, either for the Holy See or for Carafa.[1]

The seizure of the Colonna territory was effected quite
quietly under the protection of the Papal troops ; nevertheless, not only Rocca di Papa, but Paliano as well, were
strongly fortified, regardless of Alba's protest that he could
not allow such a proceeding in the neighbourhood of the
Neapolitan frontier.[2]

After both the legates had received the cross on May 11th,[3]
Carafa left for Civitavecchia on the 19th, and set sail from
there two days later.[4]

[1] Besides Navagero's letter of May, 16, 1556, in BROWN, VI.,
1, n. 484, cf. in the *Avviso di Roma of May 11, 1556, (Cod.
Urb. 1038, p. 137 seqq. Vatican Library) and the *report of
Camillo Paleotti of May 13, 1556 (State Archives, Bologna) ;
see also MASIUS, Briefe, 258 ; COLA COLEINE, *Diario, in the
Chigi Library N. II. 32.   The text of the bull of investiture in
PASSARINI, 197 seqq.

[2] See BROWN, VI., 1, n. 484 and 492 ; cf. also RIESS, 107 seqq.,
who erroneously places Rocca di Papa, which is in the Alban
hills, at the entrance to Civitavecchia !

[3] See MASSARELLI, 291.

[4] The statement of Massarelli, that Carafa started on the 11th
(Mél. d'archéol., XXII., 100), or 18th of May, is erroneous ;
Navagero (in ANCEL, Sienne, 15), the *Avviso di Roma of May
23 (Cod. Urb. 1038, p. 139. Vatican Library), a letter of C.
Paleotti, dated Rome, May 20, 1556 (State Archives, Bologna),
and Gianfigliazzi in his *letter of May 23 (State Archives, Florence),
all give the 19th.

He had received 10,000 scudi from the Pope in cash, and as much in bills, for the expenses of his mission. His suite consisted of about 250 persons, many of them being Florentine and Neapolitan exiles. The most distinguished members were Pietro Strozzi and his brother Roberto, Paolo Giordano Orsini, the Archbishops of Cosenza and S. Severino, and several other prelates, such as the Bishop of Pola, and the auditor of the Rota, Ugo Boncompagni.[1]

The legate, whose place in Rome was filled by the Duke of Paliano,[2] was to present to the king a consecrated sword and hat, and to the queen the Golden Rose ; he also made several other presents, among which were some pieces of antique sculpture.[3]

Diplomatists in Rome at once concluded that the mission of Carafa was by no means intended to bring about peace, but was, on the contrary, undertaken with a view of leading to a repudiation of what had been decided on at Vaucelles.[4]

---

[1] See besides Navagero's letters of April 18 and 23, 1556 (BROWN, VI., 1, n. 459), the reports in COGGIOLA, A. d. Cornia, 240 seqq., ANCEL, Sienne, 16 and Nonciat., I., xxxiv. seq. ; also the *Avviso di Roma of May 23, 1556 (loc. cit.) and the *report of Sarria, dated Rome, May 21, 1556, where P. Strozzi is described as " principal consultor del card. Carafa " (Archives at Simancas, Leg. 883).

[2] See Nonciat. II., 438 n. 2.

[3] Besides the reports taken from Ancel see also the *letter of Sarria cited supra note 1.   The *brief to Carafa concerning the presents for the French royal family (cf. for this BARBIER DE MONTAULT, Oeuvres compl., I., 269, where for Paul III. we must read Paul IV.), dated April 22, 1556, in the original in the State Archives, Paris, and in draft in the Brevia ad princ. Arm. 44 t. 4, n. 352   Cf. ibid n. 353 a corresponding *brief to Henry II. of April 22, 1556, to the following effect : Ad eam enim inter vos concordiam et pacem, quam praesentes indutiae nobis pollicentur, tuto conservandam, nihil esse opportunius videtur contra eos, qui eam perturbare atque omnia miscere conantur, quam iustitiae gladius et salutis galea.   Cf. ibid., n. 355, the *brief to the queen on the same day (Secret Archives of the Vatican).

[4] Lasso gives this view as early as April 11, 1556, in a *report to Ferdinand I. (Secret State Archives, Vienna).

There is, however, so far, no proof that the legate had, at that time, received any instructions to that effect. Carafa himself declared later on, during the course of his trial, that it was only after his arrival at the French court, that he received any such orders. As it would have been very advantageous for him, who had been made responsible for the violation of the armistice, to be able to point to such instructions, his statement seems worthy of belief. The first reports of the legate, who reached Fontainebleau on June 16th, concerning his preliminary negotiations, also bear out his statement.[1] It was only when threatening news arrived from Rome with regard to the intentions of the Imperialists and the Colonna, that the position was altered, and that Carafa began to work assiduously to bring about a military invasion of Italy by the French. As Henry II. seemed to lend a favourable ear to his proposals, Carafa reported somewhat prematurely to Rome, on June 25th, that he would soon return accompanied by 30 galleys and 3,000 infantry.[2] When the French king begged the Duke of Ferrara to assist the Pope against the Colonna, in an autograph letter of June 29th, Carafa so far lost sight of all idea of seemliness, as openly to attack Philip II. on July 5th, before all the ambassadors, as the accomplice of the rebellious Colonna. As early as July 13th, the legate announced that he intended to return.[3] Cardinal Rebiba, who had only left Rome on May 30th, and had then travelled very slowly, received orders to return home, as his mission to Brussels now had no object.[4]

[1] The above is in accordance with the excellent details given by ANCEL, Sienne, 17 *seqq.* Carafa's reports from France have now been published by ANCEL in the Nonciat., II., 405 *seqq.*; the first report of June 17 had already been made known in its essentials by LÄMMER (Melet., 173 *seq.*).

[2] See ANCEL, Sienne, 20 *seqq.* Concerning the threatening intentions of the Spanish *cf.* Nonciat., II., 422 n. 2.

[3] *Cf.* BROWN, VI., 1, n. 537; RIESS, 120 *seqq.*; ANCEL, Sienne, 20 *seqq.* Ancel has corrected the date (July 13 instead of June 13) of the first letter of Carafa, published by DURUY (p. 366).

[4] See PIEPER, 88-89; HINOJOSA, 98; *cf.* RIESS, 115, who maintains strongly that Rebiba started on his journey on June

The decisive crisis took place in Rome on June 20th. On that day the Pope again indulged, in the presence of the Venetian ambassador, in the most violent language against the Emperor, " this heretic and schismatic who has always favoured false doctrine in order to oppress the Holy See, and make himself master of Rome, for he not only regards this city as his own, but the whole of the States of the Church, and indeed all Italy, Venice included." It was certain, he said, that Charles V. had the intention of again reinstating the Colonna in their possessions, of making open war on the Holy See, and, finally, of refusing his obedience even in ecclesiastical matters. " Woe to him, however, if he attempts this ! " continued Paul IV., " we shall then raise the whole world against him, deprive him of his Imperial dignity and his kingdom, and let him see what we are able to perform by virtue of the authority of Christ."[1]

A few days later the Pope again broke out, to Navagero, into the most violent complaints about the " treachery " of the " heretical " Emperor. No worse man, he declared, had lived for a thousand years, and the devil had chosen him as his tool in order to paralyse the Papal efforts at reform. " The Imperialists," continued the Pope, " may deceive others, but not us, for we have taken precautions, and God's protection will not fail us ; we have friends, for when the liberty of Italy is at stake, there can be no doubt as to the unity of all Italians. We also possess a great following in Naples. We shall only call upon Venice when events seem to promise a favourable

9 ; according to the *report of Giovan Andrea Calegari to Commendone, dated Rome, May 30, 1556, Rebiba started on May 30 (Secret Archives of the Vatican). MASIUS, Briefe, 263, also agrees with this. Concerning Rebiba's recall see Nonciat., II., 447 n. 1.

[1] See Navagero's report of June 20, 1556, in BROWN, VI., 1, 518 ; cf. also G. Aldobrandini's letter to Carafa, of June 21, 1556, used by ANCEL (Sienne, 20) in a translation, to which COGGIOLA (A. d. Cornia, 249) drew attention. Both have overlooked the fact that it had already been printed in PASSARINI, 124 seqq.

and certain result, for we are aware of the discretion which the Signoria has to exercise." In this audience, which lasted for two hours, the Pope kept on repeating his assertion that his hope was fixed on God, Who would not abandon his cause.[1]

The reconciliation which Cardinal Alvarez de Toledo had brought about at that time between the Pope and Sarria,[2] no longer sufficed to alter the course of events. The attitude of the Imperialists and the Colonna seemed so threatening to Paul IV. that he believed that precautions must be taken to ensure his own safety. The terrifying picture of the events of 1527 was always before his eyes, and the fear that he might suffer the fate of Clement VII. had taken complete possession of his imagination. "As an attack by the Imperialists is expected here," writes Navagero on June 27th, " fresh troops have arrived in Rome." When the ambassador had another audience with the Pope on July 3rd, the latter again made use of the strongest expressions against Charles V., " this miserable and sorry creature, this cripple in body and soul." If the Emperor should really begin a war against him, repeated the Pope, he would be forced to have recourse to the last and most terrible weapon which Christ had bestowed on him, that of withdrawing all ecclesiastical revenues from Charles V., and declaring his throne forfeited.[3]

The situation was daily becoming more critical. Just as the Pope was disturbed by the warlike preparations of Alba, so was the latter irritated by the precautionary measures taken by Paul IV., not only in Rome, but also on the Neapolitan frontier.[4] On July 5th, 70,000

---

[1] The *létter of Navagero of June 24, 1556, overlooked by Brown, is in the Library of St. Mark's, Venice, *loc. cit.*

[2] *Cf.* BROWN, VI., 1, n. 518 and 528, as well as the *Avviso of June 27, 1556 (Cod. Urb. 1038, p. 145. Vatican Library).

[3] See BROWN, VI., 1, n. 529 and 534 ; *cf.* MASIUS, Briefe, 267.

[4] *Cf.* the *Avviso di Roma of June 20, 1556, according to which thirteen pieces of artillery were sent to Paliano (Cod. Urb. 1038, p. 141[b], Vatican Library) ; *ibid.* p. 146 an *Avviso of July 4, 1556, concerning the prohibition of undertaking military

ducats were deposited as a war fund in the Castle of St. Angelo.[1]

During this state of tension between Rome and Naples, which was continually being aggravated[2] by the encroachments of the Spanish government on purely ecclesiastical affairs, the following incident occurred on July 7th. The governor of the frontier town of Terracina caught sight of a man who was known to him as a Spanish courier, trying to steal across the frontier on foot, and without the badges of his office. He had the suspect brought before him, and as he bore none of the distinguishing marks which, in accordance with international law, would have protected him, the governor had him searched. They found on him a petition from the Imperial post-master, Juan Antonio de Taxis, to Alba, asking him to procure for him the post agency between Terracina and Velletri, and two letters from Garcilasso de la Vega, also addressed to Alba. One was in cypher, but the other contained the statement that Sarria had been stupid enough to let himself be won over by a few friendly words from the Pope, whereas the proper way to attain anything was to send the cavalry, together with 4,000 Spaniards and 8,000 Italians, by forced marches on Rome, and to have the war-ships set sail for Nettuno and Civitavecchia.[3]

---

service under foreign princes without permission from the Pope ; this prohibition was issued when Camillo Orsini declared " esser ubligato al duca di Ferrara." Concerning the fortification of the Borgo see Bull. bas. Vat., III., 26.

[1] MASSARELLI 292 ; cf. Studi e docum., XIII., 304.

[2] The well-known theologian M. Cano was accused in Rome, and in a sharp letter of April 21, 1556, ordered to appear before the court within 60 days under penalty of severe punishment. The Spanish government declared, however, that this summons had not been served on Cano, and that he and the Bishop of Lugo, who had likewise been summoned to Rome, were to remain in Spain ; see CABALLERO, M. Cano, 502 seqq., 506 seqq. ; cf. Histor. Zeitschrift., XXXIX., 288.

[3] Cf. the *report of G. A. Fachinetti to Cardinal Farnese of July 8, 1556 (State Archives, Parma) and that of Navagero of

This important document was handed to the Duke of Paliano in the late evening of July 7th, when the Pope had already retired. The Duke therefore, on his own responsibility had the post-master de Taxis arrested during the night, and his possessions seized ; he hoped in this way to be able to decipher the code letter, which was afterwards sent to experts in Venice.[1]

The Duke of Paliano informed the Pope of the discovery which he had made. While the two were deliberating on July 9th, Navagero, with Garcilasso and Sarria, arrived in the anti-camera ; the two latter were only aware of the arrest of de Taxis, but had not yet learned of the capture of the courier. The Pope received only Navagero and Sarria, and when Garcilasso was about to leave the Vatican with the latter, he was arrested and taken to the Castle of St. Angelo ;[2] his fate was shared by Girolamo Capilupi, the agent of Cardinal Ercole Gonzaga,[3] on July 10th. The palace of Cardinal Pacheco, where Garcilasso lodged, was thoroughly searched.[4] "It is believed that war has already broken out," writes the Venetian ambassador, Navagero, after Garcilasso's arrest, and when he had an audience on the following day he found

July 9, in BROWN, VI., I, n. 540 ; see also NORES, 71 seqq. ; RÜBSAM, J. B. von Taxis, Freiburg, 1889 19 ; COGGIOLA, A. d. Cornia, 266, 268 seqq.

[1] See Navagero in BROWN, VI., I, n. 540 ; Fachinetti in the Nonciat. II., 426 n. 4 ; TURNBULL, Cal., n. 522 ; cf. ROSEO, I., 6, p. 304.

[2] See besides the report of Navagero mentioned supra p. 128, n. 3, and the letter of Fachinetti in COGGIOLA, loc. cit., 271 seqq. and Nonciat. II., 427 n. 2, as well as the *Avviso di Roma of July 11, 1556, Cod. Urb. 1038, p. 143 b (Vatican Library).

[3] See the report in INTRA, Ipp. Capilupi : Arch. stor. Lomb., XX. (1893), and in COGGIOLA, loc. cit. 272 seq. ; cf. also Quellen und Forschungen d. Preuss. Inst., III., 134 seq. and the *Avvisi di Roma of July 15 and di Bologna of July 18, 1556, in the correspondence of Madruzzo in the Vice-regal Archives, Innsbruck.

[4] See the *Avviso di Roma of July 11, 1556, mentioned supra n. 2.

the Pope, who had just then received good news concerning the help of France, determined to proceed to all lengths. " We have discovered their treachery " said Paul IV., " and we shall learn yet more from those who have been arrested. They have recommended a march on Rome, and a division of our territory, but the Lord God still lives ! They will perhaps be forced to defend their own dominions ; mighty princes are on our side, and should the Spaniards attack us they will repent it ; the tyrant, the Emperor, need no longer be taken into consideration, for his possessions are like an old house, which, when a single stone is removed, falls to pieces ; when we, here in Italy, give him a slight blow, everything will be laid in ruins." Amid the most bitter complaints of the devilish wickedness of Charles, the Pope made much of his hope that Venice, too, would not fail to join in the struggle against the tyranny of Spain.[1]

On July 11th, all the Cardinals and ambassadors were summoned to the Vatican. The Pope, who spoke in Italian on this occasion, gave praise to Providence for having discovered the designs of his enemies, dwelt on the guilt of Garcilasso, and justified his proceedings against the Colonna, and the elevation of his nephew to the Dukedom of Paliano. On the advice of the Cardinals, he then appointed a commission to deliberate anew concerning a peaceful issue to the matter. The Pope declared that greatly as he detested war, he must, nevertheless, in any case take measures for his defence, especially after the discovery of the treasonable designs of the Imperialists. " If we must venture on war, which, in view of the deceitful nature of the Spaniards, is very much to be feared," he said to Navagero two days later," then we shall pronounce such a fearful sentence that the sun shall

---

[1] See BROWN, VI., 1, n. 540 ; cf. n. 540 and ROMANIN, Storia di Venezia, VI., 234 n. ; the letter of Buoncambi in COGGIOLA, A. d. Cornia, 277 seqq. ; Navagero's report in BROWN, VI., 1, n. 541 ; Summarii, 347 ; *letter of C. Paleotti, dated Rome, July 11, 1556 (State Archives, Bologna) ; the *Avviso di Roma of July 11, loc. cit. and the *Acta consist (Consistorial Archives).

thereby be darkened, and the Emperor and his son, who have been found guilty of felony and rebellion, shall be made our vassals, deprived of all their kingdoms, their subjects released from their allegiance, and their dominions divided among those who occupy them. We shall then invest the French king with Naples, and besides that give back to the Republic the ports which she formerly possessed in Apulia and Sicily."[1]

Paul IV. was, at this time, more possessed than ever by the fixed idea that the Spaniards, these Marani, as he called them, were threatening Rome with another Sack. He declared, however, that he would anticipate them ; he intended to conquer Naples, even should he have to go there in person, with his cross borne before him ; he would, moreover, have the " devilish " secret letter printed, so that everyone should recognise the treachery of the Imperialists. Those who had been arrested should be tortured until they named their accomplices.[2]

On July 25th the Pope again gave free vent to his passion against the Spaniards in the presence of Navagero. He would not, he declared, allow these traitors and heretics to do to him, under the cloak of peace, what they had permitted themselves to do to Clement VII. He had discovered their attempts at murder ; they had intended to perform even worse acts than in 1527. He would rather die than suffer such humiliations as his predecessor, Julius III. It was impossible to endure meekly such tyrannical oppression from the lowest nation on earth. "Once," he continued, "we saw in these ultra-montanes in Italy, nothing but cooks, bakers and ostlers, but now, to our ruin and disgrace, they are the masters. Where-ever they rule, as in Naples and Milan, we see lamentable tragedies. The Emperor, the tyrant and schismatic, is striving after a universal monarchy. He has promoted heresy in order to crush the Papacy and make himself master of Rome, that is to say, master of Italy and the world." Then

---

[1] BROWN, VI., 1, n. 546 ; cf. Nonciat. II., 456 n. 2.

[2] See BROWN, VI., 1, n. 549. Taxis had an arm broken under torture. See RIESS, 124, n. 35 ; cf. MASIUS, Briefe, 277, 291.

Paul IV. pointed out to the ambassador the dangers which threatened Venice from the Spaniards. Tuscany was already in their hands, and now they intended to seize upon the rest of the peninsula. Should Venice enter the war on the side of the Pope, she would thereby gain great advantages and win much celebrity, and the celestial harmony which once had existed would be once more restored, and the whole world would tremble at the name of Italy. The moment was favourable, and he himself would make every sacrifice to free Italy from her oppressors. The reserve with which Navagero received these confidences did not damp the ardour of the Pope, and he returned again and again to the dangers which accompanied the rule of the Imperialists in Naples. The Sack and the ruin of Italy had resulted from it. " But God will help us," he cried, " whosoever makes war on the Pope loses, as a schismatic, all the benefits he has received from the Holy See. From those benefits the King of Spain draws a greater revenue than from all his other kingdoms, but we shall deprive him of all those revenues. We know that the same thing cannot happen in Spain as has happened in Germany ; there are very many good people there, who will not follow him."[1]

Meanwhile a protest had arrived from Alba against the arrest of Garcilasso.[2] This and the admissions of the two prisoners increased both the anger and the fear of the Pope. He continued his preparations for war with feverish activity.[3] Camillo Orsini, who had arrived on July 18th, was ordered to put the capital into a state of defence. The Borgo was fortified, the city walls repaired, new troops for the garrison

[1] *Letter of Navagero of July 25, 1556 (St. Mark's Library, Venice, *loc. cit.*).

[2] Brought by G. de Urea ; see BROWN, VI., 1, n. 550.

[3] *Cf.* for the following especially the *Avvisi di Roma of July 11, 18 and 25, 1556. In that of July 25 it is stated : *Si fortifica il Borgo et si riparano le mura di Roma (Vatican Library). See also the report in COGGIOLA, A. d. Cornia, 282, 284 *seq.* and the *letter of A. Capilupi, dated Rome, July 18, 1556 (Gonzaga Archives, Mantua).

levied, the export of gold and precious metals forbidden ; and the war-chest in the Castle of St. Angelo increased to 100,000 ducats. People wondered how the Pope could get so much money together, considering the expense of the 10,500 soldiers already in his service.[1] The Duke of Urbino received orders to raise a further 10,000 men.[2]

Among those accused of having treasonable relations with the Emperor, Ascanio della Corgna, to whom the defence of Velletri had been entrusted, had been named. On July 23rd, the Pope ordered him to come to Rome, in order to vindicate himself. As he delayed in putting in an appearance, the suspicion against him was increased, and orders were at once issued to arrest him and bring him to Rome. Cardinal Fulvio della Corgna heard of this in good time, so that he was able to inform his brother of the threatened danger ; the latter, therefore, succeeded in escaping to Nettuno, which he delivered to the Colonna, and thence by sea to Naples.[3] Paul IV. was not the man to suffer this from a member of the Sacred College, and when Cardinal Fulvio appeared at the consistory of July 27th, he was taken to the Castle of St. Angelo. In the consistory, the Pope spoke first of this occurrence, after which the advocate and the procurator of the Apostolic Camera, Alessandro Pallantieri and Silvestro Aldobrandini appeared and read a legal document to the following effect : It is notorious that several persons in the Kingdom of Naples have, with the knowledge of Philip II. or Charles V., conspired against the Holy See, which is a transgression of the oath of

[1] See MASSARELLI, 292 ; *cf.* BROWN, VI., 1, n. 558 and TURN-BULL, n. 522.

[2] See the *Avviso of July 25, *loc. cit.*, p. 148 [b].

[3] See, besides the important reports in COGGIOLA, A. d. Cornia, 293 *seqq.*, MASSARELLI, 293, the *report of C. Paleotti of July 29, 1556 (State Archives, Bologna) and the *Avviso di Roma of August 1, 1556 (Cod. Urb. 1038, p. 150. Vatican Library), which gives many details concerning the flight. According to the thorough investigations of Coggiola the suspicion against the Condottiere was unfounded and the proceedings against him, to say the least, too hasty.

allegiance sworn by the rulers of Naples before Popes Julius III. and Paul IV. It is also notorious that the Spanish king, as well as the Emperor, have assisted the excommunicated Colonna, who are condemned for high treason, with money and troops against the Holy See, whereby they have ipso facto laid themselves open to the penalties of the major excommunication, and of high treason, and to the loss of all their dignities. The Pope took note of this pronouncement, but declared that he would not come to a decision until he had discussed the matter with the Cardinals.[1]

After this demonstration, Sarria informed the Pope that he had received instructions from his government to leave Rome, Paul IV. was much embarrassed by this announcement, as he, so far, had received so few definite pledges of sufficient help from France, that Carafa was obliged to prolong his stay there. Pope, therefore, endeavoured to postpone the rupture and to retain the ambassador. When Sarria left the city on August 8th, his departure took the form of leave of absence for the arrangement of his personal affairs.[2]

To the complaint presented by the Count of S. Valentino in the name of Alba, the Pope gave a reply which had been laid before the consistory on August 7th, and which Domenico del Nero, who was sent to Naples five days later, took with him. This denied the truth of all the accusations of the Viceroy, and, with regard to Garcilasso, declared that the latter, by his plotting against the Pope, had forfeited the inviolability of an ambassador.[3]

Although eight French galleys, with 600 Gascons, had

---

[1] See *Acta consist. cancell., VII., 37-39[b] (Consistorial Archives); cf. Navagero and Massarelli loc. cit.; Lünig, Cod. Ital. dipl., IV., 255 seq.; Nores, 110 seq.; Passarini, 137 seqq.; Riess, 132 seq.; Nonciat., II., 453.

[2] Cf. Massarelli, 293-294; Brown, VI., 1, n. 572; Coggiola, A. d. Cornia, 310, n. 1; Riess, 135; Nonciat., I., xcii.; II., 452, n. 1; cf. also the *report in the Acta consist., VII. (Consistorial Arch).

[3] See the instruction of August 11, 1556, in Nores, 394 seq.; cf. Massarelli, loc. cit.; Brown, VI., 1, n. 572.

arrived at Civitavecchia on July 25th, and the preparations for war in Rome were being carried on with the greatest activity,[1] Paul IV. did not by any means feel himself secure and sought in every way to induce Venice to ally herself with him. Antonio Carafa, who had, a little time before, been raised to the dignity of Marquis of Montebello,[2] was sent, with this object, to the city of the lagoons, but was not successful in accomplishing anything.[3] Nevertheless, Paul IV. still hoped to persuade the Venetians to abandon their neutrality.

On August 13th he discussed the matter after dinner with Navagero, and again complained in the most excited terms of the treasonable practices of the Imperialists. Should these schismatics and heretics succeed in driving him out of Rome, he would take refuge on an island, and carry on his office from there. He hoped, however, to witness the downfall of the Spanish tyranny ; Venice must know best what she ought to do, for " on our ruin, yours will necessarily follow. We, however, shall not be the slaves of the Spaniards like former Popes, but we shall bravely fight against them, be the consequences what they may."[4]

Now as before, Paul IV. considered himself personally threatened by the Spaniards, and he caused precautions to be taken against any attempt to poison him.[5] Being in such a

---

[1] *Cf.* concerning this the reports in COGGIOLA, A. d. Cornia, 292 and 318. Card. du Bellay discusses the military position of Rome in a letter of July 25, 1556, in RIBIER, II., 650 *seqq.*

[2] See MASSARELLI, 292. Antonio Carafa received, on his elevation to the marquisite, the lands confiscated from the insubordinate Count of Bagno. *Acta consist. cancell. VII. (Consistorial Arch.) *Cf.* COGGIOLA, *loc. cit.* 98, 120 *seq.,* 127 *seq.,* 136 *seq.,* 143 *seq.*

[3] *Cf.* Note 1 in NORES, 69 and Nonciat., II., 438, n. 3.

[4] See Navagero in BROWN, VI., 1, n. 578.

[5] *Da tre giorni in qua si è ristretto molto il servitio che si fa al pontefice alla tavola, perchè vogliono che tre soli camerieri soi parenti portino le vivande. Si dubita che habbi suspition di veneno. Navagero on August 15, 1556 (Library of St. Mark's, Venice).

frame of mind, it was in vain that Cardinal Medici again advised him, in the strongest terms, to refrain from war, above all on account of the insufficiency of his troops, for the Papal army would take to flight at the mere sight of the enemy, for, since the invasion of Charles VIII. not a single battle had been won by an army composed entirely of Italian troops.[1]

Every prospect of a peaceful solution of the dispute disappeared with the answer which Alba signed on August 21st, and sent to the Pope by special courier. It was to the effect that after the unjust statements in the consistory of July 27th, nothing else was possible for the Emperor and the King of Spain except to do what was permitted to every obedient son, whose father attacked him with a naked weapon, which was to take the weapon out of his hand.[2]

This ultimatum was handed to the Pope on August 27th by Pirro dell' Offredo, the third ambassador of Alba. As Offredo·expressed himself in terms still stronger than those of the document, such a violent dispute arose that the maestro di camera closed the outer doors, so that those outside might not hear the quarrel.[3]

The preparations for war had, in the meantime, advanced in Rome, and the Pope dreamed of being able to raise his army to as many as 30,000 men.[4] On August 15th, 1,200 more Gascons arrived in Rome, brave but dissolute and thieving soldiers.[5] New taxes had to be imposed in order to meet the expenses. This, as well as the ruthless destruction of the

[1] See Navagero in BROWN, VI., I, n. 582.

[2] This letter, in Spanish and French, is in REISS, Pap. de Granvelle, IV., 666 seq., in Italian in the supplement to NORES, 400 seqq. ; ibid. a similar letter to the College of Cardinals. Cf. RIESS, 138 seqq. ; BALAN, VI., 467.

[3] See Navagero in BROWN, VI., I, n. 589 and the **Avviso di Roma of August 29, 1556 (Cod. Urb. 1039, p. 156, Vatican Library).

[4] See the **Avviso mentioned in the preceding note.

[5] Cf. Navagero in BROWN, VI., I, n. 577, and in ALBÈRI, 401 seqq.

villas and vineyards lying outside the city walls, caused great dissatisfaction among the people. In this work, carried out under the direction of Camillo Orsini, neither churches nor monastries were spared. As had been done in the Borgo, fortifications were also constructed in Trastevere, and new outworks were added to the Castle of St. Angelo.[1] All this, however, was not sufficient to resist a serious attack, for, although so many defences had been begun, none of them were finished. It was still more unfortunate that the Papal troops were completely scattered all over the Campagna, since the Pope, inexperienced as he was in the art of war, refused to leave any fortified place without a garrison, or to risk anything that belonged to him.[2]

In a consistory on September 4th, 1556, the Pope and the Cardinals continued to discuss the answer to be given to Alba's letter, and to consider the possibility of a peaceful solution.[3] The news arrived, however, during the following night that Alba had crossed the frontier with his troops, and had already invested Pontecorvo.[4]

[1] Besides MASSARELLI, 295, cf. Navagero in BROWN, VI., 1, n. 588; *Summarii*, 350 seqq., and especially the **Avvisi di Roma of August 8, 15, 29, and September 5, 1556 (Vatican Library, loc. cit.). Cf. also BICCI, Not. d. famiglia Boccapaduli, Roma, 1762, 112, and PAGLIUCCHI, 128 seq., concerning the works on the Castle of St. Angelo at the time, and also at a later period. As to the cost, Navagero *reports on August 22, 1556 : " Qui si fa conto chel pontefice habbi una spesa di c. 80,000 scudi al mese ne si vede come possa lugamente sostenerla " (Library of St. Mark's, Venice).

[2] See the reports of Navagero in BROWN, VI., 1, n. 646 ; VI., 2, n. 685, as well as in RIESS, 146.

[3] MASSARELLI, 295. BROWN, VI., 1, n. 596, 600. Bonfigliazzi in NORES, 122, n. 1.

[4] MASSARELLI, 295. BROWN, VI., 1, n. 603. M. ROSEO, 519 seq. Nonciat., II., 470.

CHAPTER VI.

THE WAR WITH SPAIN.

THE decision to proceed against the Pope by force of arms had not been easily arrived at by Charles V., Philip II. and Alba, for not only political, but religious considerations as well, had stood in the way of their making it. The Spanish government had caused a special legal opinion to be obtained from the University of Louvain ; this confirmed Philip II. in his view that he would neither sin against his duty as a loyal son of the Church, nor against the obligations appertaining to his title of Catholic King, if he anticipated a threatened attack by beginning the war.[1]   Even then, however, Alba

---

[1] *Cf.* Michiel's report of 1557 in BROWN, VI., 2, n. 1062 ; *ibid.*, n. 687 ; BALAN, VI., 468-469, and RIESS, 134.   The (incorrectly printed by RIESS, p. 440 *seqq.*) " Memoriale dato da parte de S.M.ta alli teologi circa il procedere di Paolo IV. sopra il regno di Napoli," is moreover identical with the Spanish " Consulta a los teologos sobre el procedere de Paolo IV.," which has long been printed in F. CABALLERO, M. Cano, Madrid, 1871, 508 *seq.* The same document, under the title " Memorial que da parte de la Md cath. del Rey Felipe II. se dió a los teologos " is in manuscript in the archives of the Spanish embassy in Rome. Riess does not mention that Philip II. laid this complaint against Paul IV. before the Spanish theologians and jurists in a meeting summoned to Valladolid, and that he asked their opinion as to whether he would be allowed to carry on a war against the Pope under the existing circumstances, and what means he should employ in so doing.   Almost all of them answered the question in a sense favourable to the king.   The opinion of M. Cano, dated November I., 1556, was especially pleasing to the latter, as it drew a sharp distinction between the Pope as head of the Church, and as a secular prince, though it also contained words

138

still hesitated, and it was only on the third order of Philip II., who somewhat blamed him for his disobedience,[1] that he at last started from Naples on September 1st, 1556. His force only amounted to 12,000 men, but these were well-disciplined, and were commanded by generals who were bent on vengeance, among whom were Marcantonio Colonna and the Count of Popoli, who, although a relative of the Pope, had been dismissed from the Papal army on account of his Spanish sympathies. It made a great difference to the rapid progress made by Alba's troops that they advanced in a single body, whereas the Papal army was divided among many places. In this way Frosinone, Veroli and Bauco were soon lost. Alba then marched against Anagni, whereupon Piperno, Terracina, Acuto, Fumone, Ferentino and Alatri also surrendered. The Spanish Viceroy took possession of the places conquered in the name of the College of Cardinals, with the express declaration that he was prepared to deliver them up again to the Sacred College, or to the future Pope.[2]

The action of Alba, who had thus suddenly invaded the States of the Church without any declaration of war, placed Paul IV. in a position of the greatest danger, for he was unable to cope with the power of Spain either from a military or a financial point of view. At his advanced age, and with his imperfect knowledge of business, which made him unsuited for all political affairs, he was even less fitted to direct a war.[3]

and expressions little fitted to a Dominican (see CABALLERO, 277 seqq., 395 seq., 513 seqq.; cf. also LANGWITZ, Carranza, 42). Cano's opinion is printed in the Jugement impartial sur des lettres de la Cour de Rome en forme de Bref, II., Madrid, 1770, 491 seqq.

[1] See Navagero in BROWN, VI., 1, n. 758.

[2] Cf. MASSARELLI, 297; Summarii, 355, 357 seq.; see NORES, 125 seq.; ibid., 405 seq., the letter of du Bellay, Dean of the Sacred College, to Alba on September 13, and Alba's answer on September 16.

[3] Cf. PALLAVICINI, 13, 19, and especially BROSCH, I., 201 seqq. regarding the unsatisfactory state of the Pope's financial and military affairs. On September 6 Paul IV. assembled the

More acutely than ever did he now miss his experienced nephew, and he was therefore exceedingly glad when Cardinal Carafa left the French court on August 11th,[1] and arrived in Rome in the evening of September 7th. He brought great promises from the French king, as well as a considerable sum of money, and was also able to announce the arrival of 1500 Gascons, who had come with him by sea.[2]

Carafa found the Eternal City in a state of indescribable confusion. Had the gates not been closed, most of the inhabitants would have fled.[3] Great dissatisfaction prevailed in Rome on account of the stern measures which the outbreak of war always brings, and the people complained bitterly of the new impositions and the want of consideration shown by Camillo Orsini in the construction of the new fortifications. As the Porta del Popolo appeared to be especially threatened, on account of the Pincio, about a hundred buildings were pulled down there, among others the Augustinian convent in which

Cardinals, complained of Alba's invasion, of the attitude of the commission of Cardinals, and called Offredo to account because of the breach of the peace ; when the latter was about to depart, he was arrested and placed in the Castle of St. Angelo. See MASSARELLI, 295 seqq.; Navagero in BROWN, VI., 1, n. 607; Summarii, 358 seqq. and the *letter of C. Paleotti of September 7, 1556 (State Archives, Bologna).

[1] See the report of Lanssac, ed. SAUZÉ, 488.

[2] See MASSARELLI, 296, where details are given of Cardinal Rebiba's entry on September 9; cf. also BROWN, VI., 1, n. 607; ANCEL, Sienne, 22 and Nonciat., I., xxxvi. (the date of his return is here erroneously given as September 11).

[3] See Navagero in BROWN, VI., 1, n. 609, and the *letter of C. Paleotti of September 14, 1556 (State Archives, Bologna). Many Romans had already left the city by the end of August. Navagero writes on August 29, 1556 : *In somma siamo qui tra li tamburi et le armi et ogni dì si sentono natural et proprie insolentie delli soldati di questi tempi et molti dicono palesamente che tra la ruina che portera seco la fortification et la spesa et le ingiurie che fanno li soldati Roma si potrà reputar mezza sacchegiata et che dalli inimici non si potrà espettar peggio (Library of St. Mark's, Venice).

Luther had once lived ; at one time, indeed, they even thought
of demolishing the costly church which was the burial place
of the Rovere !¹ The arrival on September 15th of the soldiers
from Gascony, who had sailed with Carafa, somewhat raised
the hopes of the Romans², but their disappointment was all the
greater when the whole of the troops at their disposal were
assembled in review ; on paper they had 17,000 men, but in
reality, however, there were only 9000. In addition to this,
the news arrived that on September 15th the fortified town of
Anagni had been taken and plundered by the Spaniards. Rome
was seized by panic, for the inhabitants well knew that the
feeble garrison was not to be depended on, and that many of
the mercenaries would be the first to take advantage of the
opportunity of plundering together with the enemy. " The
terror of the inhabitants," writes Massarelli in his journal,
" is everywhere very great ; the women have received
permission to leave the city, while the men, who are
obliged to remain, are bringing all their valuables into a place
of safety."³

The only person who kept his head amid the general confusion was Cardinal Carafa. He displayed during those
critical days an extraordinary activity in carrying forward his
warlike preparations, in drawing up manifestos to the Christian

---

¹ *Cf.* the **Avvisi of August 29, September 5 and 19 (Anagni
lost. " La città sta in gran spavento et si fa un gran sgombrar."
Vatican Library) as well as MASSARELLI, 297 ; Bonfigliazzi
in NORES, 125 n. 1 ; NAVAGERO-ALBÈRI, 394 ; *Summarii*, 359 ;
M. ROSEO, 515. The report that they were about to pull down
the basilicas of St. Paolo and S. Croce (see BROWN, VI., 1, n.
631) was also current. Concerning the works of that time for
the fortification of Rome see ROCCHI, 52 *seq.*, 59 *seq.*, and tav.
8 ; RODOCANACHI, St. Ange, 157.

² See the *letter of C. Paleotti of September 16, 1556 (State
Archives, Bologna).

³ See MASSARELLI, 297 ; TURNBULL, n. 538 ; *Summarii*, 359 ;
Navagero in BROWN, VI., 1, n. 609 and in ALBÈRI, 394 ; *cf.*
also ANDREA, 41 *seq.* ; RIESS, 142 *seq.* ; Arch. stor. Napolit.
XXXV., 562.

princes in justification of the action of Paul IV.,[1] in making
efforts for the definite conclusion of an alliance with France,
and in attempts to obtain new allies.   In order to win over the
Signoria of Venice, who still adhered to their neutrality, one
of the most talented members of the Papal chancery, Francesco
Commendone, Bishop of Zante, was deputed to go there.   This
envoy also received instructions to ask for help in Urbino,
Ferrara and Parma.[2]   As had been the case before, however,
Carafa was eagerly employed in attempting to secure a principality for his family.   The very man who was stirring up
people all over the world against Spain, and who was working
with feverish energy for the formation of a great anti-Imperial
coalition, and who even aimed at getting help from the Turks,[3]

---

[1] *Cf.* concerning the manifestos, *Propugnatore A. VIII.*, 1875,
I., 345 *seq.*, 347 *seq.*;   II., 153 *seqq.*;   see also PASSARINI, 213 *seq.*,
226 *seqq.*

[2] *Cf.* BROWN, VI., 1, n. 616;   GRATIANUS, 57 *seq.*;   ANCEL,
Sienne, 31 *seqq.*   The correspondence of Carafa with Com-
mendone in the Lett. di princ. XXII.ᵃ (Secret Archives of the
Vatican);   *cf. Nonciat.*, II., 480 n. 1, 495 n. 1.

[3] The advantage which an attack by the Turkish fleet would
give at the outbreak of the war against Spain was pointed out
in the secret memorandum drawn up by Casa in May, 1556
(see MARTINETTI in the Riv. Europ., 1877, IV., 229 and *Ancel*,
in the Nonciat., II., 602).   Nothing was at first said to the Pope
about the matter (see the details by ANCEL in the Nonciat.,
I., lxxxviii., whereby the statements of BROSCH [Mitteil. des
Österr. Inst., XXV., 483], that the idea had originated with
the Pope are contradicted).   Paul IV. only heard of it in September, 1556 (see ANCEL, Disgrâce, 120).   In consequence of the
uncertainty of French help the position had become so grave
that a second sack was feared for Rome.   Cesare Brancaccio, who
had been sent to France at that time, therefore received instructions from Cardinal Carafa on October 23, 1556, that he was to
tell Henry II. to have the Turkish fleet advance quickly in case
of need (DURUY, 377. *Nonciat.*, II., 479).   Later on, in the
legal proceedings, Carafa endeavoured to deny everything;
it was, however, proved that he had repeatedly called for the
assistance of the Turks (see the documents of the case in the

was at the same time carrying on secret negotiations with the enemy in order to gain his own personal ends, in the event of his plan of a great war falling through, owing to the fickleness of Henry II.[1]

Circumstances had been for some time very favourable to Carafa in the carrying out of this most difficult part of his programme. In view of the actual occupation of the greater part of the Campagna, which had been as rapid as it was easy,

appendix to NORES, 483 *seqq.*, and especially 500). In a letter written during his imprisonment in February, 1561, to Pius IV., Carafa acknowledged that he had not only begged help from the Protestants, but had also proposed to the Sultan, Soliman I., in March, 1557, that he should give up his war against Hungary, and throw himself with all his power against Naples and Sicily ; he maintained, however, that all this had been ordered by Paul IV. (BROMATO, II., 369 n.). In reality the Pope had begun by remonstrating with the French ambassador on account of the alliance with the Turks (RIBIER, II., 615), but he afterwards became more reconciled to receiving indirect help from them as his position grew more critical on account of Alba's invasion, and as the representations of Carafa became more urgent (*cf.* BROWN, VI., 1, n. 600 ; RIESS, 161). Often as the Pope afterwards spoke of getting help from the Turks, it was always only a question of indirect help, through the alliance of France with them, which Paul IV., in his blind passion against the Spaniards, undoubtedly sanctioned and promoted, because he hoped by this means to bring about an improvement in his own painful position (see BROWN, VI., 3, n. 1163 ; RIBIER, II., 718). I have been unable to find any trace of a direct alliance between Paul IV. and the Turks, a thing which is maintained by many, but denied by BROMATO (II., 308). I am assured that the latter is right by Ancel, who is the best authority on the history of Paul IV. The rumour that the Pope had eagerly sought after and had obtained help from the Turks was soon circulated in all directions (see HOSII epist., II., 801, 845). These were actually the *horrenda* of which Canisius writes on July 28, 1557, that they were being spread everywhere against the Pope (see BRAUNSBERGER, II., 108).

[1] *Cf.* ANCEL, Sienne, 35 *seqq.* ; see also RIESS, 180.

the peace party in Rome gained adherents every day. Not only Cardinal Juan Alvarez de Toledo, but also the Frenchman, du Bellay and the French ambassador, who was by no means satisfied with Henry II.'s resolve to enter upon a great war, exhorted the Pope to come to an agreement.[1] As Carlo Carafa and his brother Giovanni, as well as Pietro Strozzi, were also working for the same end, Paul IV. consented to negotiate with Alba. The Dominican, Thomas Manrique,[2] repaired to Anagni on September 16th. In order to examine the proposals of Alba, the Pope appointed a commission of Cardinals consisting of seven members on September 17th. On the evening of the same day Manrique again went to Alba, to return again on the 19th, accompanied by Pacheco, the secretary of the Viceroy, with new proposals. The commission of Cardinals deliberated on these on September 20th, 21st, and 22nd, on the last occasion in the presence of the Pope. Paul IV. agreed that Cardinals Juan Alvarez de Toledo and Carafa should personally confer with Alba at Grottaferrata on the 26th.[3]

It appeared to Carafa that his object of securing a principality in any case for his family had been brought much nearer through his negotiations with the Imperialists ; he had not, however, reckoned with the sudden changes in his uncle's character. At the last moment Paul IV. withdrew his consent to the conference with Alba.[4]

[1] See BROWN, VI., 1, n. 621. On September 14, 1556, C. Paleotti states : *Tutto hoggi sono stati con S.Sta li rev^{mi} S. Jacomo et Parisi per tal effetto (Peace negotiations). State Archives, Bologna. Cf. also CAVALCANTI, Lettere, 206.

[2] Professor of theology at the Roman University ; see the ** Rotulo dello studio of 1559 in the Secret Archives of the Vatican, Arm. 11, t. 45, p. 84.

[3] Cf. BROWN, VI., 1, n. 616, 620 ; MASSARELLI, 297 seqq. ; Summarii, 360 ; *Letter of C. Paleotti of December 21, 1556 (loc. cit.) ; NORES, 129 seqq., 360 seqq. ; CAVALCANTI, Lettere, 207 seq. ; COGGIOLA, A. d. Cornia, 235 ; ANCEL, Sienne, 36 seqq. ; RIESS, 150 seqq. ; Nonciat., II., 466, 482 seq.

[4] Cf. BROWN, VI., 1, n. 630 ; *Avviso di Roma of September 26, 1556 (Cod. Urb. 1038, p. 162 ; Vatican Library) ; ANCEL, Sienne, 37.

In Rome, where great hopes had been built on the result of this meeting,[1] the disappointment at its frustration was very great.[2] They now prepared themselves more than ever for a siege : all the members of the religious orders were obliged to work at the fortifications. " One can scarcely describe in words," writes Massarelli in his diary, " how the Romans are trembling ; they think only of flight."[3] In order to reassure the people, Carafa removed on September 24th to the palace of S. Marco, inconvenient though he must have found its distance from the Vatican, where he had to work every day with the Pope. The Cardinal was assisted by Pietro Strozzi and the Duke of Somma.[4] On September 25th, 350 mercenaries arrived in Rome from Montalcino, under Blaise de Montluc, the brave defender of Siena ; they were well exercised in war, but were mostly German Lutherans, who mocked at the Mass and the pictures of the Saints, and only saw in the Pope the prince who paid them. Paul IV. had to endure things from these " defenders " which he would otherwise have punished in the most severe manner. The Romans also had to suffer greatly from these mercenaries, and when they kept their windows lighted all through many nights, this measure of defence was not only directed against the enemy before the walls, but also against possible attempts at pillage on the part of the garrison.[5]

[1] *Si sta in speranza grandissima di pace, writes C. Paleotti, when he announces the impending conference on September 23, 1556 (State Archives, Bologna).

[2] See the *letter of C. Paleotti of September 26, 1556 (State Archives, Bologna).

[3] MASSARELLI 298. *Letter of C. Paleotti of September 26 1556 loc. cit. BROWN, VI., I, n. 631. *Avviso di Roma of September 26, 1556, loc. cit.

[4] These three, as it states in an *Avviso of November 7, 1556, " sono quelli che fanno et governano ogni cosa." loc. cit., p. 173.

[5] See Navagero in BROWN, VI., I, n. 620, 631 and in ALBÈRI, 401, 408 ; MASSARELLI, 298 ; *Avviso di Roma of September 26, 1556 ; cf. DURUY, 193 seq. Concerning Montluc see COURT-EAULT, Blaise de Montluc, Paris, 1910.

Further discouraging news from the seat of war brought
fresh terrors to the Romans. On September 26th Alba had
invested Tivoli, while on October 1st, Vicovaro, which was
important owing to its situation, fell into his hands. Soon
afterwards Palombara and Nettuno were also lost.[1] The
enemy's troopers were now skirmishing up to the very gates of
Rome, which was sure to fall if it were seriously attacked. The
country people had the worst to suffer from both friend and
foe.[2]

With the exception of Paliano and Velletri the whole of the
Campagna had now fallen into the hands of the enemy, while
the same fate threatened the Sabina. Even more bitterly
than these blows, however, Paul IV. must have felt the fact
that the entrance of France, with all its power, into the war,
seemed doubtful even now, while in October the Farnese went
over to Spain. Ottavio Farnese received back Piacenza and
Novara, with, however, a reservation as to the Spanish right
of investiture, while Cardinal Alessandro recovered his Sicilian
revenues.[3]

While Paul IV. did not weary of giving vent in his conversation to his bitter ill-will against the Emperor and his son,[4]
Cardinal Carafa was carrying on further negotiations, through
intermediaries, with Alba. At the end of October and the
beginning of November he had meetings for this purpose with
Cardinal Santa Fiora, which were kept absolutely secret.
Venice also was working for peace through a special ambassador ; the secretary Febo Capella negotiated during the first

----

[1] *Cf.* TURNBULL, n. 545. Concerning the fate of Nettuno see
TOMASSETTI, Campagna, II., 331 *seq.*

[2] *Cf.* MASSARELLI, 298 *seq.* ; Navagero in BROSCH, I., 203,
210 ; *Summarii*, 365 seq ; *Letter of C. Paleotti of September
30 and October 7, 1556 (State Archives, Bologna). According
to the *Avviso of October 3, 1556, the news of the fall of Vicovaro
arrived at midnight, *loc. cit.*, p. 148 ; *ibid.*, p. 169 an *Avviso of
October 24, in which it is stated :   La Campagna anderà vacua "
(Vatican Library).

[3] See ANCEL, Sienne, 30 *seq.*

[4] *Cf.* Navagero's report in BROWN, VI., 2, n. 669, 674, 695.

half of October with both Alba and the Pope, but without any success.[1]

On November 18th, the battles round Ostia ended by this strong fortress falling into the hands of the Spaniards, thereby cutting off Rome's connection with the sea.[2] Alba then offered a ten days' armistice, which Carafa accepted, without informing the French ambassador in Rome of the fact.[3] It was not without difficulty that he succeeded in getting his uncle, who was filled with the deepest distrust of the Spaniards, and who was, just at that time, indulging in the bitterest denunciations against them, to agree to fresh peace negotiations, by representing to him the necessity of gaining time until the French assistance came. Paul IV. did not himself believe in the success of these attempts,[4] but the Romans, on the other hand, flattered themselves that the end of the war was in sight.[5]

The Isola Sacra, situated between the branches of the Tiber near Ostia, was the place chosen for the meeting between Alba

[1] *Cf.* BROWN, VI., 1, n. 659 *seq.*; VI., 2, n. 684, 701; ANCEL, Sienne, 38 *seq.*; RIESS, 165 *seq.*

[2] *Cf.* MASSARELLI, 299-300; BROWN, VI., 2, n. 701, 711, 713; COLA COLEINE, *Diario (Chigi Library); ANDREA, 61 *seq.*; 72 *seq.*; CABRERA, Filipe II., 11.2, c. 15; CARINCI, Lett. di O. Caetani Roma², 1893, 212 *seq.*; PRATESI in Arte e Storia, XXVIII.; RIESS, 174 *seq.*; *ibid.*, 156 *seq.*, concerning the provisioning of Rome. Jacopo Bannissio *reported to Cardinal Madruzzo on November 21, 1556, that the city " mezo assediata sta molto male " (Vice-regal Archives, Innsbruck).

[3] *Cf.* RIBIER, II., 668; *Avvisi of November 19 and 21, 1556, *loc. cit.* 175ᵇ 176 (Vatican Library); Report of Alf. Fantuzzi, dated Rome, November 21, 1556 (State Archives, Bologna); see also COGGIOLA, A. de Cornia, 339 *seq.* The text of the " Tregua " in the Appendix to NORES, 410 *seq.*; PASSARINI, 135 *seq.*; *cf. Nonciat.*, II., 502 n. 2.

[4] See BROWN, VI., 2, n. 695, 707, 713, 714. Distinct promises from Henry II. arrived in Rome on October 18, 1556; see *Corresp. de Lanssac*, 515 *seq.*

[5] According to the *Avviso di Roma of November 21, 1556, they were betting 7 to 3 in favour of peace.

and Carafa. The negotiations were carried on with the greatest assiduity on November 24th, 25th, and 27th, and there is not the least doubt that, in the discussions with regard to the return of Paliano to Marcantonio Colonna, Carafa demanded Siena as compensation for it ; in this respect he was quite willing to take the part of the Spaniards. As Alba declared that he had no power to conclude a transaction of such import-ance, it was agreed that his secretary, Pacheco, and a confi-dential representative of Carafa, should go to Philip II. In order to give time for an answer, the armistice was prolonged for forty days, *i.e.* from November 28th to January 9th.[1]

While the Romans were once more losing hope of peace,[2] France and Ferrara, the powers who had so far been on the side of the Pope, were filled with grave misgivings.[3] At this critical moment Carafa displayed all the cunning of his Machiavellian policy. Hitherto he had worked with so much skill that friend and foe alike were eager to win his favour,[4] but the time was now at hand when his double-dealing might be exposed. The Cardinal did everything he could to avoid this. He declared to the ambassadors of France, Ferrara and Venice that the negotiations and the armistice had been arranged in order to gain time for the arrival of help from Henry II.[5] When Federigo Fantuccio left on December 11th

---

[1] See the extracts from Alba's reports from the *originals in the Archives at Simancas in RIESS, 446 *seq.* and *Nonciat.*, I., XCVII. ; II., 502, 504, 645 *seq.*, 647 *seq.* The statement of PIEPER (p. 90) that Carafa had at that time " suddenly " thought of the acquisition of Siena, proves that this investigator, other-wise so trustworthy, has not seen through Carafa's plans. The Cardinal's demand is sharply and justly criticised by PALLAVICINI (13, 20). *Cf.* also PRATESI, Un storico incontro tra il card. Carafa e il duca Alba : Arte e Storia, 1910.

[2] See the **Avvisi of December 6 and 12, 1556 (Vatican Library).

[3] See *Corresp. de Lanssac*, 533 *seqq.* ; *cf.* ANCEL, Sienne, 41 *seq.* and *Nonciat.*, I., XCVI. *seq.* ; II., 507, n. 515, 523 *seq.*

[4] *Cf.* ANCEL, Sienne, 46, n. 3.

[5] *Ibid.* 41 *seq.*

as the representative of Carafa at the court of Philip II., in accordance with the arrangement made between Alba and the Cardinal, Giulio Orsini had already started on the previous day for France, in order to set the fears of Henry II. concerning the armistice at rest, to gain assurance with regard to the intentions of France towards Spain and in the matter of Siena, and to come to a decision between war and peace in accordance with what he should learn there, for Carafa himself did not yet know whether it would be more advantageous to direct his intriguing policy towards the one or the other.[1]

The mission of Fantuccio was not made in the name of the Pope, but in that of Carafa ; his official instructions for concluding peace, based on the negotiations at Ostia, were only drawn up for form's sake ; in reality, his task was to find out whether Philip II., in view of the danger of an anti-Spanish coalition, was willing to invest the Cardinal's brother with Siena. In the event of an answer in the affirmative, Carafa and his whole family were prepared to go over to the side of Spain.[2]

At the same time Carafa, who liked to have two irons in the fire, prepared another scheme. On the morning of December 15th he left Rome with a large suite ; nobody knew what he was about to do.[3] Only on the following day did the Pope inform the Sacred College that his nephew had gone to Venice to thank the Signoria for their good offices in furthering the armistice, to beg their continued mediation, and to find out whether, as was reported, Philip II. had called upon the Venetians to arbitrate. In a meeting of the Cardinals, which took place on December 20th, Carafa was appointed as legate for

---

[1] Concerning the mission of Fantuccio and Orsini see PIEPER, 91 seq. ; RIESS, 454 seq. ; ANCEL, Sienne, 45 seq., 49 seq. and Nonciat. I., xxxviii. seq. ; II., 520 seq.

[2] Cf. the thorough investigations of ANCEL, Sienne, 49. The official instructions for Fantuccio in the publication of NORES (p. 412 seq.).

[3] Cf. the reports of the ambassadors of Bologna and Ferrara in ANCEL, Sienne, 50 and Nonciat., II., 537.

the whole of Italy, and especially, according to the consistorial records, for the bringing about of peace !¹

This was, however, not generally believed, especially as the Pope, in spite of all his assertions that he was longing for peace, continued to emphasize the fact that the dignity of the Holy See must, at the same time, be maintained. Of this dignity Paul IV. had such an exaggerated idea that he considered every offence against it as an insult to God, and would rather have suffered martyrdom than forego one jot of it.

Cardinal Morone therefore informed Alba's secretary before his departure that he must always bear three things in mind : first, that the Pope, even should he be taken prisoner and à knife held at his throat, would never consent to the Colonna being reinstated at Paliano, for it appeared to him unfitting that he should, as a prince, be faced with force in his own house, or that a King of Naples, the vassal of the Church, should offer him, as Pope, such an insult ; secondly, that Paul IV. felt himself, both as an ecclesiastical and a secular ruler, so deeply offended by the invasion of the territory of the Church, that the Spanish king ought to send a special ambassador to ask for pardon ; and thirdly, that the restoration of the places belonging to the States of the Church, which had been seized, was an absolute necessity. If the dispute could not be arranged on these terms, then, according to Morone, the worst was to be expected, the excommunication and deposition of Philip II., in spite of the fact that the defection of Spain and England would follow. Even should the French help not arrive, said Morone in a letter to Pole, and the Pope be abandoned by everybody, he would not give up the claims which he considered his due ; even the influence of Carafa would be of no avail in this matter. In the same letter Morone lays stress on the fact that Paul IV. had no confidence in the Spaniards, for, he says, he looks at deeds, and not at words,

¹ See Navagero's report in BROWN, VI., 2, n. 763, 766, 767, 768 and Acta consist. cancell., VII. (Constitutional Archives).
*A letter of credence for Carafa, addressed to the Duke of Ferrara, of December 14, 1556, is in the State Archives, Modena.

and is always afraid, now as ever, that the negotiations are only for form's sake, in order to get possession of the remainder of the States of the Church.[1]

In order to prevent matters from getting into a desperate condition, Paul IV. took great pains to gain the powerful alliance of Venice. Peace, he exclaimed on November 11th, to the representative of the Republic of St. Mark, would only be possible for Italy when the barbarians were driven out ; Venice and the Holy See alone were capable of effecting this. Hundreds of years might pass, he continued, without another Pope appearing who would be as intent as he was on the liberation of Italy.[2]

It was in keeping with this aim that Carafa, who had arrived in Venice on December 21st, had instructions to propose an offensive and defensive alliance to the Signoria. The shrewd Venetians, however, clung fast to their neutrality, tempting as were the offers which were made to them. When Carafa left the city of the lagoons on January 12th, 1557, he was obliged to admit to himself, that although he had been honoured there as though he had been a crowned king, he had not attained the object with which he had been sent.[3]

Giulio Orsini, who had arrived at the French court on January 2nd, 1557, had great trouble in allaying the misgivings of Henry II., and in spite of all his efforts did not completely succeed in doing so. On the other hand he was able to induce the still hesitating king to take decisive action. At the end of January Henry broke off diplomatic relations with Philip II., and prepared to make war on the Spaniards in Italy, as

[1] See in Appendix Nos. 34 and 35 the important *letters of Morone of November 28 and December 12, 1556 (Secret Archives of the Vatican).

[2] *Cf.* the reports of Navagero and F. Capella in BROWN, VI., 2, n. 755.

[3] *Cf.* Corresp. polit. de Dominique du Gabre, éd. A. VITALIS, Paris, 1903, 204 ; NORES, 156 n. 1 ; DURUY, 208 *seqq.*, 382 *seq.* ; Mitteil. des Österr. Inst., XXV., 482 ; ANCEL, Sienne, 51 *seq.* ; RIESS, 184 *seq.*, 189 *seqq.* ; *Nonciat.*, I., xcix. ; II., 539 *seq.*, 544 *seq.*

well as in Flanders. Philip was completely taken by surprise
at this sudden turn of affairs.[1]

So few precautions had been taken by Alba during the
armistice, that Pietro Strozzi, who was henceforth commander-
in-chief of the Papal troops, easily succeeded in retaking Ostia,
and soon afterwards Tivoli, Vicovaro and the Marittima.[2]

This astonishing success made such an impression that
Alba's peace offers were declined, especially as Paul IV. did
not trust the Spaniards.[3] He hoped, with the help of France,
to win a complete victory over them, and to drive this mixture
of Jews, Marani and Lutherans, as he called them, out of
Naples, and indeed, out of the whole of Italy.   On February
12th, 1557, he appointed a special congregation to institute a
suit against Charles V. and Philip II. on a charge of felony and
rebellion.[4]

The French anxiliary army, under the Duke of Guise, had in
the meantime, advanced through Piedmont, and, while the
Farnese were observing a doubtful neutrality, through the
Duchy of Parma, and Piacenza, as far as Reggio.   Here the
Duke of Ferrara received from Guise, on February 16th, the
bâton of commander-in-chief of the allied army.   Cardinal
Carafa, who was now forced to abandon his double dealing,
and to place himself definitely on the side of the French,
although he had little confidence in them, was present at this

---

[1] See ANCEL, Sienne, 55 ; RIESS, 207 seqq. ; Nonciat., I., c.
seq.

[2] Cf. MASSARELLI, 302 ; TURNBULL, n. 572, 573 ; ROSEO,
535 seq. ; the *Avvisi di Roma of January 9, 16, 23, 30, and
February 6, 13, 20, 1557 (Cod. Urb. 1038, Vatican Library)
and the *reports of Alf. Fantuccio, dated Rome, January 27 and
February 12, 1557 (State Archives, Bologna).   Concerning the
state of the war at Ostia, cf. the rare engraving, Il vero disegno
del sito di Hostia e di Porto con li forti fatti dal campo di S.S.tà
et delli Imperiali, quali si resero a di 24 Gennaio ; see NORDEN-
SKIÖLD, Facsimile-Atlas (1889), p. 21, n. 114.

[3] Cf. Soranzo in ALBÈRI, Ser. 1, II., 449.

[4] See Navagero in BROWN, VI., 2, n. 798, 812 ; NAVAGERO-
ALBÈRI, 397 ; MASSARELLI, 303 ; ANCEL, Sienne, 57 seq.

ceremony.[1] At Reggio a council of war was held, in order to consider which point the army should attack first. Opinions were very divided, but at last it was decided, to the great vexation of the Duke of Ferrara, who was thus left without defence, that the French army should advance into the Romagna ; whether it should then turn against Tuscany, as Carafa strongly urged, or advance through the Marches on the Kingdom of Naples, was to be decided by the Pope.[2]

While the troops were being set in movement for the Romagna, Guise and Carafa hastened to Rome, and arrived there on Shrove Tuesday, March 2nd. A magnificent reception awaited the honoured guest, who took up his residence in Carafa's apartments in the Vatican. In spite of the violence with which Carafa now expressed himself against Spain, and the determination of the Pope to ally himself with France, Guise found that the preparations for the war fell far below his expectations ; many differences of opinion and personal disputes also soon became apparent.[3]

Carlo Carafa was destined to experience a disappointment of another kind. The nephew had returned to Rome in the belief that the powerful influence he had formerly exercised over the Pope was unchanged. Very soon, however, he discovered that he no longer possessed the same power over his uncle, who was so susceptible of new impressions. The Car-

[1] Cf. ANCEL, Sienne, 56, 58 and Nonciat., I., cii.

[2] See Corresp. de D. du Gabre, éd. VITALIS, 155 ; NORES, 162 seq. and the excellent details in ANCEL, Sienne, 61 seq., 64 seq. ; cf. also the briefs to Ercole in RAYNALDUS, 1557, n. 6 (also in FONTANA, Renata, I., 554 seq.) and DURUY, 356 seq.

[3] See MASSARELLI, 303 seq. ; RIBIER, II., 678 seq. ; BROWN, VI., 2, n. 825 ; TURNBULL, n. 580 ; the *reports of the " vescovo di Anglona " dated Rome, March 3, 6, and 7, 1557 (State Archives, Modena) and COLA COLEINE, *Diario (Chigi Library). Concerning the fortifications ordered on March 6, 1557, for the protection of the gates of Rome, see LANCIANI, III., 153 seq.

dinal should never, in the opinion of his best friends, have gone
so far away from the Pope.[1]

The first discovery which Carafa made in Rome was that
Silvestro Aldobrandini, who had been, since the death of della
Casa, his first private secretary and the confidant of all his
plans, had completely lost the Pope's favour. Carafa tried
in every way to save his faithful assistant, but Paul IV. was
inexorable. " When I have given an order," he informed his
nephew in an imperious manner, " there is good reason for it.
You, my lord Cardinal, have to carry out my wishes." On
the following day the Pope held a conference, at which, besides
Carafa and Guise, Strozzi and the French ambassador were
present. On this occasion Paul IV. again referred to Aldobrandini, whom he accused of having sown discord between
Giovanni and Carlo Carafa, and also of not having said a word
to him about certain legal proceedings which he had instituted
against persons guilty of grave immorality. " Yes, yes," he
said, " certain persons take too much upon themselves, and
forget that I, who have elevated them, can again degrade
them." Speaking still more clearly, he then turned in an
excited manner to Carafa, exclaiming : " You are perhaps
one of those persons ! " Although the Pope and his nephew
were reconciled the same evening, the fact remained that
Aldobrandini lost his office.[2]

Carafa found the Pope just as firm regarding the question
where the war should begin, regardless of the fact that his
nephew wished for an expedition against Tuscany, on account
of Siena. Paul IV. insisted that the Kingdom of Naples
should be the point of attack.

It was no less bitter for Carafa that his brother, the Duke
of Paliano, and the other members of his family, should, just
at this time, have rebelled against his authority.[3] Friendly

---

[1] *Letter of the Bishop of Anglona of March 7, 1557 (State
Archives, Modena) ; see ANCEL, Sienne, 72.

[2] Cf. the cypher report of Navagero in BROWN, VI., 2, n. 831,
and for details of Aldobrandini's fall ANCEL, Secrét, 22 seq.

[3] ANCEL, Sienne, 72, 78. BROSCH'S (I., 213) view that Carafa
had urged the Neapolitan enterprise is quite erroneous.

relations had never existed among the brothers ; Giovanni, as well as Antonio Carafa, could never reconcile themselves to the fact that their younger brother, although they were obliged to admit his superior talents, should far excel them in influence and authority. Cardinal Carafa had hoped to conciliate them and attach them to himself, by persuading his uncle to elevate the one to the dignity of Duke of Paliano, and to name the other Marquis of Montebello. Things showed that this hope had been vain, for now, as before, they grudged their younger brother his great influence, and their old love for Spain was not long in being re-awakened. As he had already done in September, 1555, so now in February, 1557, did the Duke of Paliano openly urge an agreement with Philip II. ; he had also taken a great part in bringing about the fall of Aldobrandini.[1]

Even at the time when Carafa enjoyed the full confidence of the Pope, the latter had kept purely ecclesiastical affairs out of his hands. Nevertheless, he hoped that consideration for the necessity of the help of France would decide Paul IV. to fall in with the rather extensive wishes of Henry II. at the impending creation of Cardinals. He was destined, however, to be disappointed in this matter as well, when the appointment took place on March 15th, 1557. This was all the more painful for Carafa as he had, on his own responsibility, made the most lavish promises to the French king with regard to this very matter.[2]

The dissatisfaction of Henry II. at the non-fulfilment of his wishes at the creation of Cardinals on March 15th, was increased by the reports of Guise from Rome. Everything, he said, was lacking, and above all money for the troops ; the supply of provisions, too, was very badly organized. In addition to this there were differences of opinion with regard to the plan of campaign which completely divided the allies. While the

---

[1] *Cf.* NAVAGERO-ALBÈRI, 386 *seq.* and the important embassy reports in ANCEL, Disgrâce, 20. DURUY (p. 46) makes much less of these disputes, and even speaks of a " triumvirat fraternal," which, however, only existed in the imagination of this author.

[2] ANCEL, L'activité réformatrice, 22 *seq.*

Duke of Ferrara wished to proceed against Milan, and Guise to attack Tuscany with the whole of his army, Paul IV. insisted, above everything else, on first assuring the safety of Rome by an immediate attack on the Kingdom of Naples.[1] By reason of these differences of opinion and their mutual recriminations, much valuable time was lost, of which Philip II. and Alba made good use in taking decisive measures for resistance.[2]

By the end of March they were at last of one mind in Rome ; the Pope's view had been accepted. The joy of the Spanish king was great, says Navagero, that they had adopted the very plan of campaign which was the least dangerous for him.

On April 5th, Guise, discouraged, and without feeling any certainty of success, repaired to the army ; on the 9th he was followed by the Marquis of Montebello, Antonio Carafa.[3] On the same day, April 9th, Paul IV. announced in a consistory the recall of all his agents, nuncios and legates, including Cardinal Pole, from the dominions of Charles V. and Philip II.[4]

This very decisive measure, as well as the preliminary arrangements for the legal proceedings with regard to the deposition of Philip II., which caused the greatest sensation, was in answer to the recall, which had been ordered by the Spanish king, of all Spaniards from Rome. In accordance with a decree of the Council of State, these

[1] ANCEL, Sienne, 65 seq., 71 seq. and L'activité réformatrice, 27 seq. ; cf. also RIESS, 236 seq. A long report from Rome of March 31, 1557, about the conduct of the war in upper Italy is in FILLON, Invent. d'autographes, Paris, 1877, n. 2658.

[2] See DURUY, 223 seq. and RIESS, 227 seq., 251, who very properly emphasizes the importance of gaining over England.

[3] See NAVAGERO-ALBÈRI, 396, and MASSARELLI, 306. The *Avviso di Roma of April 10, 1557, announces that the Pope said to Guise, who was dining with him on Sunday evening : " Va figliulo mio, che tu sia benedetto, va pur, che altro cavallier mai non tentò la più santa ne la più honorata impresa et dopo molte invective contra heretici gli donò un diamante di 3000 scudi " (Loc. cit. p. 213. Vatican Library).

[4] See PIEPER, 102 ; BIAUDET, 24.

were in future to apply to a supreme ecclesiastical court, which was about to be set up in Spain, instead of the Papal Rota, while the jurisdiction over all revenues, first fruits and " spolia " accruing to the Curia was to be withdrawn from the Holy See. Paul IV. did not allow himself to be intimidated by such measures. On Maundy Thursday the Bull *In Coena Domini* included some additions against the assailants of the Holy See, while, on Good Friday, the usual prayers for the Emperor were omitted from the liturgy.[1]

On April 27th Paul IV. gave a fearful example of his severity, when he ordered the destruction of a place called Montefortino, in the neighbourhood of Velletri, the inhabitants of which had long been notorious as rebels and bandits.[2] Shortly before this, 1500 Frenchmen had arrived at Civitavecchia as a first reinforcement. They were intended to serve for the protection of Rome,[3] but were very soon taken to strengthen the army of Guise.

During the long hesitation of the enemy, Alba had completed his preparations for the impending attack.[4] When

---

[1] *Cf.* BROWN, VI., 2, .n. 855, 856, 859, 865 ; the Portuguese report in SANTAREM, XII., 451 ; *Avvisi di Roma of April 17 and 24, 1557 (Vatican Library) ; MASSARELLI, 306-307 ; RIESS, 218 *seq.* Concerning the legal proceedings against Philip II. see GORI, Archivio, I., 209. The consistorial decision with regard to the recall of the ambassadors is erroneously placed by GULIK-EUBEL (III., 37) on March 30. All other authorities give April 9th as the date, as do the *Acta consist. cancell., VII. (Consistorial Arch.).

[2] R. DE LA BLANCHÈRE in the Rev. hist., XXII., 364. Rebuilt later, Montefortino received the name of Artena in 1873. The change of name was of little avail, for the place remained a nest of robbers (see Sighele in FERRERO's Mondo Criminale, 1897). The conquest of Montefortino was effected, according to Cola Coleine's *Diario (Chigi Library) on April 22, 1557 ; see also ROSEO, 539 *seq.*

[3] *Cf.* the *report of Delfino of April 17, 1557 (Secret State Archives, Vienna).

[4] *Discorso sopra la guerra di p. Paolo IV. con M. A. Colonna (Cod. D. 21 of the Santa Croce Archives, Rome).

this at last took place, it was evident that the Papal-French army was no match for the Spaniards. Since April 24th the struggle had turned on the siege of Civitella, which had been effectively fortified by Alba, and was bravely defended by the Count of Santa Fiora. He had aroused the enthusiasm of the inhabitants, even of the women, for the defence, and had been successful in repulsing repeated attacks.[1]

As is usually the case in disastrous operations in war, there was no want of mutual recrimination,[2] and on May 1st Guise and Antonio Carafa had so violent a dispute that the latter left the camp the same evening.

Sittings of the Inquisition were being held in Rome at the same time, in which the Pope wished to proceed at once to pronounce excommunication and deposition against Philip II. ; it was, however, pointed out to him that such penalties could not be inflicted without previous citation.[3] The Duke of Paliano and the Papal commander-in-chief, Strozzi, were ordered to proceed to the seat of war on May 12th, in order to get a clear understanding as to the state of affairs there. The prospects before Guise soon became so unsatisfactory that he raised the siege of Civitella on May 15th, thereby relinquishing the enterprise against Naples. At the end of May the Pope learned that the French commander had very nearly betaken himself to Ferrara. The ambassador of Ferdinand I. in Rome thought the Pope would have to conclude peace,

---

[1] See ANDREA, 222 *seq.* ; ROSEO, 541 *seq.* ; CABRERA, Filipe II., 1.3, c. 9 ; *cf.* PITTALUGA in the Riv. milit. ital., XLI. (1896) and FEDELE in the Riv. Abruzzese, XI. (1896) ; see also the reports mentioned in the *Nonciat.*, II., 569, n 3.

[2] See Navagero in BROWN, VI., 2, n. 878 and the *Avviso of May 8, 1557 (Vatican Library).

[3] See Navagero in BROWN, VI., 2, n. 879, 888 ; VI., 3, n. 167 ; *cf.* Mitteil. des Österr. Inst., XXV., 485, n.1. The draft of the Bull of deposition which was prepared at that time in DÖLLINGER, Materialien, I., 218 *seq.* Philip II. had already taken steps to prevent the circulation of the bull in his dominions ; see *ibid.* 217, and the letter of July 10, 1557, in CABRERA, I., 79.

as the military superiority of Alba was now evident.[1]

Paul IV. could not yet grasp the fact that his noble aim of liberating Italy and the Holy See from foreign domination, from the " barbarians," had miscarried. The representations of both his secular nephews, especially those of the Marquis of Montebello, who spoke very bitterly of the French, and very violently against the war policy, fell on deaf ears. Paul IV. still believed in the success of his policy, if only the great power of Venice would enter the war on his side. He employed all his eloquence at this time to win over the representative of the republic ; in his usual way, he went far back and referred to the times of Charles VIII., " when that unlucky gate was opened to the barbarians, which he now wanted to close." " We shall not regret," he exclaimed in excited tones, " to have done what we could, and perhaps even more than we could." For all future time those who did not assist him would be disgraced, when it should later on be told how there had once been a weak old man of eighty years of age, who, when people had thought that he would run into a corner to bemoan his feebleness, had come forward as the champion of Italy's freedom. " You will repent it, my lords of Venice," he exclaimed, " as well as all you others, who did not make use of this opportunity of ridding yourselves of this past. It began under a king who was bearable on account of his good qualities, but then came this new race, a mixture of Flemings and Spaniards, in whom there is no trace of royal dignity or of Christianity, which sticks like a burr, wherever it gets fast. The French are different ; they break off in the middle of a work, and would not remain, even were they bound. We have seen them as masters of Naples and as masters of Milan, and then they were gone ; they are inconstant. Noble ambassador ! we speak to you in confidence as we should speak to his magnificence the Doge, and to the councillors and heads of

[1] *Cf.* Navagero in BROWN, VI., 2, n. 889 ; MASSARELLI, 309 ; the letter of the ambassador of the Este in ANCEL, Secrét, 52, n. 3, and the *report of Delfino of May 29, 1557 (Secret State Archives, Vienna).

Christendom, for we know that we have laboured through these short remaining years of our life for the honour of God and for the salvation of this poor Italy, and that we have led a life of drudgery, without rest or repose." On another occasion the Pope again said to Navagero : " Mark well what I say to you ; we are old and we shall one of these days go hence, when God shall will. But the time will come when you will recognize that we have told you the truth ; God grant that it may not be to your hurt ! They are barbarians, both of them, Frenchman as well as Spaniard, and it would be a good thing if they remained at home, and that no other language were spoken in Italy than our own."[1] At the beginning of June it transpired that Guise had already received orders from his king to return to France, whereupon Strozzi was once more sent to the French camp. The result of this was the dispatch of Strozzi to the French king. On June 15th, the marshall left Rome ; he took with him the only son of the Duke of Paliano, for the French had demanded the child as a hostage, because, in consequence of Carafa's intrigues to acquire Siena, they no longer trusted their ally.[2]

The depressed state of feeling in the Eternal City was some-what relieved by the news that several thousand Swiss were about to arrive on June 12th. Paul IV. declared to Cardinal Carpi, who courageously stood out for peace, that he could agree to nothing without his ally, the King of France.[3]

In the meantime the burden of the war was pressing more and more heavily. On May 18th, the Pope decided, in spite of the opposition of certain Cardinals, such as Carpi, that a tax of one and a half per cent. should be levied on all real estate in the States of the Church. He had chosen this tax out of con-sideration for those who had only small means, but although it had been introduced long ago elsewhere, the subjects of the

[1] See the letters of Navagero of May 21 and June 28, 1557, in the Appendix to NORES, 307-308.

[2] See DURUY, 229 ; ANCEL, Sienne, 82 seq. ; Nonciat., I., xxxix. ; II., 573 n.

[3] Cf. the *report of Delfino of June 12, 1557 (Secret State Archives, Vienna).

States of the Church seemed to look upon it as something unheard of, and there was the greatest difficulty in collecting it; here and there, indeed, the attempt met with violent opposition. The Romans endeavoured to protect themselves by proposing that, instead of this tribute, a meat tax should be introduced, which would yield 100,000 scudi. The Pope considered this sum too small, and at length they agreed upon 130,000 scudi; the clergy had also to pay 50,000 scudi.[1]

While the position at the seat of war was getting more and more hopeless for the Holy See, Carafa was continuing his former intrigues for the acquisition of Siena. And end, however, was put to all his plotting by the action of Cosimo I., who, at the beginning of July, succeeded in obtaining Siena from the Spaniards, though not without a considerable sacrifice. The first news of this turn of affairs, which was a most painful blow to Carafa, reached Rome on June 25th; on July 3rd, the agreement was signed by which the Duke of Florence was invested with the territory of Siena as a Spanish fief.[2]

A very dangerous enemy of the Romans had arisen in the person of Marcantonio Colonna. He conquered Valmontone on June 29th, and also invested Palestrina; in the first days of July, he advanced to within five miles of the Eternal City.[3]

[1] *Cf.* Navagero in BROWN, VI., 2, n. n. 893, 907, 932, 941; RAYNALDUS, 1557, n. 8; MASSARELLI, 309, 311; *Letters of Tommaso Cospio to Bologna, dated Rome, June 9 and 12, 1557 (State Archives, Bologna); *Avvisi of May 29, June 5, 12 and 18, 1557 (Cod. Urb., 1038. Vatican Library); Cola Coleine, *Diario (Chigi Library). A copy of the rare publication the *Bulla Pauli IV. subsidii dimidii et unius scuti respective pro centenario,* dated *Romae,* 1557, XV., Cal. Iun. A.° 2°, in the Colonna Archives, Rome. It begins with the words: " Ubique terrarum . . . notissimum credimus quam impie et violenter superiori anno hostes Romanae ecclesiae, qui se christianos profitentur, re vero Turcis immaniores et efferatiores existunt, statum ipsius ecclesiae invaserint, etc."

[2] *Cf.* REUMONT, Toskana, I., 222 *seq.*; ANCEL, Sienne, 85; *Nonciat.,* I., cvi.

[3] See MASSARELLI, 312, and *Avviso di Roma of July 3, 1557 (Vatican Lib).

" Rome is in danger," wrote the ambassador of Ferdinand I.
on July 3rd, " but in spite of this the Pope fears nothing ; he
is waiting for the answer which Strozzi is to bring back from
France." It then transpired that Alba had offered peace on
the basis of the conditions considered in the previous November, but the Pope declared that he could settle nothing without
Henry II.[1] The people of Rome longed for the speedy return
of Strozzi. On July 19th the 2000 Swiss whose coming had
been announced some time previously by the nuncio Raverta,
arrived in Rome ; they were fine soldiers, though badly armed.
The Pope welcomed them as angels sent by God for his liberation, and invested their leaders with gold chains and knightly
rank.[2] He sent them, strengthened by Italian troops, to the
relief of the sorely pressed Paliano. The expedition ended on
July 27th in the utter defeat of the Papal troops.[3]

On July 30th, almost at the same time as this terrible news,

[1] See the *report of Delfino of July 3, 11, and 17, 1557 (Secret
State Archives, Vienna).

[2] *Cf*. PLON, Cellini, 394 *seq*.

[3] See the Spanish *account in the State Archives, Naples,
C. Farnes : the *report of Delfino of July 24, 1557 (Secret State
Archives, Vienna) and the *Avviso di Roma of July 24, 1557
(Vatican Library) ; BROWN, VI., 2, n. 969, 972, 976, 978 ; MAS-
SARELLI, 312 ; ANDREA, 273 ; NORES, 201 ; CABRERA, III.,
139. The statement contained in Cabrera, and accepted by
Ranke, that all the standards of the allies were lost in the en-
counter, with the exception of two, is erroneous ; five were saved,
and one was torn in pieces by the ensign to prevent its falling
into the hands of the enemy (see LÜTOLF, Schweizergarde, 58,
and FELLER, Ritter Melchior Lussy, I., Stans, 1906, 1 ; *cf*. also
WYMANN, Aktenstücke aus dem Römerkriege von 1557 :
Schweizer Geschichtsfreund, LXIV. (1909, 277 *seqq*.) It is an
exaggeration to say as does BROSCH (Mitteil. des Österr. Inst.,
XXV. 485) that the Swiss auxiliaries amounted to 4,000 men.
NAVAGERO-ALBÈRI (p. 401) says distinctly " quattro milla
Svizzeri in voce et forse in pagamento ma non più di due milla
in essere." *Cola Coleine (Chigi Library) also gives 2,000 ;
Bernardino Pia says in a *report to Cardinal Gonzaga, dated
Rome, July 30, 1557, that the " rotta " of the Papal troops

Strozzi returned to Rome; he brought a much more favourable report than anyone in the Curia had dared to hope. Henry II. was prepared to hold out on the Pope's side, and the latter was to decide how long Guise was to remain in Italy.[1]

Paul IV., like Carafa, now again placed all his hopes in the French. The Duke of Paliano, who had always hated the whole war, thought otherwise. He spoke more decidedly than ever in favour of peace, and fearlessly blamed even the Pope, and much more so the dangerous policy of his brother. He had a violent scene with the latter at the beginning of August, at the vigna of the Carafa in Trastevere, concerning the provisioning of Paliano. Strozzi was present when this took place. The Duke, who was enraged at the double-dealing of the Cardinal, accused him of being the cause of all their misfortunes, because he thought only of himself. When the old Pope died, he would still remain a Cardinal, but what was to become of him, and all the other members of the family? The excitement of both of them kept on increasing. "Monsignor," cried the Duke, "you are deceiving the Pope, and the King of France and his ministers. You are ruining the world, devastating Italy, destroying our family and especially myself, for to me you have done the worst of all possible things, you have robbed me of my only son. Hitherto I have restrained myself, but I can do so no longer. I shall tell the Pope everything and show him the sort of person you really are." Carlo answered him furiously, "You need not imagine that my Cardinal's hat will cause me to show you any consideration; I shall throw it off, and expose you as the stupid brute that you are." The Duke then stepped back in order to draw his sword, whereupon the Cardinal, casting his hat on the ground, was about to seize his brother by the throat, when Strozzi succeeded in separating them. The Duke of Paliano then went away, bursting with rage, and crying out: "This traitor was born

on July 27 has ensued "più tosto per imperitia et delli capitani et de soldati che d' altro" (Gonzaga Archives, Mantua). P. Segmüller is preparing a special work at Einsiedeln concerning the battle of Paliano.

[1] See ANCEL, Sienne, 85; Nonciat., I., cvii.

for the ruin of the world ! " The Cardinal begged Strozzi to hurry after him, to prevent the Pope hearing of the occurrence. Strozzi succeeded in calming the infuriated Duke, so that only a very mild account of the whole scene was communicated to Paul IV. "One sees," writes the Florentine ambassador, " how the truth is kept from the Holy Father."[1]

As Henry II. had expressly ordered Guise to comply with all the Pope's requests, he was forced to pay attention to the latter's cry for help. As soon, however, as the French army was set in motion, Alba left the Abruzzi and advancing through the valley of the Sacco, marched on Rome for the second time. It therefore appeared as if a decisive battle was to be fought near the Eternal City, where a painful scarcity of provisions was already beginning to make itself felt.[2] Then, like a flash of lightning from a clear sky, the news arrived on August 23rd of a great victory which the Spaniards had won against the French on August 10th at St. Quentin. Next morning a courier from Guise announced that he had received orders to take his troops back to France as soon as possible. The principal counsellors of the Pope, Cardinal Carafa, the Duke of

[1] *Cf.* the report of Navagero of August 3, 1557, in BROWN, VI., 2, n. 980 and the letter of Gianfigliazzi of August 18 in ANCEL, Disgrâce, 20, n. 5.

[2] According to an *Avviso di Roma of February 13, 1557, the imports of provisions were even then so limited, that orders were issued that no married man, and no one with a household of his own, was to take meals in an osteria, as otherwise those who had nowhere else to go for their food would suffer. Paul IV. said at the time to the Romans who were complaining : " cose incredibili " (Cod. Urb. 1038, p. 194). An *Avviso of August 7 speaks of the fear of a " gran carestia," for which reason the Pope should have corn brought in : " Si ragiona che si caccierano di questa città le cortegiane, il poveri et gli giudei et ogni altro sorte di bocche inutili." An *Avviso of August 21 announces : " Qua si patisce d'ogni sorte di viver ne si puo comprar cosa alcuna senza bolettino et è andato il bando che tutte le genti inutili scombrino . . . et si ragiona di cacciar ancora una parte delle famiglie de cardinali " (Loc. cit., p. 253, 257. Vatican Library).

Paliano and Strozzi had met for a conference in the night between August 23rd and 24th, which lasted until four o'clock in the morning. Then the Duke and Strozzi hastened to Guise ; they only succeeded, however, in getting from him a promise that the French army, under the command of the Duc d'Aumale, should remain from ten to twelve days longer, in order to give the Pope time to conclude peace with Alba.[1]

At that time it seemed as though very little would be required to plunge Rome once more into the horrors she had suffered in the fatal year of 1527. On August 25th Alba had advanced as far as La Colonna, situated on one of the last spurs of the Alban hills. During the following night 3000 Spaniards started for the Porta Maggiore, taking with them ladders in order to scale the walls near the gate. When they approached the city, however, they found Rome all lit up, and heard the cries of command and the beating of drums. They were prepared for an attack inside the city, for a spy had given warning to Carafa ; thereupon Alba resolved to return to La Colonna, and afterwards marched on Paliano.[2]

It is very much open to question, however, whether Alba refrained from the attack solely on account of Carafa's preparedness for defence, especially as there was all the more likelihood of success from the fact that the Romans were very

---

[1] Cf. BROWN, VI., 2, n. 999 ; ANCEL, Sienne, 87-88 ; Nonciat., I., cviii. ; MALAGUZZI, La battaglia di S. Quintino, Modena, 1890 ; ROMIER, Jacques d'Albon de St. André (1909). According to a letter of the Cardinal of Lorraine of August 21 (see Revue des quest. hist., XXXII., 477), Henry II. was willing to leave a portion of the troops for the protection of the Pope.

[2] Besides MASSARELLI, 313, see NAVAGERO-ALBÈRI, 398 seq. ; Carafa in DURUY, 390 ; ANDREA, 306 seq. and NORES, 336 ; cf. the *Avviso of August 28, 1557 (Vatican Library). *Il sig. duca d'Alba, writes Delfino on August 28, 1557, to Ferdinand I., " si è molto avicinato con le genti sue a questa città et se l'altra notte buona diligentia non ci aiutava questa città rimaneva in preda degl' inimici " (Secret State Archives, Vienna). According to Cola Coleine, *Diario (Chigi Library) the Imperialists advanced as far as Acqua Bulicante.

tired of the war and longed for peace at any price. It is much more probable that Philip II.'s generalissimo was also kept back by religious[1] and political reasons from inflicting on the capital of Christendom the terrible fate of being sacked and pillaged, which in those days was always the consequence of a victory by force of arms. As Charles V. had done thirty years before, so now would Philip II. draw down upon himself the hatred of the whole Catholic world. The restrained manner in which Alba had hitherto conducted the war—his own soldiers complained that they were led into the field against smoke or a mist—agrees very well with the supposition that the Viceroy merely wished to show the Pope, by a demonstration of his strength, how completely he held him in his power.[2]

However difficult it was for such a self-assured man as Paul IV., who was so unshakably convinced of his right and of God's protection,[3] to enter upon peace negotiations, he was forced to do so, as he stood almost defenceless before a well-armed and powerful enemy.[4] The war, indeed, was voluntary, as Navagero wrote, but the peace was enforced.[5] It was due, above all, to the skilful mediation of Venice, that an agreement was reached in a comparatively short time. On September

[1] *Cf.* NAVAGERO-ALBÈRI, 407. According to this well-informed authority, Cardinal Juan Alvarez de Toledo, Alba's uncle, is said to have pointed out to his nephew the bad end to which all those came who had taken part in the Sack of 1527.

[2] That was the opinion of Navagero ; see SAMM, Une question italienne au XVI.ᵉ siècle, 258 ; DURUY, 239 ; *Cf.* Arch. stor. Napolit., XXXV., 561, 566.

[3] *Cf.* his remarks at the end of July in BROWN, VI., 2, n. 963, 972 ; see also ALBÈRI, 390, and MANAREUS, 125. Concerning the scene with Cardinal Ghislieri see, in Appendix No. 40, the *Avviso of September 4, 1557.

[4] According to MASSARELLI, 314, the withdrawal of the Gascons from Rome began on September 4, which caused Paul IV. the greatest excitement ; see the report of the Este of September 7, 1557, in the *Annales de S. Louis*, IX., 251.

[5] NAVAGERO-ALBÈRI, 400. Concerning the peace negotiations *cf.* SAMM, Question 262 *seq.* ; DURUY, 241, 390 *seq.* ; RIESS, 271 *seq.*, 463 *seq.*

8th Cardinals Carafa, Santa Fiora and Vitelli repaired to the town of Cave, situated on a vine-clad hill about a mile from Palestrina. Under one of the large walnut trees, in which that neighbourhood is specially rich, they met the Duke of Alba. The moderation and compliance which the victors displayed in the negotiations at Cave showed how very strongly the Spaniards considered it desirable to effect a reconciliation with the Pope ; it was also no doubt of advantage to Paul IV. that the French army had not yet gone. The principal difficulty lay in the return of the confiscated estates of Marcantonio Colonna and Ascanio della Corgna, demanded by Alba, but to which Paul IV. would not agree. A final decision was hastened by the news, which arrived on September 11th, that the fortress of St. Quentin had fallen into the hands of the Spaniards. This announcement made the deepest impression on all, including the Pope. Should the news be confirmed, said Guise, then all the chains in the world would not be strong enough to keep him back.[1]

The treaty which was agreed upon on September 12th, settled the following conditions : Alba was to make, in the name of the Spanish king, that act of submission and obedience which was necessary for the forgiveness of the Pope. For this purpose Philip was also to send a special ambassador. On his part the Pope promised to receive the Spanish king once more as a good and obedient son, to give up the French alliance, and to remain neutral. Philip was to restore the cities and territories belonging to the Holy See. All punishments were to be remitted, except those pronounced against Marcantonio and Ascanio Colonna, the Marquis of Bagno, and other rebels. Paliano was to be handed over to a trusted agent of both parties, Bernardino Carbone, who was to take an oath of allegiance both to Paul IV. and to Philip II., and to observe all the arrangements which Alba and Cardinal Carafa had specially drawn up regarding this matter. This latter clause referred to a secret sub-treaty, of which, as Carafa informed his brothers

[1] See the letter of the Duke of Paliano to Carafa of September 12, 1557, in RIESS, 468.

and confidants, the Pope was unaware. According to this secret agreement, which was signed only by Alba and Cardinal Carafa, the Spanish king was to buy from Giovanni Carafa, against suitable indemnification, the right of naming the future possessor of Paliano, who, however, must not be an enemy of the Holy See. Should this indemnification not be paid within six months, then Bernardino Carbone was to deliver up the place to Giovanni Carafa. In any case the fortifications were to be demolished.[1]

Cardinal Vitelli brought the peace treaty to Rome on September 12th. The Duke of Paliano went to meet him at S. Croce, and then informed the Pope of all that had been done. Paul IV. then at once signed the public treaty, and the secret agreement on September 14th.[2] On the same day Cardinal Carafa returned to Rome, where the people welcomed him

---

[1] The public capitulation in NORES, 216 seq. and THEINER, Cod. III. 539, seq., Pallavicini, had the secret treaty before him. COGGIOLA (Paolo IV. e la capitulazione segreta, 10 seq.) procured a copy from the *Cod. 468 of the Palatine Library, Parma, comparison with which shows that Pallavicini has reported correctly, and that the statement of DURUY (p. 246 seq.) who believes with RANKE (I.[6] 194) that the secret agreement was kept hidden from the Pope is not founded on fact. Even the letters written during the negotiations by the Duke of Paliano to Cardinal Carafa (in the *Cod. Pal. 468 Parma) show that Pallavicini is right (COGGIOLA, 14, 20 seq.). Riess has overlooked the work of Coggiola as well as all the researches of Ancel. The latter differs considerably from Coggiola, while acknowledging his indebtedness to him. Concerning the supposed keeping secret of the treaty, he sums up the result of his investigations as follows : " Carafa donna connaissance au pape de la capitulation secrète mais il laissa croire à ses freres et à ses plus intimes amis que le pape n'en savait rien. Ce fut une confidence qui n'eut pas de témoins qui ne fut divulguée que lors de l'instruction du procès " (Disgrâce, 21 ; cf. ibid., 126 seq., 136 seq.) . The inscription concerning the peace at Cave in MAROCCO, Monumenti, VIII., 169.

[2] Cf. COGGIOLA, loc. cit., 30, 35 seq.

joyfully ; he at once went to the Pope, who fixed a consistory for the following day.[1]

This consistory, however, could not be held, for at midnight the Tiber broke its banks and inundated a great part of the unfortunate city. The catastrophe took place quite suddenly, so that no one had time to save their possessions. In the vineyards near the Castle of St. Angelo, many houses, the inhabitants of which had taken refuge on the roofs, were carried away by the rush of the river. Very little more was needed to raise the inundation to the level of that of 1530 ; in St. Peter's Square, the people were getting about in boats. After 24 hours the water began to subside, and then the damage done could be estimated. The Ponte S. Maria (Ponte Rotto) and nine of the mills on the Tiber were completely destroyed ; the Ponte Fabricio, the passage leading from the Castle of St. Angelo to the Vatican, and the new fortifications of the city had also suffered greatly ; the church and monastery of S. Bartolomeo on the island in the Tiber, as well as very many houses and palaces were threatened with destruction, while such quantities of grain, wine and oil had been destroyed that a famine was to be feared. The streets and squares were full of mud and filth, in many places the water was standing, a pestilential stench poisoned the air, and disease of all kinds was rife. The Venetian ambassador thought that the catastrophe would hardly have been greater had the city been sacked.[2]

---

[1] See MASSARELLI, 314. Guise left Rome during the night between September 14 and 15 (see BROWN, VI., 2, n. 1034). The brief addressed at the time to Henry II. in RAYNALDUS, 1557, n. 16.

[2] See Navagero in BROWN, VI., 2, n. 1036, 1042 ; Carne in TURNBULL, n. 664 ; *Avvisi di Roma of September 18 and 25, 1557 (Vatican Library) ; *letter of T. Cospio, dated Rome, September 16, 1557 (State Archives, Bologna) ; *letter of B. Pia of September 22, 1557 (Gonzaga Archives, Mantua) ; Lett. de' princ., I., 193 seq. ; TARDUCCI, 79 seq. ; L. LATINIUS, Lucubrat., II., 57 ; MASSARELLI, 315 ; MASIUS, Briefe, 299, 300 ; Cola Coleine in CANCELLIERI, Mercato, 21 ; ADRIANI, V., 267 seqq. ; NORES, 219, n. 1, 339 ; FABRICIUS, 166 ; BACCI, Del Tevere;

A further result of the inundation was an alteration in the bed of the Tiber, which was now more than a thousand metres distant from Ostia.[1]

On the evening of September 19th, Alba, accompanied by Cardinal Carafa, the Duke of Paliano and the Marquis of Montebello, rode into Rome. He crossed the Ponte S. Angelo, where he was greeted by the thunder of the cannon, and proceeded straight to the Vatican. He was conducted through the Loggie of Raphael to the Hall of Constantine ; here the Pope, surrounded by twenty-one Cardinals, received his conqueror. Alba knelt and kissed the Pope's foot, and with great reverence and humility begged for pardon. The Pope bade him rise, and then they both occupied themselves in courtesies and reciprocal apologies. After Alba had saluted the Sacred College, he retired to the apartments of Cardinal Carafa, which had been magnificently decorated for him.[2]

251 seq. ; OLDRADI, Aviso della pace tra la S. di N. S. Paolo IIII. ed il re Philippo con la narratione del Diluvio che è stato in Roma, con le gran ruine dei ponti, chiese, palazzi, vigne et il numero delle gente morte et le perdite de fromenti, vini et olii con altri succesi e particolarità. In Rome, per Ant. Blado, stampator camerale, 1557 (German translation : " Warh. neue Zeitung," etc. s.l., 1557, 4to, 8ll.). See further, in FORCELLA, I., 146, the inscription, still preserved, on the façade of S. Maria sopra Minerva. Concerning the annotation to Bufalini's plan, cf. Riv. Europ. XXII. (1880), 8 seq., 361 seq. See also FANFANI, Spigol., 141 seq. ; Bull. arch. com. (1895), 299 seq. ; LANCIANI, Scavi, II., 23 seq. ; DE WAAL, Campo Santo, 87 ; Atti dei Lincei, V., 5, p. 5 ; RODOCANACHI, S. Ange, 157 ; PAGLIUCCHI, 132. A. F. RAINERIO published a Sonetto sopra l'inondatione del Tevere, s.l., 4to. Concerning the letters of Andrea Speciale see TESSIER in the publication Buonarotti, Ser. 3, I., and Giorn. stor. d. lett. Ital., I., 511.

[1] GUGLIELMOTTI, Pirati, II., 317, and Spiaggia Rom., passim.

[2] See Navagero in BROWN, VI., 2, n. 1039 ; Carne in TURNBULL, n. 666 ; NORES, 219, n. 1 ; MASSARELLI, 315 seq. ; Report of A. Babbi, dated Rome, September 20, 1557, in ANCEL, La nouvelle de la prise de Calais à Rome : Annales de St. Louis, IX. (1904), 252 seqq. ; *Avviso di Roma of September 25, 1557 (Vatican

The official intimation of the reconciliation with Spain was made to the Cardinals in a secret consistory on September 20th. On this occasion, the Pope announced his intention of sending legates in the interests of a general peace to the two monarchs ; to Philip II. Cardinal Carafa, and to Henry II. Cardinal Trivulzio.[1] On the same day, Garcilasso de la Vega, Camillo Colonna, Pirro Offredo, Juan de Taxis, Capilupi, Giuliano Cesarini and others were released from their captivity in the Castle of St. Angelo. Next day there was a Te Deum in the Papal chapel, after which the Pope gave a banquet to the Cardinals, at which Alba was also present. On September 22nd the Viceroy, to whom every possible honour was shown, left Rome, the Pope bestowing on his consort the Golden Rose.[2]

Paul IV., who had been compelled to seek for peace at all costs, could indeed, be thankful that Alba had made such moderate use of his victory. It can, however, easily be understood that he suffered greatly in seeing the frustration of his grand plans for the liberation of the Holy See and Italy from the Spanish yoke. The war had lasted a whole year, and a great part of the States of the Church, and especially the Campagna, had been devastated,[3] the finances and the status of

Library). The numerous statements that Alba entered the city without any pomp is contradicted in the last named publication. B. Pia also states expressly in his *report to Cardinal E. Gonzaga : " Domenica a sera et quasi di notte entrò in Roma il s. duca d'Alba con mons. ill. Caraffa accompagnato da tutta Roma a lume con torcie." He also mentions the heavy thunder of the cannon, such as had not been heard for years, and the reception by the Pope " alegrimente " (Gonzaga Archives, Mantua).

[1] See Acta consist. in PIEPER, 97. See here also (p. 197) the instructions for both Cardinals.

[2] MASSARELLI, 316-317. BROWN, VI., 2, n. 1039, 1041. *Avviso of September 25, 1557, and the report of the ambassador of Bologna, T. Cospio of September, 22, 1557, in the State Archives, Bologna.

[3] Cf. MOCENIGO-ALBÈRI, 47, and DE CUPIS, 144. The French allies had ravaged almost as badly as the enemy ; see the complaints from the Marches in the Docum. di storia ital. publ. d. deput. di storia patria per Toscana, IV., 198.

the Pope as a secular power[1] greatly injured,[2] and the very
thing which Paul IV. wished to prevent, had been brought
about.

Marcantonio Colonna, whom the Pope specially hated, had
won so great renown in the war, that he was looked upon as one
of the first commanders in Italy.   The domination of the Spaniards in Milan and Naples was stronger than ever, and they
could now reckon on the Farnese, who had received Piacenza,
as surely as on Cosimo de' Medici, who, now that he was in
possession of Siena, was in a position to make things very
dangerous for the Holy See.[3]

Paul IV. had begun the struggle in the style of a great power ;
at the conclusion of peace, he must have been glad that he had
been successful in keeping at least the territory previously
possessed by the Holy See.   But this could now only constitute
him a power of the second rank ; no Pope could again think of
adopting a policy of war for the overthrow by force of foreign
domination.

[1] *Cf.* Soranzo in ALBERI, Ser. 2, IV., 89, who brings out the
fact that the Pope's enterprise had displayed the weakness of
the States of the Church to the whole world.

[2] According to NAVAGERO-ALBÈRI, 400, the war had cost
1½ million ducats ; *cf.* also BROWN, VI., 2, n. 707.   The national
debt was considerably increased by the erection of new Monti.
In 1556 the *Monte Novennale* was established, and in the same
year the *Monte Religione* and the *Monte Allumiere*.   See COPPI,
Finanze, 4.   The figures given there are not correct (200,000,
200,000 and 60,000 sc.), for in a presumably authentic *inventory
in the Secret Archives of the Vatican (Arm. 11, t. 91 : *De reform.
curiae*) we find (p. 11b.) : *Monte Novennale non vacabile*, by
Paul IV., *paga* 400,000 *scudi.   Monte delle Lumiere vacabile*,
by Paul IV., *paga l'anno* 7,000 *sc.*   Concerning the first Monte
cf. Nonciat., II., 417 n ; *ibid.* 418 n. concerning the financial
operations during the summer of 1556 ; concerning the erection
of the *Monte Religione*, not mentioned there, see the *report of
Navagero of October 12, 1556 (Library of St. Mark's, Venice).
With regard to the sums taken from the Papal treasure in the
Castle of St. Angelo see Studi e docum., XIII., 304.

[3] *Cf.* NAVAGERO-ALBÈRI, 406 *seq.*

However greatly the private feelings of Paul IV. rebelled, he quickly accommodated himself to his new position. The old ideas, indeed, appeared now and again, but he no longer dared to attempt to meddle with the unavoidable fact of Spanish supremacy.[1]

Secular affairs, as far as the Pope was concerned, took for the future a quite subordinate place. Although he was determined to heal, as far as it lay in his power, the heavy wounds which his mistaken policy had inflicted on the States of the Church, he wished above all in future (as he had already pointed out in the consistory of September 20th, 1557[2]) to

---

[1] ANCEL (La nouvelle de la prise de Calais à Rome, loc. cit., 254 seq.) shows how the Spanish almost completely kept the upper hand in Rome even after the departure of Alba, and how quickly the Imperialist Cardinals, della Corgna, Fano and Santa Fiora were again received into favour. At this time the suppression of the Rime of the poet Pasquale Malespini, who was friendly to the French, took place; it is commented on by S. BONGI in the Atti d. Accad. di Lucca, XXX. (1898). Better times for the French did not come until the end of January. 1558. The news then reached Rome that Guise had succeeded in capturing Calais from England, which was allied with Spain. The French party in Rome celebrated the event with great pomp. The Pope, who could not conceal his satisfaction at this blow dealt at his old enemy, put no difficulties in their way, and the Spanish reaction in Rome now came to an end. At the same time, however, Paul IV., as well as his nephew, the Duke of Paliano, took good care not to take the side of France (see ANCEL, 264 seq.). The Pope no longer took any part at all in political affairs, even if he did repeat his old view, in confidential conversation, that the French kings had always been the protectors, and the Spanish kings the enemies of the Holy See (cf. the report of the Bishop of Angoulême of June 11, 1558, in RIBIER, II., 744 seq.). The conclusion of the peace of Cateau Cambrésis, which was unfavourable to the French, must therefore have affected Paul IV. painfully (see RIBIER, II., 798); he also greatly lamented the unexpected death of Henry II. (see ibid., 810 seq.).

[2] *Affino che fusse poi più facile mediante il concilio generale riformar la chiesa et estirpar le heresie. Avviso of September 25, 1557, loc. cit. p. 266. Vatican Library.

devote himself entirely to the spiritual duties of his high
priestly office, to the reform of ecclesiastical conditions, and
the eradication of heresy.   All his care should henceforth be
devoted to these weighty matters.

CHAPTER VII.

Reform Measures of Paul IV.—Renewal of the Sacred College.

In many of the letters of congratulation which Paul IV. received from all parts of Christendom on his elevation to the Supreme Pontificate, the hope was strongly expressed, while they deplored the premature death of Marcellus II., that his successor would not fail to show his zeal in beginning and carrying into effect that most important work, the reform of the Church from within.[1]   Most of these hopes were founded on the fact that Gian Pietro Carafa had been the first to enter upon the right way of carrying out an improvement in ecclesiastical conditions, and that he had steadily pursued this high aim.[2]   A very religious Catholic layman, Girolamo Muzio, reminded Paul IV. of a saying of Marcellus II., which embodied a profound truth.   Marcellus, who had always been of one mind with Carafa, had said to Muzio, before he started for Rome for the conclave, that no Pope who did not take the work of reform in hand at the beginning of his reign, need hope to be able to effect anything later on.[3]

[1] Almost all the *letters of congratulation addressed to Paul IV. are preserved in the Papal Secret Archives, Castle of St. Angelo, Arm. 8, ordo 2, t. I., n. 2.   The first volume of this priceless collection of autograph letters contains for the most part the letters of the princes, the second the *obedientia* addresses, the congratulatory letters of the clergy as well as of the laity, and several poems, as, for instance, *one by Lelius Capilupus on p. 137, and *one by Franciscus Modestus on p. 139.

[2] See Pole's letter of June 6, 1555, in the *Nonciat.* I., 232 *seq.*, and *that of Paolo Sadoleto, Bishop of Carpentras, dated Id. Iunii 1555, in the above-mentioned collection of autograph letters, II., 173.

[3] See Appendix No. 14 (Secret Archives of the Vatican).

175

Paul IV. was himself deeply convinced of this. His first steps in the direction of reform, in the summer of 1555, showed that he was determined not to move a hair's breadth from his old principles, and that he would, now that he was in possession of the supreme power, display the greatest rigour.[1]

One of the first questions which the new Pope had to decide was whether the great legislative work which Julius III. had prepared, but had not been able to bring to an end, should now be completed. To make such use of the work of another did not appeal to the self-assured character of Paul, and although he did think of not doing so for a short time,[2] he soon changed his mind. It is certain that in doing so he was influenced by very able friends of the reform movement, who represented to him from the very beginning of his reign, that it was now much less a question of issuing new decrees, than of the strict and thorough application of those already in existence, an idea which had already been expressed in the opinion of the Cardinals in the year 1537.[3] The Bishop of Sessa, Galeazzo Florimonte, pointed out in his letter of congratulation, that Marcellus II. had also been thoroughly persuaded that in future practice should be preferred to theory, and that the necessary reform measures must first be carried out, and that only then should steps be taken to commit them to writing.

---

[1] Cf. supra p. 90.

[2] I infer this from the draft of a *bull which I found in the Secret Archives (Castle of St. Angelo Arm. 5, caps. 2, n. 18). In this document, which begins with the words : " Varietas temporum," the " Bulla super reformatione conclavis " and the " Constitutio Julii III. pro securitate episc. resident." are inserted. According to a presumably contemporaneous note on the reverse side, the document belongs to the year 1555. It here continues : " R^{mis} dom. Ostien. Portuen. Tuscul. Alban. mittatur per manus." The contents have, however, been written in a later hand : " Copia nonnullorum canonum super ordinatione cleric. et praelat. cum relat. qualit. quae in cardinalibus creandis et in promovendis ad cathed. vel alias ecclesias concurrere debent ex decret. concilii et consist. excerpt."

[3] Cf. Vol. XI. of this work, p. 165.

Florimonte also reminded Paul IV. of a letter written to him by Marcellus II., ordering him to make out a list of the men best fitted for bishoprics, so that the most worthy could easily and quickly be chosen to fill the vacant sees.[1]

Another friend of reform, the worthy Luigi Lippomano, Bishop of Verona, who drew for the Pope an appalling picture of the ecclesiastical corruption of the time, likewise remarked that enough reforms had so far been most solemnly promised, and that now it was, above all, a question of taking care that these did not prove to be merely idle words.[2]

These views exactly corresponded with those of the Pope. The very earliest measures that he adopted proved that he intended to proceed in just such a manner as was demanded by the most zealous friends of reform. There had already been conferences, discussions and decisions concerning ecclesiastical affairs on the most extensive scale, and it seemed to the practical sense of Paul IV. that the moment had now come to take the work in hand.[3] He was therefore, from the first, not inclined to continue the Council ; he considered that such an assembly involved too many difficulties in itself, and, in addition to this, proceeded much too slowly. He also probably felt that his dominating nature was little suited to such an assembly, which, moreover, necessitated an understanding with all the Catholic powers.[4] In accordance with his impetuous character, the Pope, who had always been a strong man of action, wished to begin at once with the abolition of abuses, and to insist, with the utmost rigour, on the observance of the decrees already issued.

From the first days of his reign, the proceedings of Paul IV. had been in conformity with this resolve. The very

---

[1] See the text of the **letter, in the collection mentioned *supra* *p.* 175, n. 1 (II., 156-157ᵇ, Secret Archives of the Vatican).

[2] See the letter (in a translation) in ANCEL, Concile, 4-5.

[3] See the Pope's speech in Navagero's letter of October 8, 1555, in BROWN, VI., 1, n. 242 ; *cf.* also Navagero's report of December 7, 1555, in ANCEL, Concile, 5, n. 3.

[4] *Cf.* DEMBINSKI, 13.

strict measures of the summer of 1555,[1] were followed by others of a similar nature during the autumn and the winter. The relaxed Conventuals in the district of Florence were replaced by Observants, and the Bishop of Syracuse was appointed to inspect the convents of Sicily, and a Jesuit given to him as his assistant.[2] Envoys were appointed for Spain to bring about the reform of the Benedictine congregation of the Olivetans.[3] The granting of marriage dispensations was limited,[4] as was also the method of holding monasteries " in commendam," which was so harmful.[5] The terrible severity of the new Pope was shown in an edict of the governor of Rome, issued in the year 1555, which threatened truly draconian punishments, such as the galleys, hanging, scourging, loss of property and banishment, for the moral abuses then prevalent in Rome. All participation in conspiracies, as well as the carrying of arms, was threatened with the gallows, while the right of sanctuary was

---

[1] *Cf. supra* p. 90.

[2] *Cf.* Mon. Ign. I., x, 220 *seq.*; POLANCO, V., 103. Ignatius was at that time promoting the reform of the Spanish Conventuals. At Saragossa the Conventuals were afterwards replaced by the Observants ; see POLANCO, V., 407.

[3] Besides the brief of November 8, 1555, quoted by BROMATO (II., 277), see the *briefs of December 1, 1555, for " Ioannes princ. Portug. gub. Hisp., Nunt. in Hispania and Consiliariis regiis Hisp." in Arm. 44, t. 4, n. 280-282, and *ibid.*, n. 283, *brief of December 2, 1555, " generali et monachis O.S.B. congreg. Vallis Oliveti " (Secret Archives of the Vatican). A brief of September, 1555, concerning monastic reform in Ferrara in FONTANA, Renata, II., 549.

[4] See Bull. VI., 507 *seq.*; *cf.* BROMATO, II., 482 *seq.* To understand how disinclined the Pope was to concessions of any kind, see the characteristic *letter of G. Aldrovandi, dated Rome December 24, 1555 (State Archives, Bologna). Paul IV. said indignantly to Aldrovandi's successor, C. Paleotti : *Qui non si comprano le gratie de sudditi con vescovati. *Letter of C. Paleotti of October 3, 1556, *loc. cit.*

[5] See *Acta consist. cancell., VI., 277^b-278 (December 16, 1555). Consistorial Archives.

suspended.[1] Special regulations affected the abuses which took place during the carnival, in connection with the impunity afforded by masks.[2]

The great creation of Cardinals of December, 1555, is significant of the manner in which Paul IV. intended to carry out his ecclesiastical reforms. It appeared to him to be much more important to procure fitting instruments for the execution of the ecclesiastical laws, to choose men who, in their lives and actions, represented reform itself, than to enter upon new discussions and to issue new regulations by means of a Council. Paul III. had at first adopted this course with great success, but under Julius III. several quite unsuitable elements had succeeded in gaining admission to the College of Cardinals.[3] The great turning point had, in this respect, now arrived with Paul IV. Purely ecclesiastical considerations should, for the future, alone be taken into account in the choice of the members of the Sacred College. Regardless of all the claims of secular policy, the Pope refused all the requests made by the Venetian, Imperial and French ambassadors.[4] He also paid no attention to the wishes of his nephews[5] with regard to matters pertaining to the government of the Church.

It is very remarkable that none of the candidates recommended by the French were considered, although the whole

[1] See the text of the *Bando generale (Secret Archives of the Vatican) in Appendix No. 15. That these severe punishments were inflicted is seen from the case reported by CALVI in the N. Antologia Ser. 5, CXLII., 591, of the year 1556.

[2] These Papal instructions to the governor of the city (not mentioned in Clementi's work) are cited by PADIGLIONE, La Bibl. del Museo naz. di S. Martino, Naples, 1876, 303.

[3] Cf. our particulars in Vol. XI. of this work, p. 159 seq., 173 seq., 215 seq., and Vol. XIII., pp. 70, 71.

[4] Cf. the *brief to Charles V. of December 24, 1555, in which Paul IV. justifies his non-consideration of the Emperor's wishes (Arm. 44, t. 4, n. 309. Secret Archives of the Vatican).

[5] Cf. concerning this the *report of Navagero of December 14, 1556, (Library of St. Mark's, Venice).

secular policy of Paul IV. was, at that time, directed to an
alliance with France. It is not to be wondered at, therefore,
that the requests made by the Imperialist Cardinals, Alvarez
de Toledo, Truchsess and Morone, were not granted. No
one knew upon whom the choice would fall.[1] The Pope
expressed himself in merely general terms.[2]

At the consistory of December 18th, Paul IV. made his
appearance with visible signs of excitement ; the ambassador
of the Este said : " His eyes flashed fire."[3] The Pope declared to the Dean, Cardinal du Bellay, that he would grant
no audiences before the beginning of the consistory. When
Cardinal Alvarez de Toledo endeavoured, in spite of this, to
obtain one, he was refused in violent terms. After the Cardinals had taken their places, the Pope laid before them,
with characteristic and unsparing bluntness, his reasons for
wishing to increase the Sacred College. It had come to his
knowledge, he said, that several Cardinals had declared that
he would not dare to appoint more than four new members,
because this would be contrary to the election capitulation,
which had been sworn to by him. In contradiction to this
view he explained at considerable length, appealing to the
Holy Scriptures and the opinions of standard canonists, that
the absolute power of the supreme head of the Church could
not be limited in any such manner, just as other persons were
not obliged to keep their promises, if it should prove, in
course of time, that these were disadvantageous to the common good. Should any of them fear excommunication, he
could absolve them from it. He, the supreme head of the
Church, intended to make use of his right to appoint Cardinals,
and he would not suffer any opposition ; the members of the
Sacred College possessed no decisive vote, but merely an
advisory one.

[1] *Cf.* the reports of the ambassadors of Venice, Ferrara and
Florence in ANCEL, L'action réform., 7.

[2] Concerning the early history of the promotion see *Nonciat.*
II., 274 *seq.*

[3] See ANCEL, *loc. cit.* 8, n. 4.

The Cardinals, already taken aback by this declaration, were to hear something yet stronger. Necessity, Paul IV. insisted, forced him to summon new members to the senate of the Church, as he could see no suitable persons among them ; had they not all their party and their following ?   Therefore he would, by the inspiration of the Holy Ghost, appoint several good, learned, and independent persons, in whom he could place confidence, and whom he could employ for current business, and above all for reform.   He would be directed in his choice of these, neither by ties of blood nor by any recommendations made to him.   If the Cardinals had any-thing to say to him concerning this matter he would willingly listen to them, but only to each one by himself.   He was aware that new appointments were not desired by the Car-dinals who were without means, as the maintenance of many required more than that of a few.   He would, however, take the necessary steps with regard to this, and would not permit the secular princes either to bestow or to refuse to bestow benefices on members of the Sacred College, as this violated the liberty of the Church.[1]

The Pope expressed himself in still stronger terms on the following day to the Venetian ambassador, to whom he was so fond of opening his heart.[2]   He had never in his life, he said, been so pestered with petitions and demands as now. He was, however, resolved to appoint no one on the recom-mendation of the princes or at the request of others ; he would not hesitate to choose foreigners, if only they were independent.[3]   " What a disgrace " exclaimed Paul IV. " that princes should have servants in the Sacred College !

---

[1] See the **letter of Navagero of December 18, 1555 (Library of St. Mark's, Venice) ; *cf.* Seripando, ed. HÖFLER, 354. Paul IV. had confirmed the election capitulation by a bull, which contained even more stringent measures ; see LULVES in the Quellen und Forsch. des Preuss. Histor. Inst., XII., 225.

[2] See the **letter of Navagero of December 19, 1555 (Library of St. Mark's, Venice).

[3] See the **letter of Navagero of March 14, 1556 (Library of St. Mark's, Venice).

How can secrecy be kept or impartiality be hoped for from persons in such a dependent position ? To speak plainly, what sort of people have already received the purple on such terms ? As the removal of these unsuitable persons, all at once, is impossible, we shall, by the appointment of good and capable men, gradually provide a counter-weight to them. Whenever we discover one who is worthy we shall appoint him, unexpectedly and out of the usual time." In conclusion the Pope made much of the fact that the elevation of capable Cardinals was of more value than a Council in increasing the respect felt for the Church and in carrying out the work of reform. The Pope also informed Cardinals Tournon and Lorraine that, in the coming creation, he would only consider the honour of God and his own conscience. Carafa, who, in conjunction with the French, made incredible efforts on behalf of his favourite, Giovanni della Casa, only received from his uncle the reply : " No such people ! "[1]

The seven who were appointed on December 20th, 1555, were, as Cardinal Armagnac had predicted,[2] for the most part unknown men, partly belonging to the religious orders, and partly theologians. They belonged to various nations, were recommended solely by their virtues, were all far removed from political intrigues, and, in the matter of reform, were all true representatives of the views of the Pope.[3] For the most part they had been well known to Paul IV. in earlier days, as for example, Giovanni Bernardino Scotti, the first novice of the Theatine order, who had always been devoted to study and prayer, and who still wished now to preserve

---

[1] Cf. RIBIER, II., 622 ; BROMATO, II., 259 seq. 284 ; ANCEL, L'action réform., 10 ; Studi stor., XVII., 197. The non-inclusion of della Casa was perfectly justified, as his conduct left much to be desired from a moral point of view.

[2] See TAMIZEY DE LARROQUE, Lett. inéd. du card. d'Armagnac, Paris, 1874, 79-80.

[3] Cf. concerning the different cardinals, PETRAMELLARIUS, 23 seqq. ; CIACONIUS, III., 845 seq. ; CARDELLA, IV., 342 seq. ; GULIK-EUBEL, III., 38 seq.

his poverty.[1] The same was the case with Scipione Rebiba, who had been for many years in Carafa's service, and since 1549 his representative in the archdiocese of Naples, and afterwards governor of Rome. Paul IV. had also closely followed the activities of the Gascon, Giovanni Suario Reumano, Auditor of the Rota ; he was chosen, as well as Giovan Antonio Capizuchi, who also belonged to the Rota, because there was a want of learned canonists in the Sacred College.[2] The fifth of the new Cardinals, Diomede Carafa, did not owe the purple to his relationship to the Pope, but to the fact that he had been managing his diocese of Ariano in the most exemplary manner since 1511.

If France was represented in the new appointments by Reumano, so was Germany by the learned Johannes Gropper, the saviour of the church in Cologne against the assaults of the religious innovators, and Spain by Juan Siliceo, Archbishop of Toledo. The appointment of this learned and zealous man,[3] proves how thoroughly the Pope preserved his independence in spiritual matters in all directions, even with regard to his French allies.

Scotti and Diomede Carafa were already dwelling in the Vatican, and the Pope now assigned apartments there to Cardinals Reumano, Rebiba and Capizuchi ;[4] he wished these men, as well as Gropper, to be near him, for the settlement of ecclesiastical affairs, and above all for questions of reform. The honour of living in the Vatican was therefore also bestowed

---

[1] Cf. the **letter of Navagero of January 4, 1556 (Library of St. Mark's, Venice) and the statements in the Nonciat. II., 275, n. 6. A *Vita B. card. Scotti by J. Silos is preserved in the general archives of the Theatines in Rome.

[2] See the letter of the Cardinal of Lorraine in RIBIER, II., 622. Concerning Rebiba cf. MASIUS, Briefe, 250 ; BOGLINO, 47 seq. and Nonciat. II., 405, n. 1.

[3] Cf. the *brief to Philip II. of December 24, 1555, in Arm. 44, t. 4, n. 310 and ibid. the *brief to the newly-appointed Cardinal himself of December 29, 1555 (Secret Archives of the Vatican).

[4] See the **letter of Navagero of January 4, 1556 (Library of St. Mark's, Venice).

on Gropper when he came to Rome at the end of September, 1558. This worthy champion of Catholic interests in Germany,[1] had hitherto, in his humility, refused to accept the purple ; he was now, however, forced to do so by Paul IV. Cardinal Carlo Carafa had done everything in his power to keep this eminent man away from the Pope. It was he who set on foot, through Delfino, a wretched intrigue, and even cast suspicion on the faith of the ardent apologist. Gropper however, was able to defend himself so well before the Inquisition that the case against him was quickly brought to an end. This excitement, and the unaccustomed climate of Rome, however, so affected his strength that his health broke down, and he died on March 13th, 1559, aged only 56 years. On the following day, the funeral took place in the German national church, S. Maria dell' Anima. Paul IV. pronounced the funeral oration himself, an honour which is unique in the history of the Popes. He exclaimed repeatedly : " Gropper has by no means departed from us, he has only gone before us to God."[2] Not content with this, Paul IV. referred again to the merits of Gropper in the consistory of March 15th, 1559, sternly rebuking the calumniators of this admirable

---

[1] See the praise in the letter of Adolphus, Elector of Cologne, to Cardinal Farnese, in SCHWARZ, Der päpstl. Nuntius K. Gropper, Münster, 1911, 10, n. 1.

[2] *Cf.* SCHWARZ in the Histor. Jahrbuch, VII., 396 *seqq.* ; GULIK, Gropper, 158 *seq.* ; MASIUS, Briefe, 248, 315 ; ESSER, S. Maria dell' Anima, Rome, 1899, 56 ; SCHMIDLIN, Gesch. der Anima, 294 *seqq.* ; Rev. Bénédict. XXIV., 285 *seq.* The slab covering Gropper's grave, with coat of arms, Cardinal's hat, and a high-flown inscription (FORCELLA, III., 458) had to be removed from its old place in the imperfectly understood interests of the decoration of the church of the Anima, and was lost ; it was renewed in 1885 (see LOSCHI, Il card. G. Gropper, Udine, 1896, 80) and is now in the right aisle of the Benno chapel. Extensive literature concerning Gropper in PASTOR, Reunionsbestrebungen, 166 ; JANSEN, VII.[14], 575 ; GULIK, *loc. cit.* and in HERZOG's Realenzyklopädie, VII.[3], 191.

man ; he also bestowed on his relatives all the benefices rendered vacant by his decease.[1]

The attempt, which played so great a part in the creation of Cardinals in December, 1555, to put an end to the undue influence exercised by the secular princes in purely ecclesiastical affairs, was one reason for the disinclination of the Pope to continue the Council. In addition to this, there was the remembrance of the proceedings at Basle and Constance, which were exceedingly hateful to Paul IV.[2] If it should happen that a Council could not be avoided, it should, in his opinion, under no circumstances be held in German territory, " in the midst of Lutherans," but under his own eyes in Rome. This intention, as well as the almost complete exclusion of the secular princes from such a meeting, appeared to many of the Cardinals, as for example Medici, to lay the Church open to the danger of a schism.[3] Probably, however, Paul IV. did not seriously think of holding a Council in Rome ; he wished rather to arrange the necessary conferences in such a manner that they would resemble a Council, without involving the disadvantages connected with such assemblies in the XVth century. This was clearly shown by the measures which he adopted at the beginning of the year 1556.

In a consistory on January 10th, 1556, the Pope, in a long address, unfolded his plan for undertaking a thorough reform of the Roman Curia. For sixty years, he said, this had been talked of ; he was going at last to carry it out, energetically, and without respect of persons, as one chosen by God for the purpose, and he would make a beginning with the Roman Curia itself. In witness thereof, he alluded to the orders given a few days previously to Cardinals Scotti, Rebiba and Reumano, for the reform of the Dataria. If, in doing this, he closed his chief source of revenue, this did not trouble him, and he would know how to stint himself. The others must follow in his footsteps, as he did not intend to content himself

[1] See the Diario in LAEMMER, Melet., 210.
[2] Cf. ANCEL. Concile, 7.
[3] Cf. ibid., 8-9.

with this one measure. He intended to reform in the same way the Chancery, the Penitentiary, the Signatura, the College of Cardinals, and the whole state of affairs with regard to benefices, each one in turn, and without the least consideration for the secular princes.[1] It would be seen that Paul IV. meant to proceed in accordance with his old motto, that justice should begin with the House of the Lord.

In January, 1556, he formed a special congregation, consisting of twenty Cardinals, seven prelates of the Curia, twelve referendaries of the Signatura, six Auditors of the Rota, the generals of the Dominicans, Franciscan Observants and Conventuals, nine officials of the Curia, and five theologians (Michele Ghislieri, as commissary of the Inquisition, Lainez, of the Society of Jesus, Giovan Battista Calderini of the Servites, and two secular priests) to confer about a comprehensive reform of the Roman Curia.[2]

These sixty-two members assembled in the Hall of Constantine in the Vatican in the afternoon of January 20th. The Pope himself opened the first session of the reform congregation with a speech in which he emphasized his wish to abolish the abuses which had crept into the Church of God, owing to the wickedness of the times, and enumerated the troubles which former Popes had had to contend with in this respect, even with the assistance of a General Council. Although no success had crowned their efforts hitherto, he nevertheless hoped that this time, with the help of God, they might attain some result. He himself would do all in his power,

---

[1] The short statements in the *Acta consist. (Consistorial Archives; see Appendix No. 16) are supplemented by Navagero's *report of January 11, 1556 (Library of St. Mark's, Venice, see Appendix No. 17). *Cf.* the **report of Navagero of January 4, 1556, concerning the new arrangement of the Dataria; see also, the letter of Casa of January 8, 1556, in COGGIOLA, A. d. Cornia, 125, and MASIUS, Briefe, 235.

[2] See the list of persons in the *rough draft made by Massarelli (Secret Archives of the Vatican, Concilio 79, p. 33ᵇ, 34) ANCEL (Concile, 12), was the first to draw attention to this source, overlooked by MERKLE (II., 287, n.1).

and would spare no effort, even to the loss of his life, to ensure a favourable result to their labours. As, however, the whole work of reform must start with the complete abolition of the simoniacal evils which formed the chief obstacle, the axe must be ruthlessly laid to the root of the evil.

Massarelli, who, in his official report of the session, gives the speech of the Pope, records the statement of Paul IV. that the head of the Church must eradicate simony, all the more so as all calumniators and heretics declared that this was the actual and almost the only reason why no reform had been effected hitherto, as the Popes had put difficulties in the way on the account of the loss of revenue from the Dataria. The present Pope, however, considered all gain and worldly advantage as nothing, had only God and the salvation of souls before his eyes, and was determined to carry out a reform at all costs, and above all things to eradicate simony. The justice of this report of Massarelli is evident from the fact that Paul IV., in the same session, exhorted the Cardinals, in the most earnest manner, in virtue of the obedience which they owed him, to state the plain truth without any evasions, especially concerning this most important question, whether a temporal advantage or gain could be accepted for the exercise of that power which Christ bestowed upon the Apostle Peter as head of His Church. The answer to this question was to be handed in by the Cardinals in writing.[1] Navagero relates that the Pope spoke with extraordinary power and eloquence about simony ; his words made the deepest impression on all present, and the justice of his view convinced them that the real reform of the Church consisted above all in bringing about a radical change in this respect.[2]

The question which Paul IV. now laid before the new congregation was one which had already occupied the attention of the reform commission of the Farnese Pope. At that

---

[1] See the *rough draft (Secret Archives of the Vatican) in Appendix No. 19.

[2] See in Appendix No. 20 Navagero's *report of January 24, 1556 (Library of St. Mark's, Venice).

time, however, so many differences of opinion had arisen
between the strict and the moderate advocates of reform,
that the prudent Paul III. thought it better to refrain from
any drastic measures.[1]   Paul IV. again took the matter up,
when it had come to a standstill, because he believed simony
to be at the root of all the evil.[2]   Although he held firmly, as
he had always done, to the strict conception of the Papal
power which he had always held as Cardinal, yet even he did
not venture to proceed in the matter without once more
carefully weighing it in the balance.

How very much the Pope was, at this time, filled with zeal
for reform is best seen in the letters of Navagero.   The ambassador had an audience on January 11th, in which Paul IV.
spoke with the greatest frankness about his political as well
as his ecclesiastical programme.   He especially emphasized
his intention of beginning the reform with himself, by renouncing the revenue which he received from the Dataria.
It was only on this very considerable sum that the Pope
could reckon for his personal expenditure, he said, nevertheless
it must be abolished.   " Who can doubt that God will help
me, if I act in conformity with that saying of Christ : Freely
have you received, freely give.   When I gave up everything,
and founded the Theatine order, I was able, without possessing
any guarantee for my maintenance, to lead a bearable life
for many years.   As Cardinal I had for a considerable time
no revenues, the tyrants having prevented me from taking
possession of the archbishopric of Naples, but I would not
utter a single word in order to acquire it.   In all these critical
positions the necessary means have never been wanting to
me.   Why then should I fear that it will be otherwise now ?
Even should God allow me to come to a state of actual want,
I would rather beg alms than lead a comfortable life on unlawful revenues."   " This very day," he remarked later, " I
have ordered several Auditors of the Rota to consider care-

[1] Cf. Vol. XI. of this work, pp. 155 seqq.
[2] See in Appendix No. 18 Navagero's *report of January 18,
1556, loc. cit.

fully with the other members of the reform commission what needs to be done, and not to allow themselves to be deceived. We have been thoroughly instructed by theologians and canonists concerning simony, and the teaching of St. Thomas has determined us to make truly Christian resolutions with regard to this and all other matters."[1] On January 24th Navagero speaks of a consistory in which Paul IV. showed the Cardinals that a true and exhaustive reform would also be of great benefit to themselves. On the following day the the Pope declared to the Venetian ambassador his determination to carry out the reform, even if by so doing· he should ruin his bodily health. In his drastic manner he declared that he would skin himself, and then, with equal ruthlessness, would proceed to skin the others, priests as well as laymen, if by so doing he could effect a reform. He particularly insisted that he would not deceive the world with fine-sounding bulls, nor with futile councils and useless conferences, but would perform deeds by means of the reform commission. He intended to strengthen the congregation by adding other eminent persons, to such an extent that it would appear to be a council, without bearing the name. Finally the Pope spoke at length of simony, which might, he said, on account of its consequences, be described as a heresy, in such impressive terms, that it was clear, even to the cold Venetian diplomatist, that his words came from the fulness of his heart.[2]

In accordance with this announcement, besides the sixty-two actual members, many other persons took part in the second special session of the reform commission, which took place on January 29th ; all the prelates and generals of orders then in Rome, numerous officials of the Curia and the city, as

---

[1] *Cf.* in Appendix No. 18 the *letter of Navagero of January 18, 1556. (Library of St. Mark's, Venice).

[2] *Cf.* in Appendix Nos. 20 and 21 the *letters of Navagero of January 24 and 25, 1556 (Library of St. Mark's, Venice), and the *Avviso di Roma of January 25, 1556 (Vatican Library). In January, 1556, Paul IV. requested the King of Portugal to inform him of the ecclesiastical abuses in his kingdom, as he wished to abolish them all ; see SANTAREM, XII., 440.

well as many theologians—200 people in all—were present.
Before the Pope proposed to those assembled the manner in
which the deliberations should take place, he spoke once more
of the evil of simony. To Cardinal Tournon's question, as
to which kind of simony he referred to, that forbidden by the
divine or the positive law, Paul IV., in view of the object
he was endeavouring to attain, energetically repudiated any
such distinction, and advised him in future to spare him such
empty remarks and to keep to the point. Then the method
recommended by the Pope for the discussions was sanctioned.
According to this, the members of the commission were
divided into different sections, as if in a Council, which were
to meet separately. Each section was to consist of a corresponding number of archbishops, bishops, prelates and theologians. The result of the deliberations of each section was
to be laid before the Pope in a general meeting, and he was
to arrive at the final decisions with the Cardinals alone.

On the following day, after consultation with the Cardinals,
the Pope decided on three sections, each with a Cardinal as
president. On February 2nd he caused the bishops present
in Rome to choose twenty-four of their number for the reform
commission in a secret election. Three days later he in-
dicated to the twenty-four Cardinals in Rome their place in
the three sections, the presidents of which were to be, according to their seniority, Cardinals du Bellay, Cesi and Scotti.[1]

On February 24th, the Pope, who wished to carry on the
work of reform regardless of the clouds on the political horizon,[2]
added twenty-one more prelates to the twenty-four already
chosen, and on March 2nd, he decided on the theologians,
canonists and officials of the Curia for the three sections, in
conformity with the proposals of the three Cardinal presidents.

---

[1] See in Appendix Nos. 22, 23, 24, and 25 the information
contained in the rough draft of Massarelli, and the *letters of
Navagero of February 1 and 8, 1556; cf. also ANCEL, Concile
12, and the *Avvisi di Roma of February 1 and 8, 1556, in the
Cod. Urb. 1038, p. 116, 129. Vatican Library).

[2] See the *letters of Navagero of February 15 and 16, 1556
(Library of St. Mark's, Venice). Cf. Appendix No. 27.

The whole commission now numbered 144 members, 48 in each section. Among the theologians of the first section was James Lainez of the Society of Jesus ; among those of the second, the Master of the Sacred Palace, together with a member of the Society of Jesus, and Guglielmo Sirleto, the custos of the Vatican Library ; among the canonists of this section were Ugo Boncampagni and Ercole Severoli. The Capuchin, Francesco Soleto, sat among the procurators of orders, in the third section, and Silvestro Aldobrandini among the canonists.[1]

After the business arrangements for the deliberations of the reform commission had been settled,[2] the assembly, which, with its members amounting to almost 150, actually presented the appearance of a Council, could begin its work.

Previously to this, however, on March 11th, the Pope summoned all the members to the Vatican. The Cardinals assembled in an apartment near the Hall of Constantine, and here the Holy Father informed them that the moment had now arrived to take measures against the " simoniacal heresy " and therewith to exterminate, root and branch, this source of all the evil ; he then proposed, amid universal approbation, the following question for consideration : Could an ecclesiastical superior accept voluntary gifts, or ask for such gifts, or insist upon them by means of the withdrawal of spiritual benefits, in return for the official use of his spiritual powers, without falling into the sin of simony ? The prelates were then called in, and a similar communication was again made to them by the Pope himself. They then repaired to the Hall of Constantine, where the other members of the com-

---

[1] See *Concilio, 79, f. 41[b] seqq. ; cf. ANCEL, Concile, 13 seq. Navagero says of the 21 newly appointed in his *letter of the last day of February, 1556 : " Questi non sono stati elletti con le fave come li primi, ma racordati dalli rev[mi] decano, Cesis et Trani, presidenti delle tre classe per età al pontefice et dal medesimo confirmati di modo che con tanto numero le cose saranno più longhe et havera forma quasi de concilio " (Library of St. Mark's, Venice).

[2] See *Concilio, 79, f. 50-51 ; cf. ANCEL, Concile, 14 seq.

mission were assembled. To these the Pope addressed a
third speech, in which he skilfully set forth, in other words,
what he had already said to the Cardinals and prelates.[1]
The article for deliberation was then at once printed and
presented to all the members of the commission. Several of
them, as for example Lainez, at once began to draft out their
opinions.[2]

We learn from a very interesting conversation which he
had with Navagero on March 13th, 1556, the motives which
actuated the Pope at that time. In this Paul IV. emphasized
the fact that he was spending so much time on reform because
he wished it to be a success ; in such an important matter
he would not act solely according to his own ideas, but wished
also to hear the views of others. The more strongly these
expressed themselves the better he would be pleased, as he
desired to arrive at the truth. Then he again returned to
the subject of the extirpation of simony. " Illustrious ambassador," he continued, " this has been in our thoughts for
years, for we saw many things taking place in the House of
the Lord, which would horrify you. Everyone who desired
a bishopric went to a bank, where a list was to be found, with
the price of each, and in the case of an appointment as Cardinal
it was calculated how best to draw profit from every slightest
circumstance. As soon as God had bestowed this dignity upon
us, without any effort on our part, we said to ourselves : We
know what the Lord requires of us ; we must perform deeds,
and pull out this evil by the roots. If we did not do this at
once, it was because we wished first to appoint Cardinals who

[1] See *Concilio, 79, f. 48[b] seqq. (Secret Archives of the Vatican) ;
cf. MASSARELLI, 289, the first letter of Navagero of March 14,
in BROWN, VI., 1, n. 424 and ANCEL, Concile, 15 seq.

[2] Cf. LAINEZ, Disput. Trid. (ed. Grisar), II., 325 seq. ; cf.
Histor. Jahrbuch, VIII., 725. •The treatises on simony by
G. Sirleto and P. Draco, which ANCEL (Concile, 16, n. 3) quotes,
belong to the same period. Sirleto was appointed protonotary
by Paul IV. (see BROMATO, II., 485) and entrusted with the education of his young relatives, Alfonso and Antonio. His treatise
on simony is also in the *Cod. Vat. 3511 of the Vatican Library.

were fitted to help us in this work. Now we shall carry out this reform, even at the risk of our life. If people say that in order to do so, we shall have to give up too much, and shall not, in the event, be able to make both ends meet, that does not frighten us in the least, as we are certain that He Who created all things out of nothing, will not leave us in want. It is marvellous, my lord ambassador, how this Holy See has maintained its existence, although our predecessors have done all in their power to destroy it, but it is built on so firm a rock that nothing need be feared. Should we be granted no complete success, we shall nevertheless be satisfied to have at least purified this See, so blessed by God, and then to die. To be absolutely frank with you, this new commission will have the power of a Council. We have had the article concerning simony printed, for then, although we disdain to have it sent to the universities, as it is not seemly that the Holy See should ask the opinion of others, it may still come into their hands in the course of circulation, for we desire to hear the views of everyone, so as to be able to arrive at a better decision."

In the further course of conversation the Pope remarked that his reform would entail great consequences, and that he intended showing the princes that more simony was perhaps to be found in their courts than in Rome. " But we shall put an end to that," he continued, " for we have authority over them as well as over the clergy. If necessary we shall summon a Council, and, what is more, in this illustrious city, as there is no need to go elsewhere, and, as is well known, we were never in favour of holding an assembly of the Church at Trent, in the very midst of the Lutherans."[1]

In a session of the first section of the reform commission, which was held in the house of Cardinal du Bellay, on March 26th, the article on simony was very carefully discussed. No fewer than sixteen speakers expressed their views, and

[1] See in Appendix No. 28 the *letter of Navagero of March 14, 1556 (Library of St. Mark's, Venice). *Cf.* also MASIUS, Briefe, 239.

very great differences of opinion came to light. Several, especially the Bishop of Feltre, Tommaso Campegio, defended the view that the acceptance of pecuniary compensation for the exercise of spiritual power was allowable. Others, such as the Bishop of Sessa, vigorously combated this view. A third opinion, that of the Bishop of Sinigaglia, Marco Vigerio della Rovere, was to the effect that the acceptance of pecuniary compensation was indeed permitted, but not always and only under certain conditions. It was night before the session, which had lasted for fully four hours, was brought to a close.[1]

The next meeting was to be held after Easter, but it never took place. The Pope, who was burning with eagerness to settle this important question as speedily as possible, found this great divergence of opinion so undesirable that he suspended the sittings of the commission. He thought for a time of proceeding quite independently,[2] and of issuing an absolute prohibition to the clergy to accept any gifts at all, even from voluntary donors, for spiritual advantages. Finally, however, the Pope appears to have become reconciled to the idea of a Council, under the influence of the impression made by the claims of the Polish king.[3] The danger of holding a General Council of the Church, from which the secular powers should be completely excluded, had in the meantime been made clear to him. At the reception which he held after the banquet on the anniversary of his coronation, the Pope remarked, among other things, that he would cause the Council, which he intended should be held in Rome, to be announced

---

[1] See MASSARELLI, 289, and *Concilio, 79, p. 53 seq. (Secret Archives of the Vatican); also Navagero's *letter of March 28, 1556 (Library of St. Mark's, Venice); see Appendix No. 29.

[2] Cf. the letter of Navagero of April 18, 1556, in the *Cod. Marc. 9445, p. 162b; translated in BROWN, VI., 1, n. 459.

[3] See the instructions for Rebiba in the Secret Archives of the Vatican *Polit. 78, p. 145 seq., with which the " commessioni publiche " for Carafa coincided ; see LAEMMER, Melet. 173, and Nonciat., II., 601 ; cf. also HOSII epist., II., 736.

to the secular princes, although there was no obligation on his part to do so.[1]

It was a great disadvantage for the work of reform, that just now, in the summer of 1556, when some decisive steps in this direction were generally expected,[2] the political troubles should have been steadily growing more acute, and the war with Spain becoming more probable. The Pope, however, never lost sight of the question of reform during this critical time. It deserves to be fully recognised that Paul IV. did not make the slightest concession to political considerations, either in this respect, or in the matter of the creation of Cardinals. Important as was the support of the Duke of Ferrara, and numerous as were the intercessors for Cardinal d'Este, that unworthy prince of the Church had to remain in exile.[3] In conformity with the principles of reform contained in the opinion of the Cardinals in 1537, Paul IV. in the summer of 1556 took measures against the absence of Cardinals from Rome. It was enacted at the time that all Cardinal Priests were to be ordained within three months.[4]

[1] See Navagero in BROWN, VI., 1, n. 499, and also the *report of the Genoese ambassador of May 28, 1556 (State Archives, Genoa).

[2] On June 3, 1556, G. A. Calegari informs Commendone from Rome : *Si aspetta da tutti la publicatione de la bolla rigorosa de la riforma (Lett. de' princ. 23, n. 3. Secret Archives of the Vatican).

[3] As early as October 2, 1555, Ercole of Ferrara had addressed an autograph letter to Paul IV. (in the collection of congratulatory letters in the Papal Secret Archives, II., p. 191, mentioned *supra* p. 175, n. 1) in which he announces the arrival of a special ambassador to intercede for his brother. It was believed that proceedings would also be taken against other unworthy Cardinals. Navagero *reports on January 4, 1556 : " Si dice per cosa certa che si attende a former processo contra la vita et costumi del card. de Monte " (Cod. 9445 of Library of St. Mark's, Venice).

[4] *Cf.* Acta consist cancell. for July 17, 1556 (Consistorial Archives) ; *cf.* GULIK-EUBEL, III., 37 and Bull, VI., 513 *seq.* I have found the *original briefs to the absent Cardinals, dated Rome, July 16, 1556, beginning : " Cogit nos " and all in similar

The Pope also made very searching enquiries concerning the
state of the monasteries, and the abuses in the hospitals,[1] as
he wished to make improvements in all these matters.   The
firm determination with which he kept his great aim before
his eyes is proved by the fact that he carried out a thorough
reform of the Dataria, which cost him two-thirds of his revenue, and that at a moment when the preparations for war
and for the defence of the States of the Church required more
money than ever.   The Datary appointed in July, Francesco
Bacodio, received strict orders that all petitions for favours
were to be granted gratuitously.   The Venetian ambassador,
as the representative of a commercial city, reckoned up the
large sums which were thereby lost to the Pope,[2] but this
did not trouble Paul IV. in the slightest degree.   He had
purposely made a beginning with the Dataria, the revenues
of which came to him personally, in order to show how seriously he meant to keep his promise of beginning the reform
with himself, and because he had discovered simony in the
former proceedings of the Dataria, he introduced there a
rigorous change.   Although he was fully aware of the danger
of such a diminution of his income, just on the very eve of
the war with Spain, he nevertheless carried out the measure,
for he trusted in God, Who had always helped him.   He
reminded the Venetian ambassador how he had once arrived
in Venice quite poor, with his Theatines, and yet had made
his way.   " And now," he exclaimed, " that we have been

terms, in the Papal Secret Archives, (Castle of St. Angelo, Arm.
5, caps. 3).   In all there are 15 briefs, addressed to Cardinals
Alessandro and Ranuccio Farnese, Ricci, Mendoza, E. Gonzaga,
Durante, Tagliavia, Cicada, C. del Monte, Crispi, Dandino,
Madruzzo, Doria, Mercurio and G. della Rovere.

[1] See the *Memoria per la cura delle cose spirituali pertinenti
al vicariato di Roma in the Papal Secret Archives, Arm. 8, ordo
2, t. 5, p. 5 *seq.* ; see *ibid.* p. 23 *seq.*, the *Informationi* concerning
the hospital of S. Spirito.

[2] See the letter of Navagero of July 11, 1556, in ANCEL, Concile, 18, n. 2 ; *cf.* MOCENIGO-ALBÈRI, 29, and *ibid.* 87, the account
of Soranzo ; ROSEO, III., 501.

raised to the throne of St. Peter, are we to be brought to want ? If we feared this, we should deserve to be punished by God ! "[1]

On August 21st, 1556, the Pope took a further step, which showed with what constancy he pursued his aims of reform. A decree, published in the consistory on that date, laid the axe at the root of one of the worst abuses in the matter of ecclesiastical benefices. Besides the uncanonical resignation of ecclesiastical offices, against which Paul III. had already taken steps, the so-called " Resignatio cum regressu " had developed to an ever-increasing extent, especially since the end of the XVth century. This was a resignation with the reservation that the benefice resigned should, under certain circumstances, as for example, the previous death of the acquirer, again revert to the original holder.[2] With perfect right, Paul IV. would not, under any pretext, allow of this or of the similar acts of resignation, called the " Ingressus " and the " Accessus." He looked upon them as merely inventions of the devil.[3]

He had already begun to take measures against such abuses in the first year of his reign, but had been obliged to make certain far-reaching exceptions in the case of the Cardinals.[4] Now, however, (August 21st, 1556), every " Accessus " to a benefice, by whomsoever it was made, or whatsoever conditions it might contain, was completely done away with and annulled. With regard to the " Regressus " it was decreed that the Cardinals resident in Rome should, within fifteen

[1] See Navagero's report of August 22, 1556, in BROWN, VI., 1, n. 583.

[2] Cf. HINSCHIUS, III., 283.

[3] See the characteristic conversation of Paul IV. with Navagero in his *letter of October 28, 1557 (Court Library, Vienna) ; see also BROWN, VI., 2, n. 937, 954.

[4] Cf. the report of Navagero of September 7 and 11, 1555, in COGGIOLA, A. d. Cornia, 99, and ANCEL, Concile, 25, also in Appendix Nos. 43-45 the *letter of Cardinal Vitelli of December 3, 1555 (Vatican Library) and the Acta consist. in GULIK-EUBEL, III., 37.

days, hand in to the Datary a list of the resignations of this kind possessed by them. The Cardinals who were living in Italy were to do the same within a month, and those who were beyond the Alps were given three months to comply with the order. " When we shall have received all these statements," declared the Pope, " we shall say to those who possess more than one of these ' Regressus ' : This is not lawful ; choose one of them, and give up the others. In this way, and step by step, we intend to carry out the reform. In spite of all its assaults, hell will not be able to do anything to harm this good work, which will secure for us a place in heaven."[1]

This measure was carefully and rigorously carried out. The Papal Secret Archives still preserve the lists of " Regressus " which all the Cardinals had to hand in ; at their head we find Alessandro Farnese, with a terribly long list.[2] The financial loss with which certain Cardinals were threatened was considerable, and there was no lack of vigorous complaints. The Pope, however, remained quite firm.[3]

At the end of September, Paul IV. announced further reforms, especially a prohibition for the bishops to possess any other benefice whatsoever. The objections which the Cardinals made by no means convinced the Pope that it was impossible to carry out such a measure. At the beginning

---

[1] See Navagero in BROWN, VI., 1, n. 583, and Acta consist. in GULIK-EUBEL, III., 37. A copy of the *decree of August 21, 1556, in the *correspondence of Madruzzo in the Vice-regal Archives, Innsbruck.

[2] After the period fixed had been extended for 15 days on September 4, 1556 (*Acta consist. in the Consistorial Archives) all the Cardinals handed in the prescribed lists more or less quickly ; *most of them are contained in the Papal Secret Archives, Castle of St. Angelo, Arm. 8, ordo 2, t. 6 ; the *list of Card. A. Farnese is dated 18 Cal. Octobr. 1556.

[3] Besides Navagero's reports in BROWN, VI., 2, n. 954, 1067, see his **letters of August 14 and October 28, 1557 (Court Library, Vienna) ; it is clear, at the same time, why the Acta consist. for reform matters are insufficient.

of October he again repeated that it was his fixed intention to continue on the path of a vigorous reform. He would not, like other Popes, act for form's sake, but would proceed in earnest, a thing of which he had given proof by renouncing the hundreds of thousands which the Dataria had brought him in. The devil had brought about the war with Spain in order to make any progress on the path on which he had entered impossible. He was not, however, going to be led astray, but would every day do away with some of the many abuses.[1]

The Pope's intentions were certainly of the best, but circumstances were stronger than he. In September, 1556, Alba invaded the States of the Church. The war with Spain naturally pushed the reform question more and more into the background, even though the Pope, with characteristic tenacity, was, at its commencement, still occupied with the extermination of the numerous abuses.[2] New measures on a more extensive scale, however, could not be carried out during the war, but it should always be remembered that Paul IV., at the time of his most desperate financial need, always held fast to the reform of the Dataria, as well as to the limitation of the sale of offices, and preferred to impose oppressive and unpopular taxes rather than give up any of his reforming principles.[3]

How faithfully he kept true to these principles in other respects is best seen in the creation of Cardinals of March 15th, 1557.

The French diplomatists and Cardinal Carafa had endeavoured, even more urgently than at the previous creation of Cardinals, to influence the decision of the Pope on this occasion. Although the French allowed it to appear that the duration of their military aid was dependent upon the

---

[1] See Navagero's reports of September 30 and October 2, 1556, in BROWN, VI., I, n. 636, 641.

[2] Cf. ibid.

[3] See Navagero's despatch of May 8, 1557, in BROSCH, I., 202 seq.

consideration shown to their candidates, and although Guise, Cardinal Carafa and the ambassador of the Duke of Ferrara left no means untried, they nevertheless did not attain their end.[1] The Pope preserved his complete independence and would not be influenced by anything but ecclesiastical considerations. " The dignity of a Cardinal is of such a nature," Paul IV. said to Navagero, " that a man who is fitted for it should be begged to accept it. We should seek such men with a lighted candle in our hand. Any recommendation of candidates will be of no avail."[2]

As had been foreseen by well-informed persons.[3] the majority of those who were raised to the purple on March 15th were representatives of reform, and men of lowly origin. The most distinguished of the ten newly appointed Cardinals[4] was the Dominican, Michele Ghislieri, who was considered a saint, and whom Paul IV. had for many years learned to value as Inquisitor. Virgilio Rosario and Consiglieri were also old acquaintances of the Pope. Rosario, who was born in Spoleto, had served him faithfully in financial matters ;[5] he became vicar-general of Paul IV., in which office he displayed great severity.[6] The Roman, Giovan Battista Con-

---

[1] Cf. ANCEL, L'action réform., 22 seq.

[2] See in Appendix No. 36 the *letter of Navagero of March 12, 1557 (Library of St. Mark's, Venice).

[3] In the *Avviso of March 6, 1557, it says : " Questi Franzesi dicono che il Papa farà buon numero di cardinali et alcuni vogliono che la maggior parte siano Chietini di poca considera-tione " (Vatican Library).

[4] Cf. concerning them PETRAMELLARIUS, 26 seq. ; CIACONIUS, III., 854 seqq. ; CARDELLA, IV., 353 seqq. ; BROMATO, II., 352 seqq. ; GULIK-EUBEL, III., 39 seq.

[5] Cf. the *Diurnale di tutti danari et entrate dell' ill. et rev. card. di Napoli che perverranno in mano di me Virgilio R° (Ms. 140 of the National Library in the Certosa di S. Martino at Naples).

[6] As in the case of the Roman vicariate, that is to say the place of representation of the Pope in Rome, the municipal offices of the Inquisition, and of the regent of the exchequer were in future, in accordance with the Pope's wishes, only to be bestowed on

siglieri, was a relative of that Paolo Consiglieri who, like
Carafa, belonged to the Oratory of Divine Love, had joined
with him in founding the order of Theatines,[1] and had then
become his maestro di camera. The Pope offered this admirable man the purple, but the humble Paolo firmly refused
the honour, and recommended Giovan Battista Consiglieri
instead of himself. The latter had originally been a layman,
and had been twice married ; Paul IV. had known him for a
long time, and particularly valued his piety.[2]

Lorenzo Strozzi had, as a layman, been the zealous opponent of the Calvinists ; the same was true of the Archbishop of Sens, Jean Bertrand, who was the only Frenchman
who at this time received the purple.[3]

Taddeo Gaddi, Archbishop of Cosenza, Vitellozzo Vitelli,
Bishop of Città di Castello, and the nuncio in Venice, Antonio
Trivulzio, who had represented the Holy See in France under
Julius III., all greatly distinguished for their learning, were
among those appointed on March 15th. Trivulzio and
Lorenzo Strozzi, Bishop of Beziers were the only two chosen
out of the long list of Henry II.[4]

Cardinals ; see MASSARELLI, 327 ; *cf.* MORONI, XCIV., 65, 67,
82, 94 (with wrong date).

[1] *Cf.* Vol. X. of this work, pp. 407, 411.

[2] RIESS (p. 238) calls G. B. Consiglieri a man of loose character,
without giving any proof of his assertion. *Delfino says the
opposite ; *cf. infra* p. 202, n. 2.

[3] Concerning his appointment see the *brief to Henry II. of
March 16. 1557 (Arm. 44, t. 2, p. 61. Secret Archives of the
Vatican).

[4] *Cf.* ANCEL, L'action réform., 27 and *Nonciat.*, II., 342 n ;
cf. ibid., 357 *seqq.* Cardinal Vitelli (died 1568 ; *cf.* Anecd. litt.
I., 436 *seqq.*) has rendered great service to history since he was
one of the first to take in hand one of those collections of historical
manuscripts which afterwards became the fashion in Rome.
He received permission from Paul IV. to make copies in the
Archives of the Castle of St. Angelo as well as in the Vatican
Library (see MERCATI, Bibl. Apost., 77 n.). Not a few of the
Italian manuscripts which reached German libraries, as, for ex-
ample, Berlin, Frankfort, Gotha, Wolfenbüttel, and later on

To the eight named, the Pope added the learned general of the Minorites, Clemente Dolera,[1] who was very zealous for reform, and Alfonso Carafa, the son of Antonio, Marquis of Montebello. Alfonso was only eighteen years old, but as the greatest expectations were built on the virtue of this youth, the Pope considered his elevation justified. The young marchese, who received the administration of the archdiocese of Naples on April 9th, 1557, became the avowed favourite of Paul IV., who always recited his office with him. The hopes with which able critics welcomed the new Cardinals were fulfilled, except in the case of Vitelli. That the latter followed another path was, however, concealed from the Pope by his nephew.[2]

In the meantime the war with Spain was going on, and the Pope felt very deeply the hindrances which this fact placed in the way of his reforming activities. He allowed, however, no doubts to be entertained as to his firm resolve to continue his work for the improvement of the state of the Church,[3] showing, at the same time, his readiness to listen to all the

Sweden (Stockholm, Upsala, Lund) originally belonged to his collection (RANKE, Fürsten und Völker, I. [1827] x. *seq.* DUDIK, Forsch. in Schweden, 244). Vitelli was also a keen collector of antiquities ; see LANCIANI, Scavi, III., *170 seq.*

[1] *Cf.* Soranzo in ALBÈRI, 102 ; LAUCHERT, 646 *seq.*

[2] It is certain that Vitelli led an immoral life (see GRAF, Cinquecento, 265). Paul IV. was unaware of the fact partly because Vitelli favoured the Theatines, who were, therefore, very prodigal in his praises (see CARACCIOLO, *Vita, 4, 13. Casanate Library, Rome). Delfino sent, together with his *letter of March 22, 1557, a list of the new Cardinals, with remarks as to their characters. Of Vitelli he only says : " è dotto et pieno di spirito." Trivulzio is praised as " nobilissimo, dottissimo et modestissimo," Gaddi as " persona morigeratissima," Bertrand as " homo di gran maneggio " ; Delfino gives prominence to the good lives led by Rosario, Dolera and Consiglieri (Court and State Archives, Vienna).

[3] See Navagero's *letter of May 15, 1557, and the report in BROWN VI. 2 n. 946, 954.

complaints and difficulties of his subjects, by a regulation of January 23rd, 1557, which arranged for public audiences.[1] In February, 1557, he issued new regulations against immorality in Rome,[2] and in June decreed that, for the future, no fees should be tendered at the bestowal of the pallium.[3] In the following month, in the midst of the greatest stress of war, Paul IV. took a step from which the greatest hopes were entertained in the matter of reform. The powers of the Inquisition, which already extended beyond the actual domain of matters of faith, and included the punishment of grave offences against morality, now received a further extension. Everything which the Pope referred to as " simoniacal heresy " was assigned to this tribunal on July 15th, 1557. Orders were given at the Penitentiary, the Chancery, the Signatura, and the office of the Auditors, that they were no longer to occupy themselves with such matters. The Pope wished, by the help of the Inquisition, to put an end, once for all, to some of the worst abuses, such as the payment of money for the administration of the sacraments, the ordination of those under age, the sale of benefices, and all unlawful contracts. As Paul IV. trusted no tribunal as he did the Inquisition, he was convinced that he had, by this regulation, laid a firm foundation upon which he could afterwards build with a sure hope of success.[4]

[1] One would conclude from Massarelli (302 *seq.*) that the regulation was decreed on January 27, on which day it was first carried into effect. This was, however, not the case. According to the *Acta consist., VII., p. 56, a *congregatio generalis* took place on January 23, 1557, at which the *institutio audientiae publicae* was settled. *Ibid.* the *decree relating to this " Cupiens quorumvis, etc." (Consistorial Archives). *Cf.* also in BROWN, VI., 2, n. 799 and n. 807, the description of such a public audience.

[2] *Cf.* the *Avviso di Roma of February 13, 1557 (Vatican Library).

[3] See Acta consist. in GULIK-EUBEL, III., 37.

[4] See Navagero's *report of July 16, 1557, (Court Lib. Vienna), and the *Avviso of July 24, 1557, in Appendix No. 38. In the *Acta consist. which are very incomplete, the order is not entered.

The Pope allowed no doubts to be entertained as to his firm determination to do away with the sale of benefices, and the numerous abuses in the Chancery and Penitentiary. He was quite aware that in so doing, the interests of many persons would be seriously affected ; he, was, nevertheless, of opinion that this bore no comparison to the advantages which would follow from such a step, as the Lutherans could then no longer refer to the abuses of the Curia.[1]

In his reforms Paul IV. attached special importance to the fact that he would make no exceptions, for he had convinced himself that it had been owing to these that the many salutary regulations of his predecessors had not borne the fruit expected from them.[2] How firmly he clung to his rigorous principles, the ambassadors were to learn only too frequently. Among the reports of the Venetian ambassador is one which, in this respect, is extremely characteristic of the whole procedure of Paul IV. An audience of Navagero on August 16th, 1557, is there described in detail. The ambassador, in accordance with the instructions of his government, earnestly begged the Pope's sanction for the resignation of a Venetian bishop in favour of a candidate who enjoyed the fullest confidence of the Signoria. The Pope refused the petition immediately, on the ground that bishops are bound to their church by a bond which is as indissoluble as that of marriage. " In spite of this," continued Paul IV., " dispensations have been issued by the Holy See in this matter, but my holy teacher, Thomas, and others who agree with him, are of opinion that Popes have, in such cases, no power to dispense." The Pope then enlarged, with great detail, on the dignity of the episcopate, and then, mentioning the Primacy, he quoted the saying of Homer : " One is Master." He complained bitterly of the carelessness shown in Rome, hitherto, in the

[1] See in Appendix No. 38 the *Avviso of July 24, 1557 (Vatican Library) ; cf. also the almost identical *Avviso from Rome of July 24, 1557, in the Vice-regal Archives, Innsbruck (with Madruzzo's correspondence of 1555).

[2] See Navagero's *letter of June 26, 1557 (Court Library, Vienna).

choice of the chief shepherds of the Christian flocks; he would not be found wanting in this respect, for he very well understood how much the salvation of souls depended upon it. Then, completely departing from the subject under discussion, the Pope launched forth into a long dissertation concerning the destiny of the Church, which had, in the beginning, to suffer so many persecutions at the hands of unbelievers, and had, at all times, to fight against impious heretics and other enemies, but in spite of this the little ship of Peter had never suffered shipwreck, for Christ directed and guided it. While the sectarians allowed their followers freedom from all moral restraints, Christianity demanded all manner of privations, and firm faith in such great miracles as the Incarnation of Christ in the womb of the Virgin Mary, and the transformation of bread into the true body of Our Lord. Navagero, who understood the Pope's way, listened to him quietly, and without interrupting him, as he went on to enlarge further on the mysteries of the Catholic faith, discussing the ordination of priests and the sacraments, and explaining that a Christian must make use of the means of grace possessed by the Church. After Paul IV. had given free course to his eloquence, as he dearly loved to do, he suddenly returned to the original subject of their conversation, explaining that he would gladly render any service to the Signoria, as long as this did not affect the honour of God or lie heavy on his own conscience. He would appoint bishops with whom everyone in Venice, from the Doge to the humblest gondolier, would be pleased. Only the best men, he said, were worthy of receiving the mitre. The shrewd ambassador appeared to be satisfied, and indeed thanked the Pope for the instruction he had given him.[1]

[1] See Navagero's *report, dated Rome, August 16, 1557 (Court Library, Vienna).

CHAPTER VIII.

THE FALL OF THE CARAFA.

THE longer the struggle with Spain was drawn out, the more keenly did the Pope feel the futility of his efforts for reform. " Should God be so gracious," he said to the Venetian ambassador at the beginning of September, 1557, " as to deliver us from this war, as we so earnestly desire, we would promise to devote all the years of our life to the service of His Divine Majesty, and to perform deeds which will give joy and comfort to the world, for we wish to begin with ourselves and then to reform others."[1]

The unhappy war ended soon afterwards, and Paul IV. returned with all the more vigour to his original and natural activities. He concentrated, as much as possible, on purely ecclesiastical matters, and made reform so completely the central point of his endeavours, that one may almost say that the actual reign of the Theatine Pope only began at this point.

On October 1st, 1557, he assembled the Cardinals in consistory, and explained to them, in a long address, that he looked upon their previous sufferings, the war and the inundation of the Tiber, as a punishment from God, and an earnest exhortation to reform. He admonished the Cardinals as to the whole matter of reform, and declared that it must now be carried into effect, and that he himself would be the first to take it in hand. A decree was then published by which the investiture of monasteries in commendam was absolutely forbidden, and no exemption with regard to this was to be allowed for the future, even to the Cardinals.[2] Soon afterwards a reform was

[1] See Navagero in BROWN, VI., 2, n. 1015 ; *cf.* 1017.

[2] See Acta consist. in GULIK-EUBEL, III., 37 and SANTAREM, XIII., 3, as well as the *Avviso of October 2, 1557 (Vatican Library) ; *cf.* also the second *letter of Navagero of October 9, 1557 (Court Library, Vienna).

also introduced in the Penitentiary.[1] The abuses in the
Signatura were also abolished at the same time. To the congratulations of the Venetian ambassador, Paul IV. replied that
all this was of only small importance, but that from now
onwards he would seek after nothing so much as a real reform.[2]
It was understood that a strict bull for the removal of abuses
in the matter of the system of benefices was being prepared.[3]
This dócument was remodelled at the last moment, but was
finally drawn up on November 27th, 1557, and was at once
made public.[4]

Paul IV. had already announced to the Cardinals in the
consistory of October 1st, 1557, his intention of forming a
commission from among their number, to examine into the
usefulness of the reforms already undertaken, and, under the
personal direction of the Pope, to make arrangements for those
still necessary.[5] This plan, which had been first thought of
in August, 1556, was carried into effect in a consistory of
December 3rd, 1557, in such a manner that the Cardinals of

[1] See in Appendix No. 41 the Avviso of October 16, 1557
(Vatican Library) ; cf. also CARACCIOLUS, 88 and GÖLLER, II.,
I, 125.

[2] Cf. the second *letter of Navagero of October 9, 1557. The
words of the Pope were : " Magnifico ambasciatore questo è
niente se bene è quel tanto che voi conoscete, nelle signature
non sono più ammesse quelle cose che passavano per l'ordinario
et hora a nessun altra cosa pensamo più che ad una vera riforma "
(Court Library, Vienna).

[3] See in Appendix No. 42 the *Avviso of November 13, 1557
(Vatican Library).

[4] The Motu Proprio " contra eos qui pro obtinendis beneficiis
se ipsos pro aliis supponunt vel annuas pensiones offerunt aut
beneficia impetrant pro aliis, ut ab eis aliquid consequantur, vel
pro se ipsis, ut aliis postea cum pensione resignent " in the Bull.,
VI., 528 seq. Cf. also the *Avviso of December 11, 1557 (Vatican
Library).

[5] Concerning the consistory of October 1, see the *report of
Navagero of October 2 (Court Library, Vienna) ; cf. the **Avviso
of October 2, 1557 (Vatican Library).

the Inquisition found themselves also charged with the question of reform.[1]

In the same consistory of December 3rd, 1557, the proceedings concerning the suppression of the Regressus for the Cardinals were brought to an end. More than one such Regressus was no longer to be allowed. It was ordained at the same time, with regard to the filling of vacant bishoprics, that nomination and appointment could no longer be made in the same consistory.[2] In thus separating the two things Paul IV. wished to have time to examine the candidates. In so doing he proceeded with such scrupulous observance of the decrees of the Council of Trent, that in October, 1558, no less than fifty-eight bishoprics were unoccupied.[3] The Pope, who had such a high ideal of the episcopal dignity,[4] repeatedly took occasion to exhort the newly elected bishops to perform the duties of their office faithfully, and to be consecrated as soon as possible.[5] Hosius, the eminent Bishop of Ermland, was to be summoned to Rome in the interests of reform ; in the brief concerning this, mention was also made of the holding of a

[1] What ANCEL (Concile, 19) shrewdly supposed, is proved to be a fact by the *Acta consist. of December 3, 1557 (Consistorial Archives).

[2] Acta consist. in GULIK-EUBEL, III., 37 ; cf. Bull., VI., 530 seq. ; MASSARELLI, 318 and the *letter of Cardinal Vitelli of December 1, 1557 (Vatican Library), see Appendix Nos. 43-45. The brief of December 4, 1557, concerning the Regressus in the Casanate Library, Editti, I., 102.

[3] See the report of Ces. Gonzaga in ANCEL, Concile, 24, n. 6. It had already been stated in an *Avviso di Roma of April 18, 1556, with regard to the application of the decrees of the Council of Trent to the filling of bishoprics, that Paul IV. would make no exceptions in so doing : *Et in queste concessioni questo papa è il più scrupuloso di tutti i passati (Cod. Urb. 1038, p. 134. Vatican Library).

[4] Cf. the conversation of Paul IV. with Navagero in the latter's *report of October 9, 1557 (Cod. 6255 of the Court Library, Vienna). See also supra p. 204.

[5] See MASSARELLI, 319.

Council,[1] but Rome was the only place thought of in connection with this.[2]

On December 14th, secrecy regarding consistorial discussions was decreed under threat of the most severe punishments.[3] A thorough visitation and reform of all the secular and regular clergy in Naples was arranged for and carried out.[4] On December 1st Cardinal Vitelli informed Carlo Carafa, who was staying with Philip II., that the Pope had arranged some most excellent reforms, and was still continuing to do so ; he thought and pondered on nothing else. On December 17th and 24th Vitelli repeated the same statements ; congregations were being held every day, and salutary decrees being issued ; the Pope was quite indefatigable in this respect.[5]

Paul IV. marked the beginning of the new year 1558 with fresh drastic measures against the keeping and dissemination of lampoons and heretical writings, and in special cases procuration was made punishable by death.[6] On January 18th the Pope again exhorted the Cardinals to lead blameless lives.[7] At the beginning of February he again spoke of holding a Council in Rome to further the cause of reform ; he hoped by means of this to adopt decisive measures which would everywhere be accepted with approval. As he had been a resident bishop himself, he well knew with what eagerness everything was carried to Rome, where the bishops were hampered in the exercise of their authority by the many exemptions in favour of hospitals and confraternities, so that very often they were unable to take proceedings against bad priests. This was, the

[1] Cf. RAYNALDUS, 1557, n. 37 ; EICHHORN, I., 298 ; Hosii epist., II., 907, 931, 933.

[2] Cf. as to this BROWN, VI., 2, n. 931.

[3] See MASSARELLI, 319, and the *Acta consist. (Consistorial Archives).

[4] Cf. TACCHI VENTURI, I., 454 seq.

[5] See these *letters (Vatican Library) in Appendix Nos. 42-45.

[6] See the *Avvisi di Roma of January 1 and 8, and February 5, 1558 (Vatican Library) ; cf. Bull., VI., 537 and also HINSCHIUS, V., 826 ; see also CLEMENTI, 214.

[7] See Navagero in BROWN, VI., 3, n. 1148.

Pope considered, one of the principal causes of the ecclesiastical corruption.[1] At the end of March a commissary was sent to Istria, Friuli and Dalmatia to reform the clergy there.[2] Unfortunately, the eighty-five year old Pope, who, generally speaking,[3] had hitherto enjoyed wonderful vigour and activity, began, in an unmistakable manner, to feel, for the first time, the frailties of old age. At the Curia they complained that all business, with the exception of that of the Inquisition, was at a standstill ; even the Datary and Barengo, who otherwise had free access to the Pope, now often had to wait for twenty days before they could get an audience. At the beginning of April, the French ambassador was still waiting for the audience which he had asked for four weeks before. The patience of Cardinal del Monte was tried still more severely, for he was no nearer his object of obtaining an audience with the Pope after having waited for three months.[4] In the middle of April it was reported that the condition of the Pope, which had hitherto been fairly satisfactory,[5] was causing anxiety. His strength was decreasing, and people thought that he was only waiting for the return of Cardinal Carafa in order to withdraw completely from political affairs and leave them entirely to his nephew.[6] The longed for return of Carafa took place on April 23rd, 1558.[7]

[1] BROWN, VI., 3, n. 1162.

[2] Besides the brief of March 24, 1558, in FONTANA, 447, see also *the brief to the Doge of April 2, 1558 (Arm. 44, t. 2, p. 111. Secret Archives of the Vatican).

[3] The Pope had suffered in August from want of appetite and sleeplessness, but had again recovered ; cf. the *reports of Navagero of August 5, 7, 14, and 16, 1557, in the Cod. 6255 of the Court Library. Vienna.

[4] See the *Avviso di Roma of April 2, 1558 (Vatican Library).

[5] *Sta bene, Lippomano announces to Cardinal Carafa from Rome on April 2, 1558 (Cod. Barb. lat., 5715 of the Vatican Library).

[6] See the *Avviso of April 16, 1558 (Vatican Library).

[7] See Massarelli, 322, the report in COGGIOLA, Capitolazione, 103, and the *report of Jacobo Bannissio to Cardinal Madruzzo dated Rome, April 23, 1558 (Vice-regal Archives, Innsbruck).

Carlo Carafa had been fully six months absent from Rome. Although he had received the legate's cross as early as October 6th, 1557, he had only set out on his way to Philip II. on the 22nd.[1] This delay was caused by the Cardinal's wish to take measures so that he might not be in danger of losing ground in Rome on this occasion, as had been the case with his legation at the beginning of the year. He could not, however, take such effective counter-measures as he had intended, but he succeeded in obtaining what appeared to him to be the principal thing. Full of mistrust of his elder brother, Giovanni, the Duke of Paliano, who was very discontented with the previous course of politics, he succeeded in obtaining that Cardinals Rebiba and Alfonso Carafa should be associated with the Duke in the direction of political affairs.[2] To these were also added Camillo Orsini, Luigi Lippomano, Bishop of Verona, and several other prelates. This council of state, which was to relieve the Pope, as much as possible, of the charge of political business, held its first sitting on October 23rd.[3]

In Brussels, where Cardinal Carafa arrived on December 12th, 1557, he was made welcome as far as the peace negotiations were concerned, but with regard to his private aims, which he considered of far greater importance, he found from the first that he had very little to expect. This was all the more the case, because his deadly enemies, Ascanio della Corgna and Garcilasso de la Vega had been actively employed in filling the mind of Philip II. with mistrust of the Cardinal.[4]

---

[1] See MASSARELLI, 318 ; cf. also COGGIOLA, Capitolazione, 46.

[2] See the *reports of Navagero of October 16 and 23, 1557 (Court Library, Vienna). RIESS, 288, must be amended in accordance with this.

[3] Cf. MASSARELLI, 318. Concerning the value of this alteration, at that time only theoretical, see ŠUSTA, in the Mitteil. des Österr. Inst., Erg.-Bd., VI., 552 seq.

[4] Concerning Carafa's Brussels legation, cf. PIEPER, 98 ; COGGIOLA, Cornia, 354 seq. and Capitolazione 70 seq. ; RIESS, 288 seq. ; ANCEL, Disgrâce, 21 seq. As Cardinal Carafa was furthering his own private interests in the first place, the peace negotiations which he was carrying on at the same time in France were bound

At the end of November, 1557, Bona Sforza, dowager Queen of Poland, died at Bari, after having appointed Philip II. as her sole heir.   Carafa at once formed the plan of obtaining the Duchy of Bari as a compensation for the Duke of Paliano. An envoy, Leonardo di Cardine, pointed out to the legate that he ought to take steps for this purpose in Brussels.[1]   Cardine had, on his way, communicated the plan to the Duke of Alba, but found in him no advocate, but rather a bitter opponent. It was owing to Alba's influence that Philip II. gave an evasive answer when, on New Year's Day, 1558, Carafa made an official application.   It is true that during the time that followed the Spanish court continued to overwhelm the nephew with honours, but all this outward pomp in no way corresponded to the treatment of the question of compensation, which continued to develop in a more and more unfavourable sense for Carafa after the arrival of the Duke of Alba in Brussels. All the attempts on the part of the legate to procure a more favourable consideration of his wishes remained without success.   This, however, did not prevent the worldly-minded prelate from distracting his mind, after the trying negotiations, with banquets, festivities and hunting parties.[2]   The final offer of the Spanish king was officially presented during the last days of February.   In accordance with this, Giovanni Carafa was to receive, as compensation for Paliano, the Duchy of Rossano, which would bring in an annual income of from 5000 to 6000 crowns, and besides this a yearly revenue of 10,000 crowns

to fail (see PIEPER, 100 seq.).   In correction of the statements of GOTHEIN, Ignatius, 478 and 755, the following must be noted : Paul IV. appointed Salmeron as adviser to Carafa ; Ribadeneira attached himself to Salmeron, probably to make use of the opportunity of travelling (ASTRAIN, II., 371. Epist. Salmeronis, I., xv., where details are also given concerning the return journey). Carafa took the Swiss nuncio Raverta with him to Brussels, where his nunciature also came to an end ; cf. concerning the latter, REINHARDT-STEFFENS, xiv-xx.

[1] See the Duke of Paliano's instructions for Cardine in the Appendix to NORES, 432.

[2] Cf. Firmani Diaria, 512.

from the silk duty in the kingdom of Naples ; Carlo Carafa was to receive a yearly pension of 12,000 crowns. The Cardinal, who had dreamed of much greater things, refused this offer. Even though Philip II. consented to refer further negotiations concerning the possession of Paliano to Rome, the legate was forced to admit to himself that his mission had been a complete failure. As a skilful diplomatist, he avoided an open rupture, but began his return journey in the middle of March, a profoundly disappointed man.[1]

It was believed for a long time that this fruitless mission to Brussels had destroyed Carafa's standing in the eyes of his uncle ; the truth is that exactly the opposite was the case.[2] Sick of political affairs, and more than ever anxious to devote all his powers to ecclesiastical reform, the aged Pope had awaited with longing the return of his nephew. The latter[3] had hardly arrived, when his brother, the Duke of Paliano, had to retire into the background, which fact was outwardly expressed by his removal from the Vatican to SS. Apostoli.[4]

---

[1] See COGGIOLA, Capitolazione, 102. L. Firmanus remarks concerning the return journey : *12 Martii 1558 legatus cum tribus suis familiaribus incognitus nemine sciente discessit per portas cum maxima diligentia quia transire opportebat per loca suspecta Lutheranorum (Diaria, XII., 29. Secret Archives of the Vatican).

[2] The view that the fall of the nephews took place on political grounds, and that it was especially in consequence of the failure of Carafa's legation to Brussels, has been so confidently put forward by RANKE (Päpste, I.,[6] 195) that it has been followed by all later writers. In contradiction to this COGGIOLA (Capitolazione, 104 seq.) proves, and still more does ANCEL, (Disgrâce, 23 seq.) who is supported by incontestable reports, that this is quite erroneous, and that Cardinal Carafa was never more powerful than during the time between April and December, 1558.

[3] This is especially evident from the *letters of Cardinal Vitelli to Cardinal C. Carafa, dated Rome, November 8, December 1 and 17, 1557 (cf. Appendix Nos. 42 to 45. Vatican Library), and from the report of Buoncambi to O. Farnese, dated Rome, March 26, 1558 (State Archives, Parma).

[4] See the reports in ANCEL, Disgrâce, 27, n. 2 ; cf. COGGIOLA, Capitolazione, 108.

All that concerned political, administrative, financial and judicial affairs was now entrusted to Carafa by his uncle. He surrounded the Pope with men who were devoted to his own interests, so that the old man only learned what his nephew wished him to know.[1] Paul IV. limited his own activities entirely to ecclesiastical matters. He appeared regularly only at the consistories and the sittings of the Inquisition, and devoted the remainder of his time to reform and his spiritual exercises. His inseparable companion was the young Cardinal Alfonso Carafa. Every morning the Pope went from his apartments in the Vatican, through the long corridor of Bramante, to the Belvedere, where he spent two-thirds of the day. Private audiences were now much more difficult to obtain than before, and the carrying out of current business was much more tedious. People only knew of the Pope, who had become almost invisible, that he was always occupied with the affairs of the Inquisition and with matters of reform.[2]

No one rejoiced more than Cardinal Carafa at this isolation of the Pope, and the complete restriction of his activities to ecclesiastical affairs, as he was able, in all other matters, to do as he thought fit. The less chance of success there was for his grand plans for the establishment of the Carafa family on a princely standing, the more eagerly did he endeavour to enrich himself and those belonging to him, and to enjoy life as a great noble. He much preferred to stay at his vigna in Trastevere, which he lavishly adorned with antique statuary, than in the magnificent rooms of the Borgia apartments. At the vigna he gave his friends, among whom were several worldly-minded Cardinals, such as Vitelli, Sermoneta and Ranuccio Farnese, splendid banquets, after which they gambled for high stakes. One can recognize the old soldier, above all, in Carafa's passion for the chase. Pleasures of this kind, however, were blameless in comparison with others. There can be no doubt that Carlo Carafa led a continuously immoral life.[3]

[1] Cf. GRATIANUS, 63.

[2] See ANCEL, Disgrâce, 23 seq.; cf. also Secrét, 12 seq. and COGGIOLA, Capitolazione, 109.

[3] Cf. contempory witnesses in ANCEL, Disgrâce, 25 seq.; see also GRAF, Cinquecento, 265, 281; Studi stor., VIII., 254.

What a contrast between the dissolute behaviour of a corrupt Renaissance prelate, and the simple lonely monk's life led by the Pope ! The activities of the two moved in entirely different worlds ; the Pope lived and had his being in the reform of the Church, while his nephew returned once more to the worst days of the Renaissance.[1] Carlo, however, displayed great skill in concealing his scandalous proceedings and his riotous living in Rome[2] from the Pope, and in immediately dispelling any suspicion against him.

In the summer of 1558 Paul IV. was occupied with the issue of a general reform bull, which was to include all the separate regulations. The appearance of such a document had been expected as early as June, 1556, but it transpired that it was being once more redrafted.[3] On August 8th, 1558, the Pope again referred to it in a consistory.[4] A few days later he complained in another consistory that the question of a Council

Carafa's passion for the chase was so great that he kept over 1,300 dogs, of which 400 belonged to the Cardinal, " il che da da dire non poco in questa carestia che hora regna," says an *Avviso of December 3, 1558 (Cod. Urb. 1038, p. 355[b]. Vatican Library).

[1] Even in reports which deal rather with external matters, this often appears in glaring contrast. Thus an *Avviso di Roma of October 8, 1558, first speaks of the reforming activity of the Pope, and then continues : " Li signori Caraffa attendono alle caccie et piaceri " (Cod. Urb. 1038, p. 342[b]. Vatican Library).

[2] The taxes, complains the Portuguese ambassador on December 10, 1558, are increasing, there is a want of provisions, justice is almost at a standstill, and the Pope takes no steps ; see SANTAREM, XIII., 13 ; cf. ibid. 8, 10, 22 concerning the isolation of Paul IV., with whom it was exceedingly difficult to get an audience. Concerning the " carestia " at the beginning of 1558 see CLEMENTI, 214.

[3] See the letter of G. A. Calegari in ANCEL, Concile, 23, n. 1.

[4] See *Acta consist. (Consistorial Archives) : " S.D.N. primo loco multa commemoravit quae sunt necessaria ut fiat reformatio universalis ecclesiae, postea vocatus d. Barengus ad formandam bullam super translatione festivitatis s. Dominici." Cf. concerning this infra p. 242.

could not be settled before on account of the war, but that he
would now take this matter up earnestly.[1] Two measures of
reform, which caused quite a sensation, were adopted in the
late autumn.   On October 21st, the Pope ordered that no one,
not even any of the Cardinals, should open any of the letters
addressed to him by the princes regarding questions of patronage.[2] On November 28th he decided that in future no money
should be taken for the pallium under pain of excommunication.[3] At the same consistory he united the auditorship of
the Exchequer with the office of Regent of the Exchequer,
recently established by him, and entrusted the virtuous Cardinal Alfonso Carafa with both these posts.[4] Further regulations of reform were expected and spoken of.[5]

The reform of the monasteries gave Paul IV. a great deal of
trouble during the whole of his reign.[6] The dissolution and

----

[1] *Avviso di Roma of August 13, 1558; " Lunedi si fece
consistorio, ma non si fece parola di dar la croce al r^mo di Pisa.
S.S.^tà parlò di reforma, dicendo che non havendo per le guerre
potuto congregar un concilio, non voleva più tardar a farlo (Cod.
Urb. 1038, p. 330. Vatican Library).

[2] See *Acta consist. cancell. (Consistorial Archives) and MAS-
SARELLI, 326.

[3] See *Acta consist. cancell. in GULIK-EUBEL, III., 37.

[4] See the *Avviso of December 3, 1558, in GULIK-EUBEL,
III., 37 (Vatican Library), and MASSARELLI, 327, where details
are also given concerning the abolition of this post by Pius IV.

[5] Beside the letter of Pasino di Giusti in ANCEL, Concile,
23, n. 1, cf. especially the *Avvisi di Roma of November 19
(the Pope announces three bulls in this congregation, at which
he remains for three hours : against the " sfratati," concerning
the Inquisition, and against the sons of priests) and November
26, 1558 (the bulls are ready to be printed). Cod. Urb. 1038,
p. 351, 352. Vatican Library).

[6] Concerning the reform of the Dominicans in Naples, see in
Appendix No. 49 the *brief of July 25, 1558 (Secret Archives of
the Vatican).   To this also belongs the *brief to Angelo de Medio-
lano et Augustino de Papia ord. praed. concerning the reform of
the " monachi heremit. S. Hieros. ordin." of April 4, 1559 (Arm.
44, t. 2, p. 135) and that of December 2, 1558, in FONTANA, 448.

corruption to which many of these had become a prey, is best shown by the scandalous conduct of the " vagrant monks," who by means of dispensations partly obtained from the Penitentiary and Dataria, and partly obtained surreptitiously from their superiors, and often indeed without permission at all, and under all sorts of pretexts, lived out of their monasteries, many of them even going about in secular dress. Most of these people caused the greatest scandal by their loose manner of life and their false doctrines. Paul IV. had already met with this abuse in Venice in the time of Clement VII., and had demanded that energetic steps should be taken against it;[1] in the same way he had endeavoured to put an end to it under Paul III. and Julius III. The severe regulations of the latter, and the special decrees issued by Paul IV. himself as Pope, had not, however, proved effectual.[2] It transpired in June, 1558, that decisive measures of the most severe kind were impending against these " vagrant monks " or " apostates." On July 20th a bull relating to this abuse was considered, which was published on August 3rd.[3]

In this document, which, together with the decree issued on December 16th, 1555, against the bestowal of monasteries in commendam, forms an important landmark in the history of reform of religious orders, the Pope ordains as follows ;—

1. Whoever is bound by the vows of an order, and then under any pretext, lives outside the monastery of his order, loses all the benefices and revenues of the order, as well as all academic degrees in any faculty, and all ecclesiastical offices. He shall

---

[1] *Cf.* Vol. X. of this work, p. 420 *seq.*

[2] Concerning Julius III. see Vol. XIII., p. 162 ; concerning Paul IV.'s special regulations see the *letter of Navagero of May 22, 1557 : " Mando a V.S. la bolla in stampa contra li sfratati del ordine dei frati minori ; il medesimo si aspetta anco dell' altre religioni " (Court Library, Vienna) ; Diario di N. Turinozzi, 8.

[3] The *Avviso di Roma of June 25, 1558, says : " E commessa una bolla gagliardissima contra gli sfrattati." On July 20, 1558, the bull (printed in Bull. VI., 538 *seq.*) was drafted (*cf.* *Avviso of July 23, 1558. Vatican Library) and published on August 3 ; see Gianfigliazzi in ANCEL, Concile, 26, n. 3.

be incapable in future of possessing any benefice, degree, etc.
He shall, moreover, be suspended from the performance of any
ecclesiastical duties, and especially those of a priest. The
benefices which he possesses shall be regarded as vacant, and
must be occupied by somebody else ; all reservations of benefices must come to an end. By this decree, the " apostates "
could acquire no ecclesiastical benefice during their lifetime,
fill no ecclesiastical office, and receive no ecclesiastical revenues
or pensions ; they could have no cure of souls or perform any
ecclesiastical duties, dispense no sacraments and say no mass ;
their pensions, benefices in commendam, and reservations
became null and void, and they could draw no fruits from them.
Whosoever, in face of this prohibition, should exercise the duties
of a cure of souls, or any spiritual duties, dispense the sacraments or say mass, would incur the punishment prescribed.
2. No one may shelter an " apostate " or maintain him, or
afford him assistance in keeping out of his monastery ; otherwise, after previous admonition has proved ineffectual, he
becomes liable to excommunication.
3. No patron of a living may present an " apostate " to such,
otherwise, in this particular case, he forfeits the right of
presentation.
4. The competent superiors of orders, or the bishops, may, by
force, and with the assistance of the secular arm, compel the
" apostate " to return to his monastery, or afford him maintenance in a suitable place near his monastery, or in another
monastery of the same order, so that he may do penance.
Should the " apostate " refuse to obey, he thereby incurs the
sentence of the major excommunication.
5. The " apostate " must always wear a black cap with a
finger-wide white linen band.
6. Whosoever has renounced his vows and afterwards maintains that he was not properly a member of his Order, and
believes that he can live outside his monastery, or makes an
attempt to do so, must lay the permission he has obtained
from the Pope or the Penitentiary before the Cardinal-Pro-
tector at the Curia and the Procurator-General of his order, and
proceed with his case before them.

7. The permission to enter another Order is invalid, even when obtained from the Pope or the Penitentiary, unless it is a case of entering another Order of equal or greater severity.

8. Whosoever has entered another Order and refuses to return, loses the administration of ecclesiastical benefices, offices and prelacies. Whatever sums may have been obtained by monks living outside their monasteries belong to their monasteries.

9. As experience has shown that the right, bestowed on almost all the Orders, of receiving members of other Orders, has given the " apostates " an opportunity of wandering about outside their monasteries, especially as many superiors of Orders receive such " apostates," give them the habit, and then permission to live outside their monasteries, the right of doing so is withdrawn from the Orders ; only the Carthusians and the Camaldolese Hermits, if they really live as hermits, may retain it.[1]

In accordance with his principle of at once and ruthlessly carrying into effect the reforms decided upon, Paul IV. now acted promptly. In the evening of August 22nd, all the gates of Rome were closed, and during the night the police made a comprehensive raid on all the vagrant monks. About a hundred of them were arrested.[2] Although the Pope was very unwell just at the time,[3] he insisted on the severe punishment of those who persisted in disobedience ; some of them were imprisoned, and some sent to the galleys, while many fled. The position of the person concerned was no protection ; even such a learned man as Basilio Zanchi, custos of the Vatican Library, was thrown into prison.[4] On September 3rd the

---

[1] Bull., VI., 538 *seqq.*

[2] *Cf.* besides the reports quoted by ANCEL (Concile, 26, n. 4), the *Avviso di Roma of August 27, 1558 (Cod. Urb. 1038, p. 335[b]. Vatican Library).

[3] See the *Avviso of September 3, 1558, *loc. cit.*, 333[b].

[4] *Cf.* CARACCIOLUS, 84 ; BROMATO, II., 491 *seq.* ; POGIANI, Epist., I., 25 n. ; IV., 361. B. Zanchi died in prison (see the *Avviso of October 8, 1558, *loc. cit.* 342[b].) Cardinal A. Carafa reports concerning the proceedings against the " apostates." *Fece darsene notamento da tutte le religioni per sapere quali non obedivano, et se di questi tali alcuno se le fosse presentato avanti

number in Rome of those who shared his fate amounted to
more than 200.   After the capital had been cleansed, the same
stern measures were extended to the whole of the States of the
Church.[1]

Draconian punishments of a similar kind were also to be
inflicted on unworthy secular priests.   It was expected that
the bull relating to this would be so severe that many would
prefer to escape the penalties by voluntarily leaving Rome.[2]
The Pope, who had previously taken the reform of the breviary
in hand,[3] wished to bring this matter also to a conclusion by
the end of the year.[4]

Owing to the great age of the Pope, and his unsatisfactory
state of health at this time,[5] the question of the next election
had, of late, been very eagerly discussed.   Cardinal d'Este in
particular was intriguing for his own election in a most scandalous manner.   Carafa, in his zeal for reform, had stood out
against him at the last conclave, comparing him to Simon
Magus.   As Este, as well as other Cardinals, were at this time
taking all possible measures to secure votes at the next conclave, as they had done before, Paul IV. issued a bull on
December 16th, 1558, obviously with reference to these
intrigues, in which he forbade any kind of negotiations concerning the future election during the lifetime of the reigning
Pope and without his knowledge, whether by the Cardinals or

---

che fosse stato suo caro amico mentre era in religione, lo ributtava
ne volea più vederlo dicendo che non lo conesceva (Apologia
Cod. X.F., 55 of the National Library, Naples).

[1] *Avviso of September 3 and October 8, 1558, *loc. cit.*, 333[b],
342[b]; *cf.* BERTOLOTTI, Màrtiri, 21 *seqq.*

[2] " S'aspetta bolla di riformatione contra li preti, la quale
si dubita che sarà tanto strana et rigorosa che molti cercheranno
di partirsi da Roma."   *Avviso of October 29, 1558, *loc. cit.*, 348.

[3] On August 8, 1558, Paul IV. forbade the breviary of Quiñones
(see MASSARELLI, 325, and Tüb. Quartalschrift, 1884, 481 *seq.*).
BÄUMER, Gesch. des Breviers (Freiburg, 1895, p. 415) gives the
wrong date, August 10, 1555.

[4] See the *Avviso of November 26, 1558, *loc. cit.*, 352.

[5] *Cf. infra* p. 222.

by anybody else, whatever their rank might be, under pain of the severest ecclesiastical and secular punishments.[1]

In his Christmas allocution to the Cardinals the Pope said that they need not wonder that no new appointments had been made at the Ember Days, for the Sacred College was well filled, while, in addition, he had found no candidates who possessed the necessary qualifications for such a dignity.[2]

This was, at the same time, a direct rebuff to the Pope's nephews who, just at that time, were importuning their uncle with recommendations of their favourite candidates. As had been the case before, Paul IV. would allow his family no influence in purely ecclesiastical affairs. All the more inconsiderately, therefore, did Cardinal Carafa and his brother use the power bestowed on them in secular matters ; in this sphere they ruled with a despotism that was all the greater as it was absolutely without control of any kind. Their unscrupulous baseness and insolent extortions were beyond all bounds. Owing to the Pope's isolation, his own self-assurance and his violent temperament, this state of things lasted for a very long time before any of the shameful doings of his nephews reached his ears. The first who had the courage to tell him anything unfavourable of Cardinal Carafa was a Theatine, whose name is unfortunately not known. The Pope was exceedingly astonished, thanked him for his information, and caused the accused Cardinal to be at once summoned to his presence.

Carafa showed the greatest coolness before his uncle, who was breathing vengeance, and denied everything. He displayed such skill in representing himself as the victim of

[1] See Bull., VI., 545 seq. ; cf. HINSCHIUS, V., 729 seq. ; SÄGMÜLLER, Papstwahlen, 14 seqq. and Papstwahlbullen, 40 seq. ; see also LORENZ, Papstwahl und Kaisertum, Berlin, 1874, 133 seqq. The bull was published on February 3, 1559 (see TURINOZZI, 12), but the sale of it was forbidden ; see Avviso of February 4, 1559 (Cod. Urb. 1039, p. 8. Vatican Library).

[2] See in Appendix No. 51 the *Avviso of December 24, 1558 (Vatican Library). Cardinal B. de la Cueva informed Cardinal Madruzzo of the continued reform work of Paul IV., in a *Letter dated Rome, January 8, 1559 (Vice-regal Archives, Innsbruck).

calumny that the aged Pope believed him once more. After
this occurrence, concerning which the Florentine ambassador
wrote home on August 13th, 1558, people feared, even more
than before, to bring any accusations against the Pope's
nephews.[1]

In September, 1558, Paul IV.was attacked by a severe illness,
and his life was despaired of, but his powerful constitution
overcame the crisis with a rapidity which astonished everybody.[2] Cardinal Carafa could now enjoy his favoured position
undisturbed for a few months longer, and continue to abuse
it. But quite suddenly, in January, 1559, catastrophe overwhelmed, not only the Cardinal, but also his brothers.

A comparatively trifling incident set the ball rolling. On
New Year's Day, 1559, a scandalous dispute, which almost
ended in bloodshed, arose during a banquet between the
brother of Cardinal Carpi and the Duke of Paliano's nephew,
Marcello Capece. Cardinal Carafa endeavoured to conceal the
affair from the Pope, but it nevertheless reached his ears, and
on January 6th he had Capece incarcerated in the Castle of St.
Angelo.[3]

Another occurrence took place at the same time which led
to the Pope's eyes being fully opened. The Florentine
ambassador, Bongianni Gianfigliazzi, had endeavoured in vain
for a long time to speak to the Pope on important business ;
on making a fresh attempt to obtain an audience, he was on
January 6th, 1559, repulsed in an offensive manner by Cardinal
Carafa. On the following day Gianfigliazzi managed to get in

---

[1] Concerning the first denunciation, and the tragedy of Plautilia
del Lante, see ANCEL, Disgrâce, 30 seq.

[2] Cf. MASSARELLI, 326, and the *Avvisi di Roma of August 27,
September 3, 10, 17, and 24, and October 1, 1558, in the Cod.
Urb. 1038 (Vatican Library ; cf. Appendix No. 50) ; see also
the reports in COGGIOLA, Capitolazione, 127, and the *letter of
Ansaldo Giustiniani to Genoa, dated Rome, Septembe 19, 1558
(State Archives, Genoa).

[3] Cf. the *reports of Gianfigliazzi of January 6 and 13, 1559
(State Archives, Florence) also used by ANCEL, Disgrâce, 32
seq., which differ from those in Nores ; cf. also CLEMENTI, 216.

to the Pope, told him of the insults he had received, and by skilful hints raised doubts in the mind of the old man, who had hitherto had blind confidence in his nephews.[1]

Paul IV. had been made suspicious by Carafa's attitude with regard to the scandal caused by Capece, and he began to make inquiries as to the life of his all-powerful nephew. First of all he summoned the Theatine, Father Geremia Isachino, who was honoured as a saint, and ordered him, under pain of excommunication, to tell him everything he knew concerning his nephew. Father Geremia knew only too much, especially through Cardinal Vitelli, who, until the autumn of 1558, had been closely associated with Cardinal Carafa, but had afterwards broken with him. The Pope now had to listen to things which filled him with all the more horror and disgust as he had not had the faintest idea of them. He then summoned Cardinal Ghislieri, less to hear further details as to the disgraceful proceedings of his nephews, than to reproach him for never having revealed the true state of affairs to him.[2]

[1] See the *report of Gianfigliazzi of January 7, 1559 (State Archives, Florence) used by ANCEL, Disgrâce, 34 seq., which is confirmed by an Avviso of January 21, 1559 (ibid. 35. n, 2).

[2] The statements of Campana, Thuanus and Adriani concerning the part played by Father Geremia in the fall of Carafa, which Silos and others have accepted, are quite incorrect. Ancel, who was the first to throw light on these matters, has corrected them from reports of the Florentine ambassador (Disgrâce 29). The story in Nores, which is adhered to by many, as by RANKE (Päpste, I[6]., 196) and DURUY (p. 298) of a remark made by Cardinal Pacheco on January 5, 1559, at a sitting of the Inquisition : " Holy Father, we must begin the reform with ourselves . . . " is rejected by RIESS (p. 365, n. 25) as a " later psychological explanation of the astonishing occurrence." The Diario di diverse cose notabili (Inf. polit., VIII., 401 seq. of the Royal Library, Berlin, and Addit. Ms., 20,045 of the British Museum) which is quoted by Riess (p. 363, n. 22) has already been highly praised by Ranke. Riess also over-estimates it, and sees in it " the best authority." The Diario, composed by the Roman, Vincenzo Bello, is often to be found in manuscript, as in Florence (Bibl. naz., Cod. CXXI.) in Paris (Bibl. nat. Ms. Ital., 10,059,

The revelations of Father Geremia put the aged Pope into a state of feverish excitement ; he struggled with himself for a short time, and then made up his mind. When Cardinal Carafa, who was quite unsuspicious of anything unusual, made his appearance on the morning of January 9th, 1559, for his usual audience, he had to wait for several hours, only to learn then that His Holiness would not receive him. The same answer was given him on January 12th, when he made another attempt to see the Pope, and at the same time orders were sent to the treasurer not to honour any payments bearing the signature of Cardinal Carafa.[1]

The news that the nephew who had, until now, been all-powerful, had fallen into disgrace, caused the greatest sensation in Rome. Everyone believed, however, that the Cardinal, skilled as he was in the arts of deception and persuasion, would soon succeed in again winning his uncle's favour. This, however, was not the case. On January 17th Cardinal Carafa was ordered to leave the Borgia apartments, and on the 23rd he was forbidden to appear in future at the consistory.[2]

From day to day the dreadful discoveries which the Pope was to make concerning the conduct of his nephews increased. It was said that a list had been given to him which contained 1300 unjust sentences which his relatives had pronounced. Paul IV. was completely overwhelmed, and to bitter complaints there succeeded hours of silent melancholy. The sorely tried old man sought and found consolation in prayer ; he was to be seen visiting the seven principal altars in St. Peter's with streaming eyes.[3]

n. I, 10,075, n. 5 and 10,077 [Colbert] ; cf. MARSAND, II., 167), in Rome in the Corsini Library (Cod. 128) and the Library of S. Croce in Gerusalemme. From this last manuscript it was in part published by LÄMMER, (Melet., 207 seq.) which has escaped Riess.

[1] See the Florentine and Este reports in ANCEL, Disgrâce, 33 seq.

[2] See the ambassadorial reports, ibid.

[3] See the *Avviso di Rome of January 14, 1559, in the Cod. Urb. 1039, p. 1, Vatican Library.

All the Cardinals, with the exception of Cardinal Carafa, were summoned to a consistory at the Vatican in the evening of January 27th, 1559.[1] On the appearance of the Pope at the assembly, it could be seen from his face that something unusual had taken place. In a long address he set forth with passionate emotion the " crimes of his nephews," in doing which he made not the slightest reference to their political activities, but only stigmatized their moral conduct. He called God to witness that he had not had the faintest idea of the wicked lives of his relatives, that he had had a " veil before his eyes " since the beginning of his reign, and had always been deceived ; he would now, however, cleanse his house. He ordered all three nephews to leave Rome within twelve days, and deprived them of all their offices. Carlo Carafa retained only his dignity of Cardinal ; he lost, not only the legation of Bologna, but also his supreme position as director of all the political affairs of the

[1] Concerning the consistory of January 27, 1559, cf. MASSARELLI, 329 ; Firmani Diaria in MERKLE, II., 513 seq. ; MASIUS, Briefe, 315 ; *Avviso di Roma of January 28, 1559, in the Cod. Urb. 1039, p. 4 (Vatican Library) ; Diario di N. Turinozzi, 10 seq. ; the Relazione in the Arch. d. Soc. Rom., XXXII., 222 seqq. ; the Relazione of G. Salvago in the Atti Lig., XIII., 754 seq. and the reports of the ambassadors of Florence and Ferrara of January 27 and 28, 1559, in drawing upon which ANCEL (Disgrâce, 40) points out that : " Dans aucun de ces documents authentiques on ne trouve une allusion permettant d'affirmer que Paul IV. ait voulu punir ses neveux en tant qu'hommes politiques, c'est-à-dire les punir d'erreurs dans lesquelles il avait sa large part de reponsabilité." In the *Acta consist. cancell., VII., 144, the following entry is to be found concerning the consistory of January 27, 1559 : " In dicto consistorio fuerunt enunciate certe revocationes et decreta privationum que papa tribus secretariis vid. D. Bergomen., Barengo et Lavellino iussit et commisit annotari et ad se deinde adferri. Itaque de his nihil scribere potui neque iudicio meo debui ad quos tamen et eorum acta habeatur relatio." In the *Acta consist. camer., IX., it only says : " S.D.N. Paulus papa IV. acri sermone usus est contra suos nepotes " (Consistorial Archives).

Holy See and of the States of the Church. The Duke of Paliano was, with the exception of his duchy, deprived of the position of Captain-General of the Church, and of the command of the troops and the galleys, as well as all his other offices, which brought him in an annual revenue of 72,000 scudi. The Marquis of Montebello lost the governorship of the Leonine City, and the command of the Papal body-guard.

When the Pope, whose voice was almost inaudible from pain and indignation, had finished, six cardinals approached the throne, two from each order, led by the Cardinal Dean, du Bellay, who petitioned for a mitigation of this severe sentence. Paul IV. refused the petition most decisively, and forbade, for all time, any such attempts. He then had Camillo Orsini, Ferrante di Sanguine and the Marquis of Montesarchio brought before him, and entrusted them forthwith with all military affairs. Then the Governor of the city, the Datary and the first secretary were called in, and forbidden, in the strictest terms, to obey the Pope's nephews in anything. Decrees corresponding to all these matters were at once to be drawn up. At the end of the sitting, which had lasted for two and a half hours, the Pope said to Cardinal Ranuccio Farnese that his father would not have been so foully murdered had Paul III. given a similar example of severity against his nephews. He ordered Cardinal Vitelli, who had had intimate relations with Carafa, to leave the Vatican, and caused a box to be placed there, into which everyone could put his complaints in secret.[1]

Even before the expiration of the twelve days Carlo Carafa had to go into banishment to Civita Lavinia, and his brothers to Gallese and Montebello. The whole of their following, their wives and children, and even their aged and quite guiltless mother, were also sent out of Rome. No defence was allowed to them, accused as they were of such grave crimes ; they never saw their uncle again. Diomede Carafa also was deprived of his office of castellan of the Castle of St. Angelo.[2]

[1] See the *Avviso of January 28, 1559, loc. cit. and the *letter of G. Aldrovandi, dated January 28,1559 (State Archives,Bologna).
[2] See PAGLIUCCHI, 133.

Only one exception was made ; Cardinal Alfonso Carafa, against whom nothing blameworthy could be proved, was allowed to remain in the Vatican, but he had to be most careful to make no attempt to intercede for his guilty relatives, against whom the Pope constantly expressed himself in the most severe terms, without, however, naming them.

The fall of the nephews had taken place so suddenly, and the lot of the men who in one night had sunk to the position of helpless and penniless exiles was so pitiable, that, especially as every sort of moral support was wanting to them, they could not resign themselves to their fate. All three hoped that the anger of their deeply offended uncle would, in time, pass over, and that they would then obtain forgiveness.[1] They had always been at variance with one another, and now, in their day of misfortune, they were more so than ever. The weak-minded Duke of Paliano lost his head completely and spent his time in vain longing at his castle of Gallese, divided between grief, fear and empty hopes. Carlo Carafa, who had been hit the hardest, kept his presence of mind even now, and before everything else, saw to the safety of his correspondence.[2] He had to live in a miserable little house at Civita Lavinia, a small place, in which all comfort was wanting. There, in view of the melancholy Campagna, he had plenty of time to enter into himself, but he did not think, even now, of doing so. All his thoughts and plans were directed to regaining, by any means, even the worst, his forfeited position. He still intended to do his utmost in the attempt to again deceive his old uncle, and move his heart to forgiveness ; but everything, the inter-

---

[1] The view that the nephews had again been taken into favour still prevailed in Rome at the end of February, 1559 (see a *letter to Cardinal Madruzzo in connection with this, dated Venice, March 4, 1559. Vice-regal Archives, Innsbruck). Cardinal Medici regretted in a *letter to Carafa, dated Milan, February 22, 1559, that he had not been present in Rome at the time, to prevent a rupture : " hora io voglio ben sperare che le cose s'accomodino " ; he offers his help in doing so. Original in the Cod. Barb. lat. 5698, p. 20. Vatican Library.

[2] Cf. the reports in ANCEL, Secrét., 40 and Nonciat., I., viii.

cession of the great powers, and especially Philip II., a simulated conversion, as well as a sham illness, were to prove vain.[1]

Paul IV., whose health was much affected[2] by grief and excitement, appeared to have completely effaced the remembrance of his nephews from his mind.[3] He remained inexorable, and indeed was bound to do so, since he had brought about the fall of his nephews, not on political, but on moral grounds. The more thoroughly he investigated the matter, the more convinced he became of the moral depravity of the brothers, of their disgraceful insolence, and of the way in which they had abused his confidence and compromised his government, and, above all, his reform work. Instead of his anger growing less with time, it, on the contrary, increased. The strict party, which was now coming much more into evidence, after having had so long to witness, with suppressed bitterness, the proceedings of the nephews, confirmed him in his resolution of leaving the guilty parties in banishment, of clearing out all their supporters, and of completely reorganizing the whole system of state affairs. Now only did he feel himself free from all worldly considerations. It was in this sense that Paul IV. remarked that the current year, 1559, was the first of his pontificate.[4] He wished to grant an audience every week to the envoys from the States of the Church, in order that he might hear all complaints himself. No one was allowed to write to his nephews, and they were not to know what he was doing. He provided himself with a special book in which he entered all their misdeeds. He took away the keys of the Borgia apartments, in order to keep them himself, and it was said that he

---

[1] The above is according to the very excellent account of ANCEL, Disgrâce, 42 seq., 55 seq. ; see also RIESS, 368 seq. It is also certain that Carafa continued to lead an immoral life after his fall ; see Studi stor., VIII., 255.

[2] See the *Avvisi di Roma of February 4 and 11, 1559 (Cod. Urb. 1039, p. 7 and 8. Vatican Library).

[3] Cf. SALVAGO in the Atti Lig., XIII., 757.

[4] See CARACCIOLUS, Collactanea, 65 ; cf. for this the remark reported by Pacheco in ANCEL, Disgrâce, 182.

intended to bless these rooms anew with holy water, as evil spirits had dwelt there.[1]

A complete reorganization of the council of state, appointed in the autumn of 1557, had already been effected by January 31st, 1559 ; at the head of this new body were Cardinals Scotti and Rosario, as well as the aged and disinterested Camillo Orsini, and to these were added distinguished prelates, such as Luigi Lippomano and Ugo Boncampagni. The Pope appointed bishop Angelo Massarelli as secretary. Orsini, who was as energetic as he was distinguished, immediately proceeded to clear away the Neapolitan toadies and parasites, with whom Carafa had filled all the offices ; most of these richly deserved to be subjected to a criminal investigation.[2]

On February 17th Paul IV. received the Roman Senators and the representatives of the States of the Church in the Hall of Constantine. In this assembly of about a hundred persons, he once more frankly acknowledged his previous errors. Incapable as he was at his advanced age of bearing the burden of government alone, and having always been completely ignorant of financial matters, he had allowed his nephews to manage affairs freely and they had shamefully abused his trust. Now, however, that he had been enlightened as to their corruption, he proposed to inaugurate a complete change ; those assembled, therefore, should lay all their complaints before him without fear. This was done in the fullest measure. When the Pope learned the amount of the new taxes, he cried out indignantly : " Dear sons ! I knew absolutely nothing of all this. Do not, however, be astonished at this, for those infamous nephews kept me shut up in my apartments, and only allowed me to know what suited them." To show his good will, he declared a part of the new taxes abolished. The Romans, who had already, in October, 1555, erected a statue

---

[1] *Avviso di Roma of February 8, 1557, loc. cit.

[2] Cf. Šusta's excellent treatise " Der Versuch einer Verfassung sreform im Kirchenstaat unter Paul IV." in the Mitteil. des Österr. Inst., Erg.-Bd. VI., 557 seq.

in honour of the Pope on the Capitol, now caused this to be adorned with a suitable inscription.[1]

In the course of February, the council of state undertook a thorough reorganization of the officials in Rome, and in the following month the provinces also had their turn. All the creatures of the nephews here also were replaced by new and trustworthy persons. The vice-legates were the next to be changed, a process which in many places was effected in a quite unusual manner. For example, the new governor, Giambattista Castagna, Archbishop of Rossano, arrived in Perugia at a late hour of the night, and without waiting for the dawn, he instantly summoned the council, presented his letters of credence, took the oath, and arrested the former governor. The lower posts in the government were also everywhere filled with new officials, most of whom enjoyed Orsini's confidence.[2] This admirable man did not propose to change the staff alone, but also the system of administration ; he planned a complete change in the constitution of the States of the Church, and a thorough reform of the finances. The deficit, which, hitherto, had been steadily increasing, was to be removed, partly by a discreet increase of the revenues.[3] Orsini, the soul of this political reform, also had the duty of watching the banished nephews. When he fell ill on March 31st, and died on April 4th, it was generally declared that his death had been caused

[1] See MASSARELLI, 330 and the *report of Gianfigliazzi of February 18, 1559, used by ANCEL, Disgrâce, 44. Concerning the statue on the Capitol, a work of Vincenzo de' Rossi, see the Decrees, dated 1555, XVI. Cal. Oct. and 1558, V. Cal. Nov. in the Cod. G-III.-58, p. 231 seq. of the Chigi Library ; cf. also RODOCANACHI, Capitole, 111, and LANCIANI, III., 206.

[2] See Susta loc. cit. 557 seq., who has also made use of the interesting *Diarium of an unknown member of the curia in the Cod. Urb. 852 of the Vatican Library. See also the Diario di N. Turinozzi, 13 seq. ; BONAZZI, Storia di Perugia, II., 224.

[3] For this cf. the excellent details given by Susta, loc. cit. The *Diminutione delle spese del state ecc^co fatte nel mese di Marzo 1559 dal s. consiglio coram papa, in Arm. 10, t. 45, p. 100 seq. (Secret Arch. of the Vat.)

by poison, which Carlo Carafa had caused to be administered to him. New suspicions were awakened on May 22nd, by the sudden death of the strict Cardinal Rosario.[1] Cardinals Reumano and Consiglieri, who were appointed on May 27th as members of the council of state, in place of the deceased, did not possess the necessary energy or expert knowledge. The choice of Gian Antonio di Gravina,[2] on April 3rd, as the successor of Camillo Orsini as Captain-General of the Church, was still more unfortunate. It is no wonder that the esteem with which the council of state was regarded, grew visibly less. This suited Cardinal Alfonso Carafa only too well; apart from a temporary break with the Pope, he still enjoyed his uncle's confidence and an ever increasing influence.[3]

Paul IV., therefore, did not gain a complete victory over nepotism; it is, however, owing to him, that nepotism on a large scale, which had done so much harm since the time of Callixtus III., and even more since Sixtus IV., received a decisive blow. In this way, one of the worst growths of the Renaissance days was uprooted, and the way laid open for the

[1] See ANCEL, Disgrâce, 57 seq. In addition to the sources given there, see also the Diario di N. Turinozzi, 15 seq., and the *Avviso di Roma of April 8, 1559 (Vatican Library, loc. cit.). According to this, April 4 is given as the date of Orsini's death. NORES (p. 271) wrongly gives April 2, following MASSARELLI (p. 330). Rosario's grave is in the church of the Minerva; see BERTHIER, 401.

[2] See MASSARELLI, 331.

[3] Cf. ŠUSTA, loc. cit., 563. During the Brussels legation of Cardinal Carafa, Alfonso Carafa had already partly replaced him as secretary of state (see ANCEL, Secrét., 25). Concerning the temporary loss of favour by Alfonso Carafa at the end of March, see Diario di N. Turinozzi, 15. The formal transference of all functions seems to have taken place at midsummer. On August 5, 1559, G. A. Aldrovandi reports: *Il card. di Napoli è adesso al governo delle cose appartenenti al stato (State Archives, Bologna).

Catholic reformation.   The Pope, after the fall of his nephews, worked for this with a lighter heart and undiminished zeal.[1]

[1] RIESS (p. 373) disputes the view, also held by RANKE (I[6]., 198) that Paul IV. after the fall of his nephews, " returned to his former intentions of reform," and in the last six months of his life " devoted himself passionately to the reform of the Church " as " not being testified by contemporary witnesses." It is a sufficient answer to this that Riess overlooked the treatise of ANCEL, Paul IV. et le Concile, which is so rich in matter, and which appeared as early as 1907, and in which (p. 25 *seq.*) proof is given that Paul IV., precisely in March, 1559, carried out " une réforme capitale," viz., that dealing with the duty of residence of the bishops.   Other proofs are also given in the present account, *infra*, Chap. IX., pp. 233 *seqq.*

CHAPTER IX.

FURTHER REFORM REGULATIONS.—THE NEW ORDERS.— PAUL IV. AND THE SOCIETY OF JESUS.

So strict a method of government was introduced into the Eternal City after the fall of the nephews, that the Jesuit, Nadal, was able to write that the reform of morals was accomplished.[1] New regulations concerned the precept of fasting,[2] and the restriction of public immorality ;[3] all offences of this nature were made punishable, in the case of both clergy and laity, with imprisonment and the galleys.[4] Paul IV. even forbade lawful pleasures, such as hunting and dancing, so that a correspondent wrote on January 21st, 1559 : " All pleasures have ceased here, just as if we were in the midst of Lent."[5] A Roman, who inquired of the Pope whether he would allow them to wear masks during the days of carnival, was refused with the remark : " Our nephews have put a mask on us for so long, that it will require much time to take it off.[6]"

[1] NADAL, Ephemerides,: Epist. P. H. Nadal, II., 64.

[2] *Avviso di Roma of February 4, 1559 (Cod. Urb. 1039, p. 8. Vatican Lib.).

[3] Cf. COGGIOLA, Capitolazione, 144.

[4] An *Avviso of March 11, 1559, announce that three camerieri were arrested in the Vatican with their paramours and were condemned by the Pope to " perpetua galea " (which was afterwards mitigated ; see *Avviso of April 8). The Bishop of Polygnáno was convicted of immorality, and was condemned in April, 1559, to life-long imprisonment ; he had to fast on bread and water for three months (see *Avviso of same date. Cod. Urb. 1039, f. 15, 20, 24. Vatican Library). See also CARACCIOLUS, 68 ; RODOCANACHI, S. Ange, 161 ; MASSARELLI, 334.

[5] *Avviso of January 21, 1559, loc. cit., 2[b] .

[6] " Non vi pare egli che questi nostri nepoti ci habbiano messo una mascara al volto che vi bisognera molto tempo a levarcela." *Avviso of February 8, 1559, loc. cit., 9 (wrong date in CLEMENTI, 215).

233

The most important reform which Paul IV. prepared and carried out after the fall of the Carafa concerned the episcopate. He had, for a long time past, seen, in the neglect, on the part of the bishops, of their duty of residence, a source of the gravest abuses, and he had made the most urgent representations to Clement VII. with regard to this very matter. In the great memorial of the commission of Cardinals to Paul III., in the year 1537, this part of the reform programme was also given due prominence.[1]   The Council of Trent had next, in 1547, in its sixth session, decreed that a patriarch, archbishop or bishop who was absent from his diocese unless he were lawfully prevented, or without proper and reasonable cause, should *ipso facto* lose a quarter of his annual revenues for the benefit of the poor or for repairs of churches ; should he remain absent for a further six months, he was to forfeit, in a similar manner, a second quarter of his revenues.   Should his absence be of still longer duration, he was to be denounced to the Pope in writing, by his metropolitan, or by the senior suffragan bishop of the province within three months, and the Pope would then take severe measures against him, or even depose him.[2]

In spite of all this, however, this deeply-rooted abuse was by no means eradicated.   In the letter of exhortation, in which Muzio demanded from the newly elected Pope the reform of the College of Cardinals and of the episcopate, reference was made to the many bishops who were living at the Curia without any proper reason, and the remark was made that these were useless plants in Rome, which should be set in other soil, where they might bear fruit.[3]   How fully justified this request was, is evident from the truly terrible fact that in February, 1556, there were no fewer than 113 bishops staying in Rome,[4] although they had been ordered to return to their dioceses in January, under pain of the most severe punish-

---

[1] *Cf.* Vol. X. of this work, p. 422, and Vol. XI., p. 209 *seq.*

[2] Sess. 6, de ref. c. 1.

[3] See Muzio's *letter of November 3, 1555, in Appendix No. 14 (Secret Archives of the Vatican).

[4] See ANCEL, Concile, 25.

ments.[1] In April, 1556, Paul IV. again made the most earnest representations to these prelates, who were so forgetful of their duty.[2] As all this was of no avail, he determined to adopt more severe measures.

On March 6th, 1559, all the bishops staying in Rome were summoned to a secret consistory, when the Pope communicated to them a bull, in virtue of which all bishops not actually serving the Holy See in some fixed office, had to repair to their dioceses within one month. Those who failed to obey were subject to the penalty of deposition.[3] The Pope made it perfectly plain that he intended to act in accordance with this bull. He remarked, in a threatening manner, that he would punish the disobedient more severely than the vagrant monks.[4] On March 21st he once more summoned the bishops, and again impressed this order upon them.[5] Only from ten to twelve bishops, who were engaged directly in the service of the Holy See, were allowed to remain in Rome ; all the others had to leave. By April 1st, a correspondent was able to announce that this important reform had been really effected.[6] Similar

---

[1] *Et di più che la S.S^tà . . . . voleva che tutti i vesçovi andassino a risedere ai vescovadi loro sotto protesto non vi andando privargli di vescovadi e d'ogni altra loro degnità ecclesiastica. Avviso of January 18, 1556, in the Cod. Urb. 1038, p. 125 of the Vatican Library ; cf. also ibid. the *Avviso of January 25, 1556.

[2] See in Appendix No. 30 the *report of Navagero of April 11, 1556 (Library of St. Mark's, Venice).

[3] See *Acta consist. (Consistorial Archives) ; cf. MASSARELLI, 330 ; Corpo dipl. Port., VIII., 103 ; Firmani Diaria, 514 ; Diario di V. Bello in LAEMMER, Melet., 210, and the *Avviso of March 11, loc. cit., 15.

[4] *Se non obedirano li tratterà pegio di quello ha fatto li sfratati. Avviso of March 18, 1559, loc. cit., 17^b .

[5] ANCEL (Concile, 25), only knows of this assembly, which is reported by V. Bello (loc. cit., 210 seq.) and *G. A. Calegari on March 25, 1559, to Commendone (Lett. di Princ., 23. Secret Archives of the Vatican).

[6] See the *Avvisi of March 18 and 25, and April 1 and 15, 1559 (cod. Urb. 1039, p. 17^b , 19^h , 22^b , 26. Vatican Library) ; cf. also

rules were made for the parish priests, and the Inquisition was already employed in carrying them out.[1]   In addition to this the reform of the Orders was being continued.[2]

While Paul IV. was enforcing the duty of residence on the bishops, the hand of death had already lightly touched him. The excitement caused by the unmasking and fall of his nephews had given a fatal blow to his iron constitution.[3] Since then he had become feeble in mind as well as in body. Nevertheless, he took part, in February, 1559, in the functions of Candlemas and Ash Wednesday, held congregations and granted public and private audiences.[4]   He reformed the expenditure of his court at this time by abolishing all unnecessary expenses, whereby very considerable economies were effected.[5]   At the end of the month, the consistory did not take place, as the Pope could not attend, on account of a swollen knee.[6]   His condition was still more serious in March,[7] but during Holy Week he had improved to a certain extent. Although he was still weak on his feet, he was able to be present at the functions and to pontificate in St. Peter's on Easter Sunday.   It could be seen, however, that he was suffering both in mind and body.[8]   His removal to the more airy

the *letter of Gianfigliazzi of March 29, 1559 (State Archives, Florence) and ANCEL, Concile, 25.

[1] See CARACCIOLUS, 87 ; ANCEL, loc. cit.

[2] Cf. supra p. 216 seq.

[3] Cf. supra p. 224.

[4] See in Appendix No. 52 the *Avviso of February 11, 1559 (Vatican Library).

[5] See Diario di V. Bello in LAEMMER, Melet., 209.

[6] See the *Avviso of February 25, 1559 (Cod. Urb. 1039, p. 11.   Vatican Library).

[7] See the Portuguese report of March 18, 1559, in the Corpo dipl. Port., VIII., 103.

[8] *Il Papa ha asseso alli offitii con molta sollicitudine et benchè sia debole nelle gambe non ha voluto mancare. Si vede che sta afflitto non meno della mente che dal corpo. Avviso of March 25, 1559, loc. cit., 19[b] (Vatican Library) ; cf. MASSARELLI, 330.

Quirinal, from which his friends hoped great things, could not take place on account of his feeble state.[1] In addition to all his other troubles, an irritation of the skin,[2] which so often appears in old age, now set in and deprived him of his rest at nights. On the feast of the Ascension he had to be carried to mass. All present were horrified to see him looking so ill. " He is going out," a contemporary said, " like a burning candle."[3] It was astonishing to see how he always tried to keep on his feet. When, on May 7th, the solemn procession ordered on account of the peace between France and Spain, passed through St. Peter's Square, the Pope took part in it on foot, which caused a great exhaustion of his strength.[4] He, however, was not thinking of death, as he wished to do a great deal more,[5] for he was just then issuing new and stringent regulations against immorality in Rome,[6] which led to the arrest of a great number of prostitutes.[7] On June 1st the bull against the vagrant monks, containing the strictest measures, was again enforced.[8] Paul IV. was occupied with reform literally to the very end. At the beginning of July he issued a decree to explain the last named regulation,[9] and adopted

[1] See the *Avvisi of April 15 and 22, 1559, loc. cit., 26, 28, cf. MASSARELLI, 326.

[2] The " resipilla " ; see *Avvisi of March 4 and April 22, 1559, loc. cit., 12, 28.

[3] See the *Avviso of May 6, 1559, loc. cit., 30ᵇ .

[4] See the *Avviso of May 13, 1559, loc. cit., 34.

[5] See the *Avviso of May 6, 1559, loc. cit. At the banquets to celebrate the papal election and coronation, which were held as usual and were very brilliant, the Pope begged the Cardinals to pray for his recovery. *Avviso of May 27, loc. cit., 44ᵇ .

[6] See the *Avviso of May 20, 1559, loc. cit. 36ʰ . On April 22, 1559, B. Pia reported from Rome : *Mons. Ferrantino è inquisito di simonia contratta nella risegna del vescovado d'Amelia che egli ha havuto et mi par che ci sia ordine ch'ei sia posto in prigione (Gonzaga Archives, Mantua).

[7] See COGGIOLA, Capitolazione, 144.

[8] See Editti, I., 111. Casanate Library, Rome.

[9] See the *letter of G. A. Calegari to Commendone, dated Rome, July 5, 1559 (Lett.di princ. 23, n. 2. Secret Archives of the Vatican).

measures for the reform of the monasteries in Tortona.[1] At
the end of the month he spoke of issuing a bull against those
bishops who sought to purchase a right to be present at the
Curia by relinquishing their bishoprics.[2] A month before his
death, Paul IV. issued a strict prohibition against members
of religious orders who had been consecrated bishops, receiving
offices and dignities on their return to their monasteries.
By this measure, strife among ambitious persons and many
other vexatious disputes, were once for all done away
with.[3]

The indefatigable and many sided activities in the cause of
reform displayed by Paul IV. during his reign had been
reported in terms of the highest praise to Hosius at the beginning of March, 1556, by the canon of Ermland, Samson of
Worein, who was then in Rome, and who was by no means
blind to the weaknesses of the Pope. He sets forth in a very
clear manner how the work of Catholic reformation had been
carried out, in spite of the fact that the Eternal City was, at
that time, converted into a place of arms. However much
Samson deplored the unfortunate war policy of the Pope, yet
the holy life of Paul IV., and his great severity against crime,
filled him with admiration. " Sodomites," he writes, " are
publicly burned ; on blasphemers and other criminals he
inflicts the most severe punishments. Abuses connected with
the disposal of benefices, such as reservations, the regressus
and expectancies, and similar pernicious growths, have been
completely abolished ; every kind of simony has been most
strictly forbidden, and thereby a very lucrative composition
removed ; different offices in the Curia, which had been
instituted merely as a means of providing money, have been
either entirely altered or done away with. He has further
ordered that only worthy candidates shall receive benefices,
and that nobody shall possess more than one." The canon

---

[1] See FONTANA, 451 *seq.*

[2] See the *Avvisi of July 22 and 29, 1559, *loc. cit.*, 62, 63 ; *cf.*
SANTAREM, XIII., 61.

[3] See UGHELLI, I., 763 ; Bull., VI., 565 *seq.*

further speaks of the Pope's efforts for the reform of the
breviary, the strict punishment of such as sin against the laws
of fasting, rendered still more severe by the Pope, and the
decisive measures against the Jews, those who practise illicit
intercourse, usurers, actors and buffoons.[1] Three years
later the Theatines, Geremia Isachino and Andrea Avellino,
could give the members of their Order in Naples a detailed
account[2] of the success which had already crowned the inflexible severity of Paul IV. against simonists, usurers, liber-
tines, non-observers of the laws of fasting, and the vagrant
monks. The appearance of the city was completely changed,
the people went more frequently to church and a moral
regeneration could be observed in all classes.[3]

All this was not due only to the severity of Paul IV., but also
to the example he gave. He was never absent from the sermons
which were given during Lent in the Hall of Constantine,
which all the Cardinals and prelates of the court were bound
to attend.[4] In the latter years of his life he even went so far
as to forbid entrance into the Vatican to all women. He

---

[1] Hosii epist. II., 673-674.

[2] In Italian in CARACCIOLO, *Vita di Paolo IV., in Latin in his
Collectanea, 62 seq., and in BZOVIUS, Annales, 1559, n. 34 seqq.
A document bearing the date, Rome, April 17, 1559, and the
title : *De rebus novis urbis Romanae gestis in bona fide pre-
scriptis in aulum Caesaream, in the Monastery Library at Zeitz,
is to the same effect.

[3] As in the first year of the reign of Paul IV., the regulation
issued by him that public prostitutes must attend sermons
bore good fruits, —82 of these unfortunates were converted
immediately, and more later on, of whom noble Roman ladies
then took charge—concerning this see a report of March 28,
1556, in ZIBALDONE, Notizie, anedotti, curios. et. docum. ined.,
I. (1888), n. 1 p. 4 seq. In other cities as well, e.g. Milan,
Paul IV. helped the conversion of the " meretrices " ; see his
*brief of May 2, 1558, in the Brera Library, Milan, Miscell. B. II.,
n. 32.

[4] *Report of an unknown person to Cardinal Madruzzo from
Rome, March 12, 1558 (Vice-regal Archives, Innsbruck).

observed the fasts most strictly, in spite of his great age.[1] He always took part in the festivals of the Church as far as his health permitted him. The dignified composure and simple piety which he displayed in doing so, made the deepest impression on everyone.[2] In truth he appeared on such occasions, says the Venetian ambassador, Mocenigo, as a really worthy representative òf Jesus Christ ; greater care than he displayed for the fitting observànce of divine worship was scarcely conceivable.[3]

The worldliness which had also crept into the house of God during the age of the Renaissance found an inflexible opponent in Paul IV. He forbade the disrespectful wandering about in the churches, under pain of excommunication, and especially the abuse of women being accompanied there by a following of gentlemen. He forbade, under the pain of excommunication, the begging of offerings for masses which poor priests carried on in the churches. No one could say mass in any Roman church without a written permission, which was bestowed gratis, but only after a strict investigation. Whoever dared to perform any spiritual function, without the necessary authority, was at once to be handed over to the secular power for severe punishment. The Pope had all offensive pictures removed from the churches.[4] We are reminded of his activity

[1] See *De rebus novis, etc. (Monastery Library, Zeitz) ; BROMATO, II., 489, 495, 500 seq. Concerning the Pope's strict fasts cf CARACCIOLUS, Collect., 72.

[2] See *letter of Navagero of April 4, 1556 (Library of St. Mark's, Venice) and *Avviso di Roma of January 22, 1558 (Cod. Urb. 1038, p. 287. Vatican Library).

[3] MOCENIGO-ALBÈRI, 48.

[4] Cf. CARACCIOLO, *Vita, 5, 8 ; CASTALDO, 150 seq. ; BROMATO, II., 497 seq. The proceedings taken against the " crocifissi in figura di vivi con quattro sole piaghe," and the removal of an improper picture from S. Maria Maggiore, are only mentioned here. There is no reference to the painting over of Michael Angelo's Last Judgment (cf. as to this our remarks in Vol. XII. of this work, p. 615 seq.). As tombstones in many of the churches were executed in an offensive manner, Paul IV. ordered their

in this respect by one of his medals, on which Christ is represented cleansing the Temple with a scourge.[1]

Paul IV. also endeavoured to increase the solemnity of divine worship by positive regulations. For this purpose he introduced a number of new arrangements, especially in the Papal Chapel. The adornment of the Pauline Chapel during Holy Week with a magnificent representation of the Holy Sepulchre is to be traced to him, as is also the custom of covering the streets of the Borgo with an awning of white linen on the feast of Corpus Christi, which was first done in the year 1557. In this year, as well as in the two preceding ones, and also in 1558, the Pope insisted, in spite of his great age, on carrying the Blessed Sacrament himself in the procession.[2]

Paul IV. also manifested his great devotion to the Holy Eucharist by giving orders to his fellow-countryman and court architect, Pirro Ligorio, to design a magnificent ostensorium for use at the Corpus Christi procession ; it was adorned with vine leaves of pure gold, and grapes formed of emeralds and sapphires. The Pope had intended to have a number of his ancient gold coins melted down for this purpose, had not Ligorio, to whom the destruction of these precious relics of antiquity caused the greatest sorrow, protested.[3]

The new tabernacle for the Pope's private chapel was to be of special magnificence. Giambattista da Pietrasanta had instructions to prepare four exceedingly beautiful columns of cipolino, while the ornamentation above was to be executed in bronze, after a most artistic design.[4]

removal, an order which Pius IV. carried still further ;   see CASTALDO, 150 ; SILOS, I., 417 ; RODOCANACHI, Capitole, 198.

[1] See VENUTI, 104.

[2] See MASSARELLI, 274, 291, 322, 323 ; *Report of the Genoese ambassador of May 28, 1558 (State Archives, Genoa) ; BROMATO, II., 499 seq. ; Rev. Bénédict, XXV., 62 seq. Expenses for the " Sepolcro " in the Pauline Chapel in the *Tes. segr., 1556, February and March (State Archives, Rome).

[3] CARACCIOLUS, Collect., 138 seq.

[4] See ibid., 137 ; cf. also Rev. Bénédict., XXV., 51 seq.

To Paul IV., who for the most part granted very few indulgences,[1] we owe the introduction of the indulgenced medal.[2]
The feast of St. Dominic, into whose order the Pope had wished
to enter as a young man, was transferred by him in 1558 to
August 4th, as the 5th, the day on which this feast was celebrated, was that of Our Lady of the Snow.[3] With regard to
the festival of St. Peter's Chair, Paul IV. issued a regulation,
to which he was partly led by his opposition to the false assertion of the Protestants that St. Peter had not been in Rome.
Even in the days of Leo the Great the feast of the Roman
Cathedra Petri had been celebrated in the most solemn manner
on February 22nd, in the basilica of the Prince of the Apostles.
Later on, in accordance with the two episcopal sees of St. Peter,
a distinction had been made, and the two feasts, of the Cathedra
of Antioch, as well as that of Rome, had been instituted.   The
Cathedra of Rome was, especially in the Frankish kingdoms,
kept on January 18th, while in Rome, now as before, it was
never celebrated until February 22nd, and indeed, strange to
say, for a long time as the feast of St. Peter's Chair at Antioch.
It seemed strange to Paul IV. that Rome, which owed its
unique position in the Christian world, above all, to the Prince
of the Apostles, should allow herself to be outdone in piety
and veneration for the first Pope by foreign churches.   He
therefore, on January 23rd, 1557, ordered that, for the future,
throughout Christendom, the feast of the Cathedra Romana
should be celebrated on January 18th, and that of Antioch on
February 22nd.   A bull, issued a year later, solemnly fixed
this for all time.[4]

[1] See LEA, Confession, III., 508 ; cf. 423, 555.

[2] See BROMATO, II., 499 n. On February 25, 1559, Paul
IV. again restored the old stations in S. Silvestro and S. Martino
ai Monti ; see Bull., VI., 556 seq.

[3] Bull., VI., 543 seq. and MASSARELLI, 325. The statements of
CIACONIUS (III. 831) and BROMATO (II., 500) concerning the feast
of the Assumption of Our Lady are erroneous ; see MORONI,
IX., 84.

[4] The bull " Ineffabilis " (Reg. Vat. 1851, p. 417), with correct
date in the Bull., VI., 530 seq., and a wrong one in the Bull.

Paul IV. repeatedly showed[1] how greatly he valued the old Orders, and it can easily be understood that, among the new ones, the Theatines were nearest to his heart. Marcellus II. had intended to call them to Rome, a thing which was done by Paul IV. in the first year of his reign. He assigned to them the church of S. Silvestro on the Quirinal, which was then almost entirely unbuilt upon, as a place specially suitable for the life of a strict religious order. The Dominicans, who carried on the services in this church, were removed to S. Niccolò in Campo Marzo, the care of which parish was united to that of SS. Apostoli. On November 17th, 1557, four distinguished members of the Theatine Order, Giovanni Marinonio, Bernardino Scotti, Paolo Consiglieri and Giovanni Antonio da Prato, took

bas. Vat., III., 34; cf. KRAUS, Roma sotteranea, Freiburg, 1879, 577 seq.; Freiburger Kirchenlex., II.[2], 2060 seq.; BÄUMER, Gesch. des Breviers, 416. The first ordinance from the Acta consist. (Romae die sabbati 23 Ianuarii, 1557, Congregatio generalis) in RAYNALDUS, 1557, n. 2. The bull of January 6, 1558, was decided upon in a consistory of January 7 (MASSARELLI, 320) and published on January 14, 1558. The *Acta consist. previously announce: "Primo introductus fuit dom. Guill. Sirleti [Ms: Ciurletti] protonotarius, qui legit libellibellum quendam continentem multas auctoritates, quod divus Petrus fuit Romae et ibi martirium sustinuit" (Consistorial Archives). The Pope spoke very eloquently in the consistory about the presence of St. Peter in Rome. See *letter of Cardinal Vitelli, dated Rome, January 14, 1558 (Cod. Barb. lat. 5711, p. 59. Vatican Library); see also Navagero in BROWN, VI., 3, 1143, and the Avviso published by BAUMGARTEN in the Röm. Quartalschrift, XXV., 53 *seq., but wrongly attributed to the year 1556. Paul IV. allowed the Portuguese the veneration of their queen, Elizabeth, who had died as a tertiary of St. Francis (CASTALDO, 151). When it transpired, at the beginning of April, that the body of St. Venantius had been found at Camerino, the Pope spoke of going there personally, and on foot, to show his veneration for this saint. B. Pia *reports this to Cardinal E. Gonzaga, dated Rome, April 9, 1558 (Gonzaga Archives, Mantua).

[1] Cf. Bull, VI., 490 seq.; RIPOLL-BREMOND, V., 41 seq., 44 seq., 46 seq.; BROMATO, II., 276.

possession of their new home.   The Pope bought a large garden
for the convent, and intended to rebuild the church, which was
to be joined to the Piazza SS. Apostoli by a great flight of steps,
similar to that of the Aracoeli.   The work was only begun when
Paul IV. died.[1]   There was no place where he liked to be so
well as with his Theatines on the Quirinal, and as late as April,
1559, he wished to retire thither for a longer stay.[2]   On two
occasions he honoured the convent by holding consistories
there.

The direction of the Theatine order, the privileges of which
were confirmed and added to, was undertaken by Paul IV.
himself.   On December 23rd, 1555, he dissolved the union with
the Somaschi, which had not stood the test of time.[3]   He liked,
especially in his reform work, to make use of the Theatines,
who, for the most part, kept modestly in the background.
Giovanni Marinonio was to have been made Archbishop of
Naples, but he refused so earnestly that Paul IV. had to give
way.   Bernardino Scotti also held out for a long time before
he accepted the cardinalate ; the Pope thought a great deal
of him, and Scotti rendered him great service in the work of
reform.   Paolo Consiglieri, one of the four founders of the
Theatines, was obliged to undertake the duties of maestro di
camera, but he persistently refused to accept the purple.[4]   It
is scarcely necessary to mention here that Paul IV. also promoted the interests of the houses of the Theatines in Venice
and Naples.[5]   The Pope especially valued the Theatine,
Geremia Isachino, as an outspoken counsellor, a man of prayer

[1] See SILOS, I., 325 seq. ; CASTALDO, 147 ; ANCEL, Disgrâce,
29.   The inscription in S. Silvestro in FORCELLA, IV., 42.

[2] Cf. supra p. 237, and the *Avviso of April 15, 1559 (State
Archives, Florence).

[3] *Brevia Pauli IV. Arm. 44, t. 44, n. 170 (Secret Archives
of the Vatican) ; original in the General Archives of the Theatines
in Rome.   Cf. SILOS, I., 336 seq.

[4] SILOS, I., 330 seq. ; BROMATO, 11., 274 seq.   Concerning
Scotti's relations with Paul IV. see MASIUS, Briefe, 234, 249.

[5] SILOS, I., 355. *Indulgenze di Paolo IV. per la casa de'
Teatini a Napoli. (General Archives of the Theatines in Rome).

and of the strictest penitential life. Paul IV. had summoned him to Rome from Naples in 1556,[1] and later on entrusted him with the direction of the house of the Order.[2]

After the conclave, the Barnabites resolved to send their superior to the new Pope, and to offer themselves to him for every kind of service. Paul IV., who had already supported the new Order in every way in his power, greatly appreciated this proof of devotion, and promised them his protection in all things. The reputation of the Barnabites had, at that time, been so widely spread that they received invitations to found colleges, not only from Italian cities, but also from Portugal and Ireland. These invitations, however, were not accepted, partly from want of members, and partly in accordance with the principle of the founders of the Order, not to spread the congregation outside Milan. Finally, however, in 1557, they were induced to found a college in Pavia. Paul IV. confirmed this establishment, which, to his great joy, worked entirely in the spirit of Catholic reform.[3]

Paul III. had endeavoured to allay the continual disputes between the Capuchins and the Observants. The Capuchins could only accept Observants with the permission of their superiors, and the same prohibition held good for the Observants with regard to the Capuchins. After the death of Paul III. the Capuchins regarded this regulation as having lapsed; Julius III., however, renewed it for the Capuchins, and, on their complaint, on February 15th, 1551, for the Observants as well.[4]

---

[1] See the *letter of Navagero of January 4, 1556 (Library of St. Mark's, Venice.)

[2] ANCEL, Disgrâce, 29; cf. BROMATO, II., 222.

[3] See BARELLI, 256, 258 seq., 264, 266 seq. The attempt, already made in 1552, to unite the Barnabites with the Jesuits, was again renewed in August, 1559, but again failed; cf. Arch. stor. Lomb., XXXVIII. (1911), 152 seq.

[4] Bull. Capuc., I., 24. The Congreg. ord. min. Ulixbon. was given permission by Julius III. on October 4, 1552, to wear the " cuculla " of the Capuchins; see WADDING, XVIII., 514.

Already, in the first year of the reign of Paul IV.,[1] the differences between the two Orders had grown more acute. In order to protect himself the better against the accusations of his opponents, the Vicar-General of the Capuchins, who was confirmed in his office in 1555, did not leave the Eternal City for two years ; it was only in 1557 that he began the usual visitation of his convents.[2] This Vicar-General, Thomas Tiferno, did not succeed in gaining access to Paul IV. until he had waited for six months ; he then, at last, in 1558, succeeded in getting the confirmation of the Order and of its privileges which he asked for, but the Pope only granted them orally, and without a brief. While he was absent from Rome on his journey of visitation, proceedings against the Capuchins were again going on at the Curia. His adversaries had gained the powerful Cardinal Carafa on their side ; the bull which pronounced the suppression of the Capuchins was already drafted, and there seemed no reason to doubt that Paul IV. would sign it, when the fall of the nephews took place. The chronicler of the Capuchins describes this storm against the new Order as the most severe it ever had to face, for the Capuchins had had no idea of the attack upon them, and had, therefore, been able to make no defence.[3]

The Society of Jesus had also to pass through critical days in the reign of Paul IV. On May 23rd, 1555, Ignatius of Loyola was in the middle of a conversation with P. Gonçalvez, when the sounds were heard which told that the Papal election was accomplished. It was soon known who the newly elected Pope was : Cardinal Carafa. When this name was uttered, Gonçalvez remarked that a cloud passed over the face of the

[1] Concerning the earlier relations of Paul IV. with the Italian Franciscan Observants, *cf.* the thorough and exact work of ED. D'ALENÇON : G. P. Carafa, vesc. di Chieti (Paolo IV.) e la riforma nell' ordine dei Minori dell' Osservanza, Foligno, 1912, which is rich in documentary material.

[2] BOVERIUS, 1555, n. 3 *seq.*, p. 527.

[3] BOVERIUS, 1558, n. 3, p. 552 *seq.* " Nulla hac saevior tempestas, etc." (p. 553). The Cardinal is not named, but it was certainly Carafa.

founder of the Society of Jesus. Later on Ignatius himself acknowledged to a confidant, that all the bones of his body had trembled at that moment.[1] This election might indeed be the means of destroying the whole of his life's work.

Ignatius and Carafa had got to know one another in Venice, as early as 1536, and had exchanged their views on many points of the religious life. Many differences in their opinions had thus come to light.[2] Carafa conceived a deep prejudice against Ignatius, which soon became still more bitter.[3] These two men, so essentially different in character, had yet another hostile encounter when, in the years 1553-1555, the relatives of a Jesuit novice of noble family sought to induce him to leave the Order, and Carafa procured a Papal indult for them. Ignatius, by counter-representations, succeeded in getting the indult withdrawn. Carafa must have felt all the more hurt as he had thus received a rebuff in a matter which caused a considerable sensation in Rome.[4] Even before this, the list upon which the Cardinals wrote down their contributions for the support of the German College did not contain the name of Carafa.[5]

It was, therefore, no wonder that the news of Carafa's elevation filled Ignatius with apprehension. After a short prayer, however, he quite regained his self-possession, and now did all in his power to win the heart of the new Pope.[6] On May 25th he informed his brethren of the election, and praised the very distinguished qualities of the new head of the Church.[7] A few months later he gave an account of the Pope's zeal for

---

[1] " Todos os ossos se lhe reuoluérão no corpo." Mon. Ign. Ser. 4, I., 198.

[2] Cf. Vol. XII. of this work, p. 24.

[3] Cf. Astrain, II., 29 seqq. ; Nadal, Epist., II., 15.

[4] A whole number of letters are concerned with this affair ; cf. Mon. Ign. Ser. 1, vols. 5-10, Register s. v. Cesari ; Epist. mixtae, vols. 3-5 ; Polanco, vols. 3-6, Register s. v. Cesari.

[5] Steinhuber, I., Tab. II.

[6] See Gonçalvez : Mon. Ign. Ser. 4, I., 198.

[7] Mon. Ign. Ser. 1, IX., 75 seq.

reform, and of the kindness he had so far shown to the Society of Jesus.[1]

Indeed, Paul IV. seemed as Pope to have forgotten the irritability of Cardinal Carafa. The first Jesuit who visited him was Bobadilla. The Pope received him in the most friendly manner, and embraced and kissed him. He spoke to Cardinals Morone and Truchsess in very favourable terms of the new Order. He then summoned Ignatius, insisted on his talking to him with his head covered, walked up and down with him in friendly conversation, and granted the favour which Ignatius asked.[2] His actions also corresponded to his words. The Pope appointed Salmeron to accompany the nuncio Lippomano on his mission to Poland, and discussed his plans for reform with Bobadilla, who was ordered to give him his opinion quite frankly. Paul IV. thought still more highly of Lainez; he forbade him to leave Rome, as he needed his advice, had a special room prepared for him in the Vatican, and thought of raising him to the dignity of Cardinal.[3] As members of the other Orders were allowed to preach in the chapel of the Vatican on great festivals, before the Pope and Cardinals, the Jesuits first received this honour under Paul IV.[4] It specially pleased the Pope that the Jesuits gave instruction in Christian doctrine to the poor people in the streets of Rome, he used often to praise them highly on this account.[5]

In spite of all this, however, the mistrust with which Cardinal Carafa's mind had been filled soon again got the upper hand. While the relations between Rome and Spain were daily becoming more strained, a report arose that the Jesuits, who were nearly all Spaniards, were collecting arms, in order, under certain circumstances, to come to the assistance of their countrymen, and Paul IV. ordered a search to be made at their house. Ignatius did not lose his head at this unexpected

[1] *Ibid.* 463-468.

[2] Mon. Ign. Ser. 1, IX., 359-363.

[3] *Ibid.* X., 310 *seq.*, 419.

[4] *Ibid.* X., 438 and MASSARELLI, 304, 320.

[5] NADAL, Epist., IV., 496.

suspicion. The governor of Rome wished to refrain from making the investigation, if Ignatius gave his word that there were no weapons concealed in the house. Ignatius thanked him for his confidence in him, but insisted that the house should be thoroughly searched from top to bottom. The suspicion was thereby proved to be quite unfounded.[1]

The fact that Paul IV. did not further his favourite undertaking was a far greater trial to Ignatius than this occurrence. The Pope did nothing for the Roman College, which Ignatius cherished as the apple of his eye ; it is true that at first he made promises to provide it with revenues, but all hope of getting anything from him soon disappeared.[2] Paul IV. had no sympathy with the German College ;[3] the support given by Julius III. was not continued, and in consequence most of the Cardinals withdrew the contributions they had promised. The college therefore got into terrible difficulties, and was brought by the high prices of 1555 to the very brink of dissolution.[4] Even in September, 1555, Ignatius, being unable to receive nine young Bohemians, whom King Ferdinand had sent for the Germanicum, had to give them shelter in the professed house of the Jesuits.[5] The forty-eight young men who had been promised in the autumn of 1555 for the German College, had all to be refused. For two years no German entered the college.[6] As early as February in the same year even Cardinal Otto von Truchsess, the zealous champion of the Germanicum, was so discouraged that he wished to abandon the undertaking.[7]

The inflexible firmness with which Ignatius, with steadfast trust in God, held fast to what he had once begun, was proved in the most remarkable manner in this very difficult position Prices were so high in Rome that the Cardinals and wealthy

[1] ASTRAIN, II., 32.
[2] Mon. Ign. Ser. 1, X., 533.
[3] STEINHUBER, I., 33 *seqq.*
[4] *Cf.* HOSII epist., II., 673.
[5] Mon. Ign. Ser. 4, I., 161 *seq.*
[6] STEINHUBER, I., 34.
[7] Mon. Ign. Ser. 4, I., 405.

nobles had to dismiss some of their attendants.   In addition to
the Germanicum, Ignatius had to support the Roman College,
and the professed house.   He had no money, and could obtain
no loans from his friends or from the banks, on account of the
exhausted state of credit.   In spite of this he declared to his
intimates that he would face the future with no less confidence
than when Julius III. and Marcellus II. had promised him
their support.   The Roman College, he declared, would have
overcome the worst of the present difficulties within six
months,[1] and as for the German College, the time would come
when it would possess too much rather than too little.   Filled
with this trust, he caused it to be intimated to Cardinal
Truchsess that he would take the whole burden of the German
College on his own shoulders, if the Cardinal should withdraw,
and that he would sooner let himself be sold as a slave than
give up his Germans.[2]   And indeed good friends were raised
up for him in his perplexities ; the German students whom
he could not receive in Rome, he distributed among the Jesuit
colleges in Italy and Sicily, and there they were maintained
like the other members of those houses.[3]   It is true that the
German students were, until 1558, reduced to a very small
number, but when, in that year, they began to increase, Lainez
combined a college for paying pupils of other nationalities with
the Germanicum, and from the sums received from these the
German students could be maintained[4]

It must have affected Ignatius even more painfully than the
danger to his establishments in Rome, that he was to see his
real life's work, the foundation of the Society of Jesus, just
then fully completed, endangered at the end of his days.   In
view of the peculiar ideas of Paul IV., there was always reason
to fear that he would unite the struggling Order with the
Theatines, or alter its constitutions in such a manner that the
special character of the Society of Jesus would be destroyed.

[1] Mon. Ign. Ser. 4, I., 352, 404-405.
[2] *Ibid.* 257.   STEINHUBER, I., 36.
[3] Mon. Ign. Ser. 4, I., 352, 404 *seq.*   STEINHUBER, I., 36.
[4] STEINHUBER, I., 45 *seq.*, 49 *seq.*

These fears only took a definite form after the death of Ignatius.[1] Pending the election of a new General, Lainez had been chosen as his representative. When, in September, 1556, he appeared before the Pope and begged his blessing for the impending General Congregation of the Order, Paul IV. at first received him in a very friendly manner, but soon adopted a sterner tone ; the General Congregation had to understand, he said, that they could decide nothing without the confirmation of the Pope ; too much importance should not be attached to former Papal guarantees, for what one Pope had granted. another Pope might repeal.[2] As the principal duty of the General Congregation was, apart from the election of a General, finally to arrange the constitutions of the order, it was quite plain what this remark portended. Harsh remarks of the Pope regarding the founder of the Order, who, he said, had been a tyrant, did not tend to improve matters.[3]

The Congregation had been fixed for the spring of 1557, but the Spanish Jesuits were unable to come at that time, since, on account of the war between Paul IV. and Philip II., all Spaniards were forbidden to go to Rome. The idea, therefore, occurred to the fathers assembled in Rome, of holding the Congregation in Spain.[4] This suggestion was very necessary, as it was of the greatest importance to the Order to have the constitutions, and, with them, the legal basis of its existence,

[1] *Cf.* for the following, ASTRAIN, II., 1 *seq.*, 7 *seqq.* ; NADAL, Ephemerides (Epist. II., 12-16, 50-59) and the documents in NADAL, Epist. IV., 98-147, 729-734.

[2] Astrain II., 7.

[3] NADAL, Ephemerides (Epist. II., 50) : " Erat enim minatus P. Ignatio : o colui, etc., Dixerat P. Ignatium tyrannice gubernasse societatem " (*cf. ibid.*, 54). Ignatius, he said, had been the idol of his followers (*ibid.*, 15).

[4] Already on October 28, 1556, Francis Borgia had written that they would rather have held the Congregation, say at Avignon, as Rome was too far from Spain (S. FRANC. BORGIA, III., 267). At the beginning of February, 1557, the Portuguese and Spanish Jesuits were all ready to start for Rome, when the fresh outbreak of war compelled them to remain (*ibid.*, 276, 279).

settled as soon as possible. On the other hand it was an exceedingly hazardous thing, on account of the war with Spain, to broach such a plan to the Pope. Paul IV., however, had raised no great objections when Lainez, in conversation with him, suggested the idea of a Congregation in Spain. Although most of the Jesuits assembled in Rome were at first decidedly opposed to the proposal, it was eventually almost unanimously accepted, provided the Pope did not refuse his permission.

In order to obtain this, Lainez again applied for an audience. Paul IV. received him kindly, and listened favourably to his reasons for the petition, but would not come to an immediate decision. Lainez, therefore, again presented himself at the Vatican after a few days. On this occasion, however, the Jesuit, otherwise so much respected by Paul IV., was refused admission to the presence of the Pope. He repeated his attempt a second and a third time, but the Pope was never able to receive him. At last, on June 20th, 1557, he met the Pope in a corridor in the Vatican, but Paul IV. walked past without deigning to cast a glance at him. Instead, he received orders through Cardinals Scotti and Reumano, to hand over the constitutions and rule of the Society of Jesus, as well as the Papal bulls; the Jesuits in Rome were, moreover, forbidden to leave the city without permission.

These unexpected orders came like a thunderbolt upon the house of the Jesuits, for the constitutions, the precious legacy of the founder of the Order, were in danger. Prayers and works of penance were ordered and readily undertaken, as if at the approach of a great misfortune.

The reason for this sudden change of front on the part of the Pope was to be found in one who was himself a Jesuit, Nicholas Bobadilla.

Bobadilla, one of the first companions of Loyola, was a man of difficult character, and had already caused considerable trouble ;[1] he did not approve of the constitutions of the order,

---

[1] Characteristics in NADAL, Epist. II., 52 *seqq.*; ASTRAIN, II., 12 *seq.*

as drafted by Ignatius. They appeared to him to be a " laby-rinth," and full of petty, unnecessary and over-difficult requirements,[1] and he therefore thought that they must be thoroughly revised and altered ; moreover, he was not pleased with the election of Lainez as General-Vicar. He considered that it was to be gathered from the Papal bulls that the govern-ment of the Order was to pass, after the death of Ignatius, to the whole of the original founders who were still alive. He passed sharp criticisms on the manner of administration adopted by Lainez in many of his regulations, and believed above all that it had been highly indiscreet of him to keep on returning to the proposal of transferring the Congregation to Spain. Bobadilla found a supporter in the discontented Frenchman, Cogordan, who caused a hint to reach the ears of Paul IV. that they only wished to transfer the Congregation to Spanish soil, in order to be better able to arrange the con-stitutions and the election of the General as they thought fit.[2] Hence the anger of the Pope, which was expressed by the demand for the constitutions and the other documents.

Lainez displayed great activity and zeal in meeting the threatened storm. He had the arguments of Bobadilla refuted by those who understood the institute of the Society of Jesus best, and especially by Nadal.[3] As Bobadilla desired to have the matter settled by a legal decision of the Protector of the Order, Cardinal Carpi, Lainez was quite ready to present himself before the latter for judgment. It then appeared that Bobadilla himself was beginning to lose confidence in his own cause, and sought pretexts for not having to appear before the judge. Lainez therefore claimed a decision from the Cardinal Protector, apart from any question o law ; this he received, to the effect that he was to remain General-Vicar, but with the obligation of taking counsel with the professed members of the Order in important questions. Nothing now remained for Bobadilla but an appeal to the Pope. In order to be before-

[1] NADAL, Epist. IV., 101, 110.
[2] Bobadilla's complaints *ibid.* 98 *seqq.*, 729 *seqq.*
[3] *Ibid.* 133-147.

hand with him, Lainez went himself to Paul IV. and asked him
to let a Cardinal investigate the whole matter. The Pope
listened to him very kindly, and even wished to leave the choice
of the Cardinal to him. They at last decided on Cardinal
Ghislieri.

A better choice could not have been made. Ghislieri went
himself to the house of the Order, and personally examined the
different fathers.[1] Bobadilla and Cogordan did not wait for
the decision, but contrived to be sent to Foligno and Assisi on
different work.

Paul IV. was exceedingly astonished when Ghislieri informed
him of the petty nature of Bobadilla's complaints. The
prohibition to leave Rome was now removed, and the constitutions and bulls were returned without alteration by the
Cardinals entrusted with their examination. The General
Congregation was postponed until May, 1558.

At length, after waiting almost two years, this assembly was
able to meet on June 19th, 1558, in order to give the Order a
new head.[2] At the very first ballot, thirteen of the twenty
votes fell to Lainez. Paul IV. had sent Cardinal Pacheco to
preside at the election. On July 6th, the Pope received the
whole Congregation at an audience, when he spoke most kindly
concerning the Order, and gave every father his blessing
individually.[3]

The Congregation next turned to the examination of the
constitutions of the Order. The question as to whether they
were to be altered was decided by their agreeing that the
statutes were " to be considered as fixed and binding, and
to be observed as they were entered in the original copy of

---

[1] Bobadilla's judicial examination in NADAL, Epist. IV.,
109 *seq.*

[2] Extracts from their documents (lost) in the *Institutum Soc.
Iesu*, II., Florentiae, 1893, 151-188. Memorial for the Congrega-
tion by Francis Borgia in the *Mon. hist. Soc. Iesu* : S. FRANC.
BORGIA, III., 342-353 ; Lainez' answer to it, *ibid.* 353-359.

[3] BRAUNSBERGER, II., 286-291. NADAL, Ephemerides in his
Epist. II., 62.

Father Ignatius."[1] The Congregation even went so far as to forego their right to alter any essential point in the work of Ignatius.[2] The Congregation confined itself, therefore, to unimportant details alone, and to several drafts of regulations outside the constitutions, the sanction of which had not been settled by the founder.[3]

The work of the General Congregation was already approaching its end when, on August 24th, the Pope sent an order by Cardinal Scotti that they were to consider whether prayer made in common in choir should not be introduced into the Order, and whether the term of office of the General should not be limited to three years.

The fact that Ignatius had given up prayer in choir[4] as being incompatible with the object his foundation had in view, had given offence to many people. Dominic Soto, of the Order of Preachers, maintained that a religious body without prayer in choir did not deserve the name of an Order.[5] Paul IV. personally held similar views. During the audiences which Lainez had had with him relative to the General Congregation, the Pope had several times made reference to this point. When the constitutions were handed back on June 20th, 1557, Cardinal Scotti remarked that it would perhaps be advisable to confer with regard to the introduction of a choir into the Jesuit Order.

It was also not the first time that the life term of office of the General had attracted attention. Not long before the election of the General the Pope had been anxious to have an alteration in this matter considered. As, however, he had allowed perfect liberty with regard to it, the Congregation had declared that they wished to keep to the constitutions. Cardinal Pacheco had expressly remarked before the election that the General should be chosen for life, and Paul IV. had confirmed and praised the election.

[1] Tit. 2 decr. 15.
[2] Tit. 2 decr. 16.
[3] Tit. 4 decr. 72 *seqq.*
[4] *Cf.* Vol. XII. of this work, p. 77.
[5] See ASTRAIN, I., 184.

As, therefore, no express Papal command existed, and the bulls of Paul III. and Julius III. had confirmed the giving up of the choir and the duration for life of the office of General, the Congregation replied on August 30th to the renewed proposal of the Pope that they were ready to obey, but that, in so far as it rested with them, they wished to abide by the letter of the constitutions. Lainez and Salmeron were sent to Paul IV. with a memorandum which contained this declaration.[1]

This, however, was never delivered, but an extraordinary scene took place instead. Hardly had Lainez and Salmeron been admitted when the Pope himself began to speak. At first he spoke quietly, as if to himself : Ignatius had been a tyrant ; he wished that, in future, the General's period of office should only last for three years, as was the custom of the Benedictines of S. Giustina, and those of Spain. With increasing excitement he then went on to speak about prayer in choir. The Jesuits were rebels because they would not accept it ; they placed themselves in this respect, on the side of the heretics (que ayudavamos á los herejes en esto) and he feared that a devil would one day arise from among them. Prayer in choir was essential for religious orders, and was founded on a commandment of God, since it was said in the Psalms : Seven times a day I have given praise to thee. He was therefore determined to introduce the choir among the Jesuits. He emphasized his intention in the strongest terms, and those whom he was addressing declared : " he looked at us with a curious expression of the eyes, and with visible excitement."[2]

Paul IV. continued for some time in this tone, while the fathers knelt before him, but at last he allowed the two envoys to defend themselves, and visibly calmed down during the explanations of Lainez, and at the end bestowed on the two fathers, who were returning to their provinces, some objects

[1] The letter is in the documents of the first General Congregation. *Institutum Soc. Iesu*, congr. I., decr. 47.

[2] Lainez has described the scene in a document signed by him and Salmeron ; copied in ASTRAIN, II., 613-614.

which he had blessed. Then he declared that Cardinal Alfonso Carafa would communicate his orders to the Congregation, which was done on September 8th. As the constitutions appeared in print in the same year, 1558, the Papal order with regard to the three years' duration of the office of General and to the choir, had to be added on the last page.[1]

These two regulations, however, were not yet made permanent laws ; for this the forms required for the publication of an ecclesiastical law were still wanting. They were simply orders which ceased to be in force with the death of the person who issued them.[2] On the advice of able canonists, they gave up the prayer in choir after the death of Paul IV. After three years of office Lainez declared that he was willing to resign the generalship, but in this case also they acted on the principle that after the death of Paul IV. his regulation was no longer in force.[3] Besides this, Pius IV. expressly repealed the decree

---

[1] Copy of this last page in SOMMERVOGEL, Bibl., V., 76 seq. After the death of Paul IV. this page was replaced by another.

[2] Ecclesiastical law distinguishes between laws and (general and particular) orders. A law, in the first place, relates to a *territorium* and remains in force after the death of him who issued it. A particular order relates, in the first place, to persons, and according to the general opinion of canonists, lapses with the death of the person who issued it. The proceedings of Paul IV. in this case may be explained by the fact that he hesitated to alter the bulls of Paul III. and Julius III., and therefore wished to make the Jesuits adopt prayer in choir, and a three years' period of office for the General, on their own initiative, and that he expressed his displeasure by the order of September 8, that his repeated hints to this effect had not had the desired result. He certainly must have known that he could not alter, by a merely verbal indication of his wishes, what had been confirmed by the bulls of Paul III. and Julius III., unless he first expressly repealed the regulations of his predecessors.

[3] ASTRAIN, II., 36 *seqq. Mon. hist. Soc. Iesu :* S. FRANC. BORGIA, III., 576. Bobadilla had now become quite reconciled with Lainez, and to the Constitutions. He wrote to Lainez : " My wish, with regard to the position of the General, is that it may always be for life. In the case of your reverence, may it

of Paul IV. and confirmed the constitutions of the Order.[1]

last a hundred years, and if you should happen to come back to
life after your death, may it last until the Day of Judgment ! "
ASTRAIN, II., 37.

[1] H. NATALIS, Scholia in Constitutiones, Prati, 1883, 275.
S. FRANC. BORGIA, III., 671 *seq.*

CHAPTER X.

PAUL IV. AND THE ROMAN INQUISITION.

THE fiery zeal with which Paul IV. confronted the worldliness and corruption in the Church was even surpassed by his care for the protection of the true faith. From the very first, the preservation in all its purity and the defence of this precious gift seemed to be one of the principal tasks of the supreme ecclesiastical authority.[1] Having been raised to the throne of St. Peter, he meant, as the lawful shepherd and teacher appointed by God for the preservation of the full, pure and unalloyed truth, to use the whole of his power to defend it, all the more as the dangers by which it was threatened on every side became greater.

Even more than in his measures for reform, Paul IV. displayed, in his attacks on those who deviated from the true faith, that pitiless severity and impetuous violence which were characteristic of all his actions. If one should employ every means to stamp out the plague, even to the destruction by fire of infected houses and clothing, one should proceed in like manner in fighting and extirpating the plague of the soul, which is to be prized so much more highly than the body.[2]

---

[1] Besides Vol. X. of this work, p. 371 *seq.*, and Vol. XII., pp. 504-510, and *supra* Vol. XIII., p. 215, *cf.* the testimony of Cardinal Ant. Carafa in his *Apologia (National Library, Naples) ; see also the letter of Ignatius of Loyola of August 13, 1555, in the Mon. Ign., Ser. 1, IX., 465.

[2] Paul IV. spoke repeatedly to Navagero in this sense. See the latter's *report of May 1, 1556, in which he quotes the following words of the Pope : " L'heresia è da esser perseguitata con ogni rigor et asprezza come la peste del corpo, perche ella è peste dell' anima Se si appartano, si abbrugiano, si consumano li lochi, et robbe appestate, perchè non si dee con l'istessa severità

The terrible weapons which the tribunal of the Roman Inquisition, as reorganized by Paul III., opposed to heresy, such as imprisonment, execution, and the forfeiture of the estates of those condemned to death, had been, until now, used in a comparatively moderate and merciful manner. As no permanent success had been attained in this way, Paul IV. determined to meet the efforts of the Protestant propaganda to win over Italy to its side with all the means at his command. He proceeded methodically and according to plan, displaying in so doing, a severity that no less a person than the celebrated Augustinian, Seripando, has described as inhuman.[1] These ruthless proceedings had, as a consequence, the fact that, after the death of the Pope, the fury of the populace broke out, and vented itself principally on the buildings of the Inquisition In the course of the acts of devastation carried out there, the documents of this tribunal were, for the greater part, destroyed. The authentic sources have thus been lost, and little enough remains with which to replace them. Not even the number of cases tried, or even of the executions which took place, partly in the Piazza Navona, and partly in the Campo di Fiore and the Piazza Giudea, can now be stated with any degree of accuracy.[2]

estirpar, annichilar et allontanar l'heresia, morbo dell'anima, che val senza comparatione più del corpo " (Cod. 9445, f. 180 of the Library of St. Mark's, Venice). A similar utterance of Paul IV. to Navagero in JENSEN, G. P. Caraffa, Copenhagen, 1880, 137, n. 1. Whether the four rules which, according to CARACCIOLO, *Vita 3, 5 (afterwards in RANKE, I[6]., 137, with inexact quotation) Carafa prescribed for himself, in the treatment of heretics, are authentic, appears doubtful. I consider them a later compilation.

[1] MERKLE, II., 405 ; cf. our remarks in Vol. XII. of this work, p. 508 seq. It is also quite wrong when MORONI (XXXV., 46) maintains : " dolcissima e paterna fu sempre la condotta tenuta dal tribunale di Roma."

[2] The statements of CARACCIOLA, *Vita di Paolo IV., 4, 8 (Casanate Libr.) are insufficient, and not always reliable ; they stand greatly in need of a critical investigation (cf. AMABILE, I., 138 n.). The statements of the *Libri delle giustizie della

The general decrees of the Inquisition escaped destruction
in the troubles of August, 1559 ; they are preserved in the

confraternità di S. Giovanni decollato (now in the State Archives,
Rome) upon which ORANO (p. 4 *seq.*) has drawn, are thoroughly
reliable, but not complete. According to this source, there was
executed in Rome, on the 15 Juni, 1556, Ambrogio de Cavoli
di Milano (*cf.* the *letter of G. A. Calegari to Commendone,
dated June 17, 1556 : " Domenica alli 14 fu una solenne abiura-
tione de' heretici ne la Minerva ; il lunedì seguente fu strangolato
et arso un frate Ambrosio da Milano sfratato già più anni, non
volse mai veder il crucifisso ne esser confortato." Lett. di
princ., XXIII., n. 8. Secret Archives of the Vatican ; *cf.* Arch.
stor. Napol., 593, n. 4), on August 19, 1556, Pomponio de Algerio
di Nola (*cf.* BROWN, VI., 3, App. n. 155 ; AMABILE, I., 166 *seq.* ;
DE BLASIIS in the Arch. stor. Napol., XIII., 569 *seqq.* ; BERT-
OLOTTI, Martiri, 19 ; VOLPICELLA, Racconti di stor. Napol.,
Naples, 1909, 27-88), on June 15, 1555, Gisberto di Milanuccio
Poggio di Città di Penne, on February 8, 1559, Antonio di Colella
Grosso della Rocca di Policastro, Leonardo di Paolo da Meola
da Pontecorvo and Giovanni Antonio del Bo ; one of these three,
however, was no heretic, as is evident from the *Avviso of
February 11, 1559 (see Appendix No. 52). *Cf.* also BERTOLOTTI,
Martiri, 26, and TURINOZZI, 7. The burning of a Waldensian
in 1558 is mentioned by BROMATO (II., 454). Carnesecchi was
summoned to Rome on October 25, 1557, and as he refused to
appear he was condemned in his absence on April 6, 1558. Particulars concerning him in a future volume of this work. With
regard to the action against Andrea Centani, Bishop of Limosso
and Cyprus, see, besides BUSCHBELL, 81, n. 6, the *Acta consist.
cancell., VII., of February 4, 1558 : *R. Saracenus proposuit
unam causam contra episcopum Limosien. depositionis ipsius
ab episcopatu propter heresim (Consistorial Archives). Concerning the further course of this affair see *Acta consist. of July
24 and August 9, 1559. According to Navagero (AMABILE,
I., 141) about 60 prisoners were in the dungeons of the Inquisition at the death of Paul IV. (according to BROMATO [II., 577],
there were 72). It can also be proved, not for Rome, but for
Bologna, that witches were burned there by order of Paul IV. ;
see BATTISTELLA, Il S. Officio e la riforma religiosa in Bologna,
Bologna, 1905, 168.

Archives of the Holy Office.[1] As these are, unfortunately, still closed to scientific research, a fortunate find in a private Roman library becomes all the more valuable. Two manuscripts of the princely house of Barberini contain the general decrees of the Roman Inquisition since the year 1555, from which the personnel of the tribunal and a number of important decisions may be gathered.

At the accession of Paul IV., four Cardinals, Juan Alvarez de Toledo, Carpi, Puteo and Verallo belonged to the Holy Office as Inquisitors-General. Of these, only Toledo and Carpi took part in the sitting of the Inquisition which Paul IV. held on September 1st, 1555, at his summer residence in the palace of S. Marco. On this occasion, the long trusted commissary-general, Michele Ghislieri, and the assessor, Giovanni Battista Bizzoni, received from the Pope the same full powers to conduct legal proceedings in questions of faith against all persons, no matter how high their position, as those possessed by the Cardinal-Inquisitors.[2]

Paul IV. held a specially solemn sitting of this supreme tribunal of the faith on October 1st, 1555. Of the Cardinal-Inquisitors, Toledo, Carpi and Puteo were present ; Verallo was absent on account of severe illness. The Pope had also summoned the highest officials of Rome to this sitting. Before these he made the following statement : After God had chosen him to be the head of the Church, he considered it his duty to place matters of faith before all others, for faith was the essence and basis of Christianity. He had arranged, therefore, that the Commission of the Inquisition should take precedence of all the other bodies in Rome, and its members should be respected by all the other officials accordingly. They were to

[1] *Cf.* Vol. XII. of this work, p. 508. It is evident from a manuscript in the Classense Library, Ravenna, that other documents of the said archives also escaped destruction after the death of Paul IV. This manuscript contains : *Gabrielis patriarchae Alexandrini litterae ad Paulum IV. arabice scriptae ex ipsis originalibus quae cum sua versione latina in officio s. Rom. et univ. Inquisitionis servantur transcriptae.

[2] See PASTOR, Dekrete der römischen Inquisition, 14.

afford the members of the Inquisition every assistance, including that of the secular armed force.   The favour of the Pope
would depend upon the degree in which each of them promoted
the work of the Inquisition.[1]

The three Cardinals named, as well as the commissary-
general and the assessor, had been for years tried members of
the Holy Office ; there seemed, therefore, to be every guarantee
that the tribunal would perform its duties with the severity
which Paul IV. considered necessary as a defence against the
religious upheaval.   In spite of this, however, Paul IV.
insisted on being present at all the principal sittings.   On
April 18th, 1556, the Thursday in each week was fixed for
these.[2]   Nothing was allowed to interfere with the Pope's
taking part in these sittings, an innovation which attracted
much attention.[3]   The fulfilment of this duty seemed to him
the most important of all.   Navagero reports : " Of the three
days which are devoted to the consistories, Monday, Wednesday, and Friday, and the two days for the court, Tuesday and
Saturday, the Pope misses many, but he never fails to be
present at the Thursday sitting of the Inquisition, in which he
usually takes part personally, whatever may come in the way.
I remember that at the news that Anagni had fallen, everyone
in Rome flew to take up arms, and feared that their lives and
property were in danger.   The Pope, however, remained calm ;
it was the day for the Inquisition, and he spoke quietly of the
matters that concerned it, as if there were not the slightest
thought of war, or as if the enemy were not before the gates."[4]

All the other correspondents are also agreed that nothing
lay so near to the heart of Paul IV. as his Inquisition.[5]   In

[1] *Ibid.* 15 *seq.*

[2] *Ibid.* 18.

[3] *Cf.* the *report of the Genoese ambassadors, Giustiniano
Fiesco and Lorenzo Grimaldi, dated Rome, May 28, 1556 (State
Archives, Genoa).

[4] NAVAGERO-ALBÈRI, 382.

[5] ADRIANI. (V. 239 ; *cf.* 344) says that he devoted the greater
part of his time to it.   *Il pontefice, writes Navagero on August
5, 1557, mangia ancor ritirato, pur vien detto che sta bene et

spite of the financial stress, he allotted 12,000 scudi for the renovation of the building in the Via Ripetta,[1] which was destined for it. By a Motu Proprio of February 11th, 1556, he invested this house with all the privileges enjoyed by the palaces of the Pope and the Cardinals, and gave the officials exemption from taxes.[2]

The number of the members of the tribunal was increased, in the autumn of 1556, to eight ; besides Toledo, Carpi and Puteo, Cardinals Medici, Scotti, Rebiba, Reumano and Capizuchi now belonged to it.[3] The four last named, who had been raised to the purple by Paul IV., fully shared his strict views ; Rebiba had, as commissary of the Roman Inquisition in Naples, given convincing proofs of this.[4]

It was decided on April 23rd, 1556, that whoever should prejudice the Inquisition by the violation of its secrecy should incur the sentence of excommunication, *latae sententiae*. A year later it was decreed that the members of the Inquisition who belonged to the clerical state, upon whose judgment and sentence the shedding of blood under torture or death should ensue, were liable to no censure or irregularity. On October 28th in the same year, the same exemption was extended to all the officials of the Holy Office.[5]

A witness worthy of belief testifies that Paul IV., at a sitting of the Inquisition, reminded the Cardinals how often he had made representations to Julius III. concerning the too

hoggi è stato nella congregatione sull' inquisitione fin 23 hore (Court Library, Vienna). This ardour was continually increasing.

[1] *De rebus novis urbis Romanae gestis (see *supra* p. 238). Manuscript in the Monastery Library, Zeitz.

[2] Motu Proprio of February 11, 1559 (Secret Archives of the Vatican) ; see Appendix No. 26. Concerning the situation of the house of the Inquisition see Arch. d. Soc. Rom., I., 139.

[3] *Cf.* PASTOR, Dekrete 20. MASSARELLI, 302 must be rectified in accordance with this ; he names only six Cardinal Inquisitors until January, 1557.

[4] See AMABILE, I., 214.

[5] See PASTOR, Dekrete, 18.

lenient proceedings of the tribunal.[1] Now, at any rate, exactly the opposite was the case. The Inquisition acted in such a manner that even strict Catholic critics expressed disapproval, and reminded them that in all the proceedings which their duty laid upon them charity to the sinner must not be lost sight of, a thing which Christ Himself had taught and practised.[2]

Fateful above all was the extension of the Inquisition's sphere of activity far beyond the domain of actual religious doctrine, which was given to it by Paul IV. Political matters, which, in Spain and also in many Protestant countries, were often combined with religious questions in proceedings against heretics, had hitherto been excluded from the Inquisition in Rome. Paul IV. paid no attention to this. In the war with Spain, Count Niccolò of Pitigliano, who belonged to the Orsini family, and who had commanded the Papal cavalry, was suspected of having an understanding with the enemy, and was taken to the Castle of St. Angelo as a prisoner of state. He was even kept there after the peace of Cave. The French ambassador, who, in October, 1557, intervened on behalf of the Count, learned that proceedings were to be taken against him by the Inquisition because he had had a Jewess as his mistress. On his asking whether he should be regarded as a heretic on that account, he was informed that the Count was accused of heresy because he had driven religious orders out of his territory and had held heretical opinions. The ambassador laid stress on the fact that the Count had proceeded against the religious as political traitors, and for the safety of his dominions, but not to promote heresy or to refuse respect to religion. The accusation, however, could not be proved, and the Count was eventually set at liberty.[3]

---

[1] See the declarations of Cardinal Reumano taken from the documents of the Carafa trial and quoted by BRUZZONE in La Cultura, N.S.I. (1891), 434.

[2] See Seripando in MERKLE, II., 405.

[3] *Cf.* RIBIER, II., 671, 710, 715, 720. It may be assumed that the dispute with Philip II. also came before the Inquisition

A whole number of immoral misdemeanours, which had nothing to do with a court for the preservation of the Catholic faith, were also given over to the Inquisition for treatment and punishment, which necessitated a further increase of the officials of the tribunal.   As early as October 17th, 1555, Paul IV. renewed the regulation of his predecessor, Julius III., that the crime of blasphemy should be dealt with by the Holy Office.[1]   A decree of February 1556 laid it down that all those who had sinned against the commandment of fasting should be punished by the Inquisition.[2]   The authorities also inform us that those guilty of outrages on maidens, procurers and sodomites were to be brought before the same tribunal.[3]

Not only the punishment of these and other similar crimes, but also everything which the Pope described as " simoniacal heresy," such as the sale of the sacraments, the ordination of those under age, and abuses in the matter of benefices, were all to be dealt with by the Inquisition.   " We are of opinion," said Paul IV., in July, 1557, " that no tribunal is more honourable or works with greater zeal for the glory of God than the Inquisition, and we have therefore resolved to refer everything to it that is connected with the articles of faith or can be brought into relation with them."[4]   The increase of the members of the tribunal to fifteen Cardinals was certainly in con-

(see BROWN, VI., 3, App. n. 167), as it was also connected with ecclesiastical matters ; cf. supra p. 127.

[1] See PASTOR, Dekrete, 17.

[2] Navagero reported on February 16, 1556 : *Sua Stà a fatto far un bando che siano commessi al inquisitione colloro che non farano la quadrigiesima, eccetti li amalati, a quali sia licito romperla con consenso .de' medici et con licentia delli deputati a tal cargo ; ha commesso similmente all' inquisitione li biastematori (Cod. Marc. 9445, f. 120b. Library of St. Mark's, Venice).

[3] See the *Avviso of August 21, 1557 (Vatican Library) in Appendix No. 39 and Nonciat. de France, I., xxix seq. ; also ORANO, xiv. and PASTOR, Dekrete, 18.

[4] See Navagero's *report of July 16, 1557 (State Archives, Venice), translated in BROWN, VI., 2, n. 966 ; cf. supra p. 203.

nection with this.[1] On October 21st, 1557, all the powers
which the members of the Fabbrica di S. Pietro and the Penitentiary possessed with regard to the absolution of simony were
recalled. On November 25th Paul IV. decreed that simonists
should in every case, even in questions of civil law, be treated
as heretics.[2] In December in the same year he transferred the
whole of the matters dealing with reform to the same dreaded
tribunal.[3] On July 16th, 1556, it was ordered that in future,
no one was to found an Order without permission from the
Inquisition.[4]

The Inquisition was in this way overloaded with an immense
amount of business foreign to its work ; its functions were
chiefly to act as the supreme court of morals.[5] Even a painter

[1] In the exceedingly rare *Index auctorum et librorum qui ab
officio s. Rom. et univ. Inquisitionis caveri mandantur* (RIMINI,
1559 ; *cf.* HILGERS, 492), of which only one copy (Rome, Bibl.
Alessandrina, N., f. 204) is preserved. it is stated on p. 27 that
the *Nomina ill. rev. cardinalium inquisit. general. per univers.
orb. christ. contra haeretic. pravit. a S. Sede Ap. deputatorum* are :
Carpi, Pacheco, Saraceni, Puteo, Scotti, Diomede Carafa (also
named again later on !) G. Savelli, G. Asc. Sforza, Rebiba, Reumano, Capizuchi, V. Rosario, Ghislieri, Dolera and Medici.
The oldest member of the tribunal on the list is Cardinal Juan
Alvarez de Toledo, who died on the 14/15 September, 1557.
As Cardinal Pacheco only received the title S. Balbinae, which he
bears in this list, on September 20, 1557, the list must have been
drawn up between September 15 and 20, 1557. At the end of
1558 the young Cardinal Alfonso Carafa was called into the Inquisition, which was considered a special mark of distinction :
" dove non si soleva admettere se non li vecchi." *Avviso
of December 3, 1558 (Cod. Urb. 1038, p. 355. Vatican Library).

[2] See PASTOR, Dekrete, 22 *seq.*

[3] See *supra* p. 207 *seq.*

[4] See PASTOR, Dekrete, 19 *seq.*

[5] On November 20, 1557, Bernardino Pia reports to Cardinal
E. Gonzaga from Rome : *Non heri l'altro in congregatione
d'inquisitione S.S.ta fece un ragionamento molto longo contra
a ruffiani di donne dishoneste et de' giovanetti, et vuole che
la Sma Inquisitione severissimamente proceda contra quelli et

who had designed a crucifix which appeared improper, was
summoned before the Inquisition, and tortured![1] The
greatest terror was aroused, as all the strict machinery which
was directed against heresy, was now set in motion against
the simonists.[2]   These terrors were increased when, not only
obstinate heretics, but also sodomites and polygamists were
liable to be condemned to death.[3]

If the great extent of the moral corruption which the
Renaissance period had left in Rome,[4] allows such sharp
measures on the part of Paul IV. to appear intelligible, it is
quite incomprehensible that he should also have had all matters
connected with reform placed under the Inquisition.   What
required improvement in this connection had sprung from such
complicated relations, and had branched out into so many
ramifications, that the original character of the tribunal,

massimamente contra i padri, madri e fratelli che ne fanno
professione in servigio delle loro figliuole o sorelle (Gonzaga
Archives, Mantua).

[1] See the report of the Portuguese ambassador of December
10, 1558, in the Corpo dipl. Port., VIII., 73.

[2] The Acta consist. cancell. VII. for October 11, 1557, report an
example : *Commissio causae contra Io. Franc. Poliasca, episcopum Lunen. et Sarzan. . . . Et quia materia concernebat
materiam symoniacam S^{tas} Sua cognitionem et decisionem causae
quoad symoniam commisit officio sanctissimae inquisitionis
(Consistorial Archives).

[3] See the *Avviso of February, 11, 1559 (Vatican Library).
This procedure against sodomites was transferred to the In
quisitors, Rebiba and Ghislieri, on November 25, 1557 (see PASTOR,
Dekrete, 23).   It is evident from the exceedingly rare work of
ALBITIUS : De inconstantia in iure admittenda vel non (Amstelae-
dami, 1683, 349) that a decree of Paul IV. of June 17, 1559,
laid it down " quod miscentes in sortilegiis hostiam consecratam
debent etiam pro prima vice tradi brachio seculari."

[4] Sodomy and blasphemy appeared to the Romans to be
habitual crimes, which ought not to be punished severely (see
the Avviso in Challoner's report in STEVENSON, I., n. 1287).
Cf. Giorn. stor. d. lett. Ital. II. 141 seq. to see what immoral lives
were led by the students of that period.

founded for the maintenance in purity of matters of faith, was completely lost sight of by reason of these new measures, and a quite unnatural preponderance in the ecclesiastical organization had to be conferred on it. Besides, what might not be understood under the term " simoniacal heresy ? " Was it not possible for men to be persecuted as heretics, who had really only been guilty of want of prudence ?

The right, already bestowed upon the Inquisitors by Paul III., of delegating in all places far-reaching powers to clerics who were experienced in theology or jurisprudence, was extensively employed by Paul IV. He particularly made use for this purpose of the Dominicans, to whom the task of discovering heretics had long been entrusted. He sent out Dominicans as early as June, 1555, and again in October, 1557, with the title of Commissary-General, who, limited to no fixed districts, were to take measures against the spread of heresy. They had powers to proceed against anyone whose opinions appeared to be open to suspicion, even against bishops, archbishops and patriarchs ; they were also to rouse the bishops and inquisitors who seemed to be inactive in the discharge of their duties, to a more strict observance of them.[1]

Paul IV. greatly valued the Dominican, Michele Ghislieri, whom Julius III., in 1551, had appointed as commissary-general of the Roman Inquisition. Ghislieri did everything that lay in his power to meet every danger which threatened the purity of the faith. Of the correspondence which he carried on with the Inquisitors, only that with the Inquisitor of Genoa, the Dominican, Girolamo Franchi, consisting of about fifty letters, from 1551 to 1559, has been preserved.[2] From

---

[1] See, RIPOLI, Bull. praed., V., 43 seq. ; BROMATO, II., 457.

[2] I discovered this important source, which BUSCHBELL as well as ROSI (La riforma religiosa in Liguria : Atti d. Soc. Lig., XXIV., 557 seq.) have overlooked, in the *Cod. E. VII., 15 of the University Library, Genoa. The Codex, which also contains a number of documents from the time of Pius IV., to which I shall return later, comes originally from the archives of the Genoese

these, mostly autograph letters of Fra Michele Alessandrino, as Ghislieri was called, after his birthplace, we can see how indefatigable he was in the discharge of his duties. This correspondence was concerned principally with members of the religious orders in the district of Genoa, who had wandered from the faith ; one letter is concerned with disseminators of heresy in the Island of Chios.[1] As soon as an investigation was instituted, Ghislieri directed his attention, above all, to getting acquainted with the accessories. The remark of Ghislieri's biographer, that he was exceedingly severe in obstinate cases, but mild to those who repented,[2] is borne out by these original documents. A letter of June 20th, 1556, is of interest ; in this, in agreement with the Roman Inquisition, and even with Paul IV., the punishment of the galleys is only recommended for those ecclesiastics whose flight cannot be prevented in any other way. Those concerned should be made to wear the yellow dress with the red cross for some years, deprived of the power of hearing confessions and preaching, and enclosed in a monastery, where fasting and prayer should be imposed on them as a penance. The punishment of the galleys should only be employed for the Marani, who had, for the most part, only the intention of deceiving the credulous, and for incorrigible rogues.[3]

The future saintly Pope, Pius V., gives expression to his sentiments in various letters, in which the patient bearing of calumny is recommended, as the calumniator thereby injures himself more than his victim. Whoever wishes to serve God and the Holy Office, says Fra Michele, on September 3rd, 1556, to the Inquisitor of Genoa, must not fear threats, but only God, and must keep truth and justice before his eyes, come

Inquisition, which were dispersed in 1797. Rosi (*loc. cit.*, 595) only knew of the few fragments which have reached the State Archives in Genoa ; " le altre," he says, " presero vie che non abbiamo potuto scoprire."

[1] See the **letter of November 11, 1557.

[2] MAFFEI, Vita di Pio V., I, 7, p. 35.

[3] See the *letter of June 20, 1556, in Appendix No. 31.

what may.[1] When Paul IV. raised[2] this man, who was so indefatigable in combating heresy, to the bishopric of Sutri and Nepi, on September 4th, 1556, he took care not to withdraw him entirely from his former activities.

As the office of commissary-general of the Inquisition could not be united to that of a bishop, Ghislieri was appointed prefect of the palace of the Inquisition.[3] The reception of Ghislieri into the Sacred College in March, 1557, brought with it a further change in his position, and an extension of his authority. On December 14th, 1558, Cardinal Alessandrino was raised to the position of Grand Inquisitor of the Roman Church for life. This office was, in future, like that of the Grand Penitentiary, only to be filled by a member of the Sacred College, and was, moreover, to continue after a vacancy occurred in the Papal throne. All the Inquisitors, delegates as well as bishops, were to look upon the Grand Inquisitor as their supreme head, in all matters connected with questions of faith.[4]

Anxiety for the preservation of the faith in all its purity was also the reason for the exceedingly strict regulations which Paul IV. enacted against the Jews, at the very beginning of his reign. The natural reaction against the great, and in many

---

[1] See the *letters of August 29 and September 3, 1556 (University Library, Genoa) in Appendix Nos. 32 and 33.

[2] M. Ghislieri resists the acceptance of this dignity ; see Soriano in ALBÈRI, Relaz., Ser. 2, IV., 200 seq.

[3] MAFFEI, Pio. V., 38 seq.

[4] Ghislieri was not, as BENRATH (Herzog's Realenzyklopädie, XV[3]., 439) states, appointed " Commissary-General " of the Inquisition by Paul IV., but inquisitor maior et perpetuus. The passage in question from the Acta consist. has already been quoted by MAFFEI (Pio V., 45), but with the wrong date of September 14, which is also given by BROMATO (II., 458). The correct date : die mercurii 14 Decembris, 1558, is in the *Acta consist. cancell., VII., 136[b] (Consistorial Archives). Die martis 15 decemb., 1558, in RAYNALDUS, 1555 n. 23 is an error. The taking of the oath by Ghislieri took place on December 16, 1558 (see GULIK-EUBEL, III., 38). The statement of FIRMANUS (p. 512) is thus explained.

cases certainly excessive, indulgence which the Popes of the Renaissance period, especially Alexander VI., Leo. X., and lastly Paul III., had shown to the Jews, was already making itself felt under Julius III.   Paul IV. went much further than his predecessor.   His bull of July 14th, 1555, ordained that, for the abolition of the prevailing abuses, the Jews in Rome, and in the other cities of the States of the Church, should live quite apart from the Christians, in a quarter or street possessing only one entrance and exit.   It was further decreed that not more than one synagogue should be allowed in any city ; the Jews were not allowed to acquire any real estate, and were to sell any such in their possession to Christians within a fixed period.   As a distinguishing mark they had to wear a yellow head-dress.   They were forbidden to keep Christian servants, to work in public on Christian holydays, to enter into close relations with Christians, to draw up mock contracts, to make use of another calendar, or to use any other language in their commercial affairs than Italian or Latin.   Pledges on which they had lent money were not to be sold until eighteen months after the payment had become due.   Finally the Jews were not to trade in grain or any other article for human consumption, they were not to treat Christians in the capacity of physicians, they were not to allow themselves to be addressed as Sir by poor Christians, and they were to observe strictly the communal laws of any place in which they were living.[1]

The carrying out of these strict regulations was taken in hand at once.   At the end of July, 1555, the Jews first appeared in their yellow hats, which they also had to wear in Venice. Many of them preferred to dress entirely in yellow, so that the sign might be less noticeable.   They had offered the Pope

[1] Bull. VI., 498 *seq.*   The contents of the bull are very frequently not given correctly, even in REUMONT, III., 2, 532.   *Cf.* ERLER in the Archiv für Kirchenrecht, LIII., 46 *seq.*, in which Grätz is justly reproached with having accepted the statement, which is in such bad taste, of the Jewish historian, Joseph ha Cohen. VOGELSTEIN-RIEGER (II., 152) date the bull on July 12, and complain that Paul IV. has been canonized !   The wrong date is also in BERLINER, II., 2, 3 ; *ibid.* 5 the order for carrying out the wearing of the head-dress.

40,000 scudi for the withdrawal of the bull, but in vain.[1] In the autumn, a beginning was made in Rome with the marking off of a strictly separate quarter of the city, such as already existed in Venice. This Jewish quarter, which was enclosed by walls, was situated in the low-lying river district, extending from the Theatre of Marcellus and the Ponte Quattro Capi up the river as far as the palace of the Cenci, while its width lay between the Tiber and the ruins of the Portico of Octavia.[2]

The bull was carried out in Bologna as early as August, 1555, the Ghetto there receiving the name of Inferno.[3] The sale of

[1] See the contemporary report in the Rev. des études juives, XX., 68; cf. MASIUS, Briefe, 515; BERLINER, II., 2, 7; RODO-CANACHI, 40 seq.; see also Cartas de S. Ignacio, V., 288 seq.

[2] I find in the *Introitus et exitus 1555 (State Archives, Rome) marked on p. 94: " 13 Sept. scuta 100 Silvestro de Peruzzis architecto pro fabrica muri pro claudendo Iudaeos "; p. 99: 9 Octob. " scuta 100 " to the same; p. 108: 14 November, again " scuta 100 " to the same for the same purpose (cf. BER-LINER, II., 2, 4-5; RODOCANACHI, 41). In the letter quoted supra p. 239, n. 2, *De novis, etc., in the Monastery Library, Zeitz. it is stated on April 17, 1559: " Iudaei separatim vivunt." Concerning the Roman Ghetto see MORONI, XXI., 23 seqq., who gives more details than GREGOROVIUS, Wanderjahre, I., 95 seqq. Cf. concerning the Ghetto, also Histor.-polit. Bl., LVII., 515 seq. Gregorovius derives the name Ghetto, which came into use later—the old name is vicus iudeorum—from the Talmudistic " ghet " separation. Others say it is an abbrevia-tion of " traghetto " a side street, in which the idea of separation is suggested. It is certain that the word is of Venetian origin. The Ghetto there is supposed to be the oldest (cf. ZANGWILL, Dreamers of the Ghetto, Leipsic, 1899); it was far more enclosed and separated than that of Rome, which was done away with by Pius IX., and completely pulled down in 1887. The work of NATALI, Il Ghetto di Roma (Rome, 1887) tells nothing new, but RODOCANACHI (43 seq., 49 seq.) makes many useful statements.

[3] See BATTISTELLA, S. Officio in Bologna 148. A *letter of the Bolognese concerning their Ghetto, dated January 18, 1556, in the Papal Secret Archives, Castle of St. Angelo, Arm. 8, ordo 2, t. 3, p 62.

the real estate belonging to the Jews in the States of the Church realized half a million scudi, which was only about a fifth of its real value.[1]

Paul IV. caused two learned Jewish converts, the Dominican, Sixtus of Siena, and Joseph Moro, to preach to the Jews, so that they might be converted.[2] As many Jews embraced Christianity,[3] Paul IV., in March, 1556, renewed the regulation of Julius III., that a tax should be imposed on the municipalities of the States of the Church, for the support of the Roman house of catechumens.[4]

Paul IV. had granted the Jews of Ancona some alleviations in the interests of the trade of the city.[5] As they seized upon the fortunes of the Christians by means of usury, and committed deeds of violence at their expense,[6] he caused a Ghetto to be erected there as well in February, 1556.[7] The stricter measures adopted against the Jews there[8] were connected with the proceedings of the Portuguese Marani. It had already become evident in the autumn of 1555 that many of these new Christians had only been pretended converts.[9] The Inquisition therefore decided, in a sitting of October 1st, 1555, held in the presence of the Pope, to take sharp measures against those who relapsed.[10] A Neapolitan was sent to Ancona as

[1] Vogelstein-Rieger, II., 154.

[2] Cf. Grätz, VIII., 366.

[3] See the letter quoted *supra* p. 239, n. 2, *De novis, etc., in the Monastery Library, Zeitz.

[4] See the *briefs to the Duke of Ferrara and the Duke of Urbino of March 20, 1556 (Arm. 44, t. 4, n. 343. Secret Archives of the Vatican) and the bull of March 23, 1556. Bull., VI., 509.

[5] See the *brief of September 28, 1555, in the Communal Archives, Ancona; cf. Leoni, Ancona illustr., Ancona, 1832, 291.

[6] See the *brief to Genoa of December 11, 1555 (Arm. 44, t. 4, n. 258. Secret Archives of the Vatican).

[7] Cf. Rev. des études juives, III., 95.

[8] See the brief of March 23, 1556, in Ancona illustr., Ancona, 1870, 240.

[9] See the brief (quoted *supra* n. 6) of December 11, 1555.

[10] See Pastor, Dekrete, 16.

commissary, but he allowed himself to be bribed and then took to flight.[1] On April 30th, 1556, the Roman Inquisition decided that the Marani settled in Italy, who had become converts only for show, should be punished as apostates.[2] A new commisary now made a thorough investigation in Ancona, and arrested the guilty persons ; twelve of these, and according to other authorities, twenty-four, were burned,[3] forty-two others, who were less guilty, succeeded, by paying considerable sums, in getting the death sentence commuted to the punishment of the galleys for life. A letter of the Sultan Soliman to the Pope, pointing out that there were Turkish subjects among the prisoners, and threatening reprisals on the Christians in Turkey, was not without effect.[4]

Many Marani from Ancona had fled to Ferrara and Pesaro, which belonged to Guidobaldo della Rovere, Duke of Urbino. The Duke hoped to divert trade to Pesaro by means of these. At first this seemed likely to succeed ; the Levantine Jews boycotted the port of Ancona, which suffered so severely in consequence, that the city appealed to the Pope for protection;[5] the Jews of the place also joined in the petition. Paul IV., who had already requested the Duke of Urbino to hand over to the Inquisition the Marani who had fled to his dominions,

[1] See the brief quoted *supra* p. 274, n. 6.

[2] See PASTOR, Dekrete, 18.

[3] The attempt of C. GARIBALDI (Un asserto autodafé sotto Paolo IV., Bologna, 1876) to make out that this burning is a fable, will not stand the test ; *cf.* FEROSO in the Arch. stor. per le Marche, I., 689 *seq.* and D. KAUFMANN in the Rev. des études juives, XI., 149 *seq.* They have both overlooked Navagero's statement (BROWN, VI., 1, n. 463) which gives the number of those burned as 24. A brief of May 30, 1556, to the commissary of the Inquisition in Ancona in FONTANA, 440 *seq.*

[4] The Sultan's letter (dated 9 Marzo A° del profeta 963 [— 1556], in an Italian translation of the time, in the Secret Archives of the Vatican, Castle of St. Angelo, Arm. 8, ordo 2, t. 3, p. 80 *seq.*, printed in the Lett. de' princ., I., 190 *seq.* ; *f.* MAKUSCEV, Mon. Slav. merid., I., 29 ; Nonciat. de France, II., 510 n.) gave rise to the talk of a direct alilance with the Pope ; see *supra* p. 142.

[5] The Memoriale in FEROSO, *loc. cit.*, 693 *seq.*

now made further representations to Guidobaldo della Rovere, which were only successful in 1558. The Duke of Ferrara was also requested in the same year to drive out these " faithless and deeply detestable " renegades. At the same time the Inquisitor, Ghislieri, requested the Duke to take steps against a pamphlet being circulated in Ferrara in praise of those burned at Ancona.[1] Paul IV. had also ordered the destruction of Talmudistic and anti-Christian books of the Jews. Not only in Rome, but also in Cremona, great numbers of the Talmud were seized and burned by an envoy of the Inquisition, with the permission of the Spanish government.[2]

[1] See FONTANA, 435 *seq.*; CIBRARIO, Lett. di Santi, 11 *seq.*; GRÄTZ, IX., 349 *seq.*; FEROSO, *loc. cit.*, 707 *seq.* Kaufmann has referred to the treatise in the Rev. des études juives, XI., 150 *seq.*; *cf. ibid.*, XX., 47 *seq.* concerning the attempts of the Marani in the territory of Urbino to flee to Turkey. There was also a question of pretended Christians dealt with by the Portuguese Inquisition, with the affairs of which Paul IV. had been much occupied since the beginning of his pontificate (see SANTAREM, XII., 431, 443 *seq.*). On April 18, 1559, Catherine, the Queen Regent of Portugal, addressed a letter to Paul IV., begging him to institute a reorganization of the Inquisition in Portugal (Corpo dipl. Port., VIII., 142). In accordance with this request the regulation issued by Paul III. (see Vol. XII. of this work, p. 47) was to be repealed, as Portugal had already vainly requested (see SANTAREM, XIII., 19, 23). Paul IV. at first refused absolutely (Corpo dipl. Port., VIII., 193, 195 *seq.*); finally, however, the Portuguese ambassador succeeded in inducing him to change his mind. A brief in conformity with the wishes of the Portuguese government had already been drawn up (*cf.* SANTAREM, XIII., 59) when the sharp eye of Paul IV detected a mistake in it, so that everything was once more in doubt when Paul IV. died (see Corpo, VIII., 195 *seqq.*; SANTAREM, XIII., 62); Paul IV. repeatedly ordered ecclesiastical revenues to be applied to the furtherance of the Portuguese Inquisition; see *Regesta Later. 1837, p. 240, 275 (Secret Archives of the Vatican).

[2] *Cf.* CARACCIOLO, *Vita, 4, 11; ERLER, *loc. cit.*, 49; REUSCH, I., 48; VOGELSTEIN-RIEGER, II., 156 *seq.*; BERLINER, II.,

Gian Pietro Carafa had already recommended a war of destruction on all bad books in his memorial to Clement VII., because they, in conjunction with bad sermons and an immoral manner of life, were the real source of heresy.[1] Our information as to the far-reaching efficacy of his work in this direction is not as complete as could be desired. It is evident from a letter of Michele Ghislieri, the commissary-general of the Inquisition, to the Inquisitor at Genoa on June 27th, 1557, that Ghislieri had to urge moderation. To forbid such books as Ariosto's Orlando, or the Cento Novelle, Ghislieri describes, with perfect justice, as ridiculous.[2]

In September, 1557, a very long list of heretical books, which were to be burned, was prepared by the Inquisition. The Venetian ambassador reported at this time that Paul IV. had enjoined that the destruction of these books should only be carried out by degrees, so that the booksellers should not suddenly experience too great a loss. Two Cardinals were to make inquiries into the rights of the booksellers. Among the books to be destroyed immediately were all the works of Erasmus ; also certain books not dealing with theological

2, 8 *seq.*, and Zensur und Konfiskation hebräischer Bücher im Kirchenstaat, Frankfurt, 1891, 4 *seq.*

[1] See Vol. X. of this work, p. 421.

[2] The very interesting letter is as follows :—

*Rev[do] padre. Li mando lo esamine di fra Eggidio . . . Di prohibire Orlando, Orlandino, cento novelle et simili altri libri più presto daressemo da ridere ch' altrimènte, perche simili libri non si leggono come cose a qual si habbi da credere, ma come fabule, et come si legono ancor molti libri de gentili come Luciano, Lucretio et altri simili : nondimeno se ne parlarà nella congregatione de' theologi et poi a S.S.[tà] et alli rev.[ml] Pregate il Signore che ne ispiri a fare quanto sii spediente et alle sue oratione mi racommando.

Di Roma li xxvii. di giugno M.D.L. vii.

Di V. R. P[ta] Fra Michele Alessandrino.

[Address] Al molto rev[do] padre fra Geronimo de Genova contra l'heretica pravità Inquisitore [padr.] oss°. Genova a S.[tc] Dominico (Cod. E. VII., 15 of the University Library, Genoa).

subjects, such as those of Machiavelli and Poggio's Facetiae.[1]
A first copy of the Index was prepared in 1557 by Antonius
Bladus, but was not published.[2] In February, 1558, a commission of Cardinals discussed the matter.[3] On December 21st
a Papal bull appeared, revoking all permissions granted to read
forbidden books, the only exceptions being the Inquisitors-
General, and the Cardinals to whom a special permit had been
issued by the Pope.[4]

In the meantime Bladus had prepared a new and improved
edition of the Index.   What had leaked out with regard to its
contents was of such a nature that all the booksellers were in a
state of the greatest consternation.   Representations were
made to the Inquisition from various quarters, including the
Jesuit, Nadal, in consequence of which the Inquisition issued a
decree with the new Index, which somewhat modified its
extreme severity.[5] In spite of this, the decisions, which came
into force at the turn of the years 1558-1559, were so arbitrary
that no less an authority than Canisius described the list, on
account of its strictness, as a stumbling-block.[6] This judgment was not too strong.

The new Index—" A List of Authors and Books against
which the Roman and Universal Inquisition orders all Chris-

[1] See Navagero's report of September 7, 1557, in BROWN,
VI., 2, n. 1024, which Reusch as well as Hilgers has overlooked.
Preparatory work for the Index in *Concilio LXXIV. (Secret
Archives of the Vatican) ; cf. Röm. Quartalschr., XVII., 296 seq.

[2] See HILGERS, 490 seq. ; REUSCH, The " Indices librorum
prohibitorum " of the 16th century, Tübingen, 1886, 176 seqq.

[3] *Avviso di Roma of February 5, 1558 : *Si è fatto una congregatione in casa del card. di Trani sopra le cose dell' heresia
et libri heretici. (Vatican Library).

[4] SCHELHORN, Samml. für die Gesch., I., 143. FONTANA,
448 seq. A similar regulation of April 14, 1559, with regard to
heretical books in the Editti, V., 30, 2 (Secret Archives of the
Vatican).

[5] See HILGERS, 8 seq., 198, 489 seq. and Zentralblatt für Bib-
liothekswesen, XXVIII., (1911), 118 seq., where the statements
of Reusch are corrected.

[6] BRAUNSBERGER, II., 380.

tians to be on their guard, under the threat of Censure and Punishment "—distinguishes three classes of books, each in alphabetical order. The first class contains the names of those authors who have, as it were, erred " ex professo," wherefore the whole of their works, even when they contain nothing about the faith, are absolutely forbidden. Erasmus is specially mentioned in this connection. In the second class were the names of authors, of whose books only certain ones had been condemned, because experience had shown that they occasionally led persons to heresy, to a kind of insidious atheism, or above all to intolerable errors. In the third class the names of books were given, which contained pernicious doctrines, and had, for the most part, been composed by anonymous heretics. In the introduction it was stated that all books which had been written by heretics, or should in future be written by them, or published in the name of, or under the designation of heretics, were forbidden. Further, in accordance with the decree of the Council of Trent, of April 8th, 1546, all writings which had appeared during the last forty years without stating the author, printer, and the date and place of publication, even should they not treat of religion, were forbidden ; moreover, for the future, the same was to apply to all books that were published without ecclesiastical permission. In a supplement to the Index it was decreed, with regard to a number of Latin editions of the Bible, and all translations of the New Testament into the vernacular, that they were not to be printed, read or kept, without the permission of the Inquisition. Finally, a list of sixty-one printers was added, the whole of whose publications were forbidden.[1]

---

[1] See REUSCH, I., 263 *seq.*, where details are given concerning the contents, compilers and sources of this first Roman Index ; *ibid.*, 369, concerning the prohibition of the writings of Savonarola, and the deliberations before Paul IV. previous to the prohibition (*cf.* Arch. stor. Ital., Ser. 5, XXVIII., 288 *seq.*). Machiavelli was published abroad, in consequence of the Index of 1557 (see Arch. stor. Ital., XIX. [1896], 126 *seq.*). Boccaccio's Decameron was forbidden with a similar formula " donec corrigatur " (see REUSCH, I.. 389). Concerning the proceedings

The carrying into effect of these regulations, which undoubtedly went too far, was at once begun in Rome and
Bologna.   In both cities the Inquisition caused a great number
of heretical books to be burned.[1]   Cardinal Ghislieri had
repeatedly to dissuade the Inquisitor at Genoa from measures
which were too strict and hasty ;[2] he naturally insisted, however, on the carrying out of the Index.   Where there was no
Inquisitor the bishops had to take the matter in hand.[3]

Not only the booksellers, but scholars as well, everywhere

against Erasmus see also PIRENNE, III., 487, n. 2, and Histor.
Zeitschr., XC., 176. *Cf.* JORIS in the Wissenschaftl. Beilage
der Germania, 1908, No. 48, to see how Lucian came on to the
Index of Paul IV.   Two licenses of the Inquisition in 1559 with
regard to Italian translations of the Bible in the magazine,
Romania, XXIII., 416.

[1] For Rome see FIRMANUS, 513, and TURINOZZI, 6 ; for Bologna,
Serapeum, III., 155.

[2] On January 7, 1559, Cardinal Ghislieri wrote from Rome to
G. Franchi : *I libri d' humanità de buoni autori, riconosciuti,
scholiati o commentati da altri reprobati nell' Indice, si possono
concedere deletis delendis, si come anche si concedono i libri
de santi dottori.   On February 10, 1559, the following instructions
were sent to Franchi : *Rev^{do} padre. Oltre l'altre cose mi sono
occorse scrivere a V. R.^{za} con quest' ordinario, mi rimane hora
dirle che, per non illaqueare nelle censure molte anime circa
l'esshibition de libri prohibiti per causa di un termino troppo
repentino, potraà prefigerli uno over due mesi di tempo dalla
publicatione dell' Indice, et spirato quello, prorogarli poi anco
di più quendici altri giorni, acciochè non siano escusabili se in
detto tempo mancheranno di haver fatta la purgatione et cor-
rettione debita et ubedito in tutto all' ordine di esso Indice.
On February 25 Ghislieri wrote : *A quegli che V.R. conoscerà
catholici potrà lasciare l'evangeliario et epistolario volgare
ecc. et potrà anco lasciare la Biblia volgare a ms. Agostino
Pinello.   Alla presentatione de libri debbano essere eguali,
et di lasciare quei che si possono concedere anco bisogna aprirvi
bene gli occhi (Cod. E. VII., 15, of the University Library, Genoa).

[3] *Letter to G. Franchi, dated Rome, March 10, 1555, *loc. cit.*

complained of the great prejudice to their interests.[1] The
number of suspected books delivered up was in many cases so
great that those charged with their examination could hardly
cope with the work.[2] Paul IV. and the Inquisition everywhere watched over the strict carrying out, of the new regulations. These were published in Milan and were also carried
out in Naples. The number of books burned in Venice on
the Saturday before Palm Sunday was given as more than
10,000. In Florence, where there was no Inquisitor, the Duke
made up by his zeal for what was wanting.[3] In the smaller
Italian states the governments naturally submitted, but in
some places, as for instance in Genoa, differences of opinion
arose with the Roman Inquisition.[4]

It was, however, not possible to fulfil the new regulations
completely outside of Italy. Not only the Sorbonne, but the
Spanish Inquisition as well, completely ignored the Index of
Paul IV. The Spanish Grand Inquisitor Valdes issued a list
of forbidden books of his own in 1559.[5]

In Rome and in the States of the Church Paul IV. could
make use of his own courts as he pleased, in his campaign
against the heretics.[6] In the rest of Italy he very freely called
in the assistance of the governments. He applied to Duke
Ercole of Ferrara, as early as October 1st, 1555, with a request
to arrest several persons under suspicion in questions concern-

---

[1] Cf. POGIANI, Epist., III., 149 ; DEJOB, 74 seq.

[2] See TACCHI VENTURI, I., 316.

[3] Cf. in Appendix No. 54 the very interesting letter of Cardinal
Ghislieri of March 31, 1559 (University Library, Genoa). Con-
cerning the burning of books in Naples (Sessa) see Arch. Napol.,
I., 645. For that in Tuscany cf. also CIAMPI, I., 307.

[4] Cf. Ghislieri's *letter of July 21, 1559, in Appendix No. 58.

[5] Cf. REUSCH I., 298, 300 seq.

[6] See the *brief of August 3, 1555, for the vice-legate Camillus
episc. Satrian. (ut transmittat gubernatori civit. Spoleti Hieronymum
Mediolan. qui ob haeret. pravit. causam in carcere traditur. Archives of Briefs, Rome), the brief in FONTANA, 435, and in
Appendix No. 53 that to the President of the Romagna of February 27, 1559 (Secret Archives of the Vatican).

ing the faith in Modena, and to hand them over to the vice-legate of Bologna, who would bring them before the Roman Inquisition. Two members of the Valentini family, one of whom was provost of the cathedral of Modena, the bookseller Antonio Gadaldino, and the scholar Ludovico Castelvetro, who translated the works of Melancthon into Italian, are named in this document as suspects.[1] The Duke wished to have the trial of the suspects conducted in Modena, but was obliged, owing to pressure on the part of the Pope, to issue the citation in July, 1556.[2] The conservatori in Modena now protested, while Castelvetro saved himself by flight. The provost Valentini presented himself in Bologna, and was set at liberty after he had abjured his errors. The bookseller, Gadaldino, who refused to recant in any way, was condemned to imprisonment for life.[3] On November 24th, 1555, Duke Ercole was ordered to arrest two teachers of heresy who were about to come from Germany to Ferrara, and hand them over to Rome. Similar orders were also given later on to the Duke, as for example, on February 3rd, 1559, in the case of a physician who had been arrested at Reggio.[4] The government of Lucca was summoned on March 31st, 1556, to assist the inquisitors there in their procedure against the heresy prevalent in the city and diocese. The Republic of Genoa did not need such admonitions ; on its own initiative it drove the heretical Augustinian hermits out of its territory, for which it received two Papal letters of eulogy.[5]

---

[1] The brief, in TIRABOSCHI, Bibl. Mod., VI., 59, has been again published by FONTANA (p. 434 seq.).

[2] See the ambassadorial reports from Rome in SANDONINI, L. Castelvetro, 288 seq.

[3] TIRABOSCHI, Bibl. Mod., I., 447 seq. TASSONI, Cronaca : Mon. di stor. patria, XV., 341 seq. FONTANA, Renata, II., 420 seq. SANDONINI, 295 seq. CAVAZZUTI, L. Castelvetro, Modena, 1903, 210.

[4] See FONTANA, 436, 451. This letter, however, has already been printed by RAYNALDUS, 1559, n. 22.

[5] FONTANA, 437 seq., 443 seq. Concerning Lucca see DONADONI, Di uno sconosciuto poema eretico, Naples, 1900 ; Giorn. stor.

The continuation of the Protestant propaganda in north Italy caused the greatest anxiety to Paul IV. ; the Duchy of Milan was especially in danger on account of its proximity to Switzerland. The representative of Philip II., Cardinal Madruzzo, was therefore, on May 20th, 1556, exhorted to increased vigilance. It is evident from this letter to what means the heretics had recourse ; an Augustinian hermit, convicted of heresy in Milan, had been handed over to the secular power by the Inquisitor ; by means of a forged order he had succeeded in getting out of prison, and had then been assisted in his flight by some officials of the court ; the Pope exhorted the Cardinal to more severe punishments. On August 1st, 1556, he was obliged to take steps on account of the recent arrest of a heretic, who had escaped from the prisons of the Inquisition in Milan. Two years later the Inquisition in the capital of Lombardy was removed from the monastery of S. Eustorgio and transferred to that of S. Maria delle Grazie. The Inquisitor-General in the Duchy of Milan at this time was the Dominican, Giovan Battista da Cremona.[1]

Protestantism was also by no means conquered in Venice. The Pope repeatedly exhorted the representative of the Republic to see that the government allowed no heresy to strike root in its dominions. Paul IV. also pointed out on this occasion the evil consequences which any toleration would entail for the state.[2]

d. lett. Ital., XXXVII., 420 ; TACCHI VENTURI, I., 347 ; concerning the Inquisition in Florence, cf. LE BRET, Magazin, VIII., 549. According to a memorandum, of which I was informed by Lämmer, in the *Cod. A D 9(63) of the library of S. Pietro in Vincoli, a number of citizens were, at the instance of the Bishop of Lucca, on June 4, 15, and 25, 1556, " per commissione di Roma " as " eretici publicamente citati in pergamo nella chiesa di S. Martino a costituirsi nelle carceri di Roma ad istanza de quattro cardinali inquisitori sotto pena della vita e confiscazione de' beni."

[1] See FONTANA, 438 seq., 448 and FUMI, L'Inquisizione, 211 seq.

[2] *Scrivete a quella Signoria che non lascia firmar nel stato l'heresie, perchè dopo quella viene la destruttione come si puo

In Bergamo, where even in the time of Clement VII., measures had had to be taken against the followers of Luther, Bishop Vittorio Soranzo, who belonged to a noble family of Venice, was suspended in 1552 on a suspicion of heresy, and kept imprisoned in the Castle of St. Angelo. Two years later he was declared innocent, and was reinstated in his bishopric.[1] On this occasion Julius III. gave him Canon Giulio Augusto as his coadjutor. The latter, however, incurred the penalty of excommunication on account of disobedience to the Roman Inquisition in 1556, whereupon Paul IV. deprived him of his coadjutorship on June 1st, 1556 ;[2] a year later Bishop Soranzo was again arrested on an accusation of heresy, and proceedings taken against him by the Inquisition. This ended in his being condemned to recant his errors, and being deprived of his bishopric. The sentence was pronounced by the Pope in a consistory of April 20th, 1558.[3]

---

esser chiari a mille esempi. Report of Navagero of May 1, 1556 (Library of St. Mark's, Venice). Cf. also the passage from Navagero's *report of October 30, 1557 (State Archives, Venice) in DE LEVA, Degli eretici di Cittadella, Venice, 1873, 61. Padua, wrote the Jesuit, B. Palmio, on February 11, 1558, is full of heretics, who live almost unmolested ; see TACCHI VENTURI, I., 549.

[1] See UGHELLI, IV., 292 seq. and BUSCHBELL, 15.

[2] FONTANA, 441 seq.

[3] See UGHELLI, IV., 496; BROMATO, II., 453; AMABILE, I., 140 ; cf. Acta consist. in GULIK-EUBEL, 147. The efforts which Paul IV. made to have Soranzo handed over to Rome (see BROWN, VI., 2, n. 920, 1156), were in vain. Soranzo died in Venice in 1558. The brief to the nuncio in Venice was directed against the preaching of a Spanish woman there, see RAYNALDUS, 1557, n. 52. At the visitation in Istria and Dalmatia proceedings against the heretics were also to be arranged (see the *brief to the Doge of April 2, 1558. Arm. 44, t. 2, f. 111. Secret Archives of the Vatican). A decree in support of the Inquisition in Sardinia in FONTANA, 433. Faculties for the absolution of repentant Lutherans in Brescia were issued by Paul IV. on June 16, 1559 ; see RAYNALDUS, 1559, n. 22.

The dangers with which the Protestant propaganda threatened the Catholic Church in the Kingdom of Naples were very grave. On July 20th, 1556, Paul IV. repealed a regulation of his predecessor, according to which the property of heretics in that kingdom could not be confiscated.[1] When the war with Spain broke out, the work of the Inquisition in Naples was paralysed for a whole year, until the autumn of 1557.[2] How dangerously the situation developed there is clear from the autobiography of Giulio Antonio Santorio. He had the greatest difficulties to encounter as vicar-general of the Bishop of Caserta, in repressing the Protestant agitation. Full of zeal for the Catholic religion, Santorio used his utmost efforts, and all the authority of his position, and endeavoured by fasting and prayer, as well as by public and private disputations, to preserve the unity of the faith in his native place, to strengthen the weak, and to bring back those who had strayed. " By doing so," he tells us, " I incurred a violent persecution from the heretics, who insulted me and endeavoured to kill me, as I have set forth in a little book of my own." Santorio endeavoured to strengthen himself for the struggle by prayer and fasting.[3]

After the conclusion of peace with Spain, the activity of the Inquisition in Naples was again set in movement ; at the same time it received a greater impetus in Rome than ever before.[4] In October, 1557, the number of Cardinals who belonged to the tribunal was increased by four ;[5] in November the Governor of Rome, the Archbishop of Conza and Bishop of Verona were

---

[1] FONTANA, 442.

[2] See AMABILE, I., 223.

[3] See Autobiografia del card. G. A. Santorio, ed. CUGNONI in the Arch. Rom., XII., 335.

[4] Cf. AMABILE, I., 223, 226. Seripando was also in danger at this time ; see ibid., 229.

[5] *Heri poi in concistorio aggionse alli cardinali del inquisitione li rev^mi Pacheco, S. Fiore et Savello et il giorno avanti ve haveva posto Ariano [Diomede Carafa] et Triulci, il qual Triulci ha anco fatto entrare in signatura. Navagero on October 16, 1557 (Court Library, Vienna).

also added.[1] All reports agree that the activity of the Pope's work for the Inquisition reached its highest point in the year 1558.[2] Heretics were now also sent from Naples to Rome for punishment. Several of them died at the stake, for there were many among them who obstinately refused to recant their errors.[3]

Paul IV. did not content himself with taking steps against undoubted heretics ; quite innocent persons were also proceeded against by the Inquisition. As the news concerning the spread of heresy which arrived from all parts of the world, even from Spain, was becoming more disturbing, whole families in different parts of Italy falling away from the faith, as for example in Cremona, and making their escape to Geneva or Germany,[4] the fear and anxiety in Rome increased from day to day. The lively southern imagination of the Pope magnified to an immeasurable degree the dangers with which the heretical propaganda threatened the security of the Church in the south as well as in the north of Italy, and he therefore more and more lost sight of the proper point of view, from which he ought to have combated the enemy. His quite justifiable anxiety for the preservation of the Catholic faith degenerated into a kind of pessimism, which, for the most part,

[1] *Giobbia nella congregatione del inquisitione il pontefice fece entrare in essa al numero dell' altri consultori li reverendi governatore di Roma, arcivescovo di Conza et vescovo di Verona. Navagero on November 6, 1557 (Court Library, Vienna).

[2] *Cf.* in Appendix No. 48 the *Avviso of April 2, 1558 (Vatican Library). A *report of Claudio Malopera to Cardinal Madruzzo, dated Venice, April 30, 1558, encloses a *report from Rome of April 23, which says of the Pope : " Et ha precipua cura delle cose pertinenti all' inquisitione et per meglio attendervi dicono che rimetrà tutti i negotii al card. Carafa et lui attendea solo a intervenire alle congregationi, qual si farano delli casi de l'inquisitione " (Vice-regal Archives, Innsbruck). An *Avviso of December, 31, 1558 (Vatican Library) also says how very near to the Pope's heart the Inquisition was.

[3] See AMABILE, I., 230.

[4] *Cf.* the **letter of G. Garimberto to Cardinal Carafa, dated Rome, June 18, 1558 (Secret Archives of the Vatican).

saw the greatest danger just where none at all existed. A little want of care, or an ambiguous expression sufficed to give rise to the suspicion of heresy. The hasty and credulous Pope lent a willing ear to every denunciation, even the most absurd.[1] Neither rank, nor dignity nor merit weighed in the balance in the case of anyone suspected of heresy ; he would be treated with the same ruthless severity by the Inquisition as if he were the open and declared enemy of the Church. The Inquisitors, constantly urged on by the Pope, scented heresy in numerous cases where a calm and circumspect observer would not have discovered a trace of it, however strictly it might be measured by the standard of the doctrines of the Catholic Church. The envious and the calumniator were kept hard at work snapping up suspicious words fallen from the lips of men who had been firm pillars of the Church against the innovators, and in bringing groundless accusations of heresy against them.[2] It thus came to accusations being made and proceedings being taken against bishops and even Cardinals, which are as incomprehensible as they were baseless. An actual reign of terror began, which filled all Rome with fear.[3]

It is only with great sorrow that we can look back on that time of terror, mistrust and confusion, when men were brought by false arts under the suspicion of wandering from the Catholic faith, to which they were in reality devoted, heart and soul.[4]

[1] The pious Cardinal Alfonso Carafa, who was specially trusted by Paul IV., complained bitterly in August, 1559, to the French ambassador, about the " malice de ces cagots, desquels une grande partie estoient eux mesmes heretiques et remplissoient de calomnies les oreilles et le cerveau de S.S.^té." RIBIER, II., 815.

[2] No less a person than Gropper (see Histor. Jahrb., VII., 596) whom Cardinals Truchsess and Madruzzo praised as having always been a firm pillar against the heretics in Germany ; see Zeitschr. für Kirchengesch., V., 613 seq.

[3] This is quite openly stated in the *Avvisi ; see e.g. the *Avviso of December 31, 1558. (Vatican Library).

[4] In consequence of the uncertainty and confusion, it also occasionally happened that undoubtedly guilty persons were

Many of the occurrences which took place in Rome at that time remind one of those dreadful scenes which sometimes occur in the fury of battle, when the soldier no longer distinguishes between friend and foe, and mistakenly falls upon his comrade and kills him.

interceded for by good Catholic authorities. The most striking example of this is the case of P. Carnesecchi. He was cited before the Roman Inquisition in 1557, and as he did not appear, was condemned on April 6, 1558, *in contumaciam*. On April 11, 1558, Cardinal Madruzzo recommended this man to Cardinal Carafa and the Bishop of Pola (Zeitschr. für Kirchengesch., V., 612 *seq.*). The *letter in which Carnesecchi is recommended to Cardinal Madruzzo as the friend of Pole and Morone is dated Venice, March 22, 1558; the signature is illegible. I found this letter in Cardinal Madruzzo's correspondence in the Vice-regal Archives, Innsbruck.

CHAPTER XI.

THE TRIAL OF CARDINAL MORONE.

IT was on May 31st, 1557, that a report was circulated in Rome, which occasioned the deepest sorrow in every quarter of the city.[1] One of the most respected and most virtuous members of the Sacred College, as well as one of the most zealous for reform, Cardinal Morone, had been arrested and taken to the Castle of St. Angelo.

As nuncio and legate Morone had rendered the Church most distinguished services, under the most difficult circumstances ; as Bishop of Modena he had combated error, introduced reforms, and energetically supported the Jesuits.[2] Under Julius III. he had even belonged to the Roman Inquisition. All his services, however, as well as his blameless manner of life, were alike disregarded by Paul IV. With complete disregard of all legal procedure, he caused a Cardinal to be thrown into prison who was one of the best men in the Curia. No wonder that such a proceeding caused the most painful impression, not only in Rome, but everywhere else as well, even so far off as Poland.[3]

Already, on May 22nd, Morone's maggiordomo had been arrested in his presence and thrown into the prisons of the Inquisition.[4] This proceeding was looked upon as being due

[1] Delfino testifies to this in his *report to Ferdinand I., dated Rome, June 5, 1557 (Court and State Archives, Vienna).

[2] *Cf.* Vol. XI. of this work, p. 510, and *infra* p. 295 *seq.*, also TACCHI VENTURI, I., 184, 284, 509 *seqq.*, 541 n. 5. Morone was also actively employed in reform as administrator of the Bishop of Novara ; see Appendix Nos. 46-47 ; *ibid.* Morone's care to have good Catholic preachers at Modena and Novara.

[3] See the letter of A. Patricius, dated Cracow, July 6, 1557, in MORAWSKI, A. Patrycy Nidecki, Cracow, 1884, 105.

[4] See Navagero's report in BROWN, VI., 2, n. 898, and AMABILE, I., 150.

to the fact that Morone was considered to be an Imperialist,
and unfavourable to the Carafa.   The Cardinal knew very well
that he had this reputation, nor did it escape his notice that his
orthodoxy was suspected.   In his open and straightforward
way he spoke himself to Cardinal Carafa of the charges brought
against him, and pointed out to him how groundless were the
rumours concerning him ; at the same time he also expressly
reminded Carafa of the great share he had had in bringing
about the election of Paul IV.   Cardinal Carafa answered that
he entertained no suspicions against Morone, that everyone
was free as to his political opinions, and that he was not concerned with religious questions.[1]   The conversation thus
ended to their mutual satisfaction.   Consequently Morone,
who had nothing on his conscience, felt no anxiety when on
the morning of May 31st, Cardinal Carafa again asked him to
visit him, as he had an important communication to make to
him.   Morone had hardly reached the anticamera when all the
doors were closed.   Thereupon Cardinal Carafa appeared and
informed his colleague that the Pope had ordered his incar-
ceration in the Castle of St. Angelo.   Morone replied, without
a trace of excitement : " I am not aware of having failed in any
way ; besides, I should in any case have hurried here, even
from a great distance, to obey the orders of the Holy Father."
Then the Cardinal was taken in custody through the covered
passage which connects the Vatican with the Castle of St.
Angelo.   They left him three of his servants, but placed in his
cell a guard of four soldiers, whom he had to pay out of his own
pocket.   Morone preserved, in these painful circumstances,
that peace of mind which only true piety and the consciousness
of innocence can give.   He caused his mother to be informed
by letter that she must have no anxiety on his behalf.[2]

[1] See BROWN, VI., 2, n. 913.

[2] Besides MASSARELLI, 310, and the report of Navagero of
May 31, 1557 (translated in BROWN, VI., 2, n. 910) and that of
Carne in TURNBULL, n. 625, also MASIUS, Briefe 291, see especially
the report from a very well-informed source *Captura del card.
Morone in Roma all' ultimo di Maggio 1557 (Ambrosian Library,
Milan, R. 833) used by SCLOPIS (p. 22 seq.).   BENRATH (Herzog's

On the same day the legal officials seized all the papers and books in Morone's palace, which adjoined S. Maria in Trastevere, and took his private secretary to the prison of the Inquisition. There was no doubt that an accusation of heresy was in question. Nevertheless, it was believed that for the arrest of so eminent a member of the Sacred College, who had been repeatedly named by the Imperialists as the future Pope, and who was highly esteemed by Philip II. and Mary of England, other grounds must exist. In many quarters, therefore, it was current that a question of some political offence, concerned with treasonable relations of the Cardinal with the political enemies of Paul IV.,was at the bottom of the matter.[1]

This view, however, was soon denied from an influential quarter. On June 1st, Paul IV. informed the Cardinals in a General Congregation, that he had ordered the arrest of Morone on account of a suspicion of heresy, which he had entertained against him even in the time of Paul III. The Inquisition would conduct the trial, and the sentence would be laid before the Sacred College.[2] The Pope spoke to the same effect next day to Navagero. It was not a question of a crime against the state, but of one against the faith. It had come to his knowledge that even in the Sacred College there were men infected with heresy. He had been obliged to take measures against the terrible danger which this involved. " To tell the truth," he continued, " we wish to meet the dangers which threatened in the last conclave, and to take steps during our lifetime, so that the devil may not succeed in days to come in placing one of his own on the throne of St. Peter." He said

Realenzykl., XIII.[3], 481) erroneously gives the date of Morone's imprisonment as June 12, BERNABEI (p. 70) says in June, RIESS (p. 249), May 30, AMABILE, (I., 229), June 2. Navagero expressly says in his letter of May 31 : " questa mattina " (State Archives, Venice). The bad impression made by the arrest is testified to by Delfino ; see STEINHERZ, I., xxxvii., n. 2.

[1] See the report of Navagero mentioned in the previous note.

[2] See in Appendix No. 37 the *Acta consist (Consistorial Archives) and Navagero's report of June 1, 1557, in BROWN, VI., 2, n. 913 ; cf. also Carne's report in TURNBULL, n. 625.

that if he should be found wanting in this respect, reproaches might justly be brought against him in a Council.[1]

On June 3rd the conduct of the suit against Morone was entrusted to Cardinals Rebiba, Reumano, Ghislieri and Rosario at the usual Thursday sitting of the Inquisition.[2] It then transpired that, as the Pope had at once hinted, another Cardinal as well was to be called upon to answer an accusation of heresy, and that this was Morone's intimate friend Pole, against whom, however, the Inquisition could not proceed directly, because he was still in England, under the protection of Queen Mary. To the accusation against Cardinal Pole, they also joined the introduction of a suit, undertaken at that time by the Inquisition, against the vicar of Cardinal Carpi, as well as again summoning all the Cardinals to Rome.[3] It is evident that Paul IV. considered Pole as guilty as Morone, from the fact that all the attempts of Queen Mary to have the recall of Pole from his legation in England, which had been issued on April 9th, 1557, revoked, were unsuccessful ; on June 14th, 1557, his successor was appointed in the person of the Franciscan, Peto.[4]

Two days before this the trial of Morone had begun in the Castle of St. Angelo.[5] The four Cardinals entrusted with this

[1] See Navagero's report of June 2, 1557, in BROWN, VI., 2, n. 915.

[2] *Nella congregatione passata dell' inquisitione [Thursday ; see the *Avviso di Roma of June 5, 1557. Cod. Urb. 1038, p. 234. Vatican Library] il pontefice aggiunse alli tre cardinali primi cioè Pisa, Reumano, Alessandrino il rev^{mo} Spoleti a vedere le cose del rev. Morone. Navagero on June 5, 1557 (Cod. 6255, p. 427 of the Court Library, Vienna). The remark of TACCHI VENTURI (I., 539 n. 1) with regard to the " rev. de Spoleto " is erroneous. The Motu Proprio of June 11, 1557 (see Appendix Nos. 46-47) also names four Cardinals.

[3] See Navagero in BROWN, VI., 2, n. 914, 932, 933, 938 ; cf. BERTOLOTTI, Martiri, 20.

[4] See *Acta consist. (Consistorial Archives) ; BROWN, Vl., 2, n. 937, 938 ; ZIMMERMANN, Pole, 330 seq. Cf. infra p. 300.

[5] See the *Avviso di Roma of June 12, 1557 (Cod. Urb. 1038, p. 236. Vatican Library).

painful duty expressed their regret that this task should have been imposed on them, and called upon him to make an open avowal, and thus find that the clemency of the Holy Father would not fail him, should he stand in need of clemency. Morone declared that he was willing to do so, and would truthfully tell everything he could remember. As to this he remarked to Cardinal Ghislieri that he had already, at the beginning of the pontificate of Paul IV., declared that he was ready to make such a statement, a thing of which the Pope must be aware.[1]

On June 18th, 1557, Morone gave an exhaustive written answer, in which he refuted all the accusations brought against

---

[1] Contemporary *copies of the documents in the process against Morone at Milan, in the Archives of Duke Gallarati Scotti, XLI., E. n. 5. The first to make use of these was CANTÙ, who (Eretici, II., 176 seqq.) gives the complete Difesa (more properly confessione) of Morone of June 18, 1557, and points out : " In tutto il processo non v'è menzione de tortura." Cf. also CANTÙ, Il card. G. Morone : Mem. dell' Ist. Lombardo, Ser. 3, I., fasc. 4 (1866), 1 seqq., where the Difesa is once more printed on p. 24 seq. TACCHI VENTURI (I., 533 seqq.) has given the complete evidence of Salmeron. At the first glance the date of the first part of this evidence, July 25, 1555, is startling. This date is explained as follows. Soon after his accession, on June 26, 1555, Paul IV. had appointed a commissary, in the person of the Dominican, Tommaso Scotti, to seek for witnesses for the introduction of a process against Morone. This procedure gave the defenders of Morone later on, a reason for attacking the whole action against Morone as invalid, because it was illegal. Cf. in this connection the *original documents in Appendix Nos. 46-47 which I found in the Seminary Library, Foligno. Concerning the Compendium Inquisitorum, which CORVISIERI published in the Arch. d. Soc. Rom., III., 261 seqq., 449 seqq., some perfectly false views have been disseminated by RANKE (Päpste, I.[6], 92, 96). These have been corrected by BENRATH (Histor. Zeitschr., XLIV., 461 seqq.), who at the same time shows it to be probable that it is a question in this document of an extract from the process of Morone, which Santorio drew up about 1565-1566 for his own instruction, as Consultor of the Inquisition.

him.[1] With regard to the reading of forbidden books he was able to point to the extensive faculties which he possessed as Papal nuncio, and also to the fact that he had taken proceedings against the dissemination of such literature. As far as the accusation that he had deviated from the doctrine of justification defined by the Council was concerned, Morone dealt first of all with his attitude towards the Ratisbon formula of 1541. This he had advocated, but that was before the Council had made any pronouncement. After the decision of the General Assembly of the Church he had taken the decree of Trent as his rule, although no authentic Papal confirmation had yet been issued. With regard to his intimacy with Pole and his close friend Flaminio, Morone could appeal to the fact that they were considered good Catholics, even by Paul III. The Cardinal excused himself for the mistake of circulating the pamphlet " Del Beneficio di Christo " by saying that it had not been, at that time, forbidden, and that he had found nothing wrong in the pamphlet, while at the same time, he pointed out the disorder prevailing in Italy at that time. There had not been such strict supervision in matters of faith, he continued, before the erection and strengthening of the Roman Inquisition ; people had discussed religious dogma everywhere, and religious books were sold without restriction. As many places were without an Inquisitor, and in many others the Inquisitors were of no importance, everyone could trifle with the theologians and say what they liked. With regard to the dispute in which he, as Bishop of Modena, had been involved with the Jesuit Salmeron, Morone acknowledged that, in his excitement, he had made a remark concerning good works which was open to great misconstruction ; he had made amends for this by every means in his power, however, as he

---

[1] " Articuli contra card. M. de Luteranismo accusatum et in carcarem coniectum . . . 1558," first published by Vergerio with a violent polemical " annotation " (see HUBERT, Vergerios publizist. Tätigkeit, 309), and later copied by Fricke in SCHEL-HORN, Amoenit. lit., XII., 570 seqq. ; cf. WOLF, Lect. mem., II., 655 seq. ; Arch. Rom., III., 665 seq. ; see also BERTOLOTTI, Martiri, 19 seq.

had done for everything of which he had been guilty in this dispute, and had energetically supported the Jesuits in Modena and the German College in Rome.

Morone also justified the distribution of presents to heretics, as well as the clemency which he had shown years before to several Lutherans in Trent and Bologna, by maintaining his good intention in what he had done. As far as his orthodoxy was concerned he could appeal to the testimony of his vice-legates, as well as to his regulations in religious matters, which extended over a period of four years, and had had no other object in view than the preservation of the faithful in the true religion. The accusation of refusing to venerate the saints he was also able to repudiate by pointing out his actual behaviour in this respect. The accused also repeatedly touched upon his relations to people whose mistaken views on religion had only come to light later on. He maintained that the only reproach which could be brought against him in this connection was a want of discretion. As a special proof of the purity of his faith, Morone finally stated that he had sacrificed his bishopric of Modena to his zeal, since, as he was not sufficiently learned, and could not fulfil the duty of residence, he had resigned the episcopal dignity in favour of a learned Dominican, and had exhorted him to take up the fight against the machinations of the heretics in Modena.

In a supplement to his statement, Morone also drew attention to the fact that all the incidents by which he might have aroused suspicion, or given scandal through ignorance or want of care, had taken place about ten years before, and that, as nothing of the kind had occurred since that time, it seemed to him right that His Holiness, in passing sentence, should take into consideration, not only the suspicions of former days, but also the state of affairs at the present time.

Morone's defenders could also point out that, in his bishoprics of Modena and Novara, he had only allowed pure Catholic doctrine to be preached. Proof was given of this, not only with regard to the doctrine of justification defined at Trent, but also with respect to the Catholic teaching as to the authority of the Pope, good works, and the veneration of the saints

and their relics.   There were also authentic proofs that Morone
had, from the first, taken measures against heresy in Modena,[1]
and that he had drawn the attention of the Curia to the dangers
which were threatening there.[2]   Attention was also drawn
to the fact that he had advised Paul III. to make a league with
the Catholic powers by means of which Protestantism might
be combated by force of arms.   With regard to the pamphlet
" Del Beneficio di Christo " it should be taken into consideration, in favour of the Cardinal, that this little book was on sale
everywhere, including Rome ;   that theologians, indeed, even
Inquisitors, to whom Morone had given it to read, had approved of it, but that the Cardinal, after the treatise had been
condemned by the Inquisition, had also condemned it.   Morone
could also point to the way in which, when one of his friends

---

[1] How early Morone had taken proceedings against the innovators in Modena is evident from the *letter which he wrote
from Ghent to his vicar-general in Modena on May 9, 1540.
In this he says :   " L'inquisitione contra li heretici mi piace
somamente, ma è necessario sia fatta per homini prudenti, dotti
e vivaci che habbiano forza di poterla esseguire perchè altrimenti
non si farebbe buon effetto alcuno, anzi si perderebbe la riputa-
tione."   Already on December 7, 1540, Morone *writes from Mons
to the same :   " In queste travagli publiche mi rincresce fuor di
modo il pericolo di quella città di queste nove sette et vi prego
vogliate esser diligente et aprir gli occhi, accioche si scoprino
questi principii quali, dubito siano troppo radicate, ma sappiate
che di minor favilla di questa s'è eccitato questo gran foco di
Germania et se alcuna cosa bisognerà ch'io possi far in questa
absentia avisatemi perchè sto con l'animo tutto inquieto."   On
*December 29 Morone again wrote to his vicar and enclosed a
letter to Farnese (this is printed in TACCHI VENTURI, I., 509
seq.) with detailed instructions how he was to proceed in Modena.
How very much the religious innovators were on his mind in
Ratisbon is shown by his *letters to his vicar dated February
7, April 18, and May 3, 1541.   These, and other *documents,
which go as far as 1545 (see Appendix Nos. 46-47) are in the codex
of the Seminary Library, Foligno.

[2] See Nuntiaturberichte, published by CARDAUNS, VI., xvii.,
n. 1.

had gone astray in matters of faith, he had persisted in making him abjure his errors. It was also shown how Morone had always supported the Inquisitors in Modena, Bologna and Novara, and that he had himself punished two heretics in Bologna. A suspicious utterance concerning the heretics in Bologna, to the effect that he would warn them in time, was explained by the defence as having merely been intended as an expression of courtesy, which, in any case, could not weigh in the balance against the measures actually taken by the Cardinal against the heretics.[1]

The witnesses called to testify against Morone were remarkable, several of them having entertained views that were heterodox, while others were openly hostile to him ; one of them retracted what he had previously alleged. Their credibility, therefore, was more than open to suspicion, and Morone justly protested against such witnesses. Several others, such as the Prior of the Dominicans in Modena and the Bishop of Civita Castellana, even testified in his favour, and spoke in praise of him, but these favourable pronouncements were not entered in the minutes of the trial ! This, however, was not the only injustice in the legal procedure against the Cardinal. Morone had also to complain of the fact that his defence was rendered more difficult, and even to a certain extent impossible, because the names of various witnesses and their guarantors were withheld from him, although he had earnestly requested to be informed of them ; the same applied to the statement of where and when he had been found wanting.[2]

As had been the case with the witnesses, nothing damaging to the Cardinal could be found among the books and papers confiscated in his palace ; on the contrary, the superscriptions with which Morone had provided the heretical books proved that he condemned them, and did not wish them to be read.

[1] See the extracts from the documents found by me in the Seminary Library, Foligno, in Appendix Nos. 46-47.

[2] See *ibid.* An *Avviso di Roma of March 30, 1560, states that papers had been found which had been hidden by Paul IV. because they testified in Morone's favour (Cod. Urb. 1039, p. 144. Vatican Library).

The letters of Vittoria Colonna to the Cardinal proved to be the merest business letters, in which religion was not even mentioned.[1]

It was clear from all this that there were no grounds for accusing Morone of the crime of heresy. Only a few trifling instances of want of prudence could be proved against him, and these could very easily be explained by the fact that the Cardinal had a generous and conciliatory nature, and that he personally went as far as possible to meet the heretics, and before adopting severe measures endeavoured to win them over by kindness. Errors were in this way unavoidable, since he, a prelate of the time of Leo X., had not had a thorough theological training. Even though he may in consequence have expressed himself, from time to time, in a materially erroneous sense, he had never at any time been guilty of a formal act of heresy, and therefore, according to the decision of the Council, his conduct was free from all blame.

In spite of this Paul IV. was anything but satisfied of the innocence of Morone, for a conviction to the contrary was too deeply rooted in his mind. The Cardinal remained in the strictest confinement, and was, from the first, treated more like a convicted heretic than a prisoner under examination. His request to be allowed to say mass was refused, indeed, he was not even permitted to hear mass.[2] In the middle of July the Pope deprived him of his office as governor of Sutri,[3] although so far none of the accusations against him had been

[1] See Appendix, Nos. 46-47.

[2] See Navagero's report of June 19, 1557, in BROWN, VI., 2, n. 941. An *Avviso of August 21, 1557, first mentions at this time his deprivation of hearing mass; this is, however, a mistake for the refusal to allow Morone to gain the Indulgence then published, which he had begged to do; see BROWN, VI., 2, n. 1018.

[3] *Il Papa ha levato il governo di Sutri al rev. Morone et datolo al card di Napoli. Navagero on July 17, 1557 (Cod. 6255 of the Court Library, Vienna). The villa of Morone at Sutri now belongs to the seminary there; a mantelpiece (now in the bishop's palace) bears the inscription: Io. Card. Moronus.

proved. For this reason Morone refused to purchase his freedom by an abjuration of heresy in general. He rightly understood that by so doing he would acknowledge that he had been
found wanting in matters of faith.[1]

At the beginning of August the supporters of the Cardinal
requested that he might be set at liberty. They were informed
that if he were to ask mercy of the Pope, a way of setting him
free would be found. Morone, however, could not be induced
to do this ; he declared that mercy presupposed a fault, and
that therefore he could not ask it ; the only thing he asked
was justice, even if they were to keep him in the Castle of St.
Angelo all his life.[2]

As Morone, in the consciousness of his innocence, persisted
in remaining firm on this point,[3] he had to languish in the
dark dungeons of the Castle of St. Angelo until the death of
Paul IV. It appears that, besides Morone and Pole, other
Cardinals came under the suspicion of the Inquisition. In
the last half of August, 1557, the same tribunal ordered the
arrest of Cardinal Bertano's secretary, of a member of the
household of Cardinal Farnese, and also of a theologian of
Cardinal du Bellay. These arrests were made in connection
with a charge of heterodoxy, although this seems to have been
a mistake ; on the other hand the proceedings against them
were based on grave offences against morality, of which they
had been guilty.

For a long time nothing more was heard of Cardinal Morone ;
a contemporary states that it seemed as if he had been crossed
out of the book of the living.[4] When Alba again drew atten-

[1] See Carne's report of July 2, 1557, in TURNBULL, n. 641.
The report of Masius (Briefe, 297) shows how right Cardinal
Morone was.

[2] See the **report of Navagero of August 5, 1557 (Court
Library, Vienna).

[3] See the letter of September 18, 1557, in the Lett. de' princ.,
I., 195.

[4] See in Appendix No. 39 the *Avviso di Roma of August 21
1557 ; cf. Navagero in BROWN, VI., 2, n. 996. Bernardino
Pia reports in a *letter of August 21, 1557, to Cardinal E. Gonzaga

tion to the prisoner, who was still being kept in the strictest confinement, and interceded for him, he only succeeded in getting the case taken up once more.[1]   The speedy termination of the proceedings which was promised to him,[2] was not, how-ever, realized. As the Cardinal had successfully repudiated all the charges against him, and proved that he had taken proceedings against the very persons whose heretical views he was accused of sharing,[3] his detention must be condemned in the severest terms. Paul IV. was possessed by the idea that Morone, as well as Pole, was infected with heresy, and the terrible picture of a suspected heretic one day ascending the throne of St. Peter left him no peace.[4]

Queen Mary of England had, in the meantime, offered resistance to the recall of Pole which had been ordered by Paul IV. As her earnest representations, that such a measure would seriously interfere with the Catholic movement in Eng-land, proved unavailing, she resolved to take a grave step ; an order was issued that any bearer of Papal letters should be arrested. The attitude of Pole himself was very different. Although the Papal brief had not been delivered to him, he was aware of it, and that was enough. He immediately resigned his title and the insignia of legate, and at once re-frained from every function connected with his office. In order to learn what the head of the Church really wished, and

that Cardinal Bertano had been in great trouble at first, on account of the arrest of his secretary Adriano by the Inquisition, " ma poi ch'ella è chiarita che tal captura è per interesse partico-lare del med^{mo} M. Adriano imputato per heretico et d' haver mangiato carne il venerdì ella si è consolato." The *teologo* of du Bellay, who was also arrested at that time by the Inquisition, is not mentioned here by name (Gonzaga Archives, Mantua).

[1] *Cf*. Navagero in BROWN, VI., 2, n. 1041 and 1042, the **Avviso of October 9, 1557, and TACCHI VENTURI, I., 538 *seq*., n. 3.

[2] See the *letter of B. Pia to Cardinal E. Gonzaga of September 22, 1557 (Gonzaga Archives, Mantua).

[3] *Cf*. Navagero in BROWN, VI., 2, n. 1062.

[4] See *ibid*.

also to justify himself against the accusations that had been made against him, he sent his confidential envoy, Niccolô Ormanetto, to Rome. Ormanetto, however, did not succeed in accomplishing anything. Paul IV. insisted that Pole was suspected of heresy, and that he must defend himself in person in Rome ; it was also necessary that he should at once be confronted with Morone.[1]

Cardinal Carafa received orders, before he entered upon his Spanish legation in October, 1557, that he was to justify the proceedings against the two Cardinals with Philip II., and to urge the king to deliver up Pole. It is incredible that Paul IV. could have supposed that the Spanish king would agree to such a proceeding, as the whole world knew that, if he returned to Rome, Pole could only expect the same treatment as Morone, who had been imprisoned for months in the Castle of St. Angelo, and was still kept there, although the Inquisition could fix no guilt on him at his trial.[2] Much as the Inquisitors endeavoured during the time that followed to obtain proofs against him, they could not succeed in doing so. On the contrary, documents were discovered which left no doubt as to the Catholic sentiments of Morone,[3] but in spite of this, the unfortunate Cardinal was not set at liberty.

Paul IV. looked upon Cardinal Pole as the more guilty of the two. Morone, he considered, had only been a docile pupil, who had become worse than his master. The Pope complained to Navagero that Priuli, Pole's secretary, also belonged to this accursed school, and to this house of apostates, as also did Marcantonio Flaminio, who would have been burned, had he not died. " We have had his brother, Cesare Flaminio, burned in the piazza before the church of the Minerva." Galeazzo Caracciolo had been a friend of Priuli, and at the mention of his name Paul IV. would get into a terrible state of excitement, for Caracciolo, a grandson of the Pope's sister, had

[1] *Cf.* BECCADELLI, Vita del card. R. Pole, in the Monum., II., 318 *seq.*

[2] See TURNBULL, n. 641 ; PALLAVICINI 14, 5, 2 ; ZIMMERMANN, Pole, 332, 337.

[3] See Navagero in BROWN, VI., 2, n. 1086.

fled to Geneva, leaving his family behind. " Let us be silent
about him," exclaimed Paul IV., " even if my own father were
a heretic, I would gather the wood to burn him ! "[1]   In view
of these fearful words, it is only too easy to believe that, as the
trial of Morone was prolonged into the following year, grave
fears were entertained as to his fate.[2]

In view of the terrible severity of Paul IV. it is not strange
that hardly anyone in Rome ventured to intercede for the
unfortunate Cardinal.   Among the few who energetically took
up his cause were several members of the Society of Jesus.
No less a personage than Lainez, the General of the new Order,
had a letter written to P. Ribadeneira in Brussels on January
24th, 1558, asking him, together with P. Salmeron, to apply
to the confessor of Philip II., so that, through his mediation, the king might intercede for Morone, as well as for
Pole.[3]

The less were the solid grounds for imputing guilt to Morone,
the more did the fears of Paul IV. increase that this man, whom
he considered a heretic, might be destined to succeed him.   An
obstacle must be put in the way of such an eventuality by the
issue of the most stringent regulations.   At the end of 1558
it became known that Paul IV. had prepared a bull, according
to which any Cardinal who had been convicted of heresy, or
who had even been brought before the Inquisition on a suspicion of heretical tendencies, should be deprived of their active
and passive right of voting at the conclave.[4]   On February
8th, 1559, the Pope did indeed lay such a document before the
consistory, but did not succeed in getting it approved, as the
Cardinals declared that even the best man might have an
enemy, who would say evil things of him ; before conviction

[1] See the *report of Navagero of October 23, 1557 (State
Archives, Venice), translated in BROWN, VI., 2, n. 1067 ; cf.
BERTOLOTTI, Martiri, 20.

[2] See the *Avviso di Roma of February 4, 1559 (Cod. Urb.
1039, p. 8.   Vatican Library).

[3] See Epist. P. Salmeronis, I., 235.

[4] See Carne's report of December 31, 1558, in STEVENSON, I.,
54, and the Mantua report in ANCEL, Secrét., 53 n. 1.

a Cardinal could not be excluded from the conclave.[1]   The
bull was consequently remodelled.   In the form in which it
was signed by all the Cardinals, on February 15th, it only
declared that the election of a man who had actually, at any
time, lapsed from the faith, was invalid.   At the same time the
old regulations concerning the punishment of heretics, lay as
well as clerical, even when they had held the highest dignities,
were solemnly renewed and rendered more severe, so that all
persons who were possessed of rank and dignities should, after
the first offence, be treated as having relapsed, because it had
been proved that the defection of such persons entails the most
disastrous   consequences.[2]

[1] MÜLLER (Konklave Pius IV., 25) has found out the true state
of the case from Carne's report in STEVENSON, I., 136, and from
the excerpt *ex actis consist. et diar.* in LAEMMER, Mant., 209 ;
the only thing not correct is the date, February 15, which he
holds to.   The Acta consist. cancell. VII. (Secret Archives of
the Vatican) from which the following extract is taken, clear
up this point : *Die merc. 5 [correctly 8] febr. 1559 Consistorium
S. D. N. primo iussit bullam legi per dom. Barengum secretarium
contra de heresi convictos et condemnatos vel qui convinci
aut condemnari poterunt, ad quem et eius totum tenorem prout
in illa latius continetur me refero.

[2] These are the essential points contained in the much discussed Bull *Cum ex apostolatus officio* (Bull. VI., 551 *seq*.).   In
the battles which were waged before and after the definition of
Papal Infallibility, the adversaries of the doctrine, and especially
DÖLLINGER (Janus, 405 *seq*.) endeavoured to give a dogmatic
and ex cathedra character to this bull of Paul IV.   There can
be absolutely no question of this.   The exordium of the bull
only gives the motive for the supreme authority of the Papacy.
Grounds for decisions, in themselves, are, however, never considered as actual authoritative standards in ordinary Councils,
but only the decisions themselves.   In the document we are
considering, the essence is contained in the sanction of punishment ; in the bull, it is true, we come upon the word *definimus* ;
however, this expression also occurs in non-dogmatic documents ;
see HERGENRÖTHER, Staat und Kirche, 767, where it is explained
in the clearest manner that there is no question here of a dogmatic

Paul IV., however, did not give up his original plan. On March 6th he issued a decree that no one who had even been accused of heresy, could become Pope, although such a one would not forfeit his active, but only his passive right of voting.[1] No one had any doubt that both regulations were especially aimed at Morone.[2]

At the beginning of May, 1559, it was understood that the Pope had once more offered Morone pardon, if he would ask for it. Morone's answer was the same as before ; he asked nothing but justice.[3] The four Cardinal Inquisitors again took up the proceedings against him.[4] When, on May 22nd, the severe Cardinal Rosario, one of the four, died suddenly, it was hoped that a favourable turn in the state of affairs would come for Morone.[5] On June 2nd, they did actually begin to read the process which the Inquisition had instituted against him, before the General Congregation of Cardinals. As daily

pronouncement, but only of a disciplinary act. The writer of the criticism on KRAUS, Kirchengeschicte in the Histor.-polit. Bl. ,CII., 352 seq. emphasizes that the discovery of the " Janus " party that the bull was intended to sanction the " Roman principles concerning the connection of the two powers " is absolutely false, since the document contains nothing more than simple disciplinary regulations, which pre-suppose that the public laws existing at that time had been issued for the protection of the Catholic faith, and in the interests of public order against those who infringed it. An after effect of Döllinger's error is the equally unfounded view taken by HUGO KOCH (see Histor.-polit. Bl., CXX., 849) that in the bull of Paul IV. the " hierocratic idea " is put forward. Cf. also FÈVRE, Hist. de la Papauté, VII., 275 seqq.

[1] LAEMMER, Mant., 210. MÜLLER, loc. cit.

[2] See the **Avvisi di Roma of February 18 (Si crede fatto per convincere et privare Morone) and April 8, 1559 (see Appendix No. 55). Vatican Library.

[3] **Avviso di Roma of May 6, 1559 ; ibid.

[4] See the **Avviso di Roma of May 20, 1559 (Appendix No. 56) ; ibid.

[5] See the **Avviso di Roma of June 3, 1559 (Appendix No. 57) ; ibid.

meetings of the Cardinals were now being held with regard to this matter, a speedy termination was expected. On June 15th a month was given to the Cardinal to reply once more to all the charges brought against him. He was also now allowed to discuss the matter with others.[1] At the beginning of July several defenders were appointed for him, among others Marcantonio Borghese,[2] and the Inquisitors conferred almost daily as to the affair;[3] the Pope seemed to have time for nothing else, and his proceedings inspired everyone with fear.[4]

The difficulties which the affairs of the imprisoned Cardinal, whose eyes had suffered a great deal from his confinement,[5] had to encounter, are evident from a report of Bernardino Pia to Cardinal E. Gonzaga on July 28th,.1559. Pia had shown the prisoner a copy of the letter in which Cardinal Gonzaga had begged the Emperor to intervene on behalf of Morone, and had written to him a detailed report as to his position. Morone, says Pia, was quite convinced that if the Pope died before his case was decided, he could take part in the conclave. Paul IV. and the Cardinal Inquisitors also knew this very well, and therefore the Pope was now hurrying on the conclusion of the matter. Moreover, they were making difficulties about returning to Morone the papers which testified in his favour. Morone, continues Pia, recognized that Cardinal

---

[1] See the *Avvisi di Roma of June 10 and 17, 1559 (Vatican Library). G. A. Calegari reports on June 10 to Commendone :

*E stato ogni dì congregatione d'inquisitione avanti S.S.^tà dove si sono letti sempre i processi di Morone.

[2] Al card^al Morone sonno stati dati advocati et defensori ms. Marc' Antonio Borghese et altri, fa copiar il processò per darglilo. *Avviso di Roma of July 1, 1559 (Vatican Library).

[3] So reports G. A. Calegari in a *letter to Commendone, dated Rome, July 5, 1559 (Lett. di princ., XXIII., n. 2. Secret Archives of the Vatican).

[4] See the Portuguese report of June 17, 1559, in the Corpo dipl. Port., VIII., 150.

[5] See in Appendix No. 48 the *Avviso of April 2, 1558 (Vatican Library).

Gonzaga was right in his view that it would now be better if
the proceedings could be drawn out as long as possible, and he
therefore did not press matters, but he considered that the Pope
and the judges, especially Rebiba, were too vehement.   Had
not the Pope, as Bernardino Pia goes on to relate in his report,
remarked a few days before, that a trial had not been at all
necessary, for he knew the true state of affairs, he was the
judge, and he could pronounce sentence without more ado?
Such threats did not frighten a man like Morone, who was
conscious of his innocence.   He had confidence in God, and
hoped that the Cardinals, and especially Pacheco and Puteo,
would not allow injustice to be done.   Pacheco had the
minutes of the trial copied, in order to have them at hand at
any time.   Morone hoped, if the affair followed a legitimate
course, to come out of it all completely justified.[1]

[1] S. S. R. [Morone], writes B. Pia, è chiara che se il papa morisse
prima che fosse espedita la sua causa ei potrebbe entrar in conclave et questo istesso lo sa S.S.^tà et i cardinali giudici et per
questo rispetto il papa sollecita l'espeditione con molta fretta
et se gli fanno degli aggravii et fra gli altri questo in non res-
tituirli le scritture che le tolsero fin da principio et che fanno
a suo proposito talché non hieri l'altro fu forzato a far una pro-
testa che il tempo non corresse fin che dette scritture non fossero
interamente restituite.   Conosce benissimo S.S.R. che ciò ᴓhe
V.S.I. dice che sarebbe bene che la causa andasse in longo et che
l'esempio che da di p. Paolo III. et del card. di Ravenna [B.
Accolti] serve alla pura verità et non è essa per affrettare, ma
trova tanta passione nel papa et nei giudici et fra gli altri primi
in M. Pisa [Rebiba] che non sa bene come poter ritardar la fuga
che le danno.   Dice che el papa quattro dì sono bravò gagliardamente saper i casi suoi che non occorrevano tanti processi,
scritture ne giustificationi ne servar termini che saveva benissimo
come si stesse il fatto, che esso era il giudice vero che senza altro
poteva et doveva dar la sentenza et altri simili et terribili parole,
pure spera in Dio che i cardinali habbino a non lasciar far torto
et massimamente Pacecco et Puteo, i quali hanno il processo
in mano et Pacecco lo fà copiar per tenerne copia appresso,
di se et poter vederla a tutt' hore.   Se non se le fa torto è per
S.S.R. sicuro di giustificarsi benissimo (Gonzaga Archives,Mantua).

The hour of his liberation only came for the sorely tried Cardinal, who continued to defend himself energetically,[1] as he had done from the first, when Paul IV. died. Two days later, the College of Cardinals resolved, although not without some opposition, to allow him to enter the conclave, with, moreover, the active and passive right of voting.[2] The new Pope, however, at once ordered a revision of the case against Morone. After a strict investigation by Cardinals Puteo and Ghislieri, of whom one was celebrated as a legal authority, and the other as a theologian, Pius IV. pronounced the final sentence on March 13th, 1560. This blames the proceedings of the Inquisition under Paul IV. on a number of points, both with regard to the actual facts and to the procedure. The imprisonment of Morone had been effected without the slightest legitimate grounds for suspicion. The investigation itself, as well as the whole conduct of the process, in which the prescribed and necessary forms had not been observed, was stigmatized as invalid, indiscreet and unjust. It was further established that there neither existed any reason for the condemnation of the Cardinal, nor any suspicion, however slight, as to his orthodoxy, and indeed that the very opposite of the accusation against him had come to light, and that the Cardinal must therefore be declared absolutely innocent.[3]

Such a vindication of Cardinal Pole could not take place, as he had already died on November 18th, 1558. Gentle and mild as the noble Englishman was, he nevertheless felt the

[1] See the report of Ascanio Caracciolo in MÜLLER, Konklave, 26 n. 1.

[2] See MASSARELLI, 334; Vargas in DÖLLINGER, Beiträge, I., 272; RIBIER, II., 829.

[3] See RAYNALDUS, 1560, n. 98; MASSARELLI, 343; PALLAVICINI, 14, 2-3; SICKEL, 8, 10, 46. In the *Vita di Morone (Varia Polit., XIX., 502, in the Secret Archives of the Vatican) it states that the Cardinal has been *per false calumnie et maligne persecutioni* kept in prison for 26 months. How fully the sharp criticisms on the procedure of Paul IV. are justified is clear from the documents in the Seminary Library, Foligno, in Appendix Nos. 46-47.

disgrace put upon him most deeply. He could not remember that a Cardinal, during the time of his office as legate, had ever been deposed without previous examination, on the mere suspicion of heresy. The charge brought against him appeared to him all the more strange, as, before his departure for England, he had had a long and confidential conversation with Paul IV., then Cardinal Carafa, in which he had proved his orthodoxy to the complete satisfaction of the latter. Besides this, there was the honourable testimony which the Pope himself had bestowed upon him in the consistory when he was created Archbishop of Canterbury. " Why," he asked himself, " should the Pope suspect my orthodoxy, when I have been engaged in constant battles and disputes with the heretics and schismatics, and have had great success in gaining advantages for the Catholic religion ? Because my activities have been so disagreeable to the heretics in England, nothing would give them greater pleasure than to hear me stigmatized with the name of " heretic " myself. Even supposing that I had formerly considered false doctrines to be true, which is certainly not the case, that would be no reason for taking steps against me, now that I have won such glorious victories over the heretics, saved so many souls by my efforts and struggles, and once again re-established the authority of the Holy See in England."[1]

A biographer of Pole justly remarks that he had to pass through one of the hardest tests that can be imagined for a true son of the Church, a test which was to prove whether he placed the holy cause to which he had devoted his life before his own interests and even his own person.[2] Pole stood this test with the greatest distinction. In humble obedience to the

---

[1] See STRYPE, Memorials, VI., 35, and ZIMMERMANN, Pole, 341 *seq*. Concerning the conversation between Pole and Carafa see the letter of F. Gherio to L. Beccadelli, dated Rome, April 29, 1553, in BECCADELLI, II., 348 *seq*. The groundlessness of the charge of heresy against Pole is emphasized by modern writers, especially acutely and justly by CUCCOLI, M.A. Flaminio, Bologna, 1897, 107 *seq*.

[2] KERKER, Pole 115.

supreme authority placed over him by God, he looked upon the injustice shown to him as a blow from the hand of his father, to be borne with respect and patience.

In his first excitement Pole had drafted a letter of self-vindication ; in thinking this over later, however, he felt that he had, in some places, expressed himself too bitterly concerning the weaknesses of the Pope. He therefore threw the letter into the fire with the words : Thou shalt not uncover the nakedness of thy father.[1]

Pole did not despair, however, of inducing the head of the Church to change his mind. It is characteristic of his genuine Catholic sentiments that, in the letter which he addressed to Paul IV. on March 30th, 1558, he first and above all took up the cause of his friend Priuli, and also raised his voice on behalf of the imprisoned Morone. In his own defence he remarked : " I, more than anyone else, must be the opponent of the heretics and·schismatics, for, as your Holiness well knows, among the many and heavy blows which have been dealt against me, there was not one which did not come from them, and solely for the sake of the Catholic Church. But, people may say to me, what weight can your recommendation have in a matter of this kind, if you yourself are accused of heresy before the same court ? This much, at any rate, in so far as manifest deeds on behalf of the Church and religion must be of greater weight than the mere assertions of those who can adduce neither words nor actions against me, for none such exist. But, they will say, this accusation against you was already entered upon when your confidential friend Morone was thrown into prison on the suspicion of heresy ; your deposition is a proof of your guilt.

What shall I answer to this ? First, that the words of your Holiness are more worthy of belief than any hints or strange rumours. Your Holiness has declared to the English ambassador and to my agent who was sent to Rome, that you had

---

[1] BECCADELLI, II., 325-326. A friend of Pole's had taken a copy before it was burnt, and this is still preserved ; see ZIMMERMANN, Pole, 338 *seq.*

withdrawn the legation from me, not because I had been guilty
of any fault, but because you did not consider it fitting to make
an exception in the case of England, and to leave me as legate
with a king who was carrying on war with the Pope, when all
the other legates accredited to the King of Spain had been
recalled.   I have accepted the explanation given by your
Holiness as to the reason for my deposition, although the circumstances of this kingdom are not quite the same as those of
Spanish countries.   After the reconciliation with the king, the
legations in the different parts of the Empire were again
restored, and your nephew was sent as legate to the Spanish
court ; my reinstatement, however, in spite of the urgent
requests of the queen, the petition of the College of Cardinals,
and the demands of all the estates of this realm, has always
been postponed ; indeed, your Holiness has allowed the rumour
to be circulated that an action was about to be brought against
me for heresy.   How am I to explain the proceedings of your
Holiness ?   Am I to believe that there is here a question of a
matter concerning God, as you informed the English ambassador when he pressed for an answer ?   Am I to believe that your
present course of action is based on the conviction that you
are thereby fulfilling the command of God, and performing
your duty to Him, and honouring Him ?   How can I do so ?
Does God order a son to be slaughtered ?   He did so once,
when He commanded Abraham to sacrifice his son Isaac,
whom he loved, and with whom the promise was connected.
What else does your Holiness plan but my death, since you
are trying to rob me of the glory of my orthodoxy ?   What
sort of life, I ask you, does one leave to the shepherd in the
eyes of his flock, when one has deprived him of the good name
of his orthodoxy ?   The fatal axe which you have destined
for me, will destroy me much more surely than that destined
for Isaac, who at the sight of the preparations for the sacrifice,
asked : ' Father, behold fire and wood ; where is the victim ? '
As I see the fire and the sword in the hands of your Holiness,
and my shoulders are laden with the wood for the sacrifice, I
do not need to ask where is the victim, but must, on the contrary, inquire why your Holiness, prejudiced by false sus-

picions, is thinking of slaughtering me on account of religion, me, the son who has always loved you, who is not conscious of having done anything to deserve your present disfavour, but much rather of having deserved your good will, as he has, by the grace of God, carried out the work that was expected of him, to the joy of the Church and the honour of the Holy See. Why then, is your Holiness about to pierce my soul with the sword of affliction ? If your Holiness does this in order, as you say, to fulfil a duty to God, then let the fire be laid to the victim. But I hope, if you act according to God's commands in other respects, that He will not allow the sacrifice to be accomplished, as He did not allow it in the case of Abraham."[1]

In his will, Pole solemnly declared once more that he persevered completely and firmly in the faith which his forefathers had received from the Roman Church, that he was obedient to the one, holy, Catholic Church of Christ, and to him who sat on the Apostolic chair as Roman Pontiff, and that with all due reverence he begged the blessing of Paul IV., whom he had served to the best of his ability, by seeking, in all his dealings with the Apostolic See, nothing but the honour of God and the good of the Church.[2]

There were two other prelates who, like Pole and Morone, were brought before the Inquisition to answer a groundless charge of heresy : Egidio Foscarari and Gian Antonio Sanfelice. Foscarari belonged to the Dominican Order, and enjoyed a great reputation as a theologian, no less than as a priest. Paul III. had appointed him Master of the Sacred Palace. In this capacity he had examined the Book of the Exercises of Ignatius of Loyola, and his sanction of this famous work could be seen at the beginning of the printed editions. In 1550, Foscarari was appointed Bishop of Modena,

---

[1] QUIRINI, V., 31-36.
[2] See CIACONIUS, III., 637. Giulio Gonzaga and Carnesecchi blamed this Catholic declaration as " superflua, per non dire scandolosa, in quel tempo massimamente " (AMABILE, I., 177). The comments made thereon by Amabile betray a complete ignorance of Catholic doctrine.

in succession to Morone. In the following year he took part
in the Counoil of Trent and, after his return to Modena, distinguished himself as a bishop in every way. This pious and
learned prelate now fell under suspicion and was imprisoned
in the Castle of St. Angelo on January 21st, 1558, and proceedings against him were undertaken by the Inquisition. No
proof whatever of any guilt could be found, and Foscarari
therefore demanded a solemn declaration of his innocence.
This was refused him. He only regained his freedom on
August 18th, 1558, after he had pledged himself to appear
before the Inquisition whenever required.[1]

The proceedings against the former Bishop of Cava, Sanfelice, who was arrested at the same time as Morone,[2] can, at
any rate, be explained, in so far that this hot-blooded native
of south Italy had, in 1547, at the Council of Trent, during the
deliberations concerning the doctrine of justification, vehemently advocated false views, at any rate, objectively.[3] It
could not, however, be proved that Sanfelice had obstinately
held to heretical opinions ; he had not gone beyond the
freedom of discussion allowed by the Council, and he was
liberated in July, 1559, after an imprisonment of twenty-five
months.[4]

The Augustinian, Girolamo Negri, had attracted the hatred

---

[1] *Cf.* MASSARELLI, 465 ; PALLAVICINI, 15, 11, 2 ; 24, 13, 4 ;
QUÉTIF, II., 184 *seq.* ; TIRABOSCHI, VII., 1, 271 *seq.* ; BROMATO,
II., 452 *seq.* The absolution first pronounced by Pius IV. in
CANTÙ, II., 193 *seq.*

[2] See MASSARELLI, 310.

[3] See Vol. XII. of this work, p. 341.

[4] See MASSARELLI, 350 ;· PALLAVICINI, 15, 11, 1 ; UGHELLI.
I., 618 ; VII., 177 *seq.* ; AMABILE, I., 146 ; BERTOLOTTI, Martiri,
102. RODOCANACHI (S. Ange, 160) wrongly names Sanfelice's
successor instead of himself. A well known man of letters,
Niccolò Franco, who was arrested in the summer of 1558, for
mocking at the Inquisition, had also to be set at liberty in February, 1559, as the advocacy of heretical doctrines could not be
proved against him. See GNOLI in the Raccolta di studi dedic.
a A.d'Ancona, 550 ; *cf.* Giorn. stor. d. lett. Ital., XXVI., 224 n. 3.

of the Lutherans by his successful sermons against them, and at length they spread false reports that he advocated uncatholic opinions. The consequence of these calumnies was that in 1556, by the command of the Pope, Negri was deprived of the permission to preach. The heretics were triumphant at the issuing of this prohibition, but to the Catholics it was a source of annoyance. How hasty and imprudent this step had been was proved when a thorough investigation took place, which resulted in 1557 in a solemn declaration of Negri's innocence.[1]

Paul IV. might well have said to himself that by the unjust persecution of innocent persons, he had very seriously injured his own reputation, as well as that of his much valued tribunal of the Inquisition.[2] Such an idea, however, never occurred to him. When representations were made to him on account of his excessive severity, he only replied that it was in consequence of the excessive consideration shown to others, that the Church had lost nine-tenths of her adherents.[3] Once only, in February, 1559, did he put a stop to severe proceedings against an innocent person ;[4] in this case there was question of no less a person than Johannes Gropper.

The exaggerated zeal and impetuosity of the Pope was, at last, the cause of his having a dispute and quarrel with his Grand Inquisitor.[5] The circumstances were as follows : The

[1] See TIRABOSCHI, VII., 1, 248 seq. (Roman edition).

[2] It was supposed that in this case, as in others, he had only been influenced by personal hatred ; cf. the opinions collected by MÜLLER (Konklave Pius' IV., 23, n. 1), of which it should indeed be said that they were absolutely unjust and inapplicable, as PALLAVICINI (14, 5, 3-4) has brought out against Sarpi. If anything is clear it is that Paul IV. honestly believed that Pole, Morone, and the others whom he persecuted, were infected by heresy. He had been convinced of this for a long time. It is not, therefore, just when contemporaries attribute the treatment of Pole and Morone to an intrigue of the nephews ; the latter only fanned a feeling which already existed.

[3] CASTALDO, 118.

[4] Cf. supra p. 184.

[5] There had been no lack of previous small differences of opinion. Thus Ghislieri writes to G. Franchi on March 11, 1558 :

Inquisition had been hitherto so severe in Spain that no opinions at variance with the Catholic faith could be found.[1] There now appeared to be a change for the worse. Already, in the forties of the XVIth century a community of crypto-Protestants had arisen in Seville, to which belonged several priests and monks. The following is an example of the means they employed : Constantino Ponce de la Fuente, who had been preaching in the cathedral since the end of 1555, had lately fallen under suspicion. In order to conceal himself from the Inquisition, and to be able secretly to continue his Protestant propaganda, he offered himself to the Jesuits, who had possessed a college in Seville since 1554, as a candidate for admission into the Order. He was, however, refused.[2] The Inquisition had learned of this movement in Seville, which was so dangerous to the Catholic faith, in spite of the cunning of the innovators. When, at the beginning of 1557, inquiries were made concerning several suspected persons, eleven monks from the Hieronymite monastery, S. Isidore, left their house in order to escape to Geneva. This remarkable step increased the suspicions of the Inquisition, which, in July, 1557, succeeded in coming upon the traces of the Protestant community, after the discovery of a number of anti-Catholic writings, which had been smuggled into the city. About a hundred arrests were eventually made, and five monks of S. Isidore were also imprisoned ; similar events took place at Valladolid.[3] Suspicion had also fallen on Bartolomeo Carranza, the Arch-

---

*Ho parlato a N.S. qual con suo solito santo zelo mi ribuffò con dirme che senza dar altra dilatione si dovessi procedere ne la causa (Cod. E. VII., 15 of the University Library, Genoa).

[1] Concerning the severity of the Inquisition see the report from the court of Charles V. of the year 1535 in the Histor. Jahrb., XIII., 194.

[2] See ASTRAIN, II., 94 *seqq.*

[3] See SCHÄFER, Beiträge, I., 264 *seqq.*, 348 *seqq.*, 373 *seqq.* The statements made hitherto concerning the large number of Protestants in Spain, are here reduced to their proper proportion by means of reasonable investigation. See also SCHÄFER, Sevilla und Valladolid, Halle 1903.

bishop of Toledo, during the trial of the prisoners. This man, who was distinguished for his learning and zeal for souls, had rendered great services to the Church, and had himself repeatedly taken steps against the disseminators of false doctrine ; he had also published a book in the Spanish language in 1558, entitled " Declarations concerning the Christian Catechism." In this book, it is true, he advocated Catholic doctrine on the whole, but on certain points expressed himself in an erroneous manner, or at any rate in a way liable to be misunderstood. Carranza mentioned indulgences in only one place in his book, which contained over 800 pages, and then in a contemptuous manner.[1]

The very first news of the discovery of these Protestant communities in Spain had aroused the greatest consternation in Rome.[2] The Pope forgot all his old enmity towards Charles V., and praised his watchfulness.[3] Rumour magnified the danger very considerably. The Spanish Grand Inquisitor, Fernando de Valdes, in his report to Paul IV., himself dealt with the discovery of the two communities in Seville and Valladolid, in terms which, if the extent of the evil had not been more clearly defined from another quarter, might have meant that the whole of Andalusia and Castille had been infected with the " plague of heresy."[4] As, at the same time, it transpired that heretical passages had been discovered in a work by one of the first dignitaries of the Church in Spain, Paul IV. was overcome by even greater horror and amazement.

The Pope endeavoured to stem the threatened danger by issuing a number of most severe regulations. On January 4th, 1559, he bestowed on the Grand Inquisitor Valdes, the

[1] See LAUGWITZ, Carranza, 29 seqq. The position which Carranza held with regard to Protestantism, has, indeed, never been made quite clear, but appears not to have been without objection ; see SCHÄFER, I., 265 n.

[2] See the **letter of Garimberto of June 18, 1558 (Secret Archives of the Vatican).

[3] See the *Avviso di Roma of June 25, 1558 (Vatican Library).

[4] See SCHÄFER, I., 186 ; III., 104 seqq.

exceptional powers which he asked for, authorizing him to hand over to the secular arm for punishment, all heresiarchs, teachers of heresy, and other heretics concerning whom there might be reason to suppose that they did not intend to abjure their errors from earnest and honourable motives, but only in order that they might be able, when once they were set at liberty, once more to disseminate heresy, teach it again, or otherwise promote it, thus doing injury to the work of the Inquisition ; these special powers were also to be used in the case of those who had relapsed.[1] To this decree, which superseded the usual rules, a regulation was added on the following day, with regard to the discovery and destruction of heretical books.[2] On January 7th, larger revenues were allocated to the Spanish Inquisition,[3] and on the same day the Grand Inquisitor was authorized, for a period of two years, to hold investigations concerning questions of faith, in the case of all bishops, archbishops, patriarchs and primates, to take proceedings against them, and, in the event of their being likely to escape, to arrest them and hold them in safe custody, on condition, however, that a report of everything should be at once sent to the Pope, and the guilty parties as well as the

---

[1] See RAYNALDUS, 1559, n. 18 ;   cf. LLORENTE, II., 261 ; SCHÄFER, I., 316 seq.

[2] See RAYNALDUS, 1559, n. 15.

[3] See RAYNALDUS, 1559, n. 16. When the Spanish nunciature was transferred to the Bishop of Chiusi in the spring of 1559, the latter received a special admonition, besides the instructions to protect the liberty of the Church against the encroachments of the royal power, to promote the Inquisition by every means in his power (see LAEMMER, Melet., 174 seq. ; PIEPER, 105). Concerning a brief of 1555 to the Inquisition in Granada, see LEA, Celibacy, Boston, 1884, 568. The same author remarks (Confession, I., 385) that Paul IV.'s brief to the Spanish Inquisition against sollicitation is not, as Llorente states, of 1556, but of February 18, 1559. To the end, Paul IV. was against the too great independence of the Spanish Inquisition. According to RIESS (p. 295), Paul IV. endeavoured, in the autumn of 1557, to bring to Rome all the suites of the Spanish monarchy against heresy, especially those from Sicily.

sealed acts of their trial, be sent, as soon as possible, to Rome.[1]

This brief was directed against Carranza, for whose arrest the Inquisition now made preparations. Much as Philip II. was in agreement[2] with the severe measures taken against the heretics, it was only after great hesitation that he allowed steps to be taken against Carranza, and he insisted that due respect should be shown to the prisoner.[3] The archbishop took great trouble to have his case transferred to Rome, and sent a Dominican[4] there for this purpose, who was received and supported by Cardinal Ghislieri. This excited the Pope, who in his impaired state of health, was always growing more nervous and violent,[5] to such an extent that, for half-an-hour, he hurled such violent reproaches in the consistory at the hitherto highly esteemed Cardinal, that Cardinal Consiglieri remarked that it was impossible to live or have dealings with the Pope any longer. At a second consistory Paul IV. repeated his reproaches against Ghislieri, declared that he was unworthy of his position, and said that he felt remorse of conscience for having ever bestowed the purple on him. A report of August 5th, 1559, from Rome, states that it was feared there that the Grand Inquisitor Ghislieri would be taken to the Castle of St. Angelo as a prisoner![6] It was at this time that Paul IV. said to the French ambassador that heresy was such a grave crime that, were a person even slightly infected with it, there re-

---

[1] See RAYNALDUS, 1559, n. 19 ; *ibid.*, n. 20, a brief to Philip II. of January 11, 1559, in which the king is requested to support the new Papal measures.

[2] *Cf.* the *letter of the royal confessor, Bernardo de Fresneda, to Cardinal Carafa, dated Brussels, February 12, 1559 (Lett. di princ., XI., 269. Secret Archives of the Vatican).

[3] See LAUGWITZ, 53.

[4] Fr. Hernando de San Ambrosio ; see Colección de doc. ined., V., 505, and DÖLLINGER, Beiträge, I., 259 *seq.*

[5] Paul IV.'s physician, A. Ricchi, lays special stress on this in his *account of the last illness of the Pope (Vatican Library; see Appendix No. 60).

[6] See Appendix No. 59.

mained no other remedy than to consign him at once to the flames, no matter if he belonged to the highest rank.[1] It is also characteristic of him that during the last days of his life, Paul IV. bestowed warm words of praise on his old adversary, Philip II., because the latter took severe measures against the heretics in Spain.[2] On May 21st, 1559, the first great public auto-da-fé had taken place in Valladolid. In accordance with the sentence pronounced, the greater number of the prisoners were pardoned ; thirteen, among them three priests, five women and one Jew, were handed over to the secular power for execution. All these unfortunates repented of their errors, with one exception, who, as a thoroughly obstinate heretic, was burned alive.[3]

[1] RIBIER, II., 815.

[2] RIBIER, II., 814 *seq.* According to the *Avviso di Roma of June 24, 1559, Paul IV. summoned the Inquisitors to his room on the Thursday, and pronounced a long panegyric on Philip II., on account of his punishment of the Lutherans (Vatican Library).

[3] See SCHÄFER, I., 324 *seq.* ; RIESS, 371 *seq.* ; S. FRANC. BORGIA, III., 505 *seqq.* ; Atti d. Soc. Lig., XXXVIII., 104 *seq.*

CHAPTER XII.

SPREAD OF PROTESTANTISM IN THE NETHERLANDS, FRANCE AND POLAND.

IN another part of the immense Spanish Empire, in the Netherlands, it happened, towards the end of the pontificate of Paul IV., that the Papal and royal powers found themselves united in common action in an ecclesiastical matter. The population of this country, which was highly developed both from a material and an intellectual point of view, held fast to the religion of their forefathers in the middle of the XIVth century, at least as far as the great majority was concerned.[1] It had not been possible, however, completely to master the Protestant movement in a country that was so eminently cosmopolitan. The secret Protestant propaganda in the Netherlands had become all the more dangerous during the first fifty years of the XVIth century, because the revolutionary Calvinism, which had already been introduced into the southern Walloon provinces by the English and French refugees, now began to take root in the northern provinces as well.[2] This change for the worse in the state of affairs did not escape the notice of Philip II., and if he contented himself at first with the confirmation of the regulations issued against heresy by Charles V., he nevertheless showed clearly that he was not going to tolerate the laxity with which these had hitherto been put into force.[3]

---

[1] According to the testimony of Heinrich Dionysius 1553; see HANSEN, (Akten zur Geschicte des Jesuitenordens, Bonn, 1896, 247) and Badoer (1557; see ALBÈRI, Ser. I., iii., 291) which are in agreement, there can be no doubt with regard to this; see PIRENNE, III., 452.

[2] Cf. RACHFAHL, Oranien, I., 409 seq.; PIRENNE, III., 525 seqq.

[3] See Bullet. de la Comm. Roy. d'hist., Ser. 2, XI., 231; PIRENNE, III., 461.

Proceeding rightly from the point of view that repressive measures alone would not be of much avail, he sought, by the furtherance of the Catholic reformation, to remove the numerous ecclesiastical abuses, from which not the least part of the movement of defection had originated. He gave the Jesuits permission to form settlements as early as August 20th, 1556, although Viglius, the President of the Council, opposed it.[1] The king also endeavoured in other ways to combat the grave abuses in ecclesiastical matters, as well as the serious defections from the Church ; at length he resolved to lay the axe at one of the principal roots of the ecclesiastical state of chaos.

In the seventeen provinces, the population of which was greater than that of any other European country north of the Alps,[2] there were only two real bishops of the country, those of Tournai and Arras.[3] The Bishop of Liège was an independent Prince of the Holy Roman Empire in his bishopric, and his diocese also included parts of the German Empire ; like the Bishop of Utrecht, he was under the Elector of Cologne. In the southern part of the Netherlands, Cambrai was dependent on a French archbishop. The same was the case in other parts of the Netherlands. These foreign bishops were too far away to understand the conditions there, and, moreover, they not infrequently exercised their powers there in an illegal manner, and to the prejudice of the sovereign. In addition to this, difficulties arose owing to the difference of the language, which were further increased when people had to go abroad to look after their rights or to appear before a judge. The native dioceses did not correspond to the political districts of the country, and they were so extensive and so thickly populated that one bishop was not able to look after them. In consequence of this, the gravest scandals, from a moral point of view, were able to creep in among the secular and regular clergy. Spiritual instruction, in the form of preaching and

---

[1] Cf. Vol. XIII. of this work, p. 209.

[2] Cf. PIRENNE, III., 358 seq.

[3] Cf. concerning the organization of the dioceses before 1559 LAENEN in the Annales de l'Acad. archéol. de Belgique, Ser. 5, VI., 67 seq.

catechizing, was woefully neglected, and the sacraments very carelessly dispensed. In some places the young people grew up in a state of utter neglect.[1] Even the more earnest-minded bishops were unable, in the unpractical and chaotic condition of the spiritual jurisdiction, to remedy the state of affairs.

In order to do away with this confusion, Philip II. asked from Rome a complete reorganization of the hierarchy, so that by an increase in the number of the bishops, and a diminution in the extent of the dioceses, they might be in a position to proceed, both against the ecclesiastical abuses, and the inroads of heresy. The Pope entrusted this important matter to a commission, consisting of Cardinals Pacheco, Saraceni, Puteo, Reumano, Capizuchi and Rosario. This commission recognized the good intentions of the Spanish king, who, even if he were greatly influenced by political motives, nevertheless had in view, above everything else, the futherance of the religious needs of his provinces of the Netherlands. The proposed reorganization would undoubtedly benefit them in the highest degree.[2]

After long and thorough consideration, it was decided in Rome, that, for the future, the jurisdiction of the German and French bishops should cease in the Netherlands, and that, in addition to the old dioceses, fourteen new ones should be established, namely, Namur, St. Omer, Malines, Antwerp, Ghent, Bruges, Ypres, Bois-le-duc, Roermond, Haarlem,

---

[1] See JANNSEN, Über die erste Periode der niederl. Revolution des 16. Jahrh., in the German edition of the Civiltà catt. I., Münster, 1855, 34 ; HOLZWARTH, I., 107 seq. ; cf. RACHFAHL. I., 306 seq., 610.

[2] See MIRAEUS, Opera dipl. III., 523 seq. ; cf. A. JANSEN, Het advies der commissie van zeven Kardinalen : Archief v. d. geschiedenis v. d. Aartsbisdom Utrecht, IX. (1881), 1-22 ; BROM, Archivalia, II. (1911), 147. The *Instructions for Sonnius, the envoy sent to Rome, dated Brussels, March 8, 1558, in the State Archives, Brussels. Concerning the plans of Philip II., and the justification of his proposal, see GACHARD, Corresp. de Philippe II., I., xciii. seq. ; KOCH, Abfall, 44 seq. ; HOLZWARTH, I., 69 seq. ; PIRENNE, III., 501 seq., 504.

Deventer, Leeuwarden, Groningen and Middelburg. These dioceses, which corresponded as far as possible to the frontiers of the separate provinces, and to the divisions of the two languages of the country, were placed under the three metropolitan churches of Cambrai, Utrecht and Malines. According to this arrangement, the Archbishop of Malines was to have the dioceses of Antwerp, Bois-le-duc, Ghent, Bruges, Ypres and Roermond under him ; the Archbishop of Cambrai was to have those of Tournai, Arras, St. Omer and Namur, and the Archbishop of Utrecht those of Haarlem, Middelburg, Deventer, Leeuwarden and Groningen.

For this reorganization, which was very excellent from an ecclesiastical point of view, the Pope had to make an important concession to the exertions of Philip II. on behalf of his national church. The Spanish king received the right to propose suitable candidates for the fourteen new dioceses, as well as for those of Utrecht, Tournai and Arras ; the king was to remunerate the new bishops from his own treasury, until a fixed income was allotted to them, and to choose the candidates carefully from among the doctors or licentiates of theology. In spite of this limitation, the measure meant an immense strengthening of the royal power. Whether the natives of the Netherlands, who were so jealous of their liberties, would quietly accept it, was another question. Besides this, the new bishoprics could not very well be endowed, except at the expense of the monasteries and collegiate foundations.[1] Consequently, there was considerable excitement among the nobility of the Netherlands, which spread among the influential clergy of the monasteries and foundations. Naturally, all those who were inclined to the new doctrines, regarded the prospect of an increased and more severe ecclesiastical super-

---

[1] The reasons for this compensation are explained in the judgment of the Cardinals cited *supra* p. 321, n. 2, that the " bona monasteriorum hodie non Christo, sed privatorum commodis et vitae voluptatibus serviant, eo quod in eis non admodum regulariter vivatur."

vision with great aversion. The new measure,[1] which was promulgated by a bull of May 12th, 1559,[2] proper and salutary as it was in the abstract, nevertheless contained the germ of grave complications.

In the neighbouring kingdom of France, which was so closely associated with the Netherlands by so many intellectual and material ties, Henry II. was watching, with no less decision than Philip II. was doing in his dominions, over the maintenance of the external stability of the old Church, which had brought so many advantages to the crown by means of the concordat.[3] The hopes which the reformers had built on the alliance of the French king with the German Protestant princes against the Emperor, had not been realized. Purely political reasons alone had tempted Henry II. to this course, and the persecution of the Protestants continued during the alliance just as severely as before. After the death of Julius III. it was again politics which had brought about a close union of Henry II. with the Pope.

Paul IV. did not delay in making his alliance with France useful for ecclesiastical purposes as well. If the nuncio, Gualterio, had already been active in exhorting the king to

---

[1] *Questa sera N.S. ha fatto congregatione di molti cardinali sopra la divisione et erectione dei vescovadi di Fiandra. B. Pia to Cardinal E. Gonzaga, dated Rome, April 22, 1559 (Gonzaga Archives, Mantua).

[2] Bull., VI., 559 *seqq.*; *cf.* GULIK-EUBEL, III., 38; MASIUS, Briefe, 318-319; BROWN, VII., n. 75. RIESS (p. 73) erroneously places this bull of May 12, 1559, in connection with the auto-da-fé of May 31, 1559; he also maintains that Philip II. did not obtain the right of appointment for Malines and Antwerp, which is contradicted by the text of the bull. Cambrai alone is not mentioned there. As early as August 8, 1559, Philip II. addressed a letter to the bishops of the Netherlands concerning the extirpation of heresy; see Compte rendu de la Comm. d'hist., Ser. 3, IX., 300 *seqq.*

[3] Concerning the action taken against the innovators in France since 1551, see AUBERT in the Rev. des quest. hist., LXXXIII. (1908), 107 *seq.*

take energetic steps against the innovators,[1] Cardinal Carafa lost no time, on his appearance at the French court, in proposing, in the Pope's name, the introduction of the Roman Inquisition into France.[2] The king willingly promised to do everything to suppress heresy in his kingdom. He also promised to observe the agreement regarding the concordat entered into with Julius III., which had been so often broken.[3] On account of the opposition of the Paris Parliament to the introduction of the Roman Inquisition, Henry II. and Paul IV. arranged a compromise, according to which three French Cardinals should conduct the Inquisition in France, under the direction of the Holy See. A brief of April 25th, 1557, entrusted Cardinals Lorraine, Bourbon and Châtillon with the necessary powers for so doing.[4] This arrangement, which the Parliament also resisted, lasted for so short a time that the Pope revoked it as early as June, 1558, and entrusted the work of the Inquisition once more to the diocesan bishops.[5] They, however, as well as the secular tribunals, were often wanting in decision. It is no wonder that those of the new religion were always growing bolder. Their number was constantly increasing, especially because the unprincipled king misused the privileges granted him by the concordat in the most shameful manner. Ecclesiastical benefices were used for the reward of those who had rendered services in war or at the court ; the younger nobles received them for their maintenance, for which reason the benefices were entered in a false name. It thus happened that officers serving in the army were also receiving the revenues of rich abbeys, and, what was still worse, several of

[1] See *Nonciat.*, II., 340.

[2] See RIBIER, II., 677.

[3] See *Nonciat.*, II., 354, 415, 459 ; *cf.* RAYNALDUS, 1555, n. 41.

[4] RAYNALDUS, 1557, n. 29. RIBIER, II., 677. The letter of thanks for the brief from Cardinal Lorraine to Paul IV., in the Zeitschr. für Kirchengesch., V., 611.

[5] This fact, hitherto unknown to all investigators, including HINSCHIUS (VI., 342), I have taken from an *Avviso di Roma of July 2, 1558 (Vatican Library). Concerning the resistance of the Parliament see SOLDAN, I., 252.

these holders of benefices also wanted to administer the office assigned to them. A Venetian ambassador remarked with astonishment how quickly soldiers and merchants in France were often turned into bishops and abbots. The ecclesiastical state consequently degenerated more and more, and it not infrequently happened that dioceses were abandoned by their bishops, or else possessed none at all. This neglect of their duty on the part of the superiors had the most disastrous effect on the lower clergy. In spite of all this, however, the Church still had deep roots among the people, though the great evils which had taken possession of them rendered them incapable of offering an effective resistance to the innovators.[1] A regeneration of ecclesiastical conditions might have been introduced by the Jesuits, but the University and the Parliament just at that time put the greatest obstacles in the way of any extension of their activities.[2]

The Catholics, therefore, remained weak, disunited and badly organized ; the innovators, on the other hand, kept firmly together, and steadily developed a methodical agitation, under the direction of Calvin. It is not, therefore, to be wondered at, that they were increasingly successful. Indeed, in the spring of 1559, a minority in the Parliament of Paris was favourable to them, and resisted the former severe measures against them. The king, who was more than ever inclined to a decisive resistance to heresy,[3] since the peace of Cateau-Cambrésis had been concluded with Spain in April, 1559, endeavoured to silence the opposition by appearing suddenly in the Parliament on June 10th. He had, however, to meet with violent resistance. If Parliament had hitherto attacked, in a thoroughly Gallican way, the Roman Curia as the source of all the evil, they did not now fail to turn also against the

---

[1] See Soranzo in ALBÈRI, Ser. I., II., 409 ; DE MEAUX, Luttes religieuses, 46 seqq. ; MARCKS, Coligny, 262 seq.

[2] Cf. Vol. XIII. of this work, p. 203 seq.

[3] Cf. SOLDAN, I., 266 seqq., where the decisions on the religious questions and the influence of the peace are made clear, and it is shown that no secret article concerning the extirpation of heretics existed.

king, whose loose manner of life afforded many points of attack. With unmistakable allusion to him, Anne Dubourg called out : " Adultery and debauchery swagger about unmolested, but who are those who are condemned to death ? Those whose crime consists in. having uncovered the Roman shame, and having striven to bring about a salutary reform." Henry II. answered by ordering the arrest of Dubourg, and addressing a circular to the Parliament and the courts of justice, admonishing them to the most severe measures against those who had fallen away from the faith.[1]

It was expected that Henry II. would see to the carrying out of his orders by making a tour of his kingdom, and, in alliance with the Duke of Savoy, undertaking an expedition for the destruction of Geneva, the head-quarters of Calvinism. All plans of this kind, however, were destroyed by the sudden death of the king, at the age of only forty-two ; he succumbed in July to a wound he had received in a tournament. Two months before this, the preachers of eleven heretical conventicles assembled secretly in the suburb of St. Germain, and there drew up a confession of faith, and a system of church government, both thoroughly imbued with the spirit of Calvin.[2] The number of the adherents of Calvin at this time in France amounted to 400,000,[3] if the Venetian ambassador, Soranzo, is to be believed. Under such circumstances the Parliament entrusted with the care of the country, and which was now entering upon office after the death of Henry II., would be a specially fateful one for France. Paul IV. feared that it would prove indulgent to those who had fallen away from the faith, and held up Philip II. before it as a model.[4]

[1] See DE MEAUX, Luttes relig., 56 seqq. ; cf. SOLDAN, I., 277 seq., and RANKE, Franzosische Geschicte, I.², 187 seq., Ranke erroneously makes the king appear in the Parliament as early as March 10. See also AUBERT, loc. cit., 111 seq.

[2] See HERZOG's Realenzyklopädie, III.³, 784 seq. ; VI.³, 232 seq.

[3] See ALBÈRI, Ser. I, ii., 409 ; cf. ibid., iii., 425 seq.

[4] Cf. besides RIBIER, II., 811, 815, the report of B. Pia to Cardinal E. Gonzaga, dated Rome, July 19, 1559 (Gonzaga Archives, Mantua).

The dangers which threatened the Catholic Church in Poland were no less grave than in France. The learned and eminent Bishop of Verona, Luigi Lippomano, had already been destined by Julius III. to act as nuncio at the court of the last Jagellon king, Sigismund Augustus, whose weakness and instability gave cause for the worst fears. On June 13th, 1555, Paul IV. ratified the appointment of Lippomano.[1] The nuncio, well provided with letters of recommendation from the Pope and Cardinal Farnese, who was then Protector of Poland, proceeded by way of Augsburg, where he was present at the Imperial Diet, on a special mission, from the end of July until September 7th. The learned Jesuit Salmeron was appointed by the Pope to accompany him to Poland.[2] The journey from Augsburg to Warsaw lasted thirty-two days, and from thence to Wilna, where the Polish king then resided, and which they at length reached on October 28th, another fifteen days. Salmeron drew a vivid picture of the difficulties of the long journey, and of the deprivations which the travellers had to endure, in a letter to Ignatius of Loyola. " Whoever has travelled through this country," he said, " has not only done penance for all his sins, but has also gained a plenary indulgence."[3]

When they were admitted to an audience at Wilna by the king, the latter declared to the nuncio that there were only two means of settling the religious confusion in his kingdom : either the holding of a General Council, which, under the present circumstances was impossible, or of a national council.[4] According to Catholic principles, a national council could not

---

[1] See RAYNALDUS, 1555, n. 56 ; ibid., n. 57-61 ; THEINER, II., n. 662-664 ; CARO-FARNESE, II., 314 seq. ; 326 seqq. ; cf. DEMBINSKY, Rzym, 191 ; EHRENBERG, 69 seq. ; see also L. LATINIUS, Lucubrat., I., 50 seqq., and HOSII epist., II., 597, 606. Concerning Lippomano, cf. also LAUCHERT, 570 seq.

[2] See POLANCO, V., 177. On July 12, 1555, Salmeron received ' scuta 60 pro itinere in regno Poloniae " (*Intr. et Exit., 1555. State Archives, Rome).

[3] Epist. Salmeronis, 130 ; cf. Hosii epist., II., 622.

[4] Salmeron to Ignatius on January 1, 1556, loc. cit., 132.

make a definite pronouncement with regard to matters of faith ; moreover, it contained within itself, under the circumstances then prevailing, the danger of the rise of an independent national church, and of a complete severance from the Holy See. Lippomano lost no time in pointing this out to the king, and in demanding that, instead of the previous negligence, strict measures should be adopted against the enemies of the faith. In his conversations with persons in authority, however, he found " all the doors closed."[1] The bishops also were wanting in decision and courage, and ecclesiastical conditions were in great need of improvement in every way.[2] With the exception of the eminent Hosius, and the noble Nicholas Dzierzgowski, Archbishop of Gnesen, most of the bishops were without any zeal for their office, and full of weak compliance ; several, indeed, were not free from the suspicion of having leanings towards heresy.[3] The Pope had already explained to them, on October 8th, 1555, in answer to their inquiry, that dogmas of the Catholic Church could only be decided in a General Council, but not in a provincial or national one, and at the same time had admonished them not to shrink from any danger in the defence of the faith. Repentant heretics should be forgiven, but obstinacy should be punished with great severity.[4] However, severity was not to be thought of, on

[1] *Ibid.* 133 ; *cf.* also Lippomano's report in DEMBINSKY, Rzym, 191, n. 2.

[2] *Cf.* Lippomano's report to Hosius of June 1, 1556, in CYPRIAN, Tabular. eccl. Rom., Frankfort, 1743, 67 ; Hosii epist., II., 713.

[3] *Cf.* EICHHORN, Hosius, I., 205 *seqq.* Joh. Drohojowski, bishop of Leslau (Kujawien) seemed to be especially open to suspicion ; *cf.* EHRENBERG, 74. Lippomano examined witnesses concerning him, and also concerning the bishop of Cracow, A. Zebrzydowski, and sent their evidence to Rome (see RELACYE, I., 26 *seq.* ; *ibid.* a letter of vindication from Drohojowski to Paul IV.). The Catholic parish priest, BUKOWSKI, is of opinion, in his history of the Polish Reformation (Dzieje reformacyi w Polsce, II., Cracow, 1883, n) that there were hardly three or four bishops who upheld the dignity of their position, and that, for the most part, the evil was increasing to an alarming extent.

[4] RAYNALDUS, 1555, n. 61.

account of the weakness of the good-natured king. Many influential members of the court cherished the new doctrines, some quite openly and some in secret, and used all their influence to support them. All efforts, therefore, for the defence of the Catholic Church against the attacks of the innovators, however illegal these might be, proved fruitless. The nobles could take possession of church property without molestation ; courage as well as unity were wanting to the Catholic party, and the erection of a Jesuit college, which Salmeron had wished to effect, proved quite impossible.[1]

Lippomano resolved to remain at Wilna for the present, and sent Salmeron back to Rome, so that he might report to the Pope concerning the state of affairs in Poland by word of mouth. Matters were daily growing worse, since the king allowed the nobles, in their private dwellings, to hold any form of divine service based on the Scriptures, which suited them best. It is clear from the instructions which Sigismund Augustus gave at the beginning of 1556 to the ambassador, Stanislaus Maciejowski, who was proceeding to Rome, that, in spite of all the representations of the Pope and his nuncio, the king still held fast to the idea that he could once more restore peace to his kingdom by holding a national council, and by making far-reaching concessions to the religious innovators.[2] When the ambassador arrived in Rome, in May, he was received with all due honour.[3] On May 5th he performed the solemn act of " obedientia " to the Pope.[4] The good impression which this had produced was completely destroyed, however, by the demands which Maciejowski made in the name of the king at a private audience : the marriage of priests, communion under both kinds, the saying of mass in the language of the country, and, finally, the holding of a

---

[1] Salmeron to Ignatius on January 1, 1556, *loc. cit.*, 133.

[2] DEMBINSKI, Beschickung des Tridentinums, 55 *seq.*, where details are given of the weakening of the Instructions.

[3] See Navagero's *report of May 2, 1556 (Library of St. Mark's, Venice).

[4] See *Acta consist. cancell. VII. (Consistorial Archives) ; MASIUS, Briefe, 259 ; MASSARELLI, 290.

national council, in the event of a General Council proving impossible, and should the Pope consent to it.[1]   Paul IV. was most painfully affected by the idea that a Catholic king should so far forget himself as to adopt as his own the demands of the very people whom he should have punished most severely, but he never for a moment thought of granting them. In a letter to the king, he referred him to his nuncio, who was fully instructed on all points, at the same time warning him most earnestly of the responsibility of the monarch, who would one day have to render an account before the tribunal of God's justice.[2]

Lippomano had, in the meantime, had some distressing experiences. Every day it was becoming clearer to him that it was not the king who ruled, but the great nobles, and, above all, Prince Nicholas Radziwill, who was related to the king by marriage, and who promoted the interests of the innovators in every way. In order to induce Radziwill to change his mind, Lippomano addressed a very urgent letter to him. In reply, he received a letter drawn up by the apostate Vergerio, which was full of personal insults and abuse, especially against the Pope, and was soon after circulated in print.[3] The nuncio's position grew still worse when it became known, through somebody's indiscretion, that he had advised the king, quite in accordance with the ideas of the Pope, to put an end to the religious complications in his kingdom, by having from eight to ten of the worst ringleaders put to death. Lampoons and caricatures now jeered at the Pope's representative, whose very life was threatened. Completely discouraged, Lippomano, at the beginning of April, 1556, begged to be recalled

[1] See the letter of the Duke of Paliano to Lippomano of May 30, 1556, in a Polish translation in the RELACYE, I., 29 seq.; cf. BROWN, VI., 1, n. 484.

[2] RAYNALDUS, 1556, n. 29; TURNBULL, n. 508; MASIUS, Briefe, 263 seq., 277 seq.

[3] KRASINSKI, 121. Concerning Radziwill see KONIECKI, Gesch. der Reformation in Polen, Breslau, 1872, 47; ROSTOWSKI Lituanicarum Soc. Iesu historiarum libri 10, ed. Martinov Paris, 1877, 5, 7.

from the " hell " in which he found himself. It was best, he wrote, very hastily, to leave Poland without a nuncio, since he could not remain with dignity in a place where monks and cardinals were openly mocked at, and designs were entertained against the life of the Pope's representative.[1] Lippomano had, nevertheless, to remain for almost another nine months at his very difficult post. It was especially painful to him that he found, on the part of the Catholics, not only incredible weakness, but also unfounded jealousy. When he finally succeeded, in September, in bringing together a provincial synod of the Polish clergy at Lowicz, they wanted to exclude him from the conferences, and it required all his energy and sagacity to prevent this. The synod made several salutary decisions with regard to the improvement of ecclesiastical discipline, and for the protection of the Catholics against the attacks of the heretics, and removed the immediate danger of a national council.[2] This danger, however, was by no means completely averted.

Lippomano, as well as the Pope, awaited the Diet, which was to be held in Warsaw, with great anxiety. They both feared that, in view of the weakness of the king, the fall of the Catholic Church in Poland was inevitable.

At the end of September, 1556, Lippomano had once more reported, in great detail, to Rome, the persecutions to which he was exposed on the part of the innovators. He would, he said, employ all his powers at Warsaw, for the defence of the Church, and in accordance with the commands of the Pope, but would then make use of the permission granted him, to return to Italy. It sufficed him to have shown that it was

[1] The letter of Lippomano to P. Contarini from Lowicz of April 8, 1556, in the Cod. Barb. lat. 822, p. 329 *seq.* (Vatican Library) ; also in the Library of St. Mark's, Venice, It. V., 16, p. 279 *seq.* ; in Polish in the RELACYE, I., 13 *seqq.*, Concerning the lampoons against Lippomano and the Pope see HOSII epist., II., 670, 751 ; HUBERT, 304 *seq.* ; VÖLKER, 29 *seq.*

[2] *Cf.* KRASINSKI, 116 *seq.* ; EICHHORN, I., 268 *seq.* ; RELACYE I., 33 *seq.*, 40 *seq.* ; TROSKOLANSKI, Dzieje reformacyi polskiej, 1556-1560, Lwów, 1905-1907.

neither the Pope's fault, nor his own, if matters did not improve. These matters Lippomano summed up by saying : " Here in this country, everyone acts exactly as he pleases, without fear of punishment."[1]

The following occurrence at the Diet at Warsaw shows that the nuncio was not too severe in his judgment. Paul IV., in an encyclical of December 4th, 1556, had earnestly admonished the Polish bishops to use every means to prevent disadvantageous decisions being arrived at in the assembly.[2] The result of this was that the demand for complete religious liberty, which was presented by the Prussian cities, in union with the Polish knighthood, was refused, the king declaring that the Diet must occupy itself only with the defence of the country. Before his departure, Sigismund even issued a prohibition of all religious changes ; this edict, however, was neither published nor carried out ![3]

At the beginning of 1557 Lippomano left the Polish kingdom,[4]

[1] " Ognuno fa ciò che gli piace nec est qui visitet aut qui cor rigat." Lippomano to the Duke of Paliano, dated Lowicz' September 22, 1556 (Cod. Barb. lat. 822, p. 355 of the Vatican Library, and It., V., 16, p. 292 seq. of the Library of St. Mark's, Venice). The letter in which Lippomano points out that he had not made use of his faculties, as he did not wish to take a certain Heller away with him from Poland, is in the RELACYE, I., 32-40, in a Polish translation.

[2] RAYNALDUS, 1556, n. 41.

[3] See EICHHORN, I., 273-274 ; cf. HOSII epist., II., 879.

[4] Cf. EICHHORN, I., 275 n. 1. On March 7, 1557, Lippomano *reports to Paul IV. from Verona that he is very much fatigued from the journey, and is also suffering from gout, for which reason he sends his auditor to report for the time being (Original in the Cod. Barb. lat. 5715 of the Vatican Library). In a *letter dated Verona, May 18, 1557, he expresses the hope of soon being able to go to Rome. Navagero reports concerning his arrival there on June 26, 1557 : *Gionse qui domenica il rev. di Verona ; " to-day he is only two leagues away from the Pope." ; (Court Library, Vienna, loc. cit.). Lippomano's *Relatione di Polonia (widely circulated in manuscript, e.g., in the Cod. Urb. 822, p. 634 seq. ; Ottob. 2433, p. 172 seq., 2510, p. 69 seq. Vatican

which then remained without a nuncio for six months.[1]
When, however, in the summer of 1558, another attack upon
the Catholic Church in Poland was declared to be imminent,
Paul IV. recognized that Lippomano's advice, to leave Poland
without a Papal representative, had been a mistake. On July
14th, the eminent Cardinal Rebiba was appointed legate to the
Emperor and the King of Poland. As obstacles to his departure presented themselves, the appointment of a new nuncio
for Poland was made on August 11th.[2] This was Camillo
Mentuato, who had already been in Poland under Julius III.
His experiences were no better than those of Lippomano.
Paul IV. had decided that two members of the Jesuit order,
Peter Canisius and Theodoric Gerhard, should accompany the
nuncio. Gerhard had to be replaced by another Jesuit, owing
to illness. As the latter also fell ill on the way, Canisius
arrived alone with the nuncio in Cracow, after a most difficult
journey, on October 12th, 1558. He found the Catholic
Church there flourishing externally, but dangerously threatened
with an attack by the innovators. The powerful nobles had
almost all fallen away, but the great mass of the people were

Library. Copies also in the Chigi and Corsini Libraries ;
translated in the RELACYE, I., 64 seq.) is of no great importance.

[1] WIERZBOWSKI (Synopsis legat. nuntior., etc., in Polonia,
Rome, 1880. 59) also supposes that Pamfilo Strasoldo was only
intended as nuncio in 1557. The instructions for him in the
Altieri Library, Rome, Miscell. VI., 161 seq., printed in CIAMPI,
II., 33. What horrible lies about Paul IV. were circulated in
Poland in the summer of 1557, is evident from the letter in
the Opera ined. St. Orzechowski, ed. KORZENIOWSKI, I., Cracow,
1891, 481 seq.

[2] See PIEPER, Legaten, 117 seq., where, however, the briefs
of Paul IV. concerning Mentuato's appointment, which are printed
in the RELACYE, I., 69 seq., 71 seq., are overlooked ; cf. also
L. LATINIUS, Lucubrat., I., 131 seq.; COGGIOLA, Capitolazione,
126 ; EHRENBERG, 76 seq. ; the statements in CIAMPI, I., 169
are quite erroneous. Concerning Rebiba see DEMBINSKI, Rzym,
195.

true to the old faith, and gave numerous proofs of their pious dispositions.[1]

The nuncio was not found wanting in zeal,[2] and Canisius supported him faithfully.[3] After a meeting with the Archbishop of Gnesen, he betook himself, accompanied by Canisius, to Petrikau, where the Diet was again to be held.

The longer Canisius remained in Poland, the more clearly did he understand the danger threatening the Church and her interests. " Everything here," he reports to Rome, " depends on the king and the bishops. The king has fair words for us, but nobody who knows his character more intimately expects anything from him. He puts the whole blame for the religious disasters of the last four years on the bishops ; they, in their turn, complain of the king."[4] These complaints appear to have been justified, for, as had previously been the case, no deeds followed his words.[5] The bishops themselves, however, were also much to blame. Canisius points this out, and says that it almost appeared as if, despairing of anything being possible, they had made up their minds for the worst, and thought only of one thing, which was to save what they could for themselves from the general shipwreck. Many of them, moreover, were very old men, and several of them were not to be trusted, especially a certain Uchanski, to whom the Pope had very properly refused confirmation, and from whom more was to be feared than was to be hoped from all the rest. The heretics now dared to hold divine service quite publicly, and hardly anyone, with the exception of the nuncio, raised any protest. The representatives of the Pope met everywhere with great mistrust ; Canisius had only one consolation : the newly appointed Archbishop of Gnesen, Przezembski, the

[1] BRAUNSBERGER, II., 294 seq., 301 seq., 303, 310 seq., 319 seq., 831 ; cf. ZALESKI in the publication Przeglad Powszechny, LI. (1896), 155 seq., 326 seq.

[2] BRAUNSBERGER, II., 325.

[3] Cf. Anz. der Krakauer Akad. der Wissensch., 1894, 228 seq.

[4] BRAUNSBERGER, II., 341.

[5] Cf. Lippomano's opinion in the letter of September 30, 1557, in HOSII epist., II., 879.

primate of the kingdom, came to him of his own initiative, in order to confer with him about the foundation of a Jesuit college in Poland.[1]

The principal duty of Mentuato was to prevent anything happening at the Diet which would be disadvantageous to the Church.[2] As the General Council was still in the distant future, the idea of a national synod again sprang up. Canisius endeavoured to rob the plan of its danger by proposing that the synod should be held under the presidency of a Cardinal. The fact that not only the nobles, but the cities as well, demanded the exclusion of the bishops from the forthcoming election of the king, on the ground that their oath to the Pope was not compatible with their oath of allegiance to the king,[3] shows the dangerous state of mind disclosed in the Diet. When the latter was safely concluded without any injury having resulted to the Church, the nuncio was very much to be congratulated on the fact. He did not, it is true, succeed in getting the king to prohibit heretical preaching. The reason for this was that Mentuato had now to reckon with the jealousy of the Catholic bishops, as had previously been the case with Lippomano, for they endeavoured to exclude him from their conferences, and, on the whole, adopted an ambiguous attitude.[4] On February 11th, 1559, the nuncio announced that the Diet had closed in great disorder, without having arrived at any decision.[5] This much, at least, had been gained, that the king had allowed no steps to be taken against the bishops, nor any change to be made in the religion of the country;[6] in other respects, however, heretics like Lasco could continue their propaganda undisturbed. Religious conditions, reports

---

[1] See BRAUNSBERGER, II., 341 seq., 346, 351 seq., 359.

[2] Cf. ZAKRZEWSKI, Powstanie i wzrost reformacyi w Polsce, Lipsk, 1870, 260 seq. ; DEMBINSKI, Rzym, 196 seq.

[3] See BRAUNSBERGER, II., 342, 355 ; DEMBINSKI, 196.

[4] See Mentuato's *report from Petrikau of January 28, 1559 (Lett di princ. XI., 252 seq. Secret Archives of the Vatican) ; cf. DEMBINSKI, 197 seq.

[5] *Letter of Mentuato, loc. cit., XI., 254-256.

[6] Cf. BRAUNSBERGER, II., 361.

Mentuato from Cracow on April 11th, 1559, were steadily getting worse ; he could accomplish nothing owing to the weakness of the king,[1] whom nobody wished to vex.

At the same time Paul IV. made application, in an extremely outspoken letter, to the king himself. His duty, he said, as chief shepherd of the Church, compelled him to speak frankly concerning the things which were reported to him from Poland. These were to the effect that the king favoured the heretics, whom one should not even salute, according to the precepts of the apostle, St. John ; he had them at his table, was in correspondence with them, allowed their writings to be disseminated, and permitted them to hold meetings and to preach publicly against the Catholic faith. It filled him with the deepest sorrow to think that the king, instead of defending the Church, supported its adversaries with his favour. " Have you then," said the Pope, " so far forgotten your parents and your forefathers, those celebrated kings, that you take upon yourself to favour heretics, and live on friendly terms with those people whose writings should be avoided like the plague?" The Pope specially reproached the king with having given the bishopric of Kujaiwien to that Uchanski, Bishop of Chelm, who was infected with the most detestable heresy, without waiting for the confirmation of the Holy See, and with having appointed Prince Radziwill, the open defender and leader of the heretics, as his first minister of state. The dissemination of heresy would bring about the downfall of his kingdom. There was still time, however, to change, and remove the innovations introduced into his dominions. The Pope concluded by saying that he hoped his exhortations would be listened to. Should they remain without effect, then he would not only recall his nuncio, but would also employ such means as God should inspire him to adopt.[2]

[1] *Tanto mite che difficilmente s'induce a dispiacere ad alcuno (Lett. di princ. XI., 263-264. Secret Archives of the Vatican).

[2] The undated letter in RAYNALDUS, 1556, n. 34, belongs, as the contents show, not to the year 1556, but to the spring of 1559. (Kindly pointed out to be by Dr. Kuntze). With regard to the dispute concerning the filling of the bishopric of Kujawien cf.

In Rome, where Hosius personally made a report,[1] the defection of the Polish king was already feared. Cardinal Puteo, the vice-protector of Poland in the Curia, also addressed to him an urgent letter of exhortation.[2] These fears, however, proved to be groundless. If the king, from weakness and for political reasons, did not earnestly protect the ancient church against the attacks of the religious innovators, he, at any rate, did not join them.[3]

WIERZBOWSKI, Uchanskiana, I.—V., Warsaw, 1885, and J. KORYTKOWSKI, Die Ersbischöfe von Gnesen, III., Posen, 1889 (in Polish).

[1] *Cf.* EICHHORN I., 303 *seq.* According to an *Avviso di Roma of May 13, 1559, Paul IV. detained Hosius in Rome; it was thought that he would make him a Cardinal (Cod. Urb. 1039, p. 35. Vatican Library).

[2] L. LATINIUS, Lucubrat., II., 138 *seq.*

[3] *Cf.* DEMBINSKI, Konzil, 62 *seq.* and Ryzm, 199.

CHAPTER XIII.

The Consummation of the Schism in Germany. Dispute of Paul IV. with Ferdinand I.

While the scales were still trembling in the balance in Poland, in Germany they were ever leaning more and more towards Protestantism. The decisive step was taken at the Diet of Augsburg. The Holy See was represented there by the nuncio, Delfino, as well as by the Cardinal-Legate, Morone, who, however, was summoned to Rome, together with Cardinal Truchsess, at the end of March, 1555, for the Papal election. Truchsess had, clearly in agreement with Morone, entered a protest on March 23rd, 1555, against the plan according to which the religious affairs of the Empire were to be arranged in favour of the Protestants. The importance of the influence exercised by these two men is shown by the fact that the resistance of the Catholics to the far-reaching demands of the Protestants now began to weaken.[1] From the reports of Delfino Paul IV. learned that the heretics did not even hesitate to threaten that they would break down the resistance of the Catholics by force of arms.[2] Paul IV. had, even as a Cardinal, watched the development of affairs in Germany very carefully,

[1] See MAURENBRECHER, Karl V., 332. Concerning the protest of Truchsess see STEINBERGER, Die Jesuiten und die Friedensfrage, Freiburg, 1906, 10. I take this opportunity of drawing attention to a manuscript in the Seminary Library at Trêves, (II., 14), which has not yet been examined in detail : *Protocollum actorum in Comitiis Augustanis, incipiens a. d. 31 Dec., 1554 et finiens d. 25 Sept., 1555, scriptum a quodam qui interfuit comitiis et cardinali legato ibidem praesenti fuisse videtur amicus.

[2] See Delfino's report of June 2, 1555 in MAURENBRECHER, 169*. Paul IV. made much in his *brief of thanks for the congratulations of Ferdinand I., dated June 19, 1555, of the hopes which he placed in the King of the Romans concerning the interests of religion (Brev. ad princ. Arm. 44, t. 4, n. 131. Secret Archives of the Vatican).

338

and with growing anxiety ;[1] he now resolved to do everything in his power to prevent the result of the Diet proving unfavourable to the Church. He therefore commissioned Luigi Lippomano, who was destined as nuncio to the Polish king, and who, in the last part of the life of Paul III., had been with Pighino for two years in Germany, and had a thorough knowledge of the conditions there,[2] to go first to Augsburg ; he then recalled Delfino to Rome, to give him an oral account of all that had taken place.[3]

It was pointed out to Lippomano in his instructions that he should work upon Ferdinand I. and the Catholic princes of Germany, so that the Diet might be dissolved without being brought to a formal conclusion, and without its having adopted any decisions unfavourable to the Catholics. The nuncio was specially instructed to draw the attention of the King of the Romans to the fact that if the aggressive Lutheran policy should be successful in overthrowing the Catholic bishoprics, the Protestants would before long proceed to the destruction of the Imperial house of Austria.[4] Paul IV. wrote himself in this sense to Ferdinand I., on July 6th, 1555. At the same time the Pope, in special briefs, called upon the Catholic princes of Germany, Albert V. of Bavaria, Henry of Brunswick, and William of Cleves, as well as the whole of the episcopate, to rally to the protection of Catholic interests.[5] Paul

---

[1] Carafa had been in the Netherlands in 1515 (not, as Lossen says, in 1514 ; MASIUS, Briefe, 250).

[2] Cf. Nuntiaturberichte, XI., xiii seq.

[3] See the *briefs of July 9, 1555, to Delfino and Lippomano and that of July 10 to Ferdinand I. (Brev. ad princ., loc. cit., n. 158, 159, 160. Secret Archives of the Vatican) ; cf. PIEPER, 109 ; STEINHERZ, I., xxxiv.

[4] The instructions of July 3, 1555 in MAURENBRECHER, 169*.

[5] The *brief to Ferdinand I. of July 6, 1555 in the Brev. ad princ., loc. cit., n. 148, that to Albert V. in RAYNALDUS, 1555, n. 44 ; the further *letters to the Archbishops of Mayence and Salzburg, to Henry of Brunswick and William of Cleves, as well as to different German bishops in the Brev. ad princ., loc. cit., n. 151-156 (Secret Archives of the Vatican).

IV. in particular set great hopes on Albert V., to whom he addressed a special letter of thanks and praise on July 26th, in which he acknowledged the growing importance of Bavaria in Catholic matters.[1]

The two representatives of the Holy See at Augsburg were not wanting in zeal, and if their indefatigable representations to King Ferdinand, to Albert V. and to the bishops were not more successful than was actually the case,[2] this was in no way their fault. Ferdinand I. and Albert V. by no means realized the importance of the demands of the innovators. They found themselves forced into such a position that one may be glad that, chiefly owing to the exertions of the nuncio, the worst was averted, and that those demands of the Protestants which aimed at the handing over to the new religion of the remaining parts of Germany, which were still true to the Catholic Church, were refused. At the same time, those things which the Protestants succeeded in attaining were so pregnant of results, that the victory of the religious rupture in Germany was thereby assured.[3]

While Delfino, on August 14th, was hurrying to Rome to deliver his report, Lippomano remained at Augsburg until the first week in September.[4] He handed in a resolute note setting forth that disputes in matters of faith could be decided by no other court than that of the Holy See. When the unfavourable outcome of the Diet could no longer be doubted, he left Augsburg, in order not to be a passive witness while regulations were being made which were, for the most part, highly disadvantageous to the Catholic religion.[5]

---

[1] RAYNALDUS, 1555, n. 45 ; cf. DRUFFEL, IV., 701, n. 1.

[2] See the reports of the nuncios in MAURENBRECHER, 177* seq. ; cf. WOLF, Deutsche Gesch., I., 728 seq.

[3] Cf. PASTOR, Reunionsbestrebungen, 466 seq.; JANSSEN-PASTOR, III., 17-18, 794 seqq.

[4] See the reports of the nunciatures in MAURENBRECHER, 178* seqq. The arrival of Delfino in Rome was delayed by illness ; see the *letter of Delfino dated Venice, September 7, 1555 in the Cod. Barb. lat. XLI., 23 (Vatican Library).

[5] See Delfino's Informazione infra p. 341, n. 2.

The Pope had, at the last moment, endeavoured, by means of an urgent letter on September 6th, 1555, to induce the Emperor to influence his brother,[1] but in vain. Charles V., who could not reconcile the concessions demanded by the Protestants with his conscience, nevertheless considered them inevitable, in view of the actual state of affairs, and allowed the full powers which he had conferred on Ferdinand I. to remain as they were. Exhausted by a struggle which would have worn out a will of iron and nerves of steel, he was, just at that time, making the final arrangements for withdrawing completely from the affairs of the world. The so-called religious peace of Augsburg was, therefore, arrived at on September 25th, 1555 ; by this, Ferdinand I., placed as he was in the greatest difficulties by the attitude of the Turks, the French, and the Protestant princes,[2] gave his assent to the

[1] The brief, with passages missing, according to a manuscript at Simancas, in MAURENBRECHER, 183* seq., is in full in the *Brev. ad princ., loc. cit., n. 232 (Secret Archives of the Vatican).

[2] This strained position was already brought out by both nuncios in their report of July 31, 1555 (MAURENBRECHER, 177*) ; later on Delfino specially emphasized it in his Informazione. This interesting report, which defends Ferdinand wherever possible, is frequently found in Italian libraries ; in Rome, in the Secret Archives of the Vatican, Cod. Urb. 851, P. 1, p. 14 seq., Vat. 5666, Polit. 10, p. 264 seq. ; in the Altieri Library, Miscell. XI., p. 116 seq.; in the Barberini Library, LVIII., 40, p. 38 seq. ; in the Corsini Library Cod. 677 (formerly 35— B. 6), p. 415 seq. ; in the Library of St. Mark's, Venice (see VALENTINELLI in the Abhandl. der Bayr, Akad. Histor., Kl. IX., 763) ; in the Graziani Archives at Città di Castello, Istruz. I., 389 seq., and also in the National Library, Paris, St. Germain, 278 (see MARSAND, II., 80) and Ital. 1171 (see PIEPER, 206). The copy in DÖLLINGER (Beiträge, I., 228 seq.) which is defective and full of mistakes, is the one most frequently cited. This has already been pointed out by REIMANN (Forschungen, V., 323) PIEPER (loc. cit.) STEINHERZ (I., xxxvi.) and POSTINA (Zeitschr. fur Gesch. des Oberrheins, N.F., XV. [1900], 366), but they have all overlooked the fact that long before Döllinger's edition (since 1844) there was a fairly good copy from a MS. in the Colonna Archives, in the publication Saggiatore,

Imperial recognition of the religious rupture.   The princes and states of the Empire, who professed the Confession of Augsburg, now obtained what they had so long striven after : the indefinite duration of the peace, the undisturbed possession of the church property seized before 1552, the suspension of episcopal jurisdiction in their dominions, and full liberty in the practice of the form of church government which they claimed.   Every State of the Empire, whether Catholic or professing the Confession of Augsburg, now had the right to fix the religion of its subjects ; whoever did not wish to conform was at liberty to leave the country after the sale of his property ; whoever could not or would not do so, must conform to the religion of the authorities of the state.[1]   The principle of the new national religion was this : To whomsoever the country belongs, to him also belongs its religion.   Secular absolutism had won the day in religious matters.   The innovators, however, in their joy at what they had gained, overlooked the fact that this was a two-edged weapon, which might at once be turned against themselves in the event of a prince. changing his religious opinions.   The Protestants did not consider themselves bound by the spiritual reservation, in accordance with which those who adopted the new doctrines must forfeit ecclesiastical offices and dignities, as this clause had only been introduced into the text of the religious peace as a regulation issued by Ferdinand I. in virtue of his plenary Imperial powers, and had not yet been decided by the states of the Empire.   These and similar obscurities contained in themselves the germ of new and serious disputes.   The peace was really rather a measure of expediency than a final agreement ; in more than one respect it resembled an armistice, which was used to gather fresh strength in order to renew the struggle with still greater bitterness than before.   This was

I., 2, 130 *seqq.*   The time of its composition Reimann (*loc. cit.*) rightly places at the beginning of 1559, (not 1557, as Döllinger supposed).

[1] *Cf.* PAULUS, Religionsfreiheit und Augsburger Religionsfreide : Histor-pol. BL., CXLIX., 356 *seqq.*, 401 *seqq.*

the conviction both of the Protestants and the Catholics.[1]
It was also in this sense that Paul IV. acted.   However
deeply he was pained by the injury inflicted on the Church by
the Augsburg decisions, he restrained himself after making a
solemn protest.[2]   He hoped to render this agreement, which
he considered invalid, ineffectual, by means of special negotiations, or, if this should prove impossible, to combat its harmful
results by every means in his power.   As a means to this end,
Delfino was again sent, towards the end of 1555, as a special
nuncio to Ferdinand I., who had ardently wished for the return
of this man, who was so devoted to him.[3]   Before he was sent,

---

[1] *Cf.* RITTER, Deutsche Gesch., I., 85.   How the Protestants at
once made propaganda against Paul IV. in Germany by dubbing
him Antichrist is clear from the satirical publication : *Newe
Zeytung aus Rom vom newen Babst Paul IV.*, *A*° 1555 (copy in the
Royal Library, Berlin).

[2] I can find no solemn protest in the sharp expressions of disapproval, which are to be found in the letters to Ferdinand I.
and the Bishop of Passau (see RAYNALDUS, 1555, n. 51, 53) ; a
brief would have been required for this, such as that of 1648 later
on.   It was not issued, probably because in Rome the Augsburg
decisions were not regarded as final.   There is no doubt, however,
that Paul IV. repudiated this insulting agreement, which violated
the rights of the Church in so many ways, and regarded it as
invalid.   The unfounded reproaches cast at the Pope on account
of this supposed point of view, have been contested by HERGEN-
RÖTHER (Staat und Kirche, 703).

[3] See RAYNALDUS, 1555, n. 51 ; STEINHERZ, I., xxxiv-xxxv.
Besides the letters to Ferdinand I. and the Bishop of Passau of
December 18, quoted by RAYNALDUS, *loc. cit.*, similar letters
were sent to Cardinal Madruzzo as prince bishop of Trent, to the
Archbishops of Cologne, Salzburg, Mayence and Magdeburg, the
Bishop of Brixen, Trêves, Eichstätt, Würzburg and Bamberg,s
to Albert V. of Bavaria, as well as to several members of the
House of Hapsburg (Maxim. regi Bohemiae, Ferdinando archi-
duci Austriae, Carolo archiduci Austriae ; see Brev. ad princ.
Arm. 44, t. 4, n. 158, 165).   Delfino left Rome on December 27 ;
see *report of Navagero of December 28, 1555, *loc. cit.* (Library of
St. Mark's, Venice).

there had been exhaustive deliberations with Morone, and it was the Cardinal, who was so well acquainted with conditions in Germany, who drew up the instructions for the nuncio. The task assigned to Delfino in his dealings, first with the Prince-bishops of Trent and Brixen, and then with the Duke of Bavaria, Albert V., the bishops of Salzburg, Eichstätt, Bamberg, Würzburg and Passau, and, finally with the King of the Romans himself, was, in each case, of a similar nature. In the first place the nuncio was to make remonstrances against their unlawful agreement to the fatal decisions of the Diet of Augsburg, he was to endeavour to obviate their disastrous effects, and, above all, to prevent still further decrees, unfavourable to Catholics, from being issued at the impending Diet at Ratisbon. In the second place, Delfino was to urge the carrying out of a reform in accordance with Catholic principles, in which they saw in Rome the best and most effective means of placing an obstacle in the way of the increasing defections from the Church in Germany.[1]

Delfino was also given the special commission of giving to the Duke of Bavaria, whose importance to the Catholic cause was fully realized in Rome, reasons for the refusal of the Holy See to grant the demands which the Duke had secretly laid before the Pope in the name of his subjects. Bavaria asked that the chalice might be granted to the laity, that married persons might be allowed to fill ecclesiastical offices, and that there should be a mitigation of the law of fasting.[2] If it was believed by the Bavarians that a greater leakage from the Church could be averted by the granting of these concessions, an entirely different view was held in Rome. At the end of February and at the beginning of March, 1556, Delfino explained the Pope's refusal to the Duke at Munich, and the latter gave the most convincing assurances that he would allow nothing contrary to the wishes of His Holiness, even if he thereby lost his life and his territories. When, however,

---

[1] See PIEPER, 199 seq. ; cf. ibid., 110 seq.

[2] Cf. SCHWARZ in the Histor. Jahrb., XIII., 146 seq. ; MASIUS, Briefe, 255-256.

the states renewed their demand, the weak prince gave way so far, on March 31st, that he declared, with many reservations and clauses, however, that the dispensing of Holy Communion to the laity under two kinds, and the non-observance of abstinence, were not penal.[1]

Delfino was by this time in Vienna. The experiences which he there had with Ferdinand I. were much more disheartening than those he had experienced with the Duke of Bavaria. The complaints which, by order of the Pope, he made, with regard to the concessions, so detrimental to the Catholic cause, made to the innovators at Augsburg, were sharply rejected by the King of the Romans ; he had been forced, he said, by necessity, to grant these, as well as his concessions to the Protestants in Austria.[2] The conflict then beginning between Paul IV. and the House of Hapsburg was not without its influence on this attitude. This dispute took such a grave form that, in April, 1556, the Pope spoke of the deposition of Charles V. and Ferdinand I., because they had agreed to the Augsburg decisions.[3] No one rejoiced more at this unhappy strife than the German Protestants,[4] to whom it was also of great advantage that the Catholic princes of Germany had, either from carelessness or optimism, neglected to see that the concessions made did not receive a still wider extension than the strict working of the

---

[1] Cf. RIEZLER, IV., 505 seq. Concerning the very vaccillating attitude of Albert V. towards the religious question at that time, see JANNSEN-PASTOR, IV., 15-16, 112, n. 6. A. Masius also sought to obtain in Rome the granting of the chalice to the laity from April to July, 1556, by order of the Duke of Cleves, for his dominions, but in vain (see MASIUS, Briefe, 215 seq., 241 seq., 245 seq., 266 seq., 271 seq., 277 seq.) Concerning the unfortunate development of the state of affairs in the territory of Cleves see Histor. Zeitschr., L., 16 seq.

[2] Cf. the *report of Delfino, copies of which are preserved at Simancas (Libros de Berzosa) and used by Maurenbrecher in the Histor. Zeitschr., 12 seq. Several reports of July, 1556, are printed in PIEPER, 113 n.

[3] See Badoer's report of May 31, 1556, in BROWN, VI., 1, n. 501.

[4] See BROSCH in the Mitteil. des Österr. Inst. XXV., 477 n.

Augsburg decision conferred on them. Delfino had a difficult position in Vienna, and he realized more and more how little he could accomplish. The whole question of the faith, as he reported shortly before his return on September 21st, 1556, was in the greatest danger all over the country, and especially in the hereditary Hapsburg dominions. This was caused, partly by the continued difficulties of Ferdinand I., and partly by the indifference of almost all the prelates. He therefore proposed to address an earnest exhortation to them, and also to the King of the Romans, and to all the secular princes of Germany, which, under certain circumstances, should be made public by printing it.[1] When, at the end of October, Delfino informed the Pope and a congregation of Cardinals of the impending ruin of the Catholic Church in Germany, Paul IV. was so embittered against the Hapsburgs that, with great injustice, he attributed to them all the blame for the unhappy developments in Germany.[2] It was in vain that Cardinals Medici and Morone, as well as Delfino, pointed out the evil effects which the Pope's war against Spain must exercise on the spread of Protestantism in Germany and Austria. The answer of Paul IV. consisted in his calling out to Delfino, in the presence of Morone : " Your King of the Romans is a brother of that heretic. We only suffer him, because we do not know whom we should put in his place."[3]

[1] **Report of Delfino to Paul IV., dated Vienna, September 21, 1556, in the Casanate Library XXI., 1, 36, also a copy in Simancas, Libros de Berzosa.

[2] STEINHERZ, who (I., xxxv., n. 2) very significantly rejects the words of Vergerio, so full of hatred towards Delfino's nunciature, as incredible, represents the nuncio as returning to Rome as early as July, 1556. That this is an error is plain from Delfino's **letter, cited in the previous note, which shows that he was still in Vienna on September 21, 1556. An *Avviso of October 31, 1556 (Cod. Urb. 1038, p. 171. Vatican Library) reports distinctly in addition to this that Delfino arrived in Rome on Sunday (October 25), and that the Pope lodged him in the Vatican ; on the Wednesday the nuncio made a report in the Congregation of Cardinals.

[3] See Navagero's report on January 2, 1557 in BROWN, VI., 2, n. 781 ; cf. ibid. n. 686, 695. At the beginning of December,

Under these circumstances it is not astonishing that the nunciature at the court of Ferdinand I. remained unfilled. As this unnatural state of affairs still continued after the conclusion of peace with Philip II., open opposition sprang up in the Curia. We learn from a report of the Venetian ambassador, on November 6th, 1557, of the complaints made by the Cardinals that the Pope assembled the Inquisition every Thursday for the prosecution of a single heretic, while he overlooked important matters, such as the loss of whole kingdoms, like Poland and Germany, which he left without nuncios.[1] These complaints resulted in relations with Ferdinand I. being once more resumed. On November 14th, 1557, the Papal notary, Jacobus Linterius, was appointed special ambassador to Ferdinand I., with instructions to call upon the king to close the conference on religion at Worms. At the same time the resumption of the nunciature to the King of the Romans was suggested.[2] This, however, did not actually take place until January, 1558 ;[3] the prelate who was appointed, Antonio Agostino, Bishop of Lerida, proceeded to Frankfort-on-Maine,

1556, Paul IV. appears to have thought of sending Delfino back again (see STEINHERZ, I., xxxv.) MAURENBRECHER (Histor. Zeitschrift, L., 37) erroneously supposes that he really did return to Germany.

[1] See Navagero's report of November 7, 1557 in BROWN, VI., 3, n. 1076.

[2] See the brief to Ferdinand I., of November 14, 1557, in RAYNALDUS, 1557, n. 32 ; ibid. n. 33, a brief to the *episcopus Labacensis* (not *Lubecensis* as in Raynaldus), Urban Textor, who had been confessor and court preacher to Ferdinand I. At the same time Paul IV. wrote to *Martinus Gusmanus, prepos. regii cubic.* (see Brev. ad princ., *loc. cit.*, f. 67. Secret Archives of the Vatican). Concerning the conference at Worms see, besides JANNSEN-PASTOR, IV.,,,15-16 21 *seq.* ; BRAUNSBERGER, II., 789 *seq.* and CARDAUNS, Unionsbestrebungen, 281 *seq.*

[3] The attitude of Philip II. had an influence on the Pope's decision (see BROMATO, II., 421). On December 14, 1557, the mission of Agostino was announced in the consistory ; see *Acta consist., Consistorial Archives.

where he met King Ferdinand, who was staying there, on March 6th, 1558.[1]

Besides general orders for the protection of the German Catholics, Agostino was given the special duty of watching over the Papal rights in the proposed assumption by Ferdinand I. of the Imperial dignity, which had been resigned by Charles V.[2] How unwelcome the appearance of the nuncio was to the King of the Romans may be gathered from the fact that he had refused Linterius an escort to the assembly at Frankfort.[3] As Ferdinand could not now send back the representative of the Pope, who had so unexpectedly arrived at Frankfort, he endeavoured to soothe him by declaring that the religious question would not be dealt with in the assembly.[4] This was not, however, true, for the election capitulation agreed upon at Frankfort contained a very explicit obligation to hold to the Augsburg decisions of 1555. On March 14th, 1558, Ferdinand I. swore to these in the presence of the Electors, three of whom belonged to the Protestant confession, in the electoral chapel of Frankfort Cathedral, whereupon Joachim II. of Branden-burg, as Arch-Chamberlain of the Empire, placed the golden crown upon his head. They all then betook themselves to a dais erected in front of the choir, where the documents con-cerning the resignation of the Imperial dignity by Charles V., and sanctioned by the Electors, and the acceptance of that dignity by his brother, were read aloud to the people. The proceedings were then closed by the solemn proclamation of

---

[1] See Depeschen vom Kaiserhofe, III., 17 n.

[2] As supplementary to the statements in REIMANN, Streit 301 seq., and PIEPER, 115 seq., see *Brevia Arm. 44, t. 2, p. 65 : to Ferdinand I. ; ibid, p. 88 ; to the Bohemian king, Maximilian, both dated December 18, 1557 ; p. 92 : to the Duke of Cleves, dated January 4, 1558, all relating to the mission of Agostino ; ibid. p. 105 : yet another *brief to Ferdinand I., dated February 20, 1558, whereby Agostino receives powers for the negotium ecclesiae Aquilej (Secret Archives of the Vatican).

[3] Cf. SCHMID, Kaiserwahl, 5 seq., 39 seq.

[4] Depeschen vom Kaiserhofe, III., 17 n.

Ferdinand as Roman Emperor-elect.[1] All participation in this very important act was refused to the representative of the Pope, who found himself obliged to play the part of a merely passive spectator, face to face with an accomplished fact![2] The Protestants were jubilant. Peter Martyr wrote to Calvin that by this event, the authority of the Roman antichrist had been more completely ·shattered than ever before.[3]

It is difficult to understand how Ferdinand I. could have believed that a Pope, who was so penetrated with the idea of his own position and rights, could tamely submit to such a proceeding.[4] Had not Julius III. already declared in 1551, that the transference of the Imperial dignity without the agreement of the Pope was invalid, and that the right of election belonged only to the Catholic Electors?[5]

When Maximilian, in February 1508, as the first to deviate from the old traditional custom, assumed the title of Roman Emperor-elect, he had acknowledged the Pope's right of coronation by a special declaration, thereby making it possible for Julius II. subsequently to give his approval. Charles V. had also assured himself of the consent of Leo. X. when he assumed the title of Roman Emperor-elect in 1520, and at his coronation at Bologna all the traditional formalities had been scrupulously observed.[6] Now, however, not only had the resignation of Charles V. taken place, but also the proclamation of Ferdinand I. as Roman Emperor-elect, and the Pope had on both occasions been completely ignored. Nor was this all. In 1531, at the accession of Ferdinand I. as King of the Romans, a brief had been obtained from Clement VII., so that the participation of the Protestant Elector of Saxony might

---

[1] *Cf.* J. W. HOFMANN, Sammlung ungedruckter Nachrichten, I., Halle, 1736, I *seqq.* ; HÄBERLIN, III., 404 *seqq.*

[2] See REIMANN' Streit, 301 ; SCHMID, Kaiserwahl, 6.

[3] CALVINI Opera, XVII., 144.

[4] RANKE (Deutsche Geschicte, V., 420) points out that nobody could wonder at the resistance of the Pope.

[5] See Nuntiaturberichte, XII., xlv.

[6] *Cf.* Vol.VI. of this work, p. 297, Vol. X., p 92 *seq.*, and TURBA, Beiträge zur Gesch. der Habsburger, III., Vienna, 1901, 86.

not invalidate the election.[1] But on this occasion, at the far
more important proceedings at Frankfort, three Electors had
taken part, who had fallen away from the Church, and were
engaged in a violent struggle with the Holy See. Thus a quite
abnormal situation had been created, which was quite unprecedented. If the Pope had already assisted at the deliberations concerning the election of a king, how much more should
he have done so at the proclamation of an Emperor, who was
bound to be the protector of the Holy See ! And now this new
Emperor, who had been proclaimed in such a way, had pledged
himself in his election capitulation to support the state of
affairs, so very unfavourable to Catholics, which had been
called into being by the decisions of the Diet of Augsburg.
This was, however, by no means the only reason why Ferdinand
could not be held to be a proper person to play the part of
protector of the Church. It was well known in Rome that he
had recently mitigated the severity of his former regulations
against the Protestants, and had appointed bishops in Hungary
and transferred them to other dioceses without seeking the
confirmation of the Holy See. Above all, Paul IV. reproached
Ferdinand I. with having suffered the heterodoxy of his son,
Maximilian.[2]

All this makes it easy to understand why Paul IV., who had
always been filled with mistrust and ill-will against the Hapsburgs, was greatly excited by the news of the proceedings at

[1] See BUCHOLTZ, IX., 18.

[2] *Cf.* the despatches of Pacheco, used in the Histor. Zeitschr.,
XXXII., 266, and the decisions of the Papal commission in
SCHMID, Kaiserwahl, 16 *seq.* A very detailed enumeration of the
objections regarding Ferdinand himself, originating from Delfino,
has been published by SICKEL (p. 30 *seqq.*) "One can judge,"
says REIMANN (Paul IV., 32), "among other things, how very
well informed Rome was concerning the religious conditions in the
Austrian countries, although there had been no permanent nuncio
in Vienna for years." A pendant to Delfino's report is the *Relatio
Aloysii Lippomani episc. Veron, quoad fidem* in the Graziani
Archives at Città di Castello, Instruz. I., 241 *seq.* The document
is unfortunately undated.

Frankfort. It was clear to him that he could not recognize such a renunciation of the Imperial dignity, performed in such a way, and at the same time so one-sided, when the dignity contained in itself very clearly defined duties towards the Church, solemnly undertaken by oath. He was also of opinion that he ought not to acknowledge the accession of such a man as Ferdinand I. He never for a moment thought of making a calm examination of the reasons which made it inadvisable to bring the legal standpoint into too great prominence. Yet there was not the smallest doubt that, in consequence of the great dislocation of power which had come to pass in the last twenty-five years in favour of the Protestants, no one in the Empire would trouble their heads in the least about the opposition of the Holy See to the proceedings at Frankfort. On the contrary, should the Pope wish to exclude the Hapsburgs from the possession of the Imperial dignity, which they had already seized, it could easily be foreseen that the Protestants, out of pure spite against the Roman " antichrist," would come in, with all their power, including force of arms, on the side of Ferdinand. It was, moreover, clear that Ferdinand would have to make still further concessions to the Protestants if he should have to depend upon them for the preservation of his Empire. Besides this, they had to take into consideration in Rome, that, however much Ferdinand might have been found wanting in certain respects, there was no doubt as to his personally Catholic attitude, and finally, it was notorious that all the concessions of this prince to the innovators had been made under the pressure of the direst necessity.[1]

All these considerations pointed to the advisability of limiting proceedings to a formal protest, and in other respects showing an indulgent forbearance, in order to avoid still greater evils.[2]

[1] *Cf. supra* p. 341. The demand made by the Protestant electors, that they should no longer be obliged to pledge themselves in the coronation oath to protect the Church, was successfully opposed by Ferdinand.

[2] REIMANN (Streit, 299) is of opinion that two courses might have been taken : " the Pope might either have deferred the

Unfortunately Paul IV. had not the slightest idea of doing anything of the kind. Entirely regardless of the complete change in the state of the world, and of all the evil consequences of his action, he insisted, in the most uncompromising manner, on the legal standpoint. With characteristic obstinacy, he persisted in the view that the choice of the Electors and the person chosen, were subject to examination by the Pope, and to the right of confirmation or repudiation by him, and that it was unlawful for the Emperor to carry on the government of the Empire before having received this Papal approbation. He claimed the right of sanction, not only as to the accession of Ferdinand I., but also as to the abdication of Charles V. In a secret consistory called together in March, he gave vent to his indignation at the insult offered to the Holy See ; he took up his position on the standpoint that the abdication of Charles V. was invalid, as it had been done without the consent of the Pope, and was, moreover, the act of a monarch who was no longer in possession of his senses, and finally, that the accession of Ferdinand had no legal foundation, on account of the participation of apostates in the election.

He enjoined strict silence on the Cardinals, and told them, at the same time, to consider what measures should be adopted. His next communication to the Cardinals, that the learned custodian of the Vatican Library, Guglielmo Sirleto, would lay the documents relative to the matter before them,[1] proved that Paul IV. was determined once more to open, in the fullest sense, the old disputed question of the relationship between the Empire and the Papacy. The public, also, soon learned

discussion of the question of the right of the Protestant Electors until the next election of a King of the Romans, or have at once acknowledged the good Catholic, Ferdinand, as Emperor, on the ground of the election of 1531, or, in order to proceed more surely, he might have done the latter, and made no concession to the future, by a declaration corresponding to the second brief of Clement VII. cf. supra p. 349), in which way the difficulty was afterwards overcome."

[1] See the report of du Bellay in RIBIER, II., 623, with wrong date. Cf. REIMANN, Streit, 318 seq., also SCHMID, Kaiserwahl, 7.

of the dispute between the Pope and the Emperor. On Good Friday, April 8th, 1558, the usual prayer for the secular head of Christendom was omitted.[1] A month later the recall of Agostino, who had proceeded with Ferdinand to Vienna, followed.[2] The chief chamberlain, Martin de Guzman, had started from Vienna for Rome on April 22nd, and although he learned of the Pope's attitude in Venice, he nevertheless continued his journey, and arrived in Rome during the night between May 12th and 13th. The Pope caused a communication to be conveyed to him, through Cardinal Pacheco, that he must refuse him a solemn reception as " Imperial " ambassador, and then refused him even a private audience.[3]

Matters continued in this position, all the more so as Paul IV. was supported in his attitude of hostility by the most distinguished among the Cardinals, theologians and canonists at the Curia. A commission for the consideration of the legal question had already been formed in May, and consisted of ten Cardinals (Vitelli, Rebiba, Carlo and Alfonso Carafa, Puteo, Reumano, Ghislieri, Scotti, Saraceni and Pacheco) and six prelates (Lippomano, Agostino, Sirleto, Camerario, Ugo Boncompagni and Restauro Castaldo). These were able, with more or less success, to put forward, in learned disquisitions, a great array of mediæval theologians and canonists to prove the invalidity of Ferdinand's title to the Imperial dignity.[4]

[1] *Avvisi di Roma of April 9 and 16, 1558 (Cod. Urb. 1038, p. 299, 301. Vatican Library).

[2] The *letter of recall for Agostino, dated Rome, May 9, 1558, in the Brevia Arm. 44, t. 2, p. 114 (Secret Archives of the Vatican), Concerning his departure see Depeschen vom Kaiserhofe, III., 28 seq. ; cf. SCHMID, Zeitschr. für Gesch., VIII., 4.

[3] Cf. REIMANN, Streit, 303, 321 ; Paul IV. und das Kaisertum 27 seqq. ; SCHMID, 8 seq. ; see also in the Depeschen vom Kaiserhofe, III., 51 seq.

[4] Cf. SCHMID, Kaiserwahl, 13 seq., where three opinions in accordance with Cod. Barb. XXXIII., 65, are given ; see also DAUNON, Essai hist. sur la puissance temp. des Papes, II., Paris, 1818, 156. The news in an *Avviso of May 28 (loc. cit. 310. Vatican Library) of the beginning of the opposition in the com-

Taking their stand on the laws actually in force, they proved that it was impossible to grant a public audience to Guzman as "Imperial" ambassador, and that the proceedings at Frankfort had been null and void. Even had they been valid, such a man as Ferdinand could not be entrusted with the position of Imperial protector of the Holy See, for he had not only allowed encroachments on ecclesiastical affairs, and brought suspicion on himself by suffering the irreligion of his son, but had also broken his oath to protect religion by condoning the defections from the Church, and swearing at Frankfort to what was contrary to what his former oath had pledged him to. But if Ferdinand had been in himself a suitable person, his election was invalid owing to the participation in it of heretical Electors, quite apart from the fact that the whole assembly had not been entitled to proceed to the election of an Emperor during the lifetime of his predecessor.

Among the proposals as to what had better be done at the moment, there were only two, those of Cardinals Pacheco and Puteo, which definitely advised that the altered conditions of the times should be taken into consideration, and pointed out the great dangers to which an unfriendly attitude on the part of the Holy See might give rise. As it was only a question of positive law, Puteo was of opinion that the Pope could accept the "obedientia" of Ferdinand, in so far as Charles V. remained firm in his determination to resign his jurisdiction, and the ambassador was properly accredited. With regard to the complaints made against Ferdinand personally, it would be well to see whether some excuse could not be found for him. Pacheco put forward such excuses in great detail, and entreated

mission to Paul IV., and of the questioning of learned jurists in Padua and Bologna, is not confirmed elsewhere. On the other hand, it is clear from a report from Paris of June 6, 1558, to Cardinal Farnese (Bibl. de l'École des Chartes, LXXI., 328) that Paul IV. had applied to the Sorbonne for an opinion. As to this opinion it does not depend, as Hergenröther (Staat und Kirche, 222) points out, upon the actual reasons and arguments, but on legal axioms. Commendone also composed a treatise at this time on the disputed question ; see GRATIANUS, 63 *seq.*

the Pope, by a just recognition of the circumstances and of the times, to show clemency. Philip II. also threw all his weight into the scales in favour of his uncle. It was all, how-even, in vain. The commission held firmly to the ancient rights, and finally decided that confirmation must be refused to Ferdinand, unless he proved his title and showed all due honour to the Holy See.[1] Guzman then received orders from Vienna to start his journey home, whether he had accomplished his mission or not, should he not have been granted an audience within three days of the receipt of the letter. Only on July 13th was a semi-public audience granted to him. The Pope was exceedingly gracious, and announced that he would send a special embassy to Ferdinand I., but he did not give way on the point at issue. In a consistory he laid down the following conditions for his recognition of Ferdinand : the substantia-tion of the abdication of Charles V., an examination into the life and conduct of Ferdinand, a promise on the part of the latter to abolish Lutheranism in his house and hereditary dominions, and the exclusion of heretics from future elections and all similar assemblies.[2]

Guzman left Rome on Jaly 14th ; on the same day Ugo Boncompagni was decided on as nuncio to Ferdinand I. On July 20th, Cardinal Rebiba, who had been appointed legate in Poland, received instructions to travel by way of Vienna. The departure of both, however, was delayed, because the arrival of the Spanish ambassador in Venice, Vargas, was expected. Mentuato, the nuncio destined for Poland, was, in the meantime, the only one to report in Vienna as to the claims of Paul IV.[3]

[1] See SCHMID, Kaiserwahl, 20 seqq. Sittings of the commission are also mentioned in the *Avvisi di Roma of July 9 and 16, 1558 (loc. cit. 324, 327, Vatican Library) with the notice that nothing can be learned concerning them, as silence is enjoined under pain of excommunication. Concerning the intervention of Philip II., see SCHMID, Zeitschr. für Gesch., VIII., 7 seq.

[2] Cf. RIBIER, II., 759; REIMANN, Streit, 303 seq. ; SCHMID, Kaiserwahl, 25 seq. ; Depeschen vom Kaiserhofe, III., 52 seq.

[3] See MASSARELLI, 324 ; PIEPER, 117 seq. ; cf. supra p. 335.

All the hopes which had been built on the negotiations of Vargas[1] were now to prove vain. Ferdinand I., in the meantime, prepared to take earnest measures in his own defence. On September 5th he made an official communication to the Electors concerning his quarrel with the Pope,[2] and invited them to the impending Diet. At the same time the Imperial chancellor, Seld, was instructed to draw up an official document repudiating the claims of the Pope. It is evident from this important paper to what bitterness and dangerous sentiments the attitude of Paul IV. had given rise at the Imperial court. The chancellor, who undoubtedly wished to remain a Catholic, employed in this treatise a manner of speech which only slightly differed from that of the Protestants.[3] " While, in former times," he says, " the Papal ban was more feared than death, it is now laughed at, and while formerly people considered everything that came from Rome as being divine and holy, Roman conduct and life are now known to the whole world to such a degree, that everyone, no matter what he may be, and whether he belongs to the old religion or the new, spits at them." The weaknesses of Paul IV. are mercilessly exaggerated, and all merit concerning the cause of reform is denied to him by Seld, who sums up by declaring openly : " His Holiness is, on account of his age and other circumstances, no longer responsible for his actions or in his right senses ! " Seld advises strongly against any granting of the claims put forward by Paul IV., because in that case the whole country would rebel against both Emperor and Pope. The best thing to do was not to trouble about the confirmation or repudiation of Paul IV. Should it come to the worst, Ferdinand could, in accordance with the decisions at Basle and Constance, appeal to a free Christian Council.[4]

[1] See the *Avviso di Roma of October 1, 1558, *loc. cit.* 341 (Vatican Libr.)

[2] See SATTLER, Gesch. Württembergs, IV. Beil., No. 48.

[3] So said HÄBERLIN (III., 555).

[4] The opinion is printed in GOLDAST, Polit. Reichshändel, V., 167-199, RITTER (I., 145s *eqq.*) brings into prominence the fact that Seld decidedly takes his stand on the grounds of the Basle and

The tension had just reached its highest point when the death of Charles V., on September 21st, 1558, put an end to the difficulty with regard to his abdication. An end to the whole unhappy dispute was very much to be desired, all the more so as the highly influential Gropper pointed out the dangers which a refusal to acknowledge Ferdinand would entail.[1] It was only the uncatholic attitude of Maximilian, the principal cause of the scandal, which caused Paul IV. to persist in his protest. Before the obsequies of Charles V. were held, on December 12th, the Pope warned the Cardinals and ambassadors that by holding funeral solemnities, the authority of the Holy See in the question of the abdication of the Imperial would be prejudiced, and a right would be indirectly deduced from it.[2] The nuncios were at the same time instructed to communicate this protest to the Kings of France and

Constance decisions. GRAUERT has, with his usual thoroughness, shown in the Histor. Jahrb., XVI., 519, and in the Histor.-polit. BL, CXX., 643 seq., how the Protestants at that time brought the name of Dante into the ecclesiastical and political dispute.

[1] See SCHMID, Kaiserwahl., 29 seq. The supposition put forward here that a more conciliatory tone prevailed at the Curia is confirmed by the *Avvisi of October 22 and 29, 1558 (Cod. Urb. 1038, p. 346, 348. Vatican Library).

[2] See RIBIER, II., 774; MASSARELLI, 328; FIRMANUS, 574; SCHMIDT, Zeitschr. für Gesch., VIII., 11. Concerning the rejection of the ambassador, Juan Figueroa, sent to Rome by Philip II. in November, see MASSARELLI, 327; LAEMMER, Melet., 208 seq.; *Avviso di Roma of December 10, 1558 (loc. cit. Vatican Library); REIMANN, Streit, 329 seq.; SCHMID, Kaiserwahl, 32. Concerning the adjustment of this matter, hitherto unknown, B. Pia reports to Cardinal Ercole Gonzaga from Rome, on July 19, 1559: *Fu hieri quasi all'improviso fatta congregatione inanzi a N.S. nell'anticamera dell'inquisitione per la cosa del s. Don Giov. Figheroa, il quale con molta lode che la S. S. disse di lui et col voto dei cardinali fu rimesso et admesso nella gratia di S. B. et per ambasciatore della M^{tà} Catt. (Gonzaga Archives, Mantua). The incident which led to the holding of the requiem for Charles V. at S. Giacomo in Rome, on March 4, 1559, is treated in the Annales de S. Louis, IX., 265 seq.

Poland, as well as the non-recognition of Ferdinand. This was the answer to Vargas' intimation that Ferdinand intended to submit the dispute to the Electors.[1] A sharp brief to the King of the Romans had already been drawn up,[2] when the fall of the Pope's nephews caused the dispute to recede into the background ; no settlement, however, was arrived at, in spite of a renewed Spanish attempt at mediation.[3] Fortunately no further steps were taken by the Pope, for a serious vindication of the law in this secular question against the Empire would have had the worst possible effects upon even the spiritual rights of the Holy See.

It is natural that no one should be willing to part with any rights he may possess, and therefore, from a purely human point of view, Paul IV. cannot be blamed if, as the representative of an eminently conservative authority, he would not abandon the ideally thought out relationship between the two powers, and the position held by the Holy See in the Middle Ages. Paul IV., however, should have realized that the interests of the Church in Germany would not be served by his clinging to the mediæval idea of the Imperial dignity, and the pressing of claims, the granting of which must have the effect of driving the Hapsburgs into the closest union with everything hostile, and even into close alliance with the Protestant states of the Empire.[4] How great was the danger that lay in this course of action, may best be understood from

---

[1] See SCHMID, Kaiserwahl, 31 *seq.*

[2] It is in the *Vat. 6216, p. 301 (Vatican Library). *Cf.* SCHMID, *loc. cit.* 33-34, who rightly concludes that it was never sent.

[3] *Cf.* REIMANN, Streit, 314 *seq.* In the Histor. Zeitschr., XXXII., 268 *seq.*, MAURENBRECHER maintains that Paul IV. at last declared that he was prepared to refrain from official proceedings in the matter, and would settle it amicably, and gives as his authority the report of F. v. Thurns in SICKEL, 27 *seq.*, which, however, refers to Pius IV.

[4] *Cf.* BUCHOLTZ, VII., 461.

the hopes which the innovators built on the Papal opposition to the head of the Empire, who, in spite of everything, was still the most important support of the Church in Germany.[1]

[1] See JANNSEN-PASTOR, IV.,[14-16] 69 *seq.*

CHAPTER XIV.

Mary the Catholic and the Legation of Cardinal Pole.

The reproach of unwise severity, which may, with justice, be brought against Paul IV. in his dealings with Ferdinand I., has also been made with regard to his attitude towards the Kingdom of England. In this case, however, the blame may be said to be only partly justified.

In the second week after the coronation of Paul IV., on June 6th, 1555, the " obedientia " embassy, which had been appointed in the time of Julius III., arrived in Rome.[1] An honourable reception was accorded to the ambassadors, Thirlby, Bishop of Ely, Edward Carne, and Viscount Montague, by the members of the Pope's household, the Cardinals, and the Roman nobility. The difficulty arising from the fact that in the letters of credence, the royal title was used with regard to Ireland, was overcome by the Pope's raising Ireland to be a kingdom by a bull of June 7th.[2] Then the public consistory was held on June 10th, 1555, in which the representatives of England made the solemn " obedientia " in the Sala Regia of the Vatican. The Bishop of Ely, in his speech, drew special attention to the repeal of the anti-papal laws by Parliament, and begged for reunion with the Church. Paul IV. answered graciously, praised the zeal of the sovereigns and of Cardinal Pole, and reminded his hearers that he had himself been in England as a collector of Peter's Pence, and had thus become acquainted with the generosity of the English people. He ordered that a special service of thanksgiving should be held in the church of S. Maria in Aracoeli. There was a

---

[1] Cf. Vol. XIII. of this work, p. 288. Thirlby's diary during his journey as ambassador is printed in Hardwicke, State Papers, I., 62-102.

[2] Bull. VI., 489 seq. ; cf. Bellesheim, Gesch. der Kirche in Irland, II., 108.

banquet to the ambassadors on the same day, and a magnificent illumination of the Castle of St. Angelo in the evening.[1]

Joyful demonstrations of this kind seemed to be justified, in so far as England was now once more officially united to the Holy See. Nevertheless the future of the Church there was by no means assured. An active party was at work in England, and was making use of every means, not only to drive the Catholic religion once more out of the country, but also to undermine the authority of Queen Mary, its principal supporter.

The rebellions of Northumberland and Wyatt had been, to a great extent, the work of the Protestants.[2] The calumnies and fables related concerning the Spaniards and the Spanish marriage were originated by the same party.[3] When the revolts failed, the battle against the queen was continued by pamphlets. Even in the time of Henry VIII., the Imperial ambassador, Chapuys, could report that the invectives of the German Lutheran preachers were nothing in comparison with the abuse of their English co-religionists,[4] whose printed pamphlets now went to the greatest lengths in the insults which they hurled at the queen and her ministers. These publications were circulated everywhere; one such, which bristled with aspersions on her Majesty and her ministers, and threatened her with the worst in the event of Philip's arrival, was even found, in April 1554, on the table of the royal kitchen.[5]

The principal question dealt with in these writings was the lawfulness of women being in possession of the supreme power. While the preachers had nothing to say against the sovereignty of Lady Jane Grey, in Mary's case they found it to be against the Word of God and the laws of the land, that the supreme power over men should be in the hands of a woman. Mary's

---

[1] Cf. MASSARELLI, 273, 274, 275; COGGIOLA, Farnesi, 76; PAGLIUCCHI, 134.

[2] See Vol. XIII. of this work, p. 265.

[3] See Ibid. 261 seq.

[4] GAYANGOS, V., 1, n. 26, p. 83.

[5] BREEN in the Dublin Review, CXVII., 118.

second Parliament, in April, 1554, had, therefore, to declare that it made no difference, according to the laws of the country, whether the supreme power was wielded by a king or a queen.[1] It was further widely asserted in these publications that no obedience was due to the queen, as she was a worshipper of idols. According to a treatise by Christopher Goodman, Christ and His Gospel had been abolished, and antichrist set up in His place, when the political power had been placed in the hands of a woman, who worshipped idols. " By obeying her," wrote Goodman, " you displease God, by disobeying her, you will again win God's approbation . . . through resistance to her and her godless decrees, you will again become true worshippers of God, and loyal Englishmen."[2] John Bale, Thomas Becon, and Bartholomew Traheron wrote in similar terms. The number and violence of the abusive writings of the Scotsman, John Knox, were especially remarkable. This man, who had approved of the murder of Cardinal Beaton in his native land, had in 1549 sought and found an asylum in England, but had had to escape to the continent after Mary's accession. A woman who rules over men is, according to him, a monster, and the queen is either " a cursed Jezabel " or " the godless Mary."[3] Ponet, the deposed Calvinist bishop of Winchester, who had taken part in Wyatt's rising, but soon fled, despairing of success, wrote, on the continent, a quite revolutionary treatise concerning political power,[4] in which he maintained that Mary should, according to both the divine and human law, be punished with death.[5]

As little opposition was shown by the Protestant party to abuse such as this, as to the action of those who actually attacked Catholic preachers in the pulpit, overwhelmed Catholic practices with the coarsest abuse, or incited the

[1] LINGARD, VII., 169 seq.

[2] In BREEN, loc. cit.

[3] Ibid. ; cf. Dictionary of National Biography, XXXI., 312.

[4] GAIRDNER, 332.

[5] " So that now both by God's laws and man's she ought to be punished with death." Ponet, Short Treatise on Political Power, 96, in BREEN, 119.

people against the queen by means of alleged spirit voices.[1]

The government could not put up with such a state of affairs indefinitely. Ever since Mary's marriage the question as to the best measures to be adopted had been seriously considered by the royal Council,[2] and it was finally resolved to renew the old laws against heresy which had been issued by Richard II., Henry IV. and Henry V. for the preservation of order in state and church, at the time of the trouble with the followers of Wycliffe. The enforcement of these laws was divided between the bishops and the secular courts. The bishops had to summon and examine those suspected of heresy, in order to find out if it really existed. Those who remained obstinate in their heretical errors, were to be handed over to the secular courts, and by them condemned to be burned.[3] It cannot be maintained that the majority of the royal Council which made this decision, was definitely Catholic;[4] political considerations, more than anything else, turned the scale in questions such as this.

It was not without grave reflection that the queen consented to the renewal of the penal laws, for she was, by nature, inclined to clemency. Her former adviser, the Imperial ambassador, Simon Renard, warned Philip II. that harsh measures would give the heretics an excuse for renewed revolts, and Philip himself advised against severity.[5] Cardinal Pole had recommended that clemency should be shown to heretics while he was still in Italy,[6] and he once more expressed the same sentiments when he dissolved the Convocation of the clergy in January, 1555.[7] The only objection was that there seemed

[1] See Vol. XIII. of this work, p. 270.

[2] LINGARD, VII., 189.

[3] LINGARD, IV., 331.

[4] BREEN, 115. Soranzo's report of August 18, 1554 in BROWN, V., n. 934, p. 559.

[5] GAIRDNER, 355 seq.

[6] See Vol. XIII. of this work, p. 222.

[7] GAIRDNER 355 seq. He forgave three heretics in the diocese of London when they appealed to him. GAIRDNER in the Dictionary of National Biogr., XLVI., 44; cf. Pole's letter to Otto von Truchsess of June 20, 1554 in BROWN, V., n. 901, p. 514; SPILLMANN, II., 124.

to be no way of controlling the spokesmen of the heretics, if they did not extirpate the heresy itself, which they regarded as the root of the ever recurring rebellion and disturbance in the kingdom. According to the old traditional ideas, punishment and fear were the only way of getting the upper hand of heresy. Cranmer, in his draft of a book of ecclesiastical canons, handed over obstinate heretics to the secular arm for punishment, and there could be no doubt as to what was meant by such punishment.[1] Calvin, the adviser of the English Protestants, had declared in a letter to the Protector, Somerset, that according to a strict observance of the law, extreme measures would have to be adopted against the Catholics,[2] while similar treatment had long been in force against the Anabaptists.

With the views then prevailing, it is easy to understand that the proposal to renew the old laws against the heretics should have met with hardly any opposition in Parliament. It was considered during the three days, from December 13th to the 15th, 1554, in the House of Commons, and again for three days, from December 15th to the 18th, in the Upper House ; only in the latter was there any opposition.[3]

[1] LINGARD, VII., 187 seq.

[2] " A ce que ientendz, Monseigneur, vous avez deux especes de mutins qui se sont eslevez contre le roy et lestat du royaume les ungs sont gens fantastiques qui soubz couleur de l'Evangile vouldroient mettre tout en confusion. Les aultres sont gens obstinez aux superstitions de lantechrist de Rome. Tous ensemble meritent bien destre reprimez par le glayve qui vous est commis, veu quilz sattachent non seulement au roy, mais a Dieu qui la assis au siege royal." Letter to Lord Somerset : CALVINI Opera, XIII. (Corp. Reform., XLIX.), 68.

[3] GAIRDNER, 346.   J. Gairdner, the best authority on the history of the English Reformation, admits that the persecution of the Protestants under Mary originated in political motives.   " The very mildness of Mary's beginnings," he says (p. 336) " had encouraged both heresy and treason."   " Rebellion and treason," he says (p. 353 seq.) " had been nourished by heresy, nay, heresy was the very root from which they sprang. And it was really more important in the eyes of Mary to extirpate the root than

The laws against the heretics framed during December were to come into force on January 20th, 1555. In the meantime, the fanaticism of several Protestants made a further law necessary. On January 16th, Parliament declared it high treason to pray for the death of the queen. They had recently, on January 1st, come upon the traces of nocturnal conventicles, in which such a prayer was commonly used, namely that God might turn the heart of the queen from worshipping idols, or put an end to her days. These nocturnal meetings took place in different parts of London and the neighbourhood, in order to avert suspicion ; they were very largely attended, and £10

merely to lop off the branches. She had all possible desire to show indulgence to the misguided if they could be brought to a better state of mind ; and the bishops might be trusted, especially Bishop Bonner, to do their very utmost to dissuade the obstinate from rushing on their fate. But there was to be no more tolerance for incurable perversity, for the heresy laws were now revived."
" The so-called Bloody Mary was in reality the most kind-hearted of the Tudors," says Gairdner in the English Historical Review, XXI. (1906), 373. Against the statement of A. INNES (England under the Tudors, London, 1905), that Mary's persecution of the Protestants proceeded from her intense conviction of the soul-destroying effects of heresy, no measure against which appeared to her too severe, when it was a question of saving souls, Gairdner remarks (ibid.) : " I do not know where he (Innes) finds grounds for this view. The facts are simply these : if the old religion was to be restored, it had to be protected from insult and violence, which were only too prevalent, and the renewal of the former laws against heresy seemed the only effectual means of doing so."
MAITLAND (Essays on subjects connected with the reformation in England, London, 1849), who gives extracts from the inflammatory letters of the Protestant refugees, describes as one of the principal causes of the Protestant persecution under Mary ' the bitter and provocative spirit of several of those who were very active, and took a prominent part in the furtherance of the advance of the reformation, the political opinions which they defended, the language in which they disseminated them, the furious personal attacks on those whom they regarded as their enemies, and finally, in the case of those who were really animated by

was often collected in a single night for the " Prisoners of Christ."[1]

This renewed proof of hostility was not calculated to dispose Parliament to show greater clemency to the Protestants. When, on January 18th, 1555, the political prisoners in the Tower were set at liberty, there remained a class to whom this act of clemency was not extended ; these were the Protestant preachers who were in the Tower as accomplices of Northumberland, Suffolk, or Wyatt, either for illicit preaching, or other incitement to revolt. Their imprisonment was not a harsh one ; they could circulate their writings among themselves, and were able to prepare a common declaration in which they earnestly besought Parliament " as poor prisoners of Christ, and in the name of Christ, our dear Redeemer," to enter into itself, and repent of having given its consent to the abolition of many blessèd laws with regard to religion, which had been issued by two noble kings, to the satisfaction of the whole country. Now, however, superstition was again set up, to the contempt of God and His Word, and with such open robbery, violence and cruelty as were not customary even in Turkey. They begged permission to be allowed to vindicate the homilies and the liturgy of King Edward as being truly Catholic ; should they not succeed in so doing, then they were ready for the stake.[2]

This challenge was accepted. On January 22nd, the un-

religious principles, and strove for a true reformation of the Church, the want of eagerness, to say the least, shown in dissociating themselves from an unbridled, godless and low rabble, which made common cause with Protestantism, in order to do battle with the law, the well-to-do classes, the clergy and the authorities." " It seems impossible," continues Maitland, " that a man of any reflection, even if he be led astray by biassed reports, or involved in religious prejudice, can fail to recognize the mere fact as such, that the English persecution was caused in great measure by the proceedings of co-religionists in exile [the composers of the inflammatory writings."] *Cf.* BREEN, 114.

[1] GAIRDNER, 348.
[2] *Ibid.*, 349.

happy preachers had to appear at the episcopal palace, where
Gardiner announced to them the laws which had just come into
force. On the 28th, the legal proceedings proper took place
in the church, before a great concourse of people. Of the six
who were cited, two recanted, one of whom, however, recalled
his recantation. The other four were excommunicated as
obstinate heretics, whereupon the secular tribunal condemned
them to death by fire, which they steadfastly endured in
different places at the beginning of February.[1]

On February 9th Bishop Bonner of London condemned six
other Protestants. On the following day, however, the
Franciscan, Alfonso de Castro, preached a sermon before the
queen and King Philip, in which he blamed the action of the
government and succeeded in preventing any further executions
in the country for the time being.[2]

---

[1] GAIRDNER, 349-352.

[2] According to Foxe's Book of Martyrs, de Castro " inveighed
against these executions, while he boldly explained what is true,
that the English bishops had not learned in the Scriptures to burn
heretics." Alfonso de Castro has written a whole book, *De iusta
haereticorum punitione* (Salamanca, 1547, and elsewhere) from
which one can gather his real views better than from Foxe. In
the introduction he says that there are two extreme views with
regard to the punishment of heresy, between which the truth is
to be found. The one was too hasty in inflicting punishment,
and the other maintained that no punishment at all should be
inflicted. Concerning the first view, the only one with which we
are concerned, de Castro says : Some persons, who have much
of the Pharisee in them, are so morose and severe, that, in their
opinion all heretics should be persecuted with irreconcilable hatred
and without mercy. Hatred against heretics is regarded by them
as the surest sign of an ardent zeal for the Catholic faith. Such
people do indeed possess zeal, but not enlightened zeal. St. Paul
teaches that we should reprimand those who resist the truth,
in a modest manner, if God does not grant them a change of mind,
so that they may recognize the truth. A good superior must think
of his own weakness, and judge kindly of the weakness of others,
and endeavour to free from the snares of heresy those who err by
humility and clemency, rather than drive them by severity over

While the persecution was in abeyance, the royal Council discovered the traces of a new conspiracy.[1] Protestant inhabitants of Cambridge, to whom the duties of the Catholic religion were too irksome, collected a great number of arms, and planned a revolt against the " Papists " which they hoped would meet with wide support. The conspirators thought of marching on London, and there, with the help of their co-religionists, not only to drive out all foreigners by murder and violence, but also to avenge the restoration of the old religion on the persons of the queen and her husband. As the Venetian ambassador, Michiel, wrote on March 26th, people were now prepared for severe measures on the part of the government, for everybody now clearly saw that the clemency and mildness their majesties had hitherto shown in forgiving everyone, was every day giving rise to new excesses. It had been of no avail, for example, when the government had shown mercy on the occasion of a similar conspiracy at Ipswich during the previous summer. When one of the condemned heretics had been sent to Suffolk to be burned there at the beginning of February, 1555,[2] the peasants resolved to rise at the moment of the execution and set fire to a number of houses, not only to save the condemned man, but also to avenge themselves on the Catholics.

the precipice of destruction. Even the physician does not at once have recourse to the iron (Opera Alphonsi a Castro, Parisiis 1571, 1037). Similar opinions, *ibid.* l., 1, c. 17, p. 1160 *seq.*, *e.g.* : " non tamen statim, cum deprehensus est, digna poena illi infligetur, sed prius oportet ad illius emendationem laborare, ut si possible fuerit, ab errore ad fidem catholicam prius revocetur, et sic spiritus eius in Dei iudicio salvus fiat. Blanda admonitione est opus, non severa, quia nimia severitas saepe frangere et raro corrigere solet." The other extreme view which de Castro combats, according to which no punishment at all should be attached to heresy, is, as de Castro says, only defended by the heretics themselves.

[1] Michiel on March 26, 1555, in BROWN, VI., n. 37.

[2] Michiel erroneously says Norfolk instead of Suffolk ; see BROWN, VI., p. 31, n.

Indeed, the investigations into the conspiracy were not yet
concluded when the fires of the stake were once more lighted.
On March 26th, shortly after the chief conspirator, Bowes,
had been taken to the Tower, instructions were issued to the
magistrates to guard the public peace, to arrest the disseminators of seditious writings, the preachers of heretical doctrines, the organizers of secret meetings, and to hand over
obstinate heretics to the bishops.[1]

The bishops did not show any great activity in carrying out
their thankless task, but showed clemency, as far as it was in
their power to do so.[2]   In many dioceses not a single heretic

---

[1] LINGARD, VII., 193.

[2] " It is quite untrue, as Foxe and his school have made the
world believe, that the authorities were savage or ferocious "
(GAIRDNER, 349 ; cf. supra p. 364.) Under many bishops there were
no executions at all.   Gilbert Bourne, bishop of Bath and Wells,
in the proceedings on account of heresy, did all he could for the
prisoners, " always earnestly exhorting them to save themselves
by recantation . . . In his own diocese it does not appear that
any one was put to death " (Dictionary of National Biography,
VI., 29).   Cuthbert Tunstall, of Durham " refrained as far as
possible from persecuting the protestants, and condemned none
of them to death " (ibid. LVII., 314).   Fuller says of William
Glynn of Bangor (Worthies of England, ed. NICHOLS, II., 571) :
" Though constant to his own he was not cruel to opposite judgments as appeareth by there being no persecution in his diocese "
(ibid., XXII., 11).   Many bishops had nothing to do with the persecution in their dioceses.   John Holyman, of Bristol, " though
a zealous Romanist . . . was never active in persecution." He
refused to be present when his chancellor, Dalby, sent three men
to the stake (ibid, XXVII., 215).   George Day, of Chichester,
" He is said not to have persecuted, but several persons were
burned in his diocese " (ibid. XIV., 232-233).   From other dioceses
only very few executions of Protestants are known.   Thomas
Thirlby, of Ely, had, it appears, sanctioned the execution of John
Hullier on account of heresy ; besides this case, only two others
suffered death on account of religion in his diocese, and that was
without the co-operation of Thirlby (ibid. LVI., 137).   Under
James Turberville, of Exeter, (ibid. LVII., 325), David Pole, of

was burned, and persecution was only active in three or four.[1] It was, naturally, most violent in the capital, which the Venetian ambassador describes as " the chief seat of lies, and of instigation to rebellion."[2] Bishop Bonner, however, was by no means the ruthless tyrant which a very biassed historical description would make him.[3] On May 24th, 1555, the royal Council sent him a reprimand because he showed so little zeal against the heretics ; he was requested to act in accordance with the law, " for the honour of God, and for the better preservation of peace in the kingdom."[4] Bonner thereupon

Peterborough (ibid. XLVI., 20), Antony Kitchin, of Llandaff (ibid. XXXI., 230) only one Protestant was executed. Concerning Gardiner see infra p. 371. The said work of reference makes no mention of executions, and, at the most, of participation in examinations, or at the burning of the corpses of Bucer and Fagius, in the biographies of Robert Warton, of St. Asaph (LIX., 431), Thomas Watson, of Lincoln (LX., 32), James Brooks, of Gloucester (VI., 438), Ralph Baynes, of Lichfield-Coventry (III., 456), Maurice Griffith, of Rochester (XXIII., 234), Thomas Goldwell, of St. Asaph (XXII., 97), Nicholas Heath, of York (XXV., 345), Richard Pate, of Worcester (XLIV., 11), Cuthbert Scott, of Chester (LI., 15), Thomas Stanley, of Sodor and Man (LIV., 50), Owen Oglethorpe, of Carlisle (XLII., 48), and Henry Morgan of St. David's (XXXIX., 16). Besides Bonner, John White, of Lincoln (LXI., 53), John Christopherson, of Chichester (X., 294), John Hopton, of Norwich (XXVII., 347), Robert King, of Oxford (XXXI., 154), adopted stern measures against the Protestants. Concerning the chancellor of the diocese of Oxford, John Storey, see SPILLMANN, II., 129.

[1] TRÉSAL, 322. ZIMMERMANN in the Histor. Jahrbuch, XXIII., 833.

[2] Michiel on July 9, 1555, in BROWN, VI., 1, n. 154, p. 133.

[3] Foxe shows, in his book of Martyrs, as Gairdner says, extreme desire to make out charges of cruelty against Bonner (Dictionary of National Biography, V., 359). The injustice of the accusations of Foxe, which were simply adopted by the succeeding writers of history, is proved by S. R. MAITLAND, Essays on the reformation, London, 1849, 409 ; cf. ZIMMERMANN, 98.

[4] LINGARD, VII., 194.

had to examine and sentence, by degrees, however, 120 accused persons who were sent to him. He did everything he could to save these unfortunate people, and in many cases his endeavours were successful. Indeed it was precisely the great number whom he induced to recant, that earned for him the hatred of the innovators.[1] Conversions were also reported from other quarters. When Dr. John Cheke, the former tutor of Edward VI., turned to the Catholic Church, thirty other Protestants, who were already threatened with death, followed him.[2] In one case all the prisoners were set free on their simple oath to be faithful to God and the queen.[3] Dr. John Storey was very active in London, in clearing the city of " schism, heresy and rebellion," as it is significantly described. In the middle of June, 1555, he was of opinion that conditions in the capital had decidedly improved.[4]

Bishop Gardiner had, as Lord Chancellor, taken part in the first examinations and condemnations of the heretics, but never afterwards.[5] Under Pole, as Archbishop of Canterbury, only once, on November 10th, 1558, were five Protestants executed, and that when the Cardinal was already on his death-bed, and hardly knew what was taking place.[6]

[1] ZIMMERMANN, 100.

[2] Michiel on November 2, 1556, in BROWN, VI., 2, n. 690.

[3] LINGARD, VII., 207.

[4] His letter to Courtenay of June 17, 1555, in BROWN, VI., 1, n 137.

[5] LINGARD, VII., 192 ; cf. 189 n.

[6] Ibid., 205 ; cf. MARTIN, 111 seq. Pole's envoys, who visited the universities of the country, had the bones of Bucer and Fagius removed from the principal church of Cambridge in 1557, at the request of the University, and burned (Briefe Treatise concerning the Burnynge of Bucer and Fagius, translated by Goldyng, 1562 ; cf. Dictionary of National Biography, X., 294). The remains of the nun, Catherine, who was married to Vermigli, and which had been placed in order to insult the Catholics beside the shrine of St. Frideswide, in Christ Church, Oxford, were also dug up in 1561, but were mingled with the relics of St. Frideswide and solemnly reburied in Christ Church. Cf. (I. CALFHILL) Historia de exhumatione Catherinae, nuper uxoris doctissimi theologi

It is not easy to determine what part the queen took personally in the condemnations. She wrote to Pole in November, 1555, that in her opinion great severity and violence should be avoided in dealing with the heretics, but in the treatment of the seducers of the people, justice should be allowed to take its course. The people must be made to understand clearly that no one was punished unjustly, for only in this way could many be brought to acknowledge the truth and be preserved from a relapse. She especially wished that no one should be burned in London, except in the presence of a member of the royal Council, and that during the carrying out of the sentence, good sermons should be preached in London and elsewhere, for the conversion of the people.[1] Moreover, Mary had taken but little part in public events since the beginning of 1555.[2] She was ill even at the beginning of the year, and in April she withdrew to Hampton Court, where she remained quietly for some months. A report that she was dead was widely circulated and was believed by many.[3] The people assembled in crowds, and gave signs of the greatest joy, when, on her return from Hampton Court, they were able to convince themselves that she was alive.[4] Mary had hinted, at the beginning

D. Petri Martyris ac eiusdem ad honestam sepulturam restitutione Oxonii facta III. id. Ian., 1561, Oxford, 1561 ; (KONR. HUBERT) Historia Catharinae Vermiliae P. Martyris coniugis exhumatae, Argentorati, 1561 ; Acta Sanctorum Octob. VIII., 533 seqq. (where there is a copy of Calfhill's publication) ; Dictionary of National Biography, XX., 276 ; REUSCH, Index, I., 420.

[1] BROWN, VI., 3. App. n. 136, p. 1647. LINGARD, VII., 189. The date of the MS. is clear from the contents ; cf. Pole's letter to Morone of November 11, 1555, in BROWN, VI., 1, n. 276.

[2] BREEN, 111 seq.

[3] BROWN, VI., 1, n. 85, 174, 200.

[4] Michiel on August 27, 1555, in BROWN, VI., n. 200. " No one can describe," writes Michiel, " what a mass of people crowded along the very broad road, and what signs of joy the people expressed at the sight of the queen. The joy was all the greater, as the people of London had been convinced that the queen was dead. On her appearance they ran about madly from one place to another, seeking to see better, in order to make sure that it really

of her illness, that her hope of an heir was about to be realized, but it became more clear every day that she was suffering from dropsy, and had misunderstood the signs of her disease. In September she felt better, and tried, for a short time, once more to take part in the affairs of state. Her condition, however, soon grew worse, and from that time she never again appeared at the Council of State, and could hardly have had any influence in the condemnations on account of religion.

In Foxe's Book of Martyrs the number of these condemnations is given as 277, but all those on this list did not suffer death, and many of those named were not martyrs in any sense of the word, but suffered well-deserved punishment as ordinary criminals; others again, were not martyrs for Protestantism, for they were punished for holding doctrines, for the profession of which the innovators themselves would have put them to death. Nevertheless, there remain about 200 persons who suffered a terrible death on account of their Protestant opinions,[1] and, for the most part they met their fate steadfastly.[2] It was, moreover, permitted, that those condemned should have a small bag of gunpowder between their legs or before their breast, which exploded at the first

was her. And when they had assured themselves of this fact, and that she was looking better than before, they gave still greater signs of joy by shouting and greeting her, and by every means in their power, especially as, to their great satisfaction and that of Her Majesty, King Philip sat beside the queen, and, on the other side, Cardinal Pole, who are both very popular on account of their great friendliness."

[1] LINGARD, VII., 207.

[2] This steadfastness in the victims of justice was quite usual in England. " The English," writes Litolfi, " are obstinate by nature and exceedingly courageous ; it has often been seen how they have ascended the scaffold or the stake laughing, while they made merry over such a martyrdom ; many used to boast of the number of their family who had been hanged or quartered." So writes Annibale Litolfi to Duke Guglielmo Gonzaga of Mantua, on June 20, 1557, in BROWN, VI., 3, App. n. 171, p. 1672 ; cf. anecdotes related ibid.

contact with the fire, and caused a speedy death, or at least unconsciousness.[1] It must be said, to the honour of the government, that it was not sullied with the atrocities which were practised, with such refined cruelty, on Catholics in the time of Elizabeth. In spite of this, it is upon Mary, above all others, that the accusation of cruelty has been fixed. John Foxe, who had fled to Germany before the persecution, collected the reports of the sufferings of his co-religionists, and his account, all distorted by hatred, has for hundreds of years called forth and nourished horror against Mary and the Catholic Church among English Protestants.[2]

[1] ZIMMERMANN, 103.

[2] Foxe's Book of Martyrs (Acts and Monuments) was a household word in almost every English family of Puritanical tendencies, and the principal arsenal for weapons against Catholics. Preachers took examples from it as material for their sermons ; the Convocation of the Clergy decided in 1571 that the book must be procured by every cathedral church, and in many parish churches it lay, fastened by a chain, for common use (S. L. LEE in the Dictionary of National Biography, XX., 146 seqq.) Concerning Foxe's reliability Lee says (p. 148 seq.) : " The enormous extent of Foxe's work has prevented a critical investigation of the whole. But it is plain from such examination as the work has undergone that Foxe was too zealous a partisan to write with historical precision. He is a passionate advocate, ready to accept any prima facie evidence. . . Foxe's mistakes sometimes arise from faulty and hasty copying of original documents, but are more often the result of exaggeration. John Deighton, a very friendly critic, showed that Foxe's account of the martyrdom of " John Horne and a woman " at Newent, on September 25, 1556, is an amplification of the suffering at the stake of Edward Horne, on September 25, 1558 (NICHOLS, Narratives of the reformation, 69). The errors, in date and Christian name, in the case, are very typical. Foxe, moreover, undoubtedly included among his martyrs persons executed for ordinary secular offences. He acknowledged his error in the case of John Marbeck, of Windsor, " martyr," of 1543, whom he represented in his text of 1563 to have been burned, whereas the man was condemned, but pardoned. Foxe was often less ingenuous. He wrote that one Greenwood or

The great majority of the people who had the courage to go to the stake belonged to the working classes. The nobles, among whom there were many with Protestant leanings, are only represented by nine names. The middle classes are entirely unrepresented ; sixteen of the preachers, and five of the Protestant bishops suffered death at the hands of the executioner.[1] There were only the three bishops, Cranmer, Ridley and Latimer, who were men of importance, among those who suffered death. All three had already been thrown into the Tower on account of political offences before the renewal of the penal laws.[2] In March, 1554, they were taken to Oxford, so that they might in public disputations give reasons and replies concerning their opinions.[3] As they persisted in their views, they were, on April 20th, 1554, declared to be obstinate heretics. The legal proceedings against them, however, only began in September, 1555. The sentence against Cranmer, as he was an archbishop, was reserved to the Pope.

The Bishop of Gloucester, Dr. Brooks, conducted the

Grimwood, of Hitcham, near Ipswich, Suffolk, having obtained the conviction of a " martyr," John Cooper, on concocted evidence, died miserably soon afterwards. Foxe was informed that Greenwood was alive, and that the story of his death was a fiction. He went to Ipswich to examine witnesses, but never made any alteration in his account. Later . . . a clergyman named Prick recited Foxe's story about Greenwood from the pulpit of Hitcham Church. Greenwood was present, and proceeded against Prick for libel, but the courts held that no malicious defamation was intended (CROKE, Reports, edited by LEACH, II., 91) . . . It has been most conclusively shown that his chapter on the Waldensians is directly translated from the ' catalogus ' of Illyricus, although Illyricus is not mentioned by Foxe among the authorities consulted. Foxe claims to have consulted ' parchment documents ' whereas he only knew them in the text of Illyricus. This indicates a loose notion of literary morality which justifies some of the harshest judgments passed on Foxe."

[1] ZIMMERMANN, 104.

[2] See Vol. XIII. of this work, p. 247.

[3] See *Ibid.* p. 274.

investigation on behalf of Cardinal Jacopo Puteo. On September 7th, Cranmer was granted a period of eighty days within which to vindicate himself in Rome ; on September 12th, he had to appear before Brooks.[1] The charge against him was not only that of heresy, but also that of having broken his oath of celibacy, sworn to the Pope. After the expiration of the eighty days, Paul IV., on December 4th, 1555, pronounced the sentence of excommunication and deposition against him, and ordered him to be handed over to the secular power.[2] Ridley and Latimer had to appear before Brooks and two other bishops, who acted on behalf of Pole, on September 30th, 1555. On October 16th, they were both sent to the stake at Oxford. Latimer was killed almost at once, after the lighting of the fire, by the explosion of the bag of gunpowder placed before his breast ; Ridley, however, had to suffer longer, owing to the awkwardness of his friends, who wished to make his death easier.[3]

After his imprisonment, Ridley had, for a short time, returned to the worship of the old religion, but soon repented of his declaration and recanted.[4] Cranmer proved himself ready to go still further. In his first examination, on September 12th, he adopted, it is true, an unyielding attitude, but when it was put to him that if the king is the head of the Church, then Nero at the time of St. Peter, and also the Sultan of Turkey, must equally be regarded as heads of the Church, he accepted this inference without hesitation.[5] He gradually became more pliant, and one by one signed seven declarations, in which he at last acknowledged the Pope and the Catholic

[1] GAIRDNER, 364 seq.

[2] RAYNALDUS, 1555, n. 30.

[3] After the people had been convinced that everything had been done to save them both, they were not unwilling to witness the execution (Pole, on October 26, 1555, in BROWN, VI., 1, n. 256, p. 226). Usually the people of London showed displeasure at the execution of heretics. Michiel, on June 1, 1555, ibid. n. 116 ; cf. n. 49, p. 45.

[4] LINGARD, VII., 195 seq.

[5] GAIRDNER, 365.

Church, renounced the doctrines of Luther and Zwingli, and condemned his former proceedings.[1]

All these concessions, however, were in vain. The queen had no confidence in the rectitude of this unprincipled man,[2] and the event proved that she had judged rightly. On the morning of his execution, March 21st, 1556, Cranmer signed the seventh and last recantation, which he promised to read immediately before his death. In this he declared that he accepted all the doctrines of the Catholic Church, and further that nothing lay so heavy on his conscience as what he had written against those doctrines. The first of these declarations he did actually read, even if he did not, as was soon shown, understand them in the Catholic sense. Instead of reading the second, however, he declared that nothing lay so heavy on his conscience as having been induced to make these seven recantations ; his right hand, which had signed them, should, in expiation, be the first to feel the fire. He actually stretched it out into the flames, as soon as the fire was lighted. Immediately afterwards he was dead.[3]

Many English Protestants had fled to the continent since 1554 ; it was not easy for them to find a place of refuge. They were received unwillingly in France and the German Lutherans were as much disliked by the English sacramentarians as the Catholics. Some went to Wesel, where they were very unwelcome.[4] Peter Martyr Vermigli procured an asylum for others at Strasbourg, and many went to Calvinist Switzerland. Johann a Lasco went to Poland, and Coverdale to Denmark.[5]

---

[1] *Ibid.*

[2] BROWN, VI., 1, n. 434, p. 386.

[3] *Ibid.* and GAIRDNER, 370 *seqq.*

[4] Melancthon applied to the Council of Wesel on their behalf in a document of November 19, 1556 (Corp. Reform., VIII., 908), but writes on March 29, 1557 : " Exulibus Gallicis et Anglicis doleo meam intercessionem lenissime scriptam non profuisse apud Fesulanos " (=inhabitants of Wesel ; *ibid.* IX., 121). In the same way Melancthon advised, on July 13, 1557, the English refugees in Frankfurt to be patient (*ibid.* IX., 179).

[5] GAIRDNER, 391 *seq.*

Frankfort-on-Maine was a great meeting place for the fugitives. There they received the joint use of a church with the French Protestant refugees, whereupon the question immediately arose as to whether the English Book of Common Prayer could be used also in Frankfort. At first they came to an agreement, but were once more at variance when John Knox appeared there as a preacher. Soon, however, they were reconciled for a second time, though before long the dispute was again at " boiling point." When Richard Cox arrived in Frankfort with nine more refugees, the little Frankfort community was divided into Knoxians and Coxians. John Knox preached in the pulpit against Cox, but a friend of the latter found a way of having his troublesome assailant removed from Frankfort. He complained to the magistrate of Knox, and accused him of having said in one of his publications[1] that the Emperor was no less an enemy of Christ than Nero, and that he had cursed the Queen of England.[2] Calvin, who had already taken part in the dispute,[3] made reproaches to the English community in Frankfort for having driven Knox away. They defended themselves in a letter, which, among other admissions, contains the remarkable statement that the insane and inflammatory writings of Knox had been in great measure responsible for the persecution in England.[4]

[1] Faithful Admonition of Christians, concerning the present troubles of England : Works, III., 257.

[2] CALVINI Opera, XV. (Corp. Reform., XLIII.,) 337, 370, 393, 422, 447, 523, 551, 558. Dictionary of National Biography, XXXI., 312 seq. GAIRDNER, 391 seq.

[3] Letter of January 18, 1555, loc. cit., 393 seqq.

[4] Hoc tibi affirmare possumus, vesanum illum Knoxi libellum plurimum olei igni persecutionis is Anglia addidisse. Nam ante illum editum libellum ne unus quidem ex fratribus nostris mortem fuerat perpessus : simul atque ille prodiit, in quam multos optimos viros flammis saevitum sit ad vos pervenisse non dubitamus. Angli Francofordienses Calvino, 20 September, 1555 (Opera Calvini, XV. [Corp. Reform., XLIII.,] 780 seq.) Because the English refugees everywhere, in Italy, Germany, and France spread evil rumours against the government, and the religion,

In spite of this view, however, England was again flooded in
1555 with abusive writings by the innovators. Various
wretches endeavour every day, writes Michiel on May 13th,
to disturb the peace, and where possible to cause revolts.
Several days ago, a dialogue, full of the foulest abuse of
religion, the government, and the persons of the king and
queen, was circulated.[1] Special attention was drawn at the
end of the year to a pamphlet personally directed against
Philip II. This held up a terrible picture before the eyes of
the English people, of Philip treading the rights of the inhabitants of the Kingdom of Naples under foot, and saying that if
Mary remained childless he would do away with her and make
himself master of England. The writer of this pamphlet was
supposed to be one of the English refugees in Strasbourg,
" who employ every means in their power to drive the people
to rebellion."[2]

English fugitives also worked against the queen in Italy.
When Paul IV. published his bull against the alienation of
church property,[3] they at once sent the document to England
in order to make the people believe that the concessions of
Pole with regard to the church property in England were
revoked.[4] " It is hardly credible," writes Pole to Muzzarelli,

the draft of a Bill was laid before Parliament in November, 1555,
which ordered all natives of England to return home. Michiel
on November 11, 1555, in BROWN, VI., 1, n. 274. *Cf.* R. JUNG,
Die eng. Flüchtlingsgemeinde in Frankfurt a. M. 1554 bis 1559,
Frankfurt, 1910.

[1] BROWN, VI., 1, n. 80, p. 70. King Philip asked the Emperor
by special messenger whether he should proceed against this libel.
Letter of Badoer, Brussels, May 19, 1555, *ibid.* n. 85.

[2] Letter of Badoer, Brussels, December 3, 1555, *ibid.* n. 300.
The title of the pamphlet (A Warninge for Englande, etc.) in LEE,
Dictionary of National Biography, XXXVI., 348. *Cf.* Pole's
letter of November 23, 1555 (in BROWN, VI., 1, n. 287), which
also points out that the pamphlet was from a Protestant hand.

[3] See *supra* p. 91.

[4] Michiel, Letter of September, 16, 1555, in BROWN, VI., 1,
n. 215.

" how many false reports are circulated in order to turn the
hearts of the people away from the Pope." When he spoke
concerning this to the queen, she declared with sighs and tears
that she had not the heart to repeat to him all the things that
were reported to her.[1] The courage of the revolutionary
elements increased especially after the death, on November
12th, 1555, of Gardiner, whose powerful hand had been much
feared by his adversaries.[2]

The mood which this unceasing incitement had called into
being among great numbers of the people found expression in
the most violent outbreaks of fanaticism, and in ever recurring
conspiracies and revolutionary plots. While the priest was
distributing communion on Easter Sunday, April 4th, 1555,
in the church of St. Margaret's, Westminster, an ex-monk
wounded him on the head and hand, so that he lay there like
one dead. The perpetrator of this deed asserted that he was
inspired thereto by the Holy Ghost, as a protest against the
idolatry. He had not received the courage to carry out this
enterprise at Christmas, but now he was ready " to die for
the Lord." Foxe included this raving lunatic among his
" martyrs."[3] A statue of St. Thomas of Canterbury over the
entrance to the Mercers' Chapel, had been frequently mutilated, several times during the night.[4] Churches were often
broken into and the Blessed Sacrament was frequently dese-
crated ;[5] there were many disturbances during the church
services after the death of Cranmer.[6]

In May, 1555, a young man represented himself as being
Edward VI., who was asserted not to be really dead at all ;
several people pretended to believe him, and organized a

---

[1] Pole to Muzzarelli on October 26, 1555, *ibid.* n. 255.

[2] Pole to Philip on November 23, 1555, *ibid.* n. 287.

[3] Michiel on April 15, 1555, in BROWN, VI., 1, n. 57, p. 50 *seq.*
GAIRDNER, 355.

[4] MICHIEL on March 19, 1555, in BROWN, VI., 1, n. 32, p. 28.
GAIRDNER, 355.

[5] Michiel, *loc. cit.*

[6] Michiel on March 24, 1556, in BROWN, VI., 1, n. 434, p.
386.

rising.[1] In the January of the following year a pamphlet appeared which again asserted that King Edward was still living, and in France, and was only waiting for a rising of the people to land in England.[2] Another plot set on foot at the end of 1555 by Henry Dudley, a relative of the Duke of Northumberland, was more dangerous; it was only discovered by the government at the beginning of March, 1556, through information given by one of the conspirators. It was proposed to set fire to London in different places, and in the confusion to seize upon the royal treasury, establish themselves in the Isle of Wight, and from there, arrange a rising throughout the kingdom.[3] At the trial of the numerous prisoners it was discovered that the rebels had been supported by France,[4] that the queen and all foreigners were to have been murdered,[5] and Elizabeth set upon the throne in her place.[6] Courtenay was to have been her husband and co-regent. The inquiry into the wide ramifications of this plot lasted until May.[7] It was hardly at an end when further troubles arose in June. A young man named Cleobury declared that he was Courtenay, to whom he bore a great resemblance, and proclaimed himself as king, and Elizabeth as queen, in Sussex. The people, however, would have nothing to do with him, and he was executed for high treason on September 20th.[8] An arch-heretic, well known in Germany, was mixed up with Cleobury's rising, of which Michiel gives some account in August, 1556. He lived, for safety, hidden

---

[1] Michiel on May 27, 1555, *ibid.* n. 97.

[2] Michiel on January 21, 1556, *ibid.* n. 358 ; *cf.* n. 377.

[3] Michiel on March 17 and 24, 1556, *ibid.* n. 429, 434.

[4] Michiel on March 30 and April 14, 1556, *ibid.* n. 440, 458.

[5] Michiel on April 21, 1556, *ibid.* n. 461 ; *cf.* Soranzo, April 14, 1556, *ibid.* n. 457.

[6] LINGARD, 216, *seq.* GAIRDNER, 379.

[7] Michiel on May 5, 1556, in BROWN, VI., 1, n. 477.

[8] LINGARD 219. Several of his accomplices were hanged as early as August. They died repentant, and acknowledged that they had been led to this false step by mistaken views on religion. Michiel on August 18, 1556, in BROWN, VI., 1, n. 580.

in the woods, but came to the villages from time to time in all
sorts of disguises, in order to encourage his co-religionists with
tales of better times, when religion would be established and
" slavery " at an end.[1]   In March, 1557, the French Protestants, in conjunction with the English refugees, endeavoured
to deliver the two fortresses of Hammes and Guisnes, in the
territory of Calais, into the hands of the French.[2]   The following month again brought with it a new act of treachery.
Thomas Stafford, the son of Pole's sister Ursula, had been from
the first vehemently opposed to the Spanish marriage of the
queen, and had probably taken part in Suffolk's rising.   He
escaped, however, from prison to France, and took an active
part there in the intrigues of the English Protestants.   His
object was not only to overthrow Mary, but also to make himself king.   He set sail for England with two ships given him
by the King of France, on September 18th, and summoned
the people to defend themselves against " the devilish attacks
of Mary, the unlawful queen," who would deliver her country
into the slavery of the Spaniards.   His hope that thousands
would join him proved vain, and Stafford was taken prisoner
almost without a blow having been struck, and ended his life
on May 28th, at Tyburn.[3]

Although no one benefited by these risings, they nevertheless greatly damaged the esteem in which the queen was held.
She was forced either to pronounce sentence of death on those
who were guilty, or else to confiscate their property, and her
popularity thereby suffered considerably.   " The lower classes
in England," writes the Venetian ambassador, Michele Surian,
" love risings and tumults,"[4] and his predecessor, Michiel,

[1] Michiel on August 25, 1556, in BROWN, VI., 1, n. 585,
p. 578.

[2] LINGARD 226.

[3] A. F. POLLARD on the Dictionary of National Biography, LIII.,
460.   LINGARD, 226 seq.   Surian (the Venetian ambassador in
London) on April 29, 1557, in BROWN, VI., 2, n. 870.   The King of
France denies having taken part in the conspiracy ; see ibid.
n. 896, 926 ; cf. also n. 926, p. 1150.

[4] On April 29, 1557, in BROWN, VI., 2, n. 870.

says,[1] " the instigators of rebellion are excused by everybody, and their pretexts, the banishment of the foreigners or of the faith meet with silent approval. As soon as a man of importance puts himself at the head, a revolt is sure to take place, and the life of the queen to be placed in danger."

In coming to a conclusion like this, it must not be forgotten that the ambassadors only knew the conditions in the capital at all intimately. The country people were, however, discontented, for the harvest was exceedingly bad in the years 1555-1557, and a general scarcity prevailed.[2] If, however, the rebellions of Stafford and others found but little support, it proves that the discontent of large classes of the people with the government cannot have been of so great an extent as the Venetian ambassadors believed, and that the reason for the unrest of the masses must be sought somewhere else than in the severe measures against the Protestants.[3]

While the government was defending the newly restored religion after its own fashion, by measures of violence, Cardinal Pole considered that his own duty consisted in the renewal of and care for religious life among the Catholics.

Pole could not, it is true, withdraw entirely from politics. He was not only legate for the English church, but also for the reconciliation of the contending princes, and, indeed, Marcellus II. had confirmed him in both legations shortly after his accession.[4] Pole devoted himself to the office of peacemaker with great zeal.[5] On May 23rd, the anniversary of the election of Paul IV., a peace conference was opened at Marck, near Gravelines. This unimportant village had been chosen as the scene of the negotiations because the English, French, and

---

[1] Report of May 13, 1557, *ibid.* n. 884, p. 1056.

[2] Michiel's report to the Senate of Venice, 1557, in BROWN, VI., 2, n. 884, p. 1068, 1085. Michiel on October 27, 1555, *ibid.* VI., 1, n. 258. Surian on April 21 and June 1, 1557, *ibid.* VI., 2, n. 863, 912.

[3] Nonciat. de France, II., 359.

[4] Michiel on May 6, 1555, in BROWN, VI., 1, n. 72.

[5] Michiel on August 6, 1555, *ibid.* n. 176.

Flemish territories met there.[1] The conference was dissolved on June 7th without having reached any result.[2] Paul IV. also confirmed Pole's two legations, first by word of mouth, and then in a brief of December 23rd, 1555.[3] At the new peace conference which was held at Vaucelles from December 25th, 1555, to February 5th, 1556, the English Cardinal did not, it is true, take part personally, but his envoy, Parpaglia, exercised no small influence on the proceedings.[4] Pole was actively engaged in other ways for the interests of peace, both through his intermediaries, and by his letters to the King of France, to Philip II. and to the Emperor.[5]

Towards the end of August, 1555, the legate was asked to undertake yet another political office. Before Philip left England, he spoke to Pole, in the presence of the assembled royal Council, and expressed the wish that the Cardinal should, in his absence, be a support and consolation to the queen, and exercise a sort of superintendence over the government. Pole answered in courteous terms that he could not accept such a position without the permission of the Pope.[6] For the personal consolation of the queen, however, he took up his abode for a considerable time in the royal palace,[7] but, as far as possible, took no part in secular affairs, and appears never to have assisted at the Council of State.[8]

After the departure of Philip, Pole's advice was especially sought by the queen, with regard to the still unsettled question

---

[1] Michiel on May 27, 1555, *ibid.* n. 92 ; *cf.* Michiel on May 9, 1555, *ibid.* n. 75.

[2] Priuli on June 7, 1555, *ibid.* n. 126.

[3] RAYNALDUS, 1555, n. 35 ; *cf.* Pole to Paul IV., in January, 1556, in BROWN, VI., I, n. 360.

[4] RIESS, 85 ; *cf.* BROWN, VI., I, n. 322, 363.

[5] *Cf.* BROWN, VI., I, n. 258, 269, 293, 329, 400, etc.

[6] Michiel on September 3, 1555, in BROWN, VI., I, n. 204. Pole to Carafa on October 10, 1555, *ibid.* n. 244. Paul IV. sanctioned Pole's action in the matter ; see Michiel on November 25, 1555, *ibid.* n. 289, p. 261.

[7] BROWN, VI., I, n. 200, 251.

[8] Michiel on September 3, 1555, *ibid.* n. 204, p. 178 *seq.*

of the church property. By the confiscation of the possessions
of the church under Henry VIII., the clergy had been reduced
to poverty.[1] There were, in particular, a number of benefices
entailing the care of souls, which had formerly been filled by
the religious orders, but these, since the dissolution of the
monasteries, and owing to the complete inadequacy of the
revenues, had fallen into the hands of people without learning
or moral stability.[2]

An alteration in these lamentable conditions could only be
looked for from the generosity of the faithful. Mary, on the
advice of Pole,[3] determined to be the first to give an example.
More than 800 benefices were in the possession of the Crown;[4]
Henry VIII., moreover, in his capacity as head of the church,
had claimed the tithes and first fruits for himself. Mary now
felt it on her conscience that, in spite of her having relinquished
the title of supremacy over the church, she still continued to
draw these revenues.[5] In addition to this, although Pole, at
the time of the reunion of England with Rome, had promised
that the Church would not demand her property back again,
he had nevertheless refused to make a further declaration that
the possessor of such property might continue to feel easy in his
conscience.[6]

Philip, before his departure, had very unwillingly agreed to
the immediate renunciation of the church property, and the
ministers also made difficulties since the crown was itself in
financial straits, and had just then, in October, 1555, been
obliged to ask for a subsidy from Parliament. Mary, however,
remained immovable ; she declared that the renunciation
of ten royal crowns would not be too great a sacrifice to assure
the salvation of her soul.[7] She had already promised Pole to

[1] *Cf.* BROWN, VI., 1, n. 14.
[2] Michiel on November 25, 1555, in BROWN, VI., 1, n. 289.
[3] Michiel on July 1, 1554, *ibid.* n. 150 ; *cf.* n. 14, p. 10.
[4] Michiel on November 25, 1555, *ibid.* n. 289, p. 261. *Ibid.*
n. 14, p. 11 ; the number of these benefices is given as 700.
[5] *Ibid.* p. 260.
[6] *Ibid.* n. 14 ; VI., 2, p. 1075.
[7] LINGARD, 212 *seq.*

restore the church property at the beginning of April, but experienced lawyers had pointed out that the seizure of the property had been confirmed by an Act of Parliament, and could therefore only be given back with the consent of Parliament.[1]

It was not, however, so easy to procure this consent. Parliament, which assembled on October 21st, counted among its members many who were themselves in possession of church property, and who had no wish at all that an example of generosity and self-sacrifice should be given from the throne.[2] The fear that, in spite of all concessions, they would be forced by the church to restore the stolen property, had not entirely disappeared. On the contrary, this fear had been increased by the bull of Paul IV. concerning the restitution of church property, and the enemies of the government had not been slow in making use of it.[3] A declaration from the Pope that this bull did not apply to England, was, in the opinion of Pole, absolutely necessary, and he repeatedly made application to Rome that such a declaration should be sent to him.[4] A bull, confirming the concessions of Pole, was read by Gardiner in Parliament on October 23rd. At the same time the Chancellor assured them that no one thought of requiring from others the generosity shown by the queen.[5]

The House of Lords, with only two exceptions, now agreed to Mary's wishes, but the opposition still continued in the House of Commons. Then Mary summoned sixty members of the House to her presence, and, in her deep sonorous voice, made them an impressive speech concerning her intentions.

---

[1] Pole to Morone on August 9, 1555, in BROWN, VI., 1, n. 179.

[2] Michiel on October 27 and December 3, 1555, *ibid.* n. 258, 297.

[3] *Cf. supra* p. 379 ; Pole to Muzzarelli on October 26, 1555, *ibid.* n. 255.

[4] On August 9, 18, 28, September 16, and November 11, 1555, *ibid.* n. 179, 188, 196, 217, 276.

[5] Michiel on October 27, 1555, *ibid.* n. 258. The Bull was read at St. Paul's Cross as early as September. TYTLER, Edward and Mary II., 483 ; Dictionary of National Biography, XLVI., 43 ; *cf. infra* p. 389.

Providence, she said, had placed her on the throne so that she might restore the true religion ; all her efforts so far for this end would, however, avail her nothing, if her conscience were not set free from a double injustice, the possession of the benefices, and the tithes and first fruits. If so much love had hitherto been shown for her person, she concluded, with very marked emphasis, she hoped that still greater love would now be shown for the salvation of her soul, for otherwise, no other kind of love would have any value in her eyes.[1]

After she had finished, one of the members wished to answer her, but his colleagues forced the audacious man to be silent, as only the Speaker of the House had the right to answer the sovereign. Then Pole explained that the crown would sustain no real loss by the renunciation of the tithes and first fruits, as it would then be freed from the duty of paying pensions to the monks and priests who had been expelled, and who had retired into private life and lived as laymen since the change of religion ; the emoluments of the benefices after they had been restored would be of advantage to the sons of the nobles and the people, which would be much better for the common good than if they went into the coffers of the state.[2]

Pole's speech was listened to with general approval, but the fear of the consequences which might possibly result from their acceptance of the draft of the royal bill, still continued to weigh heavily on all their minds. On December 2nd, the bill was handed over to a committee for consideration, and on December 3rd they debated it behind closed doors from break of day until 3 o'clock in the afternoon, when it was finally accepted by 183 votes against 120.[3]

The Chancellor, Gardiner, although he was already suffering from a mortal illness, had employed his last powers on behalf of the bill, and for the granting of the subsidy.[4] On November 12th he succumbed to his great exertions, to the deep grief of

---

[1] Michiel on November 25, 1555, in BROWN, VI., 1, n. 289.

[2] *Ibid.*

[3] Michiel on December 3, 1555, *ibid.* n. 297 ; on December 3, 1555, n. 298.

[4] Pole to King Philip on October 26, 1555, *ibid.* n. 256.

Pole, as well as of the queen. He had been a true and exceedingly skilful servant to his sovereign ; everybody acknowledged, Michiel informs us on the day of Gardiner's death, that
no better or more capable person could have been chosen for
the post of Chancellor.[1] On the same day Pole wrote that it
seemed as though justice and religion would die with Gardiner,
so greatly did his disappearance from public life encourage
the unruly elements against whom he had always fought so
steadfastly.[2]

On the death of Gardiner, the greater part of the nobles
wished to see the chancellorship bestowed on Pole, but the
legate declined this offer. He must, he said, devote all his
powers to the affairs of the Church, and he dared not take any
other duties upon himself.[3] Paul IV. approved this action
on the part of his legate.[4]

The purely ecclesiastical questions, indeed, offered a wide
enough field for Pole's zeal for reform. He was determined
to devote the whole of his powers to the restoration of religion
in his native land ; not even to take part in the conclave after
the death of Julius III., would the " self-forgetful ascetic "[5]
leave England,[6] although the Emperor called upon him[7] to
travel to Rome,[8] and was prepared, as was Philip, to support
him at the Papal election with all his influence.[9]

Pole's first measures and concessions in ecclesiastical affairs,[10]
had not only been verbally sanctioned by Paul IV. to the
English ambassador, but had again been expressly confirmed

[1] November 11, 1555, *ibid.* n. 274, p. 245.

[2] *Ibid.* n. 275.

[3] Michiel on November 18, 1555, in BROWN, VI., 1, n. 282, p. 252.
Soranzo on November 27, 1555, *ibid.* n. 293.

[4] Pole to Morone on February 5, 1556, *ibid.* n. 378.

[5] Michiel on April 8, 1555, *ibid.* n. 48.

[6] For reasons which kept him back, see his letter to de las Naves
on April 8, 1555, *ibid.* n. 51.

[7] Badoer on March 31, 1555, *ibid.* n. 41.

[8] Michiel on April 15, 1555, *ibid.* n. 57.

[9] Badoer on April 7, 1555, *ibid.* n. 48 ; *cf. supra* p. 2 *seqq.*

[10] See *supra* Vol. XIII. of this work, p. 287.

on June 20th, 1555, in a formal bull.[1] The giving up of the church property, as well as all the legal regulations which had been made during the schism, were to remain in force, but the clerics who had been ordained by invalidly consecrated bishops were strictly ordered to be ordained again by their various bishops. As there seemed to be some doubt as to this last point, a new Papal brief followed on October 30th, 1555, from which it was clearly to be seen that ordination according to the formulary of Edward VI. was regarded as invalid in Rome.[2] Of the seven Anglican prelates who had lost their sees in 1554, three had been deposed on account of the nullity of their consecration.[3]

Pole regarded it as his first and most important duty to fill the vacant bishoprics and cures of souls with worthy men. Julius III. had already sanctioned the election and consecration of five English bishops on July 6th, 1554.[4] Paul IV. gave the Papal confirmation to six other English prelates in a consistory on June 21st, 1555.[5] The vacancies caused by

[1] The Bull *Praeclara carissimi*, found by Gasquet in 1895 (*cf*. Civiltà catt. 1895, II., 562 *seq*.), printed in part in the American Eccles. Review XIII. (1895), 42, and complete in the Docum. ad legat. card. Poli spect. 18 *seq*., in the Tablet, LXXXVI. (1905), 499 *seq*. and in BRANDI, Delle ordinaz. anglic.[4] Roma, 1908, 171 *seq*.

[2] The brief, *Regimini*, likewise found by Gasquet in 1895, printed in the American Eccles. Review, XIII. (1895), 43 *seq*., in the Docum. ad legat. card. Poli spect. 27 *seq*., and in Katholik, 1895, II., 275; *cf*. BELLESHEIM in the Histor.-polit. Bl., CXIX., 436 *seq*.

[3] BREEN in the Dublin Review, CXVII. (1895), 109.

[4] See Vol. XIII., p. 273. They were John White, of Lincoln, Maurice Griffith, of Rochester, James Brooks, of Gloucester, Henry Morgan, of St. David's, Gilbert Bourne, of Bath and Wells. At the same time Julius sanctioned the translation of Robert Warton to St Asaph, and confirmed George Day for Chichester.

[5] RAYNALDUS, 1555, n. 25. They were John Hopton, of Norwich, John Holyman for Bristol (see Engl. Hist. Rev., XII., 1897, 303-307), James Turberville, for Exeter, William Glynn, for Bangor, Thomas Stanley, for Sodor and Man, Ralph Baynes,

death were again filled by means of new appointments.[1] On
the whole, the bishoprics under Mary were filled by capable
and learned men.[2] Christopherson of Chichester was considered to be the founder of Greek studies at Cambridge, and
wrote the first, if not a complete, translation of the Greek
church historians.[3] Baynes was one of the principal restorers
of Hebrew learning in the British Isles.[4] Glynn of Bangor
was, according to Protestant testimony, an able man of letters,
and a great Hebraist, and a good and religious man, according
to the spirit of that time.[5] Holyman of Bristol, an opponent
of the divorce of Henry VIII., had gained a great reputation
by reason of his learning and the holiness of his life. Scott
of Chester aroused the admiration of his friends, and the anger
of his enemies by the zeal which he displayed for his diocese.[6]
Christopherson, Goldwell, Glynn and Holyman had, like Scott,
distinguished themselves under Edward VI. for their fidelity
to the Church,[7] and if others, on the whole, did not pass
through that period of trial without blame, still Day, Heath,
Bonner and Gardiner had suffered imprisonment and deposition

for Coventry-Lichfield. At the same time, Nicholas Heath was
confirmed for York, and Thomas Thirlby for Ely, and Hugh
Curwin was appointed to Dublin. Goldwell was consecrated in
Rome.

[1] In 1556 Cuthbert Scott received the bishopric of Chester, in
1557 David Pole that of Peterborough, John Christopherson that
of Chichester, Owen Oglethorpe that of Carlisle, and Robert King
was transferred to Oxford.

[2] Cf. T. E. BRIDGETT and T. F. KNOX, The true history of the
Catholic hierarchy deposed by Queen Elizabeth, London, 1889;
SPILLMANN, II., 34 seqq. Concerning Goldwell see TH. KNOX in
The Month, 1876, I., 53 seqq., 129 seqq.; Histor.-polit. Bl., LXXX.
(1877), 962 seqq.; Concerning Watson see BRIDGETT in the preface
to the new edition of Watson's Sermons on the Sacraments, London, 1876: cf. Histor.-polit. Bl., loc. cit., 866 seqq.

[3] Dictionary of National Biography, X., 294.

[4] Ibid. III., 456.

[5] Ibid. XXII., 11.

[6] Ibid. LI., 15.

[7] Ibid. X., 293; XXII., 11, 97; XXVII., 214.

for their faith,[1] and, with one exception, they all afterwards proved by their steadfastness under Elizabeth, that the zeal which they had displayed under Mary for the restoration of the Catholic religion had been based on firm conviction. When, on the summons of the legate, the English bishops assembled for a synod, the Venetian ambassador, Michiel, wrote that Pole, as well as everybody else, looked on them as exemplary men ; they were learned, fulfilled their duty of residence, were assiduous in preaching and instruction, and were not wanting in zeal.[2]

The synod had been assembled in order that they might decide about the distribution of the church property ceded by the crown, as well as to remove abuses [3] In the matter of the church property, the Convocation of the higher clergy, which always held its meetings at the same time as Parliament, had already prepared the draft of a decree. The synod took a very long time in making any further arrangements in the matter. Opened on November 4th, 1555,[4] it only came to a temporary conclusion in the middle of February, when, at the beginning of Lent, the bishops had to return to their dioceses.[5] The synod, which was to have been reopened on November 10th, 1556, was, however, adjourned to May 10th, 1557, and eventually never met at all.[6] Besides the deliberations concerning church property, the assembly was chiefly occupied with the reform of the clergy. The reform decrees agreed upon were

[1] See Vol. XIII. of this work, p. 240.

[2] Michiel on November 4, 1555, in BROWN, VI., 1, n. 269.

[3] Pole himself gives this reason for the Synod (Letter to Philip on November 11, 1555, *ibid.* n. 275.)

[4] Michiel on November 4, 1555, *ibid.*, n. 269.

[5] Pole to Paul IV. (Casanate Library, Rome, XX., 1, 36. Extract in BROWN, VI., 1, n. 395, with the correct date, February 19, 1556). The speech which Thomas Watson, dean of Durham, made at the dissolution of the Synod, is published in an English translation by J. MOYES in the Dublin Review, CXIX., (1896) 415 *seqq.*

[6] Paul IV. sent a letter of approbation to the Synod and to Pole, both in RAYNALDUS, 1555, n. 33 and 34.

published at the dissolution of the synod on February 10th.[1]
They contained, for the most part, nothing new, but called
attention to the laws of the Church already in force. One of
the decrees, however, contains the germ of a very important
development, which has exercised an influence extending far
beyond the confines of England. Pole ordered the establishment of seminaries for boys, principally with the object of
supplying a remedy for the scarcity of priests. This ordinance[2]
was the pattern and model used by the Council of Trent for its
celebrated decree concerning seminaries, which has been so
fruitful of results.[3] The word " seminary " and the idea were
taken by the Council from Pole's decree.[4]

Pole and Mary also combated the prevailing want of priests
by the restoration of the destroyed monasteries. The Fran-
ciscans and Dominicans, who had fled to Flanders from the
persecution, now partly returned, and were treated with
honour by the people.[5] Sixteen Benedictines had again resumed their habit and returned in March, 1555, although, like
abbot Feckenham, they had been treated as secular priests,
and had filled lucrative posts.[6] The Franciscan convent at
Greenwich again numbered twenty-five members in November,
1555, the Benedictines received back their monastery at West-

---

[1] *Reformatio Angliae ex decretis Reginaldi Poli*, Rome, 1562,
printed in LABBE, Concilia, XIV., 1733 *seqq.* ; LE PLAT, IV.,
570 *seqq.* ; ROCCABERTI, Bibliotheca maxima Pontificia, XVIII.,
350 *seqq.* Pole himself gives a sketch of the decrees in a letter
to Morone of February 19, 1556, in BROWN, VI., 1, n. 396. *Cf.*
ZIMMERMANN, Maria, 120 *seq.*

[2] Decr. 11, ROCCABERTI, 362.

[3] Sess. 23, de ref., c. 18. The agreement between the two is
partly a matter of words. Much closer is the connection with
Pole's decree in the first draft of the decree of Trent, printed in
MARTENE-DURAND, Amplissima Collectio, VIII., Paris, 1733,
1335, translated in M. SIEBENGARTNER, Schriften und Einricht-
ungen zur Bildung der Geistlichen, Freiburg, 1902, 361, where
the points of agreement are pointed out.

[4] So says SIEBENGARTNER, *loc. cit.*, 85.

[5] Michiel on March 19, 1555, in BROWN, VI., 1, n. 32.

[6] *Ibid.* ; cf. MARTIN, Pole, 113.

minster, and the Carthusians their celebrated monastery at
Sheen, while the nuns' convent was again restored at Syon.[1]
" From day to day," writes Michiel on July 1st, 1555, " through
Pole's exertions, hospitals, monasteries and churches rise
again from among the ruins."[2]

In all the departments of religious life, Pole displayed a far-
reaching activity. He appointed visitors[3] for the Universities
of Oxford and Cambridge ; new editions of the liturgical books,
which had, for the most part, been destroyed under Edward
VI., appeared, partly in Paris and Rouen ;[4] books for the
assistance of preachers, and publications for the instruction
of Catholics, among them the works of Thomas More, were
printed.[5] On March 20th, 1557, Pole was ordained priest,
and on the 22nd, consecrated Archbishop of Canterbury. In
this capacity, he succeeded, by his clemency, sagacity and
learning, in reforming this, the most corrupt diocese of the
whole kingdom, till it was, in the opinion of the Venetian
ambassador, an example, not only to England, but also to
France and many parts of Italy.[6] The Catholic religion also
flourished, in other ways, everywhere in England. The
Protestant, Jewell, complains in a letter to Vermigli on March
20th, 1559, that in Oxford, Protestantism has so far gone back,
principally owing to the zeal of the learned Dominican, Petrus
de Soto, that hardly two Protestants are to be met with in the
city.[7] According to the testimony of Jewell many of those
who belonged to the new religion returned to the old church
under Mary, and remained steadfastly true to her during the
first years of the reign of Elizabeth.[8] The priests showed an

[1] Michiel on November 4, 1555, September 28 and November 16,
1556, in BROWN, VI., 1, n. 269, 634, 704. List of the restored
houses ibid., VI., 2, p. 1074 n.

[2] BROWN, VI., 1, n. 150.

[3] GAIRDNER, 381 seq.

[4] F. G. LEE, Reginald Pole, London, 1888, 211.

[5] ZIMMERMANN, Maria, 117.

[6] Surian on April 21, 1557, in BROWN, VI., 2, n. 863.

[7] Zurich Letters, translated by Robinson, First series, London,
1848, 10. ZIMMERMAN, Maria, 121 seq.

[8] ZIMMERMAN, 122 seq.

heroic spirit of self-sacrifice during an epidemic, while clergy and laity rivalled each other in once more decorating the restored churches, and in providing them with everything necessary for the worthy celebration of the divine mysteries.[1]

However, in spite of this very promising progress, and " although by far the greater and most influential part of the people were honestly devoted to the faith and divine worship of their forefathers,"[2] Mary found it impossible, during her short reign, to exterminate Protestantism, especially among the nobility, in London, and in the industrial and seaport towns. Michiel says in 1557,[3] speaking only of those parts of the community which he knew well, that, outwardly and to all appearance, thanks to the esteem felt for the queen and the zeal of the legate, the Catholic religion increased from day to day, and struck deeper roots. This appearance, however, was not in keeping with the reality. The English were prepared to change their religion at the will of the sovereign, and they were also capable of becoming Mahommedans and Jews to please the king. They would also in time once more really adopt the Catholic religion, if they were not afraid that the church property would some day be demanded back.

Great danger threatened the continuation of the Catholic restoration when England, in Philip's war against France and the Pope, took the side of Spain.

England had reason enough to declare war against France. The French king, or his ambassador, Noailles, had had a hand in all the revolts against the English queen, and French policy had sought to place difficulties in her way everywhere. Nevertheless it was not easy for Philip, who had once more been living in England from March 17th to July 6th, to succeed in getting war declared. The Council put forward the plea of the poverty of the crown, which did not allow of a war, and pointed to Mary's marriage contract, which expressly excluded England from participation in the wars of Spain. Then Stafford's

[1] *Ibid.*, 114, 118.
[2] Opinion of J. STEVENSON in The Month, LXXIX. (1893), 24.
[3] BROWN, VI., 1, n. 884, p. 1074 *seq.*

attempt at rebellion, supported by France, took place in April, and the ill-feeling aroused by this new and unwarrantable act of hostility, accomplished what Philip had not been able to bring about. War was declared against France, and Pole in consequence found himself in the difficult position of having the consort of his sovereign an enemy of the Pope, and his sovereign herself at war with the Pope's ally.[1]

Pole had advised against the war with France.[2] While Philip had been in England he had avoided meeting the Pope's opponent in public, and had only visited him secretly, at night and unattended.[3] But in spite of this careful attitude he found himself involved as well in the conflict which had arisen between Paul IV. and the Spaniards.

Philip had ordered all Spanish subjects to leave Rome. The Pope replied by recalling all nuncios and ambassadors from Philip's dominions, in a consistory on April 9th, 1557, so that the king might not be able to hold them as hostages. Pole was not recalled from England, but lost, as the Pope expressly stated, his position as legate. This, however, was very difficult to reconcile with his office of President of the Council of State. None of the Cardinals in the consistory was asked for an opinion as to this step, and no one dared to offer any opposition.[4]

The news of these proceedings, which soon reached England, caused a general sensation, and the greatest dismay among the friends of Pole. The queen and the bishops at once addressed

---

[1] LINGARD, 228 seq.

[2] Soranzo on February 7, 1557, in BROWN, VI., 2, n. 810.

[3] Soranzo on April 13, 1557, ibid. n. 858, p. 1015. Navagero on May 8, 1557, ibid. n. 880, p. 1039.

[4] Navagero on April 10, 1557, ibid., n. 855 ; cf. n. 856 ; see also TURNBULL, n. 586, 589 seq. Already, at the end of 1556, Paul IV. had been of opinion that Pole must leave England ; he had adhered to this opinion in spite of the counter-representations of Morone ; see the *letter of Morone to Pole, dated Rome, November 28, 1556 (Arm. 64, t. 32, p. 215 seq. Secret Archives of the Vatican).

letters to the Pope, begging him to leave Pole in his legation,[1] and the English ambassador in Rome, Edward Carne, employed all the means in his power for the same object. On May 15th he obtained an audience with Paul IV., in which he pointed out the confusion which would occur in England, should Pole no longer be legate. The Pope saw that he had been too hasty, but did not like at once to revoke what had been done publicly. When, however, Cardinal Medici asked him how the deposition of Pole was to be entered in the consistorial records, he declared that Pole retained the dignity of " legatus natus," which was always connected with the archiepiscopal see of Canterbury, and that he might enter that in the records.

So far Pole had only heard a rumour of his deposition, for the queen had caused the Papal brief concerning it to be intercepted and kept back until she had made remonstrances in Rome.[2] On May 25th, the Cardinal explained the position of affairs in England in a letter to the Pope.[3] He understood the deposition in the sense that he would lose both legations, and the dignity of " legatus a latere " as well as that of " legatus natus."[4] If, however, there were to be no legate at all in the country, this would be most disadvantageous for the progress of religion and for the reputation of the Holy See. If the Pope was not satisfied with the legate who had held that office hitherto, he should appoint another in his place ; so much depended on the presence of a legate. If the Pope agreed to this, he was ready to support and assist the new legate in every way. In a letter to Stefano Sauli of the same date, he once more gave the assurance that he would willingly obey the Pope, but that as his messenger had brought no further orders from Rome, he would wait for them.[5]

[1] Pole on May 25, 1557, in BROWN, VI., 2, n. 899.   Pole's letter of defence in ZIMMERMANN, Pole, 340.

[2] Pole's letter of defence, loc. cit.

[3] In BROWN, VI., 2, n. 899, p. 1114 ; cf. n. 900.

[4] He appears to have changed his opinion on this point later on, for he signed himself as legatus natus until his death.   LINGARD, 234 n.

[5] BROWN, VI., 2, n. 900.

The way out of the difficulty which Pole had suggested found favour with the Pope. On June 14th, in a consistory, he appointed the Franciscan, William Peto (Petow),[1] as Cardinal and legate for England. Peto, by his ecclesiastical attitude under Henry VIII., had brought upon himself the anger of that monarch, and had been living for a considerable time as an exile in Rome, but had now returned again to his convent at Greenwich. At the same time as he appointed Peto, Paul IV. sent a brief to Pole recalling him to Rome.[2] Peto's appointment was an unfortunate one in every respect, and Carne, when Cardinal Carafa informed him of it, answered with considerable indignation,[3] that Peto was a worn-out old man, incapable of any further work, and of no use for the post of legate. Peto himself refused the Cardinal's hat, as well as the dignity of legate, as being too great a burden for him.[4] Mary caused the messenger with the briefs for Pole and Peto to be detained at Calais. In common with Philip, she had again renewed her request at the end of May that the Pope would leave Pole in his office,[5] and now she wrote again. If, she said, the Pope had not listened to her before, she hoped that he would do so now, and that they would forgive her in Rome if she thought that she knew best who was qualified for the government of the kingdom.[6]

Paul IV., however, would not give way, although Peto wrote himself to the Pope, saying that he could not show himself in the streets of London without being mocked at.[7]   Paul

---

[1] Acta Consistoria in RAYNALDUS, 1557, n. 43.   Letter to the English bishops of June 20, 1557, in which Peto's appointment is communicated to them, ibid. n. 44.   The brief to Philip and Mary of the same date in TURNBULL, n. 637 ; see also MASSARELLI, 311 and CARDELLA, IV., 369 seq.

[2] Navagero on June 18, 1557, in BROWN, VI., 2, n. 937.

[3] They have made " un legno " a Cardinal.   To the Pope Carne said, Peto is " un vecchio rebambito." ibid.

[4] Navagero in August, 1557, ibid n. 981.

[5] Navagero on June 18, 1557, ibid. n. 938.

[6] Navagero on August 5, 1557, in BROWN, VI., 2, n. 981.

[7] Instructions for Stella of January 10, 1558, ibid. VI., 3, n. 1135.

IV. further insisted that Pole should come to Rome, for the affair had, in the meantime, taken quite another turn. The old accusation of heresy was again being renewed against Pole, and there could be no further question of his being legate.[1] Besides this, Pole had himself applied to the queen that the messenger with Peto's appointment should be allowed to cross the Channel, and he no longer exercised his functions as legate, although he was urged to do so.[2]

The war with France was in the meantime drawing to an end. The great victory of St. Quentin (August 10, 1557) was followed, on January 8th, 1558, by the severe blow of the loss of Calais. The place was important as a market for English commerce, and it had a still greater importance in the eyes of the English people, as it was the last trophy from the glorious Anglo-French wars of the fast disappearing middle ages.   Very great therefore was the dismay of the people and the sorrow of the queen at the news of the loss of the fortress ; it not only damaged the esteem in which Mary was held, but it also told upon the religion which she protected.   " Since the loss of Calais," wrote Count Feria to Philip,[3] " there are not more than a third of the people at church that one formerly saw there."

Calais was the last grief in Mary's life. She had been ill for a long time, and at the beginning of November, her condition became hopeless. On the 6th she sent her jewels to Elizabeth with the request that she would keep up the old religion, and take over the debts of the queen.[4]   On the morning of the 17th, while a priest was saying Mass before her, she ended her sorrowful life. Cardinal Pole only survived her a few hours ; in March he was completely broken down, so that

[1] See *supra* p. 292.

[2] Navagero on September 7, 1557, in BROWN, VI., 2, n. 1024.

[3] London, February 2, 1558, in KERVYN DE LETTENHOVE, Relations politiques des Pays-Bas et de l'Angleterre, I., 130.

[4] Christophe d'Assonville to Philip, Westminster, November 7, 1558, *ibid.* 277.

Feria wrote to King Philip that he was practically a dead man.[1]

Mary was perhaps the best of the English queens ; she was not only one of the most highly educated women of her time—she understood five languages and had an excellent knowledge of Latin literature—but she displayed, in addition to a spotless purity of life, a remarkable kindness of heart. She loved to go incognita with the ladies of her court to visit the hovels of the poor, and make inquiries about their wants and help them whenever it was in her power.[2]

As she was the best, she was also one of the most unfortunate princesses who occupied the throne of England. Apart from the early years of her childhood, her life was nothing but a chain of sorrow and anguish, which prematurely undermined her bodily strength. As a young growing girl she was obliged to witness the repudiation of a loved mother and the criminal passion of a father. In the reign of Edward she suffered persecution at the hands of her brother, and after she had ascended the throne, contrary to all expectation, she saw herself abandoned by a husband whom she adored, and entangled in a web of plots by her half-sister, and her life threatened by the very conspirators whose lives she had spared. Her popularity disappeared more and more, her ardent hopes of an heir to the throne were not realized, and even in that field to which all her thoughts and actions were directed, she was involved in disputes with the Pope, whose honour she had defended at the cost of great sacrifices, and died filled with the fear that in a few years the whole of her life's work would once again be broken in pieces. She has been condemned, even

---

[1] " Es un hombre muerto " (*ibid.* 153). Pole was buried in Canterbury Cathedral (see BONELLI, Il sepolcro del card. Polo : Rassegna d'Arte, 1907). The pontifical ring which Pole received at the reconciliation of England with Rome was to be seen in 1910 at the exhibition in connection with the Congress of English Catholics at Leeds. The news of the deaths of Mary and Pole reached Rome on December 10, 1558 ; see MASSARELLI, 328.

[2] * H. CLINTON, Life of Jane Dormer, Duchess of Feria, ed. by Estcourt and Stevenson, London, 1887, 64 *seq.*

after her death, in the accounts of biassed historians, to come down to posterity as a " bloody " memory. In spite of all this, however, Mary's life was not lived in vain. She has exercised a far-reaching influence on the religious life of England. Before her day, the position of Catholics was neither definite nor clear ; they let themselves be driven further and further, and had come at last into a state of schism and heresy, almost without having discovered it. The events of Mary's reign brought about a complete change in this respect. After her reign the Catholic Church in England can point to martyrs and confessors in great numbers. Mary also exercised an influence outside the Catholic Church ; if Elizabeth simply did not dare to establish Calvinism in England, and if the Protestantism of the present day still bears a character which in many respects accords with Catholic ideas, Mary is the person to whom this is to a great extent to be attributed, for it was she who put a stop to the gradual disappearance of Catholic thought and Catholic feeling in England.

CHAPTER XV.

IMMEDIATELY after the death of Mary, Archbishop Heath of York, as chancellor of England, announced the news to the Upper House, and, in accordance with the statute of the thirtieth year of Henry VIII., spoke of his daughter Elizabeth as the rightful heir to the throne. She was acknowledged as such without opposition. The joy with which the English people greeted the new sovereign was all the greater, as none of them would hear of the accession of Mary Stuart, the wife of the French Dauphin, and the grand-daughter of the eldest sister of Henry VIII. In view of the danger lest England should come under Franco-Scottish influence, even Catholics overlooked the fact that Elizabeth was the daughter of Anne Boleyn, and held a very doubtful position as far as her religion was concerned.

Her education had been entirely conducted on those lines, yet her Protestantism did not stand the test under Mary. The princess had, as Knox reproached her later on, denied her religion, and had bowed down before that which she had been taught to regard as the worship of idols.[1] Although Elizabeth had, after some slight opposition, professed to be a zealous Catholic,[2] during the whole of Mary's reign, hardly anyone believed in the sincerity of her conversion. The Venetian ambassador, Michiel, bears witness in his account of the year 1557, that people considered Elizabeth to be a hypocrite, who

[1] *Cf.* STRYPE, Annals, I., 2.

[2] She even went so far as to gain an indulgence published by the Pope in September, 1555 ; see MACHYN, Diary (Camden Society, London, 1848), 94.

401

secretly cherished anti-Catholic opinions more strongly than
ever. The deep aversion which Mary felt for her illegitimate
sister was still more increased by this. She would willingly
have excluded her from the succession, but was dissuaded from
this step by Philip, into whose favour Elizabeth had insinuated
herself.[1] In the spring of 1554 Elizabeth had been imprisoned
in the Tower, on a suspicion of having participated in Wyatt's
plot. She was set at liberty after two months, but was carefully watched, though in a very considerate manner, for no one
knew better than Mary the masterly way in which Elizabeth
could delude and deceive. This extraordinary gift of deception
and unfathomable subtlety,[2] as well as her boundless love of
power, and her statesmanlike and penetrating insight, the
daughter of Anne Boleyn had inherited from her father. In
every respect a genuine Tudor, she united to a passionate and
ardent temperament, the power of cool and systematic cal-
culation. Her behaviour, therefore, especially during the first
months of her reign, was exceedingly guarded and careful with
regard to the religious question.

The proclamation in which Elizabeth announced her
accession to the throne did not refer to religious matters ;
a passage at the end, however, which forbade under any
pretext the breaking or alteration of the arrangements and
customs prevailing in the country, might have been considered
as a challenge to the religious innovators. The fact that the
queen, as she had done in Mary's reign, continued to attend
Mass and Vespers, and that the Catholic worship remained
unchanged, was far more likely to set the minds of zealous
Catholics at rest. In the same way, the obsequies for Mary
were conducted according to the Catholic rites.[3]

In spite of all this, however, the Spanish Ambassador,
Feria, was not at all easy in his mind about the further course
of events, for it had not escaped him that all the new members

[1] Michiel in BROWN, VI., 2, p. 1058 seq.
[2] See MEYER, I., 11.
[3] See the reports in KERVYN DE LETTENHOVE, I., 310, 313 and
BROWN, VI., 3, n. 1287, as well as Hayward's Annals (Camden
Soc. 1840), 12.

of the Privy Council, and those newly summoned to the court, were of the Protestant persuasion. All these avoided the representative of Philip II. like " the devil." An attempt on the part of Feria to fathom the queen's real views on religion failed completely,[1] and a courtier with Protestant leanings had a similar experience when, in speaking of the amnesty given to the prisoners, he permitted himself an ambiguous reference to the furtherance of Protestant interests.[2]

Nothing however, could be further from the truth than to suppose that Elizabeth had not yet decided upon the course which she intended to adopt with regard to religion. On the contrary, she had long since determined, in order to secure the legitimacy of her succession, and to satisfy her love of power, to carry out a revolution in the religious conditions in England in an anti-Papal sense, and a well-considered plan for the overthrow of the Catholic religion was prepared.[3] The queen was much too clever to undertake this work alone ; she wished first of all to feel the ground firmly under her feet, to win popularity with the people, and to fill the court and offices of state with Protestant elements, before she let her Catholic subjects understand what they had to expect with regard to that which they prized above all else. Yet the Catholics had acclaimed her with as much loyalty as those professing the new religion.

When Christmas arrived, the queen considered that the time had come to throw aside her previous reserve, with regard to certain points. She gave orders to Bishop Oglethorpe of Carlisle, that he was to omit the elevation of the sacred host at Mass. The bishop refused ; the queen, he said, might have power over his life, but not over his conscience. In order that she might not have to venerate the sacred host, Elizabeth left the chapel before the offertory.[4] Two days

---

[1] See Feria's letter in KERVYN DE LETTENHOVE, I., 338 seq.

[2] Cf. MEYER, I., 13 seq.

[3] See BURNET, Hist. of the Reformation, ed. Pocock, V., 497 seq. ; cf. STEVENSON in The Month, LXXIX., (1893) 26 seq.

[4] Cf. the report of Feria in KERVYN DE LETTENHOVE, I., 365, and that of the ambassador of Mantua in BROWN, VII., n. 2.

later a proclamation was issued which forbade preaching for
the time being, and introduced the English language for the
Epistle and Gospel at Mass.   This innovation was immediately
carried into effect in the royal chapel.   Elizabeth appointed
married priests to serve there, who, in the prayers, omitted
the names of the Mother of God, the Saints, and the
Pope.[1]

It is not surprising that, after these occurrences, the bishops
had scruples about exercising their office at the coronation
of a princess, who by her encroachments on the rights of the
Church, proclaimed quite clearly that she was determined
to break the traditional oath which pledged her to support it.
The refusal of the bishops caused considerable perplexity
to Elizabeth, for she, as well as her chief adviser, William
Cecil, attached great importance, on account of the people,
to the coronation taking place before the new Parliament
assembled.   After long negotiations, the Bishop of Carlisle
was induced to perform the ceremony, a weakness which he
afterwards bitterly regretted.[2]

The coronation took place on January 15th, 1559, in
Westminster Abbey, amid a display of great splendour.
It is certain that many changes were introduced at the celebration of the Catholic coronation mass, the elevation, in
particular, being omitted.[3]   When insisting on this, Elizabeth
left no room for doubt that she intended immediately to
break the solemn coronation oath she had just taken, to
protect the rights of the Church.   If anyone still had any
illusions as to this, his eyes were soon to be opened by the
events that followed.   At the opening of Parliament on
January 25th, the new chancellor, Bacon, informed the
members that they would be called upon—although the
queen could do it by her own power—to decide upon a com-

---

[1] See BROWN, VII., n. 28 : KERVYN DE LETTENHOVE, I., 366.

[2] See STRYPE, Annals, I., n. 50.

[3] Cf. the essays of Bayne, Wilson and Lockhart-Ross in the
Engl. Hist. Review, XXII., 650 seqq. ; XXIII., 87 seq., 533 seqq. ;
XXIV., 322 seq.

prehensive confession of faith, and a common form of divine service, for the whole kingdom.[1]

At the beginning of February, Edward Carne, the English ambassador in Rome, received orders to break off diplomatic relations with the Pope.[2]

For hundreds of years, owing to a calumny circulated by Sarpi, it was believed that Paul IV. had hastened this turn of affairs by " his abrupt and discouraging answer " : The queen must, before everything else, submit her claims to the throne to the decision of the Holy See.[3] There can be no question of the Pope having, in this manner, himself put an end to the last possibility of an agreement.[4] After the declaration which Carne had made in the name of his government, Paul IV. could not but believe that the arrival of a large embassy for the " obedientia " was to be expected in Rome.[5] Therefore the attitude of Paul IV. towards Elizabeth was by no means unfriendly. It is evident from a report of the Bishop of Angoulême to the King of France on December 25th, 1558, that the Pope, at that time, had no idea that the defection of Elizabeth from the Church was imminent. The French endeavoured in that audience with Paul IV. to induce him to make objections to a marriage between Elizabeth and Philip II. but without success. The Pope, who spoke in a perfectly friendly manner of the queen, answered that

[1] See d'EWES, Journal of both houses, 11 seq. ; LINGARD, VII., 257 ; MEYER, I., 15 seq.

[2] See Acts of the Privy Council, VII., 50 ; State Papers. Foreign, 1558-1559, n. 299, 474 ; cf. STRYPE, Annals, I., 1, 51.

[3] So RANKE describes it, Päpste, I[6]., 203 ; cf. also RANKE, Englische Gesch., I., 301.

[4] See the thorough investigation by MAITLAND in the Engl. Hist. Review, XV., 324 seqq., by which Sarpi's account is conclusively shown to be a spiteful fabrication. With the destruction of this legend, one of the foundations of Ranke's view (Päpste, I.,[6] 202) disappears, namely that Paul IV. has " more perhaps than any of his predecessors, furthered the dissemination of Protestantism, which he hated, detested and persecuted."

[5] See MAITLAND, loc. cit., 326 seq.

he could not believe in a marriage of Elizabeth with the Spaniard ; should it, however, come to that, he could by no means agree to the proposal of the French that he should refuse the necessary dispensation for the marriage.[1] The French ambassador, as Carne reported, was also attempting to get the Pope to declare Elizabeth illegitimate.[2] When Carne presented his letters of recall on March 10th, he begged the Pope to permit him to leave Rome on the pretext that he wished to see his family again. Paul IV. refused, as he had no certain information as to the defection of the queen.[3] He openly hoped that the opposition of the Catholics in Parliament would prevent a break with Rome.

The prospects of such a break being avoided did not appear quite hopeless. By means of extensive pressure on the members, the queen had succeeded in securing a safe majority for her plans in the House of Commons, but things seemed less favourable to her in the Upper House. Convocation expressly declared its firm adherence to the Catholic doctrines of transubstantiation, the sacrifice of the mass, and the Papal supremacy, and declared that the decision concerning matters of faith, the sacraments and religious discipline did not pertain to any assembly of the laity, but only to the lawful pastors of the Church.[4]

The cession of tithes and first fruits to the crown was accomplished without any difficulty, but violent opposition was aroused by the draft of a bill regarding the royal supremacy over the Church. The bishops did not fail to make strong remonstrances against it. The venerable Archbishop Heath of York in particular, explained with calmness, lucidity, and much pertinency, the reasons which made it impossible for Catholics to acknowledge the royal supremacy. Two matters, he declared, were included in the bill : the separation

[1] RIBIER, II., 776. MAITLAND, 327.

[2] State Papers, Foreign, 1558, n. 160, 161 ; cf. KERVYN DE LETTENHOVE, I., 333, 455.

[3] Cf. MAITLAND, 328.

[4] Cf. BIRT, The Elizabethan religious settlement, London, 1907, 44 seq. ; SPILLMANN, II., 18 ; MEYER, I., 16.

from the Holy See, and the transference of the power of ecclesiastical government to the queen. As far as the rupture with the Pope was concerned, they must carefully weigh the fact that by such a step they would exclude themselves from the General Councils, from ecclesiastical privileges and, finally, from the unity of the Church of Christ. The archbishop then proceeded to prove, in an impressive manner, that according to the clearly expressed text of the Holy Scriptures, a woman could not teach in the Church, nor fulfil the duties of the supreme ecclesiastical office, and that therefore she could not be head of the Church.[1]

The force of such reasoning did not escape Elizabeth herself: She therefore had the title of " chief governor of all spiritual and ecclesiastical affairs " introduced into the bill instead of " Head of the Church."[2] In this form the bill was passed

[1] STRYPE, I., App. 6. Concerning the speech see the opinion of MEYER, I., 21.

[2] MEYER (I., 19 *seq.*) is the first to have drawn attention to the fact that the Elizabethan primacy was limited, in the XXXIX Articles, by the following supplement : " We give not to our princes the ministering either of God's Word or of the Sacraments, the which thing the injunctions also lately set forth by Elizabeth our Queen do most plainly testifie, but that only prerogative which we see to have been given always to all godly princes in holy Scriptures by God Himself, that is that they should rule all estates and degrees committed to their charge by God, whether they be ecclesiastical or temporal, and restrain with the civil sword the stubborn and evil doers." This weakening limitation, however, changed nothing in the fact that the law granted the Queen, in spiritual as well as ecclesiastical matters, the supreme power, abolished the jurisdiction and authority of the Pope, and transferred them to the crown. The enemies of Rome understood this quite well. Parkhurst wrote on May 21, 1559, to Bullinger : " The Queen will not, it is true, be named the Head of the Church, although this title was offered to her ; she, however, willingly accepts the title of a Ruler of the Church, which comes to the same thing. The Pope is once more driven out of England, to the great sorrow of the bishops, and the whole gang of shaven priests." Zurich Letters, I., n. 12. SPILLMANN, II., 28 ; *cf.* also LILLY in the Dublin Review, CIX., 14 *seq.*

on March 22nd. Parliament was then prorogued until after Easter. Except the bishops and the abbot of Westminster, only Lord Montague and the Earl of Shrewsbury remained firm in their opposition to this violent separation of the English Church from Rome. The Spanish ambassador, Feria, made an attempt, at the last moment, to restrain Elizabeth from confirming the fateful Act of Supremacy.

To his representations, the cunning queen made answer that she did not assume the title of Head of the Church, and that she would dispense no sacraments. She haughtily asked the ambassador if Philip would be angry if she had mass said in English. She left no room for doubt as to her determination to proceed in a thoroughly autocratic manner with regard to religious questions. Feria was of opinion that the Pope should now be informed of the state of affairs ; the ambassador, who may have over estimated the zeal of the English Catholics, appears to have entertained the erroneous opinion that Elizabeth would not be able to hold out, if Paul IV. should now pronounce the sentence of excommunication against her.[1]

However great the dismay at the Curia may have been at the adverse development of conditions in England,[2] they did not at once proceed to the infliction of this extreme penalty. In such circumstances the Holy See is always accustomed, with long forbearance, to exhaust all milder measures. Men of strict ecclesiastical views, such as the Jesuit, Ribadeneira, who was at the time in London, advised the Curia to show

[1] Feria's report in KERVYN DE LETTENHOVE I., 475 seqq. and 481 seq. The statement of the ambassador, that two-thirds of the English had been Catholics, is questioned by MEYER (I., 7) ; Ribadeneira also says in his report of January 20, 1559 (Précis hist., 1890, 348), that the Catholics are " Muchos mas sin comparación que los herejes." However, it may be reconciled with this estimate, the number of zealous Catholics was small ; cf. the statement of Michiels in BROSCH, VI., 453, n. 1.

[2] Cf. the information from the Diario of the Corsini Library (38—F. 6), which Maitland gives in the Engl. Hist. Review, XV., 330, but is not able to describe more closely. It is the Diario of Cola Coleine.

great caution in dealing with the new queen.[1] Philip II. also advised the Pope to wait.[2] The Spanish king, in whom the English Catholics placed great hopes, preferred to have Elizabeth on the throne, rather than Mary Stuart, who was devoted to the interests of France. Philip II. also still cherished the illusion of obtaining the hand of Elizabeth, either for himself, or for a scion of the House of Hapsburg. Paul IV. too, at the beginning of May, 1559, still hoped that the Spanish king would succeed in preserving England for the Church.[3]

Elizabeth made use of the favourable opportunity by quickly taking the second step for the establishment of the English state church. After the severance from Rome had taken place, the Catholic form of worship must also be abolished. As an introduction to this, the queen caused a religious conference to be held in Westminster Abbey during Easter week. As it was soon shown that everything had

---

[1] *Cf.* the interesting letter of Ribadeneira to Lainez, dated London, January 20, 1559, published by DELPLACE in the Précis dist., 1900, 348. In view of the close relations between Paul IV. and Lainez, it is very probable that the advice was decisive of the Pope's attitude.

[2] See KERVYN DE LETTENHOVE, I., 508 ; *cf.* SPILLMANN, II., 25 ; BROSCH, VI., 459.

[3] See the brief to Philip II. of May 4, 1559, in RAYNALDUS, 1559, n. 1. According to an *Avviso di Roma of May 13, 1559, a letter of Philip II. with reference to the conditions in England, was read at a sitting of the Inquisition of May 11 (Cod. Urb. 1039, p. 35. Vatican Library). In June, the Venetian ambassador at Brussels believed that Paul IV. would take steps against Elizabeth on account of her defection from the Church ; we know nothing for certain, however, about the intentions of the Pope at that time (see MARTIN, L'église cath. et la conversion d'Angleterre, VI., 58 *seq.*) If Paul IV. did, after further details concerning Elizabeth's defection had reached him, express his dislike for the queen, he nevertheless took no decisive steps. The story that he tried to get the English crown for Mary Stuart has been proved to be completely false, by means of a thorough investigation by POLLEN in The Month, XCVI., 392-402.

been arranged to the disadvantage of the Catholics, these refused to continue to attend. Elizabeth's answer to this was to throw the Bishops of Winchester and Lincoln into the Tower.[1] In spite of this attempt to intimidate the opposition in Parliament, the bill relating to the abolition of the mass and the introduction of the new Anglican liturgy aroused strong opposition ; in the Upper House it only passed by a majority of three.[2] Besides the clerical members, who voted with great determination against the bill, Lord Montague, the aged Marquis of Winchester, the Earl of Shrewsbury, Lords Morley, Stafford, Wharton, Rich, North and Ambrose Dudley defended the Catholic liturgy, which for almost a thousand years had been associated with the national and spiritual life of the English people. On June 24th, the Feast of St. John the Baptist, the new order of things was to come into force, and the sacrifice of the mass to cease throughout the kingdom.

The new liturgy, with several alterations, closely followed the second Book of Common Prayer of Edward VI., of the year 1553. The clergy who opposed it were at first to lose their income for one year, and be imprisoned for six months ; for a repetition of their offence they were to be deposed and imprisoned for a year, and for the third offence they were threatened with imprisonment for life. In the case of the laity, fines were to enforce attendance at the new services. Whoever should attack these services, or induce a priest to adopt another form of worship, was to be fined 100 marks on the first occasion, 400 on the second (at the present value— £2,500) and to suffer imprisonment for one year, and on the third offence to forfeit all his property and to be imprisoned for life.[3] Similar drastic punishments threatened those who refused to take the oath of supremacy, and remained faithful to the spiritual jurisdiction of the Pope. With regard to

[1] See KERVYN DE LETTENHOVE, I., 487 seq., 489 ; BROWN, VII., n. 58 ; LINGARD, VII., 261.
[2] See KERVYN DE LETTENHOVE, I., 519.
[3] Cf. SPILLMANN, II., 32.

this offence the third act of resistance was to be punished by death.

Armed with these weapons, Elizabeth now proceeded to destroy the Catholic hierarchy in England, and to force the new state church upon her subjects. She was, however, shrewd enough to avoid, at first, applying the full severity of the law. She well realized the power which lies in the " blood of the martyrs." Gradually and with great caution, the English were to be made into Anglicans, and the first thing to be done was to rob them of their bishops. In July, 1559, an official summons was issued, ordering them to observe the new laws, but only one, Antony Kitchin, Bishop of Llandaff, who had already been a schismatic under Henry VIII., a Calvinist under Edward VI., and a Catholic under Mary, gave way, and now became an Anglican. All the other bishops were true to their oath. Elizabeth took care, at the beginning, not to give the Catholics a martyr ; deposition, forfeiture of property, and imprisonment sufficed her, in order to make the bishops harmless.[1] She hoped that once the shepherds had been removed the sheep would stray.

Paul IV. had already been touched by the hand of death when these blows were dealt at the Catholic religion in England. He did not live to see the later developments in the situation. His iron constitution succumbed at last to dropsy ; although the doctors had declared this disease to be present, for a long time the Pope hoped that he would be cured.[2] His Holiness, says a correspondent on June 3rd, endeavours to appear well, and his doctor, to whom he has promised a considerable

---

[1] *Cf.* BRIDGETT-KNOX, The true history of the Cath. Hierarchy deposed by Elizabeth, London, 1889 ; GEE, The Elizabethan clergy and the settlement of religion, 1558-1564, Oxford, 1898, and especially G. E. PHILLIPS, The extinction of the ancient Hierarchy, London, 1905 ; *cf.* BELLESHEIM in Histor.-polit. Bl., CXXXVI. (1905), 891 *seqq.* The further measures of Elizabeth against English Catholics are to be dealt with in a connected manner in Vol. XV. of this work.

[2] *Cf.* the *Avvisi of May, 1559, cited *supra* p. 409, n. 3.

increase in his emoluments, does everything in his power ; his condition, however, only grows worse.[1] Although the summer heat was now very noticeable, the Pope suffered much from cold, so that his room had to be heated. The temperature was so high that Cardinal Alfonso Carafa had to be released from his duty of reciting the breviary with the Pope, and the Theatine, Father Geremia, did so in his stead. Ill as the Pope was, he appeared, nevertheless, on June 14th, at the sitting of the Inquisition, but he was so weak that he had to be carried out at the end of the deliberations. The most disquieting rumours were current ; on June 17th it was reported that the Pope was dead, a statement which was all the more readily believed as a comet was said to have appeared during the night over the Vatican. The dropsy was increasing, and two new doctors were called in. The invalid disputed with them concerning his condition, and quoted passages from Avicenna and Galen.[2] On June 22nd, the Pope had the meeting of the Inquisition held in his room, and indulged, during the sitting, in a long panegyric of Philip II., on account of his proceedings against the Lutherans in Spain. He again asserted on this occasion how much he had the extirpation of heresy at heart. He wished the regulations with regard to this, as well as those concerning the vagrant monks, to be carried out most strictly. The Pope could no longer keep on his feet, and his weakness was so great that he was only given fourteen more days to live, and the conclave was openly spoken of.[3]

There was only one person who would not believe that the end had come, and that was Paul IV. himself. " It is astonishing, and almost miraclous " says a contemporary on July 8th, " that His Holiness, in spite of all his bodily sufferings, retains his mental powers, as if he would attain to the years of Peter. He himself still has hope, and says that he will

[1]*Avviso di Roma of June 3, *loc. cit.* 47 *seq.*   (Vatican Library).

[2] *Avvisi di Roma of June 10, 17, and 24, *loc. cit.* 49 *seq. ; cf.* SANTAREM, XIII., 46, 49. Concerning the physicians of Paul IV. see MARINI, I., 420 *seq.*

[3] See the *Avvisi di Roma of June 24, and July 8, 1559.

reach the age of his father, who lived for twelve years in a similar condition, and died a centenarian." And, indeed, Paul IV. still granted audiences, signed petitions, held meetings of the Inquisition, and spoke of making a pilgrimage to Loreto in August. He gave orders to prepare for this journey, and for the prevention of revolts, and issued a strict edict against the bearing of weapons in Rome. On July 15th it was announced that the Pope was better, and had had himself carried to the Belvedere ; on Thursday the 13th he had been for two hours at a sitting of the Inquisition.[1]

Although they tried to keep the Pope's actual condition secret, it nevertheless got abroad that the dropsy was continually increasing.[2] At the end of July His Holiness again took part in a sitting of the Inquisition, which was held in his room, and consistories were also held there on the 31st of the month and on August 2nd.[3] On the latter occasion the Pope earnestly impressed upon the Cardinals the duty of impartiality in affairs of state,[4] and optimists believed

[1] *Avvisi di Roma of July 8, and 15, *loc. cit.* 58[b] . In that of July 8 it states : " Cosa veramente maravigliosa et quasi sopernaturale è quest' infirmità del Papa, che così mantiene con tanti mali che questo corpo patisse et ch'il sta tanto gagliardo d'animo che pare vi sia vita alli giorni di Pietro, ancora ch'il sia hidropico con i testicoli gonfiati, patiss' di renella et h'una gamba grossa et immobile che si cerca di purgare quanto più si può, ha poi il catarro ch'alle volte lo molesta, nondimeno con tutto questo ha speranza et dice che viverà sin'al età di suo padre, che con tal infirmità visse anni 12 et era di cent'anni quando mori." *Cf.* for this the letter of A. Verancsic in the Mon. Hung. hist. Script., XXXII., 333, and the *reports of Gianfigliazzi of July 8 and 14, 1559 (State Archives, Florence).

[2] See Selvago's report of July 10 in the Atti Lig., XIII., 757. Cardinal Medici was already thinking of travelling to Rome, says *Clara de Ems to Annibale de Ems from Milan on July 16, 1559 (Archives at Hohenems).

[3] See the *Avvisi di Roma of July 22 and 29, and August 5, *loc. cit.*, 62 *seq.* ; *cf.* the report of B. Pia, dated Rome, July 19, 1559 (Gonzaga Arch. Mantua).

[4] See Acta consist. in GULIK-EUBEL, III., 38 n.

that he would recover.[1] The end was finally hastened by a circumstance very characteristic of Paul IV. He had always kept the laws of fasting in the strictest manner, although he was dispensed from them by reason of his great age, and had repeatedly been in danger of death through abstaining from meat. But in spite of all that Cardinal Alfonso Carafa and the doctors could do, and in spite of the great heat, the Pope remained for three days without meat or any sustaining food.[2] A severe fainting fit was the forerunner of death, which took place on August 18th. Before he died the Pope recommended the affairs of the Church to the Cardinals, particularly the Inquisition and the rebuilding of St. Peter's.[3]

Paul IV. was not yet dead, although he was considered to be so, when the Roman populace, not content with the usual opening of the general prisons when a vacancy occurred in the Holy See, rushed to the buildings of the Inquisition on the Ripetta, ill-treated the officials there, destroyed many documents relating to trials, as well as confiscated books, and finally set the buildings on fire. They had set the pris-

---

[1] See the reports of G. Aldrovandi, dated Rome, August 2, 5, and 16, 1559 (State Archives, Bologna).

[2] See the *testimony of the physician A. Ricchi (Vatican Library) in Appendix No. 60.

[3] See MASSARELLI, 332 ; FIRMANUS, 516 ; *Diaro* in the appendix to NORES, 451 ; SANTAREM, XIII., 64 ; Corpo dipl. Port., VIII., 202 *seq.* ; joint *report of Gianfigliazzi and the Bishop of Cortona of August 18, 1559, in the State Archives, Florence. G. Aldrovandi *reported on August 18 ; " Questa notte passata alle 7 hore venne un accidente a N.S. chel tenne fuori di se un hora ; circa le 8 ritornò alquanto in se et è andato cosi temporeggiando fin'a quest'hora che sono le 12 nella quale ha fatto chiamare tutti li car[ll] a quali ha raccomandato questa s. sede, la inquisitione, fabrica di S. Piero el altro." A second letter of August 18 (2 h. di notte) announces the death " fra le 21 et 22 hore " (State Archives, Bologna). An *Avviso di Roma of August 19 emphasizes that the condition of the Pope had been aggravated by the death of Lippomano and the act of the Duke of Paliano (the murder of the supposed paramour of his wife). (Cod. Urb. 1039 p. 71. Vatican Library).

oners at liberty, after having made them promise to live as Catholics in future. Public opinion looked upon the personal enemies of the Pope as having been the instigators of the disturbances.[1] It was not difficult to stir up the people ; the sufferings of the war against Spain, as well as the maladministration of the hated nephews, were still only too deeply rooted in the minds of the Romans. The benefits which they owed to Paul IV. were completely forgotten.[2] On August 18th a mob of people stormed the Capitol and mutilated the statue of Paul IV. which had been erected there ; the head of the statue was left on the following day exposed to the mockery of the boys in the street. A Jew even ventured to set his yellow cap on it. At last they dragged it through the city, and finally sank it in the Tiber.[3] A decree of the Roman people on August 20th ordered the removal of all

[1] MOCENIGO, 37. *Cf.* concerning the troubles of the time, besides the authorities named in the previous note, the reports in RIBIER, II., 827 *seq.*; PARIS, Négociations relat. au règne de François II., II., 98 *seq.*; VOGELSTEIN, II., 158 *seq.*, 423 *seq.*; RULE, Inquisition, II., 206; Römische Quartalschrift, XVI., 309 ; Guidus in MERKLE, II., 606 *seq.*; " Wahrhafftige Newe Zeitung " (see MÜLLER, 18 *seq.*) ; MASIUS, Briefe, 321 ; *Avvisi di Roma of August 19 and 26, *loc. cit.*, 71 *seq.* (Vatican Library) ; *Report of E. Stanghelini, dated Rome, August 21 (Gonzaga Archives, Mantua) ; *Letters of Gianfigliazzi of August 18, and of the Bishop of Cortona of August 19, 1559 (State Archives, Florence).

[2] Such were the Pope's care that grain should be brought to Rome (*cf.* MORONI, II., 146 ; BENIGNI, 34 *seq.*) and for the extirpation of the bandits (*cf.* Cod. Barb. LVI., 29, p. 90^b *seq.*, and Cod. XXVIII., D. 11, p. 61 *seq.* of the Library of the Soc. di stor. patria at Naples).

[3] In addition to the authorities cited *supra* note 1, *cf.* also FORCELLA, I., 34 ; RODOCANACHI, Capitole, 111, 113 ; LANCIANI, III., 206 *seq.* and Cod. G. III., 78, p. 210 of the Chigi Library, Rome. E. Stanghelini *wrote on August 21, 1559 : " Et il capo d'essa [statua] hieri si vedeva per Roma in poter de'fanciulli, i quali lo sputavano et burlavano nel modo che si suol beffare M. Pasquino, al quale si havrebbe maggior rispetto."

the coats-of-arms and inscriptions of " the tyrannical house of Carafa." Lampoons and satires mocked at Paul IV. and his nephews in every possible way.[1] Pamphleteers against whose immoral books the Pope had taken measures, now took a bloody revenge.[2] The tumultuous proceedings were only to some extent brought to an end on August 22nd; the city, however, still remained in a seething condition, and disorders were rife. Every kind of rabble, refugees and bandits roved through the streets committing murders. Rome resembled, as the Venetian ambassador, Mocenigo, declared, the forest of Baccano. All the palaces were garrisoned by armed men, and no one ventured in the streets at night.[3]

The body of Paul IV. was buried at night on August 19th in St. Peter's, near the tomb of Innocent VIII, as deep as possible, and a guard set over it,[4] for fear of an outbreak on the part of the people. Here the mortal remains of the Pope remained until Pius V. had them taken to S. Maria sopra Minerva on October 2nd, 1566, and placed in the monument which he had erected, and which still adorns the beautiful chapel of Oliviero Carafa. It stands, very suitably, on the left wall, just opposite the beautiful fresco of Filippino Lippi's " Triumph of St. Thomas over the heretics." The design was made by Pirro Ligorio, who also superintended its erection. A pair of black Ionic columns, connected with one another, and adorned with a peculiar ornamentation in the form of cushions, serve to frame the monument, in which the employment of costly parti-coloured marbles is characteristic. In a rectangular niche over the sarcophagus, with its antique ornamentation, is placed the statue of Paul IV., which is more than life size, and was executed by Giacomo

---

[1] *Cf.* *Cod. Urb. 1205, p. 46 *seq.* (Vatican Library); GORI, Archivio, II., 172 *seq*; DURUY, xvi *seqq*; SICKEL, Konzil, 14 *seq.*; see also SIMIANI, 36.

[2] *Cf.* BONGI, Annali Gioliti, I., 17.

[3] MOCENIGO, 38 *seq.*

[4] See FIRMANUS, 517; *cf.* Bollet. d. Suizz. ital., VII., 35.

Cassignola. It shows the Pope seated in full pontifical state, with the right hand raised to bless, and in the left the keys of Peter. The head, true to life, reproduces most admirably the ascetic features of Carafa. The pediment over the niche is borne up by two garlanded Hermae ; on the slanting sides of the cornice, the white marble statues of Faith and Religion, executed by Tommaso della Porta, once rested, but unfortunately were removed later on, and are now preserved in the sacristy. The inscription under the sarcophagus praises Paul IV. as the vigorous punisher of everything evil, and the ardent champion of the Catholic faith.[1]

The homage which Pius V. paid to the memory of his predecessor is all the more significant when we remember that he was thoroughly acquainted with the great faults of Paul IV., and had had to suffer from them. . The Pope himself had, at the approach of death, recognized his faults and bitterly repented of them. Three days before his death he summoned the General of the Jesuits, Lainez, to his side and said to him : " How bitterly flesh and blood have deceived me ! My relatives have plunged me into an unhappy war, from which many sins in the Church of God have arisen. Since the time of St. Peter there has been no such unhappy pontificate in the Church ! I repent bitterly of what has happened ; pray for me."[2]

Even if this open confession is exaggerated, no one, however,

---

[1] See CIACONIUS, III., 834 ; VASARI, VII., 551 ; REUMONT, III., 2, 735 seq. ; MÜNTZ, III., 364 ; FRIEDLANDER, 13 ; BERTHIER, 191 seq. How very much Pius V. honoured the Carafa Pope, see SILOS, I., 401 seq. and BROMATO, II., 616 seq. The agreement with regard to the erection of the monument at the expense of the Papal exchequer (for 3000 scudi) is dated April 9, 1566. Besides Giacomo Cassignola and Pirro Ligorio, Tommaso della Porta, Giovan Pietro Annone of Como, Rocco of Montefiascone and other artists were employed on it ; see BERTOLOTTI, Art. Subalp., 99 seq. ; Studi e doc., XV., 131 seq. ; cf. also CASTALDO, 175 seq.

[2] See O. MANAREUS, De rebus Soc. Iesu, Florence, 1886, 125 seq. According to Seripandus, ed. HOFLER, 55, Paul IV. said, before his death, " se in pontif. sede non pontificem, sed servum fuisse."

need repeat the attempt of the older writers and try to defend
the serious mistakes of Paul IV. The unprejudiced historian
must not shut his eyes to the grave faults, which, as well as
the great qualities, were characteristic of the Carafa Pope ;
above all, he must appreciate all that was done in the interests
of reform during his short pontificate.

Paul IV. was undoubtedly a remarkable man, of a clearly
marked, genuine, and unusually strong and unbending
character. Sincerely pious, always blameless in his life, and
full of apostolic zeal, the co-founder of the Theatines always
stood ruthlessly for the strictest standpoint in ecclesiastical
matters. Although he was a very good classical scholar, and
by no means without feeling for art,[1] such a man could not
and would not become a Maecenas in the sense of the Renaissance Popes.[2] The saying attributed to him, that it was more

[1] *Cf.* the inventory of his estate, first published by BERTOLOTTI
in Gori, Archivio, II., 51 *seqq*, and subsequently by BARBIER DE
MONTAULT (Inventaire do P. Paul IV. en 1559, Montauban,
1879, and Oeuvres compl., I., Poitiers, 1889) in detail.

[2] It was the war with Spain, the financial distress, and the cares
concerning ecclesiastical reform, which prevented Paul IV. from
playing the traditional role of a Mæcenas. Nothing in particular
was done either for the university or the library. A costly Greek
Evangeliarium was procured for St. Peter's (see CASTALDO, 71-72).
Dedications of publications are not many, and are for the most
part concerned with treatises on ecclesiastical matters (*cf.*
LAUCHERT, 617, 619, 629, 632). *U. Folietae, De philos. et iuris
civilis inter se comparatione ad Paulum IV. libri tres*, Romae, 1555 ;
concerning the dedication of a medical work, see ROTH, Vesalius,
259. Paulus Manutius was summoned to Rome to publish
theological works directed against the Lutherans (see RODO-
CANACHI, Capitole, 115 *seq*.) SANTORO (Giampaolo Flavio da
Altovito, Pisa, 1907) treats of one of the few humanists favoured
by Paul IV. Concerning Casa, Barengo and other humanists
appointed by Paul IV., see *supra* p. 84. Concerning Sirleto see
L. LATINIUS, Lucubrat., II., 45 *seq*. 49 ; WETZER u. WELTE,
Kirchenlex., XI[2]., 360 ; TACCONE- GALLUCCI, G. Sirleto, Rome,
1909. RITTER, Gesch. der Philosophie, IX., 565, points out that
the philosopher, B. Telesio, was favoured by Paul IV. By a

necessary to fortify Rome than to adorn it with pictures, may be an anecdote,[1] but it nevertheless sums up the political

brief of July 31, 1559, the Pope agreed to the foundation of the University of Douai, at the wish of Philip II. (see LEMAN in the publication Les Questions ecclésiast., V., Lille, 1912, 43 seqq.) Paul IV. had neither time nor money for artistic undertakings. The re-building of St. Peter's lay, above all, near his heart ; concerning this, as well as his relations with Michael Angelo, I shall treat, in a connected manner, when considering Pius IV. In the Vatican, apart from restorations and some changes in the dwelling apartments, his work consisted in the completion of the Pauline Chapel (see Appendix No. 28) and the arrangement of his private chapel in the Belvedere ; cf. concerning this ANCEL in the Rev. Bénéd., XXV., 49 seqq. ; see ibid., 63 seq., concerning the Casino in the garden (cf. FRIEDLANDER, 2 seq.) and concerning the demolition which treated the Hall of Constantine ; cf. concerning these, also MASSARELLI, 325 and the *Avviso di Roma of August 13, 1558 (Vatican Library). In the Vatican to-day, nothing but an inscription in the Sala Ducale reminds us of Paul IV. (see FORCELLA, VI., 71). Among the artists employed by the Pope, Pirro Ligorio, the Pope's official architect, is the most prominent, and besides him, there were Taddeo Zuccaro and Guglielmo della Porta (see ANCEL, loc. cit., 71). Paul IV. employed the same artists as his predecessors for his coins and medals, although some new names also appear (see PLON, 394 seq. ; with regard to the coins see SERAFINI, 246 seq.) His *Motu Proprio, dated January 30, 1556, announced a plan of Paul IV's which was never carried into effect : " per quem conceditur facultas rev. gubernatori alme Urbis conducendi unum palatium magnum sumptibus Cam. Ap. in quo omnes causae pro tempore decidantur et terminentur " (Editti I. Secret Archives of the Vatican). The governor of Assisi, Marcello Tuto, had the name and arms of Paul IV. affixed to the Fontana Marcella ; this is, however, no proof that the Pope had helped this work, which still exists. His coat-of-arms also appears in the wall-paintings of the governor's palace at Assisi.

[1] We may conclude that this was a mere anecdote from the fact that Paul IV., especially in the work on the Castle of St. Angelo, was most careful with regard to the adornment of the fortress with statues ; see RODOCANACHI, St. Ange, 157.

situation, which was not favourable to the arts.   There was,
moreover, another reason.   Deeply penetrated with the
dignity of his position, Paul IV. considered it to be his principal
duty to re-establish what the moral wickedness of the Renaissance, and the violent storms of the rupture in the faith had
convulsed and broken up.   That which he had striven after,
with the aid of a few chosen spirits, amid the worldliness of the
Medici Popes, he hoped to be able to realize in a glorious manner now that he had been raised to the throne of St. Peter.
Embittered by the long delay, and naturally impatient, he
began the great work with the fiery zeal which was characteristic of him, immediately after his accession.   The reform
Pope, whom everyone awaited, seemed, judging from his
previous activity, at last to have arrived in the person of
Carafa.   If, all the same, his pontificate only partly justified
these hopes, and was, indeed, in many respects, a disappointment, this was above all the consequence of the weaknesses
which too often cast a shadow over the excellent qualities of
Paul IV.

A genuine southerner, in whom thought immediately found
expression in his words, he allowed himself, in the excitement
of the moment, to be so far carried away, as to make use of
expressions which would seem incredible, if they were not
vouched for by witnesses above suspicion.   His precipitate
actions were also in keeping with his words.   It was evident
on every side that Paul IV. was as much wanting in knowledge
of the world and of human nature, as in moderation and
sagacity, things which were more than ever necessary at such
a time of disturbance and transition.   Owing to his choleric
nature he was always inclined to drive things to extremes.   A
breath, as of red-hot molten lava, seems to emanate from his
stormy mode of action, which reminds us greatly of his
countryman, the unfortunate Urban VI.   Without con--
sideration of what must be the consequences upon his religious
and reforming activities, of a rupture with Spain, the principal
Catholic power, he flung himself against the mightiest monarch
in the world in a struggle which ended disastrously, deeply
injured Rome and the States of the Church, delayed the carry-

ing out of the work of reform, and caused open joy to the enemies of the Church, and grief to her friends. Similar feelings
were aroused by the dispute with Ferdinand I., in which Paul
IV. fought for ideals, the realization of which had become
impossible.[1] While the Pope treated the Cardinals with
unprecedented rudeness and contempt,[2] he blindly trusted his
nephew, Carlo Carafa, who was as crafty as he was unprincipled, and whose behaviour placed the head of the Church at a
great disadvantage from every point of view. Too late did the
deceived and blindfolded Pope learn of the unworthiness of
those to whom he had shown favour, and in whom he had
placed his trust. The terrible severity which he now displayed
towards them was not in itself blameworthy, but Paul IV. did
not take into consideration that he had himself placed his
nephews in their high positions, and had then let them do as
they liked, without any control whatever.[3] If his trust had
been boundless before, so now was his severity, which also
affected those who were innocent.[4] The remainder of his reign
was now exclusively devoted to the activities which had
formerly occupied the life of Carafa : reform and the Inquisition. But in this respect as well, his procedure was of such a
nature that its exaggerations greatly jeopardized the success of
what he was striving for. His successor had to mitigate the
proceedings of the Inquisition, as well as many of his reform
decrees. The shrewd Pius IV. also restored the diplomatic

---

[1] Hosius (Epist., II., 667) has made a very sharp criticism of
Paul IV's war against Spain and the Catholic Hapsburgs; later
on Pallavicini has done the same (14, 9. 5). See also DEMBINSKI,
Rzym, 13 seq. ; cf. 103, 141.

[2] To the non-observance of the election capitulation, the
*memoir of Cardinal du Bellay, composed in 1559, (Gonzaga
Archives, Mantua) attributes all the disadvantageous aspects of
the reign of Paul IV. Cf. Quellen und Forschungen des Preuss.
Inst., XII., 226.

[3] ANCEL (Disgrâce, 179) justly brings this out.

[4] *A. Ricchi also acknowledges this ; see Appendix No.
60.

relations with the powers which had been broken off under his predecessor.[1]

Nevertheless, the reign of Paul IV., in spite of its errors and defects, forms an important landmark in the history of the Catholic reformation, to the success of which he prepared the way.[2] Openly and candidly, as Adrian VI. had done on a previous occasion, he proclaimed the principle of a reform in both head and members, and took more trouble than Paul III. or Julius III. to carry it into effect. The break with the past which he effected by his refusal to nominate Cardinals at the will of the princes, the summoning of worthy men to the Senate of the Church, the ruthless fight against simony in every form, the abolition of the holding of benefices in commendam, of the " regressus " and the sale of offices, the reform of the monasteries, the Dataria and the Penitentiary, and finally, to crown all, the enforcement of the duty of residence on the bishops, were all great and permanent services rendered by Paul IV. The energy which he displayed at the fall of his nephews put an end, for a long time, to nepotism on any large scale, and was a reform of the greatest importance.[3]

Even if the unbounded violence of the character of Paul IV. awakened fear and hatred in wide circles, his otherwise pious and exemplary life called forth the greatest admiration. An aged man, " who like a born ruler, seemed to be quite penetrated with the dignity of his office, who did not allow himself to be affected, either by the weight of his eighty years or by misfortune, who stood up so fearlessly for what he considered to be right against the mightiest princes," must have made a

[1] See BIAUDET, 24. Not only the Imperial nunciature, but also those of Venice and Florence, were vacant at the death of Paul IV. Those of France, Naples, Portugal, and Poland were the only ones that were regularly working.

[2] See SEGMÜLLER, 29 ; cf. also HERRE, 18. G. Catalani, in the preface to the 10th Vol. of the Annali d'Italia, Lucca, 1764, xxxvi., has made it clear that Muratori brought out only the darker side of Paul IV., and has not done him justice.

[3] See the opinion of Cardinal A. Carafa in his *Apologia (Library at Naples ; cf. Appendix Nos. 61, 62) and ANCEL, Disgrâce, 183.

deep impression upon his contemporaries.[1] No less a person
than the historian Panvinio, who was by no means prejudiced
in favour of the Carafa Pope, said that Paul IV. was the first to
re-establish and strengthen ecclesiastical discipline, and that
many of the later salutary decrees of the Council of Trent were
to be traced back to him.[2] Guglielmo Sirleto entirely agrees
with him.[3] Well-informed contemporaries, like Giulio Pogiano,
can hardly find words to describe the change which the reforming activity of Paul IV. brought about in Rome. The Venetian ambassador was of opinion that the city had been turned
into a well-ordered monastery.[4] What the noble Dutch Pope,
Adrian VI., had in vain attempted, to break with the evil
tendencies of the Renaissance, the fiery Neapolitan had
succeeded in doing.

One must realize the abandoned conditions of the time of
Alexander VI. and Leo. X. in order to be able fully to appreciate the merits of Paul IV. The tearing out of such old and
deeply rooted abuses, which were only too firmly entwined in
the circumstances of the times, was in truth only possible by
means of a masterful procedure in which was contained all the
severity of an inexorable repression. Paul IV. was the right
man for this. His fiery soul, which flamed out in open rage,

---

[1] See MÜLLER, Konklave Pius' IV., 9.

[2] Concerning PANVINIUS, Vita, *cf.* Appendix No. 61-62.
BROMATO (II., 504 n.) has already drawn attention to the passage
in question. RANKE (1⁶., 199), REUMONT (III., 2, 529), BEAU-
FORT (Hist. des Papes, IV., Tournai, 1841, 201), and MATHIEU
(Pouvoir temp. des Papes, Paris, 1863, 504) are of the same
opinion as Panvinius. BENRATH (Jahrb. fur protest, Theol.,
1878, 123, 143) also describes Paul IV. as " a powerful intellect,
and an admirably gifted Pope," who made himself master of the
forces for a complete reaction in ecclesiastical affairs, and then
disciplined them.

[3] See SILOS, I., 393 ; *cf.* 232.

[4] See MOCENIGO-ALBÈRI, 48 and CANTU, II., 27 ; *cf. supra*
p. 238. The change also showed itself in the medals, on which
mythological representations were entirely replaced by those of a
Christian character ; see MÜNTZ, III., 119.

when an abuse of what was holy came before his eyes, could not do enough to cauterize, with red-hot iron, the wounds which a vicious age had inflicted upon the Church. The reform, built up on the authority of strictly ecclesiastical principles, which had been initiated by Paul III., the Carafa Pope continued so energetically and carried out with so much strength, that the later Popes of the time of restoration were able to go on and build successfully on his firm foundations.

APPENDIX

OF

UNPUBLISHED DOCUMENTS

AND

EXTRACTS FROM ARCHIVES.

APPENDIX.

1555, April 4, Rom.

. . . Perchè invero da Sta Croce infuori i Franzesi non hanno subbietto da potere riuscire loro, se già Dio non volessi rovinare interamente questa Sta Sede, et se bene dalla banda Imp^{le} et di casa Monte ci è poca unione, nei Franzesi, non vi è anco molta. Et questo modo di procedere che si è tenuto fino a hora di non eccettuare particularmente persona nè insistere in uno più che in un altro, come si fece nel conclavi passato, ma dire che si faccia un huomo da bene, che sia il servitio di Dio et se ne possa sperare la quiete universale, è piaciuto molto a ciascuno et credo sia stato meglio. Staremo a vedere il fine, il qual piaccia a Dio che sia conforme al desiderio dell' E.V. et stia sicura che de me non si è fatto nè farà instantia particulare nè in prò nè in contro, se non tanto quanto mi ordinerà l' E. V., giudicando che il precedere in questo negotio per questa via sia più honesto et migliore . . .

[Orig. State Archives, Florence.]

2. AVERARDO SERRISTORI TO COSIMO I., DUKE OF TUSCANY.[2]

1555, April 6, Rom.

. . . Il cardinal Sta Croce è stato molto reservato et si è governato con modestia infinita, non si sendo mai potuto scorgere nelle parole sue altro che desiderio di vedere un buon papa in questa Sta Sede, il qual modo di procedere lo fa venerando sopra ogn' altro et si vede che ha gran parte nel pontificato, perchè ancora che la maggiore parte giudichi che l' assumtione sua fussi per essere poco a proposito per il servito di S. M^{tà}, non di meno la vita sua esemplare fa che molti della banda Imp^{le} et di casa Monte vi andranno, chi per credere che habbi a essere Papa, altri per guadangnarselo per la promotione di lor medesimi et alcuni per non li parere potere ragionevolmente negargnene ; non di meno si crede, che dalla banda franzese harà delle difficultà, perchè Ferrara dicono che non

---

[1] See *supra*, p. 6, n. 3.   [2] See *supra*, p. 7, n. 1, Petrucelli, II., 74 *seq.*

andrà in lui per respetto di casa Farnese, et S. Giorgio, Sermoneta, Urbino et altri giovani, che sono avezzi a vivere licentiosi, lo fuggiranno, come uno scoglio, sendo loro tremenda la sua severità, in modo che anco il fatto suo harà delle difficultà et così ce ne potremmo facilmente andare con la creatione in lungo . . .
[Orig. State Archives, Florence.]

3. Provost Ghisi to Lodovico Strozzi.[1]

1555, April 8, Rom.

. . . La imperiale vorrebbe Fano, il qual horri è stato molto molto presso al segno, se li Francesi unitamente propongono et gagliardamente fin qui aiutano Sta Croce et Ferrara, a quali si dice ch' una parte de imperiali consentono, ma il resto per quel che s' intende tirano a traverso, acennando ad altri soggietti, et la parte de vecchi che è chiamata neutrale ecclesiastica non ha mai fin qui voluto lasciarsi intendere di voler dar voti ad alcuno delli nominati, parendo a tutti loro che a questa propositione essi sieno degni soggietti a par di qual si voglia altri di questi predetti, in modo che stando sì discordi si da materia et campo alle fationi di darne conto all' Imp^{re} et al re, et per ciò spogliati della loro propria autoritade indignamente fanno che la creatione del Papa, con molto dispiacere de tutti, vaddi così di longo in infinito. A me pare che in questi negotii del far il Papa sien tante difficultadi, diversitadi et mutationi che mal si possi giudicare chi habbia ad essere quello che gionga a questo ultimo segno . . .
[Orig. Gonzaga Archives, Mantua.]

4. Bernardino Pia to Sabino Calandra.[2]

1555, April 8, Rom.

. . . Questa notte passanta Fano è stato tanto vicino al Papato che se S. Giacomo et Theatino non si sforzavano con mille false imputationi che le danno e di Lutherano e d' altro, egli riusciva. Vogliono che si sia scoperto un buco nel muro che entrava nella sua camarella, s' intende che ha Theatino un fascio de processi contra di lui e di tutti i sogetti papabili. Sta Croce medesimamente è andato molto al basso non sendo

---

[1] See *supra* p. 3, n. 3.   [2] See *supra* p. 9, n. 1.

reuscita a un gran pezzo una pratica che fu fatta per lui non questa notte l' altra, et dicono che si è scoperta non so chè promessa di dar Camerino al Sr Baldovino, riuscendo a l' uno e l' altro Monte con tutto che habbi tanto obligo come si sa al Sr Baldovino per essere chiamato suo figliolo e aggradito da suo fratello, si è nostro contrario, et insieme S^{to} Angelo, il quale è venuto fino a parole rigorose con Sta Fiore . . .

(Orig. Gonzaga Archives, Mantua.]

5. AGOSTINO GONZAGA, BISHOP OF REGGIO, TO THE CASTELLAN OF MANTUA.[1]

1555, April 9, Rom.

. . . Questa matina si è penetrato chel cardinale Ferrara fu per essere adorato et uscire Papa dominica sera, che mons^r ill^{mo} nostro con altri amici gli diede il voto, ma essendone avertito Sta Fiore, il quale in absentia di questi altri signori imperiali ha sin qui fatto il capo della fatione imperiale, si voltò con una grossa banda alla volta di Sta Croce, et fece così fatta diversione che Ferrara non hebbe piu che vintidua, o vintitre voti, et si è saputo per certo chel cardinale di Trento concorse con Sta Fiore per divertire. Basta che mons^r di Ferrara ha fatto prova de la voluntà et animo di mons^{re} nostro ill^{mo} et che a lui ha detto il vero ; se esso corresponde per la pariglia con sua s. ill^{ma}, puotriamo havere assai presto una buona nova. Si sono ben anche dette alcune cianze in banchi del cardinale di Fano, che sia stato vicino al Papato, ma sono vanità et pratiche fatte da mercanti per conto delle scomesse.

[Orig. Gonzaga Archives, Mantua.]

6. CARDINAL E. GONZAGA TO FRANCESCO GONZAGA.[2]

1555, April 10, Rom.

Noi havemo fatto molto presto nostro Papa laudato Dio percio che non siamo stati più che 4 dì chiusi in conclave che la cosa si è risoluta nel card. di S. Croce non per via di scrutinio, ma di negotiatione, et di pratiche, et se così tosto non si conchiudeva senza dubbio riusciva Papa nello scrutinio della mattina seguente il card. di Ferrara.

M. Cervini was ever di costume grave e severo. Se sarà tale Papa quale è stato cardinale, se ne puo aspettar gran bene

---

[1] See *supra*, p. 7, n. 4. [2] See *supra*, pp. 35, n. 6 ; 37, n. 3 ; 49, n. 1

alla chiesa christiana universale. He was firmly convinced
that, for a Pope ciancie, motti ridicoli et tratenimenti piacevoli
were quite unfitting, He was the terror ot the dissolute, and
the friend ot others.

Egli è d' età di 54 o 55 anni, di persona assai grande, di viso
estenuato e di complessione delicata. E stato tenuto fin qui
di buona vita, di belle lettere et d' honesta et grave conver-
satione et poche volte è stato visto a ridere, et s' ode pur o vede
qualche cosa ridicola fa un poco di ghignetto et se la passa con
una severità catoniana. Non si è dilettato di mangiare molto
nè di feste nè di buffoni. Gli sono spiacciute le licenze pre-
tesche, ha havuto in odio gli sfratati, ha perseguitato i sospetti
di heresia et ha sempre procurata la reformatione della chiesa
sotto Pauolo et Giulio predecessori suoi. In somma egli è di
diretto il rovescio di Papa Giulio, il quale haveva messe le cose
in tal termine che si conosce chiaramente che Dio ci ha dato
questo per pietà che ha havuto della chiesa sua santa, onde . . .
possiamo sperare la reformatione et la correctione d' infiniti
scandalosi abusi . . .

Hoggi ha parlato alla sua famiglia (See *supra*, p. 37).
Desires bishops to be resident.

Al card. Nobili, che è d' età di 15 anni et tutto dato alle
lettere, ha fatto una bella esortatione dicendo : Figliuol mio,
ho inteso che voi sete su una bona via da farvi da bene, dotto
et virtuoso cardinale ; vi prego che vogliate caminar ani-
mosamente, se amate la gratia mia . . . Medesimamente ha
parlato a Monte ricordandogli che fin hora è vivuto molto
licentiosamente et che se pensava di mutar vita gli sarà in luogo
di figliuolo, se anco vorrà continuare la vita che ha fatta fin
qui non potrà S. Sta per debito suo mancar di tentar ogni via per
ridurlo alla buona strada . . .

[Copy. Cod. 2425, 4—6. University Library, Bologna.]

7. Camillo Capilupi to Ferrante Gonzaga.[1]

1555, April 10, Rom.

. . . Non essendo nel scrutinio di non hieri l' altro che fu il
primo, riuscito Papa il cardinale di Ferrara per cagione che nel
primo scrutinio non si possono dare gli accesi, et essendosi, da
gli aversarii suoi scoperto, il negocio esser tanto inanci, che se

[1] See *supra*. p. 7, n. 4.

questa matina si faceva un altro scrutinio egli riusciva Papa,
subito si voltorono a Sta Croce, al quale questi signori Imperiali
si voltorono anch' essi, giudicando più servigio di S. M^tà l'
ellegere Sta Croce che Ferrara ; fra quali, che furono li princi-
pali, fu il Camerlengo, la Ceva, Carpi, Saraceno, Napoli et
molti altri, li quali hieri sera circa alle XXIII hore andorono
per adorarlo sicome fecero.   Monsr ill^mo nostro anch' esso v' ha
parte perchè quando fu chiamato all' adoratione, rispose, che
havrebbe fatto mons^r di Trento, perciochè a lui haveva obligata
la parola sua, e però essendosi voltato Trento anche mons^r ill^mo
andò ad adorarlo molto voluntieri, havendolo per huomo da
bene et persona digna di questo carico et dignità . . . S. S^tà
ha voluto che si faccia senza sorte alcuna di pompa per fuggire
la spesa et per essere nei giorni santi.   S. S^tà non ha voluto
signare nè far₄ gratia alcuna, che le fosse dimandata nella
creatione.   Ha confirmati alcuni ufficiali, come il Datario, il
Vicario, il Barengo che è sopra i brevi et il Governatore ; ella
s' è mostrata amorevole a tutti i cardinali anche a quelli che le
sono stati contrarii, si è mostrata d' un animo composto, perchè
non ha fatto segno alcuno di mutatione per allegrezza, nè con
gesti, nè con fatti.   Pare che la corte in generale tema la
severità sua, la quale però si spera che [sia] per moderare
accompagnandola con equità . . .
[Copy in a letter of Camillo Luzzara.   Gonzaga Archives,
    Mantua.]

8. GIROLAMO MUZZARELLI, ARCHBISHOP OF CONZA, TO THE
        COLLEGE OF CARDINALS.[1]

1555, Mai 12, Brussel.
    Illustrissimi et amplissimi domini.
    Quum per unum tabellarium, quem oratores Angli, qui sunt
in Italia, et paulo post per alterum, quem huc ex Urbe caesari-
ani ministri destinarunt, auditum fuit ab ipso Caesare et a tota
eius curia de morte foe. rec. S. D. N. Marcelli II. pontificis
maximi, visa est una cuiusdam communis luctus acerbitas et
Caesaris et omnium ferme animós continuo occupare.   A me
vero potissimum nil poterat hoc tempore acerbius audiri.   Eo
in pontificem maximum electo orta simul et erecta fuit spes
dignitatis christianae reipublicae restaurandae et illustrandae.
Hoc effecit notissima ipsius vitae sanctitas et prudentia geren-

---

[1] See *supra*, p. 54, n. 2.

darum rerum. Confirmarunt eandem spem prima semina
studiorum pontificatus ipsius, quae nil prius quam splendorem
divini cultus et rectam morum institutionem constantissime
pollicebantur. Optata fruges tantorum seminum sine maxima
molestia non potuit tam repente extingui, quae cum summa
omnium laetitia et commoditate expectabatur. Hinc vero eo
amplius videtur dolendum esse, quo magis verendum est, ne
publica haec et ingens iactura extincti dignissimi pastoris
inflicta sit a divina iustitia secundum culpam indigni gregis
christiani. Inter tot aerumnas et luctus Ecclesiae catholicae,
none video quomodo mihi respirandum sit, nisi in cinere et
cilitio preces et lachrimas convertam ad Christum, ut sibi in hac
sanctissima sede vicarium constituat qui cum populum tum
clerum ecclesiasticum velit ad formam orthodoxae professionis
pio zelo et paterna solertia revocare.

Aspiret divina clementia, ita ut aliqua lux consolationis
recuperetur ex sapientissimo consensu ill^{marum} amplitudinum
vestrarum, quibus cum humillima affectus observantia me
ipsum offero et dedo illisque omnia precor foelicia in Christo
Jesu domino nostro.

Datum Bruxellae, quarto idus maii MDLV.

Ill^{marum} et r^{marum} dominationum v^{rum}

[Autogr.] Humillimus et obsequentissimus servus
f. Hieronymus episcopus Consanensis.

[Orig. Lett. di princ. XV 105.   Secret Archives of the Vatican.]

9. CAMILLO OLIVO TO SABINO CALANDRA.[1]

1555, Mai 23, Rom.

. . . La creatione sua è stata tale che manco male è tacerla o
dirla a bocca che scriverla, perciochè non è stata buona voluntà
di quei che l' hanno eletto, ma per dispetto di coloro che
praticavano di fare il Puteo e per ambitione di voler essere
quelli che facciano il Papa di lor mano, et la cosa passò con
molto tumulto e non senza scandolo de gli amatori del bene et
con pericolo di scisma, perciochè fu detto il Puteo da alcuni
et alcuni altri Chieti et da hieri alle vinti hore fin hoggi alle
dieciotto s' è stato con due Papi in conclavi. Ma la miseri-
cordia di Dio, la bontà del Puteo e la pia mente di coloro che
l' havevano eletto, accompagnata dalla facilità d' alcuni di loro
the per natura si mutano volentieri ha rimediato a tanto male,

---

[1] See *supra*, pp. 65, n. 4 ; 92, n. 3.

et concordemente sono venuti tutti i cardinali in Chieti, di cui si promette per ogniuno poco più lunga vita di quella che habbia havuto Papa Marcello, essendo in settantanove anni, che questo basta quando fosse il più sano homo senza che ha pur anch' esso catarro et alle volte patisce di flusso, il che per secondo che dicono i suoi è la sua sanità et la sua purgatione, perciochè affermano che non prese mai medicina in vita sua et con quel flusso purga tutti gli humori cativi. La patria sua è Napoli et è di casa Caraffa et zio del principe di Stigliano, onde la signora donna Hippolita nostra potrà farci con S. Stà qualche favore. Chi spera da questa eletione assai di bene et chi mon molto. La vita sua riformata di tanti anni promette riforma nella Chiesa di non molto. La vita sua riformata di tanti anni promette riforma nella Chiesa di Dio, ma la patria e la natura sono di qualche consideratione et forza. Dio benedetto, se così è suo servigio, gli dia lunga vita accioche ogni tratto non habiamo a torre su questo viaggio . . .

[Orig. Gonzaga Archives, Mantua.]

10. POPE PAUL IV. TO GIROLAMO MUZZARELLI, ARCHBISHOP OF CONZA.[1]

1555, Iuni 2, Rom.

Venerabili fratri Hieronymo achiepiscopo Consano apud ser^{mum} Caesarem nostro et Sedis Apostolicae nuntio. Paulus pp. IIII.

Venerabilis frater, salutem et apostolicam benedictionem. Cum in earum curarum et laborum partem, qui ad pastorale hoc munus nostrum obeundum a nobis sunt suscipiendi, etiam dilectum filium nobilem virum Ioannem Caraffam, comitem Montorii, nostrum secundum carnem nepotem, vocaverimus deque illius fide ac virtute rerumque tractandarum peritia plurimum nobis possimus polliceri, volumus ac tuae fraternitati mandamus ut, quoties ei ad te scribere aut internuncios mittere, quavis de re aut quavis de causa, contigerit, non minorem ei fidem per petuo habeas quam si a nobismetipsis et scriptae literae et missi internuntii essent. Datum Romae apud sanctum Petrum sub anulo piscatoris, die secunda iunii M. D. Lv, pontificatus nostri anno primo.

[Item :] Venerabili fratri Sebastiano episcopo Viterbiensi

---

[1] See *supra*, p. 84, n. 1.

apud Christianissimum regem nostro et Sedis Apostolicae nuntio.

Ven[ii] fratri Zachariae episcopo Pharensi apud regem Romanorum nostro et Apostolicae Sedis nuntio.

Ven[ii] fratri Philippo episcopo Salutiarum apud dominium Venetorum nostro et Apostolicae Sedis nuntio.

. . . provinciae nostrae Romandiolae vicelegato.

. . . civitatis nostrae Perusiae et Umbriae vicelegato.

. . . in provincia nostra Patrimonii commissario generali.

. . . provinciae nostrae Campaniae vicelegato.

. . . in provincia nostra Marchiae Anchonitanae vicelegato.

. . . Episcopo Veronensi.

[Concept. Arm. 44, t. 4, n. 113. Secret Archives of the Vatican.]

11. Consistory of June 5th, 1555.[1]

Apud sanctum Marcum.

Romae die mercurii quinta mensis iunii[2] 1555 fuit consistorium in quo . . .

Sanctissimus dominus noster dominus Paulus divina providentia papa IV, de salute animarum sollicitus, ut persone ecclesiastice absque'alicuius symonie aut ambitionis suspicione ad ecclesiarum et monasteriorum regimina promoveri et persone ipse puro corde et sincera conscientia presidere valeant, de fratrum consilio statuit et ordinavit quod de cetero futuris temporibus patriarchalibus, metropolitanis et cathedralibus ecclesiis ac monasteriis pro tempore vacantibus, de quibus consistorialiter disponi contigerit, non ad personarum promovendarum huiusmodi requisitionem supplicationem aut instantiam, sed iis, que de iure patronatus fuerint aut ad quas seu quae idonearum personarum presentatio seu nominatio ad Imperatorem, reges aut alios principes pertinuerit, ad presentationem seu nominationem Imperatoris, regum seu aliorum principum, ius patronatus seu facultatem presentandi aut

---

[1] See *supra*, p. 90, n. 3.
[2] GULIK-EUBEL (III., 37) date changed ; perfectly erroneous ; according to the redaction of the " Acta consist." in Barb. lat., 2873 the consistory took place on May 26th, 1555, which is impossible, if only for the reason that the coronation took place on this day. It is also certain that the first consistory took place only on May 29th ; see *supra* p. 80.

nominandi huiusmodi habentium, et r^{mi} cardinalis huiusmodi negocium in consistorio proponentis, aliis vero ecclesiis seu monasteriis ad solius cardinalis proponentis, aliis vero ecclesiis seu monasteriis ad solius cardinalis proponentis relationem duntaxat provideri debeat.

[Acta consist, cancell., VI., 243b—244. Consistorial Archives of the Vatican.]

12. CONSISTORY OF JULY 17TH, 1555.[1]

Apud sanctum Marcum.

Roma die mercurii decima septima mensis iulii 1555 fuit consistorium in quo haec acta sunt.

Sanctissimus dominus noster, indemnitati patriarchalium, metropolitanarum et cathedralium ecclesiarum providere cupiens, de fratrum consilio statuit atque decrevit, ut de cetero perpetuis futuris temporibus in provisione seu alia dispositione ecclesiarum earundem non dispensetur cum aliquibus super defectu etatis nisi iuxta decreta concilii Lateranensis novissime celebrati et concordata Gallie desuper cum Sede Apostolica inita, quae super hoc inviolabiliter observari voluit et expresse mandavit.

[Acta consist. cancell., VI., 250^b. Consistorial Archives of the Vatican.]

13. BERNARDO NAVAGERO TO VENICE.[2]

1555, October 12, Rom.

. . . His Holiness said to me : Quel che habbiamo a dirvi, magnifico ambasciator, è che heri il cardinal S. Iacomo, che è nostro amico antico et buono, vene à pregarne che fossamo contenti di udir l' ambasciator dell' Imperatore, che è il marchese di Sarria, l' insolentia del qual veramente non habbiamo potuto tollerar et per mostrarglielo nullum reliquimus locum, so non questo che non gli habbiamo commandato che in termine di tanti giorni uscisse del stato nostro. Noi, si ben conoscemo haver da far con gente infidele et che sempre cercha inganarci, pur havendo rispetto, non a loro, ma al grado che tenimo, che, dovendo esser noi li authori della pace, non par

---

[1] See *supra* p. 90, n. 4.   [2] See *supra*, p. 107, n. 1.

che convenga che accendiamo un focco che abbrugieria più che tutti li altri, et considerando a chi è morto per me in croce, fossemo contenti che venisse, il qual con molte parole humane et riverente ne disse non voler guerra con noi et che questa era intention delli soi principi et che havea ordine di far retirar le gente ; al che respondessemo : Si voi non volete guerra con noi, nè noi con voi. Dicendomi a questo proposito S. S^{tà} : Vi vogliamo dir liberamente, s^{or} ambasciator, da una parte ne pareria esser il più fortunato homo del mondo, quando per mezo nostro havesse piaciuto a S. M^{tà} Divina di cacciar questi barbari d' Italia, liberar il regno di Napoli, il stato di Milano, che all' hora possamo dir alla nostra ser^{ma} Signoria et alla nostra Venetia : Questa è una republica libera et grande ; siamo pregati a questo, siamo sollicitati et havessamo ancho da noi forze non contemnendae, perchè ne basteria animo di haver 20 mila fanti et 2 mila cavalli, et l' Imperatore ne volesse voltar la faccia, haveria da guardarsi le spalle, gli possamo far molto maggior danno che non pensa et non teme. Dall' altra parte siamo vecchio, ne vossamo chel nostro animo fosse vires ultra sortemque senectae. Colligarsi col rè, che lo desidera nè aspetta altro, non vogliamo, per non haver l' un inimico aperto, l' altro compagno et per questa via superiore, perchè spendendo et agiutandosi, vorria poi da noi molte cose che per aventura non sariano honeste. Vogliamo, magnifico ambasciator, star liberi, oltra che il rispetto, che habbiamo particular a quella Signoria non ci lassa entrar in guerra, perchè non si potria far senza di lei, et havuto che havesse notitia in quel medesimo tempo bisogneria che noi gli domandassemo agiuto. Le guerre non ranno per voi : sapiamo come si governa quel stato, che a longo andar bisogna ricorrer alle borse de particulari, li quali diventano poi poveri, et la pace vi arrichisse con tanti commertii quanti havete. Credete voi che ci siamo scordati quanto prontamente per la fede et religion nostra entraste con papa Paulo III et Carlo Quinto in una guerra, et come ancho fosti illusi et abandonati ? Noi per amor che vi portiamo non vi consigliessamo mai ad entrar in guerra. Questo medesimo animo habbiamo anchor noi, et se habbiamo bravato et bravamo, è che conosciamo la debolezza di questi imperiali. La summa è, per dirvi l' interno del cor nostro et in confessione, che noi non vogliamo guerra se non più che astretti. Fatte intender questo a quelli miei signori, fattelo intender per quelli cauti modi che saperete. Conchiudendo, come ha fatto tante altre volte, nella laude di quella eccrîa republica, la conservation et grandezza della quale disse desiderare come la sua istessa, dicendomi : Questa è stata una digressione un poco longa ; ritornamo à dirvi che questa matina, oltre ogni nostra esspettatione, è venuto il secretario del cardinal S^{to} Iacobo, che intendete che è qui, et ne ha dimandato che per poter scrivere all' Imperatore, l' ambasciator desidereria sapper con quanta gente armata restaremo. Vi confessiamo la verità, mag^{co} ambasciator, che se alterassemo grandemente, lo cacciassemo dal nostro conspetto, dicendoli che non conoscevimo alcun che ne potesse dar legge, et che non conoscevimo altro patron che Christo et che volemo tenir et cavalli et fanti quanti ne piacceva. . . Finito che hebbe S. S^{tà} la ringratiai con quella forma di parole che mi parve conveniente, dicendo che mi partiva sempre con maraviglia dalli prudenti et savii soi discorsi et che V. Ser^{tà} rimaneria molto consolata di tanta confidentia che nostra haver S. S^{tà} in lei. Ben disse : Parleremo sempre così con voi.come col cor nostro et con questo, abbracciatomi teneramente, mi licentiò ; et nel ussir dalla camera molti di quelli camerieri et prelati, che stano in l' anticamera, mi dissero che il card^l S^{to} Jacobo havea ditto publicamente d' esser venuto per far tutto quello che volea il pontifice . . .

[Copy. Cod. 9445, f. 9^b —10. Library of St. Mark, Venice.]

14. G. Muzio to Pope Paul IV.[1]

1555, November 3, Pesaro.

. . . Hora è il tempo, santo padre, di metter mano ad eseguire i santi pensieri ; hora è il tempo da levar col coltello dello spirito gli abusi introdutti dalla affettione della carne e del sangue. Il cardinal Marcello, che fu poi Papa Marcello precessor di V. S^{tà}, discorrendo meco in Ugubio nella materia della riformatione, il giorno avanti che egli quindi si partisse per venire a Roma, quando seguì la sua esaltatione, mi disse, tra le altre cose, che il papato è come il zambelotto, il quale sempre conserva quella piega che egli prende da principio et che qual Papa dal principio del suo papato alla iriformatione non mette mano, non bisogna che speri di poter piu far cosa

---

[1] See *supra*, pp. 175, n. 3 ; 234, n. 3.

buona. Così diceva egli et si come V. Sta con lui fu di animo conforme, credo anchora che ella sia della medesima opinione. Se nel principio adunque si ha da cominciare, si ha anche da metter mano al principio et al capo della chiesa. Il capo è Roma, dalla quale tutti gli stati et tutte le conditioni delle persone hanno da prender la regola. Et in Roma dopo V. Sta (dalla cui vita et dalla cui dottrina ogniuno si puo riformare, se vuole haverla per esempio) principale è il collegio de' cardinali ; tra quali prego il Sig^r Dio che non vi sia oppositione di vita nè di dottrina. Dopo questi sono i vescovi, i quali in Roma sono piante inutili et doverebbono esser trapiantati in terreno dove havessero da far frutto. Ma pur che non ve no sieno di quelli, che in luogo di fruttificare ad utilità de popoli, apportino mortifero veleno. Colpa di chi infino ad hora ha dato le prelature et i beneficii senza guardare a cui. Et che abuso è questo ? Ho detto abuso ? Che abominatione è introdutta nella chiesa di Dio ? Se haverò figliuoli del corpo infermi, prendero pensierò che siano medicati da persona dotta e prattica di medicina. Et che dico figliuoli ? se haverò un branco di pecore (per non dir parola più dishonesta), non lo darò, se non saprò prima che colui sia atto alla cura di quelle. Et le anime, create alla similitudine di Dio et ricomperate col santissimo sangue del signor nostro Jesu Christo, sono non raccomandate al governo, ma gittate alla tirannia di chi molte volte non sa pur regger le proprie sue mani, gli occhi suoi et la sua lingua. Et da questo inconveniente ne nasce poi quell' altro, che i vescovi, i quali sono stati creati senza considera-tione danno i sacerdotii, la amministratione de sacramenti et la cura delle anime alla feccia de gli humoini. Hanno bisogno si la Dataria, la Cancellaria et la Penitentiaria di esser riformate, et da tor via si hanno le simonie, che si fanno ne' contratti de' beneficii ; ma quella non penso che habbia da esser gran fatica, nè di molti giorni fra persone che tutto dì hanno tal materie tra le mani. Questa è la importantia che huomini di buona vita et di sana dottrina habbiano le prelature, accioche la universal chiesa di Dio sia ben regolata : chè questo è quello che leverà gli abusi et serrerà la bocca alla heretica pravità. Io parlo securamente et liberamente in questo suggetto, come colui che in me ho conosciuto et proveduto a quello che veggo et danno in altrui. Chè, essendo a me data intentione di dignità ecclesiastiche, sapendo io l' ordine de' sacri canoni

essere che per gradi a quelli si ascenda, non havendo io mai
servito la Chiesa, ne bene essendo sofficiente a governar l'
anima mia, et intendendo di quanto carico sia la dispensatione
de' beni de' poveri, mi ho eletto di starmene in vita secolare,
non volendo in me consentire a quello abuso il quale in altrui
biasimo nelle mie scritture. Et così ho anche messo silentio a
maldicenti che già andavano divulgando che io era papista,
percioche uccellava a beneficii. Et di questa buona mente, la
quale il signor Dio ha donata a me, prego la sua sempiterna
Maestà che ne faccia parte anche a molti, accioche più age-
volmente la S^{tà} Vostra possa colorire i suoi santi disegni. Et
con ogni humiltà di cuore le bacio i santi piedi.

Di Pesaro a III di novembre del M. D. L. v.

Di V. S^{tà} Humilissimo servo et devot^{ma} H. Mutio creatura

[Orig. Castel S. Angelo, Arm. 8, ord. II., t. 2, p. 244—245^b.
Secret Archives of the Vatican.]

15. EDICT OF THE GOVERNOR OF ROME, 1555.[1]

Bando generale.

Il signor governatore di Roma, volendo obviare alli abusi et
errori che si commettano in publico scandalo e vilipendio del
honor d' Iddio et provedere al honesto, quieto et pacifico
vivers di questa alma città, di espresso ordine et spetial commissione di S. S^{tà}, ordina et 'commanda che nessuna persona di
qual si voglia grado, stato, conditione, età o sesso et preminenza, ardisca in alcun modo biastemmare o dishonestamente
nominare il santissimo nome dell' onnipotente Iddio o del suo
unigenito figliuol Jesu Christo o della gloriosa sempre vergine
sua madre e regina del cielo o di qual si voglia santo o santa,
sotto pena per la prima volta a chi contrafarà di star con le
mani ligate dietro tutto un giorno alla berlina, la quale a questo
effetto si farà mettere in diversi luoghi publici, et per la seconda
volta, oltra la sopradicta pena, di esserli forata la lingua, et
per la terza sotto pena della galea per cinque anni, reservandosi
pero in ogni caso l' arbitrio d' augmentare et diminuire la pena
secondo la qualità delle persone et biastemme et si darà fede
ad un solo testimonio con il detto dello accusatore, il quale
sarà tenuto secreto. Et di più rinova ogni altro ordine fatto
sopra a cio fino al presente.

[1] See *supra*, p. 179, n. 1.

Item, che nessuna persona di qual si vogli stato, grado, preheminenza o conditione se sia ardisca o presumma accompagnare alle chiese, dove sono le stationi overo indulgenze, o nelle quali si celebri qualche festa, così dentro di Roma come fuori, cortigiane o meretrici di nessuna sorte, nè stando nè andando, parlare con loro o fare cosa alcuna lasciva o dishonesta, nè per le vie dirette di dette chiese giocare ad alcun giuogo, etiam tollerato, alla pena dę dui tratti de corda et de venticinque scudi d' applicarsi a luoghi pii da ellegersi da dicto signor governatore ; et dalle cortegiane o meretrici, che se faranno o lassaranno accompagnare, che parlaranno o faranno cosa alcuna lasciva o dishonesta, oltra la pena predetta pecuniaria d' applicarsi come di sopra, della frusta et esilio perpetuo dalla città di Roma, le qual cortigiane debbiano subito sotto la medesima pena, tolto il perdono, partirsi di chiesa et andar per li fatti loro.

Item, accioche si possano conoscere le gentildonne dalle cortigiane et meretrici, ordina che nessuna cortigiana, meretrice o donna di mala vita ardisca portare in modo alcuno, sotto pretesto di qual si voglia licenza, habito solito portarsi da gentildonne o cittadine romane ; ne meno presumma andare per Roma in carretta o in cocchio, sotto pena della frusta el del bando de Roma et di perdita del habito et confiscatione de tutti i suoi beni, d' applicarsi al monasterio delle Convėrtite di Roma ; et chi impresterà cocchio o carretta a nessuna di dette cortigiane, perdere il cocchio et quei cavalli ; et al cocchiero che condurrà il cocchio, di tre squassi di fune ; et chi ce andarà dentro in compagnia di dette cortigiane, incorrerà in pena di cinquanta scudi d' applicarsi alla rev^ma Camera apostolica et il bando perpetuo di Roma et de tre tratti di fune ad arbitrio di detto signor governatore : il quale revoca ogni et qualunque licenza data sin qui da qual si voglia persona, dechiarando che si procederà etiam ex officio, et daràssi fede ad un' solo testimonio con il giuramento. Et de più, per ordine di S. Sta, rinova ogni altro ordine fatto sin qui in questa materia di cocchi, et spetialmente che non vi possino andare huomini da dodeci anni in su insieme con donne, etiam che fossero parenti o marit loro.

Item dichiara per avertimento di ciaschuno, che nessuna persona come di sopra ardisca in alcun modo commettere il nefando et detestabil vitio della sodomia overo esserne mezano ;

il che facendo, incorrerà nella pena contenuta nelle leggii constitutioni et statuti de Roma, per le quali contro tali qual, contraverranno se procederà senza remissione alcuna.

Item che nessuna persona ardisca nè presumma di tenere o fare alcuna sorte de barattaria, giocare o fare giocare in alcuno modo di nessuna sorte de giochi illiciti, nè fare ballare o fare festini in casa o in qual si vogli altro luogo, nè ventura de qual si voglia cose o robbe, sotto la pena che se contiene nelli bandi fatti per gli altri governatori, d' applicarsi, augmentarsi o diminuirsi secondo l'arbitrio di detto signor governatore.

Item che nessuno ardisca di giocàr a palla, a maglio per le strade publiche tanto dentro come fuori di Roma et nelli luoghi dove conversano genti, sotto pena dello arbitrio di esso signor governatore.

Item commanda et prohibisce per espresso ordine di S. B^{ne} che nessuna persona, anchor che fosse duca, marchese, conte, barone, signore di città, castella, feudatario, palatino, offitiale, gentilhomo o familiar loro o di qual si voglia reverendissimo o altri signori et loro palafrenieri o qual si vogli altra persona privilegiata, dal presente giorno in poi, ardisca nè presumma, per qual si voglia causa, di portar bastoni atti ad offendere nè altr' armi che spade, pugnale et giacco, sotto pena di tre squassi de corda et de venticinque scudi d' oro et altre pene ad arbitrio del signor governatore, et, passata un' hora di notte portare spada, pugnali, cortelli più lunghi d'un palmo, bastone di grossezza atto ad offendere, rottelle, mazze ferrate, pallotte di piombo, sassi, balestre da passatori, o pallotte, polzoni, o qual si voglia sorte di armi, tanto deffensive quanto offensive, et così coperte come discoperte, sotto pena di tre squassi di fune da darsegli in publico et di cinquanta scudi d' oro oltra la perdita dell' armi da pagarsi ipso facto alla Camera Apostolica. Et siano tenuti gl' hosti alli loro hospiti et li portannari delle porte di Roma a tutti quelli ch' intraranno in Roma fargli intendere tal prohibitione del portar dell' armi, sotto la medesima pena, eccettuando impero tutti quelli i qual son ministri et prefetti sopra la iustitia et loro servitori.

Item, considerando esso signor governatore quanto sia pericoloso et tenere di schioppi et archibusi a rota piccoli, quali hanno la canna da dua palmi in giu, prohibisce et comanda ad ogni et qualunque persona, come di sopra, che da qui avanti non ardisca nè presumma tenere in casa nè portare nè far portare nè usare detti schioppi nè archibusi, nè vendergli etiam per mercanti nè fargli vender per altre persone ; anzi fra otto giorni proximi da venire ciaschuno gli debba effettualmente denuntiarli ad esso signor governatore, sotto penà a qualli i quali gli portaranno etiam disarmati e senza le rote, et gli saranno trovati addosso, della forca, et a quelli gli saranno trovati in casa, ad arbitrio di esso signor governatore ; a qual pene si procederà con ogni cellere esecutione, et a qualunque persone le terrano in casa o nelle loro botteghe o in altri luoghi et non gli haveranno denuntiati, passati detti otto giorni, incorreranno in pena di trecento scudi d'applicarsi ipso facto et senz' altra dechiaratione alla r^da Cam^a Apostolica, et della galea per dui anni o piu o meno ad arbitrio di esso signor governatore. Et si ne farà esecutione rigorosa et si procederà etiam nelle sopradecte cose per via d' inquisitione, et si starà al giuramento et detto d'un testimonio solo degno di fede ad arbitrio di esso signor governatore ; et allo accusatore, il quale sarà tenuto segreto, se gli darà la parte de la pena pecuniaria, et passati detti otto giorni, se fara cercare per il bargello et suoi essequtori senza rispetto alcuno e publicamente nelle case nelle quali parrà ad esso signor governatore.

Item, per provedere alli scandali, quali giornalmente occorrono, per l' andare che si fa per Roma con li cocchi furiosamente, prohibisce et comanda a tutti gli cocchieri di qualsivoglia persona, che da hoggi innanzi non ardisca nè presumma di giorno nè di notte andare con cocchi furiosamente per la città di Roma ne sue strade publiche, sotto pena di tre squassi di corda, alla quale se procederà senza alcuna remissione. Ma debbano andar con passo honesto et moderato, di modo che ogniuno possa antivedere et scansarsi. Et in la medesima pena incorreranno tutti gli servitori et famigli, barilari·et portatori di grano, quali senza proposito faranno correr overo andare furiosamente li lor cavalli per le strade publiche ; notificandosi che incorrendo in tal prohibitione da due volte in su, oltra le pene sopradette, se gli darà pena la galea ; et si procederà ancora per via d'inquisitione.

Item comanda a tutti homicidiali e banditi o disfidati, non solamente dalle terre, luoghi meditae vel immediate soggetti alla sancta Sede Apostolica et iurisdittione di S. Beat^ne, ma d'ogni altro luogo ancora che sia fuora della decta iurisdictione di S. Sta et Sede Apostolica, che tra dua giorni prossimi debbano effettualmente essersi partiti di Roma e suo territorio e distretto, altramente, passato decto termine, si procederà contro di loro a cattura et punitione delle persone, vista la forma di detti bandi o disfidationi et delitti commessi.

Et similmente ordina qual si voglia persona che havesse per sigurezza sua ottenuto alcuno salvo condotto o fidanza, qual non habbi presentato fin qui al decto monsignor governatore, lo debba infra sei giorni dal dì della publicatione del presente bando haver presentato avanti S. Signoria, accio ne possa far parola con S. B^{ne} et havere espresso ordine di bocca di S. S^{tà} come si debbia governare circa dette fidanze et salvi condotti ; et non le presentando tra decto termine, di commissione di S. B^{ne} Sua Sig^{la} ex nunc dechiara detti salvi condotti et fidanze per nulle et di niun vigore et fa intender che, non ostante detti salvi condotti et fidanze, si procederà contra di loro secondo che altrimente sarà di iustitia.

Item comanda a tutti li baroni di Roma, a tutte le communità et università et a qual si vogli altro signore o particolare persona et etiam alli habitanti in Roma, che non debbiano in li loro luoghi, case et habitationi, tanto in Roma come fuori, dar ricetto a detti homicidiali o banditi et diffidati, nè recettar delinquenti di qualunque sorte, nè darli da mangiare o bevere, nè aiuto o favore in qual si voglia modo, sotto le pene che si contengono nella Clementina et nelle sacre constitutioni et statuti et bandi [di] suoi predecessori, et altre pene ad arbitrio di S. S^{tà} et di esso signor governatore.

Item che qual si vogli persona vagabonda et senza essercitio o partito alcuno debbiano infra tre giorni haver disgomberato la città di Roma, altramente saranno presi et mandati in galea per quel tempo parerà ad esso signor governatore, et nella medesima pena incorreranno tutti gli mendicanti che son sani et gagliardi et gli ruffiani et giuntatori.

Item a tutti et singuli armaroli, lanciari, spadari et mercanti ancora del l' arte bianca et a tutti li altri, etiam non mercanti, a chi spettarà il presente bando, per authorita del nostro officio, per il presente tenore facciamo intendere et notifichiamo che dalla publicatione di questo, sotto pena di escommunicatione, confiscatione de' tutti et singuli lor beni et della galea et altre pene del nostro arbitrio da imponergli, non ardischino ne presummano vendere ne far vendere publicamente, ne secretamente, ne imprestare a persona alcuna, di qual si voglia stato, grado, conditione o preminenza se siano a sia, alcuna sorte d'arme defensive overo offensive senza espressa licenza.

Item il sig^r governatore dichiara quanto alle quadriglie della notte, che, oltre le pene delle armi, se alcuno sarà trovato in più di quattro con l'armi, che incorrano nella pena della galea.

Item che nessuna persona, come di sopra, ardischi d' impedire in alcun modo l'essequtioni, ancora che pretendessero che fossero ingiuste, nè far resistenza in alcun modo con fatti o con parole overo con arme a qual si voglia essecutor della corte, nè ingiuriargli in alcun modo, et che nessuno ardisca o presumma farsi ragione da se medesimo, concitare tumulti o gridare publicamente, o invocar le case de potenti o gli nomi loro, nè brugiare, rompere o imbrattare porte, fenestre, gelosie o impannate di qual si voglia persona, ancorche fossero meretrici o cortigiane, nè in alcun modo offendere le persone loro, nè ricettare delinquenti di qualunque sorte, nè dargli magnare o bere, aiuto et favore in qual si voglia modo, nè portare di giorno alcuna sorte di bastone atto ad offendere, nè fare adunanze o conventicule le pene delle leggi communi, statuti, bolle, constitutioni, reformationi et bandi altre volte fatti et publicati, da estendersi ancora sino alla pena del ultimo suplicio inclusive ad arbitrio di esso signor governatore.

Item ordina et dichiara che quello che cappeggiarà, o con armi o senza, ipso facto se intenda esser incorso nella pena della forca, et chi l' accusarà et farà che venghi in mano della corte sarà premiato di cinquanta scudi contanti, ancora che fosse compagno nel cappeggiare, al quale sara perdonato per quella volta.

Item che tutti li medici, barbieri, chirurgi, hospitalieri et altri ricettanti feriti o altri delinquenti, incontinente et senza alcuna tardanza per se o per altri fidedigni siano tenuti denunciare o fare denunciare al prefato signor governatore o suo notario del criminale, sinceramente et sanza fraude, li nomi, cognomi, qualità, patria et altri segni et contrasegni di essi feriti et delinquenti, et la verità del caso, et se detti feriti o delinquenti non volessero specificar gli nomi loro et delli offendenti, non debbiano curarli ne recettarli, anzi il tutto come di sopra notificare sotto le pene si contengono nelli bandi delli predecessori, nelle qual pene incorreranno tutti gli patrini et rettori delle chiese, i quali sotterraranno quelli che fossero stati et [sic] ammazzati, senza notificarlo come di sopra.

Item renova tutti gl'altri bandi d' ogn' altro signor governatore sopra qual si voglia materia, dechiarando per il presente bando che nessuna piazza in Roma di qual si voglia signore et potentati sarà secura et che li essequtori cercaranno et piglieranno li delinquenti, et chi se opporrà a loro o nessuno di loro incorrerà la pena della vita et perdita de beni ad arbitrio di esso signor governatore, secondo la qualità delle persone.

Item in ciaschuno delli sopradetti casi si reserva facoltà et arbitrio di potere minuire o augmentare le pene secondo la qualità del tempo, del luogo, delle persone et de casi, et fa intendere alli accusatori et spie che sarranno tenuti secretissimi et premiati ogni volta che riportaranno cosa veruna alla corte di Sua Sig^{ria} ; et ogni uno si guardi de contravenire e dalla mala ventura.

Datum etc.

[a tergo alia manu :] 14. Romana. Banno generale del modo del vivere della citta, 1555.

[Castel S. Angelo, Arm. 8, ord. II., t. 5, p. 15—18b. Secret Archives of the Vatican.]

16. Consistory of January 10th, 1556.[1]

Romae die veneris 10 ianuari, 1556.

Consistorium. . . . Postea S^{mas} longo sermone dixit, se velle procedere ad reformationem quam multi pontifices se facturos promiserant et tamen nil hactenus factum fuerat et ad id deputare intendebat personas idoneas.

[Acta consist. cancell., VII., Consistorial Archives of the Vatican.]

17. Bernardo Navagero to Venice.[2]

1556, Januar. 11, Rom.

. . . In questo consistoro,[3] dopo lunghissime audientie de cardinali, il Papa entrò a parlare della riforma e disse, che ogni giorno conosceva esser asseso in quel supremo grado per voler di Dio, perchè vedea S. Divina Maestà supplir a tutte le imperfettion sue, sì dell' animo come del corpo, che in questa età decrepita gli dava forza di soportar li travagli et fatiche

---

[1] See *supra*, p. 186, n. 1. [2] See *supra*, p. 186, n. 1, and Ancel Concile, II.
  [3] di hieri.

che porta con se il Papato et gli meteva in animo la cosa della reforma, la qual volea far in effetto così come li passati pontefici da 60 anni in qua la proponeano in parole ; che pero S. Stà reformeria prima se ; onde havea proposto li tre cardinali che gia scrissi al Datariato acciò lo regolassero, et che, se ben ella ne patirà, trazendo il suo viver da quello, pur che se restrenzerà, perchè la natura è contenta de poco ; et che, fatto questo, li altri se preparino che reformerà loro ancora, accennando la Cancellaria, Penitentiaria, la Camerlengaria, la vita de cardinali et la perpetuità de i beneficii con li regressi, accessi et altre introdutioni, aggiongendo che, reformata la corte, vorrà poi senza alcun respetto toccar li principi. Et essendo stato, secondo il solito di S. Stᵗᵉ, copioso et vehemente, messe fine al concistoro, per esser l'hora tarda. . . .

[Copy. Cod. 9445, 88ᵇ —89. Library of St. Mark,Venice.]

18. BERNARDO NAVAGERO TO VENICE.[1]

1556, Januar. 18, Rom.

At an audience on Jan. 17th with the Pope u.a. : . . . Et qui vogliamo dir a voi con molta confidentia quel che habbiamo detto più volte all' una parte et all' altra, che a componer questi doi principi non vi è altro mezo che noi, et gli habbiamo detto la causa che è questa, che cadaun de quei principi sanno per molte prove che non possono ruinar l'avversario ; possono ben l'un all' altro far de danni, de prendersi qualche città et con la guerra lunga roinar li suoi stati di danari et di homeni : che uno vinchi et abbassi del tutto l'altro deve esser già, per l'esperientia di tante cose passate, for di speranza ; ma esser quasi certo che a quella parte ove noi si accostassemo, accrescessamo tante forze che l'altro potria dubitare grandemente della universal sua ruina, et potrebbe esser, magnifico ambasciatore, che questa paura te questo modo di parlare che gli havemo fatto, gli facesse un giorno fare qualche bona deliberatione, et vi vogliamo dir che habbiamo fatto delle bravure a questo effetto et non habbiamo voluto alcun di loro per compagno, li volemo per sudditi et sotto questi piedi come si conviene et come ha voluto ch' ha edificata questa s. Chiesa et ci ha posto in questo grado, et prima che far una viltà vossamo morire, ruinar' ogni cosa et appicciar foco in tutte quattro le parti del mondo.   Li nostri

---

[1] See *supra*, pp. 69, n. 2 ; 188, n. 2 ; 189, n. 1.

predecessori pur troppo hanno abbassato questa s. Sede et col tanto temer li principi hanno fatto dell' indegnità, onde ne sono causate infiniti disordini. The complaints of the Spanish clergy would be remedied. Et per poter far meglio queste cose, vogliamo cominciarla riforma da noi et proveder al Datariato. The following passage in ANCEL, Concile, 18 bis via. Then comes the following characteristic speech of the Pope : Et perche Christo cel comanda, gratis accepistis, gratis date, parole di colui qui dixit et facta sunt, mandavit et creata sunt, che voglio dubitar io che Sua Divina M^{tà}, che mi ha notrito fino alli 80 anni, al presente mi abandoni ? Et quando io volse lassar ogni cosa, trovai una quarantena de homeni segnalatissimi et boni (che un papa non si saria sdegnato di haverli), i quali lassorono officii et beneficii et vennero a servirmi ; et molti anni mi sono intertenuto senza saper da chi mi fosse dato il vivere, et pur non ho fatte simonie, et come cardinal ancora son stato un poco d'anni senza haver niente quando non hebbi il possesso dell' arcivescovato di Napoli che mi era tenuto da tiranni, nè io mi degnai dirne pur una parola, et non mi mancò cosa alcuna. Perche voglio temere che mi habbi da mancar adesso ? Et quando per il Signor Dio volesse che al presente mi mancasse, sostenerei di andar accattando con una scudella prima che haver tutte le commodità per questa via indiretta con ruina dell' anima mia et di tanti altri che vengono dietro. Hor per concluderla, magnifico ambasciator, rengratiamo Christo (et qui si cavo la bereta) che ci ha dato quest' animo di far senza alcun rispetto l'honor di S. M^{tà} et il bene di questa Santa Sede. Noi procuraremo la causa di Dio, et S. M^{ta} procurarà la nostra. Habbiamo a punto hoggi raccordato ad alcuni auditori di Rota, che vedino et pensino bene con quest' altri dottori, che gli deputaremo, sopra queste cose, et non si lassaremo ingannar, perchè della simonia habbiamo letto quello che ne dicono theologi et canonisti, tanto che potemo dir esserne instruttissimi, et la dottrina del nostro s. Thomaso in questa come in tutte le altre cose ne ha fatto rissolver christianamente ; quando questi ne haverano referito il parer loro, gli faremo quelle provisioni che seranno necessarie. Mi disse poi S. S^{tà} che le sue genti hormai haveano occupato la maggior et meglior parte del stato del conte di Bagno, et che quel poverino si ravederia del suo mal consiglio. Et essendo durato il ragionamento di S. S^{tà} per buon spacio,

presi licentia havendola rengratiata della communicatione et
laudata de i magnanimi suoi dissegni con parole convenienti. . .

[Copy. Cod. 9445, 91—91[b]. Library of St. Mark, Venice.]

19. PROCEEDINGS OF THE PAPAL REFORM COMMISSION ON
JANUARY 20TH, 1556.[1]

Acta super reformatione Ecclesiae
sub Paulo IIII pontifice max° an. MDLVI.

Prima Congregatio.—Pontifex exponit promptitudinem
animi et desiderii sui circa universalem Ecclesiae reformationem, proponitque caput a quo sit initium auspicandum.

Cum sanctissimus in Christo pater et dominus noster dominus Paulus divina providentia papa quartue, iam inde ab
initio assumptionis suae animum adiecisset ad ea facienda
quae honori Dei et fidei suae catholicae exaltationi conducere
viderentur, nihil sibi antiquius fuit quam ut generali ipsius
Ecclesiae reformationi omne studium et operam navaret.
Quam quidem intentionem et si perpetuo ab ipso pontificatus
initio retinuerit, eam tamen ob diversa impedimenta et publicas
occupationes, quae hoc medio tempore acciderunt, executioni
hactenus, non sine animi sui ingenti dolore, demandare non
potuit. Verum, ne hoc tam sanctum et salutare Beat[is] suae
propositum diutius in ipsius Ecclesiae detrimentum et animarum dispendium differretur, ipsi reformationi absque ul-
teriori mora initium, Deo favente, dare constituit. Et licet
pontifex, Spiritu Sancto duce, ac potestate sibi a Deo tradita,
per se solum hanc provinciam absolvere potuisset, tamen,
quia ubi est multitudo sapientum ibi est salus et verum consilium, decrevit rem ipsam cum venerabilibus fratribus suis
S. R. E. cardinalibus primo, deinde cum aliquibus episcopis et
praelatis ac etiam omnis ordinis etiam inferioris sacrae theo-
logiae professoribus, nec non canonum et legum peritis, con-
ferre atque examinare, ut tandem, Deo ipso iuvante, reformatio
ipsa communi omnium voto et consilio in Ecclesia Dei
decerneretur.

Quare hodie, die lunae xx mensis ianuarii, anno a nativitate
Domini MDLvj, hora xx, vocatis ad se cardinalibus, praelatis,

_____
[1] See *supra*, p. 187, n. 1, and MASSARELLI 286.

theologis et aliis infrascriptis, ad ipsius omnipotentis Dei gloriam et religionis chistrianae incrementum, congregationem primam super ipso negocio reformationis, in palatio apostolico, in aula magna superiori, quae Constantini nuncupatur, habuit. Quibus dominis et praelatis sic congregatis Sanctitas Sua primum significavit eius pium desiderium et animum reformandi abusus in Ecclesia Dei hominum et temporum iniuria subortos ; retulitque labores, quos hactenus superiores eius summi pontifices, etiam congregatione concilii generalis, consumpserunt ; et quod, licet res ipsa frustra hucusque tentata fuerit, sperare se tamen in bonitate Dei eam aliquando praestari posse. Qua quidem in re omnem operam, omnem diligentiam et curam esse adhibituram ; et pro qua nihil laboris, nihil incommodi nihilve alterius cuiusvis oneris, etiam cum propriae vitae periculo, haud subituram esse. Cum autem caput et radicem totius reformationis esse haeresim simoniacam ostendisset, inprimis et ante omnia ad eam eradicandum et penitus evellendam omni conatu vacandum esse comprobavit Et iure quidem ac merito Sanctitas. Sua ab ipsius simoniae extirpatione initium sumit. Nam nihil profecto est quod magis Ecclesiae Dei officiat et ministerium sacerdotale commaculet atque perturbet, nihilque magis animas illaqueet et ad interitum ducat, quam simonia. Quam certo eo magis pontifex evellere debet, cum non sequutae hucusque ipsius Ecclesiae reformationis praceipuam et solam fere causam detractores et haeretici omnes in Pontifices maximos retulerint, eos scilicet reformationem hanc et noluisse et distulisse, propter lucri nescio cuius, qui in datariato fit, amissionem. At summus et vere sanctissimus noster pontifex, lucra, divitias et mundana omnia parvipendens, solum Deum et animarum salutem prae oculis habens, eam ipsam reformationem, nullius sui incommodi, nullius damni (sed neque damnum existimat amitti quod iniuste quaeritur) neque cuiusvis carnalis affectus habita ratione, omnino constituere et ab ipsius simoniae, ut dictum est, eradicatione initium sumere decrevit. In qua sane eradicatione facienda eorum patrum, qui aderant, iudicium et consilium libenter se audire velle et cupere declaravit : eos que propterea monuit et hortatus est, eis nihilominus in virute sanctae obedientiae praecipiens ut ipsi materiae explicandae et declarandae studium et diligentiam adhiberent, ita ut, suo tempore revocati, possent super ea re sententias dicere ; comminatusque est eis ut id in ipsis sententiis dicerent quod secundum Deum et conscientiam sentirent, fugerentque in omnibus vitium adulationis atque assentationis, constanter eis asseverans ut qui aliter facerent, praeter id quod a Deo dignam poenam reciperent, Sanctitatis etiam suae indignationem non effugerent : qui vero veritatem pure et syncere, iuxta eorum captum et capacitatem, dicerent, et a Deo ipso premium et a Sanctitate Sua laudem essent reportaturi. Exposuitque caput principale, super quo eorum studiis invigilare quodque discutere et examinare deberent, An videlicet usus potestatis datae a Christo domino nostro Petro, Ecclesiae suae capiti, possit cadere sub precio ; admonens iterum patres, ut lubenti animo id laboris studendi et veritatis perquirendae susciperent, et quod deinde invenissent, id verbo, suo tempore, dicere et in scriptis etiam ponere procurarent.

Quibus dictis, rogavit rever^{rum} dominorum cardinalium sententias, an videlicet super iis, quae Sanctitas Sua dixerat, aliquid ipsis patribus ulterius explicandum iudicarent. Cumque omnes proposita a Sanctitate Sua collaudassent, dimittitur congregatio et patres omnes recesserunt, hora circiter xxiii.

[Concilio, 79, 32—33. Secret Archives of the Vatican.]

20. BERNARDO NAVAGERO TO VENICE.[1]

1556, Januar. 21, Rom.

Hoggi è stato consistoro . . . In questo consistoro S. S^{tà} disse alcune parole cerca la reforma che volle far al tutto, dicendo alli rev^{mi} cardinali che non si spaventassero per ciò ; che quanto ella facea era per recuperar la prima et antica giurisdition della Sede Apostolica, accennando la riforma de principi, la qual reaquistada, ognuno saria felice et felicissimo il sacro collegio. Per poter procedere a questa riforma havea Sua S^{tà} tre giorni avanti fatto una congregatione de cardinali, auditori di Rota et altri dottori et generali delle religioni, nella quel parlò con tanta eloquentia et forza nella materia della simonia che accesse et infiammò ogni uno facendolli conoser che in questo solo stava la vera riforma della Chiesa, aggiongendo quasi li medesmi concetti che disse a me, et io le scrissi per le ultime mie. . . .

[Copy. Cod. 9445, 97^b —98. Library of St. Mark, Venice.]

¹ See *supra* pp. 187, n. 2 ; 189, n. 2.

21. BERNARDO NAVAGERO TO VENICE.[1]

1556, Januar. 25, Rom.

Report of to-day's audience.

. . . Et qui entrò[2] a confirmarmi quel che mi disse l' audientia passata, che ella non volleva cessar fino che non facea
questa riforma, et che, quando no la faci, se io la vedessi far
miracoli et ressussitar morti, non gli dovesse creder ; che
ella o la farrà over crepperà soto el peso ; che vuol comensiar
dalla sua pelle et scorticarlla et riformarlla, per poter poi
liberamente riformar li altri, non solamente prelati, ma li
imperii, li regni et signorie ; et che spera nel Sig^re Iddio che,
quando habbi reconciliata la chiesia con Christo, Sua Divina
M^ta farà che li principi fatiano la pace tra loro in quel modo
che la me disse l' altra audientia ; che ambi, temendo che
ella non se accosti all' avversario, potriano far qualche compositione a benefitio della Christianità. Et qui si dilatò nelle
cose gia dete altre volte, che non voglio replicar, con questo
particular cercha la riforma, che non volle con multiplicità di
bolle piene di belli prohemii et con finti concilii et altre desipulle
[sic] ingannar el mondo, ma far effetti ; et che per ciò havea
chiamata la congregatione de cardinali, auditori di Rota,
avocati concistoriali, capi delle religioni et altri dottori, et
impostolli che studino il caso della simonia ; et che vi aggion-
gierà delli altri grand'homeni et boni che serà come un concilio,
senza chiamarsi concilio. Et presto li convocherà a un altra
volta per dar expedition al negotio, nel quale ella non si las-
sieria struchar [sic] capelli nel gli occhi ; per che rengratiava
Iddio che in questo caso de simonia havea veduto quanto si
potea ; la qual simonia disse che è chiamata herexia per
l' effeto che fa. Et qui allegò la sententia di S. Pietro contra
Simon Mago, che volsse comprar el Spirito Santo ; et appresso
disse molte altre cose piene di dotrina con tanto adetto che si
vedea che venivano dal core . . .

[Copy. Cod. 9445, 102^b—103^b. Library of St. Mark, Venice.]

22. PROCEEDINGS OF THE PAPAL REFORM COMMISSION ON JANUARY 29TH, 1556.[3]

Congregatio 2^a. Pontifex iterum declarat firmissimam eius
intentionem circa Ecclesiae reformationem, proponitque
modum procedendi.

---

[1] See *supra* p. 189, n. 2.   [2] The Pope.   [3] See *supra*, p. 190, n. 1.

Die mercurii xxix eiusdem mensis ianuarii . . .

Primusque omnium cardinalis Bellaius sacri collegii decanus laudavit modum propositum a Sanctitate Sua ; deinde, cum cardinalis Turnonius petiisset a Sancte Sua declarari de qua simonia ipsa Beatitudo Sua intelligeret, an videlicet de ea quae iure divino prohibita est, an vero quae iure positivo uti simonia etiam prohìbetur, Pontifex ipse, multis verbis ac rationibus, improbavit ac detestatus est eam distinctionem, quam canonis- tae et alii doctores faciunt, duplicem videlicet esse simoniam, alteram iure divino prohibitam, quae prohibita est quia simonia, alteram prohibitam iure positivo, quae ideo simonia censetur, quia prohibita ut simonia ; declarans inprimis simoniacam labem non posse neque ab angelis neque ab ulla mundana potestate constitui, sed tantum ab ipso Deo : ac propterea nullam aliam esse simoniam nisi unam et eam iure divino prohibitam : id autem quod iure positive prohibetur esse quidem malum, quia prohibitum ; verum quod sit simoniacum per prohibitionem non posse fieri. Quod enim annexum est rei spirituali, id etiam sapere simoniam, et quidem iure divino prohibitam, quousque ipsi rei spirituali annexum est, etiam quod sit aliquod mere temporale, ut praedium, domus et similia, sicuti etiam declaratur in capite Si quis obiecerit, p. q. III. Si autem res ipsa temporalis a spirituali separetur (quod iure positivo fieri protest), desinet cadere sub simonia. Commonuitque iterum patres ut similes distinctiones et aniles, ut aiebat, fabulas in dicendis sententiis devitarent, idque solum dicerent quod ad rem propositam conduceret. Deinde inter- rogavit dominos et patres, an aliqui eorum vellent super modo procedendi iam proposito aliquid dicere, vel qui magis voluis- sent, cedulam in scriptis mitterent . . .

[Concilio, 79, 35—36. Secret Archives of the Vatican.]

23. BERNARDO NAVAGERO TO VENICE.[1]

1556, Februar. 1, Rom.

Il Pontifice mercore chiamò congregatione de molti rev^mi cardinali, prelati, auditori di Rota, generali delle religioni et canonisti et volsse che fussero ancho li deputati de cadauna congregatione de offitiali, di modo che assendeno al numero quasi di 200 persone. In essa congregatione disse S. Stà che

---

[1] See *supra*, p. 190, n. 1

quelli che erano stati nella precedente congregatione sapevano et li altri potevano haver intexo, la mente di Sua Beat^ne esser di far la riforma et di cominciar da se, perche questo era meter la secure alla radice et serar la bocha ad ognuno ; che gli havea chiamati per farli intender che volea che studiassero la cossa della simonia per poterne dar poi li loro voti, come fossero chiamati un' altra volta, che saria presto, et chel ponto stava qui, se per la collatione de benefitii et gratie ecclexiastiche si poteva pigliar danari, essendo in ciò la suprema authorità del Pontifice data da Christo a Pietro, che hanno costituito le compositioni et le anate ; et che ogni un se preparasse a dir liberamente quel che sentiva per l'honor di Dio, senza rispetto dell' interesse di Sua San^tà et de altri ; et che per non far confusione, ella se havea pensatto che li voti per classes fossero piu expeditte : queste classe loro chiamano li theologhi una, li canonisti unaltra, et cossi ogni professione una classe : a queste deputeria Sua S^tà cardinali della professione, li quali pigliariano li voti di cadauno della sua classe in scritura ; et per non moltiplicar in repliche de ragioni, da tutti tratteriano un summario et quello refeririano a Sua San^tà, alla quale se alcuno volesse dir altro, ella l' ascolteria et dellibereria quel che fosse il bene et honor di questa Santa Sede et di tutta la christianità. Et aggionse che, se a qualche uno non piaceva questo modo, ne racordasse un migliore. Fu risposto che piaceva quanto Sua San^tà havea detto. Ne voglio tacere che il rev^mo Grimani patriarcha de Acquileggia parlò con molta satisfatione de ogni uno, laudo la bona mente di Sua Sanc^tà, disse chel modo delli voti per classes era perfetto, et che esso nella materia proposta meteria el suo voto in scritura, secondo chel Signor Iddio gli inspirerà . . .

[Copy. Cod. 9445, p. 106—106^b. Library of St. Mark, Venice.]

24. PROCEEDINGS OF THE PAPAL REFORM COMMISSION ON FEBRUARY 2ND, 1556.[1]

Congregatio generalis.—Iniungitur praelatis ut ipsi ex eis 24 eligant pro classibus super reformatione constituendis.

Die dominica 2 februarii dicti anni 1556 in festo purificationis B. Mariae, hora circiter XVI., in aula quae Pappagalli

[1] See *supra*, p. 190, n. 1.

vulgo dicitur, antequam Pontifex iret ad audienda sacra, convenere coram Sanctitate Sua omnes praelati et alii qui in superiori cedula nominantur ; quibus praelatis Pontifex significavit mentem suam esse ut ipsi xxiiii ex eis eligerent ac deputarent, qui una cum aliis a Sanct^{te} Sua deputandis, per 3 classes distincti curam particularem suscepturi essent negocii reformationis. Ac propterea eo ipso mane post celebrationem missae congregarentur in eodem sacello et ipsam electionem facerent. Admonuitque eos ut, omni carnali affectu seposito solumque Deum et conscentiam prae oculis habentes, eos dumtaxat eligerent qui ad tantum onus suscipiendum idonei et digni fuissent. His dictis, itum est in sacellum Sixti, ubi candelae benedictae distributae sunt, sacraque ipsa, celebrante rev^{mo} domino cardinali Messanensi, peracta fuerunt.

[Concilio, 79, 37^b . Secret Archives of the Vatican.]

25. BERNARDO NAVAGERO TO VENICE.[1]

1556, Februar. 8, Rom.

. . . Desiderando Sua San^{tà} dare piu presto che si possa principio alla riforma, come havea dato deputatione de 24 cardinali per questo effetto, così ha voluto che vi siano 24 prelati et che tra loro si ellegano con voti secreti, come fecero il giorno di Nostra Donna ultimamente passato in capella dopo la messa et la cerimonia del benedir et dar le candelle, che, essendo ivi seduti al numero di 63, ellessero li 24 notati nella acclusa poliza, qual mando a V^{ra} Serenità ; et la ballotatione fu con le fave bianche de si et negre de no. Erano presidenti che contorono i votti li rev^{mi} Bellai decano primo vescovo, Moron primo prete et Ferneze primo diacono. Il terzo giorno poi Sua Sanc^{tà} chiamo congregatione de tutti li rev^{mi} cardinali, con invitarlli dopoi a disnar seco, nella qual divise li 24 cardinali eleti in tre classe, a otto per una, si come V^{ra} Ser^{tà} vederrà per la acclusa poliza ; et la divisione è fatta secondo l' ordine che cadauno siede. Simil divisione dicono che se farà delli 24 prelati, et si dice che il Pontifice accresserà cadauna di queste di soi [sic] altri theologhi et canonisti, et poi se li darano i dubii et cadauna classe li disputerà tra se, et quello che sarà discuso et concluzo referirano al Pontifice . . .

[Copy. Cod. 9445, 109^b —110. Library of St. Mark, Venice.]

[1] See *supra*, p. 190, n. 1.

26. PRIVILEGE OF POPE PAUL IV. FOR THE OFFICIALS OF
THE ROMAN INQUISITION.[1]

1556, Februar. 11, Rom.

Paulus IIII.

Privilegium apostolicum immunitatis officialium actu
inservientium S^{to} Officio a datiis et gabellis etc.

Motu proprio etc. Attendentes onera domui[2] Inquisitionis
haereticae pravitatis de Urbe incumbentia et ad grata, quae
dilecti filii ipsius domus officiales et ministri nobis et universae
reipublicae christianae quotidie impendunt, obsequia debitum
respectum habentes, eosque specialibus favoribus et gratiis
prosequi volentes, domum ipsam ac omnes et singulos illius
ac dictae Inquisitionis actu deservientes officiales et ministros,
nunc et pro tempore existentes, ab omnibus et singulis datiis,
gabellis et portarum dohanis, vectigalibus, impositionibus,
collectis, subsidiis, etiam caritativis, angariis et oneribus
ordinariis et extraordinariis tam realibus quam personalibus
etiam mixtis, ac publicis et privatis, etiam ratione vini, grani,
animalium et quarumcunque aliarum rerum cuiuscunque
generis et qualitatis existentium, tam per mare et aquam
dulcem quam per terram undecunque ad hictam Urbem pro
tempore delatarum et conductarum, quae in eadem Urbe
illiusque districtu ac alias ubicunque locorum nobis et S. R. E.
in spiritualibus et temporalibus subiectorum exiguntur et
exigi consueverunt, et quae ex quacunque causa hactenus
imposita reperiuntur, et in posterum ex quibusvis etiam quan-
tumlibet necessariis, iustissimis et urgentissimis causis, etiam
per nos et successores nostros Romanos Pontifices pro tempore
existentes imponi et exigi contigerit necnon contributionibus
in illis faciendis, tam pro eorum usu quam alias quomodolibet
et quandocunque emendo et vendendo, necnon refectione
stratarum ac viarum Urbis illiusque contributione ex certa
nostra scientia penitus eximimus et totaliter liberamus, ac
omnibus illis et eorum signulis liberos, immunes et exemptos
facimus et constituimus ac in posterum esse et censeri debere
volumus, decernimus et declaramus. Necnon datia, gabellas
et alias impositiones huiusmodi per eos a die electionis nostre
ad summi apostolatus apicem debita gratiose donamus et

---

[1] See *supra*, p. 264, n. 2.   [2] Ms. : domus.

remittimus eosque ad illorum solutionem non teneri volumus. Necnon domui illiusque officialibus et ministris predictis quod omnibus et singulis privilegiis, immunitatibus, exemptionibus, libertatibus, favoribus et gratiis, quibus nostrum et eiusdem S. R. E. cardinalium palatia et domus eoromque ministri, officiales et personae, tam circa gabellas illarumque exemptionem et refectionem viarum et stratarum huiusmodi quam alias utuntur, potiuntur et gaudent ac uti, potiri et gaudere poterunt quomodolibet in futurum, uti, potiri et gaudere valeant in omnibus et per omnia, perinde ac si illis specialiter et expresse concessa forent, concedimus et indulgemus. Ac omnibus et singulis datiorum, gabellarum, vectigalium, subsidiorum, impositionum, collectarum et onerum huiusmodi exactoribus collectoribus ac quibusvis aliis ubilibet constitutis, necnon viarum praedictarum magistris pro tempore existentibus, cuiuscunque dignitatis, status, gradus, ordinis vel conditionis existant et quacunque ecclesiastica vel mundana auctoritate seu dignitate vel praeeminentia praefulgeant, in virtute sanctae obedientiae et sub excommunicationis latae sententiae ac mille ducatorum pro una fabricae basilicae Principis Apostolorum de Urbe et altera medietatibus dictae domui Inquisitionis applicandorum et a contraventoribus irremissibiliter exigendorum poenis eo ipso, si contrafecerint, incurrendis, ne domum Inquisitionis illusque officiales et ministros huiusmodi ad aliquam solutionem premissorum onerum et impositionum occasione coarctare aut aliquid de eis exigere, vel super praemissis aut illorum usu seu possessione vel quasi, directe vel indirecte, quovis quaesito colore vel ingenio molestare, impedire, vexare aut inquietare quoquo modo audeant seu praesumant districtius inhibemus ; non obstantibus quibusvis apostolicis constitutionibus et ordinationibus, necnon dictae Urbis statutis et reformationibus etiam iuramento etc. roboratis, privilegiis quoque, indultis et litteris apostolicis quibusvis et sub quibuscunque tenoribus et formis ac cum quibusvis clausulis et decretis concessis et confirmatis etc., quibus omnibus etiamsi de eorum etc. illorum tenores etc. pari motu derogamus, caeterisque contrariis quibuscunque cum clausulis opportunis.

Concessum ut petitur in praesentia Domini nostri Papae. B. Card. Tranensis. Et cum absolutione a censuris ad effectum etc., et de exemptione, libertione, constitutione, voluntate,

decreto, declaratione, concessione, indulto, remissione, dona-
tione, inhibitone, derogatione et aliis praemissis, quae hic pro
singillatim et ad partem repetitis habeantur, latissime extend-
endis etc. etiam in forma gratiosa et ex certa scientia, etiam si
videbitur, cum opportuna deputatione executorum qui assistant
etc., cum facultate citandi etiam per edictum etc. et inhibendi
etiam sub censuris et poenis ecclesiasticis ac etiam pecuniariis,
aggravandi etc., contradictores etc. compescendo etc. invocato
etc. auxilio brachii saecularis. Et cum derogatione con-
stitutionum de una et duabus dietis, non tamen de tribus
latissime extendenda. Et quod praemissorum omnium et
singulorum etiam qualibet invocatione nominum, cogno-
minum, nuncupationum aliorumque circa praemissa quomodolibet exprimendorum maior et verior specificatio et expressio
fieri possit in litteris per breve nostrum, si videbitur, exped-
iendis, seu, si videbitur, praesentium sola signatura sufficiat
et ubique fidem faciat, regula contraria non obstante. Et
pro usu domus et ministrorum actu deservientium ipsi domui,
occasione dictae domus dumtaxat.

Datum Romae apud sanctum Petrum tertio idus februarii
anno primo.[Copy. Cod. Barb. lat. 1502, 154—158 ; 1503,
68—71. Vatican Library.]

27. BERNARDO NAVAGERO TO VENICE.[1]

1556, Februar. 15, Rom.

. . . Entrando a dirmi che li Pontifici passatti e questi
ultimi havevano cosi abbassata la grandezza di questa Santa
Sede che di essi non si tenea conto alcuno, et che per la verità
a farsi stimar bezogna viver di modo che non possi esser locco
ad alcuna vera oppositione ; et che questo non abbastava ;
che bizognava ancho saper delle cose assai, et non se dar in
preda delli ministri et creder ad ogniuno ; et finalmente esser
talle che nissun prossumi o ardischi di poterci ingannar, haver
animo grande, non temer sorte alcuna di pericollo, stimar la
vita quanto si debe stimar et niente piu, non voller prencipi
per compagni, perche sono inferiori, et con non farssi parciale
con alcuno, tenendo sempre tutti in suspetto et timore.

Al che havendo detto io che tutte queste et molte altre
singular qualità si ritrovavano in S. Santᵃ, risservata per la

---

[1] See *supra*, p. 190, n. 2.

providentia di Dio in questi così importanti tempi a grado
così eccelso et honorato, fenisse dicendo : Dio voglia, magnifico
ambasciator, che siamo tali quali voi, per l'amor che ci portiate,
credete che siamo ; soggiongendomi : Siamo tutti hora intenti
a questa riforma, perche qui sta il tutto, nè maggior accressi-
mento alla Sede Apostolicha si può far di reputatione che per
questa via ; nè ce ne impedirano li tradimenti et iniquità di
questi imperiali, che scoprimo ogni giorno, alli quali rimediamo
al meglio che potemo, et si sforciamo che non ne trovino
imparati nè disarmati. Si ha proveduto alli lochi importanti
dello stato et si va provedendo ancho a questa città : staremo
a veder quel che farano et dove tenderano ; et non ci coglierano
al improviso. Sono tristi, magnifico ambasciator, et per tante
operationi loro fatte in Itallia sanno d' esser in odio d' ogni uno.
Come sono, temono tutti, perche conoscono haver chauxa. In
somma, non bisogna fidarsi. . . .
[Copy. Cod. 9445, 116—117. Library of St. Mark, Venice.]

28. BERNARDO NAVAGERO TO VENICE.[1]

1556, Mart. 14, Rom.

. . . Non volendo io restar questa settimana senza audientia
del Pontifice, andai eri ad accompagnarlo in S. Pietro alla
statione, come fecero molti cardinalli et ambassiatori ; et
havendo speso sua Beat^ne molto tempo nelle sue dovotioni et
poi in veder la capella che prencipio Paula III et ella fa finire,
si voltò a me et con segnalato favore verso V^ra Serenità,
abbassandosi molto perchè me ero ingenochiato, mi abbracciò
et basciò et disse che volea che tornasse hoggi per poter star
longamente mecho, che all' hora si atrovava stanco. Et da
questo è avenuto che, essendovi andato hoggi al hora ordinaria,
Sua San^tà fece licentiare li rev^mi Pixani, Armignac, Trani,
Motulla et Reumano, che erano nel antecamera et fece introdur
me ; et dappoi molte parolle affetuose verso V^ra Ser^tà, delle
qual la rengratiai come conveniva, mi disse. . . .[2]

29. BERNARDO NAVAGERO TO VENICE.[3]

1556, Mart. 28, Rom.

. . . Giobbio fù congregatione della prima classe sopra la
riforma in casa del rev^mo Bellai decano. La somma fù che 17

[1] See *supra*, p. 193, n. 1.
[2] The sequel [in translation] is in BROWN, VI., 1, n. 425.
[3] See *supra*, p. 194, n. 1.

dissero li loro voti sopra il ponto gia datto e che io mandai a V^{ra} Serenità ; et forono tre opinioni : una del vescovo di Feltre, che si potesse pigliar danari per uxo della potesta spirituale ; la seconda del vescovo di Sessa, che non si possino pigliar per alcun modo ; la terza del vescovo di Sinigagli, che si possino pigliar, ma a certo tempo et con certe conditioni.[1]

[Copy. Cod. 9445, 145—145^b. Library of St. Mark, Venice.]

30. BERNARDO NAVAGERO TO VENICE.[2]

1556, April 11, Rom.

. . . Sendosi trovati uno de questi giorni al disnar del Pontifice alquanti prelati, Sua Sant^à li fece chiamar nella su camera, dove con parlar latino puro, ornato et copioso, secondo il solito, li represe che non andavano alli suoi vescovatti, che lassavano la loro sposa vidua et il grege comessolli senza il lor pastore, et che al mancho[3] fino che si facea la riforma, la qualle con maggior forza li commeteria che andassero alla loro residentia, non consumassero el tempo in visite, in bancheti et forsi in giochi, ma studiassero per saper poi ben governar le loro peccorelle ; perchè era una grandissima vergogna che nelle capelle ove sedenno tanti vescovi se levassero frati, et ancho laici, ad insegnarlli ; che per il più questi fanno li sermoni che doveriano far essi. Il qual parlar di Sua Sant^à è stato quasi una capara a questi di quel che disegna di far. . . .

[Copy. Cod. 9445, 150^b. Library of St. Mark, Venice.]

31. MICHELE GHISLIERI TO THE INQUISITOR GIROLAMO DA GENOVA.[4]

1556, Juni 20, Rom.

. . . Quanto al Bogiano vedete d' intendere da quanto tempo in qua ha parlato con fra Paterniano da Pesaro, et se potessivo havere notitia ove se ritrovi et così frate Andrea da Scansano quantunque sfratato, et intendiate si loro erano di l' istesse opinioni heretiche.

Quanto dil mandarlo in galea i r^{mi} et ill^{mi} miei patroni, anzi Sua S^{tà}, fuggeno più che possono di mandare alcuno in galea, ne li mandano, salvo quelli delli quali non si possino sigurare de fura ; ben li fanno portar l' habbitello giallo con la croce roscia

---

[1] The sequel in ANCEL, 16.   [2] See *supra*, p. 235, n. 2.
[3] Ms : mondo.   [4] See *supra*, p. 270, n. 3.

per qualche anni, gli privano di ascoltare confessione, di potere leggere ne predicare, li assegnano un convento per pregione, dandoli degiunii et orationi per penitentia, imponendoli che si confessino almen una volta la settimana, ma ne la galea li pare penitentia da disperati o da dimonii et di poco frutto ; però gli mandano questi marrani, perche da molti di loro et quasi da tutti siamo aggabbati ; gli mandano ancora certi disgratiati, vacabundi, furfanti de i quali mal possiamo fidarsi. Però considerate le qualitate, l' età del detto Bogiano et considerate quanto di lui si può sperare et fate quel che Dio vi spira ; et se lui è secramentario, privatelo perpetuamente de la messa, concedendoli che si possi communicare come i laici una volta il mese. . . .

Di V. R^{da} P^{tà}

fra Michele Alesandrino

[Address] Al r^{do} padre fra Gironimo da Genova inquisitore del' heretica pravità padre osserv^{mo} .   Genova.

[Orig. Cod. E. VII., 15 of the University Library, Genoa.]

32. MICHELE GHISLIERI TO THE VICAR-GENERAL OF THE ARCHBISHOP OF GENOA.[1]

1556, August 29, Rom.

Rev^{mo} mgr mio osservandissimo.

Hò ricevuto quelle di V. R^{ma} S^{tà} delli xix del presente, nelle quali mi chiarisce della calunnia data al rev^{do} padre Inquisitore, che habbi cercato di ritirare V, R^{ma} S. dal esamine nella causa di maestro Alesandro. Però a chi vole servire a Christo convien sopportare tale et maggior' ingiurie con pacientia et considerare che quelli che altri calumniano piu si offendono loro medesimi che quelli che son calumniati. Però dovemo pregare il Sig^r Iddio che gli levi la cecità del core e gli doni lume. Et a V. R^{ma} S. humilmente basciando le mani mi raccomando.

Di Roma il dì 29 di agosto del Lvj

Di V. R^{ma} S^{ia}   minimo servitore

fra Michele Alisandrino.

[Address] Al rev^{mo} mons^r vescovo di Cavoli vicario archiepiscopale di Genova

sig^r mio osserv^{mo}   Genoa.

[Orig. Cod. E. VII., 15 of the University Library, Genoa.]

[1] See *supra*, p. 271, n. 1.

33. MICHELE GHISLIERI TO THE INQUISITOR GIROLAMO DA GENOVA.[1]

1556 September 3, Rom.

Rev^{do} padre

Oltra la resposta comune ad rev^{mo} mos^r vicario et a V. R., gli dico che chi vol servire a Dio in questo santo offitio non conviene temere minaccie ma haver sol' Iddio, la verità et le giustitia davanti agl' occhi, et intervenga quel che si vole ; benche quelli medemi che minacciano vedendo la constantia del' animo ne rimangano edificati, si non sonno piu che maligni.

Da Roma ali 3 de settembre del 56.

Di V. R^{da} P^à

fra Michel Alisandrino.

[Address] Al R^{do} P. fra Girolamo da Genova inquisitore contro la heretica pravità padre oss^{do}

Genoa.

[Orig. Cod. E. VII., 15 of the University Library, Genoa.]

34. CARDINAL MORONE TO CARDINAL POLE.[2]

1556, November 28, Rom.

. . . Dico adunque intorno a questo trattato della pace brevemente : Se al ser^{mo} rè d'Inghilterra mette conto haver la pace con N. S^{re} et con la Sede Apostolica (come per ogni ragione della salute dell' anime, dell' honore et dell' utile proprio deve metter conto), bisogna che S. M^{tà}, come principe veramente catholico et come buon figliuolo di Dio et della Chiesa et di questa Sta Sede, senza star su li pontigli dell' honore et sopra la giustificatione delle cose passate, s' indolcisca et intenerisca verso S. S^{tà} come verso il padre proprio, anzi più, essendo la paternità spirituale più veneranda che la carnale, et a questo bisogna che S. M^{tà} indirizzi tuti i pensieri suoi, per satisfare alla grave offesa ricevuta qui da questo rompimento. Tengo per fermo che S. S^{tà} si mitigarà alquanto et ripigliarà l' animo paterno verso S. M^{tà}, procedendosi con questi modi, altrimenti se S. S^{tà} resta con scrupulo che vi vada un minimo ponto dell' honor suo, il quale essa per il luoco che tiene stima esser honor di Dio, mai s' acquetarà la christianità et più presto S. S^{tà} patirà il martirio che lasciarsi condurre alla pace senza l' honor

---

[1] See *supra*, p. 271, n. 1.   [2] See *supra*, pp. 69, n. 1 ; 151, n. 1.

suo, inteso nel modo che S. S^{tà} intende ; il qual modo S. S^{tà} fonda nella pietà verso Dio et nella conservatione dell' officio suo in terra et nella salute di tutto 'l popolo christiano, tenendo per fermo che mai si potrà far cosa buona in tanti bisogni et perturbationi della christianità, o per estirpare le heresie o per pacificare la christianità, o per riformare la Chiesa et li costumi, o per resister al Turco, o per fare qual altra cosa buona si voglia, se l' honore del Vicario di Christo et di questa S^{tà} Sede non sta sopra il capo di tutti li christiani, et massime delli gran principi, come è quel ser^{mo} rè ; et sia certa V. S. Illma, se non si attende a questo scopo, che tutte le fatiche di pacificare S. S^{tà} saranno vane, et benche il rè di Francia mancasse di aiutare, come ha promesso, et che S. S^{tà} abandonata da tutto 'l mondo fosse ridotta allo estremo, nondimeno sarà inespugnabile per altra via, et non obstante che l' ill^{mo} cardinal Caraffa doppo Dio sia l' unico mezzo a piegare S. S^{tà}, credo però che in questo Sua Sig^{la} Illma non potrà rimuovere S. S^{tà} dal detto fine, tanto maggiormente parendo secondo il mondo che noi siamo restati nella guerra inferiori con perdita et devastatione di tante città, luoghi et paesi.

Supplico adunque V. S. R^{ma} voglia, non solo per se, ma per tutti li altri mezzi che crederà esser idonei, voglia forzarsi di persuadere S. M^{tà} a questa piena satisfattione verso S. S^{tà} et di parole et d' effetti. . . .

[Orig.   Arm. 64, t. 32, fol. 215—218^b .   Secret Archives of the Vatican.]

35. CARDINAL MORONE TO CARDINAL POLE.[1]

1556, December 12, Rom.

N. S^{re} ha havuto a caro li boni uffici fatti per V. S. R^{ma} et Illma col ser^{mo} rè d' Ispagna, et ha veduto la copia delle lettere che S. M^{tà} ha scritto a quella.   Ma S. S^{tà} guarda piu alli fatti che alle parole et sta sempre con suspetto che non si vadi fittamente et a camino di usurpare il resto della Sede Apostolica, facendo il fondamento suo sopra l' insulto fatto a questo stato et l' occupatione de tanti luoghi et città d' importanza : et suspica tanto peggio quanto ogni cosa si fa col pretesto della securità del regno de Napoli ; et S. S^{tà} non puo patire ch' alcuni cuculati, come dice, habbino consigliato ch' il rè lo possi

---

[1] See *supra*, pp. 69, n. 1 ; 151, n. 1.

fare giustamente per sicurezza sua ; et sempre sta sul suo honore et dignità diquesta S^tà Sede ; il qual, come gia scrisse, S. S^tà reputa honore di Dio.

Partì alli giorni passati da qui il sig^re don Francesco Pacecco, mandato dal sig^r duca d' Alba per l' accordio, et venedo a visitarmi et dimandarmi parere, li disse queste propositione per verissime.

Primo, che, se S. S^tà fosse stata in pregione et col pugnale alla gola, che mai haveria consentito alla restitutione di casa Colonna in Palliano, parendo a S. S^tà esser troppo indegno che con li esserciti più potenti si voglia impedir l' amministratione di qual principe si voglia in casa sua, et tanto più d'un Pontifice, et da un rè di Napoli ch' è feudatario della Chiesia ; et giudicando S. S^tà che questa casa Colonna sia stata sempre nimica de Pontefici.

Dappoi, che S. S^tà si reputa gravemente ingiuriato nel' honor et nel stato, havendo li ministri di S. M^tà dannificato cosi in grosso in varii modi questo stato, et però bisognava pigliare qualche via di iscusatione et di humiliatione et reconoscimento, come sarebbe di scrivere a S. S^tà humilmente dimandandoli perdono, che come mal informato havea lasciato muover le armi, etc., et mandando qualche personaggio a posta.

Il terzo, che dovesse fare restituire li luochi occupati ; et per che tra principi non si usa altra securità che la fede, si dovesse contentare di quella ch' è comune tra li altri principi ; et che promettendoli il rev^mo Caraffa, credeva che si potesse credere alla fede et promissione sua, essendo signore ben nato et facendo professione non solo di cardinale, ma di cavalero honorato.

Ultimamente li disse che, non accordandosi le cose al mio giuditio per queste vie, teneva per fermo che S. S^tà escomunicarebbe il rè et lo privarebbe di tutti li regni et harebbe fatto ogni conato in tutte le vie contra S. M^tà et li suoi regni. Et con questo esseo signore si partì, parendoli che dicesse il vero.

Ho voluto replicar il medesimo a V. S. Illma, per che la cosa sta così in effetto, et se ben io sono poco aveduto, nondimeno stimo che, caminandosi per altra via, bisogni espettar la ruina del mondo, perche S. S^tà mi pare resolutissima. Et se a V. S. R^ma parerà bene indrizzare le cose a questo scopo, io ne la prego, perchè altrimenti mi metto avanti li occhi ogni estremità ; et se ben per altra via il rè di Spagna vincesse in questo mondo, S. S^tà pero non cederà mai nelle cose spirituali, et in tal caso non cura nè di separatione di Spagna, nè de recidiva de Inghelterra, nè di perdita d' ogni ubedientia ; perchè ha questo fondamento che non tenetur praestare culpam alienam, et che qui non erant ex nobis exierunt etc. Ma di tutti questi offici S. S^{tà} non ha mai voluto che a nome suo se parli, et però ha tenuto che non si sia venuto a particulari con lei ; ma forsi hora il rev^{mo} Caraffa li scriverà qualche cosa come da se, se ben non lo so certo. Ma l' ho raccordato, et S. S^{tà} sta su queste ch' ogniuno doveria fare il debito suo et che la recognitione di quella M^{tà} sia tanto necessaria che non habbi bisogno di raccordo.

Mons. Fantuccio andò heri alla M^{tà} Sua a nome solo del rev^{mo} Caraffa. E persona assai destra et forsi potrà fare qualche bene, quantunque io non ne speri molto, vedendo li apparati che vengono di Franza in soccorso di N. S^{re} et considerando li peccati nostri, per li quali si può temere che Dio non habbia ancora posta la mano in seno, ma stia levata col flagello suo. Qui si fano orationi continue, et è andato il giubileo per tutto per la pace : sopra la qual considerando alcuna volta mi pare vedere gran difficultà, perche N. S. stima non havere mai fatto una minima ingiuria a quella M^{tà}, per la qual meritasse esser trattata com' è stata, nelli machinamenti primi di veneni, di archibusi, di tratti etc. et poi in questa aggressione della Chiesia. Dall' altra parte il rè pensa havere havuto molte ragione da le minaccie et parole ingiuriose, da motivi d' armi, da disfavori alli suoi, da essaltatione di suoi nemici et d' un mal animo antico et fondata da molti anni. Et volendo N. S. la debita sodisfattione, et mesurandola secondo il giuditio suo, et parendo al rè di non esser tenuto, anzi di havere recevuto molti aggravi, pare difficile che 'l rè si disinganni et voglia sodisfar come S. S^{tà} disegna. Ma non si può negare che questo ultimo insulto fù troppo grave et merita satisfattione, et non si può negare che le suspitioni sono state maggiori dal canto del rè che non si conveniva per fare così gran fatto, et non si può negare, come si è veduto, che dalle parole et forze di S. S^{tà} non si dovea temere tanto che si venesse a tal rottura per assecurarsi. Et oltre di ciò non si può negare che ogni patientia del rè verso S. S^{tà} saria stata laudabile, come d' un figlio verso il padre. Però chi vuole concordia bisogna persuadere S. M^{tà} a risolversi di contentare S. S^{tà} nelle cose sopradette, altrimenti ne seguirà la ruina della christianità, et sarà fatto al fine la voluntà di Dio. . . .

[Orig. (autograph). Arm. 64, t. 32, f. 219—220. Secret
Archives of the Vatican.]

36. Bernardo Navagero to Venice.[1]

1557, Mart. 12, Rom.

Interview with Paul IV :

Mi disse che io dovea haver inteso che tutti credevono che
mercore passato si facesse promotione de cardinali, ma che
l' havea voluto differir perchè non vedea come potesse satisfar
a tutti e più a se stesso sendo questa dignità che bisogna pregar
l' huomini e andarli trovando con la candeletta, per dir la sua
parola, et non esser pregato. . . .

[Cod. 6255, 317. Court Library, Vienna.]

37. General Congregation of June 1st, 1557.[2]

Romae die martis 1 mensis iunii 1557 fuit congregatio
generalis, in qua S. D. N. fecit multa verba super causa reten-
tionis rev. et ill. cardinalis Moroni et dixit quod volebat facere
deputatos super huiusmodi causa et quod volebat aeque et
paterne procedere et similiter dixit quod volebat vocare omnes
cardinales ad curiam propter multas causas.

[Acta consist., Consistorial Archives of the Vatican.]

38. Avviso di Roma. 1557, July 24th.[3]

Sunday, congregation of the Inquisition about simony and
pensioni con clausule insolite of 4 hóurs, ,,et sempre parlo S.
Sta, che altri non disse parola, disse anco di voler annulla[r]
tutti gli uffitii soggiungendo che se bene si farà danno a 5 o 6
mila persone che hanno comprato gli uffitii che manco mal sarà
far così, et da[r]li beneficii et l' ispeditioni gratis, levando tutti
gli abusi che sono nella Cancellaria et Penitentiaria, che tener
infettato il mondo, non havendo altro i Luth^ni di che rimprove-
rar la sede apostolica se non de tale uffitii, et che si fanno morir
in un fatto d' arme 15 et 20 m. huomini, che non se ne fa conto
alcuno, che non sarà gran fatto per acconciar il mondo quelli
patiscono un poco.``

[Cod. Urb. 1038, 249^b . Vatican Library.]

[1] See *supra*, p. 200 n. 2,   [2] See *supra*, p. 291, n. 2.   [3] See *supra*, p. 203, n. 4.

39. Avviso di Roma. 1557, August 21st.[1]

. . . Giovedì fu posto prigione il segretario del cardinale di Fano in quella della inquisitione, chi dice per heresia, chi per sodomia, et fu messo ancora quel m. Pasino di Giusti Shiavone che sta col car^le Farnese pur per sodomia, et vi fu posto ancora il suo Ganimede, et si è messo ancora prigione per la inquisitione il seg^rio de Bellai. Al car^le Morone fu levato la messa, et non se ne ragiona più come sel fusse deletus de libro viventium. Molti stanno in dubio se la partita de S. Giorgio è per il desiderio delli studii che lo muova a venir costì o se l' è per il timore che forse ha per la carceratione delli sudetti. . . .

[Cod. Urb. 1038, 257^b —258. Vatican Library.]

40. Avviso di Roma.   1557, September 4th.[2]

. . . Fra Michiele card^le parlando col Papa sopra le cose della pace, gli disse che non occorreva Giubileo per pregar per la pace, stando in sua mano il farla, dove S. S^tà gli rispose bruscamente scazziandoselo dinanzi con parole molto brutte, dicendogli, ¿ate sfratato Lutherano.   Un piovan dopo l' haver publicato in chiesa il giubileo disse al popolo haverlo fatto per comandamento di S. S^tà, ma che li assicurava che della pace non ne faria niente, et subito fu preso et posto pregione.

[Cod. Urb. 1038, 261^b.   Vatican Library.]

41. Avviso di Roma.   1557, October 16th.[3]

N. S^or persiste in fermo proposito, di publicare la reforma, et però va di man in mano mozzando le gambe alla Penitentiaria, havendoli sin hora levato, che non si concedano più si in evidentem delli beni ecc^cl le dispense matrimoniale, le comutationi de voti et delli frati, che più in modo alcuno ne sotto color niuno non sono dispensati à uscir di monast^i, per il che gli uffi cii di quella gia ne sentono notabil danno ogni mese.

[Cod. Urb. 1038, 274.   Vatican Library.]

---

[1] See *supra*, pp. 266, n. 3; 299, n. 4   [2] See *supra*, p. 166, n. 3.
[3] See *supra*, p. 207, n. 1.

42. Avviso di Roma. 1557, November 13th.[1]

The Pope . . . havea fatta una bolla, nella quale sotto scomuniche, maleditioni et altre pene prohibiva che all' avenir non 'si dessero più beneficii se non a persone litterate, che non si potesse assicurar pensioni sopra beneficii d' un terzo, che niuno potesse impetrar beneficii per altri, et molti altri aggiramenti de capi et confusioni della corte, et l' havea sin data in mano de cursori che la publicassero, poi l' a fatto ripigliar et non ha lasciato che si publicasse, et non vuol admetter la resignatione del arcivescovato di Cipro nell' abbate di S. Cipriano.

[Cod. Urb. 1038, 277. Vatican Library.]

43–45.—Cardinal Vitelli to Cardinal C. Carafa.[2]

1557, December 1, 3, 17 and 24, Rom.

1) Pope very well. Ha facto et tuttavia fa bellissimi decreti sopra la riforma et mai pensa in altro che in questo. Decree that the proposals for the bishoprics are not to be settled in the same Consistory. Decree against the ' regressi.'

The Pope sempre che si parla di V. S. I. suspira et la desidera senza fine.

La signatura va tanto stretta che V. S. I. non s' il puo pensare e la fa spesso perchè in quella consiste gran parte di riforma.

Dat. Roma, 1 dicembre, 1557.

2) N. Sre hoggi ha fatto un decreto che nissuno cardinale o altri possa havere regresso se non a una chiesa havendo estinti tutti li regressi che s' havevono ad altre chiese, de la qual cosa alcuni se ne sono rallegrati et ad alcuni è molto dispiaciuto. Ha fatto ancora un altro decreto che non si possa in un med° consistoro proporre un rettore d' una chiesa et farne l' espeditione, ma che in un concistorio si proponga et nell' altro s' espedisca afinchè li cardinali habbino tanto più tempo di risolversi et d' informarsi delle qualità di quel che è proposto et dir poi quant' l' occorre, et hoggi ha dato principio a questa determinatione.

Di Roma, 3 dicembre, 1557.

3) The Pope is very well and is longing to see you. Non

---

[1] See *supra*, p. 207, n. 3.   [2] See *supra*, pp. 208, n. 2 ; 209, n. 5 ; 2   , n.

attende ad altro che a la riforma, daily congregations et decreti sancti. All regressi of chiese cathedrali et archiepiscopali to give way. The Pope speaks kindly of Philip II.

Dat. Roma, 17 dicembre 1557.

Orig. Cod. Barb. lat. 5711, 48, 196 ; 51, 53. Vatican Library.]

46-47. Concerning the Proceedings of the Roman Inquisition against Cardinal Morone.

While important information, taken from documents in the Gallarati-Scotti Archives, Milan, relating to the proceedings of the Inquisition against Morone has been published by Cantù and recently by Tacchi Venturi, other documents concerning this matter have been until now disregarded.[1] I found these in the autumn of 1906, during a short visit to Foligno, in the library of the seminary there, and was able to make full use of them later, through the kindness of Mgr. Faloci Pulignani. The MS. which contains them is coted : C. VI. 5. It is a contemporaneous volume, in 4to, bound in paper, of 152 numbered (not consecutive) pages. The heading of the 1st p. : " Processo fatto del 1557 contro il cardinale Morone, trovato poi innocente et assoluto, di Ludovico Jacobilli di Foligno," shows that it is the diligent collector mentioned here who has saved these documents for posterity.[2] The heading also indicates the principal contents, which are very clearly proved by the following description, to be a collection of documents of which use was made for the acquittal of the Cardinal.

1 Title

2—5 Blank.

6—9 Aedicta sive constitutiones rev. et ill. d. d. Ioannis tit. s. Stephani in Caelio monte S. R. E. praesbiteri cardinalis Moroni nuncupati et episcopi Novariensis perpetui administratoris et comitis. Novariae A. 1553 die XXV m. Ianuarii. (The 3 first pages, Reform statutes.) The following passage is crossed out with ink : " Item statuimus quod nullus sacerdos vel clericus teneat libros pro-

---

[1] See *supra*, p. 293, n. 1. Further information is to be expected from R. Ancel.

[2] Jacobilli, who was an eager collector of manuscripts, probably received this from his fellow-citizen, Sebastiano Porfiri, vicar-general of the Bishop of Novaro ; see Faloci Pulignani, Notizie del ven. Giov. Batt. Vitelli, Foligno, 1894, 43.

hibitos etc." ; also the passage : " statuimus et ordinavimus, ut unusquisque curatus habeat librum qui vocatur manipulus curatorum etc."

10—26. " Scriptum R^{mi}." This is the ' Confession ' of the Cardinal published by Cantù ; *cf. supra*, p. 293. Numerous underlinings and marginal notes show that we have here an original copy, which plays a rôle in the acquittal.

The most important marginal notes, from Morone himself, are the following :

At the passage relating to the passing on to others of Pole's writing (Cantù 178, Z. 4 v. u.) : " Qui feci male che non dovea darla non havendola letta prima."

Ordering the writing Del beneficio di Cristo (*loc. cit.* 180, Z. 15/16 v. o.) : " Questo fu male fatto."

Defence of the permission to circulate this writing (*loc. cit.* 180, Z. 25/26 v. o.) : " Dovea esser più cauto essendo il libro senza nome."

Expression (oral) of Paul III. (182, Z. 7 f v. o.) : " Dovea farla in scritto."

Conference with Salmeron (182, Z. 26 f v. o.) : " Questo fu mal fatto."

Morone's declaration that he had no confidence in his works (183, Z. 13 f v. o.) : " Li tempi non comportano che s'avviliscano le opere et meriti perchè si fa poco bene per il mondo."

His intercourse with suspects (185, par. " Un altra volta costui venne da me etc."). Added on the margin : " Con costui me portai male perchè dovea farlo metter in prigione."

Doubts as to Roman Relics (186, Z. 20 f v. o.) : " Non dovea dubitar ne parlarne."

Against the " varietà de ordini " (186, Z. 10 f v. u.) : "Non dovea parlarne in publico."

Expressions " de intercessione sanctorum " (186, Z. 6 f v. u.) : " Questo era voler saper troppo et gran temerità." (187, Z. 4 f. v. o.) : " Questo era ignorantia et incapacità." Some lines further on : " Non lassai mai la salutatione angelica."

Utterance concerning words of the prayer " vita, dulcedo et spes nostra " (187, Z. 18 f v. o.) : " Questa fu presumptione et temerità."

Expression " de conceptione virginis " (188, Z. 1) :
" Non dovea parlarne."

" Posso aver detto " etc. (188, Z. 9 f v. o.) : " In questo
son stato troppo inconsiderato et ignorante et libero."

Conversation concerning Justification (188, 3rd par.) :
" In questo son stato più volte ingannato benchè dovea
guardarmi meglio."

Attitude towards Villamarina (188, 4th par.) : "Non
dovea haver tanto rispetto."

Attitude towards D. Morando (188, 5th par.) : " Se in
questo son ingannato non so che me dire."

After the signature there follows a P.S. to the following
effect : Doppo ch' io ho scritto quel che si contien di sopra
havendo riletto et ben considerato ho advertito, che quasi
tutte le cose, nelle quali io posso per errore o ignorantia o
per trascuragine et inadvertentia haver dato qualche
suspition di me o scandalo, se non mi inganno sono state
da X anni indietro o poco meno.   Mi è parso con ogni
summission far di cio qui memoria perchè havendo per Dio
gratia doppo vissuto tanti anni senza queste occasioni, se
bene come homo fragile in molte et molte cose ho offeso
Dio, nondimeno potria parere meglio alla clementia di
N. S^{re} giustitiarmi intorno a queste cose secondo la
presente giustitia che secondo le sospettione delli passati
tempi.   Pur la Divina M^{tà} Sua si degni governare S. S^{tà}
et me secondo il meglio et conservarmi nella sua bona
gratia.

Last of all comes on p. 26 the covering letter which
Morone sent with his defence to the four Cardinals.

27—35. Defence of Morone against the accusations of the
Inquisition.   The accused repudiates these in general as
unfounded, and swears to his orthodoxy, referring to what
he has already declared to the four Cardinals.

In primis petit sibi dari copiam omnium inditiorum
hactenus contra eum habitorum ac concedi tempus
conveniens plurium dierum, cum tres dies sint terminus
nimis brevis, et quod restituantur seu ostendantur sibi
suae scripturae quae sunt in manibus fisci, ut possit illis
visis reducere sibi ad mentem materias super quibus com-
ponenda sunt interrogatoria, cum agatur de rebus antiquis
quindecim annorum et ultra ita quod facile est quod

exciderint ab eius memoria. Et insuper etiam petit nomina et cognomina eorum qui eum in talibus articulis accusant seu contra eum instigant et eorum qui pro testibus adducuntur sibi propalari ut iuxta eorum qualitates et circumstantias possit certius facere sua interrogatoria ad ostendendum innocentiam suam. . . . Et insuper quia non habens nomina testium examinandorum non potest certe et precise loqui, sed cogitur sub nube et per incerta incedere, nolens sibi ipsi in faciendis legitimis a iure permissis defensionibus deesse, si forte contingeret adduci contra se in testes d. Iacobum Iacomellum episc. Bellicastren. et d. Constantinum cognominatum Greghettum, episc. Chironen. et fratrem Barthol. Pergolam ord. s. Francisci et fratrem Bernardum de Parma ord. s. Dominici et Laurentium Davidicum et Bonifacium Valentinum, quia omnes praedicti iam dudum fuerunt et sunt ipsius rev. d. cardinalis infensi et inimici et aliqui ex eis alias fuerunt dicti rev. d. cardinalis accusatores et partim sunt infames et personae neque in hac neque in ulla alia causa fidedignae, prout (si opus esset) facile probari posset et probari si opus sit offertur et pro maiori parte est notorium, idcirco idem rev. d. cardinalis, quod praenominati aut aliqui ex eis pro testibus contra se in hac causa non recipiantur neque examinentur, si secus fiat similiter de nullitate et de gravamine cum omni reverentia convenienti solemniter et expresse omni meliori modo etc. protestatur.

Then follow pars. 38, 39, which are to be laid before all the witnesses, and which are also to be found in the copy of proceedings in Milan, Oct. 7th, 1557. (see Tacchi Venturi, I., 538, n. 3).

36—37. The articles of accusation against Morone (see *supra*, p. 294, n. 1) with marginal notes in two hands (one that of Morone), which contain references to the matter of the discharge which now follows.

37—46. Copia articulorum propositorum de a. 1542 per rev. et ill. card. Moronum, tunc episc. etc.

47—49. Aviso di quanto si ha da osservare dalli predicatori

nella città et diocesi di Modena per ordine del rev. et ill.
card. Morone 1551.[1]

50—52. Analogous regulations of Morone for preachers in the
city and diocese of Novara, which Morone has issued
through a letter dated, Rome, January 22nd, 1554.

53—54. Blank.

55—79. Letters chronologically arranged, mostly from
Morone, also others to him, for instance, from Contarini
relating principally to Lutherans in Modena 1539—1545,
among them several inedited ; *cf. supra*, p. 296.

80—81. Pro ill. et rev. dom. card. Morone.   Then follows the
document in question with the heading "Instructio ad
articulos fisci," reaching to 84. The most important
points from this defence of Morone's against the accusations have been brought forward above (p. 296).   The
most interesting passages are the following :

De meritis operum idem semper tenuit, tenet et tenebit
quod S. R. Ecclesia docet et praedicat, quod scilicet opera
nostra facta in gratia Dei sunt meritoria vitae aeternae,
quod tamen meritum principaliter credit fundari in sanguine Christi, et ita de eius mandato fuit praedicatum
Matinae ut patet in litteris p^{ti} vicarii sub die 1 martii 1543
et hoc ipsum expresse asserit rev. dominus in litteris suis
ad vic. praedict. dat. Bononiae die 25 maii 1554 et patet in
modo praedicandi Novariae n. 8[2] ; eum ita sentire arguunt
elemosinae et opera bona quae quotidie facit et fecit.

De bello iusto maxime contra hereticos ipse nunquam
dixit nec dubitavit quin id liceret et deberet, ut probatur
evidenter in litteris eius ad rev. card. Farnesium Viennae
datis sub die 17 Novembris 1539 et die ult. eiusdem[3] et in
voto inserto ibidem.[4]   Item in s. consistorio suasit Paulo
III bo. me. ut belli foedus iniret cum principibus
catholicis contra protestantes, de quo extant etiam plures
aliae litterae.

Against the accusation relating to the book ' Del beneficio di Christo ' the following was urged :

Liber iste eo tempore passim et publice erat venalis
Romae et ubique locorum et fuit sibi comendatus a

[1] This and the following passage I shall publish elsewhere.
[2] The said passages are in the MS., p. 70 *seq*.
[3] V, DITTRICH, Nuntiaturberichte Morones, 49 *seq*., 57 *seq*.
[4] *Cf.* MS., p. 59 *seq*.

theologis et inquisitoribus, quibus eum legendum dederat ; postquam intellexit eum reprobatum esse ab officio s. Inquisitionis ipse etiam ex tunc eum reprobavit et reprobandum censet. De favore praestito hereticis non potest rev. dominus reprehendi, cum immo semper faverit officio s. Inquisitionis ubique locorum et praecipue Mutinae, Bononiae, Novariae, et extant plures litterae rev. dom. Inquisitorum de Urbe et aliorum, qui usi sunt opera ipsius in negocio inquisitionis, et apud eorum officium procuravit hereticos plures castigari prout censet esse castigandos et puniendos, et praecipue Bononiae punivit quendam fabrum lignarium hereticum et alium inquisitum de heresi exclusit ab officio Antianorum et heretici Mutinenses habebant eum pro persecutore et inimico ipsorum. De pollicitatione illa[1] non est curandum, quia non erat obligatoria, sed forte fuerunt verba generalia et curialia.

86—103. Retrattione del Pergola fatta in Modena sopra il pulpito a dì 15 di Giugno 1544 in due prediche—was unknown up till then.[2]

104—114. Opinion of M. Antonius Burghesius[3] concerning the trial of Morone. Even the beginning is of great importance for the previous history of the legal proceedings : Et presuppono quod fel. rec. Paulus IV primis diebus suae assumptionis ad pontificatum deputavit commissarios ad diversas Italiae civitates ad querendas informationes et testes contra ill. et rev. card. Moronum et sic pro speciali inquisitione facienda, antequam precederet diffamatio nec aliqua inditia, quo casu inquisitio formari non potest et formata corruit et ex probationibus sic receptis procedi non potest. These were becoming more explicit . Borghese emphasizes : Sed nec infamia nec inditia aut suspitiones ex probatis signis precesserunt inquisitionem, merito minus valide processus inchoatus fuit presertim contra cardinalem, contra quem ut supra dictum est versatur tam grave periculum et in specie contra personam ill. cardinalis ab ineunte aetate apud omnes et religione, moribus et exemplo approbatissimam

---

[1] The accusation had made good, quod hereticis seu de heresi suspectis favit et precipue Bononiae, quibus pollicitus est, quod si mitteretur ex urbe aliqua provisio contra eos quod caperentur, quod illos premoneret asserendo illos hereticos non esse persequendos ex quo Deus ipse tolerat eos.

[2] Cf. concerning Pergola besides BUSCHBELL, 208, 315 CARCERERI, Riforma e inquisizione nel ducato di Urbino (Verona 1911), 13 seq.

[3] Cf. concerning this celebrated lawyer MORONI, VI., 37 seq. and supra, p. 305.

et in legationibus pro religione et aliis negotiis huius s.
sedis cathòlice et sine aliqua suspitione versatum que bona
apud homines existimatio tollere debuisset omnem sus-
pitionem delicti. . . . Nec obstant duo testes qui reperiuntur in principio processus, these are badly disposed
towards the Cardinal and therefore not worthy of belief ;
one has even been convicted of lying.

Ex quibus sequitur minus legitime inchoatum fuisse
iudicium et longe minus processum fuisse ad capturam
ad quam contra cardinalem non facile proceditur et deberent inditia urgenitiora concurrere quam in aliis requiratur
propter eminentiam et dignitatem et alias rationes de
quibus supra. Et quamvis stantibus premissis, que
reddunt processum nullum et invalidum, non esset ulterius
elaborandum, tamen ut innocentia prefati rev^{mi} eo clarius
in lucum prodeat dicam que sequuntur.

Borghese throws doubts on the credibility of the nine
witnesses against Morone.

As such the following were presented : 1. Quidam
frater Bernardus ord. s. Dominici ; 2. Frater Bartholomaeus Pergula ord. s. Francisci ; 3. Quidam lo. Bapt.
Scottus[1] qui omnes fatentur se hereticos et abiurasse et sic
habemus tres infames hereticos quibus nulla est fides
adhibenda, testes enim in criminalibus dębent esse omni
exceptione maiores. . . . Accedit quod prefati fr. Bernardus et fr. Bartholomaeus sunt eiusdem rev. card^{lis}
inimici . . . et constat quod fr. Bartholomaeus fuit
instante rev. cardinali coactus retractare certos articulos
de heresi suspectos in ecclesia Mutinensi. . . . Nec
omittendum est quod fr. Bernardus id quod deposuit
retractavit coram inquisitore et confessus fuit quod ea
quae in primo examine contra rev. cardinalem [dixit], non
erant vera. Then Borghese brings against A. Salmeron
as a witness the accusation that he was an enemy of
Morone. Augetur falsitas et inverisimilitudo causae quia
ipsemet attestatur quod de premissis certiorem reddidit
patrem Ignatium suum maiorem et tamen fatetur quod
Ignatius et alii sodales assidue habuerunt conversationem
cum rev. d. cardinali et singulis annis a sua rev. domina-
tione habuerunt pro eleemosyna scuta 50, quod non est

---

[1] *Cf.* BUSCHBELL, 196 *seq.*

credendum et conversasse et recepisse, si cognovissent
dom. suam rev^{am} diviare ab ecclesia sancta Dei. . . .
Quintus testis est bibliopola Mutinensis, qui est hereticus.
. . Sextus testis est Scottus Bononiensis, qui pariter est
hereticus et aliis sceleribus implicitus. . . . . Septimus
testis est falsus apertissime qui allegat contestem qui
contrarium deponit et attestatur in favorem rev. cardinalis asserens quod nihil hereticum cum eo fuit loquutus.
. . . Octavus testis est fr. Reginaldus¹ qui deponit in
favorem rev^{ml} cardinalis et cum inductus sit a fisco eius
dicta sunt admodum attendenda. The ninth witness, the
episcopus Bellicastren. [Jac. Giacomelli], is suspicious
eo quia cardinalis dum preesset gymnasio curavit eidem
testi annuam pensionem minui, he is also causa odii
at present, et ubi est causa odii et inimicitiae sufficit ad
repellendum testem. . . . Sed etiam repellendus est quia
est sibi contrarius quia in primo suo examine profitetur
cardinalem hereticum in articulo de libero arbitrio et
tamen in alio examine dixit nescire an id profiteretur
disputative vel ne et sic non concludit ad heresim quae
requirit pertinaciam. Et eo minus fides huic testi
adhibenda est quo ipse allegat contestem episcopum
civitatis Castellanae [Scipio Bongalli] qui contrarium
affirmat, ut merito excludatur omnis eius fides, et etiam
dictum suum revocavit.

116—117. The opinion of Ant. Massa as to the admission of
Morone to the conclave.

118. Brevis informatio processus (crossed out).

119—135. Brevis informatio status causae et processus per
offitium s. inquisitionis contra rev. d. Card. Moronum
agitati. Apparet ex ipso processu f. 31 quod papa Paulus
IV statim factus papa sub die 26 iunii 1555 expedivit
breve commissariatus, cuius vigore commissarius depu-
tatus circuivit diversas Italiae civitates querendo testes
pro informatione processus faciendi, et sic sumus in claro
quod non precedebat aliqua infamatio neque erant aliqua
inditia precedentia inquisitionem prout de iure precedere
debent ut processus valeat atque hinc sequitur quod totus
processus nihil valet nullaque est consideratione dignus,
nec quicquam faciunt duo testes informativi positi ante

---

¹ See BUSCHBELL, 99.

dictum fol. 31, quorum unus est Bonifatius Valentinus Mutin., alter Laurentius Davidicus, quia non habent prenotatum diem quo fuerunt examinati et sumus certi quod fuerunt examinati dudum post dictum diem 26 iunii 1555 et eorum dicta fortasse per errorem notarii fuerunt posita in principio processus et omnino nihil probant, nam ultra quod ambo sunt capitales inimici p^{ti} rev^{mi} d. cardinalis prout fuit pro eius parte allegatum quando dedit interrogatoria et postea in articulis deductum, preterea ambo sunt heretici et propter multa alia scelera infames et omnino ex eorum dictis nihil concluditur. . . .

Et sic habemus pro claro et indubitato quod processus inchoatus fuit non precedentibus inditiis neque infamia. Sequitur deinde carceratio non minus nulla quam iniusta et inimico dicti Pauli pape facta quia, ultra quod facta est iuris ordine ut praecipitur non servato, preterea non apparet cuius mandato facta fuerit, cum causa nondum haberet iudicem ; nam die XI iunii 1557, ut patet fol. 309, presentatus fuit motus proprius per quem papa narrato quod cardinalis pro nonnullis ad officium s. Inquisitionis pertinentibus in arce s. Angeli detenebatur, committit eius causam quatuor rev^{mis}, qui deberent audire et merita causae sibi referre, unde apparet quod dixi carcerationem esse factam sine mandato indicis competentis et iusuper quod nunc causa mortuo ipso papa reperitur sine iudice. Et quamvis stante nullitate predicta totus processus, ut dixi, redditur nullus et nullius considerationis, tamen, ut manifesta fiat innocentia p^{ti} rev. d. cardinalis, dicam que mihi occurrunt circa ea quae pro parte fisci praetendi possunt.

In the following the author first of all examines the witnesses : fr. Bernardus and fr. B. Pergula still in the Ripetta prison when they were interrogated ; J. B. Scottus and Antonius bibliopola Mutin. had themselves acknow ledged they had been heretics, et sic habemus 4 infames hereticos quibus nulla est prestanda fides de iure. Further reasons were adduced to show that those witnesses should be ignored, e.g., personal enmity, inconsistency, etc.

In a similar manner the testimony of Salmeron was confuted.

Secundus testis nescimus omnino quis sit, sed non refert

quia nihil dicit de sua scientia sed est relator verborum cuiusdam alterius.

Tertius testis est ill fr. Bernardus. . . .

Quartus est supranominatus fr. B. Pergula. . . .

Quintus est bibliopola Mutin.—hereticus.

Sextus est ille Scottus Bonon. pariter hereticus.

In all cases further grounds besides heresy (with quotations from the documents of the proceedings) were brought forward for disregarding the testimony of these witnesses.

Septimus nescimus quis sit . . . redditus falsus in duobus. . . .

Octavus testis est fr. Reginaldus qui nihil deponit contra cardinalem.

Nonus testis est Iac. Iacomellus ep. Bellicast. Grounds against these as above.

After repudiating these witnesses, the author remarks : We must also take into consideration quod et inter ipsos testes fisci sunt qui probant cardinalem esse catholicum et nunquam fuisse de heresi suspectum ut sunt p^{dictus} fr. Reginaldus et p^{dictus} prior s. Dominici Mutinae et dictus episcopus Civitatis Castellanae et[1] aliunde intelleximus esse examinatos alios qui multa deposuerunt ad favorem rev. cardinalis ut est mag^{cus} d. Bartholomaeus Spatafora nobilis Messanen. et alii plures, quorum tamen dicta non sunt posita in processu, nescimus si per inadvertentiam notarii vel ob aliam causam.

In the second part on the basis of Morone's depositiones et in scriptis et in examinibus factae are demonstrated nihil in eis contineri quod fisci intentionem adiuvet neque. rev. dom. quidquam in eis confiteri quod dicta testium comprobet quatenus contra ipsum deposuerunt. This is shown in each point and the inference is then drawn : Ex his igitur scriptis nihil resultat quo rev^{mus} cardinalis fateatur se sensisse aliquid hereticum vel suspectum fuisse suspitione probabili atque ideo fisci intentio super his fundari non potest.

The conclusion—again from another hand (Morone's)— is therefore :

Quod ad tertium principale genus pretensionum fisci

---

[1] The following words up to " causam " form a supplement in another hand, perhaps that of Morone himself. Elsewhere this document also shows signs of corrections in this hand, which has a great resemblance to that which has written the above-mentioned (p. 469) additional notes.

de libris hereticorum et epistolis marchionissae Piscariae
et aliorum quos fiscus habet pro hereticis, quae fuerunt
in eius domo repertae, paucis opus est.   Nam quoad libros
dictum est supra circa primum caput predicti scripti ipsius
rev. cardinalis et additur quod ex inscriptionibus, quae
sunt super ipsis libris manu eiusdem reverend^{mi} factae,
apparet quod ipse tenebat illos tamquam reprobos et
damnatos, non autem pro bonis et legibilibus.   Quo vero
ad epistolas in illis non continetur aliquod non solum
hereticum, sed neque etiam quod concernat religionem,
sed alia negocia, et marchionissa et aliae personae prae-
dictae non habebantur pro hereticis sed pro catholicis, ut
dictum est supra prox. circa XI caput scripti praedicti.

Itaque concludendo remanet quod neque ex testibus
neque ipsius aut aliorum scripturis quicquam est in actis,
unde probetur non modo crimen heresis, sed neque etiam
iusta causa quam ob rem potuerit apud bonos viros oriri
de ipso rev^{mo} suspitio talis peccati.

At last effect is given to the following[1] : Nolo praeter-
mittere quin (ad magis ostendendum quam inique fecerit
processum) hoc quoque dicam.   Quod licet de iure etiam
in causa heresis ubi offertur cautio de non offendendo
testes danda sint reo ipsorum testium nomina et pro parte
dicti rev^{mo} dicta cautio fuerit oblata ut sibi nomina ederen-
tur, tamen non potuit obtinere et sic non potuimus oppon-
ere contra personas nisi aliquorum ex ipsis testibus, quos
ex eorum dictis potuimus coniectura comprehendere qui
essent.   Imo quod peius est occultata fuerunt eodem
modo et dumtaxat per literam N notata nomina personarum quae per ipsos testes nominantur et locorum et
temporum quibus res, de quibus deponunt, gestae fuerunt.
Quod nullo iure cavetur etiam in causa heresis fieri per
iudices posse, ex quibus circumstantiis, si illas scivissemus,
verisimile est quod multo plures exceptiones potuissemus
elicere itaque defensio nobis concessa fuit magis verbalis
quam realis et omnino imperfecta et manca.

Hoc volui dixisse non quia multum referat in hac causa,
quae caret difficultate et ex praedictis redditur clarissima,
sed ut confirmarem, quod processus hic fuit instructus et
agitatus magis pro alicuius odii et vindictae prosecutione

---

[1] The same hand here again.

quam pro iustitia et zelo religionis utque etiam qui leget
habeat nos excusatos si videbimur pauca deduxisse et
quodammodo sicco pede pertransivisse.

48. AVVISO DI ROMA. 1558, APRIL 2nd[1].

Li negotii et li espedimenti di qua vano molto lenti e fredi,
eccetto quelli dell' Inquisitione, che ogni giorno si vede affisse
qualche citationi, et questo per causa dell' indispositioni del
papa circa alla vecchiezza, che non può la fatica, et il Datario
et Barengo che sogliono sempre parlar a S. Stᵃ di cose sue particular, sono tall' hora 20 giorni che non l' hanno visto, nelli
pono parlare, et l' ambasciator di Francia è un mese che ha
ricercato l' audientia, nella puo havere, et il card. di Monte
che sono 3 mesi, che sta in spettative di haverla, vi è piu lontano
adesso ch' era da principio. . . .

Il card. d' Oria è morto, et al card. Morone se li è ingrossata
la vista, che non vede, se non con li ochiali et lettera grossa per
l' aria trista del Castello.

The nephews are expected daily, but always delay their
arrival.

[Cod. Urb. 1038, 297°. Vatican Library.]

49. POPE PAUL IV. TO JOH. MANRIQUEZ, VICEROY OF NAPLES.[2]

1558, Juli 25,. Rom.

. . . Quo plus Ecclesiae Dei utilitatis attulit praedicatorum
ordo a beato Dominico institutus, eo magis providendum est,
ne ab eius ordinis professoribus sanctissimi illius patris disciplina et regularis observantia negligatur.   Sed cum omnibus
Christianis cara esse debet ordinis existimatio Dominicani, tum
iis praecipue, qui eadem in terra geniti sunt, unde illud tam
clarum et splendidum Ecclesiae lumen exortum est.   We beg
you, in your prayers to help erga gloriosum illum nationis tuae
confessorem, to bring back all convents of the Order in your
Kingdom ad regularem observantiam, and to support Thomas
Manriquez O. Pr. mag. theol. in everything he says to you in
the name of the vice-protector Card. Alexandrinus or of the
General.

[Minutae brev. ad princ. Arm. 44 t. 2 p. 119.   Secret Archives
of the Vatican.]

---

[1] See *supra*, pp. 286, n. 2 ; 305, n. 5.   [2] See *supra*, p . 216, n. .

50. AVVISO DI ROMA. 1558, SEPTEMBER 10th.[1]

Giovedì il Papa peggiorò assai della sua indispositione, essendoli venuto uno accidente assai maggiore de l' altro precedente, et il medico toccandoli il polso, il che per avanti non ha voluto concedere, trovò che haveva la febre, et giudico che per avanti l' haveva havuta ancóra. Onde il romor del male, et il pericolo di peggio fu grande quella sera, et tanto più che si diede ordine che la cavalleria ch' è alloggiata in quelli contorni venisse per la mattina tutta qua, et similmente le battaglie, et fu prohibito alle poste che non si desse cavalli a chi si fosse, et alle porte della Città, che non si lasciasse uscire alcuno, et dato ordine di pagar fanti, et furono pagati il dì seguente, che fu hieri, et ne sono 7 o 8 insegne di quelli che furono fatti per sospetto dell' armata Turchescha, et con questi altri potranno fare in tutto da 1300 incirca, ma per hora non passano 800. . . . Il Papa quella sera et hier matina si comunicò per mano del r.mo di Pisa molto divotamente, et dice non voleva morire disperato ne ostinato, ma che era apprechiato di pigliare qualche cosa per la salute del corpo, se cosi a loro paresse, cosa che per avanti non haveva voluto fare. Et se ben si disse hieri che stava meglio, non si credeva, because yesterday morning the " Caraffi " with " 50 muli " " 200 fanti " sent to Civitavecchia and yesterday evening all the halberdiers were ordered to come to the Castello. Some say he is worse, others the opposite ; the Pope non si serve se non delli suoi parenti. Et questa mattina s' ha fatto molta difficultà d' entrare, anche nelle stanze del card. Caraffa, che sono nell' appartamento del papa, et si tiene per certo che se non è morto non la farà lungo.

[Cod. Urb. 1038, 333. Vatican Libraryb.]

51. AVVISO DI ROMA. 1558, DECEMBER 24.[2]

The Pope said to the Cardinals che non si dovessero maravigliare di non haver fatto promotione de novi cardinali a queste tempora, perche vedeva il Collegoi anchora assai amplo, et da l' altro canto non haveva trovato soggetti convenienti,

---

[1] See *supra*, p. 222, n. 2. An *Avviso of September 17th announces the convalescence of the Pope, although he is still very weak (*loc. cit.*). *Ibid.* p. 340 a *Pasquinata of September 10th, 1558, about the illness of Paul IV. On October 1st an *Avviso announces : " Il papa e del tutto risanato."
[2] See *supra*, p. 221, n. 2.

et che anche loro dovessero trovarne al proposito, et non mancheria manco lui di ornare il Collegio di persone degne et meritevoli di tal grado.

[Cod. Urb. 1038, 353b. Vatican Library.]

52. Avviso di Roma. 1559, February 11th.[1]

. . . Sono stati abbrugiati 4 questa settimana, uno heretico et fu brugiato vivo, li altri tre morti, cioè uno che fatturava la gente et incantava et faceva un mondo de sceleragini, il secondo, che haveva vive 7 moglie et le andava vendendo a quest' et quello, l' ultimo anche heretico oltramontano, li altri de qui circonvicini fuor di Roman. . . .

[Cod. Urb. 1039, 7. Vatican Library.]

53. Pope Paul IV. to Pietro Donato, Bishop of Narni.[2]

1559, Februar. 27, Rom.

Venerabili fratri Petro Donato episcopo Narniensi provinciae nostrae Romandiolae pro nobis et S. R. E. praesidenti.

Venerabilis frater, salutem et apostolicam benedictionem. Mandato nostro tecum aget dilectus filius, qui has tibi litteras reddidit, Angelus de Armino ordinis praedicatorum, commissarius sacri officii Inquisitionis haereticae pravitatis, de quodam iniquitatis filio, quem is tibi nominabit, ob id crimen capiendo. Qua in re exequenda ut omnem diligentiam, curam et artem adhibeas volumus ac districte praecipimus et mandamus. Vehementer enim cupimus illum comprehendi et diligenter custoditum huc abs te quamprimum remitti. Praeterea visitari abs te volumus loca omnia, de quibus idem commissarius tecum loquetur. Quo in munere fungendo quanto maiorem diligentiam fraternitas tua adhibuerit, tanto rem nobis faciet gratiorem.

Datum Romae apud sanctum Petrum etc., die 27 februari 1559 pontificatus nostri anno 4°.

Alo. Lipomanus Bergomensis.

[Minutae brev. ad princ. Arm. 44 t. 2 f. 143. Secret Archives of the Vatican.]

[1] See *supra*, p. 260, n. 2.   [2] See *supra*, p. 281, n. 6.

54. CARDINAL M. GHISLIERI TO THE INQUISITOR GIROLAMO DA GENOVA.[1]

1559, Mart. 31, Rom.

R° in X° P. Con molto piacer di questo sacr^mo tribunale s' è inteso per la vostra delli XXVII di questo la obedientia di questa città. Il sir^r Idio l' habbi per sempre in sua protettione. Spirato il termine prefisso infin' a domenica proxima, V. R. facci arder publicamente tutti i libri prohibiti che a lei et a mons^r vicario sono stati presentati, et non sia chi ardisca di voler conservar libri del tutto prohibiti con speranza che 'l decreto di questo sacratissimo tribunale s' habbi a rilassare. Et fate intendere a mons^r. vicario che si guardi di fare mancamento in questo negocio. Non accade dar orecchi alle falsità del volgo. Milano esseguisce gagliardamente et ha stampato et publicato l' Indice. In Venetia il sabbato delle Olive publicamente si brusciorno più di X et forsi XII mila volumi libri ; et l' inquisitore ne fa tuttavia nuovi cumuli.

Firenze è vero che è mal provista d' inquisitori, ma il duca zelantissimo dà ogni favore a questo santo officio.

Napoli co 'l resto d' Italia han prontamente obedito. Non mancate, avertendo però di non brusciar quelli che si possono salvare, con gli totalmente prohibiti ; governatevi secondo l' Indice et secondo l' instruttione ; et non dubitate che 'l sig^r Idio aiuta la causa sua.

Alli librari non s' ha da far piu remissione che si facci comunemente alli altri, sapendo che per la loro ingordigia orta est haec tempestas et ruina maxima. Il partito di mandar i loro libri prohibiti a luochi de lutherani è stato proposto da alrfi et non s' è ammesso, chè non si concede il portare arme ad infideli ; ma piu presto s' accettaria il partito di spogliarli anche di quelle che hanno, quando si potesse.

Il tesoro della lingua latina ci contentiamo di concederlo al sig^r Ansaldo Giustiniano deletis delendis.

Il Testamento vecchio et nuovo fiandrese si vegga da chi l' intenda, prima che si conceda.

Le scritture di fra Giacomo s' hebbero fedelmente dalli cursori.

Intendo che si sono fatti alcuni essamini, con far citar la parte, con espresso pregiudiccio della causa nostra, procedendosi al

[1] See *supra*, p. 281, n. 3.

contrario di quel che si doveria. V. R. sollecitii ispedir gli essamini de' quali gli ho scritto circa i parrochiani o sudditi talmente all' abbadia che non ad altra cura.

Aspettarò che cosa havrà esseguito mons^r de Scribanis et mons^r rev^{do} d' Acquis et intanto mi raccomando alle vostre orationi.

Di Roma il dì ultimo di marzo MDLIX.

Di V. R.

[autograph] Il nome del giudice di la causa è mons^r Clusinense, qual è mons^r Santa Croce vescovo Clusinense.

Come fratello in Christo

Il Card^l Alisandrino.

[Address] Al r^{do} p. frate Girolamo dell' ordine de Predicatori inquisitore in Genoa a S. Domenico.

[Orig. Cod. E. VII., 15. University Library, Genoa.]

55. Avviso di Roma. 1559, April 8th.[1]

. . . E uscita la bolla che S. S^{tà} publicò alli dì passati contra li heretici o sospetti d' heresia et contra li scismatici, molto terribile, che non fa eccetion di persona alcuna in qualunque grado o dignità che sia, spirituale o temporale, privandoli d' ogni benefitio, dignità et honore, et dà libertà alli superiori, et comette che le debbino privare, et che mai piu possino essere tenuti habili ad alcuna dignità nè grado, il che tutto si crede fatto principalmente per privare cosi tacitamente il card. Morone che non possa promosso mai al pontificato.

[Cod. Urb. 1039, 24. Vatican Library.]

56. Avviso di Roma. 1559, May 20th.[2]

. . . Lunedi, martedi et mercordi passati le mattine fu fatta congregatione nelle stanze del cardinal de Pisa, insieme col quale furno Allessandrino, Rimini et Spoleti sopra la causa del cardinal Morone, et nella congregatione de giovedi coram S^{mo} si parlò ancora della medesima causa, et hieri mattina i detti cardinali fecero la medema congregatione nel detto luoco sopra la istessa causa, et per quanto si è inteso da persona che lo può

---

[1] See *supra*, p. 304, n. 2.   [2] See *supra*, p. 304, n. 4.

sapere, et per voler assignare a quel cardinale l' ultimo termine
ad defensionem et spedir quella causa. . . .

[Cod. Urb. 1039, 36.   Vatican Library.]

57. Avviso di Roma.   1559, June 3rd.[1]

. . . la onde è forza dire che la morte del card. Spoleti ha
giovato non poco al detto Caraffa, et ha prolongato l' espeditione della causa di Morone. . . .

. . . Monsr Osio è stato liberato dal Castello et mandato di
longo a Rieti al suo vescovato senza ch' el habbia potuto parlare a cardinale nè prelato alcuno et si dice che si tratta molto
strettamente la liberatione del rev^{mo} Morone, et potria essere
che le cose non passassero tanto male, come si dubitava, in
effetto dopo la morte di Spoleti si sonno discoverte assai male
operatione sue, perche nanti ch' il Papa fusse Papa cercava
ogni mezzo di mettere il cardinal de Napoli in disgratia de S.
S^{tà}, et si crede al certo che lui sia stato causa delle cose seguite
tra S. S^{tà} et li nipoti. . . .

Hieri si comminciò a legere il processo di Morone et durerà
insino a giovedi.   Si farà congregatione ogni dì in questo mezzo,
et si pensa che a l' hora faranno la determinatione. . . .

[Cod. Urb. 1039, 47.   Vatican Library.]

58. Cardinal M. Ghislieri to the Inquisitor Girolamo da Genova.[2]

1559, Juli 21, Rom.

R° in Christo Padre.   Io non posso credere che cotesti
signori voglino mancar di porgere tutto il lor favore a V. R.
nell' essecutione che resta a farsi circa i libri prohibiti, nè men
credo che voglino diventar censori de i decreti di questo sacratissimo tribunale, con voler far distintione tra' libri, la quale
non sia fatta dal santo officio.   Onde spero che V. R. li renderà
capaci a conoscere che le censure ugualmente ligano qualunque
tenga qual si vogli libro prohibito, o sia italiano o sia alemano.
In Firenze tanto braccio s' ha quanto si sa desiderare da quell'
ecc^{mo} prencipe.   Se c' è diffetto, il che non so, nascerà dalla
poca sufficcienza o diligenza de' ministri del santo officio.   A
noi è dato aviso che s' è fatta la debita essecutione, dalla quale
niun magistrato catholico può sottrahersi. . . .

---

[1] See *supra*, p. 304, n. 5.   [2] See *supra*, p. 281, n. 4.

Di Roma il dì XXI di luglio MDLIX

Di V. R.

Come fratello

['autograph] Il Card¹ Alisandrino.

[Address] Al rev. padre frate Girol° inquisitore et nostro car^mo
Genoa.

[Orig. Cod. E. VII., 15, University Library, Genoa.]

59. AVVISO DI ROMA. 1559, AUGUST 5th.[1]

Lunedi si fece consistorio . . . et poi se ne fec' un altro
mercordi, et in questo . . . S. S^tà ·fec' una grand bravat' al
card¹ Alessandrino[2] et lo fece star in pie di più d' una mezz'
hora per causa d' haver favorit' un certo frate. . . .[3]

S' intende che la causa principale del rebuffo ch' ha fatto S.
S^tà al cardinal Alessandrino sia stata che, essendosi in Spagna
dall' Inquisitione proceduto contro l' arcivescovo di Toledo
per haver dato fuor un suo libro che pecc' alquanto d' heresia
et per esser quello frate di s. Domenico desiderando di scifar'
il rigoroso procedere di quell' Inquisitione, h' appellato qui.
Poi s' intende ch' il ha mandato qui un suo frate con lettere di
cambio per 20 mila scudi et gioie, con ordine di corromper
ogniun a cio la causa sua fusse favorita, il qual frate ha fatto
qui il primo recapito in casa del card¹ Alessandrino, et lui
diffendeva la causa del detto arcivescovo quanto più poteva, in
modo tale che la cosa per via dell' altri dell' Inquisitione è
pervenut' all' orecchie di S. S^tà, onde nacque poi tal rebuffo
ch' il card¹ Conseglieri ha havut' a dire che non si può vivere
nè negotiare con S. S^tà che hora per hora li fa ribuffi di cavalli,
per haverne fatt' uno tal al cardinal Alessandrino che lo fece
restar un stecco, et non contento di questo S. S^tà fece fare per
il governatore un commandament' a quel frate ch' in termine
di 3 hore sotto pena della vita sgombrasse di questa città, et
fu esseguito quel commandamento quell' istessa mattina,
stand' il detto frate a tavola col cardinal Alessandrino a desin-
are, et mercordì in l' altro consistorio S. S^tà rifresco il detto
ribuffo chiamand' il detto cardinal indegno di quel grado et che

[1] See *supra*, p. 317, n. 6.
[2] *Cf.* the report of *Navagero of August 4th, 1559. State Archives, Venice.
[3] What is omitted does not refer to the dispute with Ghislieri.

se teniva la conscientia aggravata d' haverlo fatto card^le, et
si dubitò non lo facesse metter in Castello.[1]

[Cod. Urb. 1039, 65.   Vatican Library.]

60. Report of Agostino Ricchi concerning the mortal illness of Pope Paul IV.[2]

. . . Quum enim senex plus quam octogenarius animo
integerrimo, vita inculpata ac virtute nemini non cognita, tam
pertinaciter observans esset omnium rerum quae ad Dei
cultum ac religionem pertinerent, ut tum alias tum ἐν ἰχδυοφαγίαις
saepius seipsum ad extremum spiritum perduxisset, vix ab eo
tenuissimo victu dimoveri poterat, prius quam in summam
imbecillitatem atque in animi defectionem incidisset. At
vero, quum in maximis canicularium dierum squalloribus,
nobis invitis, trium iam dierum a carnibus abstinentiam atque
ab aliis omnibus optimi alimenti cibariis, te potissimum dis-
suadente, pertulisset, tandem illum etiamdum erectum syncope
prehendit.   Ex qua nempe Dei auxilio relatus, ubi res omnes
quae ad postremam lucem spectarent pro tanti principis dignitate ac prudentia composuisset, post paucas horas summa
cum pietate ac religione e vita excessit.

Ad ill^mum et rev^mum d. d. Alphonsum Carafam card. Neapolit.
Agustini Ricchi in historiam aegrotationis Pauli IV P. M.
praefatio.

[Cod. Barb. lat. 2567, 26 f.   Vatican Library.]

61—62. Concerning the sources and composition of the History of Paul IV.

Paul IV. had, during his lifetime, an excellent exponent of his
personality in the person of the Venetian ambassador, Bernardo Navagero. The story told by this distinguished
diplomatist is founded entirely on his own observation. It
affords a " wonderfully complete picture full of genuine feeling,
and pervaded with the fascination of a portrait drawn from
life."[3]

---

[1] According to a letter of the Cardinal of Siguenza, of July 29, 1559 (in
DÖLLINGER, Beiträge, I., 263) the expulsion of the Dominicans was due to an
error on the part of the governor of the city.
[2] See *supra*, pp. 317, n. 5 ; 414, n. 2 ; 421, n. 4.   For A. Ricchi, see MARINI,
I., 347 *seq.*
[3] See ANDREAS, Die venezianischen Relationen und ihr Verhältnis zur
Kultur der Rennaisance, Leipzig, 1908, 113.   Concerning Navagero, equally
distinguished as statesman and scholar, *cf.* CICOGNA, Iscrizioni Veneziane
(1855), Vol. VI., and SUSTA, Die Kurie und das Konzil von Trient, Vienna,
1911, III., iii., vi. *seq.*

This story, which perhaps surpasses all others in its plastic, intuitive knowledge, was circulated very early in manuscript, but was only published in 1846 in the collection of Albèri. It was quoted still earlier in historical literature by Ranke, as well as the supplementary work of Alvise Mocenigo of 1560. In the Analecta to the third volume of his " Papste " (pp. 48 *seqq*.) Ranke discusses both accounts. He also touches upon the principal error of Navagero, viz., that Paul IV. only began the war with Spain on account of his nepotic policy (389). The criticism which Cardinal Antonio Carafa[1] (d. 1591) wrote on Navagero's story in a work preserved in the National Library at Naples (X—F—55), has quite escaped the notice of Ranke. This *Apologia alla relatione del Navagero*, written in the hand of the Cardinal's secretary, is a noteworthy authority, in so far that Antonio Carafa lived, in his youth, in the Vatican with Paul IV. He could, therefore, give many interesting and valuable notes on the history of that Pope, and could also furnish several fair criticisms on Navagero, but, in general, he too frequently errs by excess. The essay is too partial, and, as one may gather from the title, too apologetic.[2]

Onofrio Panvinio fell into the opposite extreme in many passages of his *Vita Pauli IV.*, which first appeared in 1562. At that time the reaction against the measures of Paul IV. was at its height, and to this feeling Panvinio, doubtless influenced by his patron, Cardinal Farnese, has paid tribute. Panvinio himself seems to have felt later on that he had gone too far ; in later editions several passages have been altered in a noteworthy manner.[3]

[1] The printed works of the learned Cardinal are in the Catal. libr. Bibl. Casanat. II., 93 ; *cf.* BATTIFOL, Vaticane, 69 *seq.* ; *ibid.*, 63 *seq.*, concerning his life. Cardinal Antonio Carafa had previously endeavoured to have a literary monument to his uncle compiled, which the humanist Robertello was to have composed. Further details are to be found in a *letter of Flaminio Filonardi to Cardinal Antonio Carata, dated Padua, 1565, Juni 1 (Vat. 6895, 329–331, Vatican Library). The whole life of Paul IV. was to be treated in this work, and the truth told about the war against Spain. With regard to the manner of its composition, a work similar to that of Jovius on Leo X. was thought of, but Filonardi thought Robertello had better take Suetonius as a model, rather than Plutarch. Owing to the death of the Cardinal the plan came to nothing.

[2] G. B. Castaldo did not include the work in his book, in order not to irritate the Spaniards ; see PADIGLIONE, Bibl. del Museo di S. Martino, 242.

[3] In the discussion about the proceedings of Paul IV. against the vagrant monks, the groundless accusation continues, which is the Venetian edition of 1562 is expressed as follows : " Monasteriorum vero praefectos ut eos reciperent non coegit, qua re nihil iniquius." Concerning the arrest of Morone there is wanting in the later edition the addition " quem ex morum dissimilitudine oderat." The re-casting of the conclusion is most noteworthy. Instead of the passage " Felix procul dubio . . . attigisset " which Panvinio also included in his work on Papal elections (in which his judgment concerning Paul IV. is much more correct [MERKLE, II., 333]) it is given in the later editions thus : " Caeterum liberalitate, religionis tuendae conservandaeque zelo super omnes retro pontifices maxime clarus et quo pontifice primum hominum et

The Theatines have always held the memory of Paul IV. in honour, and rightly, as he was their co-founder. They felt it very much when Cardinal Antonio Carafa's idea of compiling[1] a biographical monument to Paul IV. was not carried out.[2] The Theatine, Antonio Caracciolo (d. 1642) took a great interest in supplying the deficiency. Caracciolo, who was also engaged in literary work in other directions, zealously collected information of every kind concerning Paul IV. Only a small part of his collection has appeared in print, under the title " Collectanea historica de vita Pauli IV." (Coloniae, 1642). The greater part remains in manuscript, and bears the title " Vita e gesti di Giovan Pietro Carafa cioè di Paolo IV. P.M."[3] Three manuscripts of this work, one of which is probably the autograph, are in the library of the Certosa di S. Martino in Naples (cf. PADIGLIONE, 427 seq). A very good copy of the original is in the Casanatense Library, Rome, in the Codex C. III., 43 (formerly N. 349).[4]

The work of Caracciolo had a wide circulation in manuscript ; copies are in the Secret Archives of the Vatican (Misc. Arm. 11, t. 101), in the Barberini Library (Barb. lat. 4953, 4961, 5370), in the Chigi Library (J. II, 65., J. III., 66), in the Vatican Library (Ottob. 617-619, incomplete, only reaching to the election of Paul IV.), in the Vittorio Emanuele Library (two copies from the Theatine Library of S. Andrea della Valle ; cf. ED. D'ALENÇON, G. P. Carafa e la riforma nell 'ordine dell 'osservanza, Foligno, 1912), and a copy in my private library ; other copies in the Library at Parma (Palat. 638, copy of Cas. C. III., 43), in St. Mark's Library, Venice (Ital. V., 59), in the Bertoliana Library, Vicenza, and in the British Museum (20011, 20012). The work of Caracciolo, compiled in 1613 (see ZACHARIAS, It. litt., 113) was frequently made use of by all historians of Paul IV. ; it is a most uncritical composition,[5] but is partly founded upon the original Carafa papers, of which

clericorum praesertim moribus depravatis salutaribus legibus certum remedium est adhiberi coeptum ; confirmandae enim ac restituendae ecclesiasticae disciplinae, in quam mirifice perturbatam eius pontificatus inciderat, auctor et princeps exstitit ita ut eius fonte cogitationum rationumque multa sacri Tridentini Concilii decreta profluxisse postea videantur." (Cologne, ed. of 1568, 445-446, also in the Cologne ed. of 1626, 411). Another alteration has been noted by MERKLE (II., cxxxiv., A. 5).
   [1] See supra p. 487, n. 1.
   [2] Concerning the collection of documents dealing with Paul IV. which the Theatine Valerio Pagano planned at the beginning of the XVIIth century, see PADIGLIONE, 302 seq.
   [3] Review of contents in DURUY, XXIII. seq.
   [4] Cod. XX. V. 56 (formerly n. 993) is a later copy.
   [5] Cf. AMABILE, I., 138 n.

many have now been lost, and contains a great deal of important and interesting information.

Its importance is, however, greater for the period preceding the election of Paul IV., than for the years of his pontificate, for which there are now far better sources available. Taken all in all Caracciolo is a convinced admirer of his hero, and always more of an apologist than a writer of history. This is also true of Castaldo and Silos, who sketch portraits which are almost without a dark side.[1]

Pallavicini cleared the way for a historical comprehension and estimate of Paul IV. in the second part of his history of the Council of Trent, which appeared in 1657. He was thereby drawn into a controversy with the Theatine, Francesco Maria Maggio, in which Pallavicini was victorious. (Cf. CALENZIO, Esame critico-letterario delle opere riguardenti la storia del Concilio di Trento, Romae 1869, 100 seqq.). Compared to the invectives of Maggio, who conceals himself under the name of Francesco Velli, the calmness of Pallavicini makes a good impression. He speaks to the point when he asserts that historians should not be writers of panegyrics. Although it has recently been said (see VOLPICELLA in the Archivio Napoletano, XXXV., 557) that Pallavicini had written in a hostile tone about Paul IV., this is by no means the case. Pallavicini depicts objectively the bright as well as the dark side of the Carafa Pope ; he only errs in so far as he regards the chief merit of Paul IV. to lie in the preservation of the unity of the faith in Italy, and does not do sufficient justice to the reforms carried out from 1555 to 1559. Maggio continued the controversy after Pallavicini's death, but could not find a printer for the part of his work dealing with the pontificate of Paul IV. (CALENZIO, loc. cit. 107).

Another Theatine, Bartolomeo Carrara (d. 1778) has rendered much better service than Maggio to the memory of Paul IV., by his history of the Pope in two volumes, published at Ravenna in the years 1748 and 1753, under the pseudonym Carlo Bromato. This is a very able work for that period. Although not free from an apologetic tendency and partiality,[2]

---

[1] SILOS (I., 421, 423 seq., 426 seq.) praises the " prudentia " of his hero ! He has also made use of manuscript sources, e.g., Caracciolo's collection, as well as the above-mentioned *Apologia. CASTALDO (176 seq.) softens down the choler of Paul IV., in a manner that is not historical : he is also not reliable as to details.

[2] Cf. REIMANN in the Forschungen zur deutschen Geschichte, V., 294.

Carrara nevertheless endeavours to judge Paul IV. from an objective point of view. Many of his faults, especially the raising to the cardinalate of Carlo Carafa, are severely censured (II., 233) but the original material for going more deeply into the matter was not at his disposal. He collected with great diligence all the information then obtainable, but this was mostly from derivative sources. Besides Caracciolo, the work of Pietro Nores, *Storia della guerra di Paolo IV. contro gli Spagnuoli*, already used by Pallavicini, is consulted.

The war of Paul IV. against Spain had already been treated of by Alessandro Andrea[1] and Mambrino Roseo.[2] Nores began the compilation of his work at the beginning of the reign of Clement VIII., but laid it aside because he had scruples about giving an account of the participation of Silvestro Aldobrandini, the father of Clement VIII., in the events of that time. He took the work up again at a later period ; the first book was finished in 1640, the third in 1641, and the fourth in 1644. Nores was careful to collect[3] letters and reports of contemporaries ; he drew upon (among others) Massarelli's Diarium VII,[4] and also procured information in Rome by word of mouth. The work, the publication of which A. Zeno had already recommended, appeared in 1847, as Vol. XII of the *Archivio Storico Italiano*. In this publication[5] a political tendency predominated. It was desired by its means to put forward Pius IX. and his predecessors, Julius III. and Paul IV. as prototypes of the struggle for national freedom [i.e. " United Italy."] For this purpose the history of a war, which, while absolutely unimportant in itself, is principally interesting as

---

[1] *Della guerra di campagna di Roma et del regno di Napoli*, ed. G. Ruscelli, Venetia, 1557 (1560). The Spanish translation, which I had before me, is dedicated to Philip II. (Madrid, 1589). The author is partial to Spaniards, often diffuse (see FORNERON, I., 81), but a good authority for military affairs (*cf.* PRESCOTT, Philip II., I., 80). Nores had drawn largely from him (see Arch. d. Soc. Rom., IV., 332 note). It is also well to consult the " Tratatto sopra lo stato ecclesiastico " in the Secret Archives of the Vatican (Misc. Arm. 15, t. 186) in which there is an account of the wars of the States of the Church since 1494 and which treats in a particularly detailed manner of the conflicts under Paul IV. *Lettere dirette a Bonifacio Gaetani* concerning the war between Paul IV. and Spain, in the Gaetani Archives, Rome.

[2] *Relazione della guerra suscitata del regno di Napoli da Paolo IV. nel 1556 al 1557*, Roma, 1558.

[3] Nores has drawn (among others) upon the documents in the Library, Parma, and in Cod. Mare. XI., 125, of St. Mark's Library, Venice : *cf.* COGGIOLA, Cornia, 223, 342.

[4] See MERKLE, II., xlviii., xlix., 303 n. 3.

[5] It is founded on a Codex Capponi, and was compared with two Neapolitan manuscripts. The manuscripts of Nores' work in the Alessandrina Library, Rome (214–1–183), the Vittorio Emanuele Library, Rome (Fondo Gesuitico, 323), the Trivulziana Library, Milan (Cod. 37), the Library of the Certosa di S. Martino, Naples (Cod. 364), and the Communal Library, Foggia (Cod. 7), have not been made use of.

being the last attempt of the Papal policy to free itself and Italy from a foreign yoke, seemed suitable. The publishers of Nores, Volpicella, Gar and Scarabelli, have done much to embellish their edition by the addition of unprinted documents. Notably, they obtained access to the " Istruzioni e Lettere di Monsignor della Casa a nome del Cardinal Carafa " from a manuscript in the possession of Gino Capponi.[1]

The work of Nores, which had already been praised by Pallavicini and Bromato, has long been very popular. Reumont (*Carafa*, I., 221, 517) describes it as the principal authority for the history of the Carafa family under Paul IV., and praises the author as the most reliable writer of the history of those events (*cf.* also *Gesch. Roms*, III., 2, 700). At a later period Duruy (20, 85) and Porena (*Arch. stor. Ital.* Ser 4, XIII., 354) overwhelmed Nores with praise, although Reimann (*loc. cit.* 327 *seqq.*) has already shown, in one point, how little Nores is often to be relied upon. Ancel, in his scientific studies on the history of Paul IV., has expressed in very severe terms a highly unfavourable opinion of Nores (see especially *Sienne*, I, .18, and *Disgrâce*, 36) which, however, did not prevent Campana from describing the work of Nores in the *Studi Storici* (XVII., 586) as a masterpiece. There can, however, be no doubt that Ancel is right. Nores contains very many errors ; he also sometimes allows his imagination to run riot, and draws upon merely secondary sources. The more the *Reports of Ambassadors*, which are to be regarded as of the first importance for the pontificate of Paul IV., become known, the less value will be attached to the work of Nores.

The dispatches of Bernardo Navagero are those most widely known. These invaluable reports, which supplement, and are, in many points much superior to the accounts of the ambassador, are not, it is true, preserved in the originals. Since the destruction by fire of the Venetian Archives in 1577, only copies are available ; these exist in the State Archives, Venice,[2] in St. Mark's Library (Ital. Cl. VII., Cod. 1097), in the Museo Correr, Venice (Cod. 1957), in the University Library, Pisa (Cod. 154, S. c. 2), in the National Library, Naples (Cod. X. D. 41), in the Court Library, Vienna (Cod. 6255—

---

[1] See Catalogo dei MSS. posseduti dal marchese G. Capponi, Florence, 1845, n. 831.
[2] Cod. Miscell. n. 98 (*cf.* BROSCH, I., 200, n. 1). Also the dispatches to the Council of Ten, only preserved in contemporary copies ; *cf.* ANCEL, Disgrâce, 21, n. 3.

Foscar. 163), and in the library of the Duke of Ossuna, Madrid (Cod. 93).

Nores was the first to make use of the rich treasure of the dispatches of Navagero ; later, Bertolotti published extracts in the *Atti Mod.* (3rd series, II., 155 *seqq.*) ; moreover, Rawdon Brown has published, in an English translation, all the dispatches relating to England, and also much of the actual history of Paul IV., in the *Calendars of State Papers*. The study of the Italian text is, however, by no means superfluous for, in accordance with his purpose, Brown has systematically looked only for dispatches concerned with England ; besides this, his translation is not always reliable, and, in any case, the best translation can never replace the original text. This is all the more important in the case of Navagero, as the correspondent has performed his task with such scrupulous conscientiousness that, whenever possible, he has given the utterances of the Pope in his actual words,[1] and this is very important in the case of such a strongly marked personality as that of Paul IV. The detailed reports of Navagero, who was on most confidential terms with the Pope, are an invaluable source ; intimate and many-sided, they afford, at the same time, a series of instantaneous photographs, everywhere breathing the warm life of the events they portray.

Besides the Venetian reports, there is also the correspondence of Cardinal Farnese to be studied ; this is still preserved in the State Archives, Parma. The Cardinal received exact information, through his agent, of all the events which took place in Rome. To these must be added the dispatches of the envoys of the Este and Medici families, in the State Archives at Modena and Florence. These reports offer, in addition to the Venetian ones, much that is new and valuable. While Duruy passed over these first-class sources in his otherwise faulty work,[2] Coggiola and Ancel have made diligent use of them.[3] I have also used this material for my work. We have

---

[1] *Perche io giudico che le parti d'un ambasciator siano dir, se si po, le medesime parole che dice il principe di sua bocca ; se ben molte cose sono le medesime o contrarie erepugnante l'una all 'altra, ho voluto sempre sforciarmi, et cosi farò nel avenir, di scriver le formal parole che mi ha detto il pontifice ; cosi havessi anche potuto aggiunger li gesti. Dispatch of October 12, 1555 (Library of St. Mark's, Venice, *loc. cit.* 10).

[2] *Cf.* COGGIOLA, Cornia, 80, 108, 292 *seq.*, 341, and ANCEL, Sienne, 1, 19, 22, 37, 40, 65 ; see also Deutsche Lit.-Zeitung, 1883, 1659, and Rev. d. quest. hist., 1884, Juillet, 335 *seq.*

[3] The extracts from the Florentine reports of Serristori in Canestrini are very defective and incomplete.

to thank Druffel and Riess for very many Spanish reports. The work of Riess, which appeared in 1909, represents a great advance on that of Duruy ; it also, however, is by no means complete, and contains as well many errors on particular points, such as the judgment on the whole policy of Paul IV.[1] The work of Ancel, the result of a wide range of studies among archives, is the best authority for this question ; it also clearly distinguishes between the Pope and his nephews, and completely exposes, the intrigues of Cardinal Carafa.

Brosch has, in his generally very feeble treatise,[2] on the struggle of Paul IV. with Philip II., only drawn on new material to the extent of a few dispatches of Navagero (Mitteilungen des Instituts österreichische Geschichtsforschung, XXV., 1904).

The reports of the French ambassadors with regard to Paul IV. were first published by Ribier, and later by Sauzé and Vitalis. Turnbull has published, in a translation, the reports of Carne, the English ambassador.

I was the first to make thorough use of the letters from Rome to Ferdinand I., in the Vienna State Archives, as well as of the reports of ambassadors which are in the State Archives, Bologna, and in the Gonzaga Archives, Mantua.

A source of a peculiar kind, which stands half way between the embassy reports and the gazettes, are the so-called " Avvisi " communications from intelligence bureaux, which the Fugger family had at that time in the capitals and centres of commerce. This source has lately been critically dealt with by Ancel in the *Mélanges d'Archéologie et d'Histoire*, XXVIII (1908).[3] Last but not least of the very important sources of information concerning the history of Paul IV., are his own " Acta," Briefs, Bulls, and diplomatic correspondence in the Secret Archives of the Vatican and in the Barberini Library. The Briefs have, unfortunately, not been preserved in their

[1] *Cf.* the criticisms of FRIEDENSBURG in the Hist. Vierterjahrsschrift 1911/12, 280, and of HERRE in the Hist. Zeitschr., CIX., 199 *seq.* See also *supra* pp. 117, n. 3 ; 136, n. 4 ; 168, n. 1 ; 223, n. 2 ; 232, n. 1.
[2] *Cf.* ANCEL, Sienne, 90, and COGGIOLA in the Studi storici, X., 227 *seq.* see also Hist. Zeitschr., 94, 186. Nothing new in BORALEVI, I., primi mesi del pontificato di Paolo IV., Livorno, 1888. JENKINS (Paul IV., London, 1886) mostly follows Duruy ; *cf.* Arch. d. Soc. Rom., X., 714 ; see also Arch. Napol., XII., 836 *seq.*
[3] The admirable remarks of SÄGMÜLLER in the Histor. Jahrb., XV., 304, about the gazetteers and writers of " Avvisi," also called " novellisti," have escaped the notice of Ancel. We must also add to the literature mentioned there ; SIMIANI, N. Franco, 36 *seq.* LUTOLF, Schweizergarde, 44 ; SICKEL in the Weimarischen Jahrb. für deutsche Sprache, I., Hanover 1858, 344 *seq.* Arch. d. Soc. Rom., XXXI., 421 ; XXXIII., 277 *seq.*

entirety; they nevertheless yield, according to Raynaldus, many interesting " finds." The " *Regesta Vaticana* " nn. 1805-1854 (*cf.* PALMIERI, 85 *seq.*) preserved in a complete condition, were examined by Ancel, who has published a biographical work on Paul IV. in several volumes ; they contain, however, but little for a history like the present, which is confined within narrower limits.[1] The diplomatic correspondence of Paul IV. has suffered numerous and important losses. A very great deal, however, has been preserved, as a large number of the Carafa archives were transferred to the Barberini Library, which contains précious original documents relating to Paul IV. and his nephews, in no less than 60 volumes. This material was related so thoroughly and in such detail by Pieper (189 *seqq.*) and then by Ancel (Secrét. 37-45 and Nonciat. I, II) that a mere reference to them is sufficient here. The Instructions and Letters of Giovanni della Casa appeared in print as early as the XVIIIth century.[2] Ancel has now published the *Nonciatures de France* in an admirable edition. The publication of the reports of the Polish nuncios, preserved in a very incomplete form, is shortly to be undertaken by the Cracow Academy.

[1] *Cf.* WIRZ, xxvi. ; ANCEL, Secrét. 61 *seq.* Here also see (15 n.) concerning the " Ruoli " of Paul IV.
[2] The best edition is the Neapolitan ; see PIEPER, 186 n.

INDEX OF NAMES IN VOL. XIV.